An International Directory of
Business Historians

An International Directory of Business Historians

Edited by
David J. Jeremy
Reader in Business History
Faculty of Management and Business
Manchester Metropolitan University

Edward Elgar

Published by
Edward Elgar Publishing Limited
Gower House
Croft Road
Aldershot
Hants GU11 3HR
England

Edward Elgar Publishing Company
Old Post Road
Brookfield
Vermont 05036
USA

British Library Cataloguing in Publication Data

International Directory of Business Historians
  I. Jeremy, David J.
  338.60922

Library of Congress Cataloguing in Publication Data

An international directory of business historians / edited by David J.
  Jeremy.
        p.   cm.
  Includes indexes
    1. Business historians—Directories.   I. Jeremy, David J.
  HF5341.I58   1994
  650'.09—dc20   93–49864
                                     CIP

ISBN 1 85278 920 4

Printed and bound in Great Britain by
Hartnolls Limited, Bodmin, Cornwall

Contents

v

Introduction

The development of the subject of business history, pioneered in the USA at the Harvard Business School in the 1920s and 1930s and soon followed in the UK and Japan, has received a fresh injection of interest since the 1970s with the ascendancy of market economies and the expansion of higher education. To meet new opportunities and challenges, economic and business historians in the UK formed the Association of Business Historians in 1990, complementing the older Business History Conference in the USA and the Business History Society of Japan. It is under the auspices of these three national associations that this directory, the first international listing for the profession, is published.

The directory has several purposes. First it is a 'who's who' of the majority of scholars in the profession (it cannot claim to be exhaustive since some people have either not been reached by our questionnaire or, for various reasons, have declined to be included). At any rate here will be found some indication of the academic backgrounds of a majority of those active or recently active in the field.

Secondly, it will serve as a register of research interests. Past or immediately-forthcoming publications are listed (no more than five per person) together with extent of research interests (defined by industry, business dimension, geographical limits and the period of historical specialism) and teaching and consultancy expertise. Indices to these interests are intended to increase the utility of the volume.

Thirdly, the *Directory* is a tool for international networking and co-operation across the profession. A few business historians have for some time operated in international orbits, much assisted by the organization of international meetings and conferences and the advent of the passenger jet airliner: this volume is intended to widen and advance these activities. Besides addresses, the directory lists telephone and fax numbers and institutional affiliations. These, together with the indices and entries, should facilitate and increase the number of international research and subject-teaching projects and ventures, such as international comparative studies or studies of international or global business.

This *Directory* would not have appeared but for the cooperation of all those (about 750) responding to the invitation to complete the questionnaires on which it is based. Our thanks to all of them. In addition, a number of individuals must be mentioned by name. The idea for *An International Directory of Business Historians* originated with Professor Geoffrey Jones of Reading University and the publisher Edward Elgar. For various reasons it was then set aside. After the UK Association of Business Historians was formed I found myself elected to the executive council of the ABH (1990–1993) with responsibility for publications. Shortly thereafter I succeeded Professor Jones as editor of Edward Elgar's New Business History Series (from 1992) and the *Directory* project was revived.

Ideas are one thing, implementation another. The executive council members of the ABH have given me collective support, permission to use the ABH membership mailing list and a free hand in compiling the *Directory*. In the USA Professor William Hausman kindly supplied the membership list of the Business History conference, of which he is the secretary–treasurer. In Japan Professor Takeshi Yuzawa was consulted about the shape of the questionnaire and undertook the very considerable task of circulating it to members of the Business History Society of Japan of which he was secretary and is editor. In addition he has edited the entries from Japanese scholars. Professor Dr Hans Pohl supplied names and addresses of all members of the German Economic History Society. Professor François Crouzet performed a parallel service with respect to the French Association of Economic Historians. Dr Rolv Petter Amdam has checked the text of the Scandinavian entries. Professor Luciano Segreto has checked the Italian entries and Dr Timo Myllyntaus those for Finland. Other people who have been helpful in reaching business historians in countries without a national association in the subject include:

Professor Pablo Martin-Aceña, Spain
Dr Bruno Bezza, Italy
Professor Murat Cizakca, Turkey
Dr F.M.M. de Goey, The Netherlands
Professor Jozef Faltus, Slovakia
Professor Ben Forster, Canada
Professor Barry Higman, The West Indies
Dr Ole Hyldtoft, Denmark
Dr Ken Jackson, New Zealand
Dr Stuart Jones, South Africa
Professor Gregory P. Marchildon, Canada
Professor Herbert Matis, Austria
Dr Timo Myllyntaus, Finland
Professor Ulf Olsson, Sweden
Professor Alice Teichova, Central and South-East Europe
Professor Jerzy Tomaszewski, Poland
Dr Simon Ville, Australia
Dr Elga Zalite, Latvia

At Edward Elgar Publishing, Mrs Sara Shailer, in charge of the circulation of questionnaires and of the computerization of the data, has been splendidly indefatigable in pushing the project forward. Completion of production at Edward Elgar Publishing has been efficiently overseen by Ms Julie Leppard. The keying-in of the data has been undertaken by Renate Mauri whose familiarity with several European languages has been invaluable. Heinz Tüselmann, one of my colleagues, has kindly checked the German entries. Hilary Quinn has prepared the final camera ready copy. Some handwritten questionnaires have given legibility problems and any resultant slips must be forgiven. Edward Elgar himself has also facilitated the search for people to be included and kept a keen eye on the progress of the book.

Clearly there are gaps because of the isolation or non-existence of business historians in some countries. Maybe the expansion of the subject will justify future editions. It should be noted that titles of countries are those that existed in 1992–3. Needless to say the editor and publisher are grateful to all those who have joined in the compilation of this work, and of course absolve them from any of the slips that inevitably creep into a volume of this kind.

David J. Jeremy
International Business Unit
Manchester Metropolitan University

Abbreviations

Acad.	Academy
Admin.	Administration
Agric.	Agricultural, Agriculture
Amer.	America, American
ao.	außerordentlich
Asst.	Assistant
Assoc.	Association, Associate
Bull.	Bulletin
Bus.	Business
Conf.	Conference
Co.	Company
Com.	Committee
Dept.	Department
Dipl.	Diplom
Dr	Doctorate (PhD)
Econ.	Economic, Economics
Ed.	Editor
Edit.	Editorial
Edn.	Edition
Fac.	Faculty
Grad.	Graduate
Habil.	Habilitation
Hist.	History, Historical
Hon.	Honorary
Inc.	Incorporated
Indust.	Industrial
Inst.	Institute/Institution
Internat.	International
J.	Journal
Lect.	Lecturer
Mem.	Member
Maths.	Mathematics
MC	Maître de course
MP	Member of Parliament
Metropol.	Metropolitan
O or o	Ordinary
Phil.	Philosophy
POB	Post Office Box
Pres.	President/Presidential
Prof.	Professor
Polit.	Political/Politics
Pub.	Publisher/Publication
Q.	Quarterly
Rev.	Review
Soc.	Society

Sen.	Senior
St	Saint, Street
Stats.	Statistics
Suppl.	Supplement
temp.	Temporary
Univ.	University
Vol./Vols.	Volume/Volumes

Aaronson, Susan Ariel

Consultant, National Acad. of Sciences & Professorial Lect., Maryland Univ., National Acad. of Sciences, 2101 Constitution Avenue, N.W. Washington DC 20418, Grad. School of Bus., Maryland Univ., USA. Tel.: 1 202 334 3743. Fax: 1 202 334 1751.

Year and Place of Birth 1954, Queens, USA.

Degrees and Qualifications BA (Hist.) Harpur College, SUNY, 1976; MA (Internat. Affairs) Columbia Univ., 1978; Ph.D. (Hist.) Johns Hopkins Univ., 1993.

Previous Post Professorial Lect., Internat. Bus., The Amer. Univ.

Current Offices and Honorary Posts Research Fellow, The Brookings Inst.

Major Honours Rovensky Dissertation Prize in Econ. Bus. Hist.; Truman Dissertation Fellowship; Brookings Inst. Fellowship; Leader Foundation Fellowship; Frederick Jackson Turner Travel Fellowship.

Fields of Expertise *Industry Fields:* public admin. and defence. *Bus. Dimensions:* US trade policy and bus. *Scope:* internat. *Period:* mid-twentieth century, 1940–70; late twentieth century, 1970–present. *Consultancy:* US technology strategy; US trade policy; US technology strategy; US trade policy.

Publications *Articles:* 'Without Practice or Practitioners', *Bus. & Econ. Hist.*, 2nd ser., 19, 1990; 'How Cordell Hull and the Postwar Planners Designed a new Trade Policy', *Bus. & Econ. Hist.*, 2nd ser., vol. 20, 1991; 'Serving Amer. Bus.', *J. of Bus. Hist.*, 34(1), Jan., 1992; 'For the People , but not by the People', Proceedings of the 107th Annual Meeting of the Amer. Hist. Assoc., forthcoming.

Abé, Etsuo

Prof., School of Bus. Admin., Meiji Univ., 1-1 Kanda Surugadai, Chiyodaku, Tokyo, Japan. Tel.: 03 3296 2052. Fax: 03 3296 2350.

Year and Place of Birth 1949, Tokyo, Japan.

Degrees and Qualifications MA Hitotsubashi Univ.

Fields of Expertise *Industry Fields:* metal manufacture. *Bus. Dimensions:* entrepreneurs and entrepreneurship. *Scope:* internat.; USA; UK; Germany; Japan. *Period:* twentieth century as a whole.

Publications *Books: Daiei Teikoku no Sangyo Haken* [The Indust. Supremacy of the British Empire] Yuhikaku, 1993.

Abe, Takeshi

Assoc. Prof., Fac. of Econ., Osaka Univ., 1-1 Machikaneyama-cho, Toyonaka, Osaka 560, Japan. Tel.: 06 844 1151. Fax: 06 841 6631.

Year and Place of Birth 1952, Tokyo, Japan.

Degrees and Qualifications BA Tokyo Univ.; Ph.D. (Econ.) Tokyo Univ.

Previous Post Asst. Prof., Inst. of Social Sciences, Tsukuba Univ., 1985–8.

Current Offices and Honorary Posts Mem. of edit. com., Bus. Hist. Soc. of Japan, 1989–92; Sec. for Western region, Socio-Econ. Hist. Soc. of Japan, 1988–92.

Fields of Expertise *Industry Fields:* textiles. *Bus. Dimensions:* entrepreneurs and entrepreneurship; strategy formation; bus. and technology; small bus. matters; markets and bus. *Scope:* regional; national. *Period:* nineteenth century; early twentieth century; interwar years, 1919–39; mid-twentieth century, 1940–70. *Teaching:* undergrad.; post grad. *Consultancy:* co. hist.

Publications *Books: Asakura Tsuneto Nikki* [The Diary of Tsuneto Asakura] ed., Yamakawa Shuppansha, 1982–91; *Nippon ni Okeru Sanchimen Orimonogyo no Tenkai* [The Development of the Cotton Weaving Industry in pre-War Japan] Univ. of Tokyo Press, 1989; *Keizai Seisaku to Sangyo* [Econ. Policy and Industry] ed., Yamakawa Shuppansha, 1991. *Articles:* 'From Putting-out to the Factory: A Cotton Weaving District in late Meiji Japan', *Textile Hist.*, Prof. Osamu Saito co-auth., 19(2), 1988, 143–57; 'Nippon Keizaishi 4 Sangyoka no Jidai jo' [The Age of Industrialization', *Econ. Hist. of Japan*, ed., 4, Iwanami Shoten, 1990.

Acheson, T.W.

Prof. and Chair, Dept. of Hist., Univ. of New Brunswick, POB 4400, Fredericton, New Brunswick, E3B 5A3, Canada. Tel.: 1 506 453 4621. Fax: 1 506 453 5068.

Year and Place of Birth 1936, St Stephen, Canada.

Degrees and Qualifications BA New Brunswick Univ., 1962; MA New Brunswick Univ., 1964; Ph.D. Toronto Univ., 1971.

Previous Post Visiting Assoc. Prof., Dept. of Hist., York Univ., Toronto, 1976–7.

Fields of Expertise *Industry Fields:* distributive trades. *Bus. Dimensions:* entrepreneurs and entrepreneurship. *Scope:* regional; Canada; British Empire *Period:* nineteenth century.

Publications *Books: St John: The Making of a Colonial Urban Community*, Univ. of Toronto Press, 1985. *Articles:* 'The Structure and Nature of York Commerce in the 1820s', *Canadian Hist. Rev.*, L(4), 1968, 406–28; 'The National Policy and the Industrialization of the Maritimes 1880–1910', *Acadiensis*,

I(2), 1972, 3–28; 'Changing Origins of the Canadian Indust. Elite 1880–1910', *Bus. Hist. Rev.*, XLVII, 1973; 'New Brunswick Agric. at the End of the Colonial Era: A Re-assessment', *Acadiensis*, XXII(2), 1993.

Achilles, Walter

Lindenkamp 31, D-31199 Diekholzen, Germany.

Year and Place of Birth 1927, Lutter a. Bbge., Germany.

Degrees and Qualifications Dr.sc.agr. Göttingen Univ., 1957; Habilitation, Göttingen Univ., 1970; apl. Prof., Göttingen Univ., 1976.

Fields of Expertise *Industry Fields:* agric., forestry, fishing. *Bus. Dimensions:* entrepreneurs and entrepreneurship; production management; bus. and technology; small bus. matters. *Scope:* regional; national. *Period:* early modern; eighteenth century; nineteenth century. *Teaching:* undergrad. *Consultancy:* co. hist.

Publications *Books: Vermögensverhältnisse braunschweigischer Bauernhöfe im 17. und 18. Jahrhundert*, 1965; *Die Belastung der braunschweigischen Landwirtschaft und ihr Beitrag zu den Staatseinnahmen im 17. und 18. Jahrhundert*, 1972; *Die Lage der hannoverschen Landbevölkerung im späten 18. Jahrhundert*, 1982; *Landwirtschaft in der Frühen Neuzeit*, 1990; *Deutsche Agrargeschichte im Zeitalter der Reformen und der Industrialisierung*, 1993.

Ackrill, Margaret

Part-time Lect., Dept. of Econ. Hist., London School of Econ. & part-time tutor in Postgraduate Studies, PGRS, Oxford Brookes Univ., 22 Charlbury Road, Oxford, OX2 6UU, UK. Tel.: 44 71 405 7686.

Place of Birth Perth, Australia.

Degrees and Qualifications BA Univ. of Western Australia; B.Litt. Oxford Univ.

Previous Post Research Fellow, London School of Econ., 1989–92.

Fields of Expertise *Industry Fields:* gas, electricity, water; insurance, banking, finance,; manufacturing and financial services generally. *Bus. Dimensions:* entrepreneurs and entrepreneurship; production management; co. finance and accounting; personnel management; co. admin.; marketing; research and development; strategy formation; merger movement and issues; bus. organization; bus. and technology; small bus. matters; multinational bus.; management education; bus.–state relations; markets and bus.; bus. values; co. culture; boardroom issues. *Scope:* national; Cocos (Keeling) Islands. *Period:* twentieth century as a whole; inter-war years, 1919–39; mid-twentieth century, 1940–70; late twentieth century, 1970–present. *Teaching:* undergrad.; post grad.

Publications *Books: Manufacturing Industry since 1870*, Philip Allan, Deddington, 1987. *Articles:* 'British Managers and the British Economy', *Oxford Rev. of Econ. Policy*, 4(1), Spring, 1988; 'Econ. Priorities', *Contemporary Record*, 3(3), Feb., 1990; 'The Cocos (Keeling) Islands Econ. Planning and Performance', *Indian Ocean States*, Indian Ocean Policy Papers no. 2, R.T. Appleyard & R.N. Ghosh eds., Australian National Univ., Canberra, 1990; 'Marketing in British Banking', *The Rise and Fall of Mass Marketing*, Richard Tedlow & Geoffrey Jones eds., Routledge, London, 1993.

Adelmann, Gerhard

Retired Prof. for Econ. and Social Hist., Historisches Seminar, Bonn Univ., Lessingweg 8, D-53359 Rheinbach, Germany.

Year and Place of Birth 1925, Lingen, Germany.

Degrees and Qualifications Diplomvolkswirt Bonn Univ., 1953; Dr.phil. Bonn Univ., 1961; Prof. (Econ. & Soc. Hist.) Bonn Univ., 1974.

Major Honours Johann Wilhelm Loebell Prize, Bonn Univ., 1961.

Fields of Expertise *Industry Fields:* mining and quarrying; metal manufacture; textiles. *Bus. Dimensions:* entrepreneurs and entrepreneurship; personnel management; bus.–state relations. *Scope:* regional; national; internat. continental north-western Europe. *Period:* eighteenth century; nineteenth century; twentieth century as a whole. *Teaching:* undergrad.; post grad.

Publications *Books: Quellensammlung zur Geschichte der sozialen Betriebsverfassung der Ruhrindustrie*, Hanstein, Bonn, 3 vols., 1960–8; *Die soziale Betriebsverfassung des Ruhrbergbaus vom Anfang des 19. Jahrhunderts bis zum Ersten Weltkrieg*, Röhrscheid, Bonn, 1962; *Der gewerblich-industrielle Zustand der Rheinprovinz im Jahre 1836. Amtliche Übersichten*, ed., Röhrscheid, Bonn, 1967; *Vom Gewerbe zur Industrie im kontinentalen Nordwesteuropa. Gesammelte Aufsätze zur regionalen Wirtschafts- und Sozialgeschichte*, Steiner, Stuttgart, 1986. *Articles:* 'Ausländische Kapitalbeteiligungen und Direktinvestitionen in der deutschen Wirtschaft 1914–1986 aus gesamtstatistischer Sicht', *Der Einfluß ausländischer Unternehmen auf die deutsche Wirtschaft vom Spätmittelalter bis zur Gegenwart*, H. Pohl ed., Steiner, Stuttgart, 1992.

Ahvenainen, Jorma

Prof. of General Hist., Dept. of Hist., Jyväskylä Univ., POB 35, SF-40351 Jyväskylä, Finland. Tel.: 358 41 601266. Fax: 358 41 601251.

Year and Place of Birth 1930, Helsinki, Finland.
Degrees and Qualifications Ph.D. Helsinki Univ., 1963.
Previous Post Assoc. Prof. of Econ. Hist., Jyväskylä Univ., 1971–89.
Current Offices and Honorary Posts Dean, Fac. of Humanities, 1990–; chairman, Board of Finnish Bus. Archives, Mikkeli.
Major Honours Mem., Finnish Acad. of Sciences & Letters, 1984; Honorary Prize, Oulu Hist. Soc., 1986.
Fields of Expertise *Industry Fields:* paper, printing, publishing. *Bus. Dimensions:* entrepreneurs and entrepreneurship. *Scope:* internat. *Period:* twentieth century as a whole. *Teaching:* post grad. *Consultancy:* co. hist.
Publications *Books: Kymin Osakeyhtiö 1918–1939* [The Hist. of the Kymmene Co. 1918–1939] Kuusankoski, 1972, (Swedish translation: Kymmene Aktiebolag 1918–1939); *The Hist. of Star Paper 1875–1960,* Studia Historica Jyväskyläensia 13, 1976; *Suomen Sahateollisuuden Historia* [The Hist. of Sawmills in Finland] Werner Söderström Oy, Helsinki, 1984; *The Far Eastern Telegraphs. The Hist. of Telegraphic Communications between the Far East, Europe and Amer. before the First World War,* Annales Academiae Scientiarum Fennicae B:216, Helsinki, 1981; *Enso-Gutzeit Oy 1872–1992,* Enso Gutzeit Oy, Helsinki, 1992.

Alberty, Július

Prof. of Education, Mateja Bela Univ., Fac. of Humanity & Social Science, Tajovského 40, 975 49 Banská Bystrica, Slovakia. Tel.: 42 88 34555.
Year and Place of Birth 1925, Vysná Pokoradz, Slovakia.
Degrees and Qualifications Ph.D.

(Hist.) Comenius Univ., Bratislava, 1968; Prof., Bratislava Univ., 1990.
Previous Post High School Inspector, Banská Bystrica.
Current Offices and Honorary Posts Science council mem., Matej Bel Univ.; vice-chairman, Slovak Hist. Com.
Fields of Expertise *Industry Fields:* agric., forestry, fishing; metal manufacture; vehicle construction. *Bus. Dimensions:* production management. *Scope:* national. *Period:* medieval; early modern; mid-twentieth century, 1940–70. *Teaching:* undergrad. *Consultancy:* co. hist.
Publications *Books: Ocelovy chlieb z Podbrezovej* [Hist. of Steel Factories in Podbrezová] 1968; *Hist. of TATRA Factory in Bánovce nad Bebravou,* 1975; *Steel Factory in Pohorelá,* 1982; *The Unified Farmer's Co-operative 'Pokrok' in Závada,* 1984.

Aldcroft, Derek H.

Prof. of Econ. Hist., Leicester Univ., Leicester, LE1 7RH, UK. Tel.: 44 533 522589. Fax: 44 533 522200.
Year and Place of Birth 1936, Abergele, UK.
Degrees and Qualifications BA (Econ.) Manchester Univ., 1958; Ph.D. Manchester Univ., 1962.
Previous Post Prof. of Econ. Hist., Sydney Univ., 1973–6.
Current Offices and Honorary Posts Edit. board mem., *The Economic Review;* visiting prof., Anglia Polytechnic Univ.
Fields of Expertise *Industry Fields:* transport and communication; machine tools. *Bus. Dimensions:* management education. *Scope:* national. *Period:* nineteenth century; twentieth century as a whole. *Teaching:* undergrad. *Consultancy:* investment advice.
Publications *Books: The European Economy 1914–1990,* 3rd edn., Routledge, 1993; first edn., 1978;

Education, Training and Econ. Performance 1944–1990, Manchester Univ. Press, 1992; *From Versailles to Wall St 1919–1929*, Allen Lane, 1977.

Alexander, James R.

Chairman, Division of Social Sciences & Prof. of Polit. Science, Division of Social Science, Univ. of Pittsburgh at Johnstown, Johnstown, PA 15904, USA. Tel.: 01 814 269 2983. Fax: 01 814 269 7255.

Year and Place of Birth 1945, Detroit, USA.

Degrees and Qualifications BA Colorado Univ.; MPA Colorado Univ.; Ph.D. Colorado Univ., 1973.

Fields of Expertise *Industry Fields:* metal manufacture. *Bus. Dimensions:* entrepreneurs and entrepreneurship. *Scope:* national. *Period:* nineteenth century. *Teaching:* undergrad. *Consultancy:* co. hist.

Publications *Books: The Johnson Steel St Rail Co.; A Project Report*, Historic Amer. Engineering Record [HAER], Amer.'s Indust. Heritage Project, 1988; *Jaybird; A.J. Moxham and the Manufacture of the Johnson Rail*, Johnstown Area Heritage Assoc., 1991. *Articles:* 'Technological Innovation in Steel Fabrication: Marketing and Production Considerations in the Development of the Johnson Rail', *Bus. & Econ. Hist.*, 2nd ser., vol. 20, 1991, 210–15; 'Technological Innovation in Early St Railways: The Johnson Rail in Retrospective', *Railroad Hist.*, 164, Spring, 1991, 64–85.

Amano, Masatoshi

Prof., Fac. of Econ., Kobe Univ., 2-1 Rokkodai-cho, Nada-ku, Kobe, Japan. Tel.: 81 78 881 1212. Fax: 81 78 882 4838.

Year and Place of Birth 1948, Osaka, Japan.

Degrees and Qualifications Ph.D. (Econ.), Kobe Univ., 1988.

Previous Post Prof., Fac. of Law & Lit., Ehime Univ., 1988–90.

Current Offices and Honorary Posts Council mem., Socio-Econ. Hist. Soc., 1989–90; sec., Socio-Econ. Hist. Soc., 1991–.

Major Honours The 30th Nikkei Prize.

Fields of Expertise *Industry Fields:* food, drink, tobacco; chemicals and allied industries; other manufacturing industries. *Bus. Dimensions:* production management; marketing; small bus. matters; markets and bus. *Scope:* local; regional. *Period:* early modern; eighteenth century; nineteenth century. *Teaching:* undergrad.; post grad. *Consultancy:* co. hist.

Publications *Books: Awa ai keizai-shi kenkyu: Kindai ikoki no sangyo to keizai hatten* [Econ. Hist. of the Awa Indigo Industry: Industry and Econ. Development in the Transition Period to Modern Japan] Tokyo, Yoshikawa Kobunkan, 1986. *Articles:* 'Tokushima-han ryutsu seisaku ni tsuite no ichi kosatsu' [The Econ. Policy of Tokushima-han from the Kansei to the Bunka Era], *Shakai-Keizai-Shigaku* [The Socio-Econ. Hist.] 41(2), 1975; 'Bakumatsu Meiji-shoki ni okeru zenki-teki-shihon no sonzai keitai' [A Study on the Commercial Capital in the Late Tokugawa Period and Early Meiji Era], *The Socio-Econ. Hist.*, 43 (4), 1977; 'Ishin-ki no Tokushima-han Shoho-kata seisaku' [The Econ. Policy of Tokushima-han in the Restoration Period], *Chiho-shi Kenkyu* [J. of Local Hist.] 161, 1979; 'Kindai Nihon no kogyo chitai ni okeru shokko to gijutsu-sha' [A Statistical Study of Factory Workers and Engineers in the Indust. Zones in Modern Japan], *The Kokumin-Keizai Zasshi* [J. of Econ. & Bus. Admin.] 166(1), 1992.

Amatori, Franco

Assoc. Prof. of Econ. Hist., Bocconi Univ., Via Gobbi 5, 20136 Milan, Italy. Tel.: 02 5836 5433. Fax: 02 5836 5439.

Year and Place of Birth 1948, Ancona, Italy.

Degrees and Qualifications Dottorato (Polit. Sc.), Florence Univ., 1973.

Previous Post Lect., Bocconi Univ., Milan, 1985–92.

Current Offices and Honorary Posts Founding mem. & board mem., ASSI (Assoc. for the Study of Bus. Hist., Italy); ed., ASSI annual publication Annali di Storia d'Impresa; board mem., Centre for the Hist. of Enterprise and Innovation, Milan.

Major Honours Fulbright Scholar, 1978–9, Harvard Bus. School.

Fields of Expertise *Industry Fields:* chemicals and allied industries; metal manufacture; vehicle construction; distributive trades. *Bus. Dimensions:* entrepreneurs and entrepreneurship. *Scope:* national. *Period:* twentieth century as a whole. *Teaching:* undergrad. *Consultancy:* co. hist.

Publications *Books: Proprietà e Direzione: La Rinascente (1917–1969)*, F. Angeli Editore, Milan, 1989; *Montecatini 1888–1966: Capitoli di Storia di una Grande Impresa*, with B. Bezza co-ed., Il Mulino Editore, Bologna, 1990; *Impresa e Mercato: Lancia 1906–1969*, Fabbri Editore, Milan, 1992. *Articles:* 'Cicli Produttivi, Tecnologie, Organizzazione del Lavoro: La Siderurgia a Ciclo Integrale dal Piano Autarchico alla Fondazione dell'Italsider (1937–1961)', *Ricerche Storiche*, 10(3), Sept.-Dec., 1980, 557–611; 'Forme d'Impresa in Prospettiva Storica', *Imprese e Mercati*, S. Zamagni ed., UTET, Turin, 1991, 123–54.

Ambrosius, Gerold

Prof., Konstanz Univ., POB 5560, 7750 Konstanz, Germany. Tel.: 49 7531 881.

Year and Place of Birth 1950, Bremerhaven, Germany.

Degrees and Qualifications Dr.rer.pol. Tübingen Univ., 1977; Habilitation Free Univ. Berlin, 1983.

Fields of Expertise *Industry Fields:* gas, electricity, water; transport and communication. *Scope:* local; regional; national. *Period:* nineteenth century; twentieth century as a whole. *Teaching:* undergrad.; post grad. *Consultancy:* corporate strategy.

Publications *Books: Die Durchsetzung der Sozialen Marktwirtschaft in Westdeutschland 1945–1949*, dva, Stuttgart, 1977; *Die öffentliche Wirtschaft in der Weimarer Republik*, Nomes, Baden-Baden, 1984; *Der Staat als Unternehmer. Öffentliche Wirtschaft und Kapitalismus seit dem 19. Jahrhundert*, Vandenhoeck-Rup, Göttingen, 1984; *Sozial- und Wirtschaftsgeschichte Europas im 20. Jahrhundert*, Munich, 1986; *Staat und Wirtschaft im 20. Jahrhundert*, Oldenbourg, Munich, 1990.

Amdam, Rolv Petter

Assoc. Prof., Inst. for Bus. Hist., The Norwegian School of Management, POB 580, N-1301 Sandvika, Norway. Tel.: 47 67 57 05 83. Fax: 47 67 57 08 54.

Year and Place of Birth 1953, Ørskog, Norway.

Degrees and Qualifications Cand. mag. Oslo Univ., 1981; Cand. philol. Oslo Univ., 1985.

Previous Post Research Fellow, Centre for Bus. Hist., The Norwegian National Archives, 1985–8.

Fields of Expertise *Industry Fields:* bricks, pottery, glass, cement; professional and scientific services; pharmaceutical industry. *Bus. Dimensions:* research and development; strategy formation; management education; bus.–state relations. *Scope:* national; internat.; Norway. *Period:* eighteenth century; twentieth century as a whole. *Teaching:* undergrad.; post grad. *Consultancy:* co. hist.

Publications *Books: Vel Blåst: Christiania Glasmagasin og Norsk Glassindustri 1739–1989*, co-auth., Gyldendal, 1989; *En Bedrift i Norsk Skole NKS og Norsk Fjernunder-visning 1914–1989*, co-auth., NKS-Forlaget, 1989; *For egen regning. BI og den økonomisk-administrative Utdanningen 1943–1993*, Universitetsforlaget, 1993. *Articles:* 'Industrial Espionage and the Transfer of Technology to early Norwegian Glass Industry', *Technology Transfer and Scandinavian Industrialisation*, Kristine Bruland ed, Berg Publishers, 1991, 73–93; 'Bus. Admin. in Norway 1936–1990', *Management Education in an Academic Context*, Lars Engwall ed., Uppala Univ. Press, forthcoming.

Andersen, Håkon With

Prof. of Modern Hist., Dept. of Hist., Trondheim Univ., 7055 Dragvoll, Norway. Tel.: 47 73 596440. Fax: 47 73 596441.

Year and Place of Birth 1949, Drammen, Norway.

Degrees and Qualifications M.Sc. (Engineering/Physics) Trondheim Univ., 1973; Dr.philos (Hist.) Trondheim Univ., 1987.

Previous Post Director, Centre for Technology & Soc., Spring 1990–Autumn 1992.

Current Offices and Honorary Posts Com. mem., Soc. for the Hist. of Technology; assoc. ed., *Hist. and Technology*; mem., Royal Norwegian Academy of Science.

Fields of Expertise *Industry Fields:* shipbuilding and marine engineering; metal goods; transport and communication; professional and scientific services; electronics and computers: manufacture. *Bus. Dimensions:* entrepreneurs and entrepreneurship; production management; personnel management; co. admin.; research and development; strategy formation; bus. and technology; small bus. matters; bus.–state relations; markets and bus.; co. culture. *Scope:* local; regional; national; internat.; Norway. *Period:* nineteenth century; twentieth century as a whole. *Teaching:* post grad. *Consultancy:* co. hist.; corporate strategy.

Publications *Books: Fra det Britiske til det Amerikanske Produksjonsideal. Forandringer i Teknologi og Arbeid ved Akers mek. Verksted og i norsk Skipsbyggeindustri 1935–1970* [From the British to the Amer. Ideal of Production. Aker mek Verksted and Norwegian Shipbuilding 1935–1970] Tapir publ., Trondheim, 1987; *Anchor and Balance. Det norske Veritas 1864–1989*, Cappelen forl., Oslo, 1989; *Frankensteins's Dilemma - En Bok om Teknologi, Miljø og Verdier*, with Knut H. Sørensen, Ad Notam, Oslo, 1992. *Articles:* 'Different Problems - Different Ways. Control, Calculation and Mass Data as Focal Points for the Study of a Social Hist. of Computing', *Scientica Yuogoslavica*, 15(1–2), 1989, Zagreb, 1990; 'Laggards as Leaders: Some Reflections on Technological Diffusion in Norwegian Shipping 1870–1940', *Technology Transfer and Scandinavian Industrialisation*, K. Bruland ed., Berg Publ., New York & London, chp. 12, 1991, 307–33.

Applebaum, Herbert A.

Director of Commercial Construction, Hartz Mountain Industries, 482 Country Club Road, Bridgewater, New Jersey 08807, USA. Tel.: 1 201 348 1200. Fax: 1 201 348 1767.
Year of Birth 1925.
Degrees and Qualifications BS (Hist.) Columbia Univ., 1952; MA (Sociology) Gannon Univ., 1971; MA (Anthropology) New York State Univ., Buffalo, 1975; Ph.D. (Anthropology) New York State Univ., Buffalo, 1979.
Previous Post Ed., *Anthropology of Work Rev.*, 1986–91.
Fields of Expertise *Industry Fields:* construction. *Bus. Dimensions:* entrepreneurs and entrepreneurship; production management; co. culture; bus. organization; bus. and technology. *Scope:* national; internat.; USA. *Period:* ancient; medieval; early modern; eighteenth century; nineteenth century; twentieth century as a whole. *Teaching:* undergrad. *Consultancy:* construction management.
Publications *Books: Royal Blue: The Culture of Construction Workers*, Holt, Rinehart & Winston, New York, 1980; *Work in non-Market Soc.*, State Univ. of New York Press, Albany, 1984; *Work in Market and Indust. Soc.*, State Univ. of New York Press, Albany, 1984; *Perspectives in Cultural Anthropology*, State Univ. of New York Press, Albany, 1987; *The Concept of Work: Ancient Medieval and Modern*, State Univ. of New York Press, Albany, 1992.

Arana, Ignacio

Prof. Titular, Dept. Modern Hist., Fac. of Philo., Geography and Hist., Pais Vasco Univ., c/ Marqués de Urquijo s/n, 01006 Vitoria, Spain. Tel.: 34 45 139811. Fax: 34 45 138227.
Year and Place of Birth 1953, San Sebastián, Spain.
Degrees and Qualifications Licenciado en Filosofía y Letras Navarra Univ., 1978; Ph.D. (Hist.) Navarra Univ., 1984.
Current Offices and Honorary Posts Pres., Soc. for Hist. Studies, Navarra; mem., Econ. Hist. Assoc.; mem., Contemporary Hist. Assoc.; mem., Estudios Vascos Soc. .
Fields of Expertise *Industry Fields:* metal manufacture. *Bus. Dimensions:* entrepreneurs and entrepreneurship; bus.–state relations. *Scope:* regional; national. *Period:* nineteenth century; early twentieth century. *Teaching:* undergrad.; post grad. *Consultancy:* corporate strategy.
Publications *Books: La Liga Vizcaína de Productores y la política económica de la Restauración. Sobre las relaciones entre el empresariado y el poder político*, Caja de Ahorros Vizcaína, Bilbao, 1988. *Articles:* 'Algodoneros catalanes y siderometalúgicos vascos ante la reforma arancelaria de 1841: una alianza imposibile', *IX Congreso de Estudios Vascos. Antecedentes de la sociedad vasca actual*, Sociedad de Estudios Vascos, San Sebastián, 1984, 337–9; 'Aproximación al fracaso de un ambicioso proyecto empresarial: Astilleros del Nervión', *Symbolae Ludovico Mitxelena septuagenario oblatae*, Instituto de Historia de la Antiguedad de la UPV, Vitoria, II, 1985, 1291–1301; 'El empresariado siderometalúrgico vasco y la ley de septiembre de 1896', *II Congreso Mundial Vasco. Congreso de Historia de Euskal Herria*, Txertoa, San Sebastián, V, 1988, 39–53; 'La recuperación de un sujeto histórico: el movimiento patronal en la reciente historiografía española', *V Congreso de la Asociación de Historia Económica*, San Sebastián, 29 September–1 October, 1993.

Armstrong, Christopher

Dept. of Hist., York Univ., Downsview, Toronto, M3J 1P3, Canada. Tel.: 1 416 736 5123.
Year and Place of Birth 1942, Toronto, Canada.
Degrees and Qualifications BA Toronto Univ., 1963; BA Balliol College, Oxford Univ., 1965; MA Harvard Univ., 1966; Ph.D. Toronto Univ., 1972 .
Major Honours Sir John A. Macdonald Prize, Canadian Hist. Assoc. for best book in Canadian hist., 1987.
Fields of Expertise *Industry Fields:* gas, electricity, water. *Bus. Dimensions:* bus.–state relations. *Scope:* national; Canada. *Period:* nineteenth century; early twentieth century. *Teaching:* undergrad.; post grad. *Consultancy:* regulatory agencies.
Publications *Books: Monopoly's Moment: The Organization and Regulation of Canadian Utilities*, with H.V. Nelles, Temple Univ. Press, Philadelphia, 1986; reissued Univ. of Toronto Press, Toronto, 1988; *Southern Exposure: Canadian Promoters in Latin Amer. and the Caribbean*, with H.V. Nelles, Univ. of Toronto Press, Toronto, 1988.

Armstrong, Fred H.

Prof. Emeritus, Dept.of Hist., Fac. of Social Science, Univ. of Western Ontario, London, Ontario, N6A 5C2, Canada. Tel.: 1 519 438 8700. Fax: 1 519 661 3868.
Year and Place of Birth 1926, Toronto, Canada.
Degrees and Qualifications BA Toronto Univ., 1949; MA Toronto Univ., 1951; Ph.D. Toronto Univ., 1965.
Previous Post Dept. of Hist., Univ. of Western Ontario, 1963–91.
Current Offices and Honorary Posts Council mem., Champlain Soc.
Major Honours Pres.'s Medal, Univ. of Western Ontario, 1979; Award of Merit, Amer. Soc. for State and Local Hist., 1984.
Fields of Expertise *Bus. Dimensions:* entrepreneurs and entrepreneurship. *Scope:* local; regional; national. *Period:* nineteenth century; twentieth century as a whole. *Teaching:* undergrad.; post grad. *Consultancy:* co. hist.
Publications *Books: Aspects of Nineteenth Century Ontario: Essays Presented to James J. Talman*, co-ed., Univ. of Toronto Press, Toronto, 1974; *Toronto: The Place of Meeting*, Windsor Publications, Los Angeles, 1983; *Handbook of Upper Canadian Chronology*, 2nd edn., Dundurn Press, Toronto, 1985, (1st edn. 1967); *The Forest City: An Illustrated Hist. of London*, Windsor Publications, Los Angeles, 1986; *A City in the Making: Progress, People and Perils in Victorian Toronto*, Dundurn Press, Toronto, 1988.

Armstrong, John

Prof. of Bus. Hist., Thames Valley Univ., St Mary's Road, Ealing, London, W5 5RF, UK. Tel.: 44 81 231 2396. Fax: 44 81 566 1353.
Year and Place of Birth 1944, Portsmouth, UK.
Degrees and Qualifications B.Sc. (Econ.) London Univ., 1969; M.Sc. (Econ.) London School of Econ., 1971.
Previous Post Reader, Polytechnic of West London, 1991–2.
Current Offices and Honorary Posts Hon. treasurer, Bus. Archives Council, UK; ed., *J. of Transport Hist.*; council mem., Econ. Hist. Soc., UK.
Major Honours Transport Trust Prize Essay, 1992.

9

Fields of Expertise *Industry Fields:* transport and communication. *Bus. Dimensions:* markets and bus. *Scope:* national. *Period:* nineteenth century; twentieth century as a whole. *Teaching:* undergrad.; post grad.

Publications *Books: Bus. Documents: Their Origins, Sources and Uses in Hist. Research,* with Stephanie Jones, Mansell, 1987. *Articles:* 'The Role of Coastal Shipping in UK Transport: An Estimate of Comparative Traffic Movements in 1910', *The J. of Transport Hist.,* 3rd ser., 8, 1987, 164–78; 'The Rise and Fall of the Co. Promoter and the Financing of British Industry', *Capitalism in a Mature Economy: Financial Institutions, Capital Exports and British Industry 1870–1939,* J.J. van Helten & Y. Cassis eds., New Bus. Hist. Ser., Edward Elgar, 1990; 'The Development of British Bus. and Co. Law since 1750', *Managing Bus. Archives,* A. Turton ed., Butterworth-Heinemann, 1991; 'Railways and Coastal Shipping in Britain in the later Nineteenth Century: Co-operation and Competition', *On the Move: Essays in Labour and Transport Hist. Presented to Philip Bagwell,* C. Wrigley & J. Shepherd eds., Hambledon Press, 1991.

Asajima, Shoichi

Prof. of Bus. Hist., Fac. of Management and Bus., Senshu Univ., 2-1-1 Higashimita, Tama-ku, Kawasaki City 214, Japan. Tel.: 81 44 911 0515.

Year and Place of Birth 1931, Tokyo, Japan.

Degrees and Qualifications Ph.D. (Econ.), Tokyo Univ., 1972.

Current Offices and Honorary Posts Bus. Hist. Soc. of Japan: council mem., 1979–84; auditor, 1985–86; exec. com. mem., 1987–88; exec. off.,

1989–90; mem., Science Council of Japan, 1991–.

Fields of Expertise *Industry Fields:* insurance, banking, finance. *Bus. Dimensions:* co. finance and accounting. *Scope:* national. *Period:* twentieth century as a whole. *Teaching:* undergrad. *Consultancy:* co. hist.

Publications *Books: Nihon Shintakugyo Hattenshi* [Hist. of Trust Business in Japan] Yuhikaku, 1969; *Senkanki Sumitomo Zaibatsu Keieishi* [Bus. Hist. of Sumitomo Zaibatsu] Tokyo Univ. Press, 1983; *Mitsubishi Zaibatsu no Kinyukozo* [Financial Structure of Mitsubishi Zaibatsu] Ochanomizu-Shobo, 1986; *Zaibatsu Kinyukozo no Hikakukenkyu* [Comparative Study of Financial Structure of Japanese Zaibatsu] Ochanomizu-shobo, 1989; *Honpo Seiho Shikin Unyoshi* [Investment of Life Insurance Companies in Japan] Nihonkeizai hyoronsha, 1991.

Atack, Jeremy

Prof. of Econ. & Research Assoc., National Bureau of Econ. Research, Dept. of Econ., Vanderbilt Univ., Nashville, TN 37235, USA. Tel.: 1 615 322 2871.

Year and Place of Birth 1949, Tadcaster, UK.

Degrees and Qualifications BA Jesus College, Cambridge Univ., 1971; Ph.D. Indiana Univ., 1976.

Previous Post Prof. of Econ., Illinois Univ., to July 1993.

Current Offices and Honorary Posts Trustee, Agric. Hist. Soc.; trustee, Cliometrics Soc.; trustee, Econ. Hist. Assoc.

Major Honours 1987 Theodore Saloutos Prize, Agric. Hist. Soc. for *To Their Own Soil: Amer. Agric. in the Antebellum North.*

Fields of Expertise *Industry Fields:* agric. and manufacture. *Bus.*

Dimensions: structure, organization, technology and economic performance. *Scope:* local; regional; national; UK. *Period:* nineteenth century. *Teaching:* postgrad. and undergrad.

Publications *Books: To Their Own Soil: Amer. Agric. in the Antebellum North*, with Fred Bateman, Iowa State Univ. Press, Ames, IA, 1987. *Articles:* 'Industrial Structure and the Emergence of the Modern Indust. Corporation', *Explorations in Econ. Hist.*, 22(1), Jan., 1985, 29–52; 'Economies of Scale and Efficiencies Gains in the Rise of the Factory in Amer., 1820–1900', *Quantity and Quiddity: Essays in Honor of Stanley L. Lebergott*, Peter Kilby ed., Wesleyan Univ. Press, 1987, 286–335; 'Tenants and Yeoman in the Nineteenth Century', *Agric. Hist.*, 62(3), Summer, 1988, 6–32; 'How Long was the Workday in 1880?', *J. of Econ. Hist.*, with Fred Bateman, 52(1), March, 1992, 129–60.

Austin, Barbara

Assoc. Prof. of Bus. Policy, Fac. of Bus., Brock Univ., Merritville Highway, 500 Glenbridge Avenue, St. Catherines, Ontario, L2S 3A1, Canada. Tel.: 1 416 892 7870. Fax: 1 416 984 4188.

Year and Place of Birth 1943, Fort William, Canada.

Degrees and Qualifications Dip.Ed. Lakehead Univ., 1963; BA McMaster Univ., 1966; MA Bishop's Univ., 1970; MBA Concordia Univ., 1980; Ph.D. Concordia Univ., 1985.

Current Offices and Honorary Posts Chair, Bus. Hist. Group, Administrative Sciences Assoc. of Canada; sec.-treasurer, Management Hist., Acad. of Management.

Major Honours John Mee Prize, Acad. of Management, 1988.

Fields of Expertise *Industry Fields:*

food, drink, tobacco; metal manufacture; textiles; timber, furniture; paper, printing, publishing; insurance, banking, finance. *Bus. Dimensions:* co. admin.; marketing; strategy formation; merger movement and issues; bus. organization; bus. and technology; bus.–state relations; markets and bus.; co. culture. *Scope:* national; internat. *Period:* nineteenth century; twentieth century as a whole. *Teaching:* undergrad. *Consultancy:* co. hist.; corporate strategy.

Publications *Books: The Manager's Job*, Holt Rinehart & Winston, Toronto, 1986. *Articles:* 'Strategy, Structure and Government Policy: An Industry and Case Study', *Acad. of Management Conf. Best Papers*, Frank Hoy ed., 1988, 123–7; 'Managing Marketing in a Commodities Manufacturing Firm', *Bus. & Econ. Hist.*, William Hausman ed., 16, 168–77, Bookcrafters, Fredericksburg, VA, 1989; 'Leadership in the Canadian Iron and Steel Industry', *Essays in Econ. & Bus. Hist.*, Edwin Perkins ed., X, Univ. of Southern California, Los Angeles, 1992, 56–65; 'Structural Adaptation in a Family Firm', *Canadian Papers in Bus. Hist.*, Peter Baskerville ed., 2, Univ. of Victoria Press, Victoria, 1992.

Austin, John

Management Consultant, 39 Meadow Bank Avenue, Sheffield, South Yorks, S7 1PB, UK. Tel.: 44 742 552095.

Year and Place of Birth 1947, Sheffield, UK.

Degrees and Qualifications B.Sc. (Soc. Sci.) Bradford Univ., 1968; Ph.D. Bradford Univ., 1974; MA Lancaster Univ., 1992.

Previous Post Sen. lect., Indust. Studies Unit, Stockbridge College, Sheffield, 1979–88.

Current Offices and Honorary Posts

Sen. lect., Dept. of Retailing & Marketing, Manchester Metropol. Univ.

Fields of Expertise *Industry Fields:* metal goods. *Bus. Dimensions:* bus. organization. *Scope:* regional. *Period:* nineteenth century. *Teaching:* undergrad. *Consultancy:* corporate strategy.

Publications *Books: Steel Town: Dronfield and the Wilson Cammell Co.*, with M. Ford, Scarsdale Publications, 1983.

Badurík, Jozef

Asst. Prof., Dept. of Slovak and Czech Hist., Fac. of Phil., Comenius Univ., Gondova 2, 818 01 Bratislava, Slovakia. Tel.: 42 7 304 111.

Year and Place of Birth 1946, Vinosady, Slovakia.

Degrees and Qualifications Dip., Comenius Univ., 1969; Ph.Dr. Comenius Univ., 1974.

Current Offices and Honorary Posts Director, Dept. of Slovak & Czech Hist., Comenius Univ.; comm. mem., Slovak Assoc. of Historians.

Fields of Expertise *Industry Fields:* agric., forestry, fishing; food, drink, tobacco. *Bus. Dimensions:* research and development. *Scope:* national. *Period:* early modern. *Teaching:* undergrad.; post grad.

Publications *Books: Hist. of Grape Growing in the Malé Karpaty Area (Slovakia) during the 16th Century,* Bratislava, 1990. *Articles:* 'The Wine Bus. in Slovakia during the 16th and 17th Centuries', *K dejinam obchodu na Slovensku,* Bratislava, 1987; 'Grape Growing in Slovakia during the Feudal Period', *Zbornik FFUK-Historica,* 39–40, 1989, Bratislava, 1991, 159–65.

Bamberg, James H.

Group Historian, The British Petroleum Co. plc, BP Archives, Warwick Univ., Coventry, CV4 7AL, UK. Tel.: 44 203 524544. Fax: 44 203 524523.

Year and Place of Birth 1951, London, UK.

Degrees and Qualifications Ph.D. Cantab., 1984.

Previous Post Deputy Group Historian, The British Petroleum Co. plc.

Current Offices and Honorary Posts Visiting Fellow, Reading Univ.

Fields of Expertise *Industry Fields:* coal and petroleum products. *Bus. Dimensions:* multinational bus. *Scope:* global. *Period:* twentieth century as a whole. *Consultancy:* co. hist.

Publications *Books: The Hist. of the British Petroleum Co.: Vol. 2, the Anglo-Iranian Years, 1928–1954,* CUP, forthcoming in 1994. *Articles:* 'The Rationalization of the British Cotton Industry in the Interwar Years', *Textile Hist.,* 19(1), 1988, 83–102.

Bano, Sayeeda S.

Lect., Dept. of Econ., School of Bus. Management, Univ. of Waikato, Private Bag 3105, Hamilton, New Zealand. Tel.: 64 7 856 2889. Fax: 64 7 838 4331.

Year and Place of Birth 1954, India.

Degrees and Qualifications MA Patna Univ.; BA Patna Univ.; M.Phil. (I.R.) Jawaharlal Nehru Univ., New Delhi, 1976; MA (Econ.) Univ. of Alberta, Edmonton, 1978; Ph.D. Simon Fraser Univ., Vancouver, 1985.

Previous Posts Research Economist, New Zealand Inst. of Econ. Research, Wellington, 1985–7; Visiting Prof., Ottawa Univ., 1991–2.

Current Offices and Honorary Posts
Life mem., I.H. Khan Law College, BS City, India; research associate, Global Inst. of Bus. Guidelines, Toronto.

Major Honours Canadian Commonwealth Scholarship; Indian Government Merit Scholarship; B.H.U. Merit Scholarship; Agha Khan Merit Scholarship, Merit Certificate for Essay Competition.

Fields of Expertise *Industry Fields:* food, drink, tobacco; chemicals and allied industries; metal manufacture; textiles; leather; transport and communication; bus. services; trade in services - shipment, travel, bus., government, etc. *Bus. Dimensions:* entrepreneurs and entrepreneurship; marketing; research and development; bus. and technology; multinational bus.; markets and bus. *Scope:* regional; national; internat.; global; Canada; New Zealand; OECD; India; Africa. *Period:* twentieth century as a whole; inter-war years, 1919–39; late twentieth century, 1970–present. *Teaching:* undergrad.; post grad.; internat. relations. *Consultancy:* corporate strategy.

Publications *Books: Intra-Industry Internat. Trade: The Canadian Experience;* The Academic Publishing Group, Avebury, UK, 1991, *A Bibliography of New Zealand Internat. Trade and Finance Research;* Dept. of Trade & Industry, (Econ. Directorate, New Zealand Government), 1986, 'Determinants of Tanzania's Balance of Payments: An Empirical Investigation'; *Readings in Econ. Policy*, L.A. Msambichacah & L.S Chandrase Kher eds., Scandinavian Inst. & Dar-es-Salaam Univ. Press, 1984. *Articles:* 'New Zealand-Australia Intra-Industry Trade', *The Trans-Tasman Trade and Investment*, with P. Lane; A. Bollard & M. Thompson eds., Victoria Univ. Press.

Bansal, Pradeep Kumar

Senior Lect., Dept. of Mechanical Engineering, Univ. of Auckland, Private Bag 92019, Auckland 1, New Zealand. Tel.: 64 9 3737599. Fax: 64 9 3737479.

Year and Place of Birth 1957, Raipur; India.

Degrees and Qualifications M.Sc. Roorkee, India, 1978; Ph.D. Indian Inst. of Technology, Delhi, 1981.

Fields of Expertise *Industry Fields:* mechanical engineering. *Bus. Dimensions:* research and development. *Scope:* internat. *Teaching:* undergrad.; post grad.

Publications *Books: Solar Crop Drying (Vols. 1 and 2),* with Sodha, Kumar & Malik, CRC Press, 1987; *Solar Passive Building: Science & Design,* with Sodha, Kumar & Malik, Pergamon Press, 1986; *Optionization of Steam-based Energy Transport in Distributed Solar Systems,* with Carden, Solar Energy, 1993. *Articles:* 'Performance Evaluation of Environmentally Benign Refrigerants in Heat Pumps 1 & 2: Simulation and Experimental Studies', *Internat. J. Refrigeration*, 15(6), 1992, 340–56.

Banzawa, Ayumu

Researcher, Shiga Univ., Fac. of Econ., 1-1-1 Banba hikone Shiga, Prefecture 522, Japan. Tel.: 81 749 22 5600. Fax: 81 749 27 1132.

Year and Place of Birth 1966, Osaka, Japan.

Previous Post Researcher, Osaka Univ., 1991–2.

Fields of Expertise *Industry Fields:* metal manufacture; transport and communication; insurance, banking, finance. *Bus. Dimensions:* co. finance and accounting; bus. and technology; bus.–state relations; markets and bus.

Scope: regional; national. *Period:* nineteenth century; early twentieth century. *Teaching:* undergrad.

Publications *Articles:* 'The Market Integration in Germany during the 19th Century as the Consequence of the Railway Development', *Osaka Econ. Papers*, 41(1), June 1991.

Barbezat, Daniel

Asst. Prof. of Econ., Dept. of Econ., Amherst College, Amherst, MA 01002, USA. Tel.: 1 413 542 7948. Fax: 1 413 542 2527.

Year and Place of Birth 1960, Johannesburg, South Africa.

Degrees and Qualifications Ph.D. Univ. of Illinois at Champaign, 1988.

Current Offices and Honorary Posts Mem., Bus. Hist. Conf.; mem., Amer. Econ. Assoc.; mem., Econ. Hist. Assoc.; mem., Econ. Hist. Soc.; mem., Cliometric Soc.

Major Honours Best Dissertation 20th Century Internat. Econ. Hist. Meetings, 1990; German Marshall Fund Fellowship; Jean Monnet Fellowship.

Fields of Expertise *Industry Fields:* coal and petroleum products; metal manufacture. *Bus. Dimensions:* multinational bus. *Scope:* internat. *Period:* twentieth century as a whole. *Teaching:* undergrad. *Consultancy:* corporate strategy.

Publications *Articles:* 'Belgian Domestic Steel Cartels and the Rerollers, 1933–38', *Bus. & Econ. Hist.*, 18, 1989, 218–27; 'Co-operation and Rivalry in the Internat. Steel Cartel, 1926–1933', *J. of Econ. Hist.*, XLIX, June, 1989, 435–47; 'A Price for Every Product, Every Place: The Internat. Steel Export Cartel 1933–39', *Bus. Hist.*, 33, Oct., 1991, 68–86.

Barker, T.C.

Prof. Emeritus of Econ. Hist. at London Univ., London School of Econ., Houghton St, London, WC2A 2AE, UK. Tel.: 44 71 955 7110. Fax: 44 71 955 7730.

Year and Place of Birth 1923, Manchester, UK.

Degrees and Qualifications MA Oxford Univ., 1949; Ph.D. Manchester Univ. 1951.

Previous Post Prof. of Econ. Hist., London Univ., 1976–82.

Current Offices and Honorary Posts Pres., Internat. Hist. Congress, 1990–5; chairman, Transport Hist. Research Trust, 1990–; chairman, Advisory Com., Athlone Press.

Fields of Expertise *Industry Fields:* food, drink, tobacco; coal and petroleum products; chemicals and allied industries; mechanical engineering; instrument engineering; electrical engineering; vehicle construction; bricks, pottery, glass, cement; transport and communication; distributive trades; professional and scientific services. *Bus. Dimensions:* entrepreneurs and entrepreneurship; co. finance and accounting; multinational bus.; markets and bus.; co. culture; boardroom issues. *Scope:* local; regional; national. *Period:* early modern; eighteenth century; nineteenth century; twentieth century as a whole. *Teaching:* post grad. *Consultancy:* co. hist.

Publications *Books: A History of London Transport*, with Michael Robbins, 2 vols, Allen & Unwin, 1963–74; *The Glassmakers: Pilkington 1826–1976*, Weidenfeld & Nicolson, 1977; *The Rise and Rise of Road Transport*, with Dorian Gerhold, Macmillan, 1993; *The Megalopolis in Hist.*, with Anthony Sutcliffe, Macmillan, 1993; *A Short, Illustrated and Updated Hist. of Pilkington, 1826–1992*, forthcoming.

Barsness, Richard W.

Executive Director, Iacocca Inst. & Prof. of Management, Lehigh Univ., 111 Research Drive, Iacocca Inst., Lehigh Univ., Bethlehem, PA 18015, USA. Tel.: 1 215 758 5452. Fax: 1 215 758 5423.

Year and Place of Birth 1935, Elbow Lake, USA.

Degrees and Qualifications BS Minnesota Univ., 1957; MA (Hist.) Minnesota Univ., 1958; M.A.P.A. Minnesota Univ., 1960; Ph.D. (Econ. Hist.) Minnesota Univ., 1963 .

Previous Post Dean, College of Bus. & Econ. & Prof. of Management, Lehigh Univ., 1978–92.

Current Offices and Honorary Posts Exec. sec., The Lexington Group in Transportation Hist.

Fields of Expertise *Industry Fields:* transport and communication. *Bus. Dimensions:* bus.–state relations. *Scope:* national. *Period:* twentieth century as a whole. *Teaching:* undergrad. *Consultancy:* co. hist.

Publications *Articles:* 'Policy Changes and Objectives of the Dept. of Transportation', *Q. Rev. of Econ. & Bus.*, IX, Spring, 1969, 63–76; 'Highways and Motor Vehicles: A New Era in Public Policy', *MSU Bus. Topics*, XXI, Spring, 1973, 15–26; 'Maritime Activity and Port Development in the United States since 1900: A Survey', *J. of Transport Hist.*, II, Feb., 1974, 167–84; 'Transportation in Bus. Hist.', *Bus. & Econ. Hist.*, Jeremy Atack ed., 2nd ser., XI, Bureau of Bus. & Econ. Research, Urbana, Illinois, 1982, 1–10, 1982 Pres. Address presented at the 28th annual meeting of the Bus. Hist. Conf.; 'Alan S. Boyd', 'Ben W. Heineman', 'Henry E. Huntingdon' and 'Hays T. Watkins', *Railroads in the Age of Regulation, 1900–1980*, biographical essays, Keith L. Bryant Jr. ed., Bruccoli Clark Layman, Columbia, SC, 1988, 38–42, 193–7, 219–22, 462–6.

Bartl, Július

Director, Dept. for Slovak & General Hist., Comenius Univ. of Bratislava, Dept. for Slovak & General Hist., Fac. of Education, Moskovská 3, 811 08 Bratislava, Slovakia. Tel.: 42 7 221 124/42 7 224 034.

Year and Place of Birth 1937, Zilina, Slovakia.

Degrees and Qualifications Ph.Dr. Comenius Univ. Bratislava, 1959; C.Sc. Acad. of Science Bratislava, 1968.

Previous Post Director of Archives, Comenius Univ., Bratislava, 1964–92.

Current Offices and Honorary Posts Com. mem., Slovak Hist. Soc., Bratislava; com. mem., Slovak Soc. for the Hist. of Science & Technology.

Major Honours Krizkova Medal, 1979, Ministry of Home Affairs, Archives Dept.

Fields of Expertise *Industry Fields:* agric., forestry, fishing; metal manufacture; metal goods; textiles; leather; transport and communication; drink. *Bus. Dimensions:* bus.–state relations. *Scope:* local; national; internat.; Austria; Slovakia; Hungary. *Period:* medieval. *Teaching:* undergrad.

Publications *Articles:* 'Bratislavsky obchod v stredoveku', *Historica*, J. of Fac. of Arts, CU, 21, 1970, 87–112; 'The Polit. and Social Situation in Slovakia at the Turning Point of the 14th and 15th Centuries and the Reign of Sigismund of Luxembourg', *Studia Historica Slovaca*, 9, 1979, 41–84; 'Dekréty Král'a Zigmunda z Roku 1405 a ich Vyznam pri Formovaní Mestianskeho Stavu v Uhorsku', *Historicky Casopis*, 40, 1982, Bratislava, 281–96; 'K Problému sociálnej Struktúry mestianstva v stredovekych Mestách na Slovensku', *Struktura Feudální Spolecnosti na Území Ceskoslovenska a Polska do prelomu 15. a 16. Století*, ed., Inst. of Hist. of the Czechoslovak Acad. of Sciences, Prague, 1984, 241–69;

'Obchod Trencína za Feudalizmu do Konca 16. Storocia', *Trencín, Remeslá, Tlaciarne, Architektúra*, M. Sismis ed., Bratislava, 1985, 116–33.

Bartlová, Alena

Leading Woman of Historic Science, Historicky Ústav SAV, Klemensova 19, 813 64 Bratislava, Slovakia. Tel.: 42 7 326321/42 7 325753.
Year and Place of Birth 1939, Bratislava, Slovakia.
Degrees and Qualifications Ph.Dr. J.A. Komensky Univ., Bratislava, 1962; C.Sc. Acad. of Science, Bratislava, 1968.
Current Offices and Honorary Posts Mem., Slovak Hist. Soc.
Major Honours Priceworthy Scientist, Slovak Acad. of Science, 1989.
Fields of Expertise *Industry Fields:* agric., forestry, fishing; food, drink, tobacco; textiles; gas, electricity, water; public admin. and defence. *Scope:* national. *Period:* inter-war years, 1919–39.
Publications *Books: Dejiny Slovenska Vol. V*, Veda, Vydavatelstvo SAV, Bratislava, 1985; *Andrej Hlinka*, ed., Obzor, Bratislava, 1991. *Articles:* 'Integr. proces ceskoslov. ekonomiky, 1918–1939', *Historicky Casopis*, 36(3), 1988, 360–72; 'K dejinám potravinárskeho priemyslu v r. 1918–1938', *Historicky Casopis*, 37(2), 1989, 250–73; 'Regionalizmus na Slovensku', *Ekonomicky Casopis*, 39(10), 1991, 772–85.

Barty-King, Hugh

Social & industrial historian & author, Holgate House, Ticehurst, Wadhurst, Sussex, TN5 7AA, UK. Tel.: 44 580 200557.
Year and Place of Birth 1914, London, UK.

Degrees and Qualifications BA Cambridge Univ., 1935.
Fields of Expertise *Period:* medieval; early modern; eighteenth century; nineteenth century; twentieth century as a whole; early twentieth century; inter-war years, 1919–39; mid-twentieth century, 1940–70; late twentieth century, 1970–present. *Consultancy:* co. hist.
Publications *Books: The Baltic Exchange, the Hist. of a Unique Market*, Hutchinson Benham, 1977; *Girdle Round the Earth, Cable and Wireless and Predecessors 1851–1979*, Heinemann, 1979; *The AA, the Story of the Automobile Assoc. 1905–1980*, AA, 1980; *HMSO the first 200 years of Her Majesty's Stationery Office 1786–1986*, HMSO, 1986; *Water: The Book, the Story of Britain's Fresh Water Supply & Sewerage*, Quiller Press, 1992.

Barzdevica, Margarita

Jr. Research Assoc., Dept. of Hist., Inst. of Latvian Hist. at the Latvian Univ., 19 Turgenew St, 1518 Riga, Latvia. Tel.: 7 132 226791.
Year and Place of Birth 1964, Riga, Latvia.
Degrees and Qualifications Grad. (Fac. of Hist.) Latvian Univ., 1987.
Previous Post Asst., Inst. of Latvian Hist., Latvian Acad. of Sciences, 1987–91.
Fields of Expertise *Industry Fields:* agric., forestry, fishing; food, drink, tobacco. *Scope:* local; national. *Period:* early modern; eighteenth century.

Baskerville, Peter A.

Assoc. Prof., Chair, Dept. of Hist., Univ. of Victoria, POB 1700, Victoria, British Columbia, V8X 2Y2, Canada. Tel.: 1 604 598 1092/1 604 721 7381.

Fax: 1 604 721 8772.

Year and Place of Birth 1943, Toronto, Canada.

Degrees and Qualifications BA Toronto Univ., 1965; MA Queen's Univ., 1969; Ph.D. Queen's Univ., 1973.

Current Offices and Honorary Posts Edit. board, *Histoire Sociale/Social Hist.*.

Fields of Expertise *Industry Fields:* transport and communication; insurance, banking, finance. *Bus. Dimensions:* entrepreneurs and entrepreneurship; co. finance and accounting; co. admin.; bus. organization; small bus. matters; bus.–state relations. *Scope:* national; internat. *Period:* nineteenth century; early twentieth century. *Teaching:* undergrad.; post grad.

Publications *Books: Bank of Upper Canada*, ed., Champlain Soc./Univ.of Carleton Press, 1987; *Canadian Papers in Bus. Hist.*, ed., vol. 1, Univ. of Victoria, 1990; *Canadian Papers in Bus. Hist.*, ed., vol. 2, Univ. of Victoria, 1993. *Articles:* 'Imperial Agendas & "Disloyal Collaborators": Decolonization and the J.S. Macdonald Ministries, 1862–64', *Old Ontario: Essays in Honour of J.M.S. Careless*, D.Keane et al. eds, Toronto, 1990, 234–56; 'Transportation, Social Change and State Formation in Upper Canada, 1841–64', *Colonial Leviathan: State Formation in mid-Nineteenth Century Ontario*, A. Greer et al. eds., Toronto, 1991.

Bateman, Fred

Prof. and Head of Dept. of Econ., Georgia Univ., Athens, GA 30602, USA. Tel.: 1 706 542 3692. Fax: 1 706 542 3376.

Place of Birth USA.

Degrees and Qualifications BA Tulane Univ.; MA North Carolina Univ.; Ph.D. Tulane Univ.

Previous Post Prof. of Bus. Econ.,

School of Bus., Indiana Univ., Bloomington, Indiana, 1964–91.

Current Offices and Honorary Posts Edit. board, *Managerial and Decision Econ.*; edit. board, *Agric. Hist.*.

Major Honours Theodore Saloutos Prize for best book in US agric. hist., 1987, for *To Their Own Soil*; selected by Choice as an Outstanding Academic Book in the US for 1987.

Fields of Expertise *Industry Fields:* agric., forestry, fishing; other manufacturing industries. *Bus. Dimensions:* bus. organization; industrialization. *Scope:* national. *Period:* nineteenth century. *Teaching:* undergrad.; post grad.

Publications *Books: A Deplorable Scarcity*, with Thomas Weiss, Univ. of North Carolina Press, 1981; *To Their Own Soil*, with Jeremy Atack, in the Henry A. Wallace Series on Amer. Agric. Hist., Iowa State Univ. Press, 1987. *Articles:* 'Market Structure before the Age of Big Bus.: Concentration and Profit in Early Southern Manufacturing', *The Bus. Hist. Rev.*, with Thomas Weiss, XLIV(3), autumn, 1975; 'The "Egalitarian Ideal" and the Distribution of Wealth in Northern Agric. Community: A Backward Look', *Rev. of Econ. & Stats.*, with Jeremy Atack, LXIII(1), Feb., 1981; 'How Long was the Workday in 1880?', *J. of Econ. Hist.*, with Jeremy Atack, 52(1), Mar., 1992.

Baughman, James L.

School of Journalism and Mass Communication, Univ. of Wisconsin-Madison, 821 Univ. Ave., Room 5115, Madison, WI 53706, USA. Tel.: 1 608 263 4898. Fax: 1 608 262 2150.

Year and Place of Birth 1952, Warren, USA.

Degrees and Qualifications BA Harvard Univ., 1974; MA Columbia Univ., 1975; M.Phil. 1977; Ph.D.

1981.

Major Honours Frank Luther Mott-Kappa Tau Alpha Award for best book in journalism Hist. for *Henry R. Luce and the Rise of the Amer. News Media*, published in 1987, National Journalism Scholarship Soc.; Cathy Covert Award for best article in mass communication hist., 1985, Assoc. of Education in Journalism–Hist. Division.

Fields of Expertise *Industry Fields:* mass media. *Bus. Dimensions:* bus.–state relations; markets and bus. *Scope:* national. *Period:* twentieth century as a whole. *Teaching:* undergrad.; post grad.

Publications *Books: Television's Guardians: The Federal Comunications Commission and the Polit. of Programming, 1958–1967*, Univ. of Tennessee Press, Knoxville, 1985; *Henry R. Luce and the Rise of the Amer. News Media*, Twayne, Boston, 1987; *Republic of Mass Culture: Journalism, Filmmaking and Broadcasting since 1941*, Johns Hopkins Univ. Press, 1992. *Articles:* 'Television in the Golden Age: An Entrepreneurial Experiment', *Historian*, 47, Feb., 1985, 175–95.

Major Honours Rudolf-Kellermann Prize for Technological Hist., 1983.

Fields of Expertise *Industry Fields:* vehicle construction; paper, printing, publishing; gas, electricity, water; transport and communication; bus. and the environment. *Bus. Dimensions:* bus. and technology. *Scope:* national. *Period:* early modern; eighteenth century; nineteenth century; twentieth century as a whole. *Teaching:* post grad.

Publications *Books: Wind- und Wasserkraft. Die Nutzung regenerierbarer Energiequellen in der Geschichte*, ed., Düsseldorf, 1989; *Zum Stand der Papiergeschichtsforschung.*, with Wolfgang Schlieder & Rolf Stümpel co-eds., Frankfurt/Bern/New York/Paris, 1993; *Quellen zur Umweltgeschichte*, with Ulrich Troitzsch, Göttingen, 1993. *Articles:* 'Die Papiermühle. Vorindustrielle Papiermacherei auf dem Gebiet des alten deutschen Reiches - Technologie, Arbeitsverhältnisse, Umwelt', *Geschichte und ihre Hilfswissenschaften*, 3rd ser., 260, Europäische Hochschulschriften, Frankfurt/Bern/New York/Paris, 1987.

Bayerl, Günter J.

Lect. and Scientific Colleague, Inst. of Social and Econ. Hist., Hamburg Univ., Dept. of Technology & Social Hist., Allendeplatz 1, 20146 Hamburg 13, Germany. Tel.: 49 40 4123 4351/040 4123 4351. Fax: 49 40 4123 4506.

Year and Place of Birth 1946, Augsburg, Germany.

Degrees and Qualifications MA Hamburg Univ., 1978; Dr.phil. Hamburg Univ., 1984.

Current Offices and Honorary Posts Vice-pres. Johann Beckmann-Gesellschaft.

Beaud, Claude

Lect., Paris-Sorbonne Univ., 1 rue Victor Cousin, 75230 Paris Cedex 05, France. Tel.: 33 1 45 25 08 33.

Year and Place of Birth 1929, Villeneuve, France.

Degrees and Qualifications Agrégé d'Histoire Paris Univ.-Sorbonne, 1965; maître de conférences Paris Univ.-Sorbonne, 1985.

Previous Post Maître Asst., Paris Univ.-Sorbonne, 1982.

Current Offices and Honorary Posts Préparation à l'Agrégation d'Histoire, 1989–93.

Major Honours Palmes Académiques (Chevalier).

Fields of Expertise *Industry Fields:* metal manufacture; mechanical engineering; electrical engineering; shipbuilding and marine engineering; insurance, banking, finance; armament industry (artillery)armament industry (artillery). *Bus. Dimensions:* entrepreneurs and entrepreneurship; production management; co. finance and accounting; personnel management; co. admin.; research and development; bus. and technology; multinational bus.; bus.–state relations; markets and business, Schneider Group. *Scope:* local; national; internat.; global; Russia before 1914; Czechoslovakia 1919–39; Le Creusot. *Period:* nineteenth century; twentieth century as a whole; late twentieth century, 1970–present. *Teaching:* Hist. 'Agrégation' examination preparation; Preparation for the Concours d'Agrégation d'Histoire. *Consultancy:* co. hist.

Publications *Books: Chocs et Entrechocs de l'Économie mondiale (1973–1987)*, ed., Sedes, 1988. *Articles:* 'La Stratégie de l'Investissement dans la Societé Schneider e Companie (1894–1914)', *Entreprises et Entrepreneurs XIX–XXième Siècles*, Presses de l'Université de Paris-Sorbonne, 7, 1983, (Congrés de l'Assoc. Fran. Hist. Econ., 1980); 'The Interests of the "Union Européenne"', *Internat. Bus. and Central Europe (1918–1939)*, A. Teichova ed., Leicester Univ. Press, 1983, 375–97; 'De l'Expansion internationale à la Multinationale: Schneider en Russie (1896–1914)', *Histoire, Économie e Société*, Sedes, 4, 1985, 575–602; 'Investments and Profits of the Multinational Schneider Group (1894–1943)', *Multinational Enterprise in Hist. Perspective*, A. Teichova ed., CUP, 1986, (9th Internat. Econ. Hist. Congress, Berne), 87–102.

Beck, William O.

Pres., Lakeside Writer's Group, 435 E. Main St, Suite K-4, Greenwood, IN 46143, USA. Tel.: 1 317 889 9813. Fax: 1 317 889 4382.

Year and Place of Birth 1945, Laurium, Michigan, USA.

Degrees and Qualifications BA (Hist.) Marian College, Indianapolis, 1971; grad. work, Amer. Hist., North Dakota Univ., 1971–2.

Previous Post Sen. Writer, Public Affairs Dept., Minnesota Power, Duluth, Minnesota, 1981–8.

Current Offices and Honorary Posts Admin. com. mem., Indianapolis (Indiana) Religious Hist. Project, 1992–3.

Fields of Expertise *Industry Fields:* gas, electricity, water. *Bus. Dimensions:* co. culture. *Scope:* national. *Period:* twentieth century as a whole. *Consultancy:* co. hist.

Publications *Books: Light Across the Prairies: An Illustrated Hist. of Northwestern Public Service Co.*, The Co., Huron, SD, 1989; *At Your Service: An Illustrated Hist. of Houston Lighting & Power Co.*, The Co., Houston, Texas, 1990; *The Service People: An Illustrated Hist. of Midwest Energy Co.*, The Co., Sioux City, Iowa, 1991; *Methodist Hospital: A Tradition of Caring*, The Co., Minneapolis, MN, 1992; *The Modakonians: Energizers of the Prairie - An Illustrated Hist. of MDU Resources Group Inc.*, The Co., Bismarck, ND, 1992.

Beltran, Alain

CNRS Researcher, Inst. of Modern Hist., 44 rue de l'Amiral Mouchez, 75014 Paris, France. Tel.: 33 1 45809046. Fax: 33 1 45654350.

Year and Place of Birth 1951,

France.

Degrees and Qualifications
Agrégation (Hist.); DEA; Thèse d'Etat.
Current Offices and Honorary Posts
Mem., Assoc. for the Hist. of
Electricity.
Fields of Expertise *Industry Fields:*
gas, electricity, water; transport and
communication; nuclear engineering.
Bus. Dimensions: entrepreneurs and
entrepreneurship; bus. and technology;
bus.–state relations; bus. values; co.
culture. *Scope:* national; internat.;
France; Europe (EC)European community. *Period:* nineteenth century; twentieth century as a whole. *Teaching:*
post grad. *Consultancy:* co. hist.

Publications *Books: Histoire(s) de
l'E.D.F. Comment se sont prises les
Décisions de 1946 à nos Jours,* with
J.F. Picard & M. Bungener, Editions
Dunod, Paris, 1985; *Culture
d'Entreprise et Histoire* [Corporate
Culture and Hist.] with Michèle
Ruffat, Editions d'Organisation, Paris,
1991; *Le Noir et le Bleu, 40 ans d'histoire du Gaz de France* [Black and
Blue. Forty Years of the Hist. of Gaz
de France] with J.P. Williot, Belfond,
Paris, 1992. *Articles:* 'L'Historien
entre Mémoire et Futur' [The Historian
between Memory and Future], *Revue
Pour* (Cultures Techniques, Entreprises
et Société) 122/123, Jul.-Sept., 1989,
57–62; 'Competitiveness and
Electricity: Electricité de France since
1946', *Technological Competitiveness
(Contemporary and Hist. Perspectives
on the Electrical, Electronics and
Computer Industries),* William Aspray
ed., IEE Press, New York, 1993,
315–26.

Benaul, Josep M.

Lect., Dept. of Econ. and Econ. Hist.,
Fac. of Econ. Science, Universitat
Autònoma de Barcelona, Edifici B,
08193-Bellaterra (Barcelona), Spain.

Tel.: 34 93 5811200. Fax: 34 93
5812012.
Year and Place of Birth 1951,
Sabadell, Spain.
Degrees and Qualifications BA
Autonomous Univ. Barcelona 1974;
Ph.D. Autonomous Univ. Barcelona,
1991.
Previous Post Director, Arxiu
Històric de Sabadell, 1986–1991.
Fields of Expertise *Industry Fields:*
textiles. *Bus. Dimensions:* bus. and
technology. *Scope:* national. *Period:*
nineteenth century. *Teaching:* under-
grad. *Consultancy:* co. hist.
Publications *Books: Guerra i Canvi
Econòmic. L'Impacte de la Guerra del
Francès en la Indústria Tèxtil Lanera
de Sabadell i Terrassa, 1808–1814,*
Fundació Bosch i Cardellach, 1993.
Articles: 'La Comercialització dels
Texits de Llana en la Cruilla desl Segles
XVIII i XIX. L'Exemple de l Fàbrica
de Terrassa Anton y Joaquim Sagrera,
1792–1807', *Arraona,* 2, 1988, 35–47;
'La Llana', *Historia Econòmica de la
Catalunya Contemporània,* vol. III,
Fundació Enciclopédia Catalana, 1991,
87–158; 'Los Orígenes de la Empresa
Textil Lanera en Sabadell y Terrassa en
el Siglo XVIII', *Revista de Historia
Indust.,* 1, 1992, 39–62; 'Aproximació
a la Història de la Indústria de
Terrassa, 1870–1939. De la
Industrialització a l'Economia de
Guerra', *Terrassa, Cent Anys a Ritme
de Llançadora,* Museu Textil, 1993.

Bender, Henning

Director, The Hist. Archives of
Aalborg, Peter Baggesgade 5, 9000
Aalborg, Denmark. Tel.: 45 98 12 57
93. Fax: 4598 10 22 48.
Year and Place of Birth 1944,
Copenhagen, Denmark.
Degrees and Qualifications MA
Copenhagen Univ., 1971.
Previous Post Research Fellow,

Copenhagen Univ., 1971–4.

Fields of Expertise *Industry Fields:* all industry fields. *Bus. Dimensions:* all industrial fields. *Scope:* regional. *Period:* eighteenth century; nineteenth century; twentieth century as a whole. *Teaching:* external examiner in bus. hist. at the five Danish universities.

Publications *Books: Aalborgs Industrielle Udvikling 1735–1940* [The Indust. Development of Aalborg 1735–1940] The Hist. Archives of Aalborg, 1987; *Danish Emigration to New Zealand,* The Hist. Archives of Aalborg, 1990; *Danish Emigration to Canada,* The Hist. Archives of Aalborg, 1991; *Danish Emigration to the USA,* The Hist. Archives of Aalborg, 1992.

Bennett, Neville

Senior Lect., Dept. of Hist., Univ. of Canterbury, Private Bag 4800, Christchurch, New Zealand. Tel.: 64 3 348 2233/64 3 3667 001. Fax: 64 3 3642 999.

Year and Place of Birth 1940, Lincoln, UK.

Degrees and Qualifications B.Sc. (Econ.) London School of Econ., 1961; Ph.D. London School of Econ. 1966.

Previous Post Lect., Hong Kong Univ., 1963–71.

Current Offices and Honorary Posts Pres., NZASIA.

Major Honours Japan Foundation Fellow, 1992.

Fields of Expertise *Industry Fields:* agric., forestry, fishing. *Bus. Dimensions:* production management. *Scope:* national; internat.; New Zealand. *Period:* nineteenth century; twentieth century as a whole. *Teaching:* undergrad.

Bergeron, Louis

EHESS Study Director, École des Hautes Études en Sciences Sociales, 54 Bd. Raspail, 75006 Paris, France. Tel.: 33 1 49542525. Fax: 33 1 49542399.

Year and Place of Birth 1929, Strasbourg, France.

Degrees and Qualifications Docteur ès Lettres et Sciences Humaines, Paris I Univ., 1974.

Current Offices and Honorary Posts Pres., Internat. Com. for the Conservation of the Indust. Heritage.

Fields of Expertise *Industry Fields:* textiles; insurance, banking, finance. *Bus. Dimensions:* entrepreneurs and entrepreneurship. *Scope:* local; regional; national. *Period:* nineteenth century; early twentieth century. *Teaching:* post grad.

Publications *Books: Banquiers, Négociants et Manufacturiers Parisiens du Directoire à l'Empire,* Mouton, Paris-La Haye-New York, 1978; *Les Capitalistes Français 1780–1914,* Gallimard-Julliard, Paris, Collection 'Archives', 1978; *Les Rothschild et les Autres,* Perrin, Paris, 1991. *Articles:* 'Permanences et Renouvellement du Patronat Français', *Histoire des Francais XIXe–XXe Siècle,* Yves Lequin, vol. II, Armand Colin, Paris, 1983; 'L'Espace du Capital', *L'Espace Français,* Le Seuil, Paris, 1989.

Berta, Giuseppe

Reader in Econ. Hist., Libero Istituto Universitario C. Cattaneo, C.so Matteotti 22, 21053 Castellanza (Va), Italy. Tel.: 39 331 480747. Fax: 39 331 480746.

Year and Place of Birth 1952, Vercelli, Italy.

Degrees and Qualifications BA (Fac. of Arts) Milan Univ., 1975.

Previous Post Reader in Modern & Contemporary Hist., Libero Istituto Universitario di Bergamo, 1983–6.

Current Offices and Honorary Posts Scientific adviser, Fondazione 'L. Einaudi', Turin.

Major Honours Walter Tobagi Prize for *The Hist. of Indust. Relations*, 1986.

Fields of Expertise *Industry Fields:* mechanical engineering. *Bus. Dimensions:* personnel management. *Scope:* national. *Period:* mid-twentieth century, 1940–70. *Teaching:* undergrad. *Consultancy:* co. hist.

Publications *Books: Le Idee al Potere. A. Olivetti tra la Fabbrica e la Comunità*, Edizioni di Comunità, 1980; *Lavoro, Solidarietà, Conflitti*, Officina Edizioni, 1983; *Capitali in Gioco*, Marsilio, 1990. *Articles:* 'Dalla Manifattura al Sistema di Fabbrica', *Storia d'Italia, Annali*, vol. I, Einaudi, 1978; 'Le Commissioni Interne nella Storia delle Relazioni Industriali alla Fiat', *1944–1956. Le Relazioni Industriali alla Fiat*, vol. III, Fabbri Editore, 1992.

Bigazzi, Duccio

Assoc. Prof. of Indust. Hist., Università degli Studi di Milano, Fac. of Letters & Philo., Via Festa del Perdono, 20100 Milan, Italy. Tel.: 39 2 58308008. Fax: 39 2 58305905.

Year and Place of Birth 1947, Florence, Italy.

Degrees and Qualifications Laurea Università degli Studi Milan, 1976.

Previous Post Researcher, Fac. of Letters & Phil., Università degli Studi, Milan, 1978–92.

Current Offices and Honorary Posts Scientific com. mem., Fondazione ASSI di Storia e Studi sull'Impresa; director, *Anchini e Imprese*.

Fields of Expertise *Industry Fields:* vehicle construction. *Bus. Dimensions:*

bus. and technology. *Scope:* national. *Period:* twentieth century as a whole. *Teaching:* undergrad. *Consultancy:* co. hist.

Publications *Books: Il Portello. Operai, tecnici e imprenditori all'Alfa Romeo 1906–1926*, Angeli, Milan, 1988; *La Storia d'Impresa in Italia. Saggio Bibliografico: 1980–1987*, Angeli, Milan, 1990; *Gli Archivi d'Impresa nell'Area Milanese. Censimento Descrittivo a Cura di Duccio Bigazzi*, Editrice Bibliografica, Milan, 1990.

Blackson, Robert M.

Prof., Dept. of Hist., Kutztown Univ., POB 730, Kutztown, PA 19530–0730, USA. Tel.: 1 215 683 4385. Fax: 1 215 683 4633.

Year and Place of Birth 1944, Greensburg, PA, USA.

Degrees and Qualifications BA Ursinus College, 1966; MA Pennsylvania State Univ., 1969; Ph.D. Pennsylvania State Univ., 1978.

Previous Post Asst. Prof., Dept. of Hist., Pennsylvania State Univ., Altoona Campus, 1970–81.

Current Offices and Honorary Posts Councillor, Pennsylvania Hist. Assoc. (USA).

Fields of Expertise *Industry Fields:* transport and communication; insurance, banking, finance. *Bus. Dimensions:* bus. organization. *Scope:* regional. *Period:* nineteenth century. *Teaching:* undergrad. *Consultancy:* co. hist.

Publications *Articles:* 'Pennsylvania Banks and the Panic of 1819: A Reinterpretation', *J. of the Early Republic*, 9, 1989, 335–58.

Blanken, Ivo J.

Head of Co. Archives, Phillips Internat. B.V., Afd. Historiografie, POB 218, 5600 MD Eindhoven, Netherlands. Tel.: 31 40 757486. Fax: 31 40 756858.
Year and Place of Birth 1946, Roermond, Netherlands.
Degrees and Qualifications Dr.Sociology Tilburg Univ., 1984; Ph.D. Leiden Univ., 1992.
Fields of Expertise *Industry Fields:* electronics and computers: manufacture. *Bus. Dimensions:* multinational bus. *Scope:* internat. *Consultancy:* co. hist.
Publications *Books: Geschiedenis van Philips Electronics, Vol. III, De ontwikkeling van de N.V. Philips Gloeilampen fabrieken tot electrotechisch concern,* Nyhoff, 1992.

Bläsing, Josvhim F.E.

Assoc. Prof. of Econ. and Bus. Hist., Tilburg Univ., Hogeschoollaan 225, POB 90153, 5000 LE Tilburg, Netherlands. Tel.: 31 13 662109. Fax: 31 13 663145.
Year and Place of Birth 1940, Berlin, Germany.
Degrees and Qualifications Ph.D. (Econ. Sc.).
Fields of Expertise *Industry Fields:* electrical engineering. *Bus. Dimensions:* entrepreneurs and entrepreneurship. *Scope:* internat. *Period:* nineteenth century; twentieth century as a whole. *Teaching:* undergrad. *Consultancy:* co. hist.
Publications *Books: Das goldene Delta und sein eisernes Hinterland 1815–1851. Von niederländisch-preußischen zu deutsch-niederländischen Wirtschaftsbeziehungen,* H.E. Stenfert Kroese B.V., Leiden, 1973; *Inleiding tot de elementaire economis-*
che geschiedenis. Een bijdrage aan de economisch-historische vorming van economiestudenten, Wolters-Noordhoff, Groningen, 1980; *Op het spoor van de Körver. Ontstaan, groei en transformaties van de Brabantse familie-onderneming Hendrix' Farieken Boxmeer 1979/1930, bedrijfsgeschiedkundig bekeken,* Martinus Nijhoff, Leiden, 1986; *Hoofdliunen van de moderne bedrijfsgeschiedenis,* Martinus Nijhoff, Leiden, 1990; *Mensen en spanningen. Sociaaleconomische geschieenis van de N.V. Provinciale Noordbrabantsche Elektriciteits-Maatschappij 1914–1985,* Martinus Nijhoff, Leiden, 1992.

Blicksilver, Jack

Prof. of Econ. Emeritus, Georgia State Univ., 82 Univ. Plaza, POB 4038, Atlanta, GA 30302-4038, USA. Tel.: 1 404 525 6519.
Year and Place of Birth 1926, Brooklyn, USA.
Degrees and Qualifications MA Northwestern Univ., 1951; Ph.D. Northwestern Univ., 1955.
Previous Post Georgia State Univ., 1963–91.
Fields of Expertise *Industry Fields:* textiles; clothing and footwear; transport and communication; insurance, banking, finance. *Bus. Dimensions:* entrepreneurs and entrepreneurship; merger movement and issues. *Scope:* regional; national. *Period:* nineteenth century; early twentieth century. *Teaching:* undergrad.; post grad.
Publications *Books: Cotton Manufacturing in the Southeast. An Hist. Analysis,* Georgia State College of Bus. Admin., Monograph, 1959; *Views on U.S. Econ. and Bus. Hist: Molding the Mixed Enterprise Economy,* Georgia State Univ. Press, 1984; *Defenders and Defense of Big Bus. in the United States, 1880–1900,* Garland

Pub. Inc., 1985. *Articles:* 'Kinship and Friendship in the Emergence of a Family-controlled Southern Enterprise', *Entrepreneurs in Cultural Context*, S. Greenfield, A. Strickon & R. Aubey eds., Univ. of New Mexico Press, 1979, 89–121; 'Apparel and Other Textile Products', *Handbook of Amer. Bus. Hist.*, David O. Whitten ed., Greenwood Press, 1990.

Boje, Per

Lect., Inst. of Hist., Odense Univ., Campusvej 55, 5230 Odense M, Denmark. Tel.: 45 66 15 86 96-2138. Fax: 45 65 93 29 74.

Year and Place of Birth 1946, Odense, Denmark.

Degrees and Qualifications MA Copenhagen Univ., 1972; Dr.Phil. Odense Univ., 1977.

Current Offices and Honorary Posts Co-ed., *Scandinavian Econ. Hist. Rev.*.

Fields of Expertise *Industry Fields:* food, drink, tobacco; mechanical engineering; electrical engineering. *Bus. Dimensions:* entrepreneurs and entrepreneurship; co. finance and accounting. *Scope:* local; regional; national; Denmark. *Period:* nineteenth century; twentieth century as a whole. *Teaching:* undergrad.; post grad. *Consultancy:* co. hist.

Publications *Books: Det industrielle miljø 1840–1940. Kilder og litteratur*, Akdemisk Forlag, Copenhagen, 1976; *Moderne tider. Odense bys historie 1868–1914*, with H. Nielsen, Odense Universitetsforlag, 1985. *Articles:* 'Danske provinskøbmænds vareomsætning og kapitalforhold 1815–47', Universitetsforlaget Aarhus, 1977, dissertation, with English summary; 'Working Class Housing in Odense 1750–1914', *Scandinavian Econ. Hist. Rev.*, with Hans Chr. Johansen, XXXIV(2), Bergen, 1986, 135–52; 'A Career Approach to Entrepreneurship:

The Case of Thomas B. Thrige', *Bus. Hist.*, 35(2), London, 1993, 33–44.

Bolton, Alfred A.

Prof. of Bus. Admin., Averett College, 420 W. Main St, Danville, Virginia 24541, USA. Tel.: 1 804 791 5605. Fax: 1 804 791 5637.

Year and Place of Birth 1926, Thorold, Canada.

Degrees and Qualifications BS West Virginia Univ., 1951; MA Goddard Coll., 1980; DBA Nova Univ., 1985.

Previous Post Prof. of Bus. Admin., 1990–3.

Current Offices and Honorary Posts Chairman, Management Hist. Div., Acad. of Management, 1987.

Fields of Expertise *Industry Fields:* glass; communication. *Bus. Dimensions:* co. culture. *Scope:* regional. *Period:* early twentieth century. *Teaching:* undergrad.; post grad. *Consultancy:* co. hist. Hawthorne Studies 1924–33.

Publications *Articles:* 'Hawthorne a half Century later: Relay Assembly Participants Remember', *J. of Management*, 9(2), Greenwood, Bolton & Greenwood, 1983, 217–31; 'Herman Hollheith: Inventor, Manager, Entrepreneur - a Centennial Remembrance', *J. of Management*, 15(4), Biles, Bolton & Dire, 1989, 603–15; 'Chester I Barnard: A Dimension of the Executive', *Internat. J. of Management*, 8(1), Biles & Bolton, Mar., 1991.

Bonin, Hubert

Maître de Conférences d'Histoire économique contemporaine, Michel de Montaigne-Bordeaux III Univ., Espl. Michel-Montaigne, Domaine Universitaire, 33405 Talence Cedex, France. Tel.: 33 56 84 50 50. Fax: 33

56 84 50 90.

Year and Place of Birth 1950, France.

Degrees and Qualifications ancien élève de l'Ecole normale supérieure de St-Cloud; agrégé (Hist.); docteur de troisième cycle (Econ. Hist.); thèse de doctorat d'Etat (in progress: 'Les Banques françaises dans l'entre-deux-guerres') .

Fields of Expertise *Industry Fields:* . *Bus. Dimensions:* entrepreneurs and entrepreneurship; co. finance and accounting; financial and banking hist. *Scope:* regional; national; internat. *Period:* nineteenth century; twentieth century as a whole. *Teaching:* post grad. *Consultancy:* co. hist.

Publications *Books: C.F.A.O. (Compagnie Française de l'Afrique Occidentale). Cent Ans de Compétition (1887–1987)*, éditions Economica, 1987; *Suez. Du Canal à la Finance (1858–1987)*, Éditions Economica, 1987; *L'Argent en France depuis 1990. Banquiers, Financiers et Épargnants dans la Vie Économique et Politique*, Éditions Masson, 1989; *Histoire de la Société Bordelaise de C.I.C. (1880–1990)*, éditions L'Horizon Chimérique, Bordeaux, 1991; *La Banque et les Banquiers en France du Moyen Age à nos Jours*, collection Références, éditions Larousse, 1992.

Bonke, Jens

Assoc. Prof., Copenhagen Univ., Inst. of Econ., Studiestræde 6, 1455 Copenhagen K, Denmark. Tel.: 45 35323023. Fax: 45 35323000.

Year and Place of Birth 1948, Nykøbing F., Denmark.

Degrees and Qualifications MA Copenhagen Univ., 1965.

Previous Post Senior Research Fellow, Inst. of Econ., Copenhagen, 1988–90.

Fields of Expertise *Industry Fields:*

food, drink, tobacco; building; households. *Scope:* national; internat. *Period:* late twentieth century, 1970–present. *Teaching:* post grad.

Publications *Articles:* 'Distribution of Econ. Resources: Implications of Including Household Production?', *Rev. of Income & Wealth*, 38(3), Sept., 1992, 281–93; 'Life-Time Income of Men and Women - the Case in Denmark', *J. of Consumer Studies and Home Econ.*, 16, 1992, 303–16; 'Factotum - husholdningernes produktion' [Factotum - Household Production], dissertation, Copenhagen; 'Diskrimination - lønforskelle mellem kvinder og mænd' [Discrimination - Wage Differentials between Women and Men], *Nationaløkonomisk Tidsskrift*, 13, 1992, 169–77.

Boot, H.M.

Sen. Lect. in Econ. Hist., Dept. of Econ. Hist., Fac. of Econ. and Commerce, Australian National Univ., POB 4, Canberra, ACT 2601, Australia. Tel.: 61 6 236 9266. Fax: 61 6 249 5792.

Year and Place of Birth 1939, Hull, UK.

Degrees and Qualifications B.Sc. (Econ.) London Univ., 1965; Ph.D. Hull Univ., 1979.

Previous Post Lect., Australian National Univ., 1970–89.

Current Offices and Honorary Posts Edit. com. mem., *Australian Econ. Hist. Rev.*; com. mem., Australian Econ. Hist. Soc.

Major Honours Ricketts Research Scholar, Hull Univ., 1967.

Fields of Expertise *Industry Fields:* banking. *Bus. Dimensions:* wages and wage payment systems; career expectations. *Scope:* national. *Period:* nineteenth century. *Teaching:* undergrad.; post grad. *Consultancy:* training, economist skills.

Publications *Books: The*

Commercial Crisis of 1847, Harvard Univ. Press, 1984. *Articles:* 'James Wilson and the Commercial Crisis of 1847', *Hist. of Polit. Economy*, 15(4), 1983, 567–83; 'Unemployment and Poor Law Relief in Manchester, 1845–50', *Social Hist.*, 15(2), 1990, 218–28; 'Salaries and Career Earnings in the Bank of Scotland, 1730–1880', *The Econ. Hist. Rev.*, XLIV(4), 1991, 629–53; 'Training, Wages and Human Capital', *Policy*, 8(3), 1992, 13–17.

Booth, Alan

Sen. Lect., Dept. of Econ. and Social Hist., Univ. of Exeter, Amory Building, Rennes Drive, Exeter, EX4 4RJ, UK. Tel.: 44 392 263296.

Year and Place of Birth 1949, UK.

Degrees and Qualifications BA (Econ. & Soc. Hist.) Univ. of Kent, 1972; Ph.D. Univ. of Kent, 1975.

Previous Post Lect., Dept. of Econ. & Soc. Hist., Sheffield Univ., 1976–81.

Fields of Expertise *Industry Fields:* metal manufacture; mechanical engineering; instrument engineering; electrical engineering; shipbuilding and marine engineering; vehicle construction; metal goods. *Bus. Dimensions:* bus.–state relations; management of labour. *Scope:* national. *Period:* twentieth century as a whole. *Teaching:* undergrad.

Publications *Books: British Econ. Policy 1930–1949: Was there a Keynesian Revolution?*, Harvester Wheatsheaf, 1989. *Articles:* 'Britain in the 1930's: A Managed Economy?', *Econ. Hist. Rev.*, 2nd ser., 40, 499–522.

Bostock, Frances G.

Bus. Hist. Research Fellow, Univ. of Reading, Dept. of Econ., POB 218, Whiteknights, Reading, RG6 2AA, UK. Tel.: 44 734 875123. Fax: 44 734 750236.

Year and Place of Birth 1938, South India.

Degrees and Qualifications MA (Hist.) Edinburgh Univ., 1960.

Fields of Expertise *Industry Fields:* insurance, banking, finance, inward f.d.i. generally; overseas banking. *Bus. Dimensions:* multinational business; development finance. *Scope:* internat.; Iran; Africa (ex British Colonial). *Period:* nineteenth century; early twentieth century; inter-war years, 1919–39; mid-twentieth century, 1940–70. *Consultancy:* co. hist. researcher.

Publications *Books: Planning and Power in Iran*, with Geoffrey Jones co-auth., Frank Cass, 1989. *Articles:* 'British Bus. in Iran, 1860s-1970s', *British Bus. in Asia since 1860*, with Geoffrey Jones co-auth.; R.P.T. Davenport-Hines & Geoffrey Jones eds., Cambridge, 1989, 31–67; 'State Bank or Agent of Empire? The Imperial Bank of Persia's Loan Policy 1920–23', *Iran*, 27, 1989, 103–13; 'The British Overseas Banks and Development of Finance in Africa after 1945', *Bus. Hist.*, special issue on Banks & Money: *Internat. and Comparative Finance in Hist.*, XXXII(3), July, 1991, 157–76; 'A Bank of Dual Nationality. The Origins and Strategy of the Ionian Bank before 1914', *Bankhistorisches Archiv*, forthcoming, 1993.

Bothwell, Robert

Prof., Dept. of Hist., Univ. of Toronto, Toronto, Ontario, M5S 1A1, Canada. Tel.: 1 416 978 6778.

Year and Place of Birth 1944, Ottawa, Canada.

Degrees and Qualifications BA Toronto Univ., 1966; MA Harvard Univ., 1967; Ph.D. Harvard Univ., 1972.

Previous Post Teaching Fellow, Harvard Univ., 1968–70.

Fields of Expertise *Industry Fields:* mining and quarrying; gas, electricity, water; professional and scientific services; public admin. and defence; nuclear engineering: manufacture. *Bus. Dimensions:* co. admin.; research and development; bus. organization; bus.–state relations. *Scope:* national; internat. *Period:* inter-war years, 1919–39; mid-twentieth century, 1940–70; late twentieth century, 1970–present. *Teaching:* undergrad.; post grad. *Consultancy:* co. hist.

Publications *Books: Eldorado: Canada's National Uranium Co.,* Univ. of Toronto Press, Toronto, 1984; *Nucleus,* Univ. of Toronto Press, Toronto, 1988; *Canada since 1945,* co-auth., 2nd edn., Univ. of Toronto Press, Toronto, 1989; *Pirouette,* co-auth., Univ. of Toronto Press, Toronto, 1990; *Canada and the United States,* Univ. of Toronto Press, Toronto, Twayne, New York, 1992.

Bowden, Sue

Lect. in Econ. Hist., School of Bus. and Econ. Studies, Univ. of Leeds, Leeds, LS2 9JT, UK. Tel.: 44 532 334492. Fax: 44 532 334465.

Year and Place of Birth 1951, Manchester, UK.

Degrees and Qualifications BA London Univ., 1980; Ph.D. London School of Econ., 1985.

Previous Post Research student, Dept. of Econ. Hist., London School of Econ.

Major Honours Frank Cass Prize, *Bus. Hist.,* 1991.

Fields of Expertise *Industry Fields:* electrical engineering; vehicle construction; gas, electricity, water. *Bus. Dimensions:* strategy formation; bus. organization; markets and bus. *Scope:* regional; national. *Period:* inter-war

years, 1919–39; mid-twentieth century, 1940–70. *Teaching:* undergrad.; post grad.

Publications *Articles:* 'The Consumer Durables Revolution in England, 1932–1938; a Regional Analysis', *Explorations in Econ. Hist.,* 25, 1988, 42–59; 'Credit Facilities and the Growth of Consumer Demand for Electric Appliances in England', *Bus. Hist.,* 32, 1990, 52–75; 'Demand and Supply Constraints in the Inter-war UK Car Industry; did the Manufacturers get it right?', *Bus. Hist.,* 33, 1991, 241–67; 'Productivity and Long-term Growth Potential', *Applied Econ.,* 23, 1992, 1425–32; 'The Bank of England, Indust. Regeneration and Hire Purchase between the Wars', *Econ. Hist. Rev.,* XLV, 1992, 120–36.

Boyce, Gordon

Lect. in Econ. Hist., Dept. of Econ. Hist., Victoria Univ. of Wellington, POB 600, Wellington, New Zealand. Tel.: 64 4 471 5385. Fax: 64 4 471 2200.

Year and Place of Birth 1954, Canada.

Degrees and Qualifications BA (Hist.) Brock Univ., 1975; MA (Hist.) Keele Univ., 1977; Ph.D. (Econ. Hist.) London School of Econ., 1984.

Previous Post Asst. Prof., Dept. of Econ., Acadia Univ., 1987–9.

Fields of Expertise *Industry Fields:* shipping; steel industry. *Bus. Dimensions:* bus. organization. *Scope:* national; UK. *Period:* nineteenth century. *Teaching:* undergrad.; post grad. *Consultancy:* organizational design.

Publications *Articles:* 'The Development of the Cargo Fleet Iron Co., 1900–14. Entrepreneurship, Costs and Structural Rigidity in the Northeast Coast Steel Industry', *Bus. Hist. Rev.,* 63(4), Winter, 1984, 839–76; The Manufacturing and

Marketing of Steel in Canada Dofasco Inc., 1912–1970', *Bus. & Econ. Hist.*, 18, 1989, 228–38; 'Continuity and Transition in Corporate Capability: Incentives, Management and Innovation at Dofasco Inc.', *Bus. & Econ. Hist.*, 19, 1990, 223–34; 'Corporate Strategy and Accounting Systems: A Comparison of Developments at two British Steel Firms, 1848–1914', *Bus. Hist.*, 34(1), Jan., 1992, 42–65; '64thers, Syndicates & Stock Promotions: Information Plans and Fund-raising Techniques of British Shipowners before 1914', *J. of Econ. Hist.*, 52(1), Mar., 1992, 181–205.

Boyns, Trevor

Asst. Director, Bus. Hist. Research Unit, Cardiff Bus. School, Aberconway Building, Colum Drive, Cardiff, CF1 1XL, UK. Tel.: 44 222 874000. Fax: 44 222 874419.

Year and Place of Birth 1953, Chatham, UK.

Degrees and Qualifications B.Sc. (Maths. & Econ.) Warwick Univ., 1974; Ph.D. Wales Univ., 1982.

Current Offices and Honorary Posts Asst. ed., *Accounting, Bus. & Financial Hist.*.

Fields of Expertise *Industry Fields:* mining and quarrying. *Bus. Dimensions:* entrepreneurs and entrepreneurship. *Scope:* regional . *Period:* nineteenth century; twentieth century as a whole. *Teaching:* undergrad.

Publications *Articles:* 'Growth in the Coal Industry: The Cases of Powell Duffryn and the Ocean Coal Co., 1864–1913', *Modern South Wales: Essays in Econ. Hist.*, C. Baber & L.J. Williams eds., 1986, 153–70; 'Rationalisation in the Interwar Period: The Case of The South Wales Steam Coal Industry', *Bus. Hist.*, XXIX, 1987, 282–303; 'Strategic Responses to

Foreign Competition: The British Coal Industry and the 1930 Coal Mines Act', *Bus. Hist.*, 32, 1990, 133–45; 'The Electricity Industry in South Wales to 1949', *Welsh Hist. Rev.*, 15, 1990, 79–107; 'Powell Duffryn: The Use of Machinery and Production Planning Techniques in the South Wales Coalfield', *Towards a Social Hist. of Mining*, 1992, K. Tenfelde ed., papers presented to the Internat. Mining Hist. Congress, Bochum, Fed. Rep. of Germany, Sept. 3–7, 1989, C.H. Beck Verlag, Munich, 370–86.

Braun, Hans-Joachim

Prof., Neuere Sozial-, Wirtschafts- und Technikgeschichte, Hamburg Bundeswehr Univ., Holstenhofweg 85, 22008 Hamburg, Germany. Tel.: 49 40 6541 2794. Fax: 49 40 6530 413.

Year and Place of Birth 1943, Königsberg, Germany.

Degrees and Qualifications Dr.phil. Bochum Univ, 1971.

Previous Post Privatdozent, Bochum Univ., 1979–82.

Current Offices and Honorary Posts Exec. council mem., SHOT; exec. com. mem., ICOHTEC; chairman, Hist. Council; chairman, German Assoc. of Engineers .

Fields of Expertise *Industry Fields:* mechanical engineering. *Bus. Dimensions:* bus. and technology. *Scope:* internat. *Period:* twentieth century as a whole. *Teaching:* undergrad. *Consultancy:* co. hist.

Publications *Books: Technologische Beziehungen zwischen Deutschland und England von der Mitte des 17. bis zum Ausgang des 18. Jarhunderts*, Schwann, 1974; *Wirtschafts- und finanzpolitische Entscheidungsprozesse in England in der ersten Hälfte des 19. Jahrhunderts*, Lang, 1984; *Entwicklung und Selbstverständnis von Wissenschaften*, with R.W. Kluwe,

Lang, 1985; *The German Economy in the Twentieth Century: The German Reich and the Federal Republic*, Routledge, 1990; *Energiewirtschaft, Automatisierung, Information. Propylaen Technikgeschichte, vol. 5. Seit 1914*, with W. Kaiser, Propyläen, 1992.

Broeke, W. van den

Sen. Lect. in Econ. & Social Hist., Dept. of Hist., Utrecht Univ., Kromme Nieuwe Gracht 66, 3512 HL Utrecht, Netherlands. Tel.: 31 30 536460. Fax: 31 30 536391.

Year and Place of Birth 1941, Middelburg, Netherlands.

Degrees and Qualifications Drs.Ec. Erasmus Univ., 1966; Dr.Ec. Erasmus Univ., 1985.

Current Offices and Honorary Posts Sec., Bus. Hist. Workshop.

Fields of Expertise *Industry Fields:* transport and communication. *Bus. Dimensions:* entrepreneurs and entrepreneurship; co. finance and accounting; multinational bus. *Scope:* regional; national; internat. *Period:* nineteenth century; early twentieth century. *Teaching:* undergrad. *Consultancy:* co. hist.

Publications *Books: Two Dutch Multinationals in Indonesia in the Period of Modern Imperialism 1890–1914: "Royal Dutch" and "Billiton"*, Ujung Pandang/Utrecht, 1978, Papers of the Second Indonesian-Dutch Hist. Conf.; *Financien en Financiers van de Nederlandse Spoorwegen 1937–1980*, Waanders, Zwolle, 1985, with English summary: The Financing of Railway Construction in the Netherlands, 1837–1890; *Frontier-crossing Railway Traffic and the Dutch Economy in the Second Half of the Nineteenth Century*, Firenze, 1993, Papers of the pre-Conf. on "European Networks 19th-20th Centuries", San Miniato.

Brown, Jonathan

Bus. Records Officer, Rural Hist. Centre, Univ. of Reading, Whiteknights, Reading, Berks, RG6 2AG, UK. Tel.: 44 734 318666. Fax: 44 734 751264.

Degrees and Qualifications BA Manchester Univ.; Ph.D. Manchester Univ.

Fields of Expertise *Industry Fields:* agric., forestry, fishing; food, drink, tobacco; mechanical engineering. *Bus. Dimensions:* entrepreneurs and entrepreneurship; production management. *Scope:* national; UK. *Period:* nineteenth century; twentieth century as a whole. *Teaching:* undergrad.; post grad.

Publications *Books: Agric. in England 1870–1947*, Manchester Univ. Press, 1990; *Steeped in Tradition: The Malting Industry in England since the Railway Age*, Reading Univ., 1983; *Entrepreneurship, Networks and Modern Bus.*, with Mary Rose co-ed., Manchester Univ. Press, 1993. *Articles: The Agrarian Hist. of England and Wales. Vol. VI, 1750–1850*, Cambridge, 1989, (sections on farming practices and malting).

Brown, Kenneth D.

Prof. of Econ. & Social Hist., Dept. of Econ. and Social Hist., Queen's Univ., Belfast, BT7 1NN, UK. Tel.: 44 232 245133. Fax: 44 232 247895.

Year and Place of Birth 1943, Nottingham, UK.

Degrees and Qualifications BA (Mod. Hist.) Reading Univ., 1965; MA McMaster Univ., 1966; Ph.D. Univ. of Kent at Canterbury, 1969.

Current Offices and Honorary Posts Mem., Econ. Hist. Soc. Council.

Major Honours Royal Hist. Soc. Whitfield Prize, 1978.

Fields of Expertise *Industry Fields:* other manufacturing industries. *Bus. Dimensions:* small bus. matters. *Scope:* national; UK. *Period:* nineteenth century; twentieth century as a whole. *Teaching:* undergrad.

Publications *Articles:* 'Models in Hist. A Micro-study of Late 19th Century British Entrepreneurship', *Econ. Hist. Rev.*, 42, 1989, 528–37; 'The Children's Toy Industry in 19th Century Britain', *Bus. Hist.*, 32, 1990, 180–97; 'Modelling for War? Toy Soldiers in late Victorian and Edwardian Britain', *J. of Soc. Hist.*, 24, 1990, 237–54; 'The Collapse of the British Toy Industry, 1979–84', *Econ. Hist. Rev.*, forthcoming; 'Through a Glass Darkly: Cost Control in British Industry: A Case Study', *Accounting Bus. & Finan. Hist.*, forthcoming.

Bryant, Keith L. Jr.

Prof. of Hist. & Head of Dept., Dept. of Hist., Univ. of Akron, Akron, OH 44325-1902, USA. Tel.: 1 216 972 6198. Fax: 1 216 374 8795.

Year and Place of Birth 1937, Oklahoma City, USA.

Degrees and Qualifications BS Oklahoma Univ., 1959; M.Ed. Oklahoma Univ., 1961; Ph.D. Missouri Univ., 1965.

Previous Post Prof. of Hist., Texas A&M Univ., 1976–88.

Current Offices and Honorary Posts Board of eds., *Railroad Hist.*

Major Honours George W. & Constance M. Hilton Book Award, Railway & Locomotive Hist. Soc., 1990; Edward Cadenhead Lect., Tulsa Univ., 1988.

Fields of Expertise *Industry Fields:* transport and communication. *Bus. Dimensions:* entrepreneurs and entrepreneurship. *Scope:* national. *Period:* twentieth century as a whole. *Teaching:* post grad. *Consultancy:* co. hist.

Publications *Books: Arthur Stilwell, Promoter with a Hunch*, Vanderbilt UP, 1971; *Hist. of the Atchison, Topeka and Santa Fe Railway*, Macmillan, 1974; *A Hist. of Amer. Bus.*, with Henry C. Dethloff, Prentice-Hall, 1983 & 1990; *The Railroads in the Age of Regulation*, Bruccoli Clark/Layman, 1988; *William Merritt Chase, a Genteel Bohemian*, Univ. of Missouri Press, 1991.

Buchan, P. Bruce

Assoc. Prof., School of Bus., Queens Univ., Kingston, Ontario K7L 3N6, Canada. Fax: 1 613 545 2013.

Year and Place of Birth 1932, Toronto, Canada.

Degrees and Qualifications BA Sc. Toronto Univ., 1955; M.Com. Toronto Univ., 1959; Ph.D. (Management) Michigan Univ., 1969.

Previous Post Asst. Prof., Windsor Univ., 1962–9.

Current Offices and Honorary Posts Academic Reviewer, Bus. Hist. Interest Group, ASAC, 1993.

Fields of Expertise *Industry Fields:* coal and petroleum products; insurance, banking, finance. *Bus. Dimensions:* strategy formation; boardroom issues. *Scope:* national; internat. *Period:* nineteenth century; late twentieth century, 1970–present. *Teaching:* undergrad.; post grad. *Consultancy:* corporate strategy.

Publications *Articles:* 'Boards of Directors - Adversaries or Advisors', *California Management Rev.*, Winter, 1981–2; 'Strategies for Responsible Share Ownership: Personal Reflections on the Experience at Queen's Univ.', Centre for Corporate Social Performance and Ethics, Fac. of Management, Toronto Univ., May, 1991; 'The Changing Role of the Board of Directors: Lessons from the East India Co. 1600–1830', *Proceedings*, ASAC, 1993; 'John Stuart

Mill - Contributions to the Principles of Management', *British J. of Management*, June, 1993.

Bud-Frierman, Lisa

Research Fellow, Dept. of Econ., Fac. of Letters and Social Science, Univ. of Reading, POB 218, Whiteknights, Reading, RG6 2AA, UK. Tel.: 44 734 875123. Fax: 44 734 750236.

Year and Place of Birth 1952, Los Angeles, USA.

Degrees and Qualifications BS (Conservation of Natural Resources) Univ. of California-Berkeley, 1974; MA (Hist. & Sociology of Science) Pennsylvania Univ., 1981; Ph.D. (Hist. & Sociology of Sc.) Pennsylvania Univ., expected 1994.

Previous Post Research Asst., Bus. Hist. Unit, London School of Econ., 1985–8.

Fields of Expertise *Industry Fields:* agric., forestry, fishing; bus. services; professional and scientific services; mercantile. *Bus. Dimensions:* bus. organization; bus. and technology; multinational bus.; bus.–state relations; markets and bus.; bus. information. *Scope:* national; internat.; UK. *Period:* nineteenth century; twentieth century as a whole.

Publications *Books: Information Acumen: The Understanding and Use of Knowledge in Modern Bus.*, Routledge, December, 1993.

Bugos, Glenn E.

122 Newport Drive, Oak Ridge, TN 37830, USA.

Year and Place of Birth 1961, Pittsburgh, USA.

Degrees and Qualifications B.S.F.S Georgetown Univ., 1983; Ph.D. Pennsylvania Univ., 1988.

Fields of Expertise *Industry Fields:* professional and scientific services;

genetic engineering: manufacture: aerospace. *Bus. Dimensions:* bus. and technology; bus.–state relations. *Scope:* internat. *Period:* twentieth century as a whole.

Bugra, Ayse

Assoc. Prof. of Econ., Dept. of Econ., Bogaziçi Univ., Bebek 80815, Istanbul, Turkey. Tel.: 90 1 263 15 00. Fax: 90 1 265 63 57.

Year and Place of Birth 1951, Istanbul, Turkey.

Degrees and Qualifications BA (Econ.) Laval Univ., Quebec; MA (Econ.) Laval Univ., Quebec; Ph.D. (Econ.) McGill Univ., Montreal.

Previous Post Research Fellow, Center for Developing Area Studies, McGill Univ., Montreal, 1983–5.

Fields of Expertise *Industry Fields:* . *Bus. Dimensions:* bus.–state relations. *Scope:* national; internat.; Turkey in a comparative perspective. *Period:* twentieth century as a whole.

Publications *Books: Iktisatçilar ve Insanlar: Bir Yöntem Çalismasi* [Of Economists and Men: A Study on the Methodology of Econ.] Remzi Kitapevi, Istanbul, 1989; *State and Bus. in Modern Turkey: A Comparative Study*, State Univ. of New York Press, forthcoming. *Articles:* 'Development Literature and Writers from Underdeveloped Countries', *Current Anthropology*, 26, 1985, 89–102; 'Turkish Holding Co. as a Social Institution', *J. of Econ. & Admin. Studies*, 4, Bogaziçi Univ., 1990, 35–51; 'Polit. Sources of Uncertainty in Bus. Life', *Strong State and Econ. Interest Groups*, M. Heper ed., Walter de Gruyter, Berlin & New York, 1991.

Burchardt, Jørgen

Nyborgvej 13, DK-5750 Ringe, Denmark. Tel.: 45 62 62 36 17. Fax: 45 62 62 36 55.
Year and Place of Birth 1946, Copenhagen, Denmark.
Degrees and Qualifications Cand. phil. Copenhagen Univ., 1993; grafonom, Den Grafiske Højskole, Copenhagen, 1969.
Fields of Expertise *Industry Fields:* metal manufacture; mechanical engineering; fishing; food, tobacco; bricks, cement. *Bus. Dimensions:* entrepreneurs and entrepreneurship; personnel management; bus. organization; bus. and technology; co. culture. *Scope:* local; regional; national. *Period:* early twentieth century; inter-war years, 1919–39; mid-twentieth century, 1940–70. *Consultancy:* co. hist.
Publications *Books: Fabrik,* Fremad, Copenhagen, 1982; *Provinsindustri,* Faaborg kulturhistoriske Museer, Faaborg, 1984; *Dokken. Museums - og feriecenter,* co-ed. & co-auth., Arbejdermuseet, Copenhagen, 1993. *Articles:* 'Arbejdstøj', *Nord Nytt,* 31, 40–50.

Burk, Kathleen

Reader in Modern & Contemporary Hist., Dept. of Hist., Univ. College London, Gower St, London, WC1E 6BT, UK. Tel.: 44 71 387 7050. Fax: 44 71 387 8057.
Year and Place of Birth 1946, Sanger, California, USA.
Degrees and Qualifications BA Berkeley Univ., 1969; MA Oxford Univ., 1972; D.Phil. Oxford Univ., 1977.
Previous Post Lect. in Hist. & Polit., Imperial College, London Univ., 1980–90.
Current Offices and Honorary Posts

Council mem., Royal Hist. Soc.
Fields of Expertise *Industry Fields:* insurance, banking, finance. *Bus. Dimensions:* bus.–state relations. *Scope:* national; internat. *Period:* nineteenth century; twentieth century as a whole. *Teaching:* undergrad.; post grad. *Consultancy:* co. hist.
Publications *Books: Britain, Amer. and the Sinews of War,* George Allen & Unwin, London & Boston, 1985; *The First Privatisation: The Politicians, the City and the Denationalisation of Steel,* The Historian's Press, London, 1988; *Morgan Grenfell 1838–1988; The Biography of a Merchant Bank,* OUP, Oxford, 1989; *'Goodbye Great Britain': The 1976 IMF Crisis,* with Alec Cairncross, Yale Univ. Press, London & New Haven, 1992. *Articles:* 'The House of Morgan Redivivus?: The Abortive Morgan Internat. 1972–73', *Bus. Hist.,* 33(3), July, 1991, 177–95.

Burley, David

Assoc. Prof., Dept. of Hist., Winnipeg Univ., 515 Portage Avenue, Winnipeg, Manitoba, R3B 2E9, Canada. Tel.: 1 416 786 9012. Fax: 1 416 786 1824.
Year and Place of Birth 1949, London, Ontario, Canada.
Degrees and Qualifications BA McMaster Univ., 1972; MA Trent Univ., 1974; Ph.D. McMaster Univ., 1983.
Fields of Expertise *Industry Fields:* real estate. *Bus. Dimensions:* entrepreneurs and entrepreneurship. *Scope:* regional; Canada. *Period:* nineteenth century. *Teaching:* undergrad.
Publications *Books: 'A Particular Condition in Life': Self-employment and Social Mobility in mid-Victorian Brantford, Ontario,* McGill, Queen's Univ. Press, forthcoming. *Articles:* '"Good for All He Would Ask": Credit

and Debt in the Transition to Indust. Capitalism - the Case of mid-Nineteenth Century Brantford, Ontario', *Histoire Sociale - Social Hist.*, 20, 1987, 79–100; *Dictionary of Canadian Biography*, vols. VII–XIII, Univ. of Toronto Press, Toronto, 1976–, 16 articles; 'The Keepers of the Gate: The Inequality of Property Ownership during the Winnipeg Real Estate Boom of 1881–2', *Urban Hist. Rev.*, 17, 1988, 63–76; 'Meeting in the Market Place: Information, Trust and Power among Ontario Bus.men, 1784–1984', *New Directions for the Study of Ontario's Past*, D. Gagan & R. Gagan eds., McMaster Univ., Hamilton, Ont., 1988, 151–66.

Burt, Roger

Sen. Lect. in Econ. Hist., Dept. of Econ. and Social Hist., The Amory Building, Univ. of Exeter, Exeter, EX4 4QH, UK. Tel.: 44 392 263284. Fax: 44 392 263305.

Year and Place of Birth 1942, London, UK.

Degrees and Qualifications B.Sc. (Econ.) London School of Econ., 1964; Ph.D. London School of Econ., 1971; MIMM, 1992.

Current Offices and Honorary Posts Dean of Soc. Studies, Exeter Univ.; sec., National Assoc. of Mining Hist. Organisations.

Fields of Expertise *Industry Fields:* mining and quarrying; metal manufacture; metal goods. *Bus. Dimensions:* entrepreneurs and entrepreneurship; management education. *Scope:* local; regional; national; internat.; global. *Period:* medieval; early modern; eighteenth century; nineteenth century; twentieth century as a whole. *Teaching:* undergrad.; post grad. *Consultancy:* engineering problems and land use/reuse.

Publications *Books: John Taylor, Mining Entrepreneur and Engineer*

1779–1863, Moorland, Buxton, 1977; *The British Lead Mining Industry*, Truran, Redruth, 1984; *Cornish Mines*, with Peter Waite & Raymond Burnley, Univ. of Exeter, 1988. *Articles:* 'Records of Mining: The Lead/Silver/Zinc Producers of the Coeur 'Alene District of Idaho, USA 1890–1933', *Bus. Hist.*, 32(3), 1990, 49–74; 'The Internat. Diffusion of Technology during the Early Modern Period: The Case of the British Non-ferrous Mining Industry', *Econ. Hist. Rev.*, XLIV(2), May, 1991, 249–71.

Buss, Dietrich G.

Prof. of Hist., Dept. of Hist., Biola Univ., 13800 Biola Avenue, La Mirada, CA 90639, USA. Tel.: 1 310 944 0351. Fax: 1 310 903 4748.

Year and Place of Birth 1939, Tokyo, Japan.

Degrees and Qualifications BA (Education) Biola Univ., 1963; MA (Soc. Sc.) California State Univ., Los Angeles, 1966; Ph.D. (Hist.) Claremont Grad. School, 1976.

Current Offices and Honorary Posts Vice-Chair, La Mirada Hist. Heritage Commission.

Major Honours Charles J. Kenney Award, Econ. & Bus. Hist. Soc., 1978.

Fields of Expertise *Industry Fields:* transport and communication. *Bus. Dimensions:* merger movement and issues. *Scope:* national; internat. *Period:* nineteenth century. *Teaching:* undergrad.

Publications *Books: Henry Villard: A Study of Transatlantic Investments and Interests, 1870–1895*, Arno Press, 1978. *Articles:* 'Henry Villard and Thomas Edison: Growth of Incandescent Lighting, 1878–1892', *Essays in Econ. & Bus. Hist.*, James H. Solton ed., Michigan State Univ. Bus. Studies, 1979.

Bussière, Eric

Maître de Conférences d'Histoire contemporaine, Univ. of Paris IV-Sorbonne, 1 rue Victor Cousin, 75230 Paris Cedex 05, France. Tel.: 33 1 40 46 26 25.

Year and Place of Birth 1955, Cambrai, France.

Degrees and Qualifications Maîtrise d'histoire Univ. of Paris IV, 1977; Agrégation (Hist.), 1980; Docteur (Hist.) Univ. of Paris IV, 1988.

Previous Post Researcher, CNRS, 1987–8.

Fields of Expertise *Industry Fields:* insurance, banking, finance; metal manufacture. *Bus. Dimensions:* multinational bus.; bus.–state relations. *Scope:* internat. *Period:* early twentieth century; inter-war years, 1919–39; mid-twentieth century, 1940–70. *Teaching:* undergrad. *Consultancy:* co. hist.

Publications *Books: La France, la Belgique et l'Organisation Economique de l'Europe, 1918–1935,* Comité per l'histoire économique et financière de la France, Paris, 1992; *Paribas, Europe and the World, 1872–1992,* Fonds Mercator, Antwerp, 1992; *Les Cercles Economiques et l'Europe au XXe Siècle,* E. Bussière & M. Dumoulin eds., Louvain la neuve, Paris, 1992, collection of texts. *Articles:* 'The Evolution of Structures in the Iron and Steel Industry in France, Belgium and Luxembourg: National and Internat. Aspects, 1900–1939', *Changing Patterns of Internat. Rivalry. Some Lessons from the Steel Industry,* E. Abe & Y. Suzuki eds., Univ. of Tokyo Press, 1991, 141–62; 'La Banque de Paris et des Pays-Bas et sa Strategie Industrielle, 1900–1930', *Entreprise et Histoire,* no. 2, 1992, 49–64.

Butel, Paul

Prof. of Modern Hist., Univ. of Bordeaux III, Espl. Michel-Montaigne, Domaine Universitaire, 33405 Talence Cedex, France. Tel.: 33 56 84 50 50.

Year and Place of Birth 1931, Lanildut, France.

Degrees and Qualifications Docteur-ès-lettres, Paris I Univ., 1973.

Current Offices and Honorary Posts Mem., Soc. of French Econ. Historians.

Fields of Expertise *Industry Fields:* food, drink, tobacco; shipbuilding and marine engineering; transport and communication; distributive trades; insurance, banking, finance,; bus. services. *Bus. Dimensions:* entrepreneurs and entrepreneurship; co. finance and accounting; marketing; bus. organization; multinational bus.; markets and bus. *Scope:* local; regional; national; internat.; UK; Germany; Netherlands; West Indies. *Period:* early modern; eighteenth century; nineteenth century. *Teaching:* undergrad.; post grad. *Consultancy:* co. hist.

Publications *Books: Les négociants bordelais, l'Europe et les Iles au XVIIIe siècle,* Aubier-Montaigne, Paris, 1974; *Les Caraibes au temps des flibustiers, XVIe-XVIIe siècles,* Aubier-Montaigne, Paris, 1980; *Histoire du Thé,* Desjonquères, Paris, 1989; *Les Dynasties bordelaises de Colbert à Chaban,* Perrin, Paris, 1991; *L'Economie française au XVIIIe siècles,* SEDES, 1993.

Butterworth, Susan

Partner, Applied Historians (Consultants), 1 Park Avenue, Tawa, Wellington, New Zealand. Tel.: 64 4 232 7072. Fax: 64 4 232 6373.

Year and Place of Birth 1948, Middlesborough, UK.

Degrees and Qualifications BA

Massey Univ., 1969; MA Massey Univ., 1971.

Previous Post Sen. Publications Officer, The Consumers' Inst., Wellington, New Zealand.

Current Offices and Honorary Posts Com. mem., Soc. for Research on Women, Wellington Branch.

Major Honours Univ. Senior Scholarship, 1968; Shortcliffe Fellowship, 1972; J.M. Sherrard Award in New Zealand Regional Hist., (joint winner), 1991.

Fields of Expertise *Industry Fields:* agric., forestry, fishing; food, drink, tobacco; public admin. and defence. *Bus. Dimensions:* entrepreneurs and entrepreneurship; research and development; bus.–state relations; co. culture. *Scope:* local; national; internat. *Period:* nineteenth century; twentieth century as a whole. *Consultancy:* co. hist.

Publications *Books: Petone: A Hist.*, Petone Borough Council, 1988; *The Maori Trustee*, with G.V. Butterworth, Wellington, 1991; *A Hist. of Quality Bakers New Zealand Ltd.*, 1993, forthcoming. *Articles:* 'Maori Fisheries Issues: Guide to Sources in Government Archives since 1840', Compiled for Joint Working Party on Maori Fisheries, June, 1988, supporting paper to the evidence of Robert Dowding Cooper in the Waitangi Tribunal, WA1-27, doc. no. 13; 'Evidence of Susan Margaret Butterworth on behalf of the New Zealand Fishing Industry Board and the New Zealand Fishing Industry Assoc. in the High Court of New Zealand', Dec., 1990, (in public domain but not published officially).

Caban, Wieslaw

Wyzsza Szkola Pedagogiczna, ul. Zeromskiego 5, 25-563 Kielce, Poland. Tel.: 48 486 70. Fax: 48 488 05.

Year and Place of Birth 1946, Mierzyce, Poland.

Degrees and Qualifications Magister Lódz Univ., 1970; Doktor Lódz Univ., 1980; Doktor Habilitowany Lódz Univ., 1990; Prof. Kielce Univ., 1992 .

Previous Post Sen. Lect., Dept. of Hist., Wyzsza Szkola Pedagogiczna, Kielce, 1975–92.

Current Offices and Honorary Posts Mem., Polish Hist. Assoc.

Major Honours Ministry of Education Prize, 1977, 1980 & 1984.

Fields of Expertise *Industry Fields:* agric., forestry, fishing; food, drink, tobacco; metal manufacture; public admin. and defence. *Scope:* regional; national. *Period:* nineteenth century. *Teaching:* undergrad.; post grad.

Publications *Books: Soc. and Economy 1832–1864*, Kielce, 1993. *Articles:* 'Alcohol Distillation and the Sugar Industry in the early Nineteenth Century', *The Hist. of Material Culture Q.*, 38, 1990; 'Landowners versus Progress in Agric. Science', *Kielce Studies*, 1990; 'Jewish Econ. Activity and Sources of Living', *Bull. of Jewish Hist. Inst. in Poland*, 1991; 'Agric. Production in the mid-Nineteenth Century', *Kieleckie Hist. Studies*, 10, 1992.

Cain, Louis P.

Prof., Loyola Univ. of Chicago & Adjunct Prof., Northwestern Univ., Dept. of Econ., Loyola Univ. of Chicago, 820 N. Michigan Ave., Chicago IL 60611, Northwestern Univ., 2003 Sheridan Road, Evanston, IL 60208, USA. Tel.: Loyola 1 312 915 6075/Northwestern 1 708 491 8225. Fax: Loyola 1 312 915 6432/Northwestern 1 708 491 7001.

Year and Place of Birth 1941, Chicago, USA.

Degrees and Qualifications BA

Princeton Univ., 1963; MA Northwestern Univ., 1966; Ph.D. Northwestern Univ., 1969.

Current Offices and Honorary Posts Edit. Board, *Bus. Hist. Rev.* & *J. of Econ. Hist.*; assoc. ed., *Cliometrics Soc. Newsletter.*

Fields of Expertise *Industry Fields:* food, drink, tobacco; electrical engineering; gas, electricity, water. *Bus. Dimensions:* entrepreneurs and entrepreneurship; bus. organization; bus. and technology; bus.–state relations; markets and bus. *Scope:* local; regional; national. *Period:* nineteenth century; twentieth century as a whole. *Teaching:* undergrad.; post grad. *Consultancy:* co. hist.

Publications *Books: Bus. Enterprise and Econ. Change*, with Paul Uselding co-ed., Kent State Univ. Press, 1973; *Sanitation Strategy for a Lakefront Metropolis: The Case of Chicago*, Northern Illinois Univ. Press, 1978. *Articles:* 'The Consent Decree in the Meat Packing Industry, 1920–1956', *Bus. Hist. Rev.*, 1981; 'From Mud to Metropolis: Chicago Before the Fire', *Research in Econ. Hist.*, 1986; 'Econ. and Bus. Hist.: One Discipline or Two?', *Perspectives on the Hist. of Econ. Thought*, D.E. Moggridge, ed., vol. III, Edward Elgar Publishing, 1990.

Cameron, Rondo

William Rand Kenan Univ. Prof., Emory Univ., 1635B No Decatur Road, Atlanta, Georgia 30322, USA. Tel.: 0404 727 7909. Fax: 0404 727 4639.

Year and Place of Birth 1925, Linden, USA.

Degrees and Qualifications BA Yale Univ., 1948; MA Yale Univ., 1949; Ph.D. Chicago Univ., 1952.

Previous Post Prof. of Econ. & Hist., Wisconsin Univ., 1961–9.

Current Offices and Honorary Posts Former pres., Amer. Econ. Hist. Assoc. ed., *J. of Econ. Hist.*, 1957–81; v.p., Internat. Econ. Hist. Assoc., 1986–1990; ex. com., IEHA, 1974–86; board of trustees, Bus. Hist. Conf., 1989–92.

Major Honours Phi Beta Kappa, Yale Univ., 1948; Fulbright Scholarship, 1950–1; Fulbright Visiting Prof., Glasgow Univ., 1962–3.

Fields of Expertise *Industry Fields:* insurance, banking, finance. *Bus. Dimensions:* entrepreneurs and entrepreneurship. *Scope:* global. *Period:* nineteenth century. *Consultancy:* co. hist.

Publications *Books: France and the Econ. Development of Europe*, Princeton Univ. Press, 1961; *Banking in the Early Stages of Industrialization*, OUP, 1967; *Banking and Econ. Development*, OUP, 1971; *Internat. Banking, 1870–1914*, OUP, 2 vols., 1992; *A Concise Econ. Hist. of the World from Paleolithic Times to the Present*, OUP, 2nd edn., 1993.

Campbell-Kelly, Martin

Senior Lect., Dept. of Computer Science, Univ. of Warwick, Coventry, CV4 7AL, UK. Tel.: 44 203 523193. Fax: 44 203 525714.

Year and Place of Birth 1945, North Wales, UK.

Degrees and Qualifications B.Sc. Manchester Univ., 1968; Ph.D. C.N.A.A., 1980.

Previous Post Sen. Lect., Dept. of Computer Studies, Sunderland Polytechnic.

Major Honours Wadsworth Prize, Bus. Archives Council, 1989.

Fields of Expertise *Industry Fields:* insurance, banking, finance; electronics and computers: manufacture. *Bus. Dimensions:* co. finance and accounting; research and development; strategy formation; merger movement and issues; bus. and technology. *Scope:* internat. *Period:* nineteenth century; twentieth century as a whole. *Teaching:* undergrad.

Publications *Books: ICL: A Bus. and Technical Hist.*, OUP, 1989.

Capie, Forrest H.

Prof. of Econ. Hist., Dept. of Banking and Finance, City Univ. Bus. School, Frobisher Crescent, Barbican Centre, London, EC2Y 8HB, UK. Tel.: 44 71 477 8736. Fax: 44 71 477 8880.

Year and Place of Birth 1940, Glasgow, UK.

Degrees and Qualifications BA Auckland Univ., New Zealand, 1967; M.Sc. London School of Econ., 1969; Ph.D. London School of Econ., 1973.

Previous Post Leeds Univ., 1974–9.

Current Offices and Honorary Posts Ed., *Econ. Hist. Rev.*

Fields of Expertise *Industry Fields:* insurance, banking, finance. *Bus. Dimensions:* merger movement and issues; markets and bus. *Scope:* national; internat. *Period:* nineteenth century; twentieth century as a whole; early twentieth century; inter-war years, 1919–39; mid-twentieth century, 1940–70. *Teaching:* undergrad.; post grad.

Publications *Books: Monetary Hist. of the United Kingdom, 1870–1982: Data Sources & Methods*, with A. Webber, George Allen & Unwin, 1985; *Monetary Regimes in Transition*, with M. Bordo co-ed., CUP, 1993. *Articles:* 'Conditions in which Hyperinflation has appeared', *Carnegie Rochester Public Series*, Brunner & Meltzer eds., March 1986, reprinted in *Major Inflations in Hist.* (Capie ed.); 'Structure and Performance in British Banking before 1939', *Money and Power*, Moggeridge & Cottrell, eds.; 'British Econ. Fluctuations in the late

Nineteenth Century', *Essays Trade*, Broadberry & Crafts eds.

Carlos, Ann M.

Assoc. Prof., Dept. of Econ., Colorado Univ., POB 256, Boulder, CO 80309, USA. Tel.: 1 303 492 8737. Fax: 1 303 492 8960.

Year and Place of Birth 1952, Dublin, Ireland.

Degrees and Qualifications BA Univ. College Dublin, 1973; Higher Dip. in Ed. Univ. College Dublin, 1974; MA Univ. College Dublin, 1975; Ph.D. Univ. of Western Ontario, 1980.

Previous Post Instructor, Univ. of Western Ontario, 1988–90.

Current Offices and Honorary Posts Edit. board, *J. of Econ. Hist.*, 1992–6; vice-pres., Econ. Hist. Soc., 1992–6.

Fields of Expertise *Industry Fields:* agric., forestry, fishing; transport and communication; fur trade; railroads. *Bus. Dimensions:* co. finance and accounting; merger movement and issues; bus. organization. *Scope:* national; internat.; Canada. *Period:* early modern; eighteenth century; nineteenth century. *Teaching:* undergrad.; post grad.

Publications *Articles:* 'The Making of a Joint Profit-Maximising Contract by a Duopoly: A Case Study from the North Amer. Fur Trade, 1804–1821', *J. of Econ. Hist.*, with Elizabeth Hoffman, XLVI(4), Dec., 1986; 'Giants of an Earlier Capitalism: The Early Chartered Companies as an Analogue of the Modern Multinational', *Bus. Hist. Rev.*, with Stephen Nicholas, 26(3), Autumn, 1988; 'Agency Problems in Early Chartered Companies: The Case of the Hudson's Bay Co.', *J. of Econ. Hist.*, with Stephen Nicholas, L(4), Dec., 1990; 'Managing the Manager: An Application of the Principal Agent Problem to the Hudson's Bay Co.',

Oxford Econ. Papers, with Stephen Nicholas, July, 1993; 'Bonding the Agency Problem: Evidence from the Royal African Co. 1672–1691', *Explorations in Econ. Hist.*, 1994.

Carreras, Albert

Prof., Dept. of Hist. & Civilization, European Univ. Inst., Via dei Roccettini 9, 50016-San Domenico di Fiesole, Florence, Italy. Tel.: 39 55 5092238. Fax: 39 55 5092203.
Year and Place of Birth 1955, Barcelona, Spain.
Degrees and Qualifications MA Autonomous Univ. Barcelona, 1979; Ph.D. Autonomous Univ. Barcelona, 1983.
Previous Post Titular Prof., Barcelona Univ., 1986–9.
Current Offices and Honorary Posts Edit. board mem., *Recerques, Revista de Historia Económica, Spagna Contemporanea, Revista de Historia Indust.*, and *Hist. and Technology.*
Major Honours II Prize 'Jaume Vicens Vives' for the Social Sciences 1987.
Fields of Expertise *Industry Fields:* manufacturing. *Scope:* national; Spain. *Period:* nineteenth century; twentieth century as a whole. *Teaching:* undergrad.; post grad.
Publications *Books: La Economía Española en el Siglo XX. Una Perspectiva Histórica*, co-ed., Ariel, 1987; *Estadísticas Históricas de España, Siglos XIX-XX*, ed., Fundación Banco Exterior, 1989; *Pautas Regionales de la Industrialización Española*, co-ed., Ariel, 1990; *Industrialización Española. Estudios de Historia Cuantitativa*, Espasa-Calpe, 1991. *Articles:* 'La Gran Empresa en España (1917–1974). Una Primera Aproximación', *Revista de Historia Indust.*, with X. Tafunell co-auth., 3,

1993, forthcoming.

Carreras, Charles

Assoc. Prof., School of Amer. & Internat. Studies, Ramapo College, Mahwah, NJ 07430, USA. Tel.: 1 201 529 7429. Fax: 1 201 529 7508.
Year and Place of Birth 1941, Richmond, USA.
Degrees and Qualifications BA St Vincent College, 1958; MA Univ. of North Carolina, 1967; Ph.D. Univ. of North Carolina, 1971.
Major Honours NEH, Summer, 1981; Woodrow Wilson, Seminar, Summer, 1984; Fulbright Summer Seminar, 1993.
Fields of Expertise *Industry Fields:* agric., forestry, fishing. *Bus. Dimensions:* bus.–state relations. *Scope:* internat. *Period:* twentieth century as a whole. *Teaching:* undergrad. *Consultancy:* co. hist.
Publications *Books: United States Econ. Penetration of Venezuela and its Effects on Diplomacy: 1895–1906*, Garland Publishers, NY, 1987. *Articles:* 'US Efforts to Expand Trade: The National Assoc.'s Caracas Warehouse, 1895–1901', *Inter-Amer. Econ. Affairs*, 31, summer, 1977, 51–64; 'Hist. of Nabisco in Central Amer.', *New Jersey in the World*, Global Learning, Montclair, NJ, 1987; 'The Survival of US Bus. in Revolutionary Nicaragua', *Bus. Assoc. of Latin Amer. Studies*, proceedings, 1989.

Carter, Ian R.

Prof. of Sociology, Dept. of Sociology, Univ. of Auckland, Private Bag 92019, Auckland, New Zealand. Tel.: 64 9 3737 599. Fax: 64 9 3737 439.
Year and Place of Birth 1943,

Luton, UK.

Degrees and Qualifications B.Sc. Bath Univ., 1967; MA Essex Univ., 1968; Ph.D. Aberdeen Univ., 1976.

Previous Post Director, Inst. for the Study of Sparsely Populated Areas, Aberdeen Univ., 1980–1.

Fields of Expertise *Industry Fields:* agric., forestry, fishing. *Bus. Dimensions:* labour process. *Scope:* regional. *Period:* nineteenth century. *Teaching:* undergrad.; post grad. *Consultancy:* social hist./biography.

Publications *Books: Farm Life in North-east Scotland*, John Donald, Edinburgh, 1979; *Ancient Cultures of Conceit: British Univ. Fiction in the post-War Years*, Routledge, London, 1990; *Rural Life in Victorian Aberdeenshire*, Mercat Press, Edinburgh, 1992; *Gadfly: The Life and Times of James Shelley*, Auckland Univ. Press, Auckland, 1993.

Casado Alonso, Hilario

Asst. Prof., Valladolid Univ., Dept. of Econ. Hist., Fac. of Econ. Science, 47011 Valladolid, Spain. Tel.: 34 83 423354. Fax: 34 83 423299.

Year and Place of Birth 1954, Burgos, Spain.

Degrees and Qualifications M.Litt. Valladolid Univ., 1977; Ph.D. Valladolid Univ., 1986.

Fields of Expertise *Industry Fields:* insurance, banking, finance. *Bus. Dimensions:* entrepreneurs and entrepreneurship. *Scope:* internat. *Period:* early modern. *Teaching:* post grad. *Consultancy:* co. hist.

Publications *Books: Señores, Mercaderes y Campesinos. La Comarca de Burgos a Fines de la Edad Media*, Junta de Castilla y Leon, Valladolid, 1987. *Articles:* 'Comercio Internacional y Seguros Maritimos en Burgos en la Epoca de los Reyes Catolicos', *Porto*, Universidade, 1990, 221–38; 'Relaciones Comerciales y Financieras entre Mercaderes de Burgos y de Lucca', *Lucca*, R. Mazzei & T. Fanfani eds., 109–20; 'Finance et Commerce Internat. au Milieu du XVIe. Siècle: La Compagnie des Bernuy', *Annales du Midi*, 195, Toulouse, 1991, 323–43.

Cassis, Youssef

Asst. Lect., Dept. of Econ. Hist., Geneva Univ., 102 Boulevard Carl-Vogt, 1211 Geneva 4, Switzerland. Tel.: 41 22 705 8192.

Year and Place of Birth 1952, Cairo, Egypt.

Degrees and Qualifications Licence ès Lettres Geneva Univ., 1974; Doctorat ès Lettres Geneva Univ., 1982.

Previous Post Maître asst., Dept. of Hist., Geneva Univ., 1983–92.

Current Offices and Honorary Posts Chairman, Academic Council, Assoc. for Banking Hist. (Switzerland); mem., Academic Advisory Council, European Assoc. for Banking Hist.; visiting research fellow, Bus. Hist. Unit, London School of Econ.

Fields of Expertise *Industry Fields:* insurance, banking, finance. *Bus. Dimensions:* entrepreneurs and entrepreneurship. *Scope:* national; internat.; UK; Switzerland. *Period:* twentieth century as a whole. *Teaching:* undergrad.; post grad. *Consultancy:* co. hist.

Publications *Books: Les Banquiers de la City à l'Époque Édouardienne 1890–1914*, Droz, 1984; *La City de Londres 1870–1914*, Belin, 1987; *Capitalism in a Mature Economy. Financial Institutions, Capital Exports and British Industry 1870–1939*, with J.J. Van Helten co-ed., Edward Elgar, 1990; *Finance and Financiers in European Hist. 1880–1960*, ed., CUP, 1992; *Financial Hist. Rev.*, with Philip

Cottrell co-ed., CUP, forthcoming 1994.

Casson, Mark

Prof. of Econ., Dept. of Econ., Univ. of Reading, POB 218, Reading, Berks, RG8 00J, UK. Tel.: 44 734 318226. Fax: 44 734 750236.

Year and Place of Birth 1945, Grappenhall, UK.

Degrees and Qualifications BA Bristol Univ., 1966.

Previous Post Reader in Econ., Reading Univ., 1977–81.

Current Offices and Honorary Posts Mem. of edit. advisory boards: *Bus. Hist., J. of Internat. Bus. Studies, J. of Bus. Econ., Scandinavian Internat. Bus. Rev.*

Major Honours Mem., Council of Royal Econ. Soc., 1985–90.

Fields of Expertise *Industry Fields:* transport and communication. *Bus. Dimensions:* multinational bus. *Scope:* internat. *Period:* twentieth century as a whole. *Consultancy:* corporate strategy.

Publications *Books: Econ. Theory of the Multinational Enterprise*, P.J. Buckley co-ed., Macmillan, 1985; *The Firm and the Market*, MIT Press, 1987; *Econ. of Bus. Culture*, OUP, 1991; *Enterprise and Competitiveness*, OUP, 1991; *The Entrepreneur: An Econ. Theory*, Martin Robertson, 1982, reprinted Gregg Revivals, 1991.

Chandler, Alfred D. Jr.

Straus Prof. of Bus. Hist. Emeritus, Harvard Bus. School, Cumnock Hall, Room 300, Boston, MA 02163, USA. Tel.: 0617 495 6367. Fax: 0617 495 8736.

Year and Place of Birth 1918, Guyencourt, USA.

Degrees and Qualifications BA Harvard Univ., 1940; MA Harvard Univ., 1947; Ph.D. Harvard Univ., 1952.

Previous Post Prof. of Hist., Johns Hopkins Univ., 1963–70.

Major Honours Newcomen Award, 1964, 1979; Bancroft & Pulitzer Prizes, 1978; Assoc. of Amer. Publishers Award, 1991; Melamed Prize, 1992; mem., Amer. Philosophical Soc., Amer. Acad. of Arts & Sciences, British Acad., Japan Acad.; Pres., Econ. Hist. Assoc. (USA), 1971–2; Pres., Bus. Hist. Conf., 1977–8.

Fields of Expertise *Industry Fields:* agric., forestry, fishing; food, drink, tobacco; coal and petroleum products; chemicals and allied industries; metal manufacture; mechanical engineering; electrical engineering; shipbuilding and marine engineering; vehicle construction; metal goods; textiles; bricks, pottery, glass, cement; paper, printing, publishing; transport and communication; electronics and computers: manufacture. *Bus. Dimensions:* bus. organization. *Scope:* internat. *Period:* twentieth century as a whole. *Teaching:* post grad. *Consultancy:* co. hist.

Publications *Books: Henry Varnum Poor*, Harvard Univ. Press, 1956; *Strategy and Structure*, MIT Press, 1962; *The Papers of Dwight David Eisenhower*, ed., vols. 1–5, Johns Hopkins Univ. Press, 1970; *The Visible Hand*, Belknap Press of Harvard Univ. Press, 1977; *Scale and Scope*, Belknap Press of Harvard Univ. Press, 1990.

Channon, Geoffrey

Dean of Humanities, Fac. of Humanities, Univ. of the West of England, St Mathias Campus, Oldbury Court Road, Fishponds, Bristol, BS16 2JP, UK. Tel.: 44 272 655384. Fax: 44 272 750402.

Year and Place of Birth 1944, Enfield, UK.

Degrees and Qualifications B.Sc. (Econ.) London Univ., 1966; Ph.D. London Univ., 1975.

Previous Post Head of School of Hist., Bristol Polytechnic, 1975–85.

Current Offices and Honorary Posts Exec. com. mem., Standing Conf. for Arts & Soc. Sc.; edit. board, *J. of Transport Hist.*.

Fields of Expertise *Industry Fields:* food, drink, tobacco; transport and communication. *Bus. Dimensions:* entrepreneurs and entrepreneurship; bus. organization; bus. values; co. culture. *Scope:* national; internat. *Period:* nineteenth century; twentieth century as a whole. *Teaching:* undergrad.; post grad.

Publications *Articles:* 'A Nineteenth Century Investment Decision: The Midland Railway's London Extension', *Econ. Hist. Rev.*, XXV(3), 1972; 'The Great Western Railway under the British Railways Act of 1921', *Bus. Hist. Rev.*, LV(2), 1981; 'A. D. Chandler's "Visible Hand" in Transport Hist.: A Rev. Article', *J. of Transport Hist.*, 3rd ser. (2), 1981; 'Railroad Competition and its Management in the United States and Britain before 1914', *Bus. & Econ. Hist.*, 2nd ser., 17, 1988; 'The Bristol Brewery Georges', *Studies in the Bus. Hist. of Bristol*, Charles Harvey & Jon Press eds., Bristol Academic Press, 1988.

Chapman, Stanley David

Prof. of Bus. Hist., Dept. of Bus. Hist., Nottingham Univ., Nottingham, NG7 2RD, UK. Tel.: 44 602 515941.

Year and Place of Birth 1935, Nottingham, UK.

Degrees and Qualifications B.Sc. (Econ.) London Univ., 1956; MA Nottingham Univ., 1960; Ph.D.

London Univ., 1966.

Previous Post Pasold Reader in Hist., Nottingham Univ., 1973–93.

Major Honours Nuffield Fellowship, 1982–3.

Fields of Expertise *Industry Fields:* metal manufacture; textiles; distributive trades; insurance, banking, finance. *Bus. Dimensions:* entrepreneurs and entrepreneurship; marketing; merger movement and issues; multinational bus.; co. culture. *Period:* eighteenth century; nineteenth century; twentieth century as a whole. *Teaching:* undergrad.; post grad. *Consultancy:* co. hist.

Publications *Books: Cotton in the Indust. Revolution*, Macmillan, 1972; new edn., 1987; *Jesse Boot of Boots the Chemists*, Hodder & Stoughton, 1974; new extended edn. in preparation; *Stanton & Staveley: A Bus. Hist.*, Woodhead Faulkner, 1981; *The Rise of Merchant Banking*, Allen & Unwin, 1984; *Merchant Enterprise in Britain*, CUP, 1992.

Chassagne, Serge

Prof. of Modern Hist., Fac. of Letters and Humanities, 1 rue Thomas Becket, POB 138, 76134 Mont-St-Aignan Cedex, France. Tel.: 33 35 14 61 45. Fax: 33 35 14 62 00.

Year and Place of Birth 1941, Angers, France.

Degrees and Qualifications Licence d'Histoire Rennes Univ., 1962; Maîtrise, 1963; Agrégation, 1965; Doctorat de troisième cycle Rennes Univ., 1970; Doctorat d'Etat (EHESS), 1986.

Previous Post Director, National Museum of Education, Rouen, 1979–89.

Current Offices and Honorary Posts Director, Dept. of Hist., Rouen.

Major Honours Grand Prix de l'Académie de Rouen, 1992.

Fields of Expertise *Industry Fields:*

mechanical engineering; textiles. *Bus. Dimensions:* entrepreneurs and entre-preneurship. *Scope:* regional; national; internat. *Period:* eighteenth century; nineteenth century. *Teaching:* under-grad.; post grad.

Publications *Books: La Manufacture de Toiles Imprimées de Touremine-les-Angers (1752–1820),* Klincksieck, Paris, 1971; *Oberkampf un Entrepreneur Capitaliste au Siècle des Lumière,* Aubier, Paris, 1980; *European Textile Printers. A Comparative Study of Peel and Oberkampf,* with S.D. Chapman, Heinemann Educational Books, London, 1981; *Le Coton et ses Patrons, France 1760–1840,* EHESS, Paris, 1991.

Chatov, Robert

Assoc. Prof. of Law and Policy, Dept. of Accounting and Law, School of Management, State Univ. of New York at Buffalo, Amherst, NY 14260, USA. Tel.: 1 716 645 3226. Fax: 1 716 645 3823.

Year and Place of Birth 1927, New York, USA.

Degrees and Qualifications BS (Econ. & Stats.) New York Univ., School of Commerce, 1949; MA (Econ.) Northwestern Univ., 1951; Ph.D. (sequences in Econ. Hist., Money & Banking) Northwestern Univ., 1951; JD Wayne Univ. Law School, 1957; Ph.D. (Bus. & Pub. Policy) Univ. of California at Berkeley, 1973.

Current Offices and Honorary Posts Ad-hoc Reviewer, Amer. Accounting Assoc.

Fields of Expertise *Industry Fields:* professional and scientific services. *Bus. Dimensions:* bus.–state relations. *Scope:* national. *Period:* late twentieth century, 1970–present. *Teaching:* undergrad.; post grad. *Consultancy:* corporate strategy.

Publications *Books: Corporate Financial Reporting: Public or Private Control?,* The Free Press, New York, 1975. *Articles:* 'The Possible New Shape of Accounting in the United States', *J. of Accounting & Public Policy,* guest editorial, no. 4, 1985, 161–74, (invited); 'Re-examining the Rules of the Game: The Dingell Hearings and Beyond', *Advances in Public Interest Accounting,* 1(1), 1986, JAI Press, 15–47; 'The Demand for Natural Gas, Electricity and Heating Oil in the United States', *Resources and Energy,* with Winston Lin & Yueh H. Chen, 9(3), Oct., 1987, 233–58; 'Corporate Codes of Conduct: Econ. Determinants and Legal Implications for Auditors', *J. of Accounting & Public Policy,* with M. Daniel Beneish co-auth., 12(1), Sp. 1993, Elsevier Science Publishing Co. Inc..

Cheape, Charles W.

Prof. of Hist., Dept. of Hist., Loyola College, 4501 N. Charles St, Baltimore, MD 21210, USA. Tel.: 1 410 617 2635. Fax: 1 410 323 2768.

Year and Place of Birth 1945, Charlotesville, Virginia, USA.

Degrees and Qualifications BA Virginia Univ., 1968; MA Brandeis Univ., 1974; Ph.D., Brandeis Univ., 1976.

Previous Post Oklahoma State Univ., 1983–4.

Fields of Expertise *Industry Fields:* chemicals and allied industries; bricks, pottery, glass, cement; transport and communication. *Bus. Dimensions:* strategy formation; bus. organization. *Scope:* national. *Period:* twentieth century as a whole. *Teaching:* undergrad. *Consultancy:* co. hist.

Publications *Books: Moving the Masses: Urban Public Transit in New York, Boston and Philadelphia,*

1880–1912, Harvard Univ. Press, Cambridge, MA, 1980; *Family Firm to Modern Multinational: Norton Co., a New England Enterprise*, Harvard Univ. Press, Cambridge, MA, 1985. *Articles:* 'Paternalism and Corporate Welfarism in large-scale Enterprise: The Norton Co. Experience', *Bus. & Econ. Hist.*, Jeremy Atack ed., 2nd ser., 13, 1984, 50–9; 'Not Politicians but Sound Bus.men: Norton Co. and the Third Reich', *Bus. Hist. Rev.*, 62, autumn, 1988, 444–66.

Chevalier, Jean-Joseph

Prof. of Geographic Hist., Lycée Renaudeau, 49300 Cholet, France.

Year and Place of Birth 1950, St Brieuc, France.

Degrees and Qualifications Maîtrise (Mod. Hist.) Rennes II Univ., 1974; C.A.P.E.S., 1976; DEA Rennes II Univ., 1989.

Current Offices and Honorary Posts Vice-pres., Assoc. of Friends of Cholet Textile Museum.

Fields of Expertise *Industry Fields:* textiles. *Bus. Dimensions:* entrepreneurs and entrepreneurship; small bus. matters. *Scope:* local; regional. *Period:* eighteenth century; nineteenth century; twentieth century as a whole.

Publications *Articles:* 'Du Mouchoir de Cholet au Negoce Mexicain: Trois Tentatives d'Ascension Sociale au Temps de la Révolution Industrielle', *Annales de Bretagne et des Pays de l'Ouest*, 93(3), 1986, 299–326 & 94(1), 1987, 71–85; 'La "Compagnie des Lins et Toiles de l"Ouest" et ses Promoteurs (1839–1863): L'Echec d'une Entreprise Capitaliste Choletaise au Temps de la Révolution Industrielle', *Annales de Normandie*, no. 2/3, May/Jul., 1988, 105–23; 'La "Société des onze Associés" de Cholet (1796–1806): Réconstructions

Economique et Politique au Lendemain de l'Insurrection Vendéenne', *Annales de Bretagne et des Pays de l'Ouest*, 97(3), 1990, 237–55; 'Les Ateliers et Usines de Blanchiment de Toiles dans le Choletais, de la Fin du XVIIIe a nos Jours', *Arts de L'Ouest*, 1992, 16–27.

Chiba, Junichi

Prof. of Accountancy, Fac. of Econ., Tokyo Metropol. Univ., 1-1 Minami-Ohsawa, Hachioji-City, Tokyo, Japan. Tel.: 81 426 77 1111.

Year and Place of Birth 1947, Miyagi, Japan.

Degrees and Qualifications BA (Econ.), Yokohama Nat. Univ., 1969; MA (Econ.), Tokyo Univ., 1972; Ph.D. (Econ.), Tokyo Univ., 1983.

Previous Post Assoc. Prof., Fac. of Bus. Admin., Rissho Univ., Tokyo, 1978–9.

Current Offices and Honorary Posts Edit., Staff of Year Book of Accounting Hist. Assoc. (Japan), 1985–7.

Major Honours Japan Accounting Assoc. Prize (1981); Accounting Hist. Assoc. (Japan) Prize (1992).

Fields of Expertise *Industry Fields:* shipbuilding and marine engineering; insurance, banking, finance; professional and scientific services. *Bus. Dimensions:* co. finance and accounting; co. law; bus.–state relations; co. culture. *Scope:* national; internat. *Period:* nineteenth century; twentieth century as a whole; inter-war years, 1919–39. *Teaching:* undergrad.; post grad. *Consultancy:* co. hist.

Publications *Books: Kaikei no Kiso-Kozo* [Fundamental Structure of Accounting] Moriyama Shoten, Tokyo, 1980; *Eikoku Kindai Kaikei Seido* [A Hist. of British Financial Accounting] Chuo-Keizaisha, Tokyo, 1991. *Articles:* 'The Case Law relating to British Public Accounting', *Keizaito Keizaigaku*, Tokyo Metropol. Univ.,

56, March, 1985; 'British Co. Accounting 1844–1885 and its Influence on the Modernisation of Japanese Financial Accounting', *Keizaito Keizaigaku* , Tokyo Metropol. Univ., 60, October, 1987; 'Sengo Wagakuri Shoken-Torihiki-Iinkai Koso to Kigyo-Kaikei-gensoku' [A Statement of Bus. Accounting Principles under the Scheme of Japanese SEC after World War II], *Keizai to Keizaigaku*, Tokyo Metropol. Univ., 65, March, 1990.

Chick, Martin J.

Lect., Dept. of Econ. Hist., William Robertson Building, Edinburgh Univ., 50 George Square, Edinburgh, EH8 9JY, UK. Tel.: 44 31 650 3842.

Year and Place of Birth 1958, London, UK.

Degrees and Qualifications MA Cambridge Univ., 1980; Ph.D. London School of Econ., 1986.

Fields of Expertise *Industry Fields:* coal and petroleum products; gas, electricity, water. *Bus. Dimensions:* bus.–state relations; markets and bus. *Scope:* national. *Period:* mid-twentieth century, 1940–70; late twentieth century, 1970–present. *Teaching:* undergrad.; post grad.

Publications *Books: Governments, Industries and Markets*, ed., Edward Elgar Publishing, 1990. *Articles:* 'Privatisation: The Triumph of Past Practice over Current Requirements', *Bus. Hist.*, XXIX(4), Oct., 1987, 104–16; 'Competition, Competitiveness and Nationalisation, 1945–51', *Competitiveness and the State*, G. Jones & M. Kirby eds., Manchester, 1991; 'Electricity Distribution', *The Polit. Economy of Nationalisation*, R. Millward & J. Singleton eds., Cambridge, 1994.

Childs, William R.

Assoc. Prof., Dept. of Hist., Ohio State Univ., 230 W 17th Ave, Columbus, OH 43210, USA. Tel.: 1 614 292 2674. Fax: 1 614 292 2282.

Year and Place of Birth 1951, Houston, USA.

Degrees and Qualifications BA Texas Univ., Austin, 1973; MA Texas Univ., Austin, 1976; Ph.D. Texas Univ., Austin, 1982.

Previous Post Asst. Prof., Ohio State Univ., 1984–91.

Current Offices and Honorary Posts Sec., Econ. & Bus. Hist. Soc. (USA).

Fields of Expertise *Industry Fields:* coal and petroleum products; gas, electricity, water; transport and communication; public admin. and defence. *Bus. Dimensions:* bus.–state relations; regulation in Amer. *Scope:* local; regional; national. *Period:* twentieth century as a whole. *Teaching:* undergrad.; post grad. *Consultancy:* theatre docudrama.

Publications *Books: Trucking and the Public Interest: The Emergence of Federal Regulation, 1914–1940*, Univ. of Tennessee Press, 1985. *Articles:* 'Origin of the Tefar Railroad Commission's Power to Control Petroleum', *J. of Policy Hist.*, 2(4), 1990, 353–87; 'The Transformation of the Railroad Commission of Tefar, 1917–1940', *Bus. Hist. Rev.*, 65(2), Summer, 1991, 285–344.

Christiansen, W. Kenneth S.

Part-time Lect., Auckland Univ. & Sen. Research Fellow, Massey Univ., 4/65 Campbell Road, Onehunga, Auckland 6, New Zealand. Tel.: 64 9 634 7061.

Year and Place of Birth 1925, Paris, France.

Degrees and Qualifications FRICS London Univ., 1951; Dip.T.P.

Auckland Univ., 1979; FPMI (Life), 1978.

Previous Post Assoc. Prof. & First Head of Dept. of Property, Fac. of Architecture, Property & Planning, Auckland Univ., (retired 1991).

Current Offices and Honorary Posts Vice-chairman, Univ. of the Third Age (U3A), Remuera, Auckland.

Major Honours Ralph Hanan Memorial Scholarship 1972–3; founding president, Property Management Inst., 1978–80.

Fields of Expertise *Industry Fields:* construction; insurance, banking, finance; bus. services; professional and scientific services. *Bus. Dimensions:* marketing; research and development; bus. organization; management education; estate agency. *Scope:* local; regional; national; internat. *Period:* mid-twentieth century, 1940–70; late twentieth century, 1970–present. *Teaching:* undergrad.; post grad. *Consultancy:* corporate strategy.

Publications *Books: Estate Management,* Real Estate Inst. of New Zealand, Auckland, 1973; *Fundamentals of Property Management,* Butterworth, Wellington, New Zealand, 1989; *Mahoney's Urban Land Econ.,* 3rd revised edn., New Zealand Inst. of Valuers, Wellington, 1991; *Property Lore,* Property Management Inst., Auckland, 1991. *Articles:* 'Property Management', *Urban Valuation in New Zealand Vol. II,* New Zealand Inst. of Valuers, Wellington, 1990, 8-1–8-34.

Churella, Albert John

Dept. of Hist., The Ohio State Univ., 230 West 17th Avenue, Columbus, OH 43210, USA. Tel.: 1 614 292 2674.

Degrees and Qualifications BA Haverford College, 1986; MA Ohio State Univ., 1990; Ph.D. Ohio State Univ., dissertation in progress: 'Corporate Response to Technological Change: The Amer. Railway Locomotive Industry, 1930–1965'.

Previous Post Teaching Assoc., Ohio State Univ., 1988–92.

Major Honours John E. Rovensky Fellowship in Amer. Econ. & Bus. Hist., 1993.

Fields of Expertise *Industry Fields:* mining and quarrying; other manufacturing industries; transport and communication; railroads, related equipment. *Bus. Dimensions:* co. admin.; marketing; research and development; bus. and technology; co. culture. *Scope:* national. *Period:* twentieth century as a whole. *Teaching:* undergrad.

Publications *Articles:* 'A Hist. of the Mammoth Cave Railroad', *J. of Spelean Hist.,* 20, Jul.-Sept., 1986, 51–7; 'Samuel Hallett and the Professionalization of Finance', paper presented at the Duquesne Hist. Forum, Pittsburgh, PA, 24 Oct., 1990; 'The Amer. Railway Locomotive Industry during World War II: The Limitations of Government Power', paper presented at the Duquesne Hist. Forum, Pittsburgh, PA, 24 Oct., 1991; 'The Lima Locomotive Works and the Dieselization Revolution, 1930–1950: Corporate Response to Technological Change', paper presented at the Ohio Acad. of Hist., Dayton, Ohio, April, 1992; 'Corporate Response to Technological Change: The Electro-Motive Division of General Motors during the 1930s', paper presented at the Econ. & Bus. Hist. Soc. Conf., Nashville, Tennessee, 24 Apr., 1993.

Cizakca, Murat

Prof. of Econ., Bogazici Univ., Istanbul & Prof., Internat. Inst. of Islamic Thought, Kuala Lumpur, Malaysia, Dept. of Econ., Bogazici Univ., Bebek 80815, Istanbul, Turkey. Tel.: 024

363938. Fax: 024 363938.

Year and Place of Birth 1946, Bursa, Turkey.

Degrees and Qualifications BA (Econ.) Leicester Univ., UK, 1968; MA (Econ. Hist.) Pennsylvania Univ., 1974; Ph.D. (Econ. Hist.) Pennsylvania Univ., 1978.

Previous Post Assoc. Prof., Internat. Inst. for Islamic Banking & Econ., Girne, Turkish Republic of N. Cyprus, 1982–4.

Current Offices and Honorary Posts Selection comm. mem., Islamic Development Bank Prizes on Islamic Econ. & Banking; exec. board mem., Internat. Conf. on the Econ. & Soc. Hist. of Turkey.

Fields of Expertise *Industry Fields:* textiles; insurance, banking, finance. *Bus. Dimensions:* entrepreneurs and entrepreneurship; bus. organization; small bus. matters; venture capital and Islamic partnerships. *Scope:* internat.; global; Turkey. *Period:* medieval; early modern; eighteenth century; nineteenth century; twentieth century as a whole. *Teaching:* undergrad.; post grad. *Consultancy:* corporate strategy.

Publications *Articles:* 'Price Hist. and the Bursa Silk Industry', *J. of Econ. Hist.*, XL, 1980, 533–51; 'Incorporation of the Middle East into the European World Economy', *Rev.*, VIII(3), 1985, 353–77; 'Tax Farming and Resource Allocation in past Islamic Societies', *J. of King Abdulaziz Univ, Islamic Econ.*, 1, 1989, 59–83; 'Financing Small Firms in the Middle East', Tenth Internat. Econ. Hist. Congress, A 4b Session, Leuven, 1990, 201–15; 'Financial Decentralization in the Ottoman Economy', *J. of European Econ. Hist.*, 2, 1993, forthcoming.

Clay, Christopher

Prof. of Econ. Hist., Dept. of Hist. Studies, Bristol Univ., 13 Woodland Road, Bristol, BS8 1TB, UK. Tel.: 44 272 303030. Fax: 44 272 288276.

Year and Place of Birth 1940, Oxford, UK.

Degrees and Qualifications BA Cambridge Univ., 1961; MA Cambridge Univ., 1964; Ph.D. Cambridge Univ., 1966.

Previous Post Reader in Econ. Hist., Bristol Univ., 1980–8.

Fields of Expertise *Industry Fields:* insurance, banking, finance. *Bus. Dimensions:* bus.–state relations. *Scope:* national; internat. *Period:* early modern; nineteenth century. *Teaching:* undergrad. *Consultancy:* co. hist. (freelance).

Publications *Books: Public Finance and Private Wealth, the Career of Sir Stephen Fox (1627–1716),* OUP, 1978; *Econ. Expansion and Social Change: England 1500–1700,* CUP, 1984. *Articles:* 'The Imperial Ottoman Bank in the later Nineteenth Century: A Multinational "National" Bank?', *Banks as Multinationals,* G. Jones ed., Routledge, 1990.

Coleman, D.C.

Emeritus Prof. of Econ. Hist., Cambridge Univ., Over Hall, Cavendish, Sudbury, Suffolk, CO10 8BP, UK.

Year and Place of Birth 1920, London, UK.

Degrees and Qualifications B.Sc. (Econ.) London Univ., 1949; Ph.D. London Univ., 1951; D. Litt. Cambridge Univ., 1981.

Previous Post Prof. of Econ. Hist., Cambridge Univ., 1971–81.

Current Offices and Honorary Posts Chairman of the Governors, Pasold Research Fund.

Major Honours F.B.A.; Wadsworth Prize (for *Courtaulds* Vol. 3).

Fields of Expertise *Industry Fields:* textiles. *Bus. Dimensions:* bus. organization. *Scope:* national. *Period:* early modern; eighteenth century; nineteenth century; twentieth century as a whole. *Teaching:* post grad. *Consultancy:* co. hist.

Publications *Books: The British Paper Industry 1495–1860*, OUP, 1958; *Sir John Banks: Baronet and Bus.man*, OUP, 1963; *Courtaulds. An Econ. and Social Hist.*, 3 vols., OUP, 1969, 1981; *Hist. and the Econ. Past*, OUP, 1987; *Myth, Hist. and the Indust. Revolution*, Hambledon Press, London, 1992.

Coll, Sebastián

Prof., Dept. of Econ., Fac. of Econ. Science, Cantabria Univ., Av. Castros S.A., 39005 Santander, Spain. Tel.: 34 42 20 16 51. Fax: 34 42 20 16 03.

Year and Place of Birth 1953, Madrid, Spain.

Degrees and Qualifications MA Madrid Univ., 1976; Ph.D. Madrid Univ., 1986.

Previous Post Titular Prof., Dept. of Econ., Cantabria Univ., 1992–3.

Current Offices and Honorary Posts Edit. board mem., *Revista de Historia Econ. & Anales de Administracion de Empresas y Economia*, (Santander).

Fields of Expertise *Industry Fields:* coal and petroleum products. *Bus. Dimensions:* entrepreneurs and entrepreneurship. *Scope:* national. *Period:* nineteenth century. *Teaching:* undergrad. *Consultancy:* co. hist.

Publications *Books: El Carbon en España 1770–1960: Una Historia Economica*, with C. Sudria co-auth., Turner, 1987; *Fuentos Quantitativas para la Historia Economica de España*, with J.I Portea, Banco de España, 2 vols., forthcoming. *Articles:* 'Empresas vs. Mercados un Boceto para una Historia de la Empresa', *Revista de Historia Economica*, IX(2), 1991, 263–81 & IX(3), 463–78; 'La nueva Historia Economica y su Influencia en

España', *Doce Estudios de Histografia Contemporanea*, G. Rugda ed., Cantabria Univ., 1991, 69–119; 'Riflessioni sulla Storia d'Impresa. Lo Stato della Questione in Spagna', *Annali di Storia dell'Impresa*, with Gariel Portella, 1992, 47–67.

Collins, Michael

Reader in Financial Hist., School of Bus. and Econ. Studies, Centre for Bus. Hist., Univ. of Leeds, LS2 9JT, UK. Tel.: 44 532 334493. Fax: 44 532 332640.

Year and Place of Birth 1946, UK.

Degrees and Qualifications B.Sc. (Econ.) London Univ., 1968; Ph.D. London Univ., 1972.

Current Offices and Honorary Posts Council mem., Econ. Hist. Soc.

Fields of Expertise *Industry Fields:* insurance, banking, finance. *Bus. Dimensions:* co. finance and accounting. *Scope:* national. *Period:* nineteenth century; twentieth century as a whole. *Teaching:* undergrad.; post grad. *Consultancy:* co. hist.

Publications *Books: Money and Banking in the UK. A Hist.*, Croom Helm, 1988, re-issued Routledge, 1991; *Banks and Indust. Finance in Britain, 1800–1939*, Macmillan, 1991; *Have the Banks Failed British Industry?*, with F.H. Capie, IEA, 1992; *Central Banking in Hist.*, ed., 3 vols., Edward Elgar Publishing, 1992. *Articles:* 'Long-term Growth of the English Banking Sector and Money Stock, 1844–80', *Econ. Hist. Rev.*, 36, 1983.

Collins, Theresa M.

Research Assoc., Rutgers Univ., Thomas A. Edison Papers, Van Dyke Hall, New Brunswick, NJ 08903, USA. Tel.: 1 908 932 5551.

Year and Place of Birth 1955, New York, USA.

Degrees and Qualifications BA New York Univ., 1979; M.Phil., 1987.

Current Offices and Honorary Posts Technology com. mem., Assoc. of Documentary Eds.

Major Honours John Rovensky Fellowship in Bus. & Econ. Hist., 1987–8; Research Fellow, Center for the Study of Philanthropy.

Publications *Books: Thomas A. Edison Papers: A Selective Microfilm Edn. Part III (1887–1898)*, with Thomas E. Jeffrey et al., forthcoming 1994.

Comin Comin, Francisco

Prof. of Econ. Hist., Univ. of Alcala, Madrid & Vice-Director of the Econ. Hist. Programme, Fundacion Empresa Publica, Fac. of Econ. Sciences, Dept. of Econ., Alcalá de Henares Univ., Pza. de la Victoria s/n, 28802 Alcalá de Henares (Madrid), Spain. Tel.: 34 91 577 79 09. Fax: 34 91 575 56 41.

Year and Place of Birth 1952, Obon, Spain.

Degrees and Qualifications BA (Econ.), Complutense Univ.; Ph.D. (Econ.) Alcalá Univ., 1987.

Previous Post Lect., Complutense Univ., Madrid & Valladolid Univ.

Current Offices and Honorary Posts Treasurer & board mem., Spanish Econ. Hist. Assoc.

Major Honours National Hist. Prize, Spanish Ministry of Culture, 1990.

Fields of Expertise *Industry Fields:* public admin. and defence. *Bus. Dimensions:* entrepreneurs and entrepreneurship; state companies. *Scope:* national; Spain. *Period:* nineteenth century; twentieth century as a whole. *Teaching:* undergrad.; post grad. *Consultancy:* co. hist.

Publications *Books: Fuentes Cuantitativas para el Estudio del Sector Publico en España (1800–1980)*, Instituto de Estuios Fiscales, Madrid, 1987; *Hacienda y Economia en la España Contemporanea (1800–1936)*, Instituto de Estudios Fiscales, 1988; *Las Cuentas de la Hacienda Preliberal en España (1800–1845)*, Banco de España, 1991; *Ini. 50 Años de Industrializacion en España*, with Pablo Martin Aceña co-auth., Espasa-Calpe, 1991; *Historia de le Empresa Publica en España*, with Pablo Martin Aceña co-ed., Espasa-Calpe, 1991.

Concato, Francis

Researcher, IRED (Inst. for Social Sc. Research & Documentation), Rouen Univ., 76821 Mont-St-Aignan Cedex, France. Tel.: 33 35 14 60 56. Fax: 33 35 14 69 40.

Year and Place of Birth 1949, Grand-Ouevilly (Rouen), France.

Degrees and Qualifications DEA Paris IX-Dauphine Univ., 1973; Maître d'Histoire Rouen Univ., 1974.

Fields of Expertise *Industry Fields:* mechanical engineering; textiles. *Bus. Dimensions:* entrepreneurs and entrepreneurship; production management; research and development; bus. and technology. *Scope:* regional; national. *Period:* eighteenth century; nineteenth century; early twentieth century.

Publications *Books: Eléments pour une histoire de la Chambre Consultative des Arts e Manufactures d'Elbeuf, 1801–1861*, with P. Largesse, Chamber of Industry & Commerce, Elbeuf, 1992. *Articles:* 'L'Appareil productif elbeuvion face au changement: une approche historique', *Etudes Normandes*, 2, 1987, 65–79; 'L'industrie drapière elbeuvienne sous la Révolution: homes, techniques et produits', *Annales de Bretagne et des Pays de l'Ouest*, with A. Becchia and P.

Largesse, 97(3), 1990, 207–225; Contribution to *Les Patrons du Second Empire, I – Anjou, Normandie, Maine,* D. Barjot, ed., Picard/Cénomane, Paris, 1991; 'La Manufacture de draps d'Elbeuf avant et après la révocation de l'Edit de Nantes', *Bulletin de la Société de l'Histoire du Protestantisme Français,* with P. Largesse, 138(3), 1992, 407–18.

Constant, Edward W. II

Assoc. Prof., Dept. of Hist., Carnegie Mellon Univ., Pittsburgh, PA 15213, USA. Tel.: 1 412 268 2880.
Year and Place of Birth 1943, Lake Charles, USA.
Degrees and Qualifications BA Rice Univ., 1965; MA Tulane Univ., 1971; Ph.D. Northwestern Univ., 1977.
Major Honours Dexter Prize of the Society for the History of Technology.
Fields of Expertise *Industry Fields:* coal and petroleum products. *Bus. Dimensions:* business and technology. *Scope:* national; Texas. *Period:* early twentieth century; inter-war years, 1919–39; mid-twentieth century, 1940– 70. *Teaching:* undergrad.
Publications *Books: Origins of the Turbojet Revolution,* Johns Hopkins, 1980. *Articles:* 'Causes or Consequences: Science, Technology and Regulatory Change in the Oil Bus. in Texas 1930–1975', *Technology and Culture,* 30, April, 1989, 426–55; 'Science in Soc.: Petroleum Engineers and the Oil Industry in Texas 1925–1965', *Social Studies of Science,* 19, Aug., 1989, 439–72.

Coopersmith, Jonathan C.

Asst. Prof., Dept. of Hist., Texas A&M Univ., College Station, TX 77843–4236, USA. Tel.: 1 409 845 7148. Fax: 1 409 862 4314.
Year and Place of Birth 1955, Washington DC, USA.
Degrees and Qualifications BA Princeton Univ., 1978; D. Phil. Oxford Univ., 1985.
Current Offices and Honorary Posts Mem., NASA Hist. Advisory Com., 1993–96; mem., IEEE Prize Com. of Soc. for the Hist. of Technology, 1991-3; mem., IEEE Hist. Com.
Fields of Expertise *Industry Fields:* gas, electricity, water. *Bus. Dimensions:* bus. and technology. *Scope:* global. *Period:* nineteenth century; twentieth century as a whole. *Teaching:* undergrad.; post grad. *Consultancy:* corporate strategy.
Publications *Books: The Electrification of Russia, 1880–1926,* Cornell Univ. Press, 1992. *Articles:* 'Technology Transfer in Russian Electrification, 1870–1925', *Hist. of Technology,* 13, 1991, 214–33; 'Facsimile's False Starts', *IEEE Spectrum,* Feb., 1993, 46–9.

Coopey, Richard

Research Fellow, Bus. Hist. Unit, London School of Econ., Houghton St, London, WC2A 2AE, UK. Tel.: 44 71 955 7783. Fax: 44 71 242 0392.
Year and Place of Birth 1951, Worcester, UK.
Degrees and Qualifications BA (C.N.A.A.) Worcester College, 1984; MA Warwick Univ., 1985; Ph.D. Warwick Univ., 1989.
Previous Post Research Fellow, Centre for the Hist. of Sc., Technology & Medicine, Manchester Univ., 1989–91.
Fields of Expertise *Industry Fields:* insurance, banking, finance. *Bus. Dimensions:* research and development. *Scope:* internat. *Period:* twentieth century as a whole. *Teaching:* post grad. *Consultancy:* co. hist.
Publications *Books: The Wilson Governments: 1964–1970,* with S. Fielding & N. Tiratsoo co-eds., Pinter,

1993; *Defence Science & Technology: Adjusting to Change*, with G. Spinardi & M. Uttley co-eds., Harwood, 1993.

Corley, T.A.B.

Sen. Lect. (part-time) in Econ., Dept. of Econ., Reading Univ., Whiteknights, Reading, Berks, RG6 2AA, UK. Tel.: 44 734 872211. Fax: 44 734 750236.

Year and Place of Birth 1923, London, UK.

Degrees and Qualifications MA Oxford Univ., 1949.

Previous Post Lect. in Econ., Queen's Univ., Belfast, 1958–62.

Major Honours Frank Steel Prize in Econ., Part I of Inst. of Banker's Examination, London, 1951.

Fields of Expertise *Industry Fields:* food, drink, tobacco; coal and petroleum products; chemicals and allied industries. *Bus. Dimensions:* entrepreneurs and entrepreneurship; marketing; multinational bus. *Scope:* local; regional; national; internat. *Period:* nineteenth century; twentieth century as a whole. *Teaching:* undergrad.; post grad. *Consultancy:* co. hist.

Publications *Books: Quaker Enterprise in Biscuits: Huntley & Palmers of Reading 1822–1972*, Hutchinson, London, 1972; *A Hist. of the Burmah Oil Co. 1886–1924*, Heinemann, London, 1983; *A Hist. of the Burmah Oil Co. Vol. II 1924–66*, Heinemann, London, 1988. *Articles:* 'The Entrepreneur: The Central Issue in Bus. Hist.?', *Entrepreneurship, Networks and Modern Bus.*, J. Brown & M.B. Rose eds., Manchester Univ. Press, Manchester, 1993; 'Marketing and Bus. Hist., in Theory and Practice', *The Rise and Fall of Mass Marketing*, R.S. Tedlow & G. Jones eds., Routledge, London, 1993.

Cox, Howard

Sen. Lect., Dept. of Internat. Bus., South Bank Univ., 103 Borough Road, London, SE1 0AA, UK. Tel.: 44 71 815 7712.

Year and Place of Birth 1954, London, UK.

Degrees and Qualifications BA (Econ.) Kingston Polytechnic, 1979; M.Sc. (Econ.) London Univ., 1980; Ph.D. (Econ.) London Univ., 1991.

Current Offices and Honorary Posts Visiting Fellow, Dept. of Econ., Reading Univ.

Fields of Expertise *Industry Fields:* agric., forestry, fishing; food, drink, tobacco. *Bus. Dimensions:* multinational bus.; bus. networks. *Scope:* internat.; global. *Period:* nineteenth century; twentieth century as a whole. *Teaching:* undergrad.; post grad.

Publications *Books: The Growth of Global Bus.*, with J. Clegg & G. Ietto-Gillies co-eds., Routledge, 1993. *Articles:* 'Growth and Ownership in the Internat. Cigarette Industry: BAT 1902–27', *Bus. Hist.*, 31(1), 1989, 44–67; 'International Bus. The State and Industrialisation in India: Early Growth in the Indian Cigarette Industry', *Indian Econ. & Soc. Hist. Rev.*, 27(3), 1990, 289–312.

Crompton, Gerald W.

Lect. in Econ. and Social Hist., Eliot College, Univ. of Kent at Canterbury, Kent, CT2 7NS, UK. Tel.: 44 227 764000.

Year and Place of Birth 1941, Bolton, UK.

Degrees and Qualifications BA Cambridge Univ., 1962; Cert. Ed. Cambridge Univ., 1963.

Previous Post Lect. in Econ. & Social Hist., Univ. of East Anglia, 1967–89.

Fields of Expertise *Industry Fields:* transport and communication. *Bus. Dimensions:* bus.–state relations. *Scope:* national. *Period:* inter-war years, 1919–39. *Teaching:* undergrad.

Publications *Books: Trade Unions in the Victorian Age,* ed. and introduction, 4 vols., Gregg Internat., 1973. *Articles:* 'Issues in British Trade Union Organisation 1890–1914', *Archiv für Sozialgeschichte,* XX, 1980; 'Efficient and Economical Working? The Performance of British Railway Companies 1923–33', *Bus. Hist.,* XVII, 2, 1985; 'Some Good Men, Some Doubtful Men. The Role of Railway Volunteers in the General Strike', *J. of Transport Hist.,* 9(2), 1988; 'Squeezing the Pulpless Orange: Labour and Capital on the Railways in the Interwar Years', *Bus. Hist.,* XXXI, 2, 1989.

Crouzet, François M.J.

Emeritus Prof. at the Univ. of Paris-Sorbonne, 6 Rue Benjamin Godard, 75116 Paris, France. Tel.: 33 1 45537803. Fax: 33 1 40463192.

Year and Place of Birth 1922, Monts-sur-Guesnes, France.

Degrees and Qualifications BA (Hist.) Paris Univ., 1943; MA (Hist.) Paris Univ., 1944; Ph.D. (Hist.) Paris Univ., 1956.

Previous Post Prof. of Modern Hist., Univ. of Paris-Sorbonne, 1969–92.

Current Offices and Honorary Posts Corresponding Fellow of the British Acad.; corresponding fellow of the Royal Historical Soc.; corresponding fellow of the Royal Acad. of Belgium; mem., Academia Europea.

Major Honours Hon. Commander of the Order of the British Empire (CBE).

Fields of Expertise *Industry Fields:* metal manufacture; textiles. *Bus. Dimensions:* entrepreneurs and entre-preneurship. *Scope:* national; internat.; UK; France. *Period:* eighteenth century; nineteenth century. *Teaching:* undergrad.; post grad. *Consultancy:* co. hist.

Publications *Books: L'Economie Britannique et le Blocus Continental (1806–1813),* PUF, 1958, 2 vols.; 2nd edn., Economica, 1987; *The Victorian Economy,* Methuen & Co. Ltd., 1982; *The First Industrialists. The Problem of Origins,* CUP, 1985; *Britain Ascendant. Studies in Comparative Franco-British Econ. Hist.,* CUP, 1990. *Articles:* 'The Huguenots and the English Fianancial Revolution', *Favorites of Fortune,* P. Higonnet, D.S. Landes, H. Rosovsky eds., Harvard Univ. Press, 1991, 221–66.

Daito, Eisuke

Prof., Tokyo Univ., Fac. of Econ., 7-3-1 Hongo, Bunkyo-ku, Tokyo 113, Japan. Tel.: 81 3 3812 2111. Fax: 81 3 3818 7082.

Year and Place of Birth 1940, Tokyo, Japan.

Degrees and Qualifications MA (Econ.) Tokyo Univ., 1970.

Previous Post Assoc. Prof., Tohoku Univ., 1973–81.

Current Offices and Honorary Posts Director, Japan Bus. Hist. Soc.

Fields of Expertise *Industry Fields:* chemicals and allied industries; mechanical engineering distributive trades. *Bus. Dimensions:* production management; personnel management; marketing. *Scope:* internat.; USA; Japan. *Period:* early twentieth century. *Teaching:* undergrad.; post grad. Japanese bus. hist. *Consultancy:* co. hist.

Publications *Books: Education and Training in the Development of Modern Corporations,* with N. Kawabe co-ed., Tokyo Univ. Press, 1993. *Articles:* 'Recruitment and Training of Middle Managers in Japan, 1900–1930', *Development of*

Managerial Enterprise, K. Kobayashi & H. Morikawa eds., Tokyo Univ. Press, 1986; 'Railways and Scientific Management in Japan 1907–1930', *Bus. Hist.*, 31(1), Jan., 1989; 'Technology and Labour in a Dual Economy: From Natural Rubber to Synthetic Resin', *Indust. Training and Technological Innovation*, H. Gospel ed., Routledge, 1991; 'Tokei-Kogyo no Hatten to Hattori Tokeiten no Shoyu to Keiei' [Development of the Watch Industry and Management of Seiko], *Keiei-sha no Jidai* [The Age of Managerial Enterprise], K. Morikawa ed., Yuhi-kaku, 1991.

Darroch, James L.

Asst. Prof., Fac. of Administrative Studies, York Univ., 4700 Keele St, North York, Ontario, M3J 1P3, Canada. Tel.: 1 416 736 5088. Fax: 1 416 736 5687.

Year and Place of Birth 1951, Toronto, Canada.

Degrees and Qualifications MA (Hist.) Toronto Univ., 1975; Ph.D. (Hist.) Toronto Univ., 1980; MBA York Univ., 1983; Ph.D. (Strategic Management & Internat. Bus.) York Univ., 1989.

Previous Post Asst. Prof., Wilfrid Laurier Univ., 1985–6.

Major Honours Strategic Grant, Social Sciences Humanities Research Council of Canada, 1991–4, (co-researcher I.A. Litvak).

Fields of Expertise *Industry Fields:* transport and communication; insurance, banking, finance, bus. services; public admin. and defence. *Bus. Dimensions:* strategy formation. *Scope:* global. *Period:* late twentieth century, 1970–present. *Teaching:* post grad. *Consultancy:* corporate strategy.

Publications *Books: Canadian Banks and Global Competitiveness*, McGill, Queen's, forthcoming, 1993.

Articles: 'Global Competitiveness and Public Policy: The Case of Canadian Multinational Banks', *Bus. Hist.*, 34(3), July, 1992, 153–75; 'Strategic Management in Turbulent Environments. The Canadian Banks in the 1980s', *Research in Global Strategic Management: Corporate Response to Global Change*, Alan M. Rugman ed., vol. III, JAI Press, 1992, 203–30; 'Strategies for Canada's New North Amer. Banks', *Multinational Bus.*, with I.A. Litvak, Spring, 1992, 1–13; 'Gaps Overlaps and Competition among Jurisdictions. Evolving Canadian Financial Services Policies and Regulations', *J. of World Trade*, with I.A. Litvak, 26(2), April, 1992, 119–35.

Davies, Peter N.

Emeritus Prof., Dept. of Econ. and Social Hist., The Univ. of Liverpool, 11 Abercromby Square, Liverpool, L69 3BX, UK. Tel.: 44 51 794 2412. Fax: 44 51 708 6502.

Year and Place of Birth 1927, Birkenhead, UK.

Degrees and Qualifications BA Liverpool Univ., 1961; MA Liverpool Univ., 1963; Ph.D. Liverpool Univ., 1967.

Previous Post Prof., Dept. of Econ. & Social Hist., Liverpool Univ., 1964–92.

Current Offices and Honorary Posts President, Internat. Maritime Econ. Hist. Assoc.; senior vice-pres., Internat. Commission for Maritime Hist.; chairman, British Commission, I.C.M.H.

Major Honours *From Wheel House to Counting House*: essays in maritime hist. in honour of Prof. Peter N. Davies (I.M.P.H.A. Memorial Univ., St John's, 1992).

Fields of Expertise *Industry Fields:* food, drink, tobacco; shipbuilding and marine engineering; transport and communication. *Bus. Dimensions:* entrepreneurs and entrepreneurship;

markets and bus. *Scope:* internat.; Japan. *Period:* nineteenth century; twentieth century as a whole. *Teaching:* undergrad.; post grad. *Consultancy:* co. hist.

Publications *Books: The Trade Makers: Elder Dempster in West Africa*, George Allen & Unwin, London, 1973, reissued 1980,; *Sir Alfred Jones: Shipping Entrepreneur par excellence*, Europa Library of Bus. Biography, London, 1978; *The Growth of the Modern Japanese Shipping and Shipbuilding Industries*, with Tomohei Chida, Athlone Press, London, 1990; *Musa Sapientum: Fyffyes and the Banana, 1888–1988*, Athlone Press, London, 1990; *The Man behind the Bridge: Colonel Toosey and the River Kwai*, Athlone Press, London, 1991.

Davis, Donald F.

Prof., Dept. of Hist., Univ. of Ottawa, Ottawa , Ontario, K1N 6N5, Canada. Tel.: 1 613 564 2485. Fax: 1 613 564 9599.

Year of Birth 1947.

Degrees and Qualifications BA Queen's Univ. at Kingston, 1969; MA Harvard Univ., 1971; Ph.D. Harvard Univ., 1976.

Previous Post Killam Postdoctoral Fellow, Dalhousie Univ., 1976–7.

Major Honours Wallace K. Ferguson Prize, Canadian Hist. Assoc., 1989 (for best book published in a field other than Canadian hist. in 1988 *Conspicuous Production*).

Fields of Expertise *Industry Fields:* vehicle construction. *Bus. Dimensions:* entrepreneurs and entrepreneurship; bus. and technology; bus.–state relations. *Scope:* internat.; USA Canada. *Period:* twentieth century as a whole. *Teaching:* undergrad.; post grad.

Publications *Books: Conspicuous Production: Automobiles and Elites in Detroit, 1899–1933*, Temple Univ. Press, Philadelphia, 1988. *Articles:* 'The Social Determinants of Success in the Amer. Automobile Industry before 1929', *Social Science Information*, 21, 1982, 67–93; 'Dependent Motorization: Canada and the Automobile to the 1930's', *J. of Canadian Studies*, 21, 1986, 106–32; 'Competition's Moment: The Jitney-Bus and Corporate Capitalism in the Canadian City, 1914–1929', *Urban Hist. Rev.*, 18, 1989, 103–22; 'Technological Momentum, Motor Buses and the Persistence of Canada's St Railways to 1940', *Material Hist. Rev.*, 36, 1992, 6–17.

---

de Goey, F.M.M.

Lect., Fac. of Hist. and Arts, Centrum voor Bedrijfsgeschiedenis, Erasmus Univ., POB 1738, 3000 DR Rotterdam, Netherlands. Tel.: 010 4082475. Fax: 010 452 0204.

Year and Place of Birth 1959, Curaçao.

Degrees and Qualifications BA Nijmegen Univ., 1981; MA Rotterdam Univ., 1986; Ph.D. Rotterdam Univ., 1990.

Current Offices and Honorary Posts Co-ed., Jaarboek voor de Geschiedenes van Bedrijf en Techniek [Yearbook on Bus. Hist. and Technology}.

Fields of Expertise *Industry Fields:* gas, electricity, water; transport and communication. *Bus. Dimensions:* bus.–state relations. *Scope:* national. *Period:* twentieth century as a whole. *Teaching:* undergrad.; post grad. *Consultancy:* co. hist.

Publications *Books: Geen Woorden, Maar Daden. Bedrijfsleven en Lokale Overheid van Rotterdam, 1945–1960*, Rotterdam, 1987; *Ruimte voor Industrie. Rotterdam en de Vestiging van Industrie in de Haven 1945–1975*, Rotterdam, 1990; *Bron Van Licht en Welvaart; Puem 75 Jaar*, Utrecht, 1991.

De Vries, Joh.

Stationsplein 38, 3818 LE Amersfoort, Netherlands. Tel.: 31 33 637304.
Year of Birth 1927.
Degrees and Qualifications Dr. Econ. Sciences Amsterdam Univ., 1959.
Previous Post Prof. of Econ. Hist., Tilburg Univ., 1967–92.
Current Offices and Honorary Posts Mem., Royal Dutch Acad. of Sciences, 1979–; chairman, Dutch Group for Bus. Hist., 1979–93.
Fields of Expertise *Industry Fields:* metal manufacture; insurance, banking, finance. *Bus. Dimensions:* co. finance and accounting; multinational bus. *Scope:* internat. *Period:* eighteenth century; twentieth century as a whole. *Teaching:* post grad. *Consultancy:* co. hist.
Publications *Books: The Econ. Decline of the Dutch Republic in the 18th Century,* reprint of 1959 thesis, Stenfert Kroese, 1968; *Hoogovens IJmuiden 1918–1968* [Hist. of the Dutch Steel Industry], 1968; *The Netherlands Economy in the Twentieth Century,* Van Gorcum, Assen, Netherlands, 1978; *Geschiedenis van de Nederlandsche Bank. V De Nederlandsche Bank va 1914–1948. I Visserings tijdvak 1914–1931* [Hist. of the Netherlands Bank. V The Netherlands Bank from 1914–1948. I The era of President Vissering 1914–1948], NIBE, Amsterdam, 1989. *Articles:* 'Benelux 1920–1970', *The Fontana Econ. Hist. of Europe,* Carlo M. Cipolla ed., 6(1), 1976.

De Wit, Dirk

Research Fellow, Centrum voor Bedrijfsgeschiedenis, Fac. of Hist. and Arts, Erasmus Univ. of Rotterdam, POB 1738, 3000 DR Rotterdam, Netherlands. Tel.: 31 10 4082475.

Fax: 3110 4532922.
Year and Place of Birth 1961, Amsterdam, Netherlands.
Degrees and Qualifications MA Rotterdam Univ., 1988.
Previous Post Research Fellow, Fac. of Philo. & Soc. Sciences, Technical Univ. Delft, 1989.
Fields of Expertise *Industry Fields:* chemicals and allied industries; insurance, banking, finance; electronics and computers: manufacture. *Bus. Dimensions:* research and development; bus. organization; bus. and technology bus.–state relations. *Scope:* national. *Period:* mid-twentieth century, 1940–70; late twentieth century, 1970–present. *Teaching:* undergrad.
Publications *Books: Windmill, Wieken naat de Wind Gekeerd, van Boerencooperatie naar Industrielle Organisatie,* HAR/CBG, Rotterdam, 1990. *Articles:* 'Facetten van een Automatiseringsbeleid: De Postcheque en Girodienst', *Jaarboek voor de Geschiedenis van Bedrijf Entechniek* [Yearbook on the Hist. of Bus. and Technology], 6, 1989, 234–57; 'Wat niet te Verzekeren valt: Electrologica als Casus uit de Opbouw van de Nederlandse Computerindustrie', *Jaarboek voor de geschiedenis van Bedrijf en Techniek,* 9, 1992, 261–92.

Deeks, John S.

Assoc. Prof., Dept. of Management Studies and Labour Relations, Univ. of Auckland, Private Bag 92019, Auckland 1, New Zealand. Tel.: 64 9 373 7599. Fax: 64 9 373 7477.
Year and Place of Birth 1940, Edinburgh, UK.
Degrees and Qualifications MA Cambridge Univ., 1963; Diploma in Personnel Management London School of Econ., 1964.
Previous Post Sen. Lect. in Bus. Studies, Centre for Continuing Education, Auckland Univ., 1972–4.

Current Offices and Honorary Posts
Chairperson, Auckland Univ. Press; mem., Postgraduate Degrees Com., School of Commerce & Econ., Auckland Univ.

Fields of Expertise *Industry Fields:* timber, furniture; broadcasting; communications. *Bus. Dimensions:* entrepreneurs and entrepreneurship; bus. and technology; bus.–state relations; markets and bus. values; co. culture; labour relations. *Scope:* national; New Zealand. *Period:* late twentieth century, 1970–present. *Teaching:* undergrad.; post grad.

Publications *Books: The Small Firm Owner-Manager: Entrepreneurial Behavior and Management Practice,* Praeger Special Studies in Internat. Bus., Finance and Trade, New York, Praeger, 1976; *Indust. Relations in New Zealand,* with J. Farmer, H.O. Roth & G. Scott, Methuen, Wellington, 1978, reprinted Longman Paul, 1982; *Labour Relations in New Zealand,* with P. Boxall, Longman Paul, Auckland, 1989, reprinted 1990 & 1991; *Controlling Interests: Bus., the State and Soc. in New Zealand,* with N. Perry co-ed., Auckland Univ. Press, Auckland, 1992; *Bus. and the Culture of the Enterprise Soc.,* Quorum Books, Westport, CT, forthcoming 1993.

Demizu, Tsutomu

Teacher, Fujiidera Technical High School, Fac. of Mech. Engineering, 10-1 Mifune-cho, Fujiidera City, Osaka 590-01, Japan. Tel.: 0729-55-0281. Fax: 0729 39 0098.

Year and Place of Birth 1945, Osaka, Japan.

Degrees and Qualifications BA, Osaka Inst. of Technology, 1967; MA, Osaka Pref. Univ., 1972.

Previous Post Engineer, Yosida Machine Tools Co., 1967–8.

Current Offices and Honorary Posts

Sec. Japan Indust. Archaeology Soc.

Fields of Expertise *Industry Fields:* mechanical engineering; instrument engineering; vehicle construction; transport and communication. *Bus. Dimensions:* production management; research and development; bus. and technology; co. culture. *Scope:* national; internat.; global. *Period:* nineteenth century; twentieth century as a whole early twentieth century; inter-war years, 1919–39; mid-twentieth century, 1940–'70; late twentieth century, 1970–present. *Teaching:* high school. *Consultancy:* co. hist.; technical transfer; education of technology.

Publications *Books: 19 Seiki Nihon no Joho to Shakaihendo: Gijutsujoho no Iten* [Information and Social Change in 19th Century Japan : Transfer of Technical Information], Research Inst. of the Humanities, Kyoto Univ., 1985; *Suisha no Gijutushi* [Technical Hist. of the Water-mill], Shibunkaku Press, 1987; *Gijutsu Keisei no Kokusai Hikaku: Sakai-shi niokeru Jitensha Buhinkogyo no Gijutsu-keisei* [Internat. Comparison on the Formatting Process of Technology: Technological Innovation of the Bicycle Parts Industry in Sakai], Chikuma Press, 1990; *Otobai no Okoku* [The Kingdom of the Motorcycle], Daiitchihoki Press, 1991; *Technologietransfer Deutschland-Japan von 1850 bis zur Gegenwart : Der deutsche Einfluß auf die japanishe Motorradindustrie der Nachkriegszeit,* Iudicium Verlag GmbH, Munich, 1992.

---

den Otter, A.A.

Prof. and Head of Dept., Dept. of Hist., Memorial Univ. of Newfoundland, St John's, Newfoundland, A1C 5S7, Canada. Tel.: 1 709 737 8420. Fax: 1 709 737 2164.

Year and Place of Birth 1941, Rotterdam, Netherlands.

Degrees and Qualifications BA Dordt College, Iowa, 1965; MA Alberta Univ., 1967; Ph.D. Alberta Univ., 1972.

Fields of Expertise *Industry Fields:* transport and communication. *Bus. Dimensions:* entrepreneurs and entrepreneurship. *Scope:* national. *Period:* nineteenth century. *Teaching:* undergrad.; post grad.

Publications *Books: Civilizing the West: The Galts and the Development of Western Canada,* Univ. of Alberta Press, 1982. *Articles:* 'Nationalism and the Pacific Scandal', *Canadian Historical Rev.,* LXIX, Sept., 1988, 315–39; 'A Congenial Environment: Southern Alberta on the Arrival of the Mormons', *The Mormon Presence in Canada,* Brigham Young et al. eds., Univ. of Alberta Press, Edmonton, 1990; 'Transportation, Trade and Regional Identity in the South-western Canadian Praries', *Prairie Forum,* XV, Spring, 1990, 1–24; 'Railway Technology, the Canadian Northwest and the Continental Economy', *Railroad Hist.,* Bull. 162, Spring, 1990, 5–19.

Current Offices and Honorary Posts Prof. of Social & Econ. Hist., Athens Univ.; Gen. Sec., Cultural Inst., National Bank of Greece.

Major Honours Mem., Academia Europaea.

Fields of Expertise *Industry Fields:* insurance, banking, finance. *Bus. Dimensions:* strategy formation. *Scope:* national; internat. *Period:* nineteenth century; twentieth century as a whole. *Teaching:* post grad. *Consultancy:* corporate strategy.

Publications *Books: Social Change and Military Intervention, Greece 1880–1909,* Exantas, Athens, 1977; 5th edn., 1986 (in Greek); *The Central Bank Question; Econ. and Political Strife in Nineteenth Century Greece,* Cultural Inst. of the National Bank of Greece, Athens; 2nd edn., 1988 (in Greek); *Banquiers, Usuriers et Paysans; Réseaux de Crédit et Stratégies du Capital en Grèce, XVIIIe–XXe siècle,* ed., La Decouverte, Paris, 1988; *Taxes and Power in Modern Greece,* Alexandria Publishers, Athens, 1993 (in Greek). *Articles:* 'Terre, Paysans et Pouvoir; Grèce, XVIIIe–XXe Siècle', *Annales, E.S.C.,* 2, 1992 & 1, 1993.

Dertilis, George B.

Prof. of Social & Econ. Hist., Athens Univ., 19 Homer St, Athens 10672, Greece. Tel.: 30 1 360 9035. Fax: 30 1 360 2145.

Year and Place of Birth 1939, Athens, Greece.

Degrees and Qualifications Diploma (Fac. of Law) Athens Univ., 1968; Ph.D. (Pol. Theory & Hist. of Institutions) Sheffield Univ., UK, 1976; Privat Dozent (Econ. Hist.) Athens Univ., 1980.

Previous Post Visiting Fellow, St Antony's College, Oxford Univ., 1992–3.

Dicke, Thomas S.

Assoc. Prof., Dept. of Hist., Southwest Missouri State Univ., 901 S. National Avenue, Springfield, MO 65804-0089, USA. Tel.: 1 417 836 5511. Fax: 1 417 836 5523.

Year and Place of Birth 1955, St Mary's, Ohio, USA.

Degrees and Qualifications BS Ed. Bowling Green State Univ., 1988; MA Ohio State Univ., 1983; Ph.D. Ohio State Univ., 1988.

Previous Post Georgia Univ., Athens, 1988–9.

Fields of Expertise *Industry Fields:* distributive trades. *Bus. Dimensions:* marketing; small bus. matters. *Scope:*

internat. *Period:* twentieth century as a whole. *Teaching:* undergrad. *Consultancy:* co. hist.

Publications *Books: Franchising in Amer., the Development of a Bus. Method, 1840–1980,* Univ. of North Carolina Press, 1992.

Dintenfass, Michael

Assoc. Prof. of Hist. & Urban Studies, Dept. of Hist., POB 413, Univ. of Wisconsin-Milwaukee, Milwaukee, Wisconsin 53201, USA. Tel.: 1 414 229 4749/1 414 229 4361. Fax: 1 414 229 6827.

Year and Place of Birth 1952, Philadelphia, USA.

Degrees and Qualifications BA Franklin & Marshall College, 1975; M.Phil. Warwick Univ., 1980; Ph.D. Columbia Univ., 1985.

Previous Post Asst. Prof. of Hist., Syracuse Univ., 1985–7.

Fields of Expertise *Industry Fields:* coal and petroleum products. *Bus. Dimensions:* entrepreneurs and entrepreneurship. *Scope:* national. *Period:* twentieth century as a whole. *Teaching:* undergrad.; post grad.

Publications *Books: Managing Indust. Decline: Entrepreneurship in the British Coal Industry between the Wars,* Ohio State Univ. Press, 1992; *The Decline of Indust. Britain 1870–1980,* Routledge, 1992.

Doig, Jameson W.

Woodrow Wilson School & Politics Dept., Princeton Univ., Princeton, New Jersey 08544, USA. Tel.: 0609 258 4808. Fax: 0609 258 1985.

Year and Place of Birth 1933, Oakland, USA.

Degrees and Qualifications BA Dartmouth College, 1954; MPA Princeton Univ., 1958; Ph.D. Princeton Univ., 1961.

Current Offices and Honorary Posts Mem., board of visitors, Rockefeller Center for the Social Sciences, Dartmouth College.

Major Honours Kaufman Award, Amer. Pol. Science Assoc., 1989.

Fields of Expertise *Industry Fields:* transport and communication. *Bus. Dimensions:* entrepreneurs and entrepreneurship. *Scope:* internat. *Period:* twentieth century as a whole. *Teaching:* undergrad. *Consultancy:* foundations.

Publications *Books: Leadership and Innovation,* joint auth. & ed., Johns Hopkins Univ. Press, 1987 & 1990; *Combating Corruption/Encouraging Ethics,* joint auth., & co-ed., Amer. Soc. for Public Admin., 1990. *Articles:* 'Politics and the Engineering Mind', *Yearbook of German-Amer. Studies,* 25, 1991, 151–99; 'Expertise, Politics and Technological Change', *J. of the Amer. Planning Assoc.,* 59, 1993, 31–44.

Donnelly, Tom

Head of Bus. Policy & Human Resource Management, Coventry Bus. School, Coventry Univ., Priory St, Coventry, CV1 5FB, UK. Tel.: 44 203 631313. Fax: 44 203 838251.

Year and Place of Birth 1945, Lennoxtown, UK.

Degrees and Qualifications BA Strathclyde Univ., 1968; Ph.D. Aberdeen Univ., 1975.

Previous Post Sen. Lect. in Bus. Policy, Coventry Univ., 1975–92.

Current Offices and Honorary Posts Edit. board mem., *Midland Hist.*

Fields of Expertise *Industry Fields:* mining and quarrying; vehicle construction. *Bus. Dimensions:* bus. organization. *Scope:* internat.; UK. *Period:* mid-twentieth century, 1940–70 late twentieth century, 1970–present. *Teaching:* post grad. *Consultancy:* co. hist.

Publications *Books: The Coventry Motor Industry since 1890*, with D. Thoms, Croom Helm, 1985; *Labour Relations in the Coventry Motor Industry 1896–1939*, with M. Durhum, Centre for Bus. Hist., Coventry Univ., 1991; *Pioneers and Inheritors: Top Management in the Coventry Motor Industry 1896–1977*, ed., Centre for Bus. Hist., Coventry Univ., 1992. *Articles:* 'The British and Amer. Motor Industries', *Bus. Hist.*, 32, Apr., 1990, 260–6; 'The Econ. Activities of the Aberdeen Merchant Guildry 1750–1815', *Scottish Econ. & Soc. Hist.*, 1, 1981, 68–81.

Douglas, Alan

POB 225, Pocasset, MA 02559, USA.
Year and Place of Birth 1943, Boston, USA.
Degrees and Qualifications BSEE Swarthmore College, 1965.
Fields of Expertise *Industry Fields:* electronics manufacture; radio. *Scope:* national. *Period:* early twentieth century.
Publications *Books: Radio Manufacture of the 1920's*, 3 vols., Vestal Press, 1988–91.

Downs, Jacques M.

Prof. of Hist., Univ. of New England, Dept. of Humanities, 11 Hills Beach Road, Biddeford, Maine 04005, USA. Tel.: 1 207 283 0171.
Year and Place of Birth 1926, Detroit, USA.
Degrees and Qualifications BA Univ. of California, Berkeley, 1948; MA Univ. of California, Berkeley, 1951; Ph.D. Georgetown Univ., 1961.

Previous Post Teacher, Eastern High School, 1960–1.
Major Honours Teacher of the Year, Univ. of New England, 1976, 1983, 1990.
Fields of Expertise *Industry Fields:* internat. trade. *Bus. Dimensions:* entrepreneurs and entrepreneurship; co. admin; bus. organization; markets and bus. *Scope:* internat.; USA; China. *Period:* nineteenth century. *Teaching:* undergrad.
Publications *Books: The Cities on the Saco*, Dyer Library, Saco, 1985; *Whence we Came*, South Congregational Church, Kennebunkport, 1990. *Articles:* 'American Merchants and the China Opium Trade, 1800–1840', *Bus. Hist. Rev.*, XLII(4), Winter, 1968, 418–42; 'Fair Game: Exploitive Role Myths and the Amer. Opium Trade', *Pacific Hist. Rev.*, XLI(2), May, 1972, 133–49.

Doyle, William M.

Asst. Prof. of Econ., Dallas Univ., 1845 E. Northgate Drive, Irving, TX 75062, USA. Tel.: 1 214 721 5054.
Year and Place of Birth 1958, Philadelphia, USA.
Degrees and Qualifications BA (Hist.) Colorado State Univ.; Ph.D. (Econ.) Tennessee Univ., Knoxville.
Fields of Expertise *Industry Fields:* insurance, banking, finance. *Bus. Dimensions:* co. finance and accounting. *Scope:* national; USA. *Period:* nineteenth century. *Teaching:* undergrad.

Dritsas, Margarita

Asst. Prof., Dept. of Hist. & Archaeology, Fac. of Letters, Crete Univ., 74100 Rethymnon, Crete, Greece. Tel.: 30 831 24070. Fax: 30 831 27956/30 831 20021.
Year and Place of Birth 1944,

Mansourah, Egypt.

Degrees and Qualifications M.Sc. (Econ.) Pol. Sociology, London School of Econ., 1978; Ph.D. (Hist.) Paris I Univ. (Sorbonne-Panthéon), 1986.

Previous Post Lect., Dept. of Social Anthropology, Univ. of the Aegean, Lesbos, Greece, 1987–9 & Fellow, Inst. of Financial Hist., Uppsala Univ., Sweden, 1993.

Current Offices and Honorary Posts Founding mem., Greek Econ. Hist. Assoc.; mem., Greek Com. of South East European Studies Assoc.; mem., Greek Literary & Historical Archives; mem., British Graduates Soc.

Fields of Expertise *Industry Fields:* textiles; construction; distributive trades; insurance, banking, finance; bus. services; professional and scientific services. *Bus. Dimensions:* entrepreneurs and entrepreneurship; marketing; research and development; strategy formation; merger movement and issues; bus. organization; small bus. matters; bus.–state relations; markets and bus.; bus. values; co. culture. *Scope:* national; internat. *Period:* nineteenth century; twentieth century as a whole; early twentieth century; inter-war years, 1919–39; mid-twentieth century, 1940–70. *Teaching:* undergrad.; post grad. *Consultancy:* co. hist.

Publications *Books: Banking and Industry in Interwar Greece,*, Cultural Foundation of the National Bank of Greece, Athens, 1990, (in Greek); *G. Haritakis - Works, Cultural & Technological,* ed. & auth. of introduction, Foundation of Bank of Indust. Development, Athens, 1990, (in Greek); *L'Entreprise en Europe et en Grèce XIXe–XXe Siècles*, with A. Teichova & H. Lindgren co-eds., Sofhis, Athens, 1991. *Articles:* 'Bank-Industry Relations in Inter-war Greece: The Case of the National Bank of Greece', *European Industry and Banking between the Wars*, P.L. Cottrell, H. Lindgren & A. Teichova eds., Leicester Univ. Press, Leicester,

London & New York, 1992; 'Naissance et Evolution des Entreprises Grecques au XXe Siècle', *Naissance et Mort des Entreprises en Europe XIXe–XXe Siècles*, Philippe Jobert & Michael Moss eds., forthcoming.

Dunlavy, Colleen A.

Assoc. Prof., Dept. of Hist., Univ. of Wisconsin, 455 North Park St, 4103 Humanities, Madison, WI 53706, USA. Tel.: 608 263 1854. Fax: 608 263 5302.

Year and Place of Birth 1950, South Dakota, USA.

Degrees and Qualifications BA, Univ. of California – Berkeley, 1980; Ph.D., 1988, Massachusetts Inst. of Technology.

Current Offices and Honorary Posts Board of Advisory Eds, *Technology and Culture.*

Fields of Expertise *Industry Fields: Bus. Dimensions:* bus.–state relations. *Scope:* internat.; USA; Germany. *Period:* nineteenth century. *Teaching:* undergrad.; post grad.

Publications *Books: Politics and Industrialization: Early Railroads in the United States and Prussia,* Princeton Univ. Press, forthcoming.

Dupree, Marguerite W.

Research Fellow (Core Post), Wellcome Unit for the Hist. of Medicine, Univ. of Glasgow, 5 Univ. Gardens, Glasgow, G12 8QQ, UK. Tel.: 44 41 339 8855. Fax: 44 41 307 8011.

Year and Place of Birth 1950, Boston, USA.

Degrees and Qualifications BA Mount Holyoke College, 1972; MA Princeton Univ., 1974; MA Cambridge Univ., 1979; D.Phil. Oxford Univ., 1981; Ph.D. (by incorporation) Cambridge Univ., 1982.

Previous Post ESRC Post-doctoral Research Fellow, 1984–5.

Current Offices and Honorary Posts Sen. Research Fellow, Wolfson College, Cambridge Univ.; council mem., Scottish Soc. of the Hist. of Medicine; newsletter correspondent, European Assoc. for the Hist. of Medicine.

Major Honours Research Fellow, Emmanuel College, Cambridge Univ., 1978–82; Sen. Research Fellow, Wolfson College, Cambridge Univ.; Wellcome Trust Research Project Grants.

Fields of Expertise *Industry Fields:* textiles; professional and scientific services; public admin. and defence; pottery; life insurance. *Bus. Dimensions:* bus. organization bus.–state relations. *Scope:* local; regional; national; internat.; UK. *Period:* nineteenth century; twentieth century as a whole; inter-war years, 1919–39; mid-twentieth century, 1940–70. *Teaching:* undergrad.; post grad.

Publications *Books: Lancashire and Whitehall: The Diary of Sir Raymond Streat 1931–1957*, ed., Manchester Univ. Press, 1987, 2 vols. *Articles:* 'The Community Perspective in Family Hist.: The Potteries during the Nineteenth Century', *The First Modern Soc.: Essays in English Hist. in Honour of Lawrence Stone*, A.L. Beier, J. Rosenheim & D.N. Cannadine eds., CUP, 1989, 549–73; 'The Cotton Industry, Overseas Trade Policy and the Cotton Board 1940–1959', *Bus. Hist.*, special iss., 32(4), Oct., 1990, *Competition and Strategic Response in World Textiles since 1870*, 106–28; 'A Profile of the Medical Profession in Scotland in the Early Twentieth Century: The *"Medical Directory"* as a Historical Source', *Bull. of the Hist. of Medicine*, with M.A. Crowther co-auth., 65, 1991, 209–33; 'The Cotton Industry: A Middle Way between Nationalisation and Self-government?', *The 1945 Labour Government and the Private Sector*, J. Tomlinson, H. Mercer & N. Rollings eds., Edinburgh, 1992, 137–61.

Dyer, Davis

Managing Director, The Winthrop Group Inc., 1100 Massachusetts Avenue, Cambridge, MA 02138, USA. Tel.: 1 617 497 0777. Fax: 1 617 661 6497.

Year and Place of Birth 1948, Enid, Oklahoma, USA.

Degrees and Qualifications BA Harvard College, 1970; MA Harvard Univ., 1972; Ph.D. Harvard Univ., 1979.

Fields of Expertise *Industry Fields:* diversified corporations. *Bus. Dimensions:* bus. organization. *Scope:* global. *Period:* twentieth century as a whole. *Consultancy:* co. hist.; corporate strategy.

Publications *Books: Reviewing Amer. Industry*, with Paul R. Lawrence, The Free Press, New York, 1983; *Chronicles of Corporate Change: Management Lessons from AT&T and its Offspring*, with Leonard A. Schlesinger, Thomas N. Clough & Diane Landau co-auths., Lexington Books, Lexington, MA, 1987; *Changing Alliances: The Report of the Harvard Bus. School Project on the Auto Industry and the Amer. Economy*, with Malcolm S. Salter & Alan M. Webber co-auths., Harvard Bus. School Press, Boston, 1987; *Emerson Electric Co.: A Century of Manufacturing*, with Jeffrey L. Cruikshank co-auth., privately printed, St Louis, 1990; *Labors of a Modern Hercules: The Evolution of a Chemical Co.*, with David B. Sicilia co-auth., Harvard Bus. School Press, Boston, 1990.

Eakin, Marshall C.

Assoc. Prof. of Hist., Dept. of Hist., Vanderbilt Univ., Nashville, TN 37235, USA. Tel.: 1 615 322 3328. Fax: 1 615 343 8028.

Year and Place of Birth 1952, Madisonville, USA.

Degrees and Qualifications BA (Hist. & Anthropology) Kansas Univ., 1975; MA (Hist.) Kansas Univ., 1977; Ph.D. (Latin Amer. Hist.) UCLA, 1981.

Current Offices and Honorary Posts Contributing ed., Brazilian Hist., *Handbook of Latin Amer. Studies*; chair, Projects & Publications Com., Conf. on Latin Amer. Hist.

Major Honours Tinker Foundation Post-doctoral Fellowship, 1987–8; Fulbright-Hays Dissertation Fellowship, 1979–80; NDEA Title VI Fellowship, 1976–7.

Fields of Expertise *Industry Fields:* mining and quarrying; textiles. *Bus. Dimensions:* entrepreneurs and entrepreneurship; bus. and technology; multinational bus.; bus.–state relations. *Scope:* local; regional; national; internat.; Brazil; Latin America. *Period:* nineteenth century; twentieth century as a whole. *Teaching:* undergrad.; post grad. *Consultancy:* co. hist.

Publications *Books: Technology and Change*, co-ed., Boyd & Fraser, San Francisco, 1979; *British Enterprise in Brazil: The St John d'el Rey Mining Co. and the Morro Velho Gold Mine, 1830–1960*, Duke Univ. Press, Durham, NC, 1989. *Articles:* 'The Role of British Capital in the Development of Brazilian Gold Mining', *Miners and Mining in the Americas*, William Culver & Thomas Greaves eds., Manchester Univ. Press, Manchester, UK, 1986, 10–28; 'Business Imperialism and British Enterprise in Brazil: The St John d'el Rey Mining Co. Limited, 1830–1960', *Hispanic Amer. Historical Rev.*, 66(4), Nov., 1986, 697–741; 'Creating a Growth Pole: The Industrialization of Belo Horizonte, Brazil, 1897–1987', *Americas*, 47(4), Apr., 1991, 383–410.

Edgerton, D.E.H.

Head of Hist. of Sc. & Technology, Sherfield Building, Imperial College, London, SW7 2AZ, UK. Tel.: 44 71 589 5111. Fax: 44 71 581 3689.

Year and Place of Birth 1959, Montevideo, Uruguay.

Degrees and Qualifications BA Oxford Univ., 1981; Ph.D. London Univ., 1986.

Previous Post Lect., Centre for the Hist. of Sci., Technology & Medicine, Manchester Univ., 1987–92.

Current Offices and Honorary Posts Academic Advisory Board, Inst. of Contemp. British Hist.

Major Honours T.S. Ashton Prize from Econ. Hist. Soc., 1993.

Fields of Expertise *Industry Fields:* professional and scientific services; public admin. and defence; aircraft. *Bus. Dimensions:* research and development; bus. and technology; bus.–state relations. *Scope:* national; UK. *Period:* twentieth century as a whole. *Teaching:* undergrad.; post grad. *Consultancy:* bus. archives.

Publications *Books: England and the Aeroplane: An Essay on a Militant and Technological Nation*, Macmillan, London, 1991. *Articles:* 'Technological Innovation, Indust. Capacity and Efficiency: Public Ownership and the British Military Aircraft Industry, 1935–1948', *Bus. Hist.*, 26, 1984, 247–79; 'Science and Technology in British Bus. History', *Bus. Hist.*, 29, 1987, 84–103; 'Liberal Militarism and the British State', *New Left Rev.*, 185, Jan./Feb., 1991, 138–69; 'The Prophet Militant and Indust.: The Peculiarities of Correlli Barnett', *Twentieth Century British Hist.*, 2, 1991, 360–79.

Edmondson, Michael

Ph.D. Candidate, Temple Univ., Gladfelter Hall, 9th Floor, Dept. of Hist., Philadelphia, PA 19122, USA. Tel.: 1 609 858 2286.

Year and Place of Birth 1966, Philadelphia, USA.

Degrees and Qualifications BA Cabrini College, Radnor, PA, 1988; MA Villanova Univ., 1989; Ph.D. Candidate, Temple Univ., 1993.

Previous Post Adjunct Instructor, Dept. of Hist., Cabrini College, 1990–2.

Major Honours President Herbert Hoover Fellowship and Grant Award Recipient, 1993.

Fields of Expertise *Industry Fields:* other manufacturing industries. *Bus. Dimensions:* bus.–state relations. *Scope:* internat. *Period:* inter-war years, 1919–39. *Teaching:* undergrad. *Consultancy:* co. hist.

Edwards, John Richard

Prof. of Accounting, Bus. Hist. Unit, Cardiff Bus. School, Univ. of Wales College of Cardiff, Colum Drive, Cardiff, CF1 3EU, UK. Tel.: 44 222 874000. Fax: 44 222 874419.

Year and Place of Birth 1946, Neath, UK.

Degrees and Qualifications B.Sc. (Econ.) Univ. College, Cardiff, 1968; M.Sc. (Econ.) Univ. College, Cardiff, 1975; Fellow, Inst. of Chartered Accountants in England & Wales, 1971.

Previous Post Reader, 1989–92.

Current Offices and Honorary Posts Chief Examiner, accountancy, Chartered Inst. of Bankers; ed., *Accounting, Bus. & Fin. Hist.*

Fields of Expertise *Industry Fields:* mining and quarrying; metal manufacture. *Bus. Dimensions:* co. finance and accounting. *Scope:* national. *Period:* nineteenth century; early twentieth century. *Teaching:* undergrad.

Publications *Books: Co. Legislation and Changing Patterns of Disclosure in British Co. Accounts, 1900–1940,* Inst. of Chartered Accountants in England & Wales, London, 1981; *A Hist. of Financial Accounting,* Routledge, London & New York, 1989. *Articles:* 'Dowlais Iron Co.: Accounting Policies and Procedures for Profit Measurement and Reporting Purposes', *Accounting & Bus. Research,* Spring 1979, 139–51; 'The Development of Indust. Cost Accounting before 1850: A Survey of the Evidence', *Bus. Hist.,* with Edmund Newell, Jan. 1991, 35–57; 'The Accountability of Municipal Corporations', *Abacus,* with H.M. Coombs, Mar. 1993, 27–51.

Edwards, Pamela C.

Ph.D. Candidate, Delaware Univ., Dept. of Hist., Newark, DE 19716, USA. Tel.: 1 302 368 8029.

Year and Place of Birth 1962, North Carolina, USA.

Degrees and Qualifications BS (Hist.) Appalachian State Univ., 1984; MA (Hist.) Appalachian State Univ., 1987; Ph.D. Candidate (Hist.) Delaware Univ., current.

Previous Post Archivist/Historian, Hist. Associates Inc., 1987–90.

Major Honours Hagley Fellowship.

Fields of Expertise *Industry Fields:* textiles; airconditioning. *Bus. Dimensions:* bus. and technology. *Scope:* national; USA. *Period:* twentieth century as a whole. *Teaching:* undergrad. *Consultancy:* co. hist.

Efmertová, Marcela

Scientific Worker, Archives of the Acad. of Sciences of the Czech Republic, Husova 4, 110 00 Prague 1, Czechland. Tel.: 42 235 89 83.

Year and Place of Birth 1959, Prague, Czechland.

Degrees and Qualifications Dr. (Hist.) Charles Univ. Prague, 1984; Ph.D. (Hist. of Technology), Acad. of Science Inst. for Theory & Hist., 1991.

Current Offices and Honorary Posts Mem., Internat. Com. for Hist. of Technology - Czech section; sec., Czech National Com. of Hist. of Science of Internat. Union of Hist. & Philo. of Science.

Fields of Expertise *Industry Fields:* electrical engineering; hist. of technology. *Bus. Dimensions:* research and development; bus. and technology. *Scope:* national. *Period:* inter-war years, 1919–39; mid-twentieth century, 1940–70; late twentieth century, 1970–present. *Consultancy:* co. hist.

Publications *Articles:* 'Institutionalisation of Electrotechnology Research in Czechoslovakia in the Years 1945–1965', *Studie z dejin techniky*, 1, Prague, 1988, 291–445, (in Czech); 'G. Giorgi's Jubilee inspired the Historical Study of the Development of Metrology in Czechoslovakia', *G. Giorgi and his Contribution to Electrical Metrology*, with M. Sedivy, Politecnico, Turin, 1990, 87–9; 'The Czech Physicist Jaroslav Safránek and his Television', *Social Studies of Science*, David Edge ed., vol. 22, 1992, 283–300; 'Krizík's Electric Tramway Tábor to Bechyne', *ICOHTEC-Symposium*, ÖFIT, Vienna, 1993, 161–70.

Eigner, Peter

Asst. Lect., Inst. of Econ. and Social Hist., Vienna Univ. of Econ. and Bus., Augasse 2-6, A-1090 Vienna, Austria. Tel.: 43 31336 4711.

Year and Place of Birth 1960, Vienna, Austria.

Degrees and Qualifications MA Vienna Univ., 1989.

Previous Post Scientific Collaborator, Inst. for Econ. & Social Research, Vienna, 1986–8.

Fields of Expertise *Industry Fields:* insurance, banking, finance; relationship between banks and industry. *Bus. Dimensions:* entrepreneurs and entrepreneurship; co. finance and accounting; personnel management; strategy formation; merger movement and issues; multinational bus.; network analysis of interlocking directorates. *Scope:* regional; internat.; East Central Europe; Czechoslovakia; Hungary. *Period:* nineteenth century; early twentieth century; inter-war years, 1919–39. *Teaching:* undergrad.

Publications *Books: Wiener Wirtschaftsgeschichte 1740–1938*, with Günther Chaloupek & Michael Wagner co-eds., Geschichte der Stadt Wien Bände 4,5, Jugend & Volk, 1991. *Articles:* 'The Network of Directors - Interlocking Directorates between Viennese Commercial Banks and Industry in the Interwar Period', Edward Elgar Publishing, forthcoming.

Engelbourg, Saul

Prof. of Hist., Boston Univ., 147 Bay State Road, Boston, MA 02215, USA. Tel.: 1 617 353 2551. Fax: 1 617 353 2556.

Year and Place of Birth 1927, Brooklyn, USA.

Degrees and Qualifications BA Brooklyn College, 1948; MA Yale Univ., 1949; Ph.D. Columbia Univ., 1954.

Fields of Expertise *Industry Fields:* insurance, banking, finance. *Bus. Dimensions:* entrepreneurs and entrepreneurship. *Scope:* USA. *Period:* nineteenth century. *Teaching:* undergrad.

Publications *Books: Internat. Bus. Machines*, Arno Press, 1976; *Power and Morality: Amer. Bus. Ethics, 1840–1914*, Greenwood, 1980.

Articles: 'Two "Souths": The United States and Italy since the 1860s', *J. of European Econ. Hist*, 15, Winter, 1986, 563–589; 'John Stewart Kennedy and the City of Glasgow Bank', *Bus. & Econ. Hist.*, Jeremy Atack ed., 15, 1986, 69–84; 'The Steadfastness of Econ. Dualism in Italy', *J. of Developing Areas*, 22, July, 1988, 515–26.

Engerman, Stanley L.

Prof. of Econ. & Hist., Dept. of Econ., Rochester Univ., Rochester, NY 14627, USA. Tel.: 1 716 275 3165. Fax: 1 716 256 2309.

Year and Place of Birth 1936, USA.

Degrees and Qualifications BS New York Univ., 1956; MBA New York Univ., 1958; Ph.D. Johns Hopkins Univ., 1962.

Previous Post Assoc. Prof. of Econ. & Hist., Rochester Univ.

Fields of Expertise *Industry Fields:* agric., forestry, fishing. *Bus. Dimensions:* production management. *Scope:* national; internat. *Period:* eighteenth century; nineteenth century. *Teaching:* undergrad.; post grad.

Publications *Books: Time on the Cross*, with R.W. Fogel, 2 vols., Little, Brown & Co., 1974; reissued with a new afterword by W.W. Norton, 1989; *Race and Slavery in the Western Hemisphere: Quantitative Studies*, with Eugene Genovese co-ed., Princeton Univ. Press, 1975; *Long-term Factors in Amer. Econ. Growth*, with Robert E. Gallman co-ed., Univ. of Chicago Press, 1986; *British Capitalism and Caribbean Slavery*, with Barbara L. Solow co-ed., CUP, 1987; *The Atlantic Slave Trade*, with Joseph Inikori co-ed., Duke Univ. Press, 1992.

Englander, Ernest J.

Assoc. Prof. of Bus. & Public Policy, School of Bus., George Washington Univ., Washington, DC 20052, USA. Tel.: 1 202 994 8203. Fax: 1 202 994 8113.

Year and Place of Birth 1952, Seattle, USA.

Degrees and Qualifications BA, 1974; M.Sc., 1979; MBA, 1982; Ph.D., 1984, all from Washington Univ., Seattle.

Fields of Expertise *Industry Fields:* genetic engineering: manufacture. *Bus. Dimensions:* bus.–state relations. *Scope:* national. *Period:* late twentieth century, 1970–present. *Teaching:* post grad. *Consultancy:* corporate strategy.

Publications *Articles:* 'The Inside Contract System of Organization and Control: A Neglected Aspect of the Hist. of the Firm', *Labor Hist.*, 28, 1987, 429–446; 'Technology and Oliver Williamson's Transaction Cost Economics', *J. of Econ. Behavior and Organization*, 10, 1988, 339–54; 'Structural Aspects of Issues Management: Transaction Costs and Agency Theory', *Research in Corporate Social Performance and Policy*, with Allen Kaufman & Alfred Marcus, 11, 1989, 257–71; 'Kohlberg Kravis Roberts & Co. and the Restructuring of Amer. Capitalism', *Bus. Hist. Rev.*, with Allen Kaufman, 67, 1993, forthcoming.

Eriksen, August Wiemann

Archivist, Rigsarkivet, Rigsdagsgården 9, 1218 Copenhagen K, Denmark. Tel.: 45 33 92 23 86. Fax: 45 33 15 32 39.

Year and Place of Birth 1947, Copenhagen, Denmark.

Degrees and Qualifications Ph.D. (Hist.) Copenhagen Univ.

Fields of Expertise *Bus. Dimensions:* bus.–state relations. *Scope:* national; internat. *Period:* nineteenth century; early twentieth century; inter-war years, 1919–39.
Publications *Books: Eksportrådgivning i Danmark 1910–1921. Privat eller Statslig opgave,* Administrationshistoriske studier, vol. 4, Copenhagen, 1984. *Articles:* 'Omkring handelsministeriets oprettelse og første år 1879–1924. Afvejningen af politiske interesser, faglige hensyn og økonomiske nødvendigheder', *Samspillet mellem organisationer og stat,* Birgit Nüchel Thomsen ed., Administrationshistoriske studier, vol. 13, Copenhagen, 1987.

Espeli, Harald

Researcher, Inst. of Social Research, Munthes Gate 31, 0260 Oslo, Norway. Tel.: 47 22557510.
Year and Place of Birth 1955, Drøbak, Norway.
Degrees and Qualifications Cand. philol. Oslo Univ. 1983; Dr. agric. Univ. of Agric., Aas, 1991.
Previous Post Researcher, Norwegian School of Management, 1991–3.
Fields of Expertise *Industry Fields:* agric., forestry, fishing; food, drink, tobacco; insurance, banking, finance. *Bus. Dimensions:* entrepreneurs and entrepreneurship; bus.–state relations. *Scope:* national; internat. *Period:* twentieth century as a whole.
Publications *Books: Fra hest til hestekrefter. Studier i politiske og økonomiske rammebetingelser for mekaniseringen av norsk jordbruk 1910–1960* [From Horse to Horsepower], Melding no. 2, Institutt for økonomi og samfunnsfag Ås-NLH, 1990; *Jordbruksproteksjonisme og handelspolitikk. Beslutningsprosesser*

bak utviklingen av det kvantitative importvernet for jordbruksvarer i Norge på 1900–tallet med hovedvekt på perioden 1934–1965 og forholdet til GATT, Melding no. 8, Institutt for økonomi og samfunnsfag Ås-NLH, 1992; *Industripolitikk på avveie. Motkonjunkturpolitikken og Norges Industriforbunds rolle 1975–1980,* Ad Notam Forlag Oslo, 1992. *Articles:* 'Eplekrigens forhistorie. Utviklingen av det norske importvernet for jordbruksvarer frem til 1989 med hovedvekt på perioden etter 1945', *"...det som svarte seg best" - studier i økonomisk historie og politikk,* E. Hovland, E. Lange & S. Rysstad eds., Festskrift til Stien Tveite, Ad Notam, Oslo, 1990, 129–41; 'Landbruket under krigen', *Nytt søkelys på okkupasjonshistorien,* Den Norske Historiske forening, Oslo, 1991, 65–99.

Fabricius, Miroslav

Researcher, Inst. of Hist. of the Slovak Acad. of Sciences, Klemensova 19, 813 64 Bratislava, Slovakia. Tel.: 42 7 326 321. Fax: 42 7 361 645.
Year and Place of Birth 1951, Bratislava, Slovakia.
Degrees and Qualifications Dip.Ed. Bratislava Univ., 1975; Ph.D. Inst. of Econ. of the Slovak Acad. of Sciences, Bratislava, 1984.
Previous Post Researcher, Inst. of Econ. of the Slovak Acad. of Sciences, 1980–9.
Current Offices and Honorary Posts Sec., Slovak Assoc. of Econ. Historians.
Fields of Expertise *Industry Fields:* agric., forestry, fishing; food, drink, tobacco; coal and petroleum products; mining and quarrying; chemicals and allied industries; metal manufacture; mechanical engineering; instrument engineering; electrical engineering;

vehicle construction; metal goods; textiles; leather clothing and footwear;
bricks, pottery, glass, cement; timber,
furniture; paper, printing, publishing;
other manufacturing industries; construction; gas, electricity, water; transport and communication; distributive
trades; insurance, banking, finance;
bus. services; professional and scientific
services; miscellaneous services; public
admin. and defence. *Bus. Dimensions:*
co. finance and accounting; co. law; co.
admin.; marketing; strategy formation;
merger movement and issues; bus.
organization; small bus. matters; multinational bus.; markets and bus. *Scope:*
local; regional; national; internat.;
global. *Period:* twentieth century as a
whole. *Teaching:* post grad.
Consultancy: co. hist. corporate strategy.
   Publications *Books: The Econ.
Development of Slovakia until the End
of Inter-War Czechoslovakia*, EÚ SAV
Press, 1989; *Improvement of the Views
on the Slovak Econ. Situation in inter-
War Czechoslovakia*, EÚ SAV Press,
1990. *Articles:* 'The Econ. Problems of
Slovakia in the post-War Period
1918–1920', *Ekonomicky Casopis*, 34,
1986, 1007–18; 'The Concept of
Agrarian Slovakia - Theory and
Practice', *Historicky Casopis*, 38,
1990, 331–41; 'The Creation of the
Corn Exchange in Bratislava',
Ekonimicky Casopis, 39, 1991,
877–90.

Falkus, Malcolm Edward

Prof. of Econ. Hist., Dept. of Econ.
Hist., The Univ. of New England,
Armidale, NSW 2351, Australia. Tel.:
61 67 73 2464. Fax: 61 67 73 3205.
   Year and Place of Birth 1940,
Westcliff-on-Sea, UK.
   Degrees and Qualifications B.Sc.
(Econ.) London School of Econ., 1961.
   Previous Post Sen. Lect. in Econ.

Hist., London School of Econ., until
1987.
   Current Offices and Honorary Posts
Director, Centre for Asian Studies,
Univ. of New England.
   Fields of Expertise *Industry Fields:*
gas, electricity, water. *Bus.
Dimensions:* co. hist. generally. *Scope:*
internat. *Period:* nineteenth century;
twentieth century as a whole.
Teaching: undergrad.; post grad.
Consultancy: co. hist.
   Publications *Books: The
Industrialization of Russia 1700–1914*,
Macmillan, 1972; *Always under
Pressure: A Hist. of North Thames
Gas since 1949*, Macmillan, 1988; *The
Blue Funnel Legend: A Hist. of the
Ocean Steam Ship Co., 1865–1973*,
Macmillan, 1990; *Called to Account:
A Hist. of Coopers & Lybrand in
Australia*, Allen & Unwin, 1993.

Faltus, Jozef

Ekonomická Univerzita,
Narodohospodárska Fakulta,
Dolnozemská Cesta 1, 852 19
Bratislava, Slovakia. Tel.: 42 7 849
847. Fax: 42 7 848 906.
   Year and Place of Birth 1929, Zlin,
Czechland.
   Degrees and Qualifications Ing.
(Econ.) Univ. of Econ., Bratislava,
1956; C.Sc. Univ. of Econ., Bratislava,
1964; Habilitation (Econ. Hist.), 1965;
Univ. Prof., 1991.
   Previous Post Research Fellow,
Documentation Centre, Univ. of Econ.,
Bratislava, 1970–9.
   Current Offices and Honorary Posts
Com. mem., Econ. Hist. Soc. of
Czechoslovakia, Prague; com. mem.,
Econ. Hist. Commission of the Slovak
Historians Soc., Bratislava.
   Fields of Expertise *Industry Fields:*
insurance, banking, finance; economic
hist. of Czechoslovakia and Slovakia in
the 20th century. *Period:* twentieth

century as a whole; inter-war years, 1919–39. *Teaching:* undergrad.; post grad.

Publications *Books: Povojnová Hospodárska Kríza 1921–1923 v Ceskoslovensku* [Postwar Econ. Depression 1921–1923 in Czechoslovakia], Vydavatelstvo SAV, Bratislava, 1966; *Prehlad Hospodárskeho Vyvoja na Slovensku 1918–1945* [A Survey of Econ. Development of Slovakia 1918–1945 - Part 1918–1938], with V. Prucha co-auth., Epocha Bratislava, 1969. *Articles:* 'Reformaa Rolna w Czechoslowacji po I. Wojnie Swiatowej' [The Land Reform in Czechoslovakia after the First World War], *Roczniki Dziejów Spolecznych i Gospodarczych*, XXXII, 1971, Poznan; 'Development of Capitalist Industrialisation of Slovakia and its Problems', *Studia Historica Slovaca*, XV, Veda Bratislava, 1986; 'Zamestnanie Obyvatelov Slovenska a Priemyselne Zavody na Slovensku Podla Uhorskeho Scitnaia K 31.12.1910' [Employment of Slovak Population and Indust. Enterprises in Slovakia according to the Hungarian Census of 31.12.1910], *Slovenska Archivistika*, 2, 1987.

Farnie, D.A.

31 Parksway, Swinton, Manchester, Lancs, M27 1JN, UK. Tel.: 44 61 736 4580.

Degrees and Qualifications BA Manchester Univ., 1951; MA Manchester Univ., 1953; Ph.D. Natal Univ., 1969.

Previous Post Reader in Econ. Hist., Manchester Univ., 1980–91.

Current Offices and Honorary Posts Council mem., Chetham Soc.

Major Honours English delegate to Internat. Conf. on Bus. Hist. (the Fuji Conf.), 1981; visiting lecturer, Bonn Univ., 1982.

Fields of Expertise *Industry Fields:* mechanical engineering; textiles; distributive trades. *Bus. Dimensions:* entrepreneurs and entrepreneurship; marketing; bus. and technology. *Scope:* internat. *Period:* nineteenth century; twentieth century as a whole.

Publications *Books: East and West of Suez. The Suez Canal in Hist., 1854–1956*, OUP, 1969; *The English Cotton Industry and the World Market 1815–1896*, OUP, 1979; *The Manchester Ship Canal and the Rise of the Port of Manchester, 1894–1975*, Manchester Univ. Press, 1980. *Articles:* 'John Rylands of Manchester', *Bull. of the John Rylands Univ. Library of Manchester*, 56(1), Autumn, 1973, 93–1929; 75(2), Summer, 1993, 3–93; 'The Structure of the British Cotton Industry 1846–1914', *The Textile Industry & its Bus. Climate*, Akio Okochi & Shin'ichi Yonekawa eds., proceedings of the 8th Fuji Conf., Tokyo Univ. Press, 1982, 45–91.

Fay, Michael

Sen. Lect., Dept. of Marketing, Univ. of Otago, POB 56, Dunedin, New Zealand. Tel.: 64 3 479 8038. Fax: 64 3 479 8172.

Year and Place of Birth 1941, UK.

Degrees and Qualifications BA Hull Univ., 1964; MA Lancaster Univ., 1975.

Current Offices and Honorary Posts Fac. Research Fellow, Div. of Commerce; curator, Otago Advertising Archive.

Federico, Giovanni

Life Fellow, Dept. of Hist., Pisa Univ., Pzza. Torricelli 3, Pisa, Italy. Tel.: 39 50 501012. Fax: 39 50 501017.

Year and Place of Birth 1954, Pistoia, Italy.

Degrees and Qualifications Laurea, Pisa Univ,; Ph.D. Pisa College of Higher Education.

Fields of Expertise *Industry Fields:* agric., forestry, fishing; textiles. *Scope:* national. *Period:* nineteenth century; twentieth century as a whole. *Teaching:* undergrad.

Publications *Books: The Econ. Development of Italy since 1870*, Edward Elgar ed., 1993; *Il Filo d'Oro. Una Storia Economica dell'Industrial Serica*, Marsilio, Venezia, 1993.

Feldenkirchen, Wilfried

Prof. of Econ. & Bus. Hist., Univ. of Erlangen-Nürnberg, Findelgasse 7, D-90402 Nuremberg, Germany. Tel.: 49 911 5302 608. Fax: 49 911 5302 616.

Year and Place of Birth 1947, Cologne, Germany.

Degrees and Qualifications Dissertation Bonn Univ., 1974; Habilitation Bonn Univ., 1980.

Current Offices and Honorary Posts Board mem., German Econ. Hist. Soc.

Major Honours Maier-Leibnitz Prize, 1982; Newcomen Prize, 1987.

Fields of Expertise *Industry Fields:* metal manufacture; mechanical engineering; electrical engineering; insurance, banking, finance. *Bus. Dimensions:* multinational bus. *Scope:* national; internat. *Period:* nineteenth century; twentieth century as a whole; early twentieth century; inter-war years, 1919–39. *Consultancy:* co. hist. corporate strategy.

Publications *Books: Der Handel der Stadt Köln im 18. Jahrhundert (1700–1814)*, dissertation, Bonn, 1974; *Die Eisen- und Stahlindustrie des Ruhrgebietes 1879–1914. Wachstum, Finanzierung und Unternehmensstruktur ihrer Großunternehmen*, Wiesbaden, 1982; *Articles:* 'Technologie,

Wirtschaftswachstum und Arbeitszeit im internationalen Vergleich Deutschland, Großbritannien, Frankreich, Belgien und die USA 1835–1914', *Technologie, Wirtschaftswachstum und Arbeitszeit im internationalen Vergleich*, vol. 24 of *Zeitschrift für Unternehmensgeschichte*, Hans Pohl ed., Wiesbaden, 1983, 75–155; 'Wachstum und Finanzierung deutscher Großunternehmen der chemischen und elektrotechnischen Industrie', *Beiträge zur quantitativen vergleichenden Unternehmensgeschichte*, vol. 19 of *Historisch Sozialwiss. Forschungen. Quantitative Sozialwissensch. Analysen von historischen und Prozeß-produzierten Daten*, Richard H. Tilly ed., Stuttgart, 1985, 94–125; 'Big Bus. in Interwar Germany. Organisational Innovation at I.G. Farben, Vereinigte Stahlwerke and Siemens', *Bus. Hist. Rev.*, 61, 1987, 417–51.

Feldman, Gerald D.

Prof. of Hist., Dept. of Hist., University of California, Berkeley, CA 94720, USA. Tel.: 1 510 642 1971/1 510 642 2518. Fax: 1 510 643 5323.

Year and Place of Birth 1937, New York City, USA.

Degrees and Qualifications BA Columbia Univ., 1958; MA Harvard Univ., 1959; Ph.D. Harvard Univ., 1964.

Major Honours Guggenheim Fellow, 1973–4; Fellow of the Historisches Kolleg in Munich, 1982–3; Fellow of the Inst. for Advanced Study in Berlin, 1987–8; Fellow of the Woodrow Wilson Center in Washington, 1991–2.

Fields of Expertise *Industry Fields:* mining and quarrying; insurance, banking, finance. *Bus. Dimensions:* entrepreneurs and entrepreneurship; merger movement and issues;

bus.–state relations; bus. values; co. culture. *Period:* early twentieth century; inter-war years, 1919–39. *Teaching:* undergrad.; post grad. *Consultancy:* co. hist.

Publications *Books: Army, Industry and Labor in Germany, 1914–1918,* Princeton Univ. Press, Princeton, 1966; Dietz Verlag, Bonn, 1985, (in German); reprinted by Berg Publishers, Leamington Spa, 1992; *Iron and Steel in the German Inflation, 1916–1923,* Princeton Univ. Press, Princeton, 1977; *Vom Weltkrieg zur Weltschaftskrise. Studien zur deutschen Wirtschafts- und Sozialgeschichte 1914–1932,* Vandenhoeck & Ruprecht, Göttingen, 1984; *Industrie und Gewerkschaften 1918–1924. Die überforderte Zentralarbeitsgemeinschaft,* with Irmgard Steinisch co-auth., Deutsche Verlags-Anstalt, Stuttgart, 1985; *The Great Disorder. Politics, Econ. and Soc. in the German Inflation, 1914–1924,* OUP, 1993.

Fink, Jørgen

Archivist, Danish National Bus. Archives, Vester Allé 12, 8000 Aarhus C, Denmark. Tel.: 45 86 12 85 33. Fax: 45 86 12 85 60.

Year and Place of Birth 1947, Copenhagen, Denmark.

Degrees and Qualifications Cand. mag. Aarhus Univ., 1971; Dr.Phil. Aarhus Univ., 1989.

Previous Post Sen. Research Fellow, Aarhus Univ., 1979–82.

Current Offices and Honorary Posts Ed., *Historie & Nyt Fra Historien* [Historical News]; sec., Historical Soc. for Jutland; steering com. mem., working group for Nordic Middle-class Studies; board mem., Soc. for Technological Hist.

Fields of Expertise *Industry Fields:* small bus. enterprises. *Bus. Dimensions:* small bus. matters.

Scope: national; Denmark. *Period:* twentieth century as a whole. *Teaching:* post grad.

Publications *Books: Middlestand i Klemme?* [Middle Class in Agony?], dissertation, 1988, summary in German, pub. Jysk Selskab for Historie; *Butik og Værksted* [Shop and Workshop], 1992, Selskabet for Stationsbyforskning. *Articles:* 'En Hovedorganisation, som Aldrig blev til' [A Bus. Organisation that was never established], *Erhvervshistorisk Årbog* [The Danish Bus. Hist. Yearbook], 1991, 92–141; 'Technical Education and the Indust. Development in Denmark 1850–1950', with Per Boje, 17th Internat. Congress of Historical Sciences, Madrid, 1992, vol. I, 271–90; 'Centraladminstrationen og Erhvervslivet 1890–1930' [Public Admin. and Bus. Community 1890–1930], *Forvaltningshistorisk Antologi,* Helle Blomquist & Per Ingesman eds., Jurst og Økonomforlaget, 1993.

Fitzgerald, Robert

Lect., Centre for Management Studies, Royal Holloway College, Univ. of London, Egham Hill, Egham, Surrey, TW20 0EX, UK. Tel.: 44 784 443783. Fax: 44 784 437520.

Year and Place of Birth 1959, London, UK.

Degrees and Qualifications BA London Univ., 1981; Ph.D. London Univ., 1986.

Previous Post Research Officer, Bus. Hist. Unit, London School of Econ., 1987–90.

Current Offices and Honorary Posts Ed., *J. of Far Eastern Studies.*

Fields of Expertise *Industry Fields:* agric., forestry, fishing; food, drink, tobacco; timber, furniture. *Bus. Dimensions:* personnel management;

marketing; strategy formation; bus. organization; multinational bus.; management education; co. culture. *Scope:* global. *Period:* nineteenth century; twentieth century as a whole. *Teaching:* undergrad.; post grad. *Consultancy:* co. hist.

Publications *Books: British Labour Management and Indust. Welfare, 1846–1939*, Croom Helm, 1988; *Timber: A Hist. of the Timber Trade Federation, 1892–1992*, Batsford, 1992; *Rowntree and the Marketing Revolution, 1862–1969*, CUP, forthcoming 1994; *The Birth of the Japanese Management System*, Frank Cass, forthcoming 1994; *Modern Bus. in Comparative Perspective*, Bristol Academic Press, forthcoming 1994.

Fleming, Keith R.

Asst. Prof., Dept. of Hist., Univ. of Western Ontario, London, Ontario, N6A 5C2, Canada. Tel.: 1 519 679 2111.

Year and Place of Birth 1956, Owen Sound, Canada.

Degrees and Qualifications BA Univ. of Western Ontario, 1978; MA Univ. of Western Ontario, 1979; Ph.D. Univ. of Western Ontario, 1988; M.Div. Univ. of Western Ontario, 1992.

Fields of Expertise *Industry Fields:* gas, electricity, water. *Bus. Dimensions:* production management; marketing; strategy formation; merger movement and issues; bus. organization; bus. and technology; bus.–state relations. *Scope:* regional; *Period:* twentieth century as a whole. *Teaching:* undergrad. *Consultancy:* co. hist.

Publications *Books: Power at Cost: Ontario Hydro and Rural Electrification 1911–1958*, McGill, Queen's Univ. Press, 1992.

Flesher, Dale L.

Arthur Andersen Alumni Prof. of Accountancy, Dept. of Accountancy, Univ. of Mississippi, Univ., MS 38677, USA. Tel.: 0601 232 7623. Fax: 0601 232 7483.

Year and Place of Birth 1945, Albany, USA.

Degrees and Qualifications BS Ball State Univ., 1967; MA Ball State Univ., 1968; Ph.D. Cincinnati Univ., 1975; CPA, 1968; CMA, 1974; CIA, 1985.

Previous Post Appalachian State Univ., 1973–7.

Current Offices and Honorary Posts Trustee & past pres., Acad. of Accounting Historians; ed., *Accounting Historians J.*; treasurer, Phi Kappa Phi Honorary.

Major Honours Leon Radde Award, Inst. of Internal Auditors, 1991, (a lifetime achievement award for contributions to internal auditing education); Burlington Northern Fac. Achievement Award, Mississippi Univ., 1987, (outstanding faculty member campus-wide).

Fields of Expertise *Industry Fields:* agric., forestry, fishing. *Bus. Dimensions:* co. finance and accounting. *Scope:* internat. *Period:* twentieth century as a whole. *Teaching:* post grad. *Consultancy:* co. hist.

Publications *Books: The Third Quarter Century of the Amer. Accounting Assoc.*, Amer. Accounting Assoc., Sarasota, FL, 1991; *The Inst. of Internal Auditors - 50 Years of Progress through Sharing*, The Inst. of Internal Auditors, Altamonte Springs, FL, 1991; *CMA Examination Rev.*, Gleim Publications Inc., Gainesville, FL, 2 vols., 1984, 1987, 1990, 1992; *Independent Auditor's Guide to Operational Auditing*, John Wiley & Sons, New York, 1982. *Articles:* 'The Contributions of Ivar Kreuger to USA Financial Reporting', *The Accounting Rev.*, July, 1986, 421–34.

Flik, Reiner

Scientific Asst., Eichstätt Catholic Univ., Fac. of Historical and Social Sciences, Universitätsallee 1, D-85071 Eichstätt, Germany. Tel.: 49 8421 20 355.
Year and Place of Birth 1954, Althengstett, Germany.
Degrees and Qualifications Dipl. Volkswirt Tübingen Univ., 1980; Dipl. Handelslehrer Tübingen Univ., 1982; Dr.rer.pol. Tübingen Univ., 1988.
Major Honours RWT Treuhand GmbH, Reutlingen Dissertation Prize, Tübingen Univ., .
Fields of Expertise *Industry Fields:* agric., forestry, fishing; metal manufacture; vehicle construction; textiles. *Bus. Dimensions:* production management; bus. organization; bus. and technology; multinational bus. *Scope:* regional; internat. *Period:* eighteenth century; nineteenth century; twentieth century as a whole. *Teaching:* post grad. *Consultancy:* co. hist.
Publications *Articles:* 'Textilindustrie in Calw und Heidenheim 1750–1870. Eine regional vergleichende Studie zur Geschichte der Industrialisierung und der Industriepolitik in Württemberg', *Zeitschrift für Unternehmensgeschichte*, supp. no. 57.

Fode, Henrik

Danish National Bus. Archives, Vester Allé 12, 8000 Århus C, Denmark. Tel.: 45 86 12 85 53. Fax: 45 86 12 85 60.
Year and Place of Birth 1946, Randers, Denmark.
Degrees and Qualifications Ph.D. Aarhus Univ., 1973.
Previous Post Archivist, Danish National Bus. Archives, 1974–92.
Current Offices and Honorary Posts Chairman, Danish Assoc. of Bus. Archivists.
Fields of Expertise *Industry Fields:* transport and communication. *Bus. Dimensions:* entrepreneurs and entrepreneurship; bus. and technology; small bus. matters. *Scope:* local; national. *Period:* eighteenth century; nineteenth century. *Teaching:* undergrad.; post grad.
Publications *Books: Dansk Toldhistorie Bd. 3 1814–1914* [Hist. of Danish Customs Vol. 3 1814–1914], 1989; *Fra Reformation til Folkestyre 1523–1849*, 1977; *Småskibsfarten på Århusbugten 1865–1914*, 1971.

Fohlen, Claude

Emeritus Prof. at the Sorbonne, 79 rue d'Aguesseau, 92100 Boulogne, France. Tel.: 33 1 48258610.
Year and Place of Birth 1922, Mulhouse, France.
Degrees and Qualifications Docteur ès Lettres Sorbonne, 1955.
Previous Post Prof., Paris I Univ., 1967–88.
Fields of Expertise *Industry Fields:* textiles. *Bus. Dimensions:* entrepreneurs and entrepreneurship. *Scope:* local; national. *Period:* nineteenth century.
Publications *Books: Une Affaire de Famille au XIXe siècle*, Méquillet-Nobiot, Paris, A. Colin, 1955; *L'Industrie Textile en France sous le Second Empire*, Paris, Plon, 1956; *La France de l'Entre-deux-guerres*, Paris-Tournai, Casterman, 1966; *Histoire du Travail au XIXe Siècle*, Paris, Nouvelle Librairie de France, 1960; *Qu'est-ce que la Révolution Industrielle*, Paris, Robert Laffont, 1971.

Foreman-Peck, James S.

Fellow of St Antony's College & Lect. in Econ. Hist., St Antony's College, Oxford, OX2 6JF, UK. Tel.: 44 865 274465. Fax: 44 865 274478.

Year and Place of Birth 1948, London, UK.

Degrees and Qualifications BA Essex Univ., 1970; M.Sc. (Econ.), London School of Econ., 1971; Ph.D. London School of Econ., 1978.

Previous Post Prof. of Econ. Hist., Hull Univ., 1988–90.

Current Offices and Honorary Posts Organizing sec., European Historical Econ. Soc.; edit. board mem., *Explorations in Econ. Hist.*; co-ordinator, ESRC Quantitative Econ. Hist. Study Group.

Major Honours Frank Cass Bus. Hist. Prize for 'Competition, Co-operation and Nationalisation' in *Bus. Hist.*, Jul., 1989, 81–102.

Fields of Expertise *Industry Fields:* chemicals and allied industries; shipbuilding and marine engineering; vehicle construction; gas, electricity, water; transport and communication. *Bus. Dimensions:* entrepreneurs and entrepreneurship; production management; co. finance and accounting; co. law; research and development; strategy formation; bus. organization; bus. and technology; small bus. matters; multinational bus.; bus.–state relations; markets and bus. *Scope:* internat.; UK. *Period:* nineteenth century; twentieth century as a whole. *Teaching:* post grad. *Consultancy:* co. hist.; corporate strategy; regulatory review.

Publications *Books: A Hist. of the World Economy: Internat. Econ. Relations since 1850*, Harvester, Barnes & Noble, 1983; 2nd edn., 1993; Spanish edn., Ariel SA, 1985; *New Perspectives on the Late Victorian Economy: Essays in Quantitative Econ. Hist.*, ed., CUP, 1991; *Smith & Nephew in the Health Care Industry 1856–1993*, Edward Elgar, 1994, forthcoming; *Public and Private Ownership in Britain: The Network Industries 1800–1990*, with R. Millward, OUP, 1994, forthcoming. *Articles:* 'Seedcorn or Chaff? New Firms and Indust. Performance in the Interwar Economy', *Econ. Hist. Rev.*, 38, 1985, 402–22.

Fraile Balbin, Pedro

Prof., Fac. of Econ. Hist., Dept. of Econ., Carlos III Univ., Avda. Madrid 126, 28903 Getafe (Madrid), Spain. Tel.: 034 624 9622. Fax: 34 1 624 9875.

Year and Place of Birth 1946, Palencia, Spain.

Degrees and Qualifications Licenciado (Econ.) Madrid Univ. 1974; Ph.D. (Econ.) Univ. of Texas at Austin, 1982.

Previous Post Assoc. Prof., Carlos III Univ., Madrid, 1991–2.

Current Offices and Honorary Posts Ed., *Revista de Historia Economica*.

Fields of Expertise *Industry Fields:* metal manufacture. *Bus. Dimensions:* bus. organization. *Scope:* internat. *Period:* twentieth century as a whole. *Teaching:* undergrad.

Publications *Books: Industrialización y Grupos de Presión. La Economia Política de la Protección en España, 1900–1950* [Lobbies and Industrialization. The Pol. Economy of Protection in Spain, 1900–1950], Alianza Editorial, Madrid, 1991. *Articles:* 'The World Market and the Indust. Growth of the Basque Country', *Modernization and Econ. Growth in Spain 1830–1930*, Nicolás Sánchez-Albornoz ed., New York Univ. Press, New York, 1987, 191–2.

Franaszek, Piotr

Sen. Lect., Dept. of Social and Econ. Hist. and Stats., Inst. of Hist., Jagiellonian Univ., ul. Golebia 13, 31–007 Cracow, Poland. Tel.: 48 12 22 10 33. Fax: 48 12 22 63 06.
Year and Place of Birth 1955, Malbork, Poland.
Degrees and Qualifications MA Jagiellonian Univ., 1979; Ph.D. Jagiellonian Univ., 1988.
Fields of Expertise *Industry Fields:* mining and quarrying. *Bus. Dimensions:* bus. and technology. *Scope:* regional. *Period:* nineteenth century; early twentieth century. *Teaching:* post grad. *Consultancy:* co. hist.
Publications *Books: Technological Progress in Galician Oil Drilling from 1860–1914,* Jagiellonian Univ. Press, Cracow, 1991; *Statistical Guidebook on the Social and Econ. Hist. of Galicia, vol. 10, Galician Agric. during the Period of Autonomy,* Polish Statistical Assoc., Jagiellonian Univ. Press, Cracow/Warsaw, 1992. *Articles:* 'French Capital in the Process of Centralisation of the Polish Oil Industry 1920–1939', *Studia Historyczne* [Historical Studies], XXIX, Cracow, 1986, 229–43; 'Innovatory Activities in Oil Mining Technology until 1914', *Roczniki Dziejów Spolecznych i Gospodarczych* [Annual Studies on Social and Econ. Hist.], vol. 49, Poznan, 1988, 77–97; 'Science and Technology in the Development of the Galician Oil Industry', *Studies in Social and Econ. Hist.,* 21, Leuven, 1990, 123–7.

Fraser, Maryna

Sen. Exec. Manager/Group Archivist, Barlow Rand Ltd, Head Office, POB 78-2248, Sandton 2146, Transvaal, South Africa. Tel.: 27 11 801 2185/6/7. Fax: 27 11 444 3643.
Year and Place of Birth 1941, Johannesburg, South Africa.
Degrees and Qualifications BA Witwatersrand Univ., Johannesburg, 1962; MA Witwatersrand Univ., 1974; Postgraduate Dip. Librarianship Witwatersrand Univ., 1964; Postgraduate Dip. Archival Science Dept. of Nat. Education, 1984.
Previous Post Witwatersrand Univ., 1972.
Current Offices and Honorary Posts Ex-officio chairman, Assoc. for Archivist & Manuscript Librarians; advisory com. mem. (Dip. Archival Sci.) Technicon, S. Africa; mem., National Archives Commission.
Major Honours Appointed to National Archives Commission 1992; Fellow of the S. African Inst. for Librarianship and Information Science 1968; commissioned by Van Riebeeck Soc. to edit commerative volume for Johannesburg's centenary, 1986.
Fields of Expertise *Industry Fields:* mining and quarrying. *Bus. Dimensions:* multinational bus. *Scope:* internat.; South Africa; UK. *Period:* twentieth century as a whole. *Teaching:* post grad. *Consultancy:* co. hist.
Publications *Books: All That Glittered. Selected Correspondence of Lionel Phillips, 1890–1924,* co-ed., OUP, 1977; *The Story of Two Cape Farms,* Barlow Rand, 1980 & 1982; *Johannesburg Pioneer Journals,* Van Riebeek Soc., 1985; *Some Reminiscences: Autobiography of Sir Lionel Phillips,* ed., Ad Donker, 1986; *Centenary Hist. of Rand Mines Limited,* Acorn Press, forthcoming.

French, Michael J.

Lect., Dept. of Econ. and Social Hist., Adam Smith Building, Univ. of

Fridlund

Glasgow, Glasgow, G12 8RT, UK.
Tel.: 44 41 339 8855. Fax: 44 41 330
4889.
Year and Place of Birth 1956,
Chesterfield, UK.
Degrees and Qualifications BA East
Anglia Univ., 1977; M.Sc. London
School of Econ., 1978; Ph.D Birkbeck
Coll., London Univ., 1985.
Major Honours Newcomen Special
Article Award, 1986 for *Bus. Hist.
Rev.* article.
Fields of Expertise *Industry Fields:*
vehicle construction; other manufacturing industries. *Bus. Dimensions:* marketing; bus. organization; multinational bus. *Scope:* internat. *Period:* twentieth century as a whole. *Teaching:* undergrad.
Publications *Books: The US Tire
Industry: A Hist.*, Twayne, 1990.
Articles: 'Structural Change and
Competition in the United States Tire
Industry, 1920–37', *Bus. Hist. Rev.*,
60, Spring, 1986, 28–54; 'The
Emergence of a US Multinational
Enterprise - the Goodyear Tire and
Rubber Company', *Econ. Hist. Rev.*,
2nd ser., XL(1), Feb., 1987, 64–79;
'The Growth and Decline of the North
British Rubber Co., 1856–1956', *Bus.
Hist.*, 30(4), Oct., 1988, 396–415;
'Manufacturing and Marketing:
Vertical Integration in the US Tire
Industry, 1890–1980's', *Bus. & Econ.
Hist.*, 18, 1989, 178–87.

Fridlund, Mats

Doctoral Student, Dept. of Hist. of
Science & Technology, Royal Inst. of
Technology, 100 44 Stockholm,
Sweden. Tel.: 46 8 790 8561. Fax: 46
8 246263.
Year and Place of Birth 1965,
Stockholm, Sweden.
Degrees and Qualifications M.Sc.
(Engineering Physics) Royal Inst. of
Technology, Sweden, 1992.

Previous Post Scientific Assoc.,
Microcosm, CERN, Geneva, 1991.
Fields of Expertise *Industry Fields:*
electrical engineering; public admin.
and defence. *Bus. Dimensions:*
research and development; bus. and
technology; bus.–state relations; co.
culture. *Scope:* national; internat.;
Sweden. *Period:* twentieth century as a
whole. *Teaching:* undergrad.
Consultancy: co. hist.
Publications *Books: Historiska
föremål på KTH från plasmafysikens
tidiga utveckling, 1940–ca. 1970*
[Historical Objects used at the Royal
Inst. of Technology in early Work on
Plasma Physics, 1940–ca. 1970], KTH,
Stockholm, 1989. *Articles:* 'Preserved
Objects in the Hist. of Plasma Physics
in Sweden', *Artifactory: Technology
Museums Special Interest Group
Newsletter*, 12(2), 1990, 4–5; 'The
Teaching of the Hist. of Technology in
Japan: A Survey in 1990', forthcoming, 1993; 'Aseas och Vattenfalls
utvecklingssamarbete, 1910–c. 1970:
Ett exempel på ett utvecklingspar i
svensk teknikhistoria [The
Development of Co-operation of Asea
and the State Power Board, 1910–ca.
1970: An Example of a Development
Pair in Swedish Hist. of Technology]',
Working papers from the Dept. of
Hist. of Science & Technology, 93(5),
Royal Inst. of Technology, Stockholm,
1993.

Friedricks, William B.

Asst. Prof. of Hist., Dept. of Hist.,
Simpson College, 701 North C St,
Indianola, Iowa 50125, USA. Tel.: 1
515 961 1634.
Year and Place of Birth 1958, Los
Angeles, USA.
Degrees and Qualifications BA
Univ. of California, San Diego, 1980;
MA Univ. of Southern California,
1985; Ph.D. Univ. of Southern
California, 1986.

Current Offices and Honorary Posts Assoc. ed., *Essays in Econ. and Bus. Hist.*.

Fields of Expertise *Industry Fields:* transport and communication. *Bus. Dimensions:* entrepreneurs and entrepreneurship. *Scope:* regional. *Period:* twentieth century as a whole. *Teaching:* undergrad. *Consultancy:* co. hist.

Publications *Books: Henry E. Huntington and the Creation of Southern California*, Ohio State Univ. Press, 1992, in Historical Perspectives on Bus. Enterprise Series. *Articles:* 'Capital and Labor in Los Angeles: Henry E. Huntington vs. Organised Labor, 1900–1920', *Pacific Historical Rev.*, 71, Winter, 1989, 327–34; 'A Metropol. Entrepreneur par excellence: Henry E. Huntington and the Growth of Southern California, 1898 –1927', *Bus. Hist. Rev.*, 63, Summer, 1989, 329–55.

Fujimura, Daijiro

Prof., Fac. of Commercial Sciences, Hiroshima Shudo Univ., 1717 Ohtsuka, Numata-cho, Asaminami-ku, Hiroshima 731-31, Japan. Tel.: 082 848 2121. Fax: 082 848 6051.

Year and Place of Birth 1946, Fukuoka, Japan.

Degrees and Qualifications BA, Kyushu Univ., 1971; MA Kyushu Univ., 1973.

Previous Post Asst. Prof., Fac. of Commercial Sci., Hiroshima Shudo Univ., 1983–90.

Current Offices and Honorary Posts Council mem., Japan Bus. Hist. Soc.

Fields of Expertise *Industry Fields:* metal manufacture. *Bus. Dimensions:* co. finance and accounting; co. admin. marketing; bus. organization. *Scope:* national. *Period:* nineteenth century. *Teaching:* undergrad.; post grad.

Publications *Articles:* 'Schneider et Cie. et son Plan d'Organisation

Administrative de 1913: Analyse et Interprétation', *Histoire, Économie et Société*, 2° Trimestre, 1991, 269–76.

Fujita, Nobuhisa

Assoc. Prof., Dept. of Bus. Admin., Ryukoku Univ., 67 Fukakusa-Tsukamoto, Fushimi-ku, Kyoto 612, Japan. Tel.: 075 642 1111. Fax: 075 643 8510.

Year and Place of Birth 1949, Nara, Japan.

Degrees and Qualifications BA, Ryukoku Univ., 1973; MA (Commerce), Waseda Univ., 1975.

Previous Post Lect., Hakuoh Women's Junior College, 1982–3.

Current Offices and Honorary Posts Sec., 1986–90; council mem., 1990–.

Fields of Expertise *Industry Fields:* mechanical engineering; electrical engineering. *Bus. Dimensions:* entrepreneurs and entrepreneurship; production management; co. finance and accounting; co. admin.; research and development; strategy formation; bus. organization; bus. and technology; bus.–state relations. *Scope:* national; internat. *Period:* twentieth century as a whole; inter-war years, 1919–39; mid-twentieth century, 1940–70. *Teaching:* undergrad.

Publications *Books: Syashi no kenkyu* [The Study of Co. Hist.; A Historical Study of Japanese Companies' Growth], Yuhikaku Co., 1990 *Articles:* 'Dai niji Taisen to Mitsubishi Zaibatsu' [Mitsubishi during World War II], *Nihon Keizai Shinbun-sya*, 1987; 'Ties between Foreign Makers and Zaibatsu Enterprise in Pre-war Japan : Case Studies of Mitsubishi Oil Co. and Mitsubishi Electric Manufacturing Co.', *Foreign Bus. in Japan before World War II*, T. Yuzawa and M. Udagawa eds., Univ. of Tokyo Press, 1990; 'Keieisenryaku no Tenkai' [The

Development of Bus. Strategy], *Gendai Kigyo Keieiron* [Modern Bus. Enterprise], Ryukoku Univ. ed., Chuou Keizai Co., 1985; 'Mitsubishi Denki no keieishiteki Kenkyo' [The Early Development of the Mitsubishi Electric Co., 1905–1920 : A Bus. Hist.], *Papers of Social Science*, Konan Univ. ed., 9, 1981.

Fujita, Yukitoshi

Lect., Aich Gakusen Univ., Oikecho Siotori 1, Toyota-shi, Aichi-ken 471, Japan. Tel.: 0565 35 1313. Fax: 0565 35 1677.

Year and Place of Birth 1962, Tokyo, Japan.

Degrees and Qualifications MBA Senshu Univ., 1987.

Fields of Expertise *Industry Fields:* mining and quarrying; coal and petroleum products; mechanical engineering; textiles; paper, printing, publishing. *Bus. Dimensions:* entrepreneurs and entrepreneurship; bus. organization. *Scope:* local; regional. *Period:* early modern; early twentieth century; interwar years, 1919–39. *Teaching:* undergrad. *Consultancy:* co. hist.

Publications *Articles:* 'Kanegafuchi Boseki no Hatten to Mitsui Bussan no Gyomukakudai' [Interdependence of Kanegafuchi Spinning Co. and Mitsui Bussan Kaisha in Meiji 30's], *Bull. of the Inst. of Bus. Admin.*, Senshu Univ., 92, Jul. 1990; 'Boekishosha no Keieishi teki Kenkyu ni tsuite' [A Survey of Bus. Historical Studies: The Case of Trading Companies in Japan], *Bull. of the Inst. of Bus. Admin.*, Senshu Univ., 83, Jan. 1989; 'Seishi San sha no Gappei ni okeru Fujiwara Ginziro to Okawa Heizabro' [The Rôle of Fujiwara and Okawa in the Merger of three Paper Manufacturing Companies], *Social Science Rev.*, Senshu Univ. Grad. School, 1, Sept. 1987.

Furlong, Patrick J.

Prof. of Hist., Dept. of Hist., Indiana Univ., South Bend, IN 46634-7111, USA. Tel.: 1 219 237 4491. Fax: 1 219 237 4538.

Year and Place of Birth 1940, Lexington, USA.

Degrees and Qualifications BA Kentucky Univ., 1961; MA Northwestern Univ., 1962; Ph.D. Northwestern Univ., 1966.

Major Honours Lindquist Award, Indiana Univ. South Bend; Winner of Peabody Award & TV Emmy Award for 'Less than they Promised', (Research Director, Studebaker), one hour television programme, 1983.

Fields of Expertise *Industry Fields:* vehicle construction. *Bus. Dimensions:* marketing. *Scope:* national; USA. *Period:* twentieth century as a whole. *Teaching:* undergrad. *Consultancy:* co. hist.

Publications *Books: Studebaker: Less Than They Promised*, co-auth., Arno Books, 1984. *Articles:* 'K.T. Keller [Chrysler Motors President], *Dictionary of Amer. Biography*, supplement 8, Scribner's, 1988; 'Paul G. Hoffman [Studebaker President], *Dictionary of Amer. Biography*, supplement 9, forthcoming.

Galambos, Louis

Prof. of Hist. & Ed., The Papers of Dwight David Eisenhower, Dept. of Hist., Johns Hopkins Univ., Baltimore, MD 21218, USA. Tel.: 1 410 516 7598. Fax: 1 410 516 4317.

Year and Place of Birth 1931, Fostoria, USA.

Degrees and Qualifications BA Indiana Univ., 1955; MA Yale Univ., 1957; Ph.D. Yale Univ., 1960.

Previous Post Rutgers Univ., 1970–1.

Current Offices and Honorary Posts Trustee, Bus. Hist. Conf.

Major Honours Pres., Econ. Hist. Assoc.; pres., Bus. Hist. Conf., 1991–2.

Fields of Expertise *Industry Fields:* chemicals and allied industries; textiles other manufacturing industries; transport and communication; insurance, banking, finance; professional and scientific services; public admin. and defence. *Bus. Dimensions:* entrepreneurs and entrepreneurship; production management; personnel management; co. admin.; marketing; research and development; strategy formation; merger movement and issues; bus. organization; bus. and technology; multinational bus.; bus.–state relations; markets and bus.; bus. values; co. culture; bus. networks. *Scope:* national; internat.; USA. *Period:* nineteenth century; twentieth century as a whole; early twentieth century. *Teaching:* undergrad.; post grad. *Consultancy:* co. hist.

Publications *Books: The Rise of the Corporate Commonwealth: US Bus. and Public Policy in the Twentieth Century*, with Joseph Pratt, Basic Books, 1988; *The Papers of Dwight David Eisenhower, Vols. VII–XIII,* ed., Johns Hopkins Univ. Press; *Amer. at Middle Age: A New Hist. of the United States in the Twentieth Century*, McGraw Hill, 1982; *Amerika Keiei Shigaku no Shin Choryu: Soshiki Sogo Riron* [New Trends in the Hist. of Amer. Management: The Theory of the Organizational Synthesis], Yamaguchi Kazuomi & Sunaga Kinchiburo translators & eds., Dobunkan, 1991.

Gallo, Giampaolo

Assoc. Prof. of Contemporary Econ. Hist., Dept. of Historical Science, Fac. of Pol. Science, Via Pascoli, 06100 Perugia, Italy. Tel.: 39 75 5855435.

Fax: 39 75 5855449.

Year and Place of Birth 1946, Perugia, Italy.

Degrees and Qualifications Laurea (Pol. Sc.) Perugia Univ., 1970; Specialist Diploma in Development Econ., Centre for Econ.-Agric. Specialization and Research, Naples Univ., 1972.

Previous Post Asst. Prof., Econ. Hist., 1980–5.

Current Offices and Honorary Posts Mem., Fondazione ASSI di Storia e Studi sull'Impresa, Milan; mem., Assoc. of Italian Econ. Historians.

Fields of Expertise *Industry Fields:* food, drink, tobacco. *Bus. Dimensions:* entrepreneurs and entrepreneurship. *Scope:* national. *Period:* twentieth century as a whole. *Teaching:* undergrad. *Consultancy:* co. hist.

Publications *Books: Ill.mo Sig. Direttore. Grande Industria e Società a Terni*, Editoriale Umbra, 1983; *Sulla Bocca di Tutti. Buitoni e Perugina: Una Storia in Breve*, ed., Electa Editori Umbri, 1990; *Industria è . Ipotesi per un Centro di Documentazione, Formazione e Promozione per l'Industria*, ed., Electa Editori Umbri, 1991; *B. Buitoni , Pasta e Cioccolato. Una Storia imprenditoriale*, ed., Protagon, 1992, (interview). *Articles:* 'Tipologia dell'Industria ed Esperienze d'Impresa in una Regione Agricola', *L'Umbria*, with R. Covino, Einaudi, 1989, 343–448.

Garcia-Ruiz, José-Luis

Catedrático E.U., Univ. School of Bus., Complutense Univ., Plaza de España 16, 28008 Madrid, Spain. Tel.: 34 91 2946798. Fax: 34 91 3946797.

Year and Place of Birth 1959, Madrid, Spain.

Degrees and Qualifications Dip.Ed., BA Madrid Univ., 1977; M.Litt.

Madrid Univ., 1985; Ph.D. Complutense Univ., Madrid 1990.

Previous Post Prof. E.U., 1988–92.

Current Offices and Honorary Posts Vice-Dir., Univ. Bus. School, Complutense Univ. of Madrid.

Fields of Expertise *Industry Fields:* insurance, banking, finance. *Bus. Dimensions:* bus. organization. *Scope:* national. *Period:* twentieth century as a whole. *Teaching:* undergrad. *Consultancy:* co. hist.

Publications *Books: Banca y Crisis Economica en España, 1930–1935,* ed., VCM, Madrid, 1991; *La Historia Económica de la Empresa Moderna en sus Textos,* ISTMO, Madrid, 1993. *Articles:* 'Tests de Causalidad, Dinero y Renta en España, 1905–1975', *Revista de Historia Económica,* 2, 295–311; 'Divergent, Parallel and Convergent Trajectories: The Hist. of the Banco Hispano-Americano and the Banco Central, 1901–1965', *Financial Institutions and Financial Markets in 20th Century Europe and North Amer.,* with Prof. Gabriel Tortella, 27–28 May, 1993, Zürich, Switzerland.

Garside, W.R.

Prof. of Econ. Hist., Dept. of Econ. and Social Hist., School of Social Sciences, Univ. of Birmingham, POB 363, Edgbaston, Birmingham, B15 2TT, UK. Tel.: 44 21 414 6634. Fax: 44 21 414 6625.

Year and Place of Birth 1944, Easington, UK.

Degrees and Qualifications BA (Special Studies Econ.) Leeds Univ., 1965; Ph.D. (Econ.) Leeds Univ., 1969.

Previous Post Lect. in Econ. Hist., Leicester Univ., 1968–72.

Current Offices and Honorary Posts Council mem., Econ. Hist. Soc.

Fields of Expertise *Industry Fields:*

mining and quarrying; shipbuilding and marine engineering; textiles. *Bus. Dimensions:* entrepreneurs and entrepreneurship; merger movement and issues; bus. and technology; bus.–state relations. *Scope:* regional; national; internat. *Period:* inter-war years, 1919–39; mid-twentieth century, 1940–'70; late twentieth century, 1970–present. *Teaching:* undergrad.; post grad.

Publications *Books: The Durham Miners, 1919–1960,* Allen & Unwin, 1971; *The Measurement of Unemployment. Methods and Sources in Great Britain, 1850–1979,* Oxford, 1980; *British Unemployment, 1919–1939: A Study in Public Policy,* CUP, 1991. *Articles:* 'Adjusting to Decline: Coalmining and the Rationalization Movement in Interwar Britain', *Sozialgeschichte des Bergbaus,* K. Tenfelde ed., Munich, 1992.

Gerriets, Marilyn

Assoc. Prof., Dept. of Econ., St Francis Xavier Univ., Antigonish, Nova Scotia, B2G 1C0, Canada. Tel.: 1 867 2127. Fax: 1 867 2228.

Year and Place of Birth 1947, New Jersey, USA.

Degrees and Qualifications BA San Francisco State College, 1971; MA Toronto Univ., 1972; Ph.D. Toronto Univ., 1978.

Previous Post Asst. Prof., Wilfred Laurier Univ., 1977–80.

Current Offices and Honorary Posts Director, Atlantic Canada Econ. Assoc.

Fields of Expertise *Industry Fields:* agric., forestry, fishing; mining and quarrying. *Bus. Dimensions:* bus. organization. *Scope:* regional; national. *Period:* nineteenth century. *Teaching:* undergrad.

Publications *Articles:* 'Kingship and Exchange in pre-Viking Ireland',

Cambridge Medieval Celtic Studies, 13, 1987, 39–72; 'The King as Judge in Early Christian Ireland', *Celtica*, 1988, 29–52; 'Theft Penitentials and the Compilation of the Early Irish Laws', *Celtica*, 1991, 18–32; 'The Impact of the General Mining Assoc. on the Early Development of the Nova Scotian Coal Industry', *Acadiensis*, 31(1), 1991, 53–84; selected to be reprinted in *New Approaches to the Econ. History of the Maritimes*, Kris Inwood ed., Acadiensis Press, forthcoming; 'The Rise and Fall of a Free Standing Co. in Nova Scotia: The General Mining Association', *Bus. Hist.*, 34(3), 1992, 16–48; reprinted in *Canadian Multinationals and Internat. Finance*, Gregory P. Marchildon & Duncan McDowall eds., Frank Cass, London, 1993.

Gerslová, Jana

Lect.-Research Asst., Silesian Univ., Fac. of Bus. Studies, Univerzitní Nám. 76, 733 40 Karviná, Czechland. Tel.: 42 6993 49951. Fax: 42 6993 46451.
Year and Place of Birth 1955, Martin, Czechland.
Degrees and Qualifications BA (Hist. Germ.) Palacky Univ., 1979; Ph.D. (Hist.) Palacky Univ., 1982; C.Sc. Czechoslovak Acad. of Sciences, Prague, 1986.
Previous Post Research Fellow, Silesian Inst. of the Czechoslovak Acad. of Sciences Opava, 1979–90.
Current Offices and Honorary Posts Mem., Assoc. of Bus. Historians of the Acad. of Sciences, Prague.
Fields of Expertise *Bus. Dimensions:* entrepreneurs and entrepreneurship; entrepreneurial ethics in hist. *Scope:* national; internat. *Teaching:* undergrad. *Consultancy:* co. hist.
Publications *Books: Kapitoly z dejin podnikání v Ceskoslovensku. I - 1918–1938* [Chapters from the Hist. of

Bus. Enterprise in Czechoslovakia. I - 1918–1938], with J. Steiner, Karviná, 1992. *Articles:* 'Projekt vyzkumu Promeny hospodárskych a sociálních struktur Ceskoslovenska a predpoklady podnikatelské aktivity 1918–1990' [Research Project: The Transformation of Czechoslovakian Econ. and Social Structures and the pre-Conditions of Entrepreneurial Activities 1918–1990], *Opava*, Slezky ústav CSAV, 1991, 47–61.

Giannetti, Renato

Sen. Fellow, Fac. of Letters and Philo., Dept. of Hist., Via San Gallo 10, 50129 Florence, Italy. Tel.: 39 55 2757949. Fax: 39 55 219173.
Year and Place of Birth 1948, Siena, Italy.
Degrees and Qualifications MA (Philo.) Florence Univ.
Current Offices and Honorary Posts Board mem., Italian Assoc. of Econ. Historians; scientific com. mem., ASSI (Associazione per lo Studio e la Storia dell'Impresa), Milan.
Fields of Expertise *Industry Fields:* chemicals and allied industries; electrical engineering. *Bus. Dimensions:* research and development; merger movement and issues; bus. organization; bus. and technology. *Scope:* national; internat.; Italy. *Period:* twentieth century as a whole; inter-war years, 1919–39. *Teaching:* undergrad. *Consultancy:* co. hist.
Publications *Books: Cliometria*, with Alberto Baccini co-auth., Dipartimento di Storia, Florence, 1992; *Technology and Enterprise in a Historical Perspective*, co-eds. with G. Dosi & P.A. Toninelli, Clarendon Press, Oxford, 1992. *Articles:* 'The Power Equipment Cartels. The Internat. Agreement and the Italian Case in the 1930s', *Internat. Cartels in Bus. Hist.*, T. Hara & H. Kudo eds.,

Tokyo Univ. Press, Tokyo, 1991, 190–209; 'Electrical Engineers and the Establishment of Standards in Italian Electrical Networks, 1900–1930', *Electricité et électrification dans le monde*, M. Trede ed., Presses Universitaires de France, Paris, 1992, 129–41; 'The Success of the Italian Shipbuilding Industry between the Wars: Market, Technology, Organization', *Internat. J. of Maritime Hist.*, IV(1), 1992, 143–54:

Giebelhaus, August W.

Prof., School of Hist., Technology and Soc., Georgia Inst. of Technology, Atlanta, GA 30332-0345, USA. Tel.: 1 404 894 6828. Fax: 1 404 853 0535.
Year and Place of Birth 1943, Rahway, USA.
Degrees and Qualifications BA (Hist.) Rutgers Univ., 1964; MA (Hist.) Rutgers Univ., 1970; Ph.D. (Hist.) Delaware Univ., 1977.
Previous Post Hagley Fellow, Eleutherian Mills Hagley Foundation, Greenville, Wilmington, Delaware, 1971–4 & 1975–6; Lect., Birmingham Univ. (UK), 1974–5.
Current Offices and Honorary Posts Trustee, Econ. & Bus. Hist. Soc.; edit. board mem., *Technology and Culture*, (Soc. for the Hist. of Technology).
Fields of Expertise *Industry Fields:* food, drink, tobacco; coal and petroleum products; public admin. and defence. *Bus. Dimensions:* marketing; research and development; bus. organization; bus. and technology; multinational bus.; bus.–state relations. *Scope:* national. *Period:* twentieth century as a whole. *Teaching:* undergrad.; post grad. *Consultancy:* co. hist.
Publications *Books: Bus. and Government in the Oil Industry: A Case Study of Sun Oil, 1876–1945*, JAI Press, 1980; *Energy Transitions:*

Long-term Perspectives, co-ed., Westview Press, 1981; *Engineering the New South: Georgia Tech, 1885–1985*, co-auth., Univ. of Georgia Press, 1985; *Bartlesville Energy Center: The Federal Government in Petroleum Research, 1918–1983*, co-auth., Office of Scientific and Technical Information, US Dept. of Energy, 1985. *Articles:* 'Farming for Fuel: The Alcohol Motor Fuel Movement of the 1930s', *Agric. Hist.*, 54(1), Jan., 1980, 173–89.

Gilpin, John F.

1733-27 Avenue SW, Calgary, Alberta, Canada.
Year and Place of Birth 1947, Edmonton, Canada.
Degrees and Qualifications BA Alberta Univ., 1972; MA Alberta Univ., 1977; Ph.D. Leicester Univ., 1992.
Previous Post Dept. of Hist., Univ. of Saskatchewan, 1992–3.
Fields of Expertise *Industry Fields:* insurance, banking, finance. *Bus. Dimensions:* entrepreneurs and entrepreneurship. *Scope:* global. *Period:* nineteenth century. *Teaching:* post grad. *Consultancy:* co. hist.
Publications *Articles:* 'The Poor Relation has come into his Fortune. The British Investment Boom in Canada 1905–1915', , Canada House Lecture Series, 53, 1992; 'International Perspectives on Railway Townsite Development in Western Canada 1877–1914', *Planning Perspectives*, 7, 1992.

Gingras, André

Project Director, École Nationale d'Administration Publique, 945 Avenue Wolfe, Sainte Foy, Québec, G1V 3J9, Canada. Tel.: 1 418 657

2485. Fax: 1 418 657 2616.

Year and Place of Birth 1934, Quebec, Canada.

Degrees and Qualifications Bacc. Chem. Eng. Laval Univ., Quebec, 1958; MBA Cornell Univ., 1967; Ph.D. candidate Laval Univ., 1977.

Previous Post Technical co-ordinator, UN Project BLI 85-009, Bamako, Mali, 1987–9, D.T.C.D. United Nations.

Fields of Expertise *Industry Fields:* public admin. and defence. *Bus. Dimensions:* strategy formation; management education; co. culture; boardroom issues. *Scope:* regional. *Period:* late twentieth century, 1970–present. *Teaching:* post grad. *Consultancy:* corporate strategy.

Girvan, Norman Paul

Director, Consortium Grad. School of Social Science, Univ. of the West Indies, Mona, Kingston 7, Jamaica. Tel.: 1 809 927 1234. Fax: 1 809 927 1234.

Year and Place of Birth 1941, Jamaica.

Degrees and Qualifications B.Sc. (Econ.) Univ. College of the West Indies; Ph.D. (Econ.) London School of Econ., 1966.

Previous Post Chief Technical Director, National Planning Agency, Government of Jamaica.

Current Offices and Honorary Posts Board mem., Regional Co-ordination of Econ. & Soc. Research; founder & first pres., Assoc. of Caribbean Economists, 1989.

Major Honours Student of the Year Award, Univ. College of the West Indies, 1961; Inst. of Jamaica Centenary Medal for Distinguished Contribution in the field of Hist. & Soc. Sci., 1981.

Fields of Expertise *Industry Fields:* mining and quarrying. *Bus. Dimensions:* bus. and technology;

multinational bus. *Scope:* regional; global; Latin Amer.; Caribbean. *Period:* twentieth century as a whole. *Teaching:* post grad. *Consultancy:* government policy to bus.

Publications *Books: The Caribbean Bauxite Industry,* Inst. of Social & Econ. Research, Univ. of the West Indies, Mona, 1967; *Foreign Capital and Econ. Underdevelopment in Jamaica,* Inst. of Social & Econ. Research, Univ. of the West Indies, Mona, 1971; *Copper in Chile: A Study in Conflict between Corporate and National Economy,* Inst. of Social & Econ. Research, Univ. of the West Indies, Mona, 1972; *Corporate Imperialism, Conflict and Expropriation: Transnational Corporations and Econ. Nationalism in the Third World,* Myron E. Sharpe, New York, 1976; *Technology Policies for small Developing Economies: A Study of the Caribbean,* Inst. of Social & Econ. Research, Univ. of the West Indies, Mona, 1983.

Glete, Jan

Sen. Lect., Dept. of Hist., Stockholm Univ., S-106 91 Stockholm, Sweden. Tel.: 08 16 20 00. Fax: 08 16 75 48.

Year and Place of Birth 1947, Västeras, Sweden.

Degrees and Qualifications Fil. Mag. Stockholm Univ., 1969; Ph.D. Stockholm Univ., 1975.

Previous Post Research Fellow, Dept. of Hist., Stockholm Univ., 1983–92.

Major Honours Beskowska stipendiet, 1992, Royal Acad. of Letters, Hist. and Antiquities.

Fields of Expertise *Industry Fields:* shipbuilding and marine engineering. *Bus. Dimensions:* bus. and technology. *Scope:* internat. *Period:* early modern. *Teaching:* post grad. *Consultancy:* corporate strategy.

Publications *Books:*

Kreugerkoncernen och Boliden [The Kreuger Group and the Boliden Mining Co.], LiberFörlag, 1975; *Kreugerkoncernen och krisen på svensk aktiemarknad* [The Kreuger Group and the Crisis on the Swedish Stock Market], Stockholm Studies in Hist. no. 28, 1981; *ASEA under hundra år, 1883–1983* [ASEA during 100 years, 1883–1993], 1983; *Ägande och industriell omvandling: Ägargrupper, skogsindustri och verkstadsindusri, 1850–1950* [Ownership and Indust. Transformation, Owner Groups, Forest Industry and Engineering Industry, 1850–1950], SNS Förlag, 1987; *Navies and Nations: Warships, Navies and State Building in Europe and Amer., 1500–1860*, 2 vols., Stockholm Studies in Hist, no. 48, 1–2.

Godley, Andrew C.

Lect., Dept. of Econ., Univ. of Reading, Whiteknights, POB 216, Reading, Berks, RG6 2AA, UK. Tel.: 44 734 875 123.

Year and Place of Birth 1963, Sheffield, UK.

Degrees and Qualifications B.Sc. (Econ.) London School of Econ., 1986; Ph.D. (Econ.) London School of Econ., 1993.

Major Honours Bus. Hist. Research Studentship, Bus. Hist. Unit, London School of Econ., 1987–8.

Fields of Expertise *Industry Fields:* clothing and footwear. *Bus. Dimensions:* entrepreneurs and entrepreneurship; bus. organization; small bus. matters; co. culture. *Scope:* internat. *Period:* nineteenth century; twentieth century as a whole. *Teaching:* undergrad.; post grad.

Publications *Articles:* 'Enterprise and Culture: Jewish Immigrants in London and New York, 1880–1914', Ph.D. thesis, London School of Econ., 1993.

Goebel, Erik

Sen. Research Archivist, Danish National Archives, Rigsdagsgården 9, 1218 Copenhagen K, Denmark. Tel.: 45 33 93 33 10. Fax: 45 33 15 32 39.

Year and Place of Birth 1949, Elsinore, Denmark.

Degrees and Qualifications MA Copenhagen Univ., 1979.

Previous Post Research Fellow, Inst. of Econ. Hist., Copenhagen Univ., 1979–81.

Current Offices and Honorary Posts Mem., Internat. Commission for Maritime Hist.; rev. ed., *Scandinavian Econ. Hist. Rev.*.

Fields of Expertise *Industry Fields:* transport and communication. *Bus. Dimensions:* bus. and technology. *Scope:* internat. *Period:* eighteenth century. *Teaching:* post grad. *Consultancy:* co. hist.

Publications *Books: The Danish West India Co. Records in the Danish National Archives*, Soc. of Virgin Islands Historians, St Thomas, 1989. *Articles:* 'The Danish Asiatic Company's Voyages to China, 1832–1833', *Scandinavian Econ. Hist. Rev.*, XXVII, 1979, 22–46; 'Danish Trade to the West Indies and Guinea, 1671–1754', *Scandinavian Econ. Hist. Rev.*, XXXI, 1983, 21–49; 'Vol. and Structure of Danish Shipping to the Caribbean and Guinea, 1671–1838', *Internat. J. of Maritime Hist.*, II, 1990, 103–31; 'Danish Country Trade Routes in Asian Waters in the 17th and 18th Centuries', *Asian Trade Routes: Continental and Maritime*, K.R. Hællqvist ed., Curzon Press, London, 1991, 104–116.

Gomez-Mendoza, Antonio

Prof. in Econ. Hist., Dept. of Hist. & Historical Institutions II, Fac. of Econ. Science, Complutense Univ. Madrid,

Campus de Somosaguas, 28023 Madrid, Spain. Tel.: 34 1 394 2459.

Year and Place of Birth 1952, Madrid, Spain.

Degrees and Qualifications BA Univ. Complutense, 1975; D.Phil Oxford Univ., 1981; Ph.D. Complutense Univ., 1981; Prof., Complutense Univ., 1989.

Current Offices and Honorary Posts Chair, Dept. of Econ. Hist., Fac. of Econ. Sci., Complutense Univ.; edit. staff mem., *Revista de Historia Indust..*

Major Honours Deakin Fellow, St Antony's College, Oxford Univ., 1986.

Fields of Expertise *Industry Fields:* mining and quarrying; chemicals and allied industries; metal manufacture; transport and communication. *Bus. Dimensions:* bus.–state relations. *Scope:* national. *Period:* nineteenth century; mid-twentieth century, 1940–70. *Teaching:* undergrad.; post grad. *Consultancy:* co. hist.

Publications *Books: Ferrocarriles y Cambio Económico en España (1855–1913). Una nueva historia económica*, Alianza Universidad, Madrid, 1982; *Ferrocarril, Industria y Mercado en la Modernización de España*, Espasa Calpe, Madrid, 1989; *El Gibraltar Económico. Francy y las Minas de Riotinto, 1936/54.* Articles: 'Oligopoly and Econ. Efficiency: Portland Cement in Spain (1899–1935)', *Rivista di Storia Económica*, 2nd ser., vol. 4, 1987, 76–95; 'The Cost of Francoist Econ. Policies to a British Firm: The Rio Tinto Co., 1939–1954', *Bus. & Econ. Hist.*, 2nd ser., vol. 21, 1992, 354–63.

Goodall, Francis

Fellow, Bus. Hist. Unit, London School of Econ., Houghton St, London, WC2A 2AE, UK. Tel.: 44 71 955 7109. Fax: 44 71 242 0392.

Year and Place of Birth 1931, Ruislip, UK.

Degrees and Qualifications BA Oxford Univ., 1954; MA Oxford Univ., 1958; Ph.D. London School of Econ., 1992.

Major Honours Henry Oliver Beckit Prize, 1954.

Fields of Expertise *Industry Fields:* gas, electricity, water. *Bus. Dimensions:* markets and bus. *Scope:* national. *Period:* twentieth century as a whole. *Consultancy:* co. hist.

Publications *Books: Bibliography of British Bus. Histories*, Gower, 1987. *Articles:* 'Appliance Trading Activities of British Gas Utilities', *Econ. Hist. Rev.*, 46(3), Aug., 1993.

Goodchild, John

Principal Local Studies Officer & Archivist, Wakefield Metropol. District Council, Library HQ, Balne Lane, Wakefield, Yorks, WF2 0DQ, UK. Tel.: 44 924 371231. Fax: 44 924 379287.

Year and Place of Birth 1935, Wakefield, UK.

Degrees and Qualifications Hon. degree M. Univ. (Open Univ.); mem., Soc. of Archivists.

Previous Post Curator, S. Yorks. Indust. Museum, 1966–75.

Current Offices and Honorary Posts Chairman, Local Hist. Study Section, Yorkshire Arch. Soc.; vice-pres., Wakefield Hist. Soc.

Major Honours Hon. Master's Degree, Open Univ.

Fields of Expertise *Industry Fields:* agric., forestry, fishing; mining and quarrying; food, drink, tobacco; metal manufacture; shipbuilding and marine engineering; textiles; clothing and footwear; bricks, pottery, glass, cement; paper, printing, publishing; gas, electricity, water; transport and communication; distributive trades; insurance, banking, finance; professional and scientific services; public admin. and defence; coal products. *Bus. Dimensions:* entrepreneurs and entrepreneurship; production management; co. finance and accounting; personnel management; co. law; co. admin.; marketing; research and development; strategy formation; merger movement and issues; bus. organization. *Scope:* local; regional. *Period:* ancient; medieval; early modern; eighteenth century; nineteenth century; early twentieth century. *Teaching:* university extra mural; British Assoc.; Newcomen Soc.

Publications *Books: Coal Kings of Yorkshire*, 1978; *Aspects of Medieval Wakefield*, 1991; *Attorney at Large*, 1986; *Coals from Barnsley*, 1986. *Articles: Textile Hist.*, various essays from vol. 1.

Gordon, Nancy M.

Self-employed freelance writer, POB 594, Amherst, MA 01004-0594, USA. Tel.: 1 413 253 7878.

Year and Place of Birth 1926, Chicago, USA.

Degrees and Qualifications BA Bryn Mawr College, 1947; MA Yale Univ., 1948; MS Massachusetts Univ., 1988; Ph.D. Yale Univ., 1955.

Previous Post Ed., *The Woodland Steward*, 1991–3.

Major Honours AAUW Fellowship, 1958–9; Fulbright Travel Grant to Germany, 1965–6; Amer. Philosophical Soc. Grant, 1969–70.

Fields of Expertise *Industry Fields:* agric., forestry, fishing. *Bus. Dimensions:* bus.–state relations. *Scope:* regional. *Period:* twentieth century as a whole. *Teaching:* undergrad. *Consultancy:* co. hist.

Publications *Books: The Austrian Empire: Abortive Federation?*, with Harold J. Gordon Jr. co-ed., DC Heath, Lexington, MA, 1974. *Articles:*

'Britain and the Zollverein Iron Duties, 1842–5', *Econ. Hist. Rev.*, 2nd ser., XXII(1), 1969; 'The Historic Vegetation of the Saratoga Battlefields: Lessons from an Historic Evaluation', *Science & Resource Management in Northeast National Parks*, NPS, Boston, MA, 1987; *The Woodland Steward*, 1989–93, assorted articles.

Gore, Ilga

Sen. Research Assoc., Dept. of Hist., Latvian Acad. of Sciences, 19 Turgenew St, Riga, Latvia. Tel.: 7 132 361378.

Year and Place of Birth 1952, Latvia.

Degrees and Qualifications M.Hist. Latvia Univ., 1977; Dr.Hist. Moscow Univ., 1982.

Current Offices and Honorary Posts Edit. board *Latvijas Vestures Instituta Zurnals*; principal specialist, Latvian Univ. 20th Century Hist. Group.

Fields of Expertise *Industry Fields:* agric., forestry, fishing. *Scope:* regional; internat. *Period:* twentieth century as a whole; early twentieth century; inter-war years, 1919–39.

Publications *Articles:* 'New Historical Source of Baltic Peasants until World War I', *Istorije*, 3, 1981; 'The Researching Problems of Peasants' Econ. Structure in 1913–1914 - The Questions of Baltic Agric. History', 1982; 'Models of Peasant Socio-economic Structure until World War I', *LPSR ZA Vestis*, 2, 1988; 'Mathematization of Hist. in Latvia', *Latv. Vest. Inst. Z.*, 2, 1992.

Goto, Shin

Assoc. Prof., School of Bus. Admin., Kanagawa Univ., 2946 Tsuchiya, Hiratsuka-City, Kanagawa 259-12,

Japan. Tel.: 0463 59 4111. Fax: 0463 58 9688.

Year and Place of Birth 1948, Tokyo, Japan.

Degrees and Qualifications BA Waseda Univ., 1971; MA Tokyo Univ., 1973.

Previous Post Assoc. Prof., Fac. of Econ., Kagawa Univ., 1982–1990.

Current Offices and Honorary Posts Council Mem., Bus. Hist. of Japan, 1991–2.

Fields of Expertise *Industry Fields:* shipbuilding and marine engineering; transport and communication. *Bus. Dimensions:* co. admin;. bus. and technology. *Scope:* national; internat. *Period:* nineteenth century; twentieth century as a whole. *Teaching:* undergrad.

Publications *Articles:* 'The Progress of Shipping Operators belonging to Trading Companies', *Japanese Yearbook on Bus. Hist.*, 3, 1986; 'P&O's Oriental Lines in the 1840's and 1850's', *Japan Maritime Research Inst. Bull.*, 240, 1986; 'On the Institutional Agreements in the Shipping Industry', *Hist. Study in Bus. Management*, K. Nakagawa ed., Iwanami, 1990; 'Reappraisal: The Development of the Japanese Shipbuilding Industry after the War', *Japan Maritime Research Inst. Bull.*, K. 298, 1991; 'A new Institutional Perspective on Shipping Conferences', *Study of Shipping Economy*, 25, 1991.

Gourvish, T.R.

Director, Bus. Hist. Unit, London School of Econ., Houghton St, London, WC2A 2AE, UK. Tel.: 44 71 955 7109. Fax: 44 71 242 0392.

Year and Place of Birth 1943, Leicester, UK.

Degrees and Qualifications BA King's College, London Univ., 1964; Ph.D. London School of Econ., 1967.

Previous Post Dean, School of Econ. & Social Studies, Univ. of East Anglia, 1986–8.

Current Offices and Honorary Posts Ed., Newsletter, Assoc. of Bus. Historians (UK); trustee, Bus. Hist. Conf. (USA); edit. advisor, *Bus. Hist.; Accounting, Bus. and Financial Hist.; J. of Transport Hist.*; council mem. Econ. & Hist. Soc.

Major Honours First Prize, Newcomen Soc. of North Amer. Award for Bus. Hist., 1974.

Fields of Expertise *Industry Fields:* food, drink, tobacco; transport and communication. *Bus. Dimensions:* bus. organization; bus.–state relations. *Scope:* national. *Period:* twentieth century as a whole. *Teaching:* post grad. *Consultancy:* co. hist.

Publications *Books: British Railways 1948–73. A Bus. Hist.*, WP, 1986; *Britain since 1945*, joint ed., Macmillan, 1991; *The British Brewing Industry 1830–1980*, with Richard Wilson, CUP, 1993. *Articles:* 'British Bus. and the Transition to a Corporate Economy: Entrepreneurship and Management Structures', *Bus. Hist.*, 29, 1987, 18–45; 'The Significance of British Rail's "Bus.-led" Organisation 1977–90. An Essay in Government-Industry Relations in Britain's Public Sector', *Bus. Hist. Rev.*, 64, Spring, 1990, 109–49.

Graham, Margaret B.W.

Manager of Research Information and Infrastructure, Xerox Palo Alto Research Center, Palo Alto, CA 94304, USA. Tel.: 1 415 812 4218. Fax: 1 415 812 4334.

Year and Place of Birth 1947, Sheffield, UK.

Degrees and Qualifications BA Wooster College, 1968; MA Harvard Univ., 1969; MBA Harvard Univ., 1976; Ph.D. Harvard Univ., 1976.

Previous Post Boston Univ. 1983–91.

Major Honours Broderick Prize for Research, Boston Univ. School of Management; Harvard Grad. Prize Fellowship.

Fields of Expertise *Industry Fields:* chemicals and allied industries; metal manufacture; other manufacturing industries; professional and scientific services; electronics and computers: manufacture. *Bus. Dimensions:* entrepreneurs and entrepreneurship; production management; personnel management; research and development; strategy formation; bus. organization; bus. and technology; management education; co. culture. *Scope:* internat. *Period:* medieval; twentieth century as a whole; inter-war years, 1919–39; mid-twentieth century, 1940–70; late twentieth century, 1970–present. *Teaching:* undergrad.; post grad.; executive. *Consultancy:* co. hist.; R&D and Manufacturing.

Publications *Books: R&D for Industry: A Century of Technical Change at Alcoa*, co-auth., CUP, 1990; *RCA and the Video Disc: The Bus. of Research*, CUP, 1986. *Articles:* 'R&D and Competition in England and the United States: The Case of the Aluminium Dirigible', *The Bus. Hist. Rev.*, 62, Summer, 1988; 'Corporate Research and Development: The Latest Transformation', *Technology and Soc.*, 1985; 'Industrial Research in the Age of Big Science', *Research on Technological Innovation, Management and Policy. Vol. II*, Richard S.Rosenbloom ed., 1985.

Greenhill, Robert G.

Principal Lect., Dept. of Bus. Studies, Fac. of Bus., London Guildhall Univ., 84 Moorgate, London, EC2M 6SQ, UK. Tel.: 44 71 320 1000. Fax: 44 71 320 1465.

Year and Place of Birth 1944, Barnehurst, UK.

Degrees and Qualifications BA (Hist.) Exeter Univ., 1966; Ph.D. Exeter Univ., 1971; Cert. Ed. London Univ., 1975.

Previous Post Research Fellow, St Antony's College, Oxford Univ., 1972–3.

Fields of Expertise *Industry Fields:* food, drink, tobacco. *Bus. Dimensions:* multinational bus. *Scope:* internat. *Period:* nineteenth century. *Teaching:* undergrad. *Consultancy:* co. hist.

Publications *Books: Marcellino Martins & E. Johnston: 150 Anos de Café*, with Edmar Bacha, Salamandra Press, Rio de Janeiro, 1992. *Articles:* 6 articles in *Bus. Imperialism 1840–1930: An Inquiry based on British Experience in Latin Amer.*, D.C.M. Platt ed., Clarendon Press, OUP, 1977.

Griset, Pascal

Research Asst., Institut d'Histoire Moderne e Contemporaine, Centre National de la Recherche Scientifique, 45 rue d'Ulm, 75005 Paris, France. Tel.: 33 1 44323043. Fax: 33 1 4432 3044.

Year and Place of Birth 1957, Paris, France.

Degrees and Qualifications Agrégation d'histoire, 1980; DEA (Hist.) Paris IV Sorbonne Univ., 1981.

Current Offices and Honorary Posts Chargé de cours, Paris IV Sorbonne Univ.

Major Honours Fullbright Grant, 1982; Prix du Meilleur Livre de Communication Européen, 1991 (Institut Européen des Affaires).

Fields of Expertise *Industry Fields:* transport and communication; public admin. and defence. *Bus. Dimensions:* research and development; bus. and technology; bus.–state relations. *Scope:* internat. *Period:* nineteenth century; twentieth century as a whole. *Teaching:* post grad. *Consultancy:* co. hist.

Publications *Books: La croissance économique de la France au XIX e siècle,* with A. Beltran, A. Colin, Paris, 1988; *Histoire des techniques, (XIX°-XX° siècles),* with A. Beltran, Paris Colin, 1990; *Les révolutions de la communication,* Hachette, Paris, 1991. *Articles:* 'Le développement du téléphone en France depuis les années 1950. Politique de recherche et recherche d'une politique', *XX e siècle-Revue d'histoire,* octobre-décembre, 1989, 41–53; 'The development of intercontinental telecommunications in the twentieth century', *Flux, Cahiers scientifiques internationaux Réseaux et Territoires,* juillet-septembre, 1992, 19–21.

Gueslin, André

Prof. of Contemporary Hist. & Vice-Pres. of Internat. Relations, Blaise Pascal Univ. (Clermont II), 29 Bd. Gergovia, 63037 Clermont-Ferrand Cedex, France. Tel.: 33 73 34 65 88. Fax: 33 73 40 64 31.

Year and Place of Birth 1950, France.

Degrees and Qualifications DES Economie Nancy II Univ., 1973; Doctorat Science Politique Nancy II Univ., 1977; Doctorat ès Lettres (Hist.) Nancy II Univ., 1983.

Previous Post Nancy II Univ., 1978 & 1987.

Current Offices and Honorary Posts V-P, French Assoc. of Econ. Historians; edit. com. mem., *Histoire et Entreprise;* edit. com. mem., *Genésis.*

Fields of Expertise *Industry Fields:* agric., forestry, fishing; insurance, banking, finance. *Bus. Dimensions:*

personnel management. *Scope:* national. *Period:* nineteenth century; twentieth century as a whole. *Teaching:* post grad. *Consultancy:* co. hist.

Publications *Books: Le Crédit Mutuel. De la Caisse Rurale à la Banque Sociale,* Editions COPRUR, Strasbourg, 1982; *Les Origines du Crédit Agricole 1840–1914,* Universitaires de Nancy, Paris, 1978; *Histoire des Crédits Agricoles 1910–1970,* Economica, Paris, 1984; *Limagrain. De la Limague à la Californie. Histoire d'une firme Agroalimentaire Chaffes (63 France),* Edn. Limagrain, 1992. *Articles:* 'Le Paternalisme revisité en Europe Occidentale (seconde moitié du XIXe Siècle–début du XXe Siècle), *Genésis,* 7, Mar., 1992, 201–11.

Haeberle, Eckehard

Lect. at the Universities of Kassel, Karlsruhe and Pforzheim College, Handschuhsheimer Landstr. 73, D-69121 Heidelberg, Germany.

Year and Place of Birth 1941, Heidelberg, Germany.

Degrees and Qualifications Dipl. Volkswirt Munich Univ., 1966; Dr.rer.pol. Munich Univ., 1970; habil. Kassel Univ., 1981.

Fields of Expertise *Industry Fields:* general hist. of industrialization. *Bus. Dimensions:* entrepreneurs and entrepreneurship; co. admin.; merger movement and issues; bus.–state relations. *Scope:* national; internat.; Germany; Europe. *Period:* nineteenth century; early twentieth century. *Teaching:* undergrad.; post grad. *Consultancy:* co. hist.

Publications *Books: Strukturwandel der Unternehmung. Untersuchungen zur Produktionsform der bürgerlichen Gesellschaft in Deutschland 1870–1914,* Frankfurter Abhdlgn. z. d. ges. Staatswiss., vol. I, J. Backhaus,

Frankfurt, Haag & Herchen, 1979; *Vom Fortbestand des Abendlandes. Eine Kritik an Oswald Spengler's und Alfred Weber's Kultursoziologien*, forthcoming, 1993; *Der Einsturz. Die letzte Kritik der Marx'schen Merhwertlehre*, forthcoming, 1993.

Hagimoto, Shinichro

Asst. Prof., Tokyo Internat. Univ., 1-13-1 Matoba-kita, Kawagoe, Saitama 350, Japan. Tel.: 0492 32 1111. Fax: 0492 34 3824.

Year and Place of Birth 1957, Hyogo, Japan.

Degrees and Qualifications BA Waseda Univ., 1977; MBA Meiji Univ., 1980.

Fields of Expertise *Industry Fields:* distributive trades. *Bus. Dimensions:* entrepreneurs and entrepreneurship; co. admin.; strategy formation; bus. organization; multinational bus. *Scope:* national; internat. *Period:* nineteenth century; twentieth century as a whole; early twentieth century; inter-war years, 1919–39; mid-twentieth century, 1940–70. *Teaching:* undergrad.

Publications *Articles:* 'The Ownership of Zaibatsu - on the Study of the Mitsubishi Corporation', *Meiji Bus. Rev.*, 33(3), 1986; 'The Concept of Modern Enterprise and the Joint-stock Co. in Pre-war Japan', *Tokyo Internat. Commercial Rev.*, 44, 1991; 'The Development of the Organization in the Mitsubishi Corporation 1910–1916', *Tokyo Internat. Commercial Rev.*, 45, 1991; 'The Formation of Internat. Organization and the Establishment of Transactional Rule in the Mitsubishi Corporation', *Tokyo Internat. Commercial Rev.*, 46, 1992.

Hájek, Jan

Sen. Lect., Dept. of Econ. and Social Hist., Fac. of Arts, Charles Univ., Prague, Czechland. Tel.: 42 2 228 441.

Year and Place of Birth 1954, Litomysl, Czechland.

Degrees and Qualifications Ph.Dr. Charles Univ., Prague; C.Sc. Czechoslovak Acad. of Sciences, 1985.

Previous Post Research Fellow, Inst. of Hist., Czechoslovak Acad. of Sciences, 1979–93.

Current Offices and Honorary Posts Sec., Czech Assoc. of Econ. Hist.; head of edit. board, *Hospodarské Dejiny* [Econ. Hist.].

Fields of Expertise *Industry Fields:* insurance, banking, finance. *Bus. Dimensions:* co. finance and accounting; markets and bus.; bus. values. *Scope:* national; internat.; Austria Czechland. *Period:* nineteenth century; early twentieth century. *Teaching:* undergrad. *Consultancy:* co. hist.

Publications *Books: Comparative Research into Mercantile Theories in Europe in the 16th and 17th Centuries*, Prague, 1980; *Dejiny Pojistovnictví v Ceskoslovensku do Roku 1918* [Hist. of Insurance in Czechoslovakia to 1918], *co-auth., Prague, 1989. Articles:* 'Pocátky a Rozmach Ceského Zálozenského Hnutí ve Tretí Ctvrtine 19. Století' [Beginnings and Development of the Czech Co-op Credit Bank Movement in the Third Quarter of the 19th Century], *Hospodárské Dejiny* [Econ. Hist.], 12, Prague, 1984, 26–320; 'Rozvoj Národnostne Ceskych Bank od Konce 19. Století do Roku 1914' [Development of the Czech Banks from the End of the 19th Century to the Year 1914], *Cesky Casopis Historicky,* 88, Prague, 1990, 356–68; 'Pocátky Cinnosti Postovní Sporitelny v Predlitavsu a Vyvoj jejích Úsporovych Obchodu do Roku 1914, Sekové a

Clearingov Rízení' [Beginnings of the Post Saving Bank in Cislaithania, Development of its Deposits to 1914, its Cheque and Clearing Operations', *Sborník Postovního,* 11, Prague, 1989–90, 4–70, ibid. 12, Prague, 1991, 33–57.

Hall, Roger D.

Assoc. Prof., Dept. of Hist., Fac. of Social Science, Univ. of Western Ontario, London, Ontario, N6A 5C2, Canada. Tel.: 1 519 661 3645. Fax: 1 416 925 8456.

Year and Place of Birth 1945, Regina, Saskatchewan, Canada.

Degrees and Qualifications BA Victoria Univ., 1967; MA Sussex Univ., 1968; Ph.D. Cambridge Univ., 1974.

Current Offices and Honorary Posts Ed. emeritus *The Canadian Rev. of Amer. Studies.*

Fields of Expertise *Industry Fields:* agric., forestry, fishing; insurance, banking, finance; land companies. *Bus. Dimensions:* entrepreneurs and entrepreneurship; co. admin.; bus.–state relations. *Scope:* national; Canada. *Period:* nineteenth century; early twentieth century. *Teaching:* undergrad.; post grad. *Consultancy:* co. hist.

Publications *Books: A Century to Celebrate: The Ontario Legislative Building, 1893–1993,* Dundern Press, Toronto, 1993; *The World of William Notman, a Nineteenth Century Photographer,* McClelland & Stewart Ltd, Toronto, 1993. *Articles:* 'Minding our own Bus.: Commercial Records in the United Kingdom relating to the Canada Trade, 1815–1854', *Archivaria,* Winter, 1976, 73–8; 'An Imperial Businessman in the Age of Improvement: Simon McGillivrae after the Fur Trade', *The Dalhousie Rev.,* 59(1), Spring, 1979, 51–73; 'A Canadian Context for Bus. Studies', *Canadian Issues,* 2(1), 1979, 53–7.

Hannah, Leslie

Prof. of Bus. Hist., London School of Econ., Houghton St, London, WC2A 2AE, UK. Tel.: 44 71 955 7110. Fax: 44 71 955 7730.

Year and Place of Birth 1947, Oldham, UK.

Degrees and Qualifications BA Oxford Univ., 1968, D. Phil., Oxford Univ., 1972; MA Cambridge Univ., 1975; Ph.D. (by incorporation) Cambridge Univ., 1975.

Previous Post Dir., Bus. Hist. Unit, 1978–88;Thomas Henry Carroll Ford Foundation Visiting Prof., Harvard Grad. School of Bus. Admin., 1984–5; Visiting Fellow, Centre for Bus. Strategy, London Bus. School, 1988/9.

Fields of Expertise *Industry Fields:* gas, electricity, water; insurance, banking, finance; manufacturing generally. *Bus. Dimensions:* entrepreneurs and entrepreneurship; co. finance and accounting; research and development; strategy formation; merger movement and issues; bus. organization; bus. and technology; bus.–state relations; markets and bus. *Scope:* global. *Period:* twentieth century as a whole. *Teaching:* post grad.

Publications *Books: The Rise of the Corporate Economy,* new edn., Methuen, 1983, (original Methuen & Johns Hopkins Univ. Press, 1976); *Electricity Before Nationalisation: A Study of the Electricity Supply Industry in Britain to 1948,* Macmillan & Johns Hopkins Univ. Press, 1979; *Engineers, Managers and Politicians: The First Fifteen Years of Nationalised Electricity Supply in Britain 1948–1962,* Macmillan & Johns Hopkins Univ. Press, 1982; *Inventing Retirement: The Development of Occupational Pensions in Britain,*

CUP, London & New York, 1986. *Articles:* 'Human Capital Flows and Bus. Efficiency', *Human Resource Management: People and Performance*, Keith Bradley ed., Dartmouth Aldershot, 1992.

Hansen, Per H.

Research Fellow, Dept. of Hist., Odense Univ., Campusvej 55, 5230 Odense M, Denmark. Tel.: 45 66158696. Fax: 45 65932974.

Year and Place of Birth 1957, Odense, Denmark.

Degrees and Qualifications Supplementary courses (Econ.) Copenhagen Univ., 1989; MA Odense Univ., 1990.

Fields of Expertise *Industry Fields:* insurance, banking, finance. *Bus. Dimensions:* co. finance and accounting; bus.–state relations. *Scope:* national. *Period:* nineteenth century; twentieth century as a whole. *Teaching:* undergrad.

Publications *Articles:* 'From Growth to Crisis. The Danish Banking System from 1850 to the Interwar Years', *Scandinavian Econ. Hist. Rev.*, 39(3), 1991, 20–40; 'Fyens Discontokasse 1846–1886: Passiv-og-Aktivforretninger', *Erhvervshistorisk Årbog*, 39, 1989, 98–137; 'Production versus Currency: The Lender of Last Resort Policy of the Danish Central Bank during the Banking Crisis of the 1920's', *Universal Banking in Twentieth Century Europe*, A. Teichova, T. Gourvish & A. Pogany eds., forthcoming.

Hansen, Povl A.

Assoc. Prof., Dept. of Geography, Roskilde Univ., POB 260, 4000 Roskilde, Denmark. Tel.: 45 46 75 77 11. Fax: 45 46 75 42 40.

Year and Place of Birth 1943, Tranebjerg, Denmark.

Degrees and Qualifications Fil.Kand Lunds Univ., Sweden, 1975; Fil.Dr. Lunds Univ., Sweden, 1989.

Previous Post Lector, Roskilde Univ., Denmark.

Fields of Expertise *Industry Fields:* plastics. *Bus. Dimensions:* research and development; bus. and technology. *Scope:* national. *Period:* mid-twentieth century, 1940–70; late twentieth century, 1970–present. *Teaching:* post grad.

Publications *Books: Plast - fra galanterivarer til "high-tech"*, Akademisk forlag, 1989, English summary. *Articles:* 'Innovation, Materials and Readjustment within the Plastics Industry', *Technological Innovation and Organizational Change*, with Madsen & Serin co-auths., Borum & Kristenden eds., New Social Science Monographs, Copenhagen, 1989; 'Adaptability and Product Development in the Danish Plastics Industry', *Research Policy*, with Serin co-auth., 23(3), 1993.

Hapák, Pavel

Sen. Scientific Worker & Historian, Alexander Dubcek Foundation, Zabotova 2, 83102 Bratislava, Slovakia. Tel.: 42 7 255 451. Fax: 42 7 494 621.

Year and Place of Birth 1931, Pinkovce, Slovakia.

Degrees and Qualifications Phil. Fac. Comenius Univ., 1952; Dip. Ed. EL Univ., Budapest, 1954; Dip. C.Sc. Slovak Acad. of Science, Bratislava, 1959; Dip. Dr.Sc. Slovak Acad. of Science, Bratislava, 1989.

Current Offices and Honorary Posts Com. mem., Slovak Econ. Hist. Soc.; com. mem., Alexander Dubcek Foundation.

Major Honours Slovak Acad. of Science Prize, 1974 & 1984.

Fields of Expertise *Industry Fields:* mining and quarrying; food, drink, tobacco; coal and petroleum products; chemicals and allied industries; metal manufacture; mechanical engineering; electrical engineering; metal goods; textiles; leather clothing and footwear; bricks, pottery, glass, cement; timber, furniture; paper, printing, publishing; other manufacturing industries; transport and communication; insurance, banking, finance. *Bus. Dimensions:* bus. and technology. *Scope:* national. *Period:* nineteenth century; early twentieth century. *Consultancy:* co. hist.

Publications *Books: Dejiny zeleziarskeho priemyslu na Slovensku* [Hist. of Metallurgy of Slovakia], Slovak Acad. of Science, Bratislava, 1961; *Dejiny Slovenska III 1848–1900* [Hist. of Slovakia vol. III 1848–1900 (economic and social hist. and technology)], Slovak Acad. of Science, Bratislava, 1992; *Dejiny Slovenska IV 1900–1918* [Hist. of Slovakia vol. IV 1900–1918 (economic and social hist. and technology)], Slovak Acad. of Science, Bratislava, 1986. *Articles:* 'The Technical School System in Slovakia in the Second Half of the 19th and early 20th Centuries', *Práce z dejin Ceskoslov. akad. ved,* 1989, vol. 1, ser. C, Prague,1989; 'Ekonomische Entwicklung in der Slovakei in den Bedingungen des aufkommenden Monopolkapitalismus', *Econ. Hist.,* 15, Czechoslovak Acad. of Science, Prague, 1986.

Hara, Terushi

Prof., Fac. of Commercial Sciences, Waseda Univ., 1-6-1 Nishi-Waseda, Shinjuku-ku, Tokyo, Japan. Tel.: 03 3203 4141. Fax: 03 3203 0874.

Year and Place of Birth 1943, Nagano, Japan.

Degrees and Qualifications B.Com.Sc., Waseda Univ., 1967; M.Com.Sc. Waseda Univ., 1970; Ph.D.

(Com. Sc.) Waseda Univ., 1985.

Current Offices and Honorary Posts Sec.; council mem.; executive officer.

Fields of Expertise *Industry Fields:* metal manufacture; mechanical engineering; textiles. *Bus. Dimensions:* production management; personnel management; merger movement and issues. *Scope:* national; internat.; France. *Period:* twentieth century as a whole; inter-war years, 1919–39; mid-twentieth century, 1940–70. *Teaching:* undergrad.; post grad.

Publications *Books: French Bus. Hist.,* ed., Yuhikaku, 1980; *French Capitalism - Formation and Development,* Nihonkeizaihyoron sha, 1986; *Introduction and Development of Scientific Management - Comparative & Historical Study,* ed., Showado, 1990; *Internat. Cartels in Bus. Hist.,* ed., Univ. of Tokyo Press, 1992. *Articles:* 'On the Conférences Internationales de l'Organisation Scientifique', *Japan Bus. Hist. Rev.,* 24(1), 1989.

Harada, Seiji

Prof. of Econ. Hist., Kansai Univ., 3-3-35 Yamate-cho, Suita-city, Osaka, Japan. Tel.: 06 388 1121. Fax: 06 330 3718.

Year and Place of Birth 1932, Tokushima, Japan.

Degrees and Qualifications MA (Econ.), Kansai Univ., 1958.

Current Offices and Honorary Posts Sec. (Kinnki Bukai); henshuu-iin; council mem. Socio-econ. Hist. Soc.

Fields of Expertise *Industry Fields:* vehicle construction; transport and communication. *Bus. Dimensions:* bus.–state relations. *Scope:* internat.; UK; British Commonwealth. *Period:* inter-war years, 1919–39. *Teaching:* undergrad.; post grad.

Publications *Articles:* 'Ryotaisenkan Igirisu no Shitsugyo to Keizaikaifuku'

[Unemployment and Recovery in Interwar Britain], *Socio-Econ. Hist. Soc.*, 1984; 'Igirisu ni okeru Jidosha no Hattatsu to Tetsudo' [The Effects of British Motor Transport], *Econ. & Pol. Studies Series*, Kansai Univ. Inst. of Econ. & Pol. Studies, 57, 1985; 'Ryotaisenkan Igirisu no Shitsugyo Mondai ni kansuru Oboegaki' [A Note on the Unemployment Problem in Britain between the Wars], *Econ. & Pol. Studies*, Kansai Univ. Inst. of Econ. & Pol. Studies, 68, 1989; 'Ryotaisenkan Igirisu ni okeru Choki Shitsugyo Mondai' [The Long-term Unemployment Problem in Interwar Britain], *Kansai Univ. Econ. Rev.*, 40(1), 1990; 'Kozotekitenkanki to shi te no Ryotaisenkan Igirisu' [The British Economy in the Interwar Period: A Period of Structural Readjustment], *Kansai Univ. Econ. Rev.*, 42(5), 1992.

Harasawa, Yoshitaro

Prof; Dept. of Indust. Management, Fac. of Engineering Science, Tokyo Univ., Kagurazaka, Shinjuku-ku, Tokyo, Japan. Tel.: 03 3260 4271. Fax: 03 3235 6479.

Year and Place of Birth 1928, Tokyo, Japan.

Degrees and Qualifications BA, Musashi Univ., 1961; MA, Tokyo Univ., 1964; Emeritus Prof., Tohoku Univ.

Previous Post Prof., Fac. of Econ., Tohoku Univ., 1973–92.

Current Offices and Honorary Posts Exec. com. mem. Soshiki Gakkai, 1978 to date; exec. com. mem. Nihon-keiei-Gakkai, 1983–6.

Fields of Expertise *Industry Fields:* textiles; paper, printing, publishing; transport and communication. *Bus. Dimensions:* entrepreneurs and entrepreneurship; co. admin.; bus. organization; bus. and technology; multinational bus.; co. culture. *Scope:* national;

internat. *Period:* nineteenth century; twentieth century as a whole. *Teaching:* undergrad.; post grad. *Consultancy:* co. hist.; corporate strategy.

Publications *Books: The Hist. of the Paper and Pulp Industry of Japan,* co-auth., Kojun-sha Pub., 1967; *Lectures of Japanese Bus. Hist.*, co-auth., 5, Nihon-Keizai-Shinbunsha, 1977. *Articles:* ' Innovative Decision-making of Bus. Organization; its Value Aspects', *'Keizai Gaku' Annual Report,* Tohoku Univ. Econ. Soc., 1973; 'Development of OHJI Paper Manufacturing Co. in Manshu (the North East District of China) - the Failure of Strategy under Slack Situation', *Hist. Study of Entrepreneurial Activities,* Nihon-Keizai-Shinbunsha, 1981; 'The Setting-up Process of Japanese-style Divisionalization - the Case of Canon Inc.', *'Keizai-Gaku' Annual Report,* Tohoku Univ. Econ. Soc., 1987.

Harbaugh, Larry E.

Independent Historian, 4821 Smoketalk Lane, Westerville, OH 43081-4430, USA. Tel.: 1 614 794 1272.

Year and Place of Birth 1948, Indianapolis, USA.

Degrees and Qualifications BA (Hist.) Ohio State Univ., 1986; MA (Amer. Bus./Hist.) Ohio State Univ., 1988.

Fields of Expertise *Industry Fields:* bus. services; miscellaneous services-restaurants; real estate; trade associations. *Bus. Dimensions:* entrepreneurs and entrepreneurship; production management; co. finance and accounting; personnel management; co. admin.; marketing; strategy formation; bus. organization; small bus. matters; management education; markets and bus.; co. culture; boardroom issues. *Scope:*

regional; national; USA; UK. *Period:* nineteenth century; twentieth century as a whole; early twentieth century; inter-war years, 1919–39. *Teaching:* post graduate; industrial training. *Consultancy:* co. hist.; corporate strategy.

Publications *Books: The Hist. of the Ohio Manufacturers' Assoc.: 1910–1932*, Harbaugh Histories, Columbus, Ohio, 1988; *The Hist. of Hegel, Voltaire and Ranke: The balance between the 'Particular and the Abstract'*, Harbaugh Histories, Columbus, Ohio, 1989; *The Scandal of the Reverend Theodore Parker: The Unitarian Christian Community in Boston 1839–1841*, Harbaugh Histories, Columbus, Ohio, 1991; *The Bermuda Triangle of Capitalism in the United States: Bus., Government and the Materialistic Consumer 1877–1939*, Harbaugh Histories, Columbus, Ohio, 1991; *Amer. Bus. and Culture between 1900–1932: The Bermuda Triangle of Capitalism*, Harbaugh Histories, Columbus, Ohio, 1992.

Hardach, Gerd

Prof. of Social and Econ. Hist., Dept. of Hist., Marburg Univ., D-3550 Marburg, Germany. Fax: 49 6421 282500.

Year and Place of Birth 1941, Essen, Germany.

Fields of Expertise *Industry Fields:* food, drink, tobacco; insurance, banking, finance. *Scope:* internat. *Period:* nineteenth century; twentieth century as a whole. *Teaching:* undergrad.; post grad.

Publications *Books: Weltmartorientierung und relative Stagnation*, Duncker & Humblot, Berlin, 1976; *The First World War*, Allen Lane, London, 1977; *Koening Kopra*, Steiner, Stuttgart, 1990.

Articles: 'The Marshall Plan in Germany', *J. of European Econ. Hist.*, 16, 1987.

Hardach, Karl W.

Prof., Econ. Hist., Dept. of Hist., Düsseldorf Univ., Universitätsstr. 1, D-40225 Düsseldorf 1, Germany.

Year and Place of Birth 1936, Cologne, Germany.

Degrees and Qualifications Dipl. Volkswirt Göttingen Univ., 1961; Dr.rer.pol. Frankfurt Univ., 1965.

Previous Post Rutgers Univ., New Brunswick, NJ, 1971–7.

Fields of Expertise *Industry Fields:* agric., forestry, fishing. *Bus. Dimensions:* bus.–state relations. *Scope:* national. *Period:* nineteenth century. *Teaching:* undergrad.; post grad.

Publications *Books: The Political Economy of Germany in the Twentieth Century*, Univ. of California Press, 1980.

Hart, Tom

Lect. in Econ. Hist., Dept. of Econ. and Social Hist., Glasgow Univ., 4 Univ. Gardens, Glasgow, G12 8QQ, UK. Tel.: 44 41 339 8855. Fax: 44 41 330 4889.

Year and Place of Birth 1939, Kilmarnock, UK.

Degrees and Qualifications MA (Mod. Hist.) Glasgow Univ., 1961; LL B Glasgow Univ., 1963.

Current Offices and Honorary Posts Sec., Scottish Transport Studies Group; treasurer, Checkland Fund, Econ. & Social Hist. Soc. of Scotland.

Fields of Expertise *Industry Fields:* gas, electricity, water; transport and communication; distributive trades; public admin. and defence. *Bus.*

Dimensions: merger movement and issues; bus. organization; bus.–state relations; public enterprise, public ownership and regulatory issues. *Scope:* UK; Scotland; Economic Community. *Period:* twentieth century as a whole. *Teaching:* undergrad. *Consultancy:* policy frameworks and strategies for transport.

Publications *Books: Greening Transport: Providing Acceptable Alternatives to Past Trends,* Scottish Transport Studies Group, 1990, Occasional Paper 2. *Articles:* 'Urban Growth and Municipal Government: Glasgow in a Comparative Context, 1846–1914', *Bus., Banking and Urban Hist.,* A. Slaven & D.H. Aldcroft eds., John Donald Publishers, 1982, 193–219; 'Transport, the Urban Pattern and Regional Change, 1960–2010', *Urban Studies,* vol. 29, 1992, 483–503, (also published as Chapter 7 in *Internat. Perspectives in Urban Studies,* vol. 1, R. Paddison, J. Money & B. Lever eds., Jessica Kingsley, 1993); 'Transport Investment and Disadvantaged Regions: UK and European Policies since the 1960s', *Urban Studies,* vol. 30, 1993, 417–436.

Hashimoto, Juro

Prof; Inst. of Social Sc., Tokyo Univ., 7-3-1 Hongo, Bunkyo, Tokyo 113, Japan. Tel.: 81 3 3812 2111.

Year and Place of Birth 1946, Saitama Pref., Japan.

Degrees and Qualifications Ph.D. (Econ.) Tokyo Univ., 1985.

Previous Post Prof. of Management, Hosei Univ., 1986–91.

Current Offices and Honorary Posts Ed., *Socio-Econ. Hist.;* council mem., Japan Bus. Hist. Soc.

Major Honours 'Economist' Prize (Japan), 1985.

Fields of Expertise *Industry Fields:*

chemicals and allied industries; electrical engineering; shipbuilding and marine engineering; gas, electricity, water; transport and communication; distributive trades; insurance, banking, finance. *Bus. Dimensions:* entrepreneurs and entrepreneurship; production management; personnel management; merger movement and issues; bus. organization; bus. and technology; small bus. matters; multinational bus.; bus.–state relations. *Scope:* national. *Period:* inter-war years, 1919–39; mid-twentieth century, 1940–70; late twentieth century, 1970–present. *Consultancy:* co. hist.

Publications *Books: Daikyokoki no Nihonshihonshugi* [The Japanese Economy between the two World Wars], 1984; *Ryoutaisenkanki Nihon no Cartels* [The Japanese Cartels in the Interwar Period], 1985; *Nihon keizairon* [The Japanese Economy under the 20th Century Pol.-Econ. World System], 1991; *Nihon keizaino Hatten to Kigyoshudan* [The Japanese Zaibatsu and Big Corporate Groups in the Econ. Historical Viewpoint], 1992.

Hastrup, Knud Bjarne

Univ. Lect. & Managing Director, Dane-Age Foundation, DaneAge Foundation & DaneAge Assoc., Vesterbrogade 97, 1620 Copenhagen V, Denmark. Tel.: 45 31234411. Fax: 45 31236510.

Year and Place of Birth 1945, Copenhagen, Denmark.

Degrees and Qualifications MA (Econ.) Copenhagen Univ., 1970.

Previous Post Director, Council of Crafts, Trades & Small Industries, 1972–84.

Fields of Expertise *Industry Fields:* industry in general. *Scope:* national; internat.; global. *Period:* nineteenth century; twentieth century as a whole. *Teaching:* undergrad.

Publications *Books: The Econ. Hist. of Danish Trades and Small Industries, 1879–1979,* 1979 (in Danish); *Danish Building Myths and Realities,* Schultz, 1982, (in Danish); *The Cultural Hist. of Handicraft,* ed. & auth. of vol. IV The Cultural Hist. of Craft Trades and Small Industries in Denmark, 1984, (in Danish); *Når få aar for Meget en Moderne Nordenshistorie om Velfærd* [A Hist. of Skandinavian Welfare], Amadeus Forlag, 1988.

Hau, Michel

Fac. of Historical Science, Strasbourg Univ. 2, Palais Universitaire, 67000 Strasbourg, France. Tel.: 33 88 34 40 04. Fax: 33 88 41 73 54.

Year and Place of Birth 1943, Reims, France.

Degrees and Qualifications Dip. I.E.P Univ. of Paris, 1966; Agrégé d'Histoire, 1968; Docteur, 1985.

Fields of Expertise *Industry Fields:* metal manufacture; textiles; transport and communication. *Bus. Dimensions:* entrepreneurs and entrepreneurship. *Scope:* regional. *Period:* nineteenth century; twentieth century as a whole. *Teaching:* post grad.

Publications *Books: La Croissance Économique de la Champagne de 1810 à 1969,* Presses Univ. Strasbourg, 1976; *L'Industrialisation de l'Alsace, 1803–1939,* Presses Univ. Strasbourg, 1987. *Articles:* 'Energiekosten und Industrialisierung der französischen Regionen von der Mitte des 19. Jahrhunderts bis zum 1. Weltkrieg', *Region und Industrialisierung,* Vandenhoek & Ruprecht, 1980; 'Naufrage et Redressement d'une grande Entreprise metallurgique: De Dietrich, 1789–1827', *Histoire, Economie et Société,* 1993.

Hausman, William J.

Prof. of Econ., Dept. of Econ., College of William and Mary, Williamsburg, VA 23187–8795, USA. Tel.: 1 804 221 2381. Fax: 1 804 221 2390.

Year and Place of Birth 1949, Wheeling, USA.

Degrees and Qualifications BA William & Mary College, 1971; MA Illinois Univ., 1973; Ph.D. Illinois Univ., 1976.

Previous Post Asst. Prof. of Econ., Univ. of North Carolina at Greensboro, 1976–81.

Current Offices and Honorary Posts Sec.-Treasurer, Bus. Hist. Conf.; ed., *Bus. & Econ. Hist.*.

Fields of Expertise *Industry Fields:* gas, electricity, water. *Bus. Dimensions:* bus.–state relations. *Scope:* national. *Period:* twentieth century as a whole. *Teaching:* undergrad.

Publications *Articles:* 'A Model of the London Coal Trade in the Eighteenth Century', *Q. J. of Econ.,* XCIV, Feb., 1980, 1–14; 'The English Coastal Coal Trade, 1691–1910: How Rapid was Productivity Growth?', *Econ. Hist. Rev.,* XL, Nov., 1987, 588–96; 'Engineers and Economists: Historical Perspectives on the Pricing of Electricity', *Technology and Culture,* with John Neufeld, 30, Jan., 1989, 83–104; 'The Structure and Profitability of the US Electric Power Industry at the Turn of the Century', *Bus. Hist.,* with John Neufeld, 32, Apr., 1990, 225–43; 'Property Rights versus Public Spirit: Ownership and Efficiency of US Electric Utilities prior to Rate-of-Return Regulation', *Rev. of Econ. & Stats.,* with John Neufeld, 73, Aug., 1991, 414–23.

Hawke, G. R.

Prof. of Econ. Hist. & Director, Inst. of Policy Studies, Inst. of Policy Studies, Victoria Univ. of Wellington, POB 600, Wellington, New Zealand. Tel.: 64 4 471 5307. Fax: 64 4 473 1261.

Year and Place of Birth 1942, Napier, New Zealand.

Degrees and Qualifications BA, B.Com. Victoria Univ. of Wellington, 1964; D. Phil. Oxford Univ., 1968.

Previous Post Reader in Econ. Hist., 1971–3.

Major Honours Tawney Lect., 1978.

Fields of Expertise *Industry Fields:* insurance, banking, finance. *Bus. Dimensions:* bus.–state relations. *Scope:* national. *Period:* nineteenth century; twentieth century as a whole. *Teaching:* undergrad.; post grad. *Consultancy:* policy studies.

Publications *Books: Railways and Econ. Growth in England and Wales, 1840–1870,* Clarendon Press, Oxford, 1970; *Between Governments and Banks: A Hist. of the Reserve Bank of New Zealand,* Government Printer, Wellington, 1973; *Econ. for Historians,* CUP, 1980; *The Making of New Zealand: An Econ. Hist.,* CUP, 1985.

Hawkins, Richard Adrian

Lect. in European Studies (Econ.), School of Languages & European Studies, Wolverhampton Univ., Stafford St, Wolverhampton, WV1 1SB, UK. Tel.: 44 902 322330. Fax: 44 902 322739.

Year and Place of Birth 1959, Southampton, UK.

Degrees and Qualifications BA Portsmouth Polytechnic, 1980; M.Sc. London School of Econ., 1981; Ph.D.

London School of Econ., 1986.

Previous Post Part-time lecturer in Hist., Univ. of Hertfordshire (formerly Hatfield Polytechnic), 1986.

Fields of Expertise *Industry Fields:* food, drink, tobacco. *Bus. Dimensions:* entrepreneurs and entrepreneurship. *Scope:* internat. *Period:* twentieth century as a whole. *Teaching:* undergrad.

Publications *Articles:* 'The Pineapple Canning Industry during the World Depression of the 1930s', *Bus. Hist.,* 31, 1989, 48–66; 'Socialism at Work? Corporatism, Soldier Settlers and the Pineapple Industry in South-Eastern Queensland, 1917–39', *Australian Studies,* 4, 1990, 35–59; 'Privatisation in Western Germany, 1957–1990', *National Westminster Bank Q. Rev.,* Nov., 1991, 14–22; 'Kingfisher PLC', *Internat. Directory of Co. Histories,* Adele Hast ed., vol. 5, Detroit & London, 1992; 'Qantas Airways Limited', *Internat. Directory of Co. Histories,* Adele Hast ed., vol. 6, Detroit & London, 1993.

Hawley, Ellis W.

Prof. of Hist., Dept. of Hist., Univ. of Iowa, Iowa City, IA 52242, USA. Tel.: 1 319 335 2301.

Year and Place of Birth 1919, Cambridge, USA.

Degrees and Qualifications BA Wichita Univ., 1950; MA Kansas Univ., 1951; Ph.D. Wisconsin Univ., 1959.

Previous Post Prof. of Hist., Ohio State Univ., 1968–9.

Current Offices and Honorary Posts Edit. board mem., *J. of Policy Hist.;* fellowship & grant com. mem., Hoover Library Assoc.

Fields of Expertise *Industry Fields:* public admin. and defence. *Bus. Dimensions:* bus. organization; bus.–state relations; bus. values.

Scope: national. *Period:* twentieth century as a whole; inter-war years, 1919–39. *Teaching:* undergrad.; post grad.

Publications *Books: The New Deal and the Problem of Monopoly,* Princeton Univ. Press, 1966; *The Great War and the Search for a Modern Order,* St Martin's Press, 1979 & 1992; *Herbert Hoover as Secretary of Commerce,* ed. & contributor, Univ. of Iowa Press, 1981; *Federal Social Policy,* co-ed. & contrib., Pennsylvania State Press, 1988. *Articles:* 'Herbert Hoover, the Commerce Secretariat and the Vision of an Associative State, 1921–28', *J. of Amer. Hist.,* 61, 1974, 116–40.

Hayburn, Ralph H.C.

Sen. Lect., Dept. of Hist., Univ. of Otago, POB 56, Dunedin, New Zealand. Tel.: 64 3 479 8605. Fax: 64 3 479 8429.

Year and Place of Birth 1947, Manchester, UK.

Degrees and Qualifications BA Univ. of Wales, 1967; Ph.D. Hull Univ., 1970.

Fields of Expertise *Industry Fields:* transport and communication. *Bus. Dimensions:* merger movement and issues. *Scope:* internat. *Period:* twentieth century as a whole. *Teaching:* undergrad.; post grad. *Consultancy:* co. hist.

Hazama, Hiroshi

Prof.; Dept. of Sociology, School of Literature, Waseda Univ., 1-24-1 Toyama, Sinjuku-ku, Tokyo 162, Japan. Tel.: 03 3203 4141.

Year and Place of Birth 1929, Kanagawa Pref., Japan.

Degrees and Qualifications BA Tokyo Kyoiku Univ.; M.Litt. Tokyo Kyoiku Univ.; Ph.D. (Litt.) Tokyo Kyoiku Univ.

Previous Post Assist. Prof., Dept. of Sociology, Tokyo Kyoiku Univ., 1964–76.

Major Honours Nihon Keizai Kenkyu-jo Prize, 1975; Nihon Rodo-kyokai & Yomiuri Sinbun-sha Prize, 1979.

Fields of Expertise *Industry Fields:* mining and quarrying; chemicals and allied industries; metal manufacture; mechanical engineering; instrument engineering; electrical engineering; shipbuilding and marine engineering; vehicle construction; metal goods; textiles; paper, printing, publishing; distributive trades; insurance, banking, finance. *Bus. Dimensions:* entrepreneurs and entrepreneurship; personnel management; bus. organization; bus. values; co. culture. *Scope:* national. *Period:* twentieth century as a whole; early twentieth century. *Teaching:* undergrad.; post grad.

Publications *Books: Igirisu no Shakai to Roshikankei* [British Soc. and her Indust. Relations], Nihon Rodo-kyokai, 1974; *Nihon ni okeru Rosi Kyocho no Teiryu* [The Historical Basis of Harmonisation of Labour-Management in Japan], Waseda, 1978; *Nihon no Siyosha Dantai to Rosikankei* [Employers Associations and Labour-Management Relations], Nihon Rodo-kyokai, 1981; *Keiei Shakaigaku* [The Sociology of Management] , Yuhikaku, 1989; *Nihon Romukanrishi Siryo-shu* [The Collected Documents on Labour-Management in Japan], ed., 1st ser., 1987, 2nd ser., 1989.

Heffer, Jean

Study Director, Ecole des Hautes Etudes en Sciences Sociales, Centre d'Etudes Nord-Americaines, 12-14 rue Corvisart, 75013 Paris, France. Tel.: 33 1 44 08 51 70. Fax: 33 1 45 44 93

11.
Year and Place of Birth 1933, Paris, France.
Degrees and Qualifications Doctorat d'Etat, Paris I Univ., 1984.
Previous Post Maître-Asst., Paris I Univ., 1969–84.
Current Offices and Honorary Posts Vice-pres., Assoc. Française d'Etudes Américaines; pres., Assoc. Française des Historiens Economistes (1988–91).
Fields of Expertise *Industry Fields:* transport and communication. *Bus. Dimensions:* entrepreneurs and entrepreneurship. *Scope:* internat. *Period:* nineteenth century. *Teaching:* post grad.
Publications *Articles:* 'Le Port de New York et le Commerce Extérieur Américain, 1860–1900', , Publications de la Sorbonne, 1986.

Heim, Carol E.

Assoc. Prof., Dept. of Econ., Univ. of Massachusetts, Amherst, MA 01003, USA. Tel.: 1 413 545 0854. Fax: 1 413 545 2921.
Year and Place of Birth 1955, Arlington, USA.
Degrees and Qualifications BA Yale Univ., 1976; MA Yale Univ., 1977; M.Phil. Yale Univ., 1979; Ph.D. Yale Univ., 1982.
Previous Post Asst. Prof., Dept. of Econ., Massachusetts Univ., Amherst, 1981–8.
Current Offices and Honorary Posts Edit. boards, *J. of Econ. Hist., Explorations in Econ. Hist., Social Concept.*
Fields of Expertise *Bus. Dimensions:* bus. organization. *Scope:* UK; USA, regional and urban. *Period:* twentieth century as a whole. *Teaching:* undergrad.; post grad. *Consultancy:* co. hist.
Publications *Articles:* 'Industrial Organization and Regional

Development in Interwar Britain', *J. of Econ. Hist.*, 43, 1983, 931–52; 'Limits to Intervention: The Bank of England and Indust. Diversification in the Depressed Areas', *Econ. Hist. Rev.*, 37, 1984, 533–50; 'Interest Rates and Crowding-out during Britain's Indust. Revolution', *J. of Econ. Hist.*, with Philip Mirowski co-auth., 47, 1987, 117–39; 'Government Research Establishments, State Capacity and Distribution of Industry Policy in Britain', *Regional Studies*, 22, 1988, 375–86; 'The Treasury as Developer-Capitalist? British New Town Building in the 1950s', *J. of Econ. Hist.*, 50, 1990, 903–24.

Helguera Quijada, Juan

Prof., Dept. of Hist. & Econ. Institutions, Fac. of Econ. Science, Valladolid Univ., Avda. Valle de Esgueva, 6–47011 Valladolid, Spain. Tel.: 34 983 423350. Fax: 34 983 423299.
Year and Place of Birth 1950, Palencia, Spain.
Degrees and Qualifications M.Litt. Valladolid Univ., 1975; Ph.D. Valladolid Univ., 1987.
Previous Post Asst. Prof., Dept. of Modern Hist., Valladolid Univ., 1976–85.
Fields of Expertise *Industry Fields:* metal manufacture; transport and communication. *Bus. Dimensions:* bus. and technology; bus.–state relations. *Scope:* national. *Period:* eighteenth century. *Teaching:* undergrad.; post grad. *Consultancy:* public enterprise hist.
Publications *Books: La Industria Metalúrgica Experimental en el Siglo XVIII: Las Reales Fábricas de San Juan de Alcaraz, 1772–1800*, ed., Valladolid Univ., 1984. *Articles:* 'Aproximación a la Historia del Canal de Castilla', *El Canal de Castilla*, Leon

Junta de Castillay ed., VV.AA., 1990, 9–159; 'La Real Fabrica de Vidrios de San Ildefonso', *Vidrio de la Granja*, VV.AA., ed., Ministerio de Cultura, 1988, 57–104; 'Las Reales Fabricas', *Historia de la Empresa Publica en España*, VV.AA., ed., Espasa Calpe, 1991, 51–87; 'Las Industrias Artilleras en la Epoca de Louis Proust', *La Casa de la Quimica: Ciencia, Artilleria e Ilustracion*, VV.AA., ed., Ministerio de Defensa, 1992, 97–135.

Helper, Susan

Asst. Prof. of Econ. and Research Assoc., Center for Regional Econ. Issues, Dept. of Econ., 311 Wickenden, Case Western Reserve Univ., Cleveland, OH 44106, USA. Tel.: 1 216 368 5541. Fax: 1 216 368 8842.

Year of Birth 1957.

Degrees and Qualifications BA (Econ. & Spanish) Oberlin Coll., 1979; Ph.D. (Econ.) Harvard Univ., 1987.

Previous Post Asst. Prof., Dept. of Operations Management, Boston Univ., 1987–90.

Current Offices and Honorary Posts Research assoc., Internat. Motor Vehicle Program, MIT.

Fields of Expertise *Industry Fields:* vehicle construction. *Bus. Dimensions:* bus. organization. *Scope:* national; global. *Period:* late twentieth century, 1970–present. *Teaching:* undergrad.; post grad. *Consultancy:* production management; customer/supplier relations.

Publications *Articles:* 'Maquiladoras: Mexico's Tiger by the Tail?', *Challenge*, with Philip Mirowski co-auth., Mar., 1989; 'Comparative Supplier Relations in the US and Japanese Automobile Industries: An Exit/Voice Approach', *Bus. & Econ. Hist.*, 1990; 'How Much has Really Changed between US Automakers and their Suppliers?', *Sloan Management Rev.*, Summer, 1991; 'Strategy and Irreversibility in Supplier Relations: The Case of the US Automobile Industry', *Bus. Hist. Rev.*, Winter, 1991; 'Long-term Supplier Relations and Product Market Structure', *J. of Law, Econ. & Organization*, with David I. Levine co-auth., Oct., 1992.

Henderson, William Otto

21 Roydon Court, Woodhall Farm, Hemel Hempstead, Herts, HP2 7PA, UK. Tel.: 44 442 64669.

Year and Place of Birth 1904, London, UK.

Degrees and Qualifications MA Cambridge Univ.; Ph.D. London School of Econ.; Dr.rer.pol. Tübingen Univ.

Previous Post Reader, Internat. Econ. Hist., 1947–75.

Publications *Books: The Lancashire Cotton Famine 1861–5*, Manchester Univ. Press, 1934; 2nd edn., 1969; *The Zollverein*, CUP, 1939; new edn., Frank Cass, 1959; *Life of Friedrich Engels*, 2 vols., Frank Cass, 1975; *Friedrich List*, Frank Cass, 1983; *Marx & Engels & the English Workers*, Frank Cass, 1989.

Henning, Hansjoachim

Prof., Econ. and Social Hist., Duisburg Univ., Lotharstraße 65, 47057 Duisburg, Germany. Tel.: 49 203 379 2259/49 203 379 3083. Fax: 49 203 379 2318.

Year and Place of Birth 1937, Solingen, Germany.

Degrees and Qualifications Dr.phil. Cologne Univ., 1962; Habilitation Tübingen Univ., 1970; o. Prof., Duisburg Univ., 1973.

Current Offices and Honorary Posts

Historical com. mem., Acad. of Sciences and Literature, Mainz; scientific advisor, Gesellschaft zur Erforschung historischer Führungsgeschichten.

Major Honours Corresponding mem., Acad. of Sciences & Literature, Mainz.

Fields of Expertise *Industry Fields:* miscellaneous services; public admin. and defence. *Bus. Dimensions:* bus.–state relations; entrepreneurs and entrepreneurship. *Scope:* regional; national; Germany. *Period:* eighteenth century; nineteenth century; twentieth century as a whole. *Teaching:* post grad.

Publications *Articles:* 'The Social Integration of Entrepreneurs in Westphalia 1860–1914. A Contribution to the Debate on the Position of Entrepreneurs in Imperial Germany', *German Yearbook on Bus. Hist.*, 1981; 'Handwerk und Industriegesellschaft: Zur sozialen Verflechtung westfälischer Handwerksmeister 1870–1914', *Rheinland-Westfalen am Industriezeitalter*, K. Düwell & W. Köllmann eds., vol. 2, Wuppertal, 1984; 'Juden in der deutschen Wirtschaft 1850–1939', *Das doppelte Antlitz. Zur Wirkungsgeschichte deutsch-jüdischer Künstler and Gelehrter*, Rolf Schörken et al. eds., Paderborn, 1990; 'Soziale Vernetzung an Rhein und Ruhr. Anmerkungen zur regionalen Mobilität unternehmerisch Tätiger', *Staat und Wirtschaft an Rhein und Ruhr 1816–1991*, Hein Hoebink ed., Essen, 1992; 'Soziales Verhalten jüdischer Unternehmer in Frankfurt/M and Köln 1860–1933', *Jüdische Unternehmer in Deutschland im 19. und 20. Jahrhundert. Zeitschrift für Unternehmensgeschichte*, Werner Mosse & Hans Pohl eds., supplement no. 64, Stuttgart, 1992.

Henwood, James N.J.

Prof. of Hist., Dept. of Hist., East Stroudsburg Univ., East Stroudsburg, PA 18301, USA. Tel.: 1 717 424 3262.

Year and Place of Birth 1932, Upper Darby, USA.

Degrees and Qualifications BS in Ed. West Chester Univ., 1954; MA Pennsylvania Univ, 1958; Ph.D. Pennsylvania Univ., 1975.

Current Offices and Honorary Posts Book rev. ed., *Railroad Hist.*; book rev. ed., *National Railway Bull..*

Fields of Expertise *Industry Fields:* transport and communication. *Bus. Dimensions:* co. admin. *Scope:* national. *Period:* twentieth century as a whole. *Teaching:* post grad. *Consultancy:* co. hist.

Publications *Books: A Short Haul to the Bay*, Stephen Greene Press, 1969; *Laurel Line: An Anthracite Railway*, co-auth., Interurban Press, 1986. *Articles:* 'Experiment in Relief: The Civil Works Admin. in Pennsylvania', *Pennsylvania Hist.*, Jan., 1972; 'A Cruise on U.S.S. Sabine', *Amer. Neptune*, 116(7); *Encyclopaedia of Amer. Bus. Hist. and Biography*, Bruccoli Clark Layman, 1988, (various articles).

Hernandez-Esteve, Esteban

Deputy Director General, Banco de España, Alcala 50, 28014 Madrid, Spain. Tel.: 34 338 66 41. Fax: 34 338 68 81.

Year and Place of Birth 1931, Barcelona, Spain.

Degrees and Qualifications MBA Escuela de Altos Estudios Mercantiles, Barcelona, 1954; Doktor der Wirtschaftswissenschaften, Albertus Magnus Univ., Cologne, 1964.

Previous Post Director, Dept. of

Recruitment & Training, Banco de España, Madrid, 1982–9.

Current Offices and Honorary Posts Chairman, Research Unit on Accounting Hist., Spanish Assoc. of Accounting & Bus. Admin. (AECA), Madrid.

Major Honours Acad. of Accounting Historians Hourglass Award, 1984.

Fields of Expertise *Industry Fields:* insurance, banking, finance. *Bus. Dimensions:* co. finance and accounting. *Scope:* national; Spain. *Period:* early modern. *Teaching:* doctorate occasionally. *Consultancy:* accounting, banking and public finance hist.

Publications *Books: Contribucion al Estudio de la Historiografia Contable en España*, Banco de España, Madrid, 1981; *Creacion del Consejo de Hacienda de Castilla (1523–1525)*, Banco de España, Spain, 1983; *Establecimiento de la Partida Doble en las Cuentas Centrales de la Real Hacienda de Castilla (1592), Vol. I: Pedro Luis de Torregrosa, Primer Contador del Libro de Caja*, Banco de España, Madrid, 1986; *Contribucion al Estudio de las Ordenanzas de los Reyes Catolicos sobre la Contaduria Mayor de Hacienda y sus Oficios*, Banco d'España, Madrid, 1988; *Noticia del Abastecimiento de Carne en la Ciudad de Burgos (1536–1537). Libro Mayor del Obligado de las Carnicerias*, Banco de España, Madrid, 1992.

Herranen, Timo

Researcher, Dept. of Econ. and Social Hist., Univ. of Helsinki, POB 33, SF-00 014 Helsinki, Finland. Tel.: 358 0 191 2080. Fax: 358 0 191 2180.

Year and Place of Birth 1956, Helsinki, Finland.

Degrees and Qualifications L.Soc.Sc. Helsinki Univ., 1988.

Fields of Expertise *Industry Fields:* gas, electricity, water. *Bus. Dimensions:* bus. and technology. *Scope:* national. *Period:* twentieth century as a whole. *Teaching:* undergrad. *Consultancy:* co. hist.

Publications *Books: Kaasulaitostoimintaa Helsingissä 1860–1985* [The Helsinki Gasworks 1860–1985], Espoo: Helsingin kaupungin energialaitos, 1985; *Hevosomnibusseista metroon - Vuosisata Helsingin joukkoliikennettä* [From the horse-driven omnibuses to the underground - a hundred years of collective traffic in Helsinki], Helsingin kaupungin liikennelaitos, 1988, (Helsingin kaupungin julkaisuja no. 39), English summary: *The Hist. of Public Transport in Helsinki*; *Petsamosta Hankoon - Pohjolan Liikenteen 50 vuotta* [From Pechenga to Hanko - A Hist. of the Transport Co. Pohjolan Liikenne], OY Pohjolan Liikenne AB, 1990. *Articles:* 'Effects of the First World War on the Engineering Industries of Estonia and Finland', *Scandinavian Econ. Hist. Rev.*, with Timo Myllyntaus, 32(3), 1984, 121–42; 'Metalliteollisuus' [Metal-industry], *Teknologinen muutos Suomen teollisuudessa 1885–1920* [Technological change in Finnish industry, 1885–1920], with Timo Myllyntaus, Karl-Erik Michelsen & Timo Herranen eds., Finska Vetenskaps-Societeten, 1986, 14–50.

Hertner, Peter

Prof. & Director of the Library, European Univ. Inst., Via dei Roccettini 9, 50016 San Domenico di Fiesole (FI), Italy. Tel.: 39 55 5092340. Fax: 39 55 5092283.

Year and Place of Birth 1942, Ulm, Germany.

Degrees and Qualifications Diplomvolkswirt Marburg Univ.,

1968; Dr.rer.pol. Marburg Univ., 1971; Habilitation, Darmstadt Tech. Univ., 1986.
Previous Post Prof., European Univ. Inst., Florence, Dept. of Hist. & Civilization, 1981–.

Fields of Expertise *Industry Fields:* mechanical engineering; electrical engineering; gas, electricity, water; insurance, banking, finance. *Bus. Dimensions:* bus. and technology; multinational bus.; bus.–state relations. *Scope:* national; internat.; global; Italy; Germany. *Period:* nineteenth century; early twentieth century; inter-war years, 1919–39. *Teaching:* post grad. *Consultancy:* co. hist.

Publications *Books: Il Capitale Tedesco in Italia*, Il Mulino, Bologna, 1984; *Multinationals. Theory and Hist.*, with G. Jones ed., Gower, Aldershot, 1986. *Articles:* 'Financial Strategies and Adaptation to Foreign Markets: The German Electro-technical Industry and its Multinational Activities, 1890s to 1939', *Multinational Enterprise in Historical Perspective*, M. Teichova, M. Lévy-Leboyer & H. Nussbaum eds., Cambridge/Paris, 1986, 145–59; 'The German Electrotechnical Industry in the Italian Market before the Second World War', *The Rise of Multinationals in Continental Europe*, G. Jones & H.G. Schröter eds., Edward Elgar Publishing, Aldershot, 1993, 155–72.

Hessen, Robert

Sen. Research Fellow, Hoover Inst. & Lect. in Management, Stanford Univ., Grad. School of Bus., Stanford Univ., Stanford, CA 94305, USA. Tel.: 1 415 723 4804. Fax: 1 415 723 1687.
Year and Place of Birth 1936, Bronx, USA.
Degrees and Qualifications BA Queens College, Flushing, NY, 1958;

MA Harvard Univ., 1969; Ph.D. Columbia Univ., 1969.
Previous Post Assoc. Prof., Grad. School of Bus., Columbia Univ., New York, 1966–73.

Publications *Books: Steel Titan: The Life of Charles M. Schwab*, OUP, 1975; reprinted by Univ. of Pittsburgh Press, 1990; *In Defense of the Corporation*, Hoover Inst. Press, 1979. *Articles:* 'The Transformation of Bethlehem Steel, 1904–1909', *Bus. Hist. Rev.*, XLVI(3), Autumn, 1972, 339–60; 'A New Concept of Corporations: A Contractual and Private Property Model', *Hastings Law J.*, 30(5), May, 1979, 1327–50; 'The Modern Corporation and Private Property: A Reappraisal', *J. of Law & Econ.*, 26(2), June, 1983, 273–89.

Hildebrandt, Reinhard

Prof., Dept. of Hist., RWTH Aachen, Kopernikusstr. 16, D-52074 Aachen, Germany. Tel.: 49 241 806036. Fax: 49 241 900003.
Year and Place of Birth 1937, Wilhelmshaven, Germany.
Degrees and Qualifications Ph.D. Hamburg Univ., 1966; Habilitation Free Univ. of Berlin, 1972; Prof. RWTH Aachen, 1973.
Previous Post Research Fellow, DFG, 1982–3.

Fields of Expertise *Industry Fields:* mining and quarrying; textiles; insurance, banking, finance. *Bus. Dimensions:* co. finance and accounting; personnel management; co. admin.; multinational bus. *Scope:* internat. *Period:* early modern. *Teaching:* post grad. *Consultancy:* co. hist.

Publications *Articles:* 'Die "Georg Fuggerischen Erben". Kaufmännische Tätigkeit und sozialer Status 1555–1600', *Schriften zur Wirtschafts- und Sozialgeschichte*, 6, Duncker &

Humblot, Berlin, 1966; 'I "Merchant Banker" della Germania Meridionale nell'Economia e nella Politica del XVI e XVII secolo', *La Repubblica Internazionale del Denaro tra XV e XVII Secolo*, A. de Maddalena & H. Kellenbenz eds., Molino, Florence, 1986, 211–42; 'Geschichte der Führung - Mittelalter und Frühe Neuzeit', *Handwörterbuch der Führung, Enzyklopädie der Betriebswirtschaftslehre*, A. Kieser et al. eds., vol. 10, C.E. Poeschel, Stuttgart, 1987, 1014–24; 'Banking System and Capital Market in South Germany 1450–1650. Organisation and Econ. Importance', *Banchi Pubblici, Banchi Privati e Monti de Pietà nell'Europa Preindustriale, Atti della Società Ligure di Storia Patria*, nuova serie, vol. XXI, Genova, 1991, 827–42; 'The Effects of Empire: Changes in the European Economy after Charles V', *Industry and Finance in Early Modern Hist.*, I. Blanchard et al. eds., F. Steiner, Stuttgart, 1992, 58–76.

Hiramoto, Atsushi

Assoc. Prof., Fac. of Econ., Tohoku Univ., Kawauchi Aobaku, Sendai, Japan. Tel.: 81 22 222 1800. Fax: 81 22 221 608.

Year and Place of Birth 1950, Tokyo, Japan.

Degrees and Qualifications BA Tohoku Univ., 1973; MA Tohoku Univ., 1975.

Fields of Expertise *Industry Fields:* shipbuilding and marine engineering; textiles; electronics and computers: manufacture. *Bus. Dimensions:* production management; strategy formation; bus. and technology; multinational bus. *Scope:* local; internat.; global. *Period:* early twentieth century; late twentieth century, 1970–present. *Teaching:* undergrad.; post grad.

Consultancy: co. hist.

Publications *Articles:* 'Kokai Zosen ryo Shoreiho to Zosen Shijo no Keisei' [Impact of Bounty Laws on the Formation of Japanese Shipbuilding Market], *The Keizai Gaku*, Tohoku Univ., 41(1), 1979, 1–20; 'Goshi Okaya Seishi Kaisha no Seiritsu' [The Formation of Okaya Seishi Co.], *The Formation of Big Bus. in Suwa Silk-reeling Industry*, The Keizai Gaku, Tohoku Univ., 47(2), 1985, 41–55; 'Johoka heno Kigyo Senryaku', *Impact of Information Technology on Bus. Strategy*, Dobunkan, 1990; 'Nihon Kiggo Sekai Senryaku to Jissen', *Japanese Corporation under Global Strategy*, Dobunkan, 1991; 'Subcontracting Strategies of Japanese Companies in Europe and Asia', *New Impacts on Indust. Relations*, S. Tokanaga, N. Altman and H. Demes eds., Indiciun Verlag, Munich, 1992, forthcoming.

Hodne, Fritz

Prof. of Econ. Hist., Inst. of Econ. Hist., Norwegian School of Econ. and Bus. Admin., Hellevn. 30, 5035 Bergen-Sandviken, Norway. Tel.: 47 5 95 90 00. Fax: 47 5 95 95 66.

Year and Place of Birth 1932, Bergen, Norway.

Degrees and Qualifications MA Claremont Grad. School, California, 1960; Cand.phil. Bergen Univ., 1961; Dr. Oeconomiae, Norwegian School of Econ. & Bus. Admin, Bergen, 1981.

Previous Post Norwegian School of Econ. & Bus. Admin., Autumn, 1984.

Current Offices and Honorary Posts Board mem., The Commerce Museum of Norway; vice chairman of board, Bergen Historical Soc.

Fields of Expertise *Industry Fields:* agric., forestry, fishing; food, drink, tobacco; shipbuilding and marine engineering; timber, furniture; gas, electricity, water; transport and communication; distributive trades; public admin. and defence. *Bus. Dimensions:* entrepreneurs and entrepreneurship; research and development; multinational bus.; bus.–state relations. *Scope:* national; internat. *Period:* eighteenth century; nineteenth century; twentieth century as a whole. *Teaching:* undergrad.;.post grad.

Publications *Books: Norges Økonomiske Historie 1815–1970*, J.A. Cappelens Forlag, Oslo, 1981; *The Norwegian Economy 1920–1980*, Croom Helm, London & New York, 1983; *Stortinget som markedsplass. Statens grunnlagsinvesteringer 1840–1914*, Univ. Publishers, Oslo, 1984; *Legene og samfunnet. Den norske Lægeforening 1886–1986*, with Øivind Larsen & Ole Berg, Den norske Lægeforening, Oslo, 1986; *God handel. Den norske Handelsstands Forbund 1889–1989*, Den norske Handelsstands Forbund, Oslo, 1989.

Hoffman, Kai J.

Sen. Lect., Dept. of Econ. and Social Hist., Helsinki Univ., Aleksanterinkatu 7, SF-00014 Helsinki, Finland. Tel.: 358 0 801 8129.

Year and Place of Birth 1944, Vaasa, Finland.

Degrees and Qualifications Ph.D. (Soc. Sc.) Helsinki Univ., 1980.

Previous Post Bus. Historian, Pohjolan Voima Oy, Helsinki.

Fields of Expertise *Industry Fields:* electrical engineering; distributive trades. *Bus. Dimensions:* bus. and technology. *Scope:* national. *Period:* eighteenth century; mid-twentieth century, 1940–70. *Teaching:* post grad. *Consultancy:* co. hist.

Publications *Books: Suomen sahateollisweden kasvu, rakenne ja rahoitus*, Suomen tiedeseura, 1980; *K-Kaupan Historia*, Kesko Oy, 1983; *Expert inom elektrotekniken,*

Stromberg 1889–1989, ABB Stromberg Oy, 1990; *Pohjolan Voima*, Pohjolan Voima Oy, 1993.

Hofsommer, Don L.

Prof. and Director of Public Hist., Dept. of Hist., St Cloud State Univ., St Cloud, MN 56301-4498, USA. Tel.: 1 612 255 4906. Fax: 1 612 654 5198.

Year and Place of Birth 1938, Fort Dodge, Iowa, USA.

Degrees and Qualifications BA Northern Iowa Univ., 1960; MA Northern Iowa Univ., 1966; Ph.D. Oklahoma State Univ., 1973.

Previous Post Director, Center for Western Studies, Augustana College, 1987–9.

Current Offices and Honorary Posts Ed., *Lexington Q.*, (Lexington Group in Transportation Hist.).

Major Honours Prizes for *Prairie Oasis* & *Southern Pacific*.

Fields of Expertise *Industry Fields:* transport and communication. *Scope:* national. *Period:* nineteenth century; twentieth century as a whole. *Teaching:* post grad. *Consultancy:* co. hist.

Publications *Books: Prairie Oasis*, Waukon & Mississippi Press, 1975; *Katy Northwest: The Story of a Branch Line Railroad*, Pruett Pub., 1976; *The Southern Pacific, 1901–1985*, A&M Univ. Press, Texas, 1986; *The Great Northern Railway: A Hist.*, et. al., Harvard Bus. School Press, 1988;*The Quanah Route: A Hist. of Quanah, Acme & Pacific Railway*, A&M Univ. Press, Texas, 1990.

Hogesteeger, Gerardus

Head of Bus. Hist. Dept., Netherlands Postal Museum, Zeestraat 82, 2518 AD The Hague, Netherlands. Tel.: 31

70 3307500. Fax: 31 70 3608926.

Year and Place of Birth 1947, Rotterdam, Netherlands.

Degrees and Qualifications MA Erasmus Univ., 1973; Ph.D. Erasmus Univ., 1984.

Fields of Expertise *Industry Fields:* transport and communication. *Bus. Dimensions:* bus. organization; bus.–state relations. *Scope:* national. *Period:* nineteenth century; twentieth century as a whole. *Consultancy:* co. hist.

Publications *Books: Concentratie en centralisatie bij de openhare telefonie in Nederland, 1881–1940,* The Hague, 1984; *Van lopende bode tot telematica,* Groningen, 1989; *Bellen voor de vrijheid; illegale telefoonverbindingen in de Tweede Wereldoorlog,* The Hague, 1990. *Articles:* 'Optische communicatie, iets nieuws?', *PTT-Jaarboek,* 1991, Groningen, 1992.

Hogler, Raymond L.

Prof. of Management, Dept. of Management, Colorado State Univ., Fort Collins, CO 80523, USA. Tel.: 1 303 491 5323. Fax: 01 03 491 0596.

Year and Place of Birth 1943, Durango, USA.

Degrees and Qualifications Ph.D. Colorado Univ., 1972; J. D. Colorado Univ., 1976.

Previous Post Assoc. Prof., Dept. of Indust. Relations, Pennsylvania State Univ.

Major Honours Fulbright-Hays Fellow, UK.

Fields of Expertise *Industry Fields:* metal manufacture; public admin. and defence. *Bus. Dimensions:* personnel management. *Scope:* national. *Period:* twentieth century as a whole. *Teaching:* undergrad.

Publications *Books: Public Sector Strikes,* Internat. Personnel

Management Assoc., 1988; *Employee Participation and Labor Law in the Amer. Workplace,* with G. Grenier, Quorum Press, 1992.

Hoke, Donald R.

Exec. Director/Director of Development, Outagamie County Historical Soc. Inc., 330 East College Avenue, Appleton, WI 54911, USA. Tel.: 1 414 735 9370.

Year and Place of Birth 1951, Bethesda, USA.

Degrees and Qualifications BA (Econ./Theater Arts) Beloit College, 1973; MA (Hist. of Technology) Delaware Univ., 1977; Ph.D. (Econ. Hist.) Wisconsin Univ. (Madison), 1984.

Previous Post Curator, Milwaukee Public Museum, 1977–85.

Major Honours Smithsonian pre-Doctoral Fellow; NEVINS Prize (EHA, 1985); fellow, NAWCC.

Fields of Expertise *Industry Fields:* metal manufacture; Amer. system of manufactures; watches, clocks and typewriters. *Bus. Dimensions:* bus. and technology. *Scope:* internat. *Period:* nineteenth century. *Consultancy:* co. hist.; endowment development.

Publications *Books: The Time Museum Historical Catalogue of Amer. Pocket Watches,* III, The Time Museum, Rockford, 1991; *Ingenious Yankees, the Rise of the Amer. System of Manufactures in the Private Sector,* Columbia Univ. Press, New York, 1990. *Articles:* 'The Woman and the Typewriter: A Case Study in Technological Innovation and Social Change', *Bus. & Econ. Hist., Papers Presented at the Twenty-fifth Annual Meeting of the Bus. Hist. Conf., 2–3 March 1979,* 2nd ser., 8, III, Bureau of Econ. & Bus. Research, 1979; '"Clocks"', *Internat. Encyclopaedia of Communications,* OUP, Univ. of

Pennsylvania, 1988; 'Product Design and Cost Considerations: Watch, Clock & Typewriter Manufacturing in the 19th Century', *Bus. & Econ. Hist.*, William J. Hausman ed., 2nd ser., 18, 1989, 119–28.

Holtfrerich, Carl-Ludwig

Prof. of Econ. & Econ. Hist., Free Univ. of Berlin, John F. Kennedy Inst. for North Amer. Studies, Lansstr. 7-9, D-14195 Berlin, Germany. Tel.: 49 30 838 3603. Fax: 49 30 838 2885.
Year and Place of Birth 1942, Everswinkel, Germany.
Degrees and Qualifications Dip.Volkswirt. Münster Univ., 1966; Doctorate Münster Univ., 1971; Habilitation (Econ. Hist.) Free Univ. Berlin, 1979.
Current Offices and Honorary Posts Academic advisory board mem., Inst. for Contemporary Hist., Munich; steering com. mem., Berlin Programme for Advanced German & European Studies; academic advisory board mem, German Historical Inst. in Washington, DC; academic advisory board mem., European Assoc. of Banking Hist.
Major Honours John F. Kennedy Memorial Fellow at Harvard Univ., 1975–6; visiting prof., Oxford Univ., 1982; Fellow of the Woodrow Wilson Internat. Center for Scholars, Washington, DC, 1982–3.
Fields of Expertise *Industry Fields:* mining and quarrying; insurance, banking, finance. *Bus. Dimensions:* multinational bus. *Scope:* regional; national; internat.; Germany; USA. *Period:* nineteenth century; twentieth century as a whole. *Teaching:* undergrad.; post grad. *Consultancy:* co. hist.
Publications *Books: Quantitative Wirtschaftsgeschichte des Ruhrkolebergbaus im 19. Jahrhundert. Eine Führungssektoranalyse,* Ardey,

Dortmund, 1973; *The German Inflation 1914–1923*, de Gruyter, Berlin/New York, 1986; *Interactions in the World Economy: Perspectives from Internat. Econ. Hist.*, ed., Hemel Hempstead, UK/New York: Harvester-Wheatsheaf, New York Univ. Press, 1989; *Econ. and Strategic Issues in US Foreign Policy (de Gruyter Studies on North Amer., Vol. 3)*, ed., de Gruyter, Berlin/New York, 1989.

Honeyman, Katrina

Sen. Lect., School of Bus. and Econ. Studies, Univ. of Leeds, Leeds, LS2 9JT, UK. Tel.: 44 532 334476. Fax: 44 532 334465.
Year and Place of Birth 1950, London, UK.
Degrees and Qualifications BA York Univ., 1972; PGCE Poulton-le-Fylde; Ph.D. Nottingham Univ., 1977.
Previous Post Temp. Lect. in Econ. Hist., Dept. of European Studies, UMIST, 1978–9.
Current Offices and Honorary Posts Sec., Women's Com., Econ. Hist. Soc.; council mem., Econ. Hist. Soc.
Fields of Expertise *Industry Fields:* textiles; clothing and footwear. *Bus. Dimensions:* entrepreneurs and entrepreneurship; bus. organization. *Period:* eighteenth century; nineteenth century. *Consultancy:* co. hist.
Publications *Books: Origins of Enterprise: Bus. Leadership in the Indust. Revolution,* Manchester Univ. Press, 1982; *Technology and Enterprise. Isaac Holden and the Mechanisation of Woolcombing in France, 1848–1914*, Scolar, 1986; *Gainful Pursuits. The Making of Indust. Europe 1600–1914*, with J. Goodman, Edward Arnold, 1988. *Articles:* 'La repercussion sociale du changement technologique dans l'industrie textile britannique, 1780–1830', *L'industrie textile en Europe du Nord aux XIXe siècle*, P.

Delsalle ed., Tourcoing, 1984; 'Women's work, gender conflict and labour markets in Europe 1600–1914', *Econ. Hist. Rev.*, with J. Goodman, Nov., 1991.

Horrocks, Sally M.

Research Assoc., CHSTM, Maths Tower, Manchester Univ., Manchester, M13 9PL, . Tel.: 061 275 5929/5850. Fax: 061 273 1123.

Year and Place of Birth 1966, Solihull, UK.

Degrees and Qualifications BA (Hons), Hist. and Phil. of Sci., Univ. of Cambridge, 1987; Ph.D, Univ. of Manchester, 1993.

Current Offices and Honorary Posts Council Mem., British Soc. for the Hist. of Sciences.

Major Honours Joint winner 1993 of T.S. Ashton Prize with D.E.H. Edgerton from the Econ. Hist. Soc.

Fields of Expertise *Industry Fields:* food, drink, tobacco; professional and scientific services. *Bus. Dimensions:* research and development; bus. and technology. *Scope:* national; UK. *Period:* nineteenth century; twentieth century as a whole. *Teaching:* undergrad.

Publications *Articles:* 'British Industrial Research and Development before 1945', *Econ. Hist. Rev.*, with D.E.H. Edgerton, forthcoming, 1994; 'The Bus. of Vitamins: Nutrition Science and the Food Industry in Interwar Britain', *The Science and Culture of Nutrition*, H. Kamminga and A. Cunningham (eds.), Rodopc, Amsterdam.

Howell, Paul M.

Principal, Howell & Assoc.s, 181 Abercrombie St, Darlington 2008, Sydney, Australia. Tel.: 61 2 310 3383. Fax: 61 2 310 3383.

Year and Place of Birth 1949, Berkeley, USA.

Degrees and Qualifications BA Univ. of California at Berkeley, 1972; MA Univ. of California at Berkeley; Ph.D. Univ. of California at Berkeley, 1983.

Previous Post Head ed., Institutional Research & Advisory Dept., Nomura Securities Co., Tokyo, 1985–9.

Major Honours Fulbright Fellowship, 1977–8.

Fields of Expertise *Industry Fields:* insurance, banking, finance. *Bus. Dimensions:* bus.–state relations. *Scope:* Internat. *Period:* nineteenth century. *Consultancy:* equities research and analysis.

Publications *Books: Capitalism in the Risorgimento: Joint-Stock Banking and Econ. Development in the Kingdom of Sardinia, 1843–1859*, Garland Publishing, 1992. *Articles:* 'An Italian Bank in the Railroad Boom of the 1850s', *Rassegna Storica del Risorgimento*, 77, 160–90.

Hrabovec, Ivan

Inst. of Hist., Slovak Acad. of Sciences, Klemensova 19, 813 64 Bratislava, Slovakia. Tel.: 42 7 361 645. Fax: 42 7 361 645.

Year and Place of Birth 1931, Bratislava, Slovakia.

Degrees and Qualifications Dipl.Pedag. Bratislava Univ., 1955; Rer.nat.Dr. Bratislava Univ., 1974; Ph.D. (Hist.) Slovak Acad. of Sciences.

Current Offices and Honorary Posts Mem., Soc. for the Hist. of Sci. (Germany); mem., Soc. for the Hist. of Sci. & Technology (Slovakia); mem., Botanical Soc. (Slovakia); mem. Slovak Hist. Soc.

Major Honours J.L. Holuby Memorial Medal, Botanical Soc. of the

Slovak Acad. of Sciences, 1991; K. Brancík Memorial Medal, Trencín Museum, 1985.

Fields of Expertise *Industry Fields:* agric., forestry, fishing; biology. *Bus. Dimensions:* research and development. *Scope:* national. *Period:* eightteenth century; nineteenth century; twentieth century as a whole. *Teaching:* undergrad. *Consultancy:* individual.

Publications *Books: Hist. of Botany and Zoology in Slovakia up to the first half of the 19th Century,* Series Z dejin vied a techniky na Slovensku, Bratislava, 1990. *Articles:* 'Thirty Years of Botany in the Slovak Acad. of Sciences', *Folia geobotanica et phytotaxonomica,* 19, Prague, 1964, 1–3; 'J.E. Purkyne and Slovakia', *Jan Evangelista Purkyne in Science and Culture,* Prague, 1988, 249–56; 'Biological Research in Slovakia', *Acta Historiae Rerum Naturalium Necnon Technicarum,* Sp. issue 21, Prague, 1989, 175–91; 'Textbooks on Zoology published in Slovakia in the 18th Century', *Acta Facultatis Rerum Naturalium Universitatis Comenianae. Zoologia,* vol. 35, Bratislava, 1991, 123–6.

Huberman, Michael M.

Assoc. Prof., Dept. of Econ., Trent Univ., Peterborough, Ontario, K9J 7B8, Canada. Tel.: 1 705 748 1501. Fax: 1 705 748 1630.

Year and Place of Birth 1955, Montreal, Canada.

Degrees and Qualifications BA McGill Univ., 1978; MA Toronto Univ., 1979; Ph.D. Toronto Univ., 1985.

Fields of Expertise *Industry Fields:* agric., forestry, fishing; textiles; other manufacturing industries. *Bus. Dimensions:* entrepreneurs and entrepreneurship; personnel management; bus. and technology. *Scope:* internat.

Period: nineteenth century; twentieth century as a whole. *Teaching:* undergrad.

Publications *Articles:* 'The Econ. Origins of Paternalism: Lancashire Cotton Spinning in the First Half of the Nineteenth Century', *Soc. Hist.,* 12, May, 1987, 177–92; 'Invisible Handshakes in Lancashire: Cotton Spinning in the First Half of the Nineteenth Century', *J. of Econ. Hist.,* 46, Dec., 1987, 987–98; 'How Did Labor Markets Work in Lancashire? Some Further Evidence on Prices and Quantities', *Explorations in Econ. Hist.,* 28, Jan., 1991, 87–120; 'Industrial Relations and the Indust. Revolution: Evidence from M'Connel and Kennedy, 1810–1840', *Bus. Hist. Rev.,* 55, Summer, 1991, 373–90.

Hyldtoft, Ole

Sen. Lect., Dept. of Hist., Copenhagen Univ., Njalsgade 102, DK-2300 Copenhagen S, Denmark. Tel.: 45 39690693.

Year and Place of Birth 1943, Sejstrup, Denmark.

Degrees and Qualifications Cand.mag., 1970; Dr.phil., 1985.

Previous Post Amanuensis, Inst. of Econ. Hist., Copenhagen Univ., 1971–5.

Current Offices and Honorary Posts Chairman, Danish Soc. for the Preservation of the Indust. Heritage; chairman, Danish network for the Hist. of Technology; board mem., Danish soc. for Econ. & Soc. Hist. and the Workers Museum.

Fields of Expertise *Industry Fields:* mechanical engineering; bricks, pottery, glass, cement; gas, electricity, water. *Bus. Dimensions:* bus. and technology. *Scope:* national; internat.; Scandinavia; Denmark. *Period:* nineteenth century; twentieth century as a whole. *Teaching:* post grad.

Publications *Books: Det industrielle Danmark 1840–1914*, co-auth., Systime, 1981; *Københavns Industrialisiering 1840–1914*, Systime, 1984; *Den lysende gas 1800–1890* [The Danish Gas Industry 1800–1890], forthcoming.*Articles:* 'Med vandkraft, dampmaskine og gasmotor' [Power engines in Danish industry 1840–1897], *Erhvervshistorisk Årbog*, 1987, 75–126; 'Foreign Technology and the Danish Brick and Tile Industry, 1830–1870', *Technology Transfer and Scandinavian Industrialisation*, K. Bruland ed., Berg, Oxford, 1991, 201–28.

Ichihara, Hiroshi

Assoc. Prof. of Labour Management, Fac. of Econ., Hokkai Gakuen Univ., 4-1-40 Asahimachi, Toyohiraku, Sapporo, Japan. Tel.: 011 841 1161.
Year and Place of Birth 1955, Chiba, Japan.
Degrees and Qualifications MA Tokyo Metropol. Univ., 1981.
Previous Post Asst. Prof. Fac. of Econ., Hitotusbashi Univ., 1984.
Fields of Expertise *Industry Fields:* mining and quarrying. *Bus. Dimensions:* personnel management. *Scope:* national. *Period:* twentieth century as a whole. *Teaching:* undergrad.
Publications *Books: Management and Labour of the Chikuho Mining Industry during the Post-war Period*, co-auth., Keibunsha, 1990. *Articles:* 'The Development of Indust. Relations in Copper Mining after the First World War', *J. of Hist. Studies*, 522, 1983, 1–18; 'An Essay on Tomoko', *Hokkaigakuen Univ. J. of Econ.*, 38(2), 1990, 229–48; 'The State of Korean Labour in Japanese Collieries in Wartime', *J. of Energy Hist.*, 15, 1991, 99–114; 'An Essay on the Labour Relations of Colliery Companies in Japan during the Post-war Period', *Japan Bus. Hist. Rev.*,

27(3), 1992, 1–33.

Ichijo, Junya

Lect., Miyako College, Yogieawa, 4-8-6 Miyako, Iwate 027, Japan. Tel.: 0193 64 2230.
Year and Place of Birth 1961, Aomari, Japan.
Degrees and Qualifications MA (Commerce) Chuo Univ., 1986.
Fields of Expertise *Industry Fields:* shipbuilding and marine engineering. *Bus. Dimensions:* entrepreneurs and entrepreneurship; management. *Scope:* internat.; UK; national; USA. *Period:* nineteenth century; early twentieth century. *Teaching:* undergrad.
Publications *Articles:* 'The Making of Modern Labour Management: Robert Owen in New Lanark (1), (2)', *Bull. of Grad. Studies*, Chuo Univ., 16(2), 17(2), 1986–7; 'Robert Owen Considered from the Bus. Hist. Point of View', *Inst. of Bus. Research Annual Bull.*, Chuo Univ., 8, 1987; 'The Making of Modern Management: Charles Babbege and his Management Thought', *Shougaku Ronsan*, 30(2), 31(1), 1988–9; 'British Management Thought in the 19th Century: Robert Owen and Charles Babbage', *Miyako Pref. College J.*, 1(2), 1991; 'The Modernization of Management in British Shipbuilding', *Miyako Pref. College J.*, 3(1), 1992.

Igartua, José E.

Assoc. Prof., Dept. of Hist., Quebec Univ. at Montreal, POB 8888, Succursale "A", Montréal, QC H3C 3P8, , Canada. Tel.: 1 514 987 8312. Fax: 1 514 987 7813.
Year and Place of Birth 1946, Canada.
Degrees and Qualifications BA (Hist.) Loyola College, Montreal, 1964; Licence ès lettres (Hist.) Laval

Univ, 1966; Ph.D. Michigan State Univ., 1974.

Previous Post Assoc. Prof., Dept. of Human Sciences, Quebec Univ. at Chicoutimi, 1978–81.

Current Offices and Honorary Posts Chairperson, Canadian Com. for Hist. & Computing.

Fields of Expertise *Industry Fields:* metal manufacture. *Bus. Dimensions:* entrepreneurs and entrepreneurship; merger movement and issues; multinational bus. *Scope:* regional. *Teaching:* undergrad.; post grad.

Publications *Articles:* '"Corporate Strategy" and Locational Decision-making: The Duke-Price Alcoa Merger 1925', *J. of Canadian Studies/Revue d'études canadiennes*, 20, Autumn, 1985, 82–101; 'Worker Persistence, Hiring Policies and the Depression in the Aluminium Sector: The Saguenay Region, 1925–1940', *Histoire sociale/Social Hist.*, 22, May, 1989, 9–33.

Iida, Takashi

Assoc. Prof., Social Sc. Div., Fac. of Foreign Studies, Tokyo Univ. of Foreign Studies, 4-51 Nishigahara, Kita-ku, Tokyo 114, , Japan. Tel.: 03 3917 6111. Fax: 03 3940 5967.

Year and Place of Birth 1956, Fukuoka pref., Japan.

Degrees and Qualifications BA Hosei Univ.; MA (Econ.) Hosei Univ.

Previous Post Research Assoc., Inst. of Social Sc., Tokyo Univ.

Current Offices and Honorary Posts Sec., Japan Bus. Hist. Soc., 1989–92.

Fields of Expertise *Industry Fields:* insurance, banking, finance,. *Bus. Dimensions:* co. finance and accounting; markets and bus. *Scope:* national; UK. *Period:* inter-war years, 1919–39. *Teaching:* undergrad.; post grad. *Consultancy:* corporate strategy.

Publications *Articles:* 'Igirisu ni

okeru Sangyo Shoken Ryutsu no Tenkai 1890–1910' [The Logic of Co. Formation and the Marketability of Home Indust. Securities in England 1890–1910], *J. of Social Science*, Tokyo Univ., 39(3), 1987, 1–128; 'Senkanki no London Syoken Torihikisho' [The London Stock Exchange in the Inter-war Years], *J. of Social Science*, Tokyo Univ., 40(3), 1988, 1–50; 'Senkanki no Merchant Bank' [The Merchant Banks in the Inter-war Period], *Shoken Keizai* [Financial Econ. Rev.], 177, 1991, 49–68.

Ikeda, Noritaka

Asst. Prof., Dept. of Econ., Fac. of Humanities, Hirosaki Univ., 1 Bunkyo-cho, Hirosaki, Aomori 036, , Japan. Tel.: 0172 36 2111.

Year and Place of Birth 1955, Hiroshima, Japan.

Degrees and Qualifications BA (Econ.) Ritsumeikan Univ., 1979; MA (Econ.) Rikkyo Univ., 1982.

Previous Post Instructor, Fac. of Econ., Rikkyo Univ., 1985–8.

Fields of Expertise *Industry Fields:* metal manufacture; mechanical engineering; instrument engineering; electrical engineering; shipbuilding and marine engineering; bricks, pottery, glass, cement; public admin. and defence; nuclear engineering: manufacture; electronics and computers: manufacture; genetic engineering: manufacture. *Bus. Dimensions:* entrepreneurs and entrepreneurship; production management; bus. organization; bus. and technology; bus.–state relations. *Scope:* national; internat. *Period:* nineteenth century; twentieth century as a whole; early twentieth century. *Teaching:* undergrad. *Consultancy:* co. hist.

Publications *Articles:* 'Nichirosensogo ni okeru

Kaigunheikiseisan no Kozo' [On the Munitions Industry in Japan, 1906–1913], *Shakai Keizai Shigaku* [The Socio-Econ. Hist. J.], 50(2), 1984, 31–54; 'Nichirosengo ni oekru Rikugun to Heikiseisan' [On the Military Arsenal in Japan, 1906–1913], *Tochiseidosigaku* [The J. of Agrarian Hist.], 114, 1987, 32–45; 'Senzen Nihon no Jukogyodaikeiei ni okeru Romukanri no Keisei' [On the Indust. Relations of the Naval Arsenal in Japan], *Rikkyo Keizaigakukenkyu* [Rikkyo Econ. Rev.], 42(2), 1988, 139–55; 'Kaigunkosho no Seiritsu to Keieikanrisoshiki no Tenkai' [On the Structure of the Navy Yard in Japan], *Rikkyo Keizaigakukenkyu* [Rikkyo Econ. Rev.], 44(2), 1990, 209–28.

Ikoma, Michihiro

Prof., Fac. of Commerce & Econ., Kinki Univ., Kowakae 3-4-1, Higashi, Osaka-City 577, Japan. Tel.: 06 721 2332. Fax: 06 729 2493.
Year and Place of Birth 1932, Wakayama, Japan.
Degrees and Qualifications MA (Bus. Admin.) Kobe Univ.
Previous Post Prof., Fac. of Econ., Wakayama Univ., 1987.
Current Offices and Honorary Posts Director, Soc. for the Econ. Studies of Securities (Japan).
Fields of Expertise *Industry Fields:* vehicle construction. *Bus. Dimensions:* co. finance and accounting. *Scope:* national. *Period:* twentieth century as a whole. *Teaching:* undergrad.; post grad. *Consultancy:* corporate strategy.
Publications *Articles:* 'Kabushiki Jikahakko no Riron' [The Hist. Development of Stock Financing in Japan], *Par Value Issue to Current Value Issue*, Chikura, 1986.

Imakubo, Sachio

Assoc. Prof., Fac. of Econ., Kyoto Univ., Yoshida Hon-machi, Sakyo-ku, Kyoto 606-01, Japan. Tel.: 075 753 3459. Fax: 075 751 1532.
Year and Place of Birth 1948, Kagoshima, Japan.
Degrees and Qualifications MA Kyoto Univ., 1976.
Previous Post Assoc. Prof., Fac. of Econ., Saga Univ., 1981–90.
Fields of Expertise *Industry Fields:* electrical engineering; electronics and computers: manufacture. *Bus. Dimensions:* production management; personnel management; *Co. Admin.;* bus. and technology. *Scope:* national; Germany. *Period:* nineteenth century; early twentieth century; late twentieth century, 1970–present. *Teaching:* undergrad.; post grad.
Publications *Articles:* '19 Seikimatsu doitsu-denki-kogyo ni okeru keiei-rohmu-seisaku (10)' [Factory Admin. and Labour Management in the German Electric Industry 1873–1903/4 (10)], *Saga Univ. Econ. Rev.*, 22(5), 1990, 71–118; '19 Seikimatsu doitsu-denki-kogyo ni okeru rodo-noritsu-zoshin-saku (1)', *Keizai-Ronso* [Econ. Rev.], 146 (3.4), 1990, 1–19; 'Seikimatsu doitsu-denki-kogyo ni okeru rodo-noritsu-zoshin-saku (2)', *Keizai-Ronso* [Econ. Rev.], 146(5.6), 1990, 16–36; 'Seikimatsu doitsu-denki-kogyo ni okeru rodo-noritsu-zoshin-saku (3)', *Keizai-Ronso* [Econ. Rev.], 147(1.2.3), 1991, 1–17; 'Seikimatsu doitsu-denki-kogyo ni okeru rodo-noritsu-zoshin-saku (4)', *Keizai-Ronso* [Econ. Rev.], 148(4.5.6), 1991, 22–47.

Inagaki, Yoshinari

Assoc. Prof., St Andrew's Univ., (Momoyama Gakuin Daigaku), Fac. of Bus. Admin., 237–1 Nishino, Sakai,

Osaka 588, , Japan. Tel.: 0722 36 1181. Fax: 0722 34 7276.

Year and Place of Birth 1953, Aichi, Japan.

Degrees and Qualifications BA (Bus. Admin.) Nanzan Univ., 1975; MA (Bus. Admin.) Kobe Univ., 1978.

Previous Post Lect., Sapporo Univ., 1981–4.

Fields of Expertise *Industry Fields:* vehicle construction; automobile industry. *Bus. Dimensions:* product policy. *Scope:* internat.; global; national; Germany. *Period:* twentieth century as a whole. *Teaching:* undergrad.

Publications *Articles:* 'Volkswagen no Kigyo Senryaku' [The Corporate Strategy of Volkswagen], *Kikai Yushutsu*, 34(14), 1986, 38–45; 'Volkswagen-sha ni Okeru Keiei Senryaku no Tenkan Katei, Dai I-bu' [On the Process of Strategic Change at Volkswagen, Part I], *Momoyama Gakuin Daigaku Keizai Keiei Ronshu*, 28(4), 1987, 33–63; 'Volkswagen-sha ni Okeru Keiei Senryaku no Tenkan Katei, Dai II-bu' [On the Process of Strategic Change at Volkswagen, Part II], *Momoyama Gakuin Daigaku Keizai Keiei Ronshu*, 29(1), 1987, 47–72; 'Nichi-Doku Jidosha Maker no Seihin Senryaku' [A Comparison of Product Strategies between Japanese and German Automobile Producers: Two Types of Innovation Strategy], *Sengo Nihon no Kigyo Keiei* [Japanese Bus. after World War II], Bushin-do, 1991, 409–41.

Ingham, John N.

Prof. of Hist., Dept. of Hist., Univ. of Toronto, 215 Huron St, Toronto, Ontario, M5S 1A1, , Canada. Tel.: 1 416 978 8469. Fax: 1 416 978 4810.

Year and Place of Birth 1939, Green Bay, USA.

Degrees and Qualifications BA Wisconsin Univ., 1962; MA Pittsburgh

Univ., 1963; Ph.D. Pittsburgh Univ., 1973.

Previous Post Hist. Dept., New York State Univ., Brockport, 1970–7.

Major Honours Wallace K. Ferguson Prize, Canadian Hist. Assoc., 1980.

Fields of Expertise *Industry Fields:* metal manufacture. *Bus. Dimensions:* bus. and technology. *Scope:* national. *Period:* nineteenth century.

Publications *Books: The Iron Barons: A Social Analysis of an Amer. Urban Elite, 1877–1945*, Greenwood Press, 1978; *Biographical Dictionary of Amer. Bus. Leaders*, 4 vols., Greenwood Press, 1983; *Contemporary Amer. Bus. Leaders*, with Lynne B. Feldman, Greenwood Press, 1990; *Making Iron and Steel: The Independent Mills of Pittsburgh 1850–1920*, Ohio State Univ. Press, 1991. *Articles:* 'Steel City Aristocrats', *City at the Point*, Samuel P. Hays ed., Univ. of Pittsburgh Press, 1989.

Ioku, Shigehiko

Assoc. Prof., Fac. of Bus. Econ. & Information, Setsunan Univ., 17–8 Idedanakamachi, Neyagawa City, Osaka Pref., Japan. Tel.: 0720 26 5101. Fax: 0720 26 5100.

Year and Place of Birth 1957, Hiroshima, Japan.

Degrees and Qualifications BA Keio Univ., 1980; M.Litt. Keio Univ., 1982.

Previous Post Coal Mining Research Centre, Kyushu Univ., 1986–92.

Fields of Expertise *Industry Fields:* agric., forestry, fishing; food, drink, tobacco; distributive trades. *Bus. Dimensions:* entrepreneurs and entrepreneurship; Co. admin.; marketing; small bus. matters; markets and bus. *Scope:* regional. *Period:* nineteenth century. *Teaching:* undergrad. *Consultancy:* co. hist.

Publications *Articles:* 'The Significance of the Formation of a little River Port in the latest Edo Era - a Case Study of Obayashi Village, Hitachi Province', *Shigaku, The Hist. Science*, 57(4), 1988; 'The Purchase of Raw Materials and Distribution of Finished Goods by Yamasa Shoyu located in the Town of Choshi in the latest Edo Era', *Shijoshi Kenkyu* [J. of Market Hist.], 11, 1992.

Irsigler, Franz

Prof., Fac. III, Trier Univ., D-54286 Trier, , Germany. Tel.: 49 651 2013316. Fax: 49 651 2013950.
Year and Place of Birth 1941, Großuretschlag, Czechland.
Degrees and Qualifications Promotion, Dr.Phil. Saarbrücken Univ, 1968; Habilitation Bonn Univ., 1974.
Current Offices and Honorary Posts Treasurer, internat. Commission for the Hist. of Towns; com. mem., Rheinland Hist. Science Assoc.; com. mem. Hanseatic Hist. Soc.
Fields of Expertise *Industry Fields:* agric., forestry, fishing; mining and quarrying; metal manufacture; textiles; clothing and footwear; paper, printing, publishing; distributive trades; insurance, banking, finance,; monetary history. *Bus. Dimensions:* entrepreneurs and entrepreneurship; co. finance and accounting; marketing; bus. organization; markets and bus.; putting-out systems (Verlage). *Scope:* local; regional; internat.; Germany; Netherlands. *Period:* medieval; early modern; eighteenth century. *Teaching:* undergrad.; post grad. *Consultancy:* co. hist.
Publications *Books: Untersuchungen zur Geschichte des frühfränkischen Adels*, Röhrscheid-Verlag, Bonn, 1969 & Rheinisches Archiv, vol. 70, 1981; *Getreideumsatz, Getreide- und Brotpreise in Köln 1368–1797*, with Dietrich Ebeling co-ed., 2 vols., Cologne, 1976/1977, (Mitteilungen aus dem Stadtarchiv von Köln, vols., 65 & 66); *Die Wirtschaftliche Stellung der Stadt Köln im 14. und 15. Jahrhundert. Strukturanalyse einer spätmittelalterlichen Exportgewerbe- und Fernhandelsstadt*, Steiner-Verlag, Wiesbaden, 1979; VSWG-Beihefte, vol. 65; *Bettler und Gaukler, Dirnen und Henker. Randgruppen und Außenseiter in Köln 1300–1600*, with Arnold Lassotta, Greven-Verlag, Cologne, 1982; paperback edn., DTV, Munich, 1992; Japanese translation, Orion Press, Tokyo, 1992; *Geschichtlicher Atlas der Rheinlande*, ed., ser. 1–4, Rheinland-Verlag, Cologne, 1981–92.

Ishii, Kanji

Prof. of Japanese Econ. Hist., Tokyo Univ., Fac. of Econ., 7-3-1 Hongo, Bunkyo-ku, Tokyo 113, Japan. Tel.: 81 3 3812 2111. Fax: 81 3 3818 7082.
Year and Place of Birth 1938, Tokyo, Japan.
Degrees and Qualifications BA Tokyo Univ., 1960; MA Tokyo Univ., 1965; Ph.D. (Econ.) Tokyo Univ., 1974.
Current Offices and Honorary Posts Socio-Econ. Hist. Soc.: ed., 1967–85; chief ed., 1986–9; exec. com. mem., 1983–; Agrarian Hist. Soc.: exec. com. mem., 1980–90; chairman of exec. com., 1991–.
Major Honours Nikkei Prize, 1966 (joint winner)· & 1984.
Fields of Expertise *Industry Fields:* agric., forestry, fishing; textiles; transport and communication; distributive trades; insurance, banking, finance,. *Bus. Dimensions:* co. finance and accounting; multinational bus.; bus.–state relations. *Scope:* national; internat. *Period:* nineteenth century;

early twentieth century; inter-war years, 1919–39. *Teaching:* undergrad.; post grad. *Consultancy:*.

Publications *Books: Nihon Sanshigyo-shi Bunseki* [Analysis of the Hist. of the Japanese Silk Industry], Univ. of Tokyo Press, 1972; *Kindai Nihon to Igirisu Shihon* [Modern Japan and British Capital], Univ. of Tokyo Press, 1984; *Kaikoku to Ishin* [The Opening of the Country and the Meiji Reform], Shogakukan, 1989; *Nihon keizai-shi* [Econ. Hist. of Japan], Univ. of Tokyo Press, 1991. *Articles:* 'Ginko sosetsu zengo no Mitsui-gumi *[The Crises of the Mitsui-gumi when they established the Mitsui Bank]*', *Mitsui Bunko Ronso*, 17, 1983.

Ito, Shoji

Prof; Grad. School of Liberal Arts, Yokohama City Univ., 22-2 Seto, Kanazawa-ku, Yokohama-shi 236, Japan. Tel.: 045 787 2311. Fax: 045 787 2316.

Year and Place of Birth 1937, Saitama pref., Japan.

Degrees and Qualifications BA (Econ.) Tokyo Metropol. Univ., 1960.

Previous Post Prof., IDE Advanced School, Inst. of Developing Economies, Tokyo, 1990–3.

Current Offices and Honorary Posts Mem., Advisory Editorial Board, *J. of Entrepreneurship*, Ahmedabad, India.

Fields of Expertise *Industry Fields:* . *Bus. Dimensions:* entrepreneurs and entrepreneurship; bus. organization. *Scope:* internat. *Period:* twentieth century as a whole. *Teaching:* undergrad.; post grad.

Publications *Articles:* 'A Note on the "Bus. Combine" in India with Special Reference to the Nattukottai Chettiars', *The Developing Economies*, Sept., 1966; 'On the Basic Nature of the Investment Companies in India',

The Developing Economies, Sept., 1978; 'Technology Transfer from Japanese to Indian Firms', *Econ. & Polit. Weekly (Bombay)*, Special Issue, Nov., 1985; 'Modifying Imported Technology by Local Engineers; Hypotheses and Case Study of India', *The Developing Economies*, Dec., 1986.

Itoh, Takashi

Assoc. Prof., Dept. of Econ., Saitama Univ., 255 Shiookubo, Urawa-shi, Saitama-ken 338, Japan. Tel.: 048 852 2111.

Year and Place of Birth 1952, Hokkaido, Japan.

Degrees and Qualifications BA Hokkaido, 1976; MA Hokkaido Univ., 1979.

Fields of Expertise *Industry Fields:* coal and petroleum products; chemicals and allied industries. *Bus. Dimensions:* marketing; multinational bus. *Scope:* internat.; global; UK; USA. *Period:* nineteenth century; twentieth century as a whole. *Teaching:* undergrad.

Publications *Articles:* 'Standard Oil Co. (New Jersey) in the United Kingdom after World War II', *Japan Bus. Hist. Rev.*, 24(2), Jul. 1989, 33–67; 'Standard Oil Co. (New Jersey) in the United Kingdom from after World War II to the late 1960s', *The Social Science Rev.*, 76–77, Jul. 1992, 91–131.

Jackson, Kenneth E.

Senior Lect., Dept. of Econ., Auckland Univ., Private Bag 92019, Auckland, New Zealand. Tel.: 64 9 3737599. Fax: 64 9 3737427.

Year and Place of Birth 1945, Merton, UK.

Degrees and Qualifications BA Univ. of Kent at Canterbury, 1968; Ph.D. Univ. of Kent at Canterbury, 1978.

Previous Post Research Asst., Southampton Univ., Oct.–Dec. 1971.

Current Offices and Honorary Posts Policy com. mem., Centre for Bus. Hist., Auckland Univ.

Fields of Expertise *Industry Fields:* agric., forestry, fishing; timber, furniture; construction; gas, electricity, water; insurance, banking, finance. *Bus. Dimensions:* bus. and technology; bus.–state relations. *Scope:* national; New Zealand. *Period:* nineteenth century; twentieth century as a whole. *Teaching:* undergrad. *Consultancy:* corporate strategy.

Publications *Articles:* 'Research Use and the Value of Bus. Archives', *Archivista: Bull. of the Archives and Records Assoc. of New Zealand,* April, 1991, 14–20; 'Corporate Hist. as a Management Training Tool: Being a Reply to Henry Ford's "Hist. is Bunk"', *Training Manager for Tomorrow's Challenge,* Kerr Inkson, Bob Berg & Pam Oliver eds., vol. 2, 1989, Auckland Univ., Auckland, GSB; 'Electricity Provision and the Concept of Service in New Zealand: An Hist. Example of Pricing Policies', *Electricité et Electrification dans le Monde,* Monique Trede ed., 1992, Presses Universitaire de France, Paris, 411–19; 'Forest Policy and Trade: The New Zealand Experience', *Changing Pacific Forests: Hist. Perspectives on the Forest Economy of the Pacific Basin,* J. Dargavel & R. Tucker eds., Forest Hist. Soc./Duke Univ. Press, Durham, NC, 1992, 126–38.

Jacoby, Sanford M.

Prof. of Hist. and Management, Anderson School of Management, Univ. of California Los Angeles, Los Angeles, CA 90024-1481, USA. Tel.: 1 310 825 2505. Fax: 1 310 206 2002.

Year and Place of Birth 1953, New York City, USA.

Degrees and Qualifications BA Pennsylvania Univ., 1974; Ph.D. Univ. of California-Berkeley, 1981.

Major Honours Nevins Prize, Econ. Hist. Assoc.; Terry Book Award, Acad. of Management.

Fields of Expertise *Industry Fields:* other manufacturing industries; distributive trades. *Bus. Dimensions:* personnel management; bus. organization; bus.–state relations; Bus. values. *Scope:* national; internat.; USA; Europe; Japan. *Period:* nineteenth century; twentieth century as a whole. *Teaching:* post grad.

Publications *Books: Employing Bureaucracy: Managers, Unions and the Transformation of Work in Amer. Industry, 1900–1945,* Columbia Univ. Press, 1985; *Masters to Managers: Hist. and Comparative Perspectives on Amer. Employers,* ed., Columbia Univ. Press, 1991. *Articles:* 'Employers and the Welfare State: The Role of Marion B. Folsom', *J. of Amer. Hist.,* Autumn, 1993.

Jaeger, Hans

General Ed., Neue Deutsche Biographie, Bayerische Akademie der Wissenschaften, Marstallplatz 8, 80539 Munich 22, Germany. Tel.: 49 89 23031154. Fax: 49 89 23031245.

Year and Place of Birth 1935, Gelsenkirchen, Germany.

Degrees and Qualifications Ph.D. Bonn Univ., 1966.

Fields of Expertise *Industry Fields:* insurance, banking, finance. *Bus. Dimensions:* bus.–state relations. *Scope:* internat. *Period:* twentieth century as a whole. *Teaching:* undergrad.

Publications *Books: Unternehmer*

in der deutschen Politik, 1890–1918,
Bonn, 1967; *Geschichte der
amerikanischen Wirtschaft im 20.
Jahrhundert*, Wiesbaden, 1973; *Big
Bus. and the New Deal*, Stuttgart,
1974; *Geschichte der Wirtschafts-
ordnung in Deutschland*, Frankfurt,
1988; *Geschichtliche Grundbegriffe 6*,
ed., Stuttgart, 1990.

Jakovleva, Marite

Junior Research Assoc., Inst. of
Latvian Hist., Latvian State Univ., 19
Turgenew St, 1524 Riga, Latvia. Tel.:
42 132 226791.
   Year and Place of Birth 1964, Riga,
Latvia.
   Degrees and Qualifications Fac. of
Hist. Grad., Latvian State Univ., 1987.
   Previous Post Asst., Inst. of Latvian
Hist., Latvian Acad. of Sciences,
1987–91.
   Fields of Expertise *Industry Fields:*
mining and quarrying; metal manufac-
ture; metal goods. *Bus. Dimensions:*
production management; personnel
management. *Scope:* local; regional;
national. *Period:* early modern; eighteenth century.
   Publications *Articles:* 'The Iron
Manufactures of Kurzeme Dukes', *Inst.
of Hist. J.*, 4, 1992, 29–48.

Jakubec, Ivan

Senior Asst., Dept. of Econ. and Social
Hist., Fac. of Philo., Charles Univ.,
Nám. J. Palacha 2, 116 38 Prague 1,
Czechland. Tel.: 0228 441 261.
   Year and Place of Birth 1960,
Prague, Czechland.
   Degrees and Qualifications Ph.Dr.
(Hist.) Charles Univ., 1984; C.Sc.
(Hist.) Charles Univ., 1990.
   Previous Post Humboldt Research
Fellow, Münster Univ., Germany,

1992–3.
   Current Offices and Honorary Posts
Mem., Czecho-Slovak Scientific-
Technical Soc.
   Fields of Expertise *Industry Fields:*
transport and communication;
European Econ. history. *Bus.
Dimensions:* research and develop-
ment; bus. and technology. *Scope:*
national; internat.; Central Europe.
Period: nineteenth century; twentieth
century as a whole. *Teaching:* undergrad. *Consultancy:* co. hist.
   Publications *Books: Texty k
dejinám ved a techniky I* [Textbook of
Hist. of Sciences and Technology],
with V. Gula, Prague Univ., 1989;
*Vyvoj ceskoslovenskych a nemeckych
drah 1929–1937* [The Development of
Czechoslovak and German Railways
1929–1937], Acta Universitatis
Carolinae, Prague, 1992, German summary; *Hamburk a jeho úloha v
ceskoslovenském zahranicním obchodu
meziválecného období* [Hamburg and
her Role in Czechoslovakian Foreign
Bus. during the Interwar Years], Econ.
Hist. of the Czechoslovakian Acad. of
Sciences, 1992.

Jancík, Drahomír

Senior Lect., Charles Univ., Fac. of
Philo., Nám. Jana Palacha 2, 116 38
Prague 1, Czechland. Tel.: 42 2
228441/42 2 228291. Fax: 42 2
325016.
   Year and Place of Birth 1948,
Olomouc, Czechland.
   Degrees and Qualifications Dip.Ed.
Prague Univ., 1972; Ph.Dr. Charles
Univ., 1975; C.Sc. Charles Univ.,
1989.
   Previous Post Sen. Lect., Fac. of
Pedagogy, Charles Univ., 1976–81.
   Fields of Expertise *Industry Fields:*
bus. services. *Bus. Dimensions:* bus.
organization; bus.–state relations.
Scope: national; internat.;

Czechoslovakia; Middle Europe. *Period:* inter-war years, 1919–39. *Teaching:* undergrad.

Publications *Books: Nemecko a Malá dohoda. Hospodárské pronikání Nemecka do Jugoslávie a Rumunska v 1. pol. 30. let* [Germany and the Little Entente. Germany's Econ. Penetration into Yugoslavia and Rumania in the First Half of the '30s], Charles Univ., 1990.

Jenkins, Reese V.

Prof. of Hist. & Director & Ed., Thomas Edison Papers, Rutgers Univ., New Brunswick, NJ 08903, USA. Tel.: 1 908 932 8511. Fax: 1 908 932 6763.

Year and Place of Birth 1938, Muncie, USA.

Degrees and Qualifications BA Rochester Univ., 1960; MS Wisconsin Univ., 1963; Ph.D. Wisconsin Univ., 1966.

Previous Post Asst. & Assoc. Prof., Program in Hist. of Science & Technology, Case Western Reserve Univ., 1967–78.

Current Offices and Honorary Posts Soc. for Hist. of Technology: exec. council mem. & chairman, Awards Com.; Assoc. for Doc. Editing: Chair, Butterfield Award & mem., Sites Com.

Major Honours Dexter Prize, Soc. for the Hist. of Technology, 1978; Outstanding Academic Book of the Year in Bus. & Econ., Amer. Assoc. of Publishers, 1989; Patricia Wise Lect., Acad. of Motion Picture Arts & Sciences.

Fields of Expertise *Industry Fields:* chemicals and allied industries; electrical engineering; gas, electricity, water; photography. *Bus. Dimensions:* entrepreneurs and entrepreneurship; research and development; merger movement and issues; bus. and technology. *Scope:* internat.; USA; UK; Germany; Belgium; France. *Period:*

nineteenth century; early twentieth century. *Teaching:* undergrad.; post grad. *Consultancy:* co. hist.

Publications *Books: Images and Enterprise, Technology and the Amer. Photographic Industry 1839–1925,* Johns Hopkins Press, 1975 & 1979; paperback edn., 1987; *The Thomas A. Edison Papers, A Microfilm Edn.,* with others, 2 parts, Univ. Publications of Amer., 1985, 1987; *The Papers of Thomas A. Edison,* with others, 2 vols., Johns Hopkins Press, 1989, 1992.

Jensen, Jakob B.

Curator, Danish Museum of Printing/Danish Press Museum, Brandts Passage 37, 5000 Odense C, , Denmark. Tel.: 45 66 12 10 20. Fax: 45 66 12 10 63.

Year and Place of Birth 1944, Horsens, Denmark.

Degrees and Qualifications MA Århus Univ., 1974.

Previous Post Curator, Museum of Industry, Horsens, 1976–89.

Fields of Expertise *Industry Fields:* food, drink, tobacco; bricks, pottery, glass, cement; paper, printing, publishing. *Bus. Dimensions:* bus. and technology. *Scope:* national. *Period:* nineteenth century. *Consultancy:* co. hist.

Publications *Articles:* articles on paper and printing industry, co-operative bacon factories, brick-making.

Jequier, François

Prof., Dept. of Hist., Fac. of Letters, Lausanne Univ., UNIL BFSH II, 1015 Lausanne-Dorigny, Switzerland. Tel.: 41 21 692 46 06.

Year and Place of Birth 1941, Lausanne, Switzerland.

Degrees and Qualifications Licence en Science Politique Lausanne Univ., 1965; Licence ès Lettres Lausanne

Univ., 1966; Docteur ès Lettres Lausanne Univ., 1972.

Previous Post Prof. of Contemporary Hist., 1976–93.

Fields of Expertise *Industry Fields:* watch industry. *Bus. Dimensions:* entrepreneurs and entrepreneurship; small bus. matters; co. culture. *Scope:* local; regional; national; internat.; Switzerland. *Period:* nineteenth century; twentieth century as a whole. *Teaching:* undergrad. *Consultancy:* co. hist.

Publications *Books: Une Entreprise horlogère du Val-de-Travers: Fleurier Watch Co SA. De l'Atelier familial du XIXe aux Concentrations du XXe Siècle*, Neuchâtel, La Baconnière, 1972; *De la Forge à la Manufacture horlogère (XVIIIe–XXe Siècles)*, Bibliothèque Historique Vaudoise, Lausanne, 1983; *Charles Veillon (1900–1971). Essai sur l'Émergence d'une Éthique patronale*, Société d'Études en Matière d'Histoire économique, Zurich, 1985. *Articles:* 'Les Archives d'Entreprise: ce que l'Historien désire obtenir', *Revue européenne des Sciences Sociales et Cahiers Vilfredo Pareto*, XV(40), 1977, 87–118; 'L'Histoire des Patrons est-elle réactionnaire?', *Etudes de Lettres*, Lausanne, Apr.-June., 1979, 15–48.

Jeremy, David J.

Reader in Business History, Internat. Bus. Unit, Fac. of Management & Bus., Manchester Metropol. Univ., Aytoun St, Manchester, M1 3GH, UK. Tel.: 44 61 247 3911. Fax: 44 61 247 6313.

Year and Place of Birth 1939, Didcot, UK.

Degrees and Qualifications Dip. Ed., BA Keele Univ., 1961; M.Litt. Bristol Univ., 1967; Ph.D. London School of Econ., 1978.

Previous Post Research Fellow, Bus.

Hist. Unit., London School of Econ., 1980–7.

Current Offices and Honorary Posts Membership sec. & publications, Assoc. of Bus. Historians (UK), 1990–93; edit. panel mem., *Accounting, Bus. & Financial Hist.*, 1993–.

Major Honours Visiting Research Associate, National Museum of History and Technology, Smithsonian Institution, 1969–70; Newcomen Special Award for article in *Bus. Hist. Rev.*, 1977; Dexter Prize from the Soc. for the Hist. of Technology, 1981; John H. Dunning Prize from the Amer. Hist. Assoc., 1982.

Fields of Expertise *Industry Fields:* textiles. *Bus. Dimensions:* entrepreneurs and entrepreneurship; co. culture; technology transfer. *Scope:* regional; national; internat.; USA; Japan; UK. *Period:* twentieth century as a whole. *Teaching:* undergrad.; post grad. *Consultancy:* co. hist.; corporate strategy.

Publications *Books: Transatlantic Indust. Revolution: The Diffusion of Textile Technologies between Britain and Amer. 1790–1830s*, MIT Press, 1981; *Dictionary of Bus. Biography*, ed., 6 vols., Butterworths, 1984–6; *Capitalists and Christians: Bus. Leaders and the Churches in Britain, 1900–1960*, Clarendon Press, OUP, 1990; *Internat. Technology Transfer: Europe, Japan and the USA, 1700–1914*, ed., Edward Elgar, 1991; *Dictionary of Twentieth Century British Bus. Leaders*, with Geoffrey Tweedale, Bowker Saur, 1994.

Jimenez, Juan Carlos

Prof. Avudante, Dept. of Applied Econ., Fac. of Econ., Alcalá Univ., Plaza de la Victoria 2, 28802 Alcalá de Henares (Madrid), Spain. Tel.: 34 91 885 4241. Fax: 34 91 885 4206.

Year and Place of Birth 1959, Madrid, Spain.
Degrees and Qualifications Grad. (Econ. & Bus. Studies) Complutense Univ. Madrid, 1981; Ph.D. (Econ.) Alcalá Univ., 1990.
Fields of Expertise *Industry Fields:* insurance, banking, finance. *Bus. Dimensions:* bus.–state relations. *Scope:* national. *Period:* twentieth century as a whole. *Teaching:* undergrad. *Consultancy:* co. hist.
Publications *Books: Historia del Banco de Crédito Indust.*, with Prof. G. Tortella, Aliana Editorial, 1986. *Articles:* 'El Banco de Crédito Indust. en su Perspectiva Histórica: Lecciones para el Futuro', *El Sector Terciario de la Economia Española*, J. Velarde et al. eds., Colegio de Economistas de Madrid, 1987, 197–204; 'La Intervención del Estado en la Financiación Indust.: el Papel histórico de la Banca pública en España', *Relaciones Banca-Industria: La Experiencia Española*, A. Torrero ed., Espasa-Calpe, 1991, 55–76; 'El Crédito oficial en España: Una Visión retrospectiva', *Revista de Economia*, 12, 1992, 80–4; 'Problemas actuales de la Empresa pública en España', *Papeles de Economia Española*, with P. Martin Aceña & F. Comin, 52/53, 1992, 231–46.

Jindra, Zdenek

Prof.; Head of Dept. of Econ. & Social Hist., Charles Univ., Fac. of Philo., Nám. J. Palacha 2, 116 38 Prague 1, Czechland. Tel.: 42 228441/42 228291. Fax: 42 2325016.
Year and Place of Birth 1931, Chlum u Trebone, Czechland.
Degrees and Qualifications Prom. Historian Prague Univ., 1955; Cand. Hist. Sc. Prague Univ., 1961; Ph.Dr., 1966.
Previous Post Docent, Dept. of Econ. & Soc. Hist., Charles Univ.,

1990–3.
Current Offices and Honorary Posts Mem. of Directory Com., Assoc. of Econ. Hist., Prague; Head of Econ. & Soc. Hist. Dept.; ed., *Prague Econ. & Social Hist. Papers.*
Fields of Expertise *Industry Fields:* metal manufacture; metal goods; insurance, banking, finance; weapon industry. *Bus. Dimensions:* entrepreneurs and entrepreneurship; multinational bus.; bus.–state relations. *Scope:* national; internat.; Germany; Austro-Hungary (to 1918). *Period:* nineteenth century; early twentieth century. *Teaching:* undergrad.; post grad.
Publications *Books: Germany and the Slavs in Central Europe*, Prague, 1961; *Dejiny novoveku vol. I–III 1640–1918* [World Hist. vols. I–III 1640–1918], Prague, 1969, 1973, mem of edit. collective & author of 316 pages; *První svetová* [The First World War], Prague, 1984 & 1987; *Der Rüstungskonzern Fried. Krupp AG 1914–1918. Die Kriegsmateriallieferungen für das deutsche Heer und di deutsche Marine*, Prague, 1986. *Articles:* 'Über die ökonom. Grundlagen der Mitteleuropa-Ideologie des deutschen Imperialismu', *Probleme der Ökonomie und Politik in den Beziehungen zwischen Ost- und Westeuropa vom 17. Jh. bis zur Gegenwart*, K. Obermann ed., Berli/Ost, 1960, 139–62.

Jobert, Phillippe

Prof. of Legal Hist., Bourgogne Univ., Fac. of Law, 4 Bd Gabriel, 21000 Dijon, France. Tel.: 33 80 39 53 35. Fax: 33 80 39 56 48.
Year and Place of Birth 1939, La Tronche, France.
Degrees and Qualifications Doctorate (Legal Hist.) Dijon Univ., 1971.
Previous Post Prof., Franche-Comté

Univ., Besançon, 1983–6.

Fields of Expertise *Industry Fields:* bankruptcies (all fields). *Bus. Dimensions:* entrepreneurs and entrepreneurship; co. law; small bus. matters; bankruptcies. *Scope:* regional; national; France. *Period:* nineteenth century. *Teaching:* undergrad.; post grad.

Publications *Books: The Birth and Death of Companies. An Hist. Perspective*, with Michael Moss co-ed. & co-auth., The Parthenon Publishing Group, Carnforth, UK, 1990; *Les Patrons du Second Empire. T.3, Bourgogne*, ed. & co-auth., Picard, Paris, 1991; *Les Entreprises aux XIXe et XXe Siècles*, ed. & co-auth., coll. Annuaire Statistique de l'Économie Française au XIXe et XXe Siècles , Presses de l'École Normale Supérieure, Paris, 1991. *Articles:* 'L'Incompatibilité entre Brevet d'Invention et Société Anonyme sous la Révolution et l'Empire', *La Révolution Française et le Développement du Capitalisme*, G. Gayot & J.P. Hirsch eds., special issue of *Revue du Nord*, 1989, 227–41; 'Jean-Baptiste Mollerat, un Pionnier de la Chimie Française', *Histoire, Economie et Société*, 2, 1991, 245–68.

Johannessen, Finn Erhard

Research Fellow, for Bus. Hist. Norwegian School of Management, POB 580, N-1301 Sandvika, Norway. Tel.: 47 67 57 05 81. Fax: 47 67 57 08 54.

Year and Place of Birth 1955, Skien, Norway.

Degrees and Qualifications Cand. philol. Oslo Univ., 1983.

Fields of Expertise *Industry Fields:* leather; gas, electricity, water; postal service. *Bus. Dimensions:* public bus. (electricity and post). *Scope:* national. *Period:* eighteenth century; nineteenth century. *Teaching:* undergrad.

Consultancy: co. hist.

Publications *Books: Challenge and Change. The History of Protan from 1939 to 1989*, Lillehammer, 1989; *Lær og Skinn i Tykt og Tynt. Den Norske Garveri-Industris Historie* [The Hist. of the Norwegian Tanning Industry], Ad Notam, Oslo, 1991; *I Støtet. Oslo Energi gjennom 100 år 1892–1992* [The Hist. of the Electricity Utility of Oslo], Ad Notam, Gyldendal, Oslo, 1992.

Johansen, Hans Christian

Inst. of Hist., Odense Univ., Campusvej 55, 5230 Odense M, Denmark. Tel.: 45 66 15 86 00. Fax: 45 65 93 29 84.

Year and Place of Birth 1935, Aarhus, Denmark.

Degrees and Qualifications MA (Econ.) Aarhus Univ., 1963; Ph.D. (Econ. Hist.) Aarhus Univ., 1968.

Previous Post Sen. Lect., Aarhus Univ., 1964–70.

Current Offices and Honorary Posts Pres., Danish Assoc. for Econ. & Soc. Hist.; exec. com. mem., internat. Econ. Hist. Assoc.

Fields of Expertise *Industry Fields:* food, drink, tobacco; bricks, pottery, glass, cement. *Bus. Dimensions:* production management. *Scope:* national. *Period:* eighteenth century; mid-twentieth century, 1940–70. *Teaching:* undergrad.; post grad.

Publications *Books: Dansk Økonomisk Politik i Årene efter 1784*, Universitetsforlaget, Aarhus, 1968; *Nøring og.Bystyre*, Odense Univ. Press, 1983; *The Danish Economy in the Twentieth Century*, Croom Helm, London, 1987; *Gennem Forandring til Fremskridt, Aalborg*, Portland, Aalborg, 1989; *En Koncern I Udvikling, ALM. Brand*, Copenhagen, 1992.

John, Richard R.

Asst. Prof., Hist. Dept. (M/C 198), POB 4348, Univ. of Illinois at Chicago, Chicago, IL 60680, USA. Tel.: 1 312 996 3141. Fax: 1 212 996 6377.

Year and Place of Birth 1959, Lawrence, USA.

Degrees and Qualifications BA Harvard Univ., 1981; MA Harvard Univ., 1983; Ph.D. Harvard Univ., 1989.

Previous Post Post-doctoral Fellow, Commonwealth Center for the Study of Amer. Culture, College of William and Mary.

Major Honours Allan Nevins Prize for best dissertation on Amer. hist., 1990; Herman E. Kroos Prize for best dissertation in bus. hist., 1990.

Fields of Expertise *Industry Fields:* transport and communication. *Bus. Dimensions:* entrepreneurs and entrepreneurship. *Scope:* internat. *Period:* nineteenth century. *Teaching:* post grad.

Publications *Books: Managing Big Bus.: Essays from the Bus. Hist. Rev.,* with Richard S. Tedlow co-ed., Harvard Bus. School Press, 1986; *Information Acumen: The Understanding and Use of Knowledge in Modern Bus.,* Lisa Bud-Frierman co-ed., Routledge, forthcoming. *Articles:* 'Out of Control', *Isis,* Dec., 1988; 'Taking Sabbatarianism Seriously: The Postal System, the Sabbath and the Transformation of Amer. Polit. Culture', *J. of the Early Republic,* Winter, 1990; 'Communications and Information Processing', *Encyclopaedia of Social Hist.,* Macmillan, 1993.

Johnman, Lewis

Senior Lect. in Econ. Hist., School of Social Sc., Univ. of Greenwich, Woolwich Campus, Churchill House, Wellington St, Woolwich, London, SE18 6PF, UK. Tel.: 44 81 316 8907. Fax: 44 81 316 8905.

Year and Place of Birth 1954, Kirkcaldy, UK.

Degrees and Qualifications BA Stirling Univ., 1980; Ph.D. London School of Econ., 1987.

Previous Post Senior Lect. in Econ. Hist., Thames Polytechnic, 1986–7.

Fields of Expertise *Industry Fields:* shipbuilding and marine engineering. *Bus. Dimensions:* bus.–state relations. *Scope:* national. *Period:* inter-war years, 1919–39; mid-twentieth century, 1940–'70. *Teaching:* undergrad.; post grad.

Publications *Articles:* 'The Large Manufacturing Companies of 1935', *Bus. Hist.,* XXVII(2), 1986; 'The Econ. of the Suez Crisis, 1956', *British Hist. since 1945: Themes and Perspectives,* L. Johnman & W. Scott Lucas eds., Pinter, 1989; 'The Labour Party and Indust. Policy, 1940–1945', *The Attlee Years,* N. Tiratsoo ed., Pinter, 1991; 'Shipbuilding', *Labour Governments and Private Industry: The Experience of 1945–1951,* N. Rollings & J. Tomlinson eds., Edinburgh Univ. Press, 1992; 'The Conservatives in Opposition, 1964–1970', *The Wilson Years,* R. Coopey, S. Fielding & N. Tiratsoo eds., Pinter, 1993.

Johnson, David

Managing Director, Horticom Services (New Zealand) Ltd, POB 18250, Glen Innes, Auckland 6, New Zealand. Tel.: 64 9 5766234. Fax: 64 9 5763593.

Year and Place of Birth 1941, Palmerston North, New Zealand.

Degrees and Qualifications B.Com. Canterbury Univ., New Zealand, 1964; Assoc., New Zealand Soc. of Accountants, 1963.

Previous Post Chairman XIVth Commonwealth Games, 1988–9.

Current Offices and Honorary Posts
Trustee (& past chairman), Auckland Maritime Museum; trustee, N. Archives & Records Trust.

Fields of Expertise *Industry Fields:* transport and communication. *Bus. Dimensions:* boardroom issues. *Scope:* internat. *Period:* eighteenth century; nineteenth century; twentieth century as a whole. *Consultancy:* co. hist.; corporate strategy.

Publications *Books: New Zealand's Maritime Heritage*, Bateman/Collins, 1987; *Wellington by the Sea*, Bateman, 1988; *Auckland by the Sea*, Bateman, 1988 & 1992; *Auckland City Life*, Bateman, 1991;*Christchurch: A Pictorial Hist.*, Canterbury Univ. Press, 1992.

Johnson, G. Wesley

Prof. of Bus. Hist., Marriott Grad. School of Management, Brigham Young Univ., Provo, UT 84602, USA. Tel.: 1 801 224 9456.

Year and Place of Birth 1932, Mesa, USA.

Degrees and Qualifications BA (Hist.) Harvard Univ., 1957; MA Columbia Univ., 1961; Ph.D. Columbia Univ., 1967.

Previous Post Prof. of Hist., Univ. of California, Santa Barbara, CA 93106, 1972–86.

Current Offices and Honorary Posts Consulting: vice-pres., Timpanogos Research Assoc.s, Salt Lake City (consulting firm for bus., corporate & governmental histories); sen. partner, Ashby & Johnson, Hist. Consultants, Provo, Utah (consulting firm for bus. & corporate histories).

Major Honours Series ed. for *Corporate Hist.*, Jostens Pub. Group, Encino, California.

Fields of Expertise *Industry Fields:* computers and software. *Bus. Dimensions:* entrepreneurs and entrepreneurship. *Scope:* national. *Period:*

late twentieth century, 1970–present. *Teaching:* post grad. *Consultancy:* co. hist.

Publications *Books: Emergence of Black Polit. in Senegal*, Stanford Univ. Press, Stanford, California, 1971; *The Public Historian Q.*, ed.-in-chief, Univ. of California Press, Berkeley, 1978–7; *Phoenix and Valley of the Sun*, Continental Publishing, Tulsa, Oklahoma, 1982; *Double Impact: France and Africa in the Age of Imperialism*, ed., Greenwood Press, Westport, Conn., 1985; *Phoenix in the Twentieth Century*, ed., Univ. of Oklahoma Press, Norman, Oklahoma, 1993.

Jones, Charles A.

Senior Lect. in Internat. Studies, Dept. of Polit. & Internat. Studies, Univ. of Warwick, Coventry, CV4 7AL, UK. Tel.: 44 203 524131. Fax: 44 203 524221.

Year and Place of Birth 1949, Waterloo, UK.

Degrees and Qualifications BA (Moral Sciences. & Hist.) Cambridge Univ., 1970; Ph.D. (Econ. Hist.) Cambridge Univ., 1974; MA (Phil.) Warwick Univ., 1987.

Previous Post Research Officer, Inst. of Commonwealth Studies, London Univ., 1974–7.

Fields of Expertise *Industry Fields:* gas, electricity, water; distributive trades; insurance, banking, finance,. *Bus. Dimensions:* strategy formation; multinational bus.; bus.–state relations. *Scope:* internat.; global. *Period:* nineteenth century; early twentieth century. *Teaching:* undergrad.; post grad. *Consultancy:* co. hist.; corporate strategy; product hist.

Publications *Books: Britain and the Dominions: A Guide to Bus. and Related Records in the United Kingdom concerning Australia,*

Canada, New Zealand and South Africa, G.K. Hall & Co., Boston, MA., 1978; *Internat. Bus. in the Nineteenth Century: The Rise and Fall of a Cosmopolitan Bourgeoisie*, Wheatsheaf, Brighton, 1987. *Articles:* 'Great Capitalists and the Direction of British Overseas Investment in the late Nineteenth Century: The Case of Argentina', *Bus. Hist.*, 22(2), Jul., 1980, 152–69; 'Competition and Structural Change in the Buenos Aires Fire Insurance Market: The Local Board of Agents, 1875–1921', *The Historian and the Bus. of Insurance*, Oliver Westall ed., Manchester Univ. Press, 1984, 114–29; 'The Fiscal Motive for Monetary and Banking Legislation in Argentina, Australia and Canada before 1915', *Argentina, Australia and Canada: Studies in Comparative Development, 1870–1965*, D.C.M. Platt & Guido Di Tella eds., Macmillan, London, 1985.

Jones, Edgar

Senior Research Fellow, Bus. Hist. Unit, London School of Econ., Houghton St, London, WC2A 2AE, UK. Tel.: 44 71 405 7686.

Year and Place of Birth 1953, Beckenham, UK.

Degrees and Qualifications BA Oxford Univ., 1975; MA Oxford Univ., 1979; D.Phil. Oxford Univ., 1982.

Major Honours Hourglass Award, Acad. of Accounting Historians, 1985.

Fields of Expertise *Industry Fields:* accountancy. *Bus. Dimensions:* bus. organization. *Scope:* internat. *Period:* nineteenth century. *Teaching:* post grad. *Consultancy:* co. hist.

Publications *Books: Accountancy and the British Economy 1840–1980: The Evolution of Ernst & Whinney*, B.T. Batsford, 1981; *Indust. Architecture in Britain, 1750–1939*,

B.T. Batsford, 1985; *A Hist. of GKN, Vol. One, Innovation and Enterprise 1759–1918*, Macmillan, 1987; *A Hist. of GKN, Vol. Two, The Growth of a Bus. 1918–1945*, Macmillan, 1990; *The Memoirs of Edwin Waterhouse*, B.T. Batsford, 1988.

Jones, Geoffrey

Prof. of Bus. Hist., Dept. of Econ., Reading Univ., Whiteknights, Reading, Berks, RG6 2AA, , UK. Tel.: 44 734 318129. Fax: 44 734 750236.

Year and Place of Birth 1952, Birmingham, UK.

Degrees and Qualifications BA Cambridge Univ., 1974; MA Cambridge Univ., 1978; Ph.D. Cambridge Univ., 1978.

Previous Post Lect. in Econ. Hist., London School of Econ., 1981–8.

Current Offices and Honorary Posts Pres., Assoc. of Bus. Historians (UK).

Major Honours Newcomen Award, 1985.

Fields of Expertise *Industry Fields:* insurance, banking, finance. *Bus. Dimensions:* multinational bus. *Scope:* internat. *Period:* twentieth century as a whole. *Teaching:* post grad. *Consultancy:* co. hist.

Publications *Books: The State and the Emergence of the British Oil Industry*, Macmillan, 1981; *The Hist. of the British Bank of the Middle East*, 2 vols., CUP, 1986, 1987; *British Multinationals: Origins, Management and Performance*, ed., Gower, 1986; *Planning and Power in Iran*, with F. Bostock, Frank Cass, 1989; *British Multinational Banking 1830–1990*, OUP, 1993.

Jones, Stephen R.H.

Assoc.-Prof., Dept. of Econ., Auckland Univ., Private Bag 92019, Auckland, New Zealand. Tel.: 64 9 3737999.

Fax: 64 9 373727.

Year and Place of Birth 1942, Gloucester, UK.

Degrees and Qualifications B.Sc. (Econ.); Ph.D. London Univ.

Current Offices and Honorary Posts Director, Centre for Bus. Hist., Univ. of Auckland.

Fields of Expertise *Industry Fields:* food, drink, tobacco; metal goods; textiles; bricks, pottery, glass, cement. *Bus. Dimensions:* entrepreneurs and entrepreneurship; merger movement and issues; bus. organization; bus. and technology; markets and bus. *Scope:* national; New Zealand; UK. *Period:* early modern; eighteenth century; nineteenth century; twentieth century as a whole. *Teaching:* undergrad.

Publications *Articles:* 'Price Assoc.s and Competition in the British Pin Industry 1814–1840', *Econ. Hist. Rev.*, 2nd ser., XXVI, May 1973, 237–53; 'Development of Needle Manufacturing in the West Midlands before 1750', *Econ. Hist. Rev.*, 2nd ser., XXXI, Aug., 1978, 354–68; 'The Organisation of Work: A Hist. Dimension', *J. of Econ. Behaviour & Organisation*, 3, 1982, 117–37; 'Technology, Transactions Cost and the Transition to Factory Production in the British Silk Industry 1700–1870', *J. of Econ. Hist.*, XLVII, 1987, 71–96; 'Concentration and Regeneration in the New Zealand Brewing Industry 1870–1970', *Australian Econ. Hist. Rev.*, XXI, Sept., 1991, 64–94.

Jones, Stuart

Univ. of South Africa, Dept. of Econ., POB 392, Pretoria 0001, South Africa. Tel.: 27 12 429 4464. Fax: 27 12 429 3221.

Year and Place of Birth 1933, Manchester, UK.

Degrees and Qualifications Ph.D.

Univ. of British Columbia, 1975.

Previous Post Sen. Lect., Head of Division of Econ. Hist., Witwatersrand Univ., 1969–93.

Current Offices and Honorary Posts Ed., *South African J. of Econ. Hist.*; past pres., Econ. Hist. Soc. of Southern Africa.

Fields of Expertise *Industry Fields:* insurance, banking, finance,. *Bus. Dimensions:* entrepreneurs and entrepreneurship. *Scope:* national. *Period:* nineteenth century; twentieth century as a whole. *Teaching:* undergrad.

Publications *Books: Banking and Bus. in South Africa*, ed., Macmillan, London, 1988; *Financial Enterprise in South Africa*, ed., Macmillan, London, 1992; *The South African Economy, 1910–90*, with André Müller, Macmillan, London, 1992; *Econ. Interpretations of Nineteenth Century Imperialism*, ed., special issue of the *South African J. of Econ. Hist.*, March, 1988. *Articles:* 'The Apogée of the Imperial Banks in South Africa: Standard and Barclays, 1919–1939', *English Hist. Rev.*, 409, Oct., 1988, 892–916.

Jonker, Joost P.B.

Ed., Documents on Dutch Foreign Relations, 1919–1930, Netherlands Hist. Inst., POB 90755, 2509 LT The Hague, Netherlands. Tel.: 31 70 3814771. Fax: 31 70 3854098.

Year and Place of Birth 1955, Amsterdam, Netherlands.

Degrees and Qualifications BA (Law) Free Univ. Amsterdam 1975; BA (Hist.) Free Univ. Amsterdam, 1979; MA (Soc. & Econ. Hist.) Free Univ. Amsterdam, 1987.

Previous Post Lect. in Soc. & Econ. Hist., Free Univ. Amsterdam, 1992–3.

Current Offices and Honorary Posts Sec. to edit. board, *NEHA-Bull.*.

Fields of Expertise *Industry Fields:*

public admin. and defence; insurance, banking, finance. *Bus. Dimensions:* co. finance and accounting; co. culture. *Scope:* national; internat. *Period:* eighteenth century; nineteenth century; early twentieth century; inter-war years, 1919–39. *Teaching:* undergrad.; post grad. *Consultancy:* co. hist.

Publications *Articles:* 'Koopman op een dwaalspoor. De Seehafen-ausnahmetarife in de betrekkingen tusen Nederland en Duitsland aan het begin van de jaren twintig', *Jaarboek van het ministerie van Buitenlandse Zaken 1988–1989*, Den Haag, 1989, 181–201; 'Lachspiegel van de vooruit-gant, het historiografische beeld van de Nederlandse industriefinanciering in de negentiende eeuw', *NEHA-Bull.*, 5, 1991, 5–23; 'Sinecures or Sinews of Power? Interlocking Directorships and Bank-Industry Relations in the Netherlands, 1910–1940', *Econ. & Soc. Hist. in the Netherlands*, 3, 1991, 119–32; 'Kassierspapier', *Gids van de papiergeldverzameling van het Nederlandsch Economisch-Historisch Archief*, J. Lucassen ed., Amsterdam, 1992, 107–20.

Just, Flemming

Assoc. Prof., Dept. of Co-operative & Agric. Research, South Jutland Univ. Centre, Niels Bohrs Vej 9, DK-6700 Esbjerg, Denmark. Tel.: 45 79 14 11 11. Fax: 45 79 14 11 99.

Year and Place of Birth 1957, Grimstrup, Denmark.

Degrees and Qualifications MA (Hist.) Aarhus Univ., 1982; Dr.Phil. Aarhus Univ., 1992.

Previous Post Research Fellow, Danish Research Council for Humanities, 1989–92.

Fields of Expertise *Industry Fields:* agric., forestry, fishing. *Bus. Dimensions:* bus.–state relations. *Scope:* national; internat. *Period:*

twentieth century as a whole. *Teaching:* post grad.; courses. *Consultancy:* co. hist.

Publications *Books: Banen fri for fremtiden* [The Struggle for Co-operative Legislation 1909–1917], Esbjerg, South Jutland Univ. Press, 1986; *Co-operatives and Farmers' Unions in Western Europe*, ed., Esbjerg, South Jutland Univ. Press, 1990; *Landbruget, staten og eksporten 1930–1950* [Agric., the State and Exports, 1930–1950], dissertation, Esbjerg, South Jutland Univ. Press, 1992. *Articles:* 'La gestion d'une agric. intensive', *Les syndicats agricoles en Europe*, Bertrand Hervieau & Rose-Marie Lagrave eds., Paris, Editions l'Harmattan, 1992, 49–71; 'Agriculture and Corporatism in Scandinavia', *Critical Perspectives on Rural Change*, Philip Lowe & Terry Marsden eds., vol. 5, London, David Fulton Pub. Ltd.

Kaczynska, Elzbieta

Warsaw Univ., Inst. of Applied Social Sciences, PL-00-046 Nowy Swiat 69, Warsaw, Poland. Tel.: 48 22 26 21 84. Fax: 48 22 26 21 84.

Year and Place of Birth 1934, Warsaw, Poland.

Degrees and Qualifications Magister Warsaw Univ., 1955; Doktor Warsaw Univ., 1962; Doktor (Sc.) Warsaw Univ., 1973; Titular Prof., 1986.

Previous Post Prof., Inst. of Sciences, Polish Acad. of Sciences, 1978–92.

Major Honours Five prizes (1st & 2nd degree) from Polish Ministry of Science & Education; Prize, Polish Acad. of Sciences.

Fields of Expertise *Industry Fields:* mining and quarrying; coal and petroleum products; metal manufacture; mechanical engineering; metal goods .

Bus. *Dimensions:* production management; co. finance and accounting; bus. and technology; small bus. matters. *Period:* nineteenth century until World War I. *Teaching:* undergrad.; post grad. *Consultancy:* co. hist.; social relations in the factory.

Publications *Books: Dzieje Robotników Przemyslowych w Polsce pod Zaborami* [Hist. of Polish Indust. Workers in Partitioned Poland], Warsaw, 1970; *Polska Klasa Robotnicza - Studia Historyczne* [The Polish Working Class - Hist. Studies], ed., vol. X., Warsaw, 1983. *Articles:* 'Tkacze w Ydunskiej Woli i Turku w Koncu XIX Wieku' [Weavers in Zdunska Wola and Turek at the end of the XIX Century], *Spoloczenstwo Królestwa Polskiego* [The Soc. in Kingdom of Poland], W. Kula ed., Warsaw, 1968, 337–96; 'Sila Robocza w Przemysle ciezkim Królestwa Polskiego 1870–1900' [The Labour Force in heavy Industry in the Kingdom of Poland], *Polska Klasa Robotnicza* [The Polish Working Class], S. Kalabinski ed., vol. I, Warsaw, 1970, 92–148; 'Bürgertum und städtische Eliten', *Bürgertum im 19. Jahrhundert*, J. Kocka ed., Munich, vol. III, 1988, 466–88.

Kaelble, Hartmut

Prof. of Social Hist., Inst. of Hist., Unter den Linden 6, 10099 Berlin, Germany. Tel.: 49 30 2093 2236. Fax: 49 30 2093 2797.

Year and Place of Birth 1940, Germany.

Degrees and Qualifications Dr.Phil. Free Univ. of Berlin, 1966; Habilitation Free Univ. of Berlin, 1971.

Previous Post Prof. of Social Hist., Free Univ. of Berlin, 1971–91.

Fields of Expertise *Industry Fields:* . *Bus. Dimensions:* entrepreneurs and entrepreneurship. *Scope:* internat. *Period:* nineteenth century; twentieth century as a whole. *Teaching:* undergrad.; post grad.

Publications *Books: Social Mobility in the 19th and 20th Centuries: Europe and Amer. in Comparative Perspective*, Berg Publishers, Leamington Spa, 1985; *Industrialisation and Social Inequality in 19th Century Europe*, Berg Publishers, Leamington Spa, 1986; *A Social Hist. of Western Europe, 1880–1980*, Gill & Macmillan/Savage, Dublin; Barnes & Noble, USA, 1990; *Income Distribution in Hist. Perspective*, with Y.S. Brener & M. Thomas co-eds., CUP, Cambridge, 1991; *Nachbarn am Rhein: Entfremdung und Annäherung der französischen und deutschen Gesellschaft seit 1880* [Neighbours on the Rhine: Divergences and Convergences between French and German Soc., 1880 to the Present], Beck, Munich, 1991.

Kahn, Robert

Pres., Robert Kahn & Assoc.s, POB 249, Lafayette, CA 94549, USA. Tel.: 1 510 254 4434. Fax: 1 510 284 5612.

Year and Place of Birth 1918, Oakland, USA.

Degrees and Qualifications BA Stanford Univ., 1938; MBA Harvard Bus. School, 1940; Hon. LL D Franklin Pierce College, 1977.

Current Offices and Honorary Posts Ed. & pub., *Retailing Today*.

Major Honours First Award for Outstanding Article in *J. of Management Consulting*.

Fields of Expertise *Industry Fields:* distributive trades; retailing. *Bus. Dimensions:* co. admin. *Scope:* internat. *Period:* twentieth century as a whole. *Consultancy:* corporate strategy.

Kajimoto, Motonobu

Asst. Prof., Fac. of Econ., Tezukayama Univ., 7-1-1 Tezukayama Nara City, Nara Prefecture, Japan. Tel.: 0742 45 4701. Fax: 0742 48 9811.

Year and Place of Birth 1948, Itami City, Japan.

Degrees and Qualifications BA Kansai Univ., 1971; MA Kansai Univ., 1973.

Fields of Expertise *Industry Fields:* transport and communication. *Bus. Dimensions:* Econ. development and transport. *Scope:* regional; global. *Period:* nineteenth century; twentieth century as a whole; early twentieth century; inter-war years, 1919–39. *Teaching:* undergrad.

Publications *Articles:* 'Minami Wales seikitan yushutsu to igirisu kaiungyo no hatten' [South Wales Coal Exports and the Development of British Shipping], *Econ. Rev. of Kansai Univ.*, 39(2), 1989; 'Jyukyuseikinakaba niokeru Minami Wales no unga to tetsudo' [A Welsh Canal and a Railway in the mid-19th Century], *Senriyama Keizaigaku*, 23(1.2), 1990; 'Jyukyuseiki Kouhan Minami Wales ni okeru Tetsudo to Sekitan Yuso no Hatten' [Railways and the Development of Coal Transport in late 19th Century South Wales], *Tezukayama Econ. Papers*, 1, 1992; 'Cardiff Kaiungyo no hatten 1870-1910' [A Study of the Development of Cardiff Shipping 1870-1910], *Econ. Rev. of Kansai Univ.*, 42(6), 1993.

Kaku, Sachio

Prof., Fac. of Econ., Hokkaido Univ., Kita 9 Nishi 7, Kitaku, Sapporo 063, Japan. Tel.: 011 716 2111. Fax: 011 747 8849.

Year and Place of Birth 1944, Tokyo, Japan.

Degrees and Qualifications BA (Econ.) Kyoto Univ., 1976; MA (Econ.) Tokyo Univ., 1970; Ph.D. (Econ.) Tokyo Univ., 1987.

Previous Post Assoc. Prof., Fac. of Econ., Shiga Univ., 1976–9.

Current Offices and Honorary Posts Mem. of edit. com., Bus. Hist. Soc. of Japan, 1987–90.

Fields of Expertise *Industry Fields:* chemicals and allied industries. *Bus. Dimensions:* entrepreneurs and entrepreneurship; co. finance and accounting; personnel management; research and development; bus. organization; bus. and technology; management education. *Scope:* regional; national; internat.; Germany. *Period:* nineteenth century; twentieth century as a whole. *Teaching:* undergrad.; post grad.

Publications *Books: Doitsu Kagaku Kogyoushi Josetsu* [An Introduction to the Hist. of the German Chemical Industry], Minerva Press, 1986. *Articles:* 'The Development and Structure of the German Coal-tar Dyestuffs Firms', *Development and Diffusion of Technology (The Internat. Conf. on Bus. Hist. 6)*, A. Okochi & H. Uchida eds., Tokyo Univ. Press, 1980, 77–94; 'Die finanzielle Entwicklung der deutschen Teerfarbenunternehmen in den Jahren von 1880 bis 1913', *Scripta Mercaturae*, 23 Jg., Heft 1/2, 1989, 132–66.

Karonen, Petri K.

Asst., Dept. of Hist., Jyväskylä Univ., Seminaarinkatu 15, 40100 Jyväskylä, Finland. Tel.: 358 41 601254. Fax: 358 41 601251.

Year and Place of Birth 1966, Hämeenlinna, Finland

Degrees and Qualifications BA, 1991; L., 1993.

Fields of Expertise *Industry Fields:* paper, printing, publishing; transport and communication. *Bus. Dimensions:*

bus. and technology; bus.–state relations; bus. values. *Scope:* national; internat. *Period:* mid-twentieth century, 1940–70; late twentieth century, 1970–present. *Teaching:* undergrad.

Publications *Books: Enso-Gutzeit Oy laivanvarustajana: Oy Finnlines Ltd ja Merivienti Oy vuosina 1947–1982. Enso-Gutzeit Oy. Historia - ja Perinnejulkaisuja 9.* [Enso-Gutzeit Oy as a Shipowner. Oy Finnlines Ltd and Merivienti Oy, 1947–1982], Imatra, 1992.

Karsten, Luchien

Sen. Lect., Fac. of Management and Organisation, Univ. of Groningen, POB 800, 9700 AV Groningen, Netherlands. Tel.: 31 50 633848. Fax: 31 50 633850.

Year and Place of Birth 1947, Groningen, Netherlands.

Degrees and Qualifications M.Econ. Groningen Univ., 1977; DEA Ecole des Hautes Etudes, Paris, 1978; M.Phil. Groningen Univ., 1980; Ph.D. (Hist.) Groningen Univ., 1989.

Current Offices and Honorary Posts Project Manager for co-operation with the Econ. Dept. of Ouagadougou Univ., Burkina Faso.

Fields of Expertise *Industry Fields:* paper, printing, publishing. *Bus. Dimensions:* entrepreneurs and entrepreneurship; personnel management; management education; organisations and time. *Scope:* internat. *Period:* nineteenth century; twentieth century as a whole. *Teaching:* undergrad.; post grad. *Consultancy:* management and time.

Publications *Books: De 8 Urendag* [The Eight Hour Day, the Hist. of Shortening Labour Time 1817–1919], IISH (internat. Inst. of Social Hist.) Studies & Essays no. 14, Amsterdam, 1990. *Articles:* 'Academic Management Education in the Netherlands', *Management Studies in an Academic Context*, with H. de Man co-auth., L. Engwall ed., Uppsala, 1993.

Katoh, Kozaburo

Prof.; Fac. of Econ., Senshu Univ., 2-1-1 Higahsi-Mita, Tama Ward, Kawasaki City, Kanagawa Pref. 214, Japan. Tel.: 81 44 911 1034/81 44 911 1266. Fax: 81 44 911 1299.

Year and Place of Birth 1930, Tokyo, Japan.

Degrees and Qualifications BA Tokyo Univ. of Education, 1953; MA Tokyo Univ. of Education, 1955.

Previous Post Asst. Prof., Fac. of Econ., Senshu Univ., 1966–72.

Current Offices and Honorary Posts Council mem., Bus. Hist. Soc. of Japan; exec. mem., Agrarian Hist. Soc., 1990–3; council mem., Socio-econ. Hist. Soc., 1991–3.

Fields of Expertise *Industry Fields:* agric., forestry, fishing; mining and quarrying; coal and petroleum products; textiles; clothing and footwear. *Bus. Dimensions:* co. finance and accounting; multinational bus.; markets and bus. *Scope:* regional; internat. *Period:* nineteenth century; twentieth century as a whole; early twentieth century; inter-war years, 1919–39; mid-twentieth century, 1940–70. *Teaching:* undergrad.; post grad. *Consultancy:* co. hist.

Publications *Books: Sen-i* [Japanese Textile Industry in Pre-Wartime Japan], with M. Kaji Nishi et al. co-eds., Koujyunsha Press, 1964, (in Japanese). *Articles:* 'Zaibatsu-Shinon' [Formation of a Finance Capital in the Meiji Period], *Study of the Japanese Indust. Revolution (1)*, with K. Ohishi, Tokyo Univ. Press, 1975, 219–89 (in Japanese); 'Yamonobe Tako to Kindaiteki Boseki-gyo' [Yaman obe Takeo, Founder of the Toyo Spinning Co. and the Modern Japanese Cotton Spinning Industry in the Meiji Era], *Koza Nihon Gijutsu no Shakaishi,*

Bekkan 2 [Social Hist. of Japanese Technology], K. Nagahara & K. Yamaguchi eds., Nihon-hyouronsha, 1986, 189–218 (in Japanese); 'G. wagunero to Shokusan - Kogyo no Ninaitetachi' [G. Wagner and Tragers of Japanese Indust. Policy in the early Meiji Period], *Koza Nihon Gijutsu no Shakaishi, Bekkan 2* [Social Hist. of Japanese Technology], K. Nagahara & K. Yamaguchi eds., Nihon-hyouronsha, 1986, 63–90 (in Japanese).

Katz, Jorge M.

Regional Advisor on Indust. and Technological Development, Production, Productivity & Management Division, ECLAC, Casilla 179–D, Santiago, Chile. Tel.: 56 2 2085051. Fax: 56 2 2080252.

Year and Place of Birth 1940, Buenos Aires, Argentina.

Degrees and Qualifications Licendiado en Economia, Univ. of Buenos Aires, 1964; D.Phil. (Econ.) Oxford Univ., 1968.

Previous Post Prof. of Indust. Econ., Univ. of Buenos Aires, 1975–1992.

Current Offices and Honorary Posts Sen. Research Fellow, National Research Council, Buenos Aires.

Fields of Expertise *Industry Fields:* indust. organization in general. *Bus. Dimensions:* research and development; bus. organization; bus. and technology; co. culture. *Scope:* regional; Argentina; Latin Amer. in general. *Period:* twentieth century as a whole; mid-twentieth century, 1940–70; late twentieth century, 1970–present. *Teaching:* undergrad.; post grad. *Consultancy:* corporate strategy.

Publications *Books: Production Functions, Foreign Investment and Growth*, North Holland Publishing Co., Amsterdam, 1969; *Importación de Tecnología, Aprendizaje e Industrialización Dependiente*, Fondo

de Cultura Económica, México, 1976; *Technology Generation in Latin Amer. Manufacturing Industries*, Macmillan, London, 1987; *Biotecnología y Economía - Estudios del Caso Argentino*, with Néstor Bercovich co-auth., Centro Ed. de América Latina, 1990; *Estructura y Comportamiento de las Mercados Principales de la Salud*, prelim. title, with Hugo Arce y Alberto Muñoz co-auth., fondo de Cultura Económica, Buenos Aires, 1993.

Katzenellenbogen, Simon E.

Senior Lect. in Econ. Hist., Dept. of Hist., Univ. of Manchester, Oxford Road, Manchester, M13 9PL, UK. Tel.: 44 61 275 3112. Fax: 44 61 275 3098.

Year and Place of Birth 1939, Trenton, USA.

Degrees and Qualifications BA Michigan Univ., Ann Arbor, 1961; D.Phil., Oxford Univ., 1969.

Previous Post Research Fellow, Dept. of Econ. Hist., Leicester Univ., 1968–70.

Current Offices and Honorary Posts Hon. sec., Third World Econ. Hist. & Development Group; asst. sec., Manchester Assoc. of Univ. Teachers.

Fields of Expertise *Industry Fields:* mining and quarrying; transport and communication; mining finance. *Bus. Dimensions:* entrepreneurs and entrepreneurship; co. finance and accounting; multinational bus. *Scope:* internat.; global; South Africa and others. *Period:* nineteenth century; twentieth century as a whole. *Teaching:* undergrad.; post grad.

Publications *Books: Railways and the Copper Mines of Katzanga*, Oxford Studies in African Affairs, Clarendon Press, 1973; *South Africa and Mozambique: Labour Railways and Trade in the Making of a Relationship,*

Manchester Univ. Press, 1983. *Articles:* 'British Bus.men in German Africa', *Great Britain and her World, 1750–1914*, B.M. Ratcliffe ed., Manchester Univ. Press, 1975, 237–62; 'Cyanide and Bubbles: Patents and Technological Change in Gold and non-Ferrous Metals Treatment', *Sozialgeschichte des Bergbaus im 19. und 20. Jahrhundert*, Klaus Tenfelde ed., C.H. Beck, 1992, 519–37; 'Southern African Mining Interests in Australia befoe 1939', *Bus. Hist.*, 32(3), July, 1993, 120–32.

Kaufhold, Karl Heinrich

Inst. for Econ. and Social Hist., Göttingen Univ., Platz der Göttinger Sieben 3, 37073 Göttingen, Germany. Tel.: 49 551 397236.

Year and Place of Birth 1932, Hildesheim, Germany.

Degrees and Qualifications Dr.rer.pol., 1968; Habilitation (Econ. & Social Hist.), 1973.

Current Offices and Honorary Posts Vice-chairman, Econ. & Soc. Hist. Assoc.; scientific advisory mem., Bus. Hist. Soc.

Fields of Expertise *Industry Fields:* mining and quarrying. *Bus. Dimensions:* entrepreneurs and entrepreneurship. *Scope:* national. *Period:* early modern. *Teaching:* post grad. *Consultancy:* co. hist.

Publications *Books: Das Gewerbe in Preußen um 1800*, Schwartz, 1978; *Das Handwerk der Stadt Hildesheim im 18. Jh.*, 2 edn., Schwartz, 1980; *Statistik des preußischen Berg-, Hütten- und Salinenwesens vor 1850*, with W. Sachse, Scripta Mercaturae, 1989; *Aufgaben und Entwicklung der preis- und lohngeschichtlichen Forschung in Deutschland*, Vandenhoeck & Ruprecht, 1991; *Bergbau und Hüttenwesen im und am Harz*, ed., Hahn, 1992.

Kawabe, Nobuo

Prof. of Bus. Hist., School of Commerce, Waseda Univ., 1-6-1 Nishiwaseda, Shinjukuku, Tokyo 169–50, Japan. Tel.: 81 3 3203 4141. Fax: 81 3 3203 0874.

Year and Place of Birth 1945, Mihara, Japan.

Degrees and Qualifications BA Waseda Univ., 1969; MA Waseda Univ., 1972; Ph.D. Waseda Univ., 1976; Ph.D. Ohio State Univ., 1980.

Previous Post Assoc. Prof., Fac. of Integrated Arts & Sciences, Hiroshima Univ., 1982–90.

Current Offices and Honorary Posts Standing mem., Board of Trustees, Bus. Hist. Soc. of Japan.

Fields of Expertise *Industry Fields:* distributive trades. *Bus. Dimensions:* multinational bus. *Scope:* global. *Period:* twentieth century as a whole. *Teaching:* undergrad.; post grad. *Consultancy:* co. hist.

Publications *Books: Education and Training in the Development of Modern Corporations*, with Eisuke Daito co-ed., Univ. of Tokyo Press, 1993. *Articles:* 'The Development of Overseas Operations by General Trading Companies, 1868–1945', *Bus. Hist. of Trading Companies*, Shin'ichi Yonekawa & Hideki Yoshihara eds., Univ. of Tokyo Press, 1987; 'Japanese Bus. in the United States before World War II', *Hist. Studies in Internat. Corporate Bus.*, Alice Teichova et al. eds., CUP, 1989; 'Overseas Activities and their Organization', *General Trading Companies*, Shin'ichi Yonekawa ed., United Nations Universities, 1990; 'Problems of and Perspectives on Japanese Management in Malaysia', *Japanese Bus. in ASEAN*, Shoichi Yamashita ed., Univ. of Tokyo Press, 1991.

Kawamura, Terumasa

Asst. Prof., Fac. of Commerce, Senshu Univ., Higashimita 2-1-1, Tama-ku, Kawasaki-shi, Japan. Tel.: 044 911. Fax: 044 911 1231.
Year and Place of Birth 1946, Shiga-ken, Japan.
Degrees and Qualifications BA (Commerce), Waseda Univ., 1969; MA (Commerce), Waseda Univ., 1975.
Fields of Expertise *Industry Fields:* textiles. *Bus. Dimensions:* entrepreneurs and entrepreneurship; production management; co. finance and accounting; co. admin.; marketing. *Scope:* local; regional. *Period:* early modern; eighteenth century; nineteenth century; early twentieth century. *Teaching:* undergrad.
Publications *Articles:* 'Bakumatsu-ki no Ashikaga-machi' [A Study of the Social Structure of Ashikaga town in the Bakumatsu Era], *Chihishi Kenkyu*, 167, 1980; 'Bakumatsu - Meiji Shonen ni okeru Motobata Keiei no Doukou' [A Study of the Operation of a Clothier in the Ashikaga District in the Bakumatsu and early Meiji Era], *Senshu Shogaku Ronshu* [Commercial Rev. of Senshu Univ.], 41, 1986; 'Meiji-ki Motobata Keiei ni okeru Shushi Kouzou ni kansuru Ichi Kensatsu' [Analysis of the Income and Expenditure of a Clothier in the Meiji Era], *Senshu Shogaku Ronshu* [Commercial Rev. of Senshu Univ.], 43, 1987; 'Meiji Shonen Kiryu Kinuori Sanchi ni okeru Shakaiteki Bungyo no Tenkai ni tuite' [A Study of the Social Division of Labour in the Kiryu District in the early Meiji Era], *Senshu Daigaku Shogaku Kenkyushoho* [Occasional Papers of the Inst. for Commercial Sciences], 83, 1991; 'Orimono Sanchi no Kakaeru Shomondai' [Difficulties of the Weaving Industry in the Change of National Indust. Structure : A Case Study of Kiryu District], *Shogaku*

Kenkyu Nenpou [The Annual Bull. of Commercial Sciences], 17, 1992.

Kawanami, Yoichi

Assoc. Prof., Fac. of Econ., Kyushu Univ., 6-19-1 Hakozaki, Higashi-ku, Fukuoka 812, Japan. Tel.: 81 92 641 1101. Fax: 81 92 632 1157.
Year and Place of Birth 1951, Amagi, Japan.
Degrees and Qualifications BA Kyushu Univ., 1976; M.Econ. Kyushu Univ., 1976.
Previous Post Asst., Fac. of Econ., Kyushu Univ., 1981-3.
Fields of Expertise *Industry Fields:* insurance, banking, finance,. *Bus. Dimensions:* co. finance and accounting. *Scope:* internat. *Period:* interwar years, 1919-39; mid-twentieth century, 1940-70. *Teaching:* undergrad.; post grad. *Consultancy:* co. hist.
Publications *Articles:* 'Financial Innovation and "Market Forces"', *J. of Econ.*, 52(1-4), Oct., 1987, Kyushu Univ., 211-33; 'The Process of Inroads into Retail Banking by Amer. Commercial Banks: An Aspect of Penetration of Bank Credit under the Managed Currency System (1) (2) (3)', *Securities Economy, The Japan Institute of Securities Economy*, 173, Sept., 1990, 97-120; 'Credit Extension and the Development of Collateral System: Hist. Development of Bus. Loans by Amer. Commercial Banks (1)', *J. of Econ.*, 56(6), Kyushu Univ.; 'Genesis of Consumer Installment Credit and the Finance Co.', *J. of Econ.*, 56(1-2), Mar., 1991, Kyushu Univ., 221-50; 'Two Concepts of "Money-Capital and Real-Capital" Marx and Veblen', *J. of Econ.*, 58(1), Sept., 1992, Kyushu Univ., 49-68.

Kawano, Aizaburo

Lect., Fac. of Commerce, Kumamoto Univ. of Commerce, 2-5-1 Oe Kumamoto 862, , Japan. Tel.: 096 364 5161. Fax: 096 363 1289.

Year and Place of Birth 1955, Kyoto, Japan.

Degrees and Qualifications BA (Econ.) Doshisha Univ., 1978; MA (Commerce) Doshisha Univ., 1985.

Fields of Expertise *Industry Fields:* insurance, banking, finance,. *Bus. Dimensions:* entrepreneurs and entrepreneurship. *Scope:* local. *Period:* early twentieth century. *Teaching:* undergrad.

Publications *Articles:* 'Mitsui Ginko no Keieiseisaku ni kansuru ichikosatsu' [A Study of the Management Policy of the Mitsui Bank], *Doshisha Grad. Students Bus. Rev.*, 20, 1985; 'Hayakawa Jidai ni okeru Mitsui Ginko shuyo eigyoten no kosatsu' [A Study of the Major Offices of the Mitsui Bank], *Doshisha Grad. Students Bus. Rev.*, 21, 1986; 'Hayakawa Jidai ni okeru Mitsui Ginko chiho shiten' [Local Branches of the Mitsui Bank under Hayakawa], *The Social Sciences*, 41, Doshiha Univ., 1988.

Kazusa, Yasuyuki

Prof. of Accounting, Soc. of Commerce, Meijo Univ., 1-501 Shiogamaguchi Tenpaku-ku, Nagoya 468, Japan. Tel.: 052 832 1151. Fax: 052 833 4767.

Year and Place of Birth 1944, Hyougo, Japan.

Degrees and Qualifications BA Ritsumeikan Univ., 1972; Ph.D. Kyoto Univ.

Major Honours Dexter Prize (Accounting Hist. Assoc.), 1989.

Fields of Expertise *Industry Fields:* food, drink, tobacco; chemicals and allied industries; mechanical engineering; electrical engineering; textiles; transport and communication; electronics and computers: manufacture. *Bus. Dimensions:* co. finance and accounting; co. admin.; merger movement and issues. *Scope:* national; USA. *Period:* nineteenth century; twentieth century as a whole. *Teaching:* undergrad.; post grad.

Publications *Books: Amer. Kanri Kaikei Shi* [A Hist. of Management Accounting in the USA], Dhobunkan, Tokyo, 1989, 2 vols. *Articles:* '1950 Nendai ni okeru General Electric Co. no Yosankanri, Kaikeishi Gakkainenpou' [The Budgetary Control of the General Electric Co. in the 1950's: A Typical Case of Participative Budgeting], *Hist. Assoc. Accounting Year Book*, 4, 1985, 21–35; 'Short-term Profit Management Using Marginal Income in Amer. Big Bus.: A Case of Direct Costing Practice in the 1950's', *J. of Commerce & Econ.*, Meijo Univ., 77(2), 1987, 38–63; 'Railroad Accounting of Amer. Railroads in the 1850's', *J. of Commerce & Econ.*, Meijo Univ., 78(1), 1988, 90–132.

Keenan, Michael G.

Sen. Lect., Dept. of Accounting and Finance, Univ. of Auckland, Private Bag 92019, Auckland 1, New Zealand. Tel.: 64 9 3737599. Fax: 64 9 3737406.

Year and Place of Birth 1945, Auckland, New Zealand.

Degrees and Qualifications BA Auckland Univ., 1967; B.Com. Auckland Univ., 1976; MA Auckland Univ., 1969; Dip.Val. Auckland Univ., 1982; Ph.D. St Andrews Univ., 1977.

Previous Post Temp. Lect., Dept. of Philo., Auckland Univ., 1978–82.

Current Offices and Honorary Posts Sub-dean, Fac. of Commerce, Auckland Univ.; Book Rev. Ed., *Pacific*

Accounting Rev..

Fields of Expertise *Industry Fields:* gas, electricity, water. *Bus. Dimensions:* strategy formation. *Scope:* regional. *Period:* nineteenth century. *Teaching:* post grad. *Consultancy:* corporate strategy.

Publications *Articles:* 'Interest Group Lobbying on Accounting Standards: Some Internat. Evidence for a Unifying Hypothesis', *Pacific Accounting Rev.*, 4(1), 1992, 97–114.

Kelly, Eileen P.

Chair of Management Dept., Ithaca College, School of Bus., Ithaca, NY 14850, USA. Tel.: 1 607 274 3341. Fax: 1 607 274 1137.

Year and Place of Birth 1955, USA.

Degrees and Qualifications BS College of Steubenville, 1978; MA Cincinnati Univ., 1979; Ph.D. Cincinnati Univ., 1982.

Previous Post Chair of Management & Marketing Dept., College of Bus. Admin., Louisiana State Univ. in Shreveport, 1988–93.

Current Offices and Honorary Posts Program Chair & Pres. Elect, Management Hist. Division of the National Acad. of Management.

Fields of Expertise *Industry Fields:* bus. services. *Bus. Dimensions:* personnel management. *Scope:* national. *Period:* nineteenth century; twentieth century as a whole. *Teaching:* undergrad.; post grad. *Consultancy:* co. hist.

Publications *Articles:* 'Employee Ownership and Indust. Democracy: The Pursuit of Free Enterprise', *Proteus*, vol. 5, 1988, 18–22; 'Managing Customer-Broker Conflict in the Securities Industry', *Internat. J. of Conflict Management*, vol. 1, 1990, 281–92; 'Ethical and Legal Perspectives on the Use of Arbitration in the Securities Industry', *Creighton Law Rev.*, vol. 25, 1992, 1311–32; 'Sex-stereotyping in the Workplace: A Manager's Guide', *Bus. Horizons*, 36, 1993, 25–31; 'Worker Ownership in the United States: An Emergent Response to Cultural Forces', *Internat. J. of Public Admin.*, 16(3), 1993, 325–40.

Kemmerer, Donald L.

Prof. of Econ. Emeritus, 1006 W. Armory Avenue, Champaign, IL 61821, , USA. Tel.: 1 217 352 2632.

Year and Place of Birth 1905, Manila; Philippines.

Degrees and Qualifications BA (Econ.) Princeton Univ., 1927; MA (Amer. Hist.) Princeton Univ., 1931; Ph.D. (Hist.) Princeton Univ., 1934.

Previous Post Prof. of Econ. Hist., Univ. of Illinois, 1937–73.

Current Offices and Honorary Posts 2nd. Vice-Pres., Midwest Econ. Assoc., 1952; Pres., Bus. Hist. Conf., 1956; Pres., Economists Nat. Com. on Monetary Policy, 1967–70; Pres., Com. on Monetary Research & Education, 1970–80.

Fields of Expertise *Industry Fields:* banking; monetary history. *Bus. Dimensions:* monetary stability; capital creation. *Scope:* national; internat. *Period:* eighteenth century; nineteenth century; twentieth century as a whole. *Teaching:* undergrad.; post grad. *Consultancy:* investment by mutual funds.

Publications *Books: ABC of the Federal Reserve System*, with E.W. Kemmerer, Harper & Bros., New York, 1950; *Amer. Econ. Hist.*, with C. Clyde Jones, McGraw-Hill Book Co., New York, 1959; *The Life of John E. Rovensky, Banker and Industrialist*, Stipes Pub. Co., Champaign, Illinois, 1977; *The Life and Times of Edwin Walter Kemmerer,*

1875–1945 and how he became an Internat. Money Doctor, Stipes Pub. Co., 1993. Articles: 'A Hist. of Paper Money in Colonial New Jersey, 1668–1775', Proceedings of the New Jersey Hist. Soc., LXXIV, 1956, 107–44.

Kennedy, Charles J.

Pres., Chas. Kennedy Archives, Chas. Kennedy Archives, 6335 0 St, Unit 240, Lincoln, NE 68510, USA. Tel.: 1 402 486 2381. Fax: 1 402 486 2456.

Year and Place of Birth 1911, Homestead, USA.

Degrees and Qualifications BA Hastings Univ., 1933; MA Nebraska Univ., 1936; Ph.D. Wisconsin Univ., 1940.

Previous Post Prof. of Econ. & Bus. Hist., Nebraska-Lincoln Univ., 1946–82.

Current Offices and Honorary Posts Pres. & treasurer, Econ. & Bus. Hist. Assoc.s (and sub-division Ebha Press); pres. & ed., Midwest United Church of Christ Historians.

Major Honours Distinguished Teaching Award, College of Bus. Admin., Nebraska-Lincoln Univ., 1977; annual award in honour of Charles Kennedy for best paper read at Econ. & Bus. Hist. Soc. conferred by the society annually, (since 1977).

Fields of Expertise Industry Fields: transport and communication. Bus. Dimensions: measuring demonstrated top management ability. Scope: national; USA. Period: nineteenth century. Teaching: undergrad.; post grad. Consultancy: co. hist.

Publications Books: Chapters on the Hist. of the Boston and Maine Railroad System, 2 vols., CBA, Nebraska, 1978–80; A New Approach to the Hist. of the Amer. Bus. System, CBA, Nebraska, 1979; Lectures on the Hist. of the Amer. Bus. System, vol. I,

CBA, Nebraska, 1979, 1981; The Technique of Appraising Entrepreneurial and Managerial Ability in Railroad Hist., essay, Nebraska, 1974; revised as first essay in Railroad Hist.: Essays on Entrepreneurial Ability and Performance by C.J. Kennedy et al., Ebha Press, 1993.

Kerr, K. Austin

Prof. of Hist., Dept. of Hist., Ohio State Univ., 230 W 17th Avenue, Columbus, OH 43210, USA. Tel.: 1 614 292 2674. Fax: 1 614 292 2282.

Year and Place of Birth 1938, St Louis, USA.

Degrees and Qualifications BA Oberlin College, 1959; MA Iowa Univ., 1960; Ph.D. Pittsburgh Univ., 1965.

Previous Post Ohio State Univ. Fac., 1965–93.

Current Offices and Honorary Posts Pres., Bus. Hist. Conf.

Fields of Expertise Industry Fields: food, drink, tobacco; chemicals and allied industries. Bus. Dimensions: bus.–state relations. Scope: national. Period: twentieth century as a whole. Teaching: undergrad.; post grad. Consultancy: co. hist.

Publications Books: Amer. Railroad Polit., 1914–1920, Pittsburgh Univ. Press, 1965; Organized for Reform: A New Hist. of the Anti-saloon League, Yale Univ. Press, 1985; Bus. Enterprise in Amer. Hist., 3rd edn., Houghton Miflin, forthcoming; Local Bus.es, Amer. Assoc. for State and Local Hist., 1990; Hist. Perspectives on Bus. Enterprise, ed., Ohio State Univ. Press, 1990, on-going series.

Khan, Zorina B.

Asst. Prof. Finance Group, 413 Hayden Hall, College of Bus., Northeastern Univ., Boston, MA 02115, USA. Tel.: 0617 373 4707. Fax: 0617 373 8798.
Year and Place of Birth 1959, Guyana.
Degrees and Qualifications B.Sc. (Econ. & Stats.) Univ. of Surrey, UK, 1981; MA (Econ.) McMaster Univ., Canada, 1982; Ph.D. (Econ.) Univ. of California, 1991.
Previous Post Lect. in Bus. Admin., Amer. College, Los Angeles, 1988–90.
Major Honours Fulbright Scholarship.
Fields of Expertise *Industry Fields:* insurance, banking, finance. *Bus. Dimensions:* bus. and technology. *Scope:* national; USA. *Period:* nineteenth century. *Teaching:* post grad.; MBA. *Consultancy:* co. hist.
Publications *Articles:* 'The Democratization of Invention during early Industrialization', *J. of Econ. Hist.*, L(2), June, 1990, 363–78; '"Schemes of Practical Utility": Entrepreneurship and Innovation among "Great Inventors" in the US', *J. of Econ. Hist.*, LIII(2) June, 1993; 'Entrepreneurship and Technological Change in Hist. Perspective', *Research in Entrepreneurship & Innovation*, forthcoming, 1993.

Kiesewetter, Hubert

Prof. of Econ. & Social Hist., Catholic Univ. of Eichstätt, Ostenstraße 26–28, D-39596 Eichstätt, Germany. Tel.: 49 84 21 20 505. Fax: 49 84 21 20 365.
Year and Place of Birth 1939, Dessau, Germany.
Degrees and Qualifications Ph.D. Heidelberg Univ., 1973; Habilitation Free Univ. Berlin, 1985.

Previous Post German Visiting Fellow, St Antony's College, Oxford Univ., 1989–90.
Fields of Expertise *Industry Fields:* other manufacturing industries. *Bus. Dimensions:* entrepreneurs and entrepreneurship. *Scope:* regional. *Period:* nineteenth century. *Teaching:* post grad.
Publications *Books: Industralisierung und Landwirtschaft*, Böhlau, Cologne/Vienna, 1988, (Mitteldeutsche Forschungen, vol. 94); *Industrielle Revolution in Deutschland 1815–1914*, Suhrkamp, Frankfurt, 1989. *Articles:* 'Econ. Preconditions for Germany's Nation-Building in the Nineteenth Century', *Nation-Building in Central Europe*; 'Region und Nation in der europäischen Industralisierung, 1815–1871', *Deutscher Bund und deutsche Frage 1815–1866*, H. Rumpler ed., Vienna/Munich, 1990, 162–85; 'Competition for Wealth and Power. The Growing Rivalry between Indust. Britain and Indust. Germany', *J. for European Econ. Hist.*, vol. 20, 1991, 271–99.

Kikkawa, Takeo

Prof.; Inst. of Social Sc., Tokyo Univ., 7-3-1 Hongo, Bunkyo, Tokyo 113, Japan. Tel.: 81 3 3812 2111
Year and Place of Birth 1951, Wakayama, Japan.
Degrees and Qualifications BA Tokyo Univ., 1975.
Current Offices and Honorary Posts Sec., Bus. Hist. Soc. of Japan, 1984–7.
Fields of Expertise *Industry Fields:* coal and petroleum products; chemicals and allied industries; gas, electricity, water. *Bus. Dimensions:* entrepreneurs and entrepreneurship; co. finance and accounting; co. law; marketing; bus. organization; bus.–state relations. *Scope:* national; internat. *Period:* twentieth century as a whole.

Teaching: undergrad. *Consultancy:* co. hist.

Publications *Articles:* 'Management and Regulation of the Electric Power Industry in Japan: 1923–1935', *Japanese Yearbook on Bus. Hist.*, 3, Japan Bus. Hist. Inst., 1986; 'On the Rapid Growth of Mitsui Fudosan [the Mitsui Real Estate Development Co.], *Aoyama Bus. Rev.*, 12, Aoyama Gakuin Univ., 1986; 'How and Why did Sogo Shosha [General Trading Companies] Develop in Japan? Rev. Essay on the Thirteenth internat. Conf. on Bus. History', *Aoyama Bus. Rev.*, 13, Aoyama Gakuin Univ., 1987; 'Bus. Activities of the Standard-Vacuum Oil Co. in Japan prior to World War II', *Japanese Yearbook on Bus. Hist.*, 7, Japan Bus. Hist. Inst., 1991; 'How did Privatisation Develop in Japan? Comparisons between the Electric Power Industry and the Telecommunications Bus.', *Électricité et Électrification dans le Monde*, Assoc. pour l'Histoire de l'Électricité en France, Paris, 1992.

Publications *Articles:* 'The Provincial Stock Exchanges, 1830–1870', *Econ. Hist. Rev.*, W.A Thomas co-auth., 2nd ser., 23, 1970, 96–111; 'Die industrielle Revolution in den Vereinigten Staaten von Amerika', *Die Vereinigten Staaten von Amerika*, W.P. Adams ed., Fischer Weltgeschichte, Frankfurt, 30, 1977, 1991–1993, 125–83; 'The Transformation of Cotton Marketing in the late Nineteenth Century: Alexander Sprunt and Son of Wilmington N.C., 1884–1956', *The Bus. Hist. Rev.*, 55, 1981, 143–69; 'The Transformation of the Atlantic Economy in the late Nineteenth Century', *Themes in British and Amer. Hist.: A Comparative Approach, c. 1760–1970, Econ. Development in Britain and Amer., 1860–1970*, Open Univ., 1984, 39–46; 'Specialised and General Firms in the Atlantic Cotton Trade, 1820–1980', *Bus. Hist. of General Trading Cos., Internat. Conf. on Bus. Hist.*, S. Yonekawa & H. Yoshihara eds., 13, Univ. of Tokyo Press, Tokyo, 1987, 65–8, 239–66, 271–2.

Killick, John Roper

Lect. in Econ. Hist., School of Bus. and Econ., Leeds Univ., Leeds 2, LS2 9JT, UK. Tel.: 44 532 676808.

Year and Place of Birth 1939, Newquay, UK.

Degrees and Qualifications BA Oxford Univ., 1958; MA Oxford Univ., 1968.

Major Honours Charles W. Ramsdell Award (Southern Hist. Assoc.).

Fields of Expertise *Industry Fields:* textiles; insurance, banking, finance. *Bus. Dimensions:* entrepreneurs and entrepreneurship; multinational bus.; markets and bus. *Scope:* internat.; USA. *Period:* eighteenth century; nineteenth century; twentieth century as a whole. *Teaching:* undergrad.

Kimura, Masato

Assoc. Prof., Fac. of Law & Diplomacy, Kanto Gakuen Univ., 200 Fujiaku, Ohta, 373 Gunma, Japan. Tel.: 0276 31 2718. Fax: 0276 31 2708.

Year and Place of Birth 1952, Kanagawa, Japan.

Degrees and Qualifications BA Keio Univ., 1975; MA Keio Univ., 1977; Ph.D. Keio Univ., 1989.

Current Offices and Honorary Posts Council mem., Japan Assoc. of Internat. Relations.

Fields of Expertise *Industry Fields:* transport and communication; insurance, banking, finance; public admin. and defence. *Bus. Dimensions:* entrepreneurs and entrepreneurship; bus. organization; bus.–state relations. *Scope:* internat. *Period:* twentieth century as a whole; early twentieth century; inter-war years, 1919–39. *Teaching:* undergrad.

Publications *Books: Nichibei Minkan Keizai Gaiko, 1905–1911* [Japan-US non-Governmental Econ. Diplomacy, 1905–1911], Keio Tsushin, 1989; *Shibusawa Ei'ichi: Minkan Keizai Gaiko no Soushisha* [Shibusawa Ei'ichi: A Founder of non-Governmental Econ. Diplomacy, Chuo Koron, 1991. *Articles:* 'Panama Unga Kaitsu (1914) to Nichibei Kankei' [The Opening of the Panama Canal and Japanese-Amer. Relations], *Kindai Nihon Kenkyu* [J. of Modern Japanese Studies], 11, Yamakawa, 1989; 'Nihon no Tai Kanminkankeizai Gaiko' [Japanese non-Governmental Econ. Diplomacy towards South Korea], *Kokusai Seiji* [Internat. Relations], 92, 1989; 'London Kokusai Keizai Kaigi (1933) to Nichibei Kyocho' [The World Monetary and Econ. Conf. of 1933 and Co-operation between Japan and the United States], *Kokusai Seiji* 97, 1991.

King, Frank H.H.

Visiting Prof., Univ. of Reading & Prof. Emeritus, Univ. of Hong Kong, Dept. of Econ., Univ. of Reading, Whiteknights, Reading, Berks, RG6 2AA, , UK. Tel.: 44 865 242102.

Year and Place of Birth 1926, London, UK.

Degrees and Qualifications BA Stanford Univ., 1948; MA Stanford Univ., 1949; BA Oxford Univ., 1952; MA Oxford Univ., 1956; D.Phil. Oxford Univ., 1961.

Previous Post Distinguished Visiting Prof., New Mexico Military Inst., 1989–91.

Current Offices and Honorary Posts

Hon. Research Fellow, Centre of Asian Studies, Honk Kong Univ.

Major Honours Rhodes Scholarship, 1949.

Fields of Expertise *Industry Fields:* insurance, banking, finance,. *Bus. Dimensions:* co. culture. *Scope:* internat. *Period:* nineteenth century; early twentieth century. *Teaching:* undergrad.; secondary school.

Publications *Books: The Hist. of the Hong Kong and Shanghai Banking Corporation*, 4 vols., CUP, 1987–91; *Survey our Empire! A Bio-bibliography of Robert Montgomery Martin 1801(?)–1868*, Centre of Asian Studies, Hong Kong Univ., Hong Kong, 1979; *A Research Guide to China-coast Newspapers, 1822–1911*, Harvard East Asian Studies Center, Cambridge, MA, 1965; *Money and Monetary Policy in China, 1845–1895*, Harvard Univ. Press, Cambridge, MA, 1965; *The New Malayan Nation - A Study of Communalism and Nationalism*, Inst. of Pacific Relations, New York, 1957.

Kipping, Matthias

Management Consultant, Braxton Associés, 113 Avenue Charles de Gaulle, 92200 Neuilly-sur-Seine, , France. Tel.: 33 1 46 37 16 16. Fax: 33 1 46 37 59 90.

Year and Place of Birth 1961, Siegen, Germany.

Degrees and Qualifications Maîtrise d'Histoire, Paris-Sorbonne Univ., 1988; MPA, Harvard Univ., 1990; Dr.Phil. Munich Univ, 1993.

Major Honours German National Scholarship Foundation Mem., 1985–8; John J. McCloy Scholar for two studies at the J.F. Kennedy School of Government, Harvard Univ., 1988–90.

Fields of Expertise *Industry Fields:* vehicle construction. *Bus. Dimensions:* bus.–state relations. *Scope:* internat.

Period: twentieth century as a whole.
Consultancy: corporate strategy.

Publications *Books: Zwischen Kartellen und Konkurrenz. Der Schuman-Plan und die Ursprünge der europäischen Einigung, 1944–52,* German Ph.D. Thesis, forthcoming 1994; *Le Plan Schuman et la Compétitivité de l'Industrie Française,* Entreprises et Histoire; 5, forthcoming 1993. *Articles* 'Reaganomics und Wettbewerbsfähigkeit - deutsche und europäische Lektionen aus einem amerikanischen Experiment', *Die USA am Beginn der neunziger Jahre. Politik, Wirtschaft, Recht,* Jakobeit, Sacksofsky & Welzel eds., Leske & Budrich, Opladen, 1993, 157–75.

Kirby, Maurice W.

Reader in Econ. Hist., Dept. of Econ., Lancaster Univ., Gillow House, Lancaster, LA1 4YX, UK. Tel.: 44 524 594232. Fax: 44 524 594244.

Year and Place of Birth 1946, Darlington, UK.

Degrees and Qualifications BA (Econ.) Newcastle Univ., 1967; Ph.D. Sheffield Univ., 1971.

Previous Post Lect. in Econ. Hist., Stirling Univ., 1973–85.

Fields of Expertise *Industry Fields:* coal and petroleum products; mechanical engineering. *Bus. Dimensions:* entrepreneurs and entrepreneurship. *Scope:* national. *Period:* nineteenth century. *Teaching:* undergrad.

Publications *Books: The British Coalmining Industry, 1870–1946: A Polit. and Econ. Hist.,* Macmillan, 1977; *The Decline of British Econ. Powers since 1870,* Allen & Unwin, 1981; *Men of Bus. and Polit.: The Rise and Fall of the Quaker Pease Dynasty of North-East England, 1700–1943,* Allen & Unwin, 1984; *The Origins of Railway Enterprise: The Stockton and Darlington Railway,*

1821–1863, CUP, 1993. *Articles:* 'Institutional Rigidities and Econ. Decline: Reflections on the British Experience', *Econ. Hist. Rev.,* 45, 1992, 637–60.

Kita, Masami

Prof. of Econ. Hist., Fac. of Econ., Soka Univ., 1-236 Tanghi-cho, Hachioji, Tokyo, Japan. Tel.: 81 426 91 2211. Fax: 81 426 91 2039.

Year and Place of Birth 1945, Himeji, Japan.

Degrees and Qualifications BA Wakayama Univ., 1967; MA Wakayama Univ., 1969; Ph.D. (Econ.) Osaka Univ., 1988.

Current Offices and Honorary Posts Socio-Econ. Hist. of Japan: sec. 1978–82, council mem. 1986–; Bus. Hist. Soc. of Japan: mem. of internat. relations 1980–6, mem. of Fuji Conf. on Bus. Hist. (2nd ser.) 1980–5, mem. of a branch com. in Japan Science Council 1984–8.

Publications *Books: Kindai-Sukkotrando-Shakaikeizaishi-kenkyu* [A Study of Scottish Socio-Econ. Hist. in Modern Times], Doubunkan, 1988; *Ippan-Keizaishi* [Theory of General Econ. Hist.], Soka Univ. Press, 1989, rep. 1991; *Kokusai-Nippon-o-Hiraita-Hitobito* [The Success of Japanese Learning Modern Technology from Scotland in the late 19th Century], Doubunkan, 1986; *Technological Transfer of Shipbuilding through Education from Scotland to Japan in the late 19th Century,* Centre of Japanese Studies of Philipps Univ. at Marburg, Germany, 1991. *Articles:* 'The Scottish Banking Invasion of England 1874–1992', *Soka Econ. Papers,* 7(1), 1977.

Kitabayashi, Masashi

Assoc. Prof., Fac. of Commerce, Sapporo Gakuin Univ., Bunkyodai, Ebetsu 069, Japan. Tel.: 011 386 8111. Fax: 011 386 8115.

Year and Place of Birth 1951, Kyoto, Japan.

Degrees and Qualifications MA (Commerce) Chuo Univ.

Fields of Expertise *Industry Fields:* insurance, banking, finance. *Bus. Dimensions:* multinational bus. *Scope:* internat. *Period:* nineteenth century; twentieth century as a whole. *Teaching:* undergrad. *Consultancy:* co. hist.

Publications *Articles:* 'Ginka geraku ki ni okeru Igirisu Shokuminchi Ginkou' [Anglo-Colonial Banks under the Depreciation of Silver], *J. of Commerce*, Chuo Univ., 24(3), 1982; '19 Seikimatsu niokeru Igirisu Shokuminchi Ginkou no kawasegyomu to pond ritsukikawase' [The British Colonial Banks and the Sterling Bills], *Japan Bus. Hist. Rev.*, 21(4), 1987; 'Igirisu Shokuminchi Ginkou no tai Ginka geraka Selsaku' [The Hongkong Bank's Even Keel as a Defence Policy for the Depreciation of Silver], *Japan Bus. Hist. Rev.*, 26(4), 1992.

Kiuchi, Kaichi

Pres., Kyoto Gakuen Univ., Nanjo Sokabi-cho, Kameoka City, Kyoto 621, Japan. Tel.: 07712 2 2001. Fax: 07712 4 8150.

Year and Place of Birth 1921, Miyazaki, Japan.

Degrees and Qualifications BA Kobe Univ., 1944; MA Osaka Univ., 1958.

Previous Post Prof., Matsuyama Univ. & Osaka Univ.

Current Offices and Honorary Posts

Director, Japan Accounting Assoc.

Major Honours Ota Prize - Japan Accounting Assoc., 1958.

Fields of Expertise *Industry Fields:* miscellaneous services. *Bus. Dimensions:* co. finance and accounting; small bus. matters. *Scope:* regional . *Period:* late twentieth century, 1970–present. *Teaching:* post grad. *Consultancy:* corporate strategy.

Publications *Books: Balance Sheet*, Dobunkan Press, 1972; *Budget Control*, Dobunkan Press, 1974; *Bus. Report*, Chuokeizaisha Press, 1982; *Corporate Accounting Law*, Chuokeizaisha Press, 1984; *Accounting System and Business Finance*, Kyoto Gakuen Ronshu, 1989.

Kjærgaard, Thorkild

Curator, Museum of National Hist., Frederiksborg Castle, 3400 Hillerød, , Denmark. Tel.: 45 42260439. Fax: 45 48240966.

Year and Place of Birth 1945, Felding, Denmark.

Degrees and Qualifications Dip. Eur. Studies Collège d'Europe, Bruges, 1969; cand.mag. Copenhagen Univ., 1976; Dr.phil. Copenhagen Univ., 1991.

Previous Post Visiting Assoc. Prof., Dept. of Hist., Kansas Univ., USA, 1987.

Current Offices and Honorary Posts Pres., Assoc. of Castles & Museums around the Baltic Sea; mem., Danish Soc. of Agrarian Hist.

Major Honours Gold Medal, Copenhagen Univ., 1973.

Fields of Expertise *Industry Fields:* agric., forestry, fishing; paper, printing, publishing; environment and econ. development. *Scope:* national; Europe. *Period:* early modern; eighteenth century; nineteenth century; twentieth century as a whole.

Publications *Books: Le Danemark*

et la Révolution Française, Copenhagen, 1989; *Den danske Revolution 1500–1800. En økohistorisk tolkning* [The Danish Revolution 1500–1800. An Ecohistorical Interpretation], Copenhagen, 1991, English edn. under preparation, (CUP). *Articles:* 'The Farmer Interpretation of Danish History', *Scandinavian J. of Hist.*, 1985, 97–118; 'Origins of Econ. Growth in European Societies since the 16th Century: The Case of Agriculture', *J. of European Econ. Hist.*, 1986, 591–8; 'Press and Public Opinion in Eighteenth Century Denmark-Norway', *Scandinavian J. of Hist.*, 14, 1990, 215–30.

Klassen, Henry C.

Assoc. Prof., Dept. of Hist., Univ. of Calgary, 2500 Univ. Drive N.W., Calgary, Alberta, T2N 1N4, , Canada. Tel.: 1 403 220 6058. Fax: 1 403 282 8606.

Year and Place of Birth 1931, Coulter, Canada.

Degrees and Qualifications BA Manitoba Univ., 1959; B.Ed. Manitoba Univ., 1961; MA Manitoba Univ., 1963; Ph.D. Toronto Univ., 1970.

Previous Post Asst. Prof., Dept. of Hist., Ottawa Univ., 1966–8.

Major Honours J.S. Ewart Memorial Award, 1962; Province of Ontario Grad. Fellowship, 1964–6; Canada Council Research Grants, 1973–6.

Fields of Expertise *Industry Fields:* agric., forestry, fishing; food, drink, tobacco; transport and communication; distributive trades; insurance, banking, finance. *Bus. Dimensions:* entrepreneurs and entrepreneurship; production management; co. finance and accounting; personnel management; marketing; bus. organization; small bus. matters; multinational bus.;

bus.–state relations; markets and bus.; bus. values; family. *Scope:* local; regional; national; internat.; USA; Canada. *Period:* nineteenth century; twentieth century as a whole; early twentieth century; inter-war years, 1919–39. *Teaching:* undergrad.; post grad.

Publications *Articles:* 'Lawyers, Finance and Econ. Development in Southwestern Alberta, 1884–1920', *Essays in the Hist. of Canadian Law Beyond the Law: Lawyers and Bus. in Canada, 1830–1930*, Carol Wilton ed., vol. IV, The Osgood Soc., Toronto, 1990, 298–319; 'The Conrads in the Alberta Cattle Bus., 1875–1911', *Agric. Hist.*, 64(3), Summer, 1990, 31–59; 'Scottish Capital on the Canadian Frontier, 1876–1920', *Scottish Tradition*, 16, 1990/91, 56–75; 'Shaping the Growth of the Montana Economy: T.C. Power & Bro. and the Canadian Trade, 1869–93', *Great Plains Q.*, 11(3), Summer, 1991, 166–80; 'Entrepreneurship in the Canadian West: The Enterprises of A.E. Cross, 1886–1920', *The Western Hist. Q.*, 22(3), August, 1991, 313–33.

Klebaner, Benjamin Joseph

Prof. of Econ., City College of the City Univ. of New York, Dept. of Econ., New York, NY 10031, USA. Tel.: 1 212 650 6212.

Year and Place of Birth 1926, Brooklyn, NY, USA.

Degrees and Qualifications BS City College, New York Univ., 1945; MA Columbia Univ., 1947; Ph.D. Columbia Univ., 1952.

Previous Post Rutgers Univ., 1951–4.

Major Honours Assoc. ed. *J. of Money, Credit and Banking*, 1975–9.

Fields of Expertise *Industry Fields:* insurance, banking, finance,. *Bus. Dimensions:* merger movement and issues; bus.–state relations; econ. history. *Scope:* USA. *Period:* twentieth century as a whole. *Teaching:* undergrad.; post grad. *Consultancy:* co. hist.; corporate strategy; USA, Controller of the Currency; regional econ. adviser.

Publications *Books: Public Poor Relief in Amer.: 1700–1860*, Arno Press, 1976; *Amer. Commercial Banking: A Hist.*, Twayne Publishers, 1990. *Articles:* 'Potential Competition in Banking and the Supreme Court', *Banking Law J.*, 92, 1975, 545–605; 'Commercial Bank Branching in New York City, 1898–1933', *Internat. Rev. of the Hist. of Banking*, 30–31, 1985, 125–48; 'The Manufacturers Hanover Decision and New York City Banking since 1945', *Internat. Rev. of the Hist. of Banking*, 32–33, 1986, 86–109.

Klein, Daniel

Asst. Prof. of Econ., Dept. of Econ., Univ. of California-Irvine, Irvine, CA 92717, USA. Tel.: 1 714 856 6363. Fax: 1 714 725 2182.

Year and Place of Birth 1962, Hackensack, USA.

Degrees and Qualifications BS (Econ.) George Mason Univ., 1983; Ph.D. (Econ.) New York Univ., 1989/90.

Major Honours Best econ. dissertation for 1988–9, New York Univ.; Hoiles Post-doctoral Fellowship (Inst. for Humane Studies), 1988–9; Arthur H. Cole Grant-in-Aid (Econ. Hist. Assoc.), 1990.

Fields of Expertise *Industry Fields:* transport and communication. *Scope:* national. *Period:* nineteenth century.

Publications *Articles:* 'The Voluntary Provision of Public Goods? The Turnpike Companies of Early America', *Econ. Enquiry*, 28, Oct., 1990, 788–812; 'Economy, Community and Law: The Turnpike Movement in New York, 1797–1845',

Law & Soc. Rev., with J. Majewski, 26(3), Autumn, 1992, 469–512; 'Private Toll Roads: Learning from the Nineteenth Century', *Transportation Q.*, with G.J. Fielding, Jul., 1992, 321–41; 'Market and Community in Antebellum Amer.: The Plank Roads of New York', *J. of Econ. Hist.*, with J. Majewski & Christopher Baer, 53(1), Mar., 1993, 106–22; 'From Trunk to Branch: Toll Roads in New York, 1800–1860', *Essays in Econ. & Bus. Hist.*, with C. Baer & J. Majewski, forthcoming.

Klein, Maury

Prof. of Hist., Dept. of Hist., Rhode Island Univ., Kingston, RI 02882, USA. Tel.: 1 401 792 4790. Fax: 1 401 792 5615.

Year and Place of Birth 1939, Memphis, USA.

Degrees and Qualifications BA Knox College, 1960; MA Emory Univ., 1961; Ph.D. Emory Univ., 1965.

Current Offices and Honorary Posts Director, Honors Program, Rhode Island Univ.

Fields of Expertise *Industry Fields:* transport and communication. *Bus. Dimensions:* entrepreneurs and entrepreneurship; strategy formation; Bus. values; co. culture. *Scope:* national. *Period:* nineteenth century; early twentieth century; inter-war years, 1919–39. *Teaching:* undergrad.; post grad. *Consultancy:* Hist. background for legal action.

Publications *Books: Prisoners of Progress: Amer. Indust. Cities, 1850–1920*, with A. Kantor, Macmillan, New York, 1976; *The Life and Legend of Jay Gould*, Johns Hopkins Univ. Press, Baltimore, 1986; *Union Pacific: The Birth, 1862–1893*, Doubleday & Co., New York, 1987; *Union Pacific: The Rebirth, 1894–1969*, Doubleday & Co., New

York, 1990; *The Flowering of the Third Amer.*, Ivan R. Dee Ing., Chicago, 1993.

Kobayashi, Hiroshi

Assoc. Prof., Fac. of Econ., Nara Sangyo Univ., Tatsuno-kita 3-12-1, Sango-cho, Ikoma-gun, Nara 636, Japan. Tel.: 0745 73 7800. Fax: 0745 72 0822.
Year and Place of Birth 1951, Okayama, Japan.
Degrees and Qualifications BA (Commerce) Waseda Univ., 1974; MA (Commerce) Waseda Univ., 1978; MA (Hist.) Ohio State Univ., 1984.
Previous Post Assoc. Prof., Fac. of Econ., Nara Sangyo Univ., 1988–92.
Fields of Expertise *Bus. Dimensions:* marketing; trade assoc. *Scope:* national; USA. *Period:* nineteenth century; early twentieth century; inter-war years, 1919–39. *Teaching:* undergrad.
Publications *Articles:* 'Purokutah ando Gyanburu: Kindai-teki Mahketingu no Hajimari' [Procter & Gamble: The Beginning of Modern Marketing], *J. of Indust. Econ.*, Nara Sangyo Univ., 1(2), 1986, 35–58; 'Zenkoku Dentoh Kyokai no Shi-teki Tenkai; Amerika no Dentohgyo ni okeru Gyokai Dantai Katsudo' [The Development of the National Electric Light Assoc.; Trade Assoc. Activities in the Amer. Electric Power Industry], *J. of Indust. Econ.*, Nara Sangyo Univ., 1(3), 1986, 47–72; 'Soshiki-ka sareta Joho Katsudo; Amerika ni okeru Keizai Gyokai Dantai Katsudo' [Organized Information Activities; Econ. and Trade Assoc. Activities in Amer.], *J. of Indust. Econ.*, Nara Sangyo Univ., 1(4), 1987, 25–40; 'Purokutah ando Gyanburu; Kindai-teki Mahketingu no Kakuritsu' [Procter & Gamble; The Establishment of Modern Marketing], *J. of Indust. Econ.*, Nara Sangyo Univ.,

2(2), 1987, 17–36; '1920 nendai no Pih ando Gih ni okeru Hanbai Yohin Kanri' [Sale Force Management of Procter & Gamble in the 1920s], *J. of Indust. Econ.*, Nara Sangyo Univ., 6(4), 1992, 59–78.

Kobayashi, Kesaji

Prof., Fac. of Bus. Adminstration, Ryukoku Univ., Fushimi-ku, Kyoto, Japan. Tel.: 075 642 1111. Fax: 075 643 8510.
Year and Place of Birth 1929, Saitama pref., Japan.
Degrees and Qualifications Ph.D. Waseda Univ., 1979.
Previous Post Prof. of Bus. Hist., Fac. of Bus. Admin., Ryukoku Univ.
Current Offices and Honorary Posts Chairman, internat. Exchange Com., Japan Bus. Hist. Soc.
Fields of Expertise *Industry Fields:* agric., forestry, fishing; electrical engineering; textiles. *Bus. Dimensions:* entrepreneurs and entrepreneurship; research and development; bus. and technology; small bus. matters. *Scope:* internat. *Period:* nineteenth century; twentieth century as a whole. *Teaching:* undergrad.; post grad. *Consultancy:* co. hist.
Publications *Books: Amerika Kigyoukeieishi Kenkyu* [Studies on the Development of Amer. Bus.], Yuhikaku, Tokyo, 1979. *Articles:* 'Amerika kigyou ni okeru Keieirinenno Rekishiteki Ichikousatsu' [A Study on the Bus. Ethos in Amer. Bus.], *Waseda Shogakukenkyuka Kiyou*, 14, 1982, 39–52; 'Another Relationship between Bus. and Government in Japan', *Ryukoku Daigaku Shakaikagaku Kenkyunenpo*, 18, 1988, 37–57; 'Armstrong Inspection to George Perkins', *Ryukoku Daigaku Keizai Keiei Ronshu*, 30(1), 1990, 70–80; 'Gendaikigyou Seirituki ni okeru Kinyukigyoka no yakuwari to sono Keieirinen' [The Role and Ideology of

the Financial Entrepreneur in the Formative Era of Modern Bus. Enterprise], *Kigyoukeiei no Rekishiteki Kenkyu* [Hist. Studies on Bus. Enterprise], K. Nakagawa ed., Iwanami Shoten, Tokyo, 1990, 144–62.

Kobayashi, Tadashi

Prof., Chiba Univ. of Commerce, 1-3-1 Konodai, Ichikawa-shi, Chiba 272, Japan. Tel.: 0473 72 4111.
Year and Place of Birth 1930, Yokohama, Japan.
Degrees and Qualifications Ph.D. Chuo Univ., 1991.
Previous Post Archivist, Meiji Mutual Life Co.
Current Offices and Honorary Posts Exec. com. mem., Japan Econ. Policy Assoc.; exec. com. mem., Nippon Acad. of Management Education.
Fields of Expertise *Industry Fields:* transport and communication; insurance, banking, finance; bus. services. *Bus. Dimensions:* entrepreneurs and entrepreneurship; co. finance and accounting; personnel management; co. admin.; marketing; bus. organization; management education; co. culture. *Scope:* internat.; global. *Period:* eighteenth century; nineteenth century. *Teaching:* post grad. *Consultancy:* co. hist.
Publications *Books: Nippon Hoken shiso no Seiseito Tenkai* [Origin and Development of Japanese Insurance Thought], Toyokeizai Shinposha, 1989; *Hoken Shisoka Retsuden* [Biographies of Insurance Thinkers], Hoken-Mainichi shinbunsha, 1991; *Kinsei senshin chitai Kidai ni Okeru 'Tanomoshi Ko' no ichi kosastu* [A Study of 'Tanomoshi' [Mutual Financial Assoc.] in the Late Tokugawa Period],; *Hokenshiso no Juyo Kozo* [Acceptance Structure of Insurance Thought in the Meiji Era],; *Meiji ki Nagasaki ni okeru Seimei*

Hoken Kaisha no Eigyo Kastudo [Activities of Life Insurance Companies in Nagasaki during the Meiji Era].

Kobayashi, Yoshiaki

Prof. of Econ. Hist., Fac. of Econ., Nihon Univ., 1-3-2 Misaki, Chiyodaku, Tokyo, Japan. Tel.: 03 3219 3463.
Year and Place of Birth 1932, Kobe-shi, Hyogo-ken, Japan.
Degrees and Qualifications B.Litt. Tokyo Univ., 1956; M.Econ. Osaka Univ., 1968; Ph.D. Osaka Univ., 1977.
Previous Post Prof., Fac. of Commerce, Doshisha Univ., 1978–90.
Fields of Expertise *Industry Fields:* mining and quarrying; coal and petroleum products; metal manufacture; insurance, banking, finance. *Bus. Dimensions:* entrepreneurs and entrepreneurship; co. admin. *Scope:* national. *Period:* eighteenth century; nineteenth century. *Teaching:* undergrad.; post grad. *Consultancy:* co. hist.
Publications *Articles:* 'France ni okeru Indokaisha no Seiritsu to seisan' [The Establishment and Liquidation of the India Co. in France], *Doshisha Bus. Rev.*, Kyoto, 1968; 'France ginko no Kigen' [The Origin of the Bank of France], *Doshisha Bus. Rev.*, Kyoto, 1969; 'Anzin Tankokaisha to France Kakumei' [The Anzin Coal Mining Co. and the French Revolution], *Doshisha Bus. Rev.*, Kyoto, 1978; 'France Tekko-o Wendel to Meiji Ishin no Kaishaku' [Wendel, King of the Steel Industry in France and Interpretation of the Meiji Restoration in Japan], *Study of Econ. & Bus. Hist.*, Osaka Econ. Univ., 1984; 'France ni okeru Rothschild Ginko to Keiretsu Kaisha' [The Rothschild Bank in France and Affiliated Companies], *Doshisha Bus. Rev.*, Kyoto, 1985.

Kocka, Jürgen

Prof., of Hist. of the Indust. World, Dept. of Hist., Free Univ. of Berlin, Habelschwerdter Allee 45, 14195 Berlin, Germany. Tel.: 49 30 838 45 38. Fax: 49 30 838 45 38.

Year and Place of Birth 1941, Haindorf, Sudetenland.

Degrees and Qualifications MA (Polit. Sc.) Chapel Hill Univ., 1965; Ph.D. Free Univ. of Berlin, 1968; Habilitation Münster Univ., 1972; Dr.h.c. Erasmus Univ. Rotterdam, 1988.

Previous Post Prof. of Social Hist., Bielefeld Univ., 1973–88.

Current Offices and Honorary Posts Permanent Fellow, Wissenschaftskolleg zu Berlin; mem., Academie Europaea Cambridge; mem., Berlin-Brandenburgische Akademie der Wissenschaften.

Major Honours Leibnitz Prize, Deutsche Forschungsgemeinschaft, 1992.

Fields of Expertise *Industry Fields:* electrical engineering. *Bus. Dimensions:* entrepreneurs and entre-preneurship. *Scope:* national. *Period:* nineteenth century. *Teaching:* post grad. *Consultancy:* co. hist.

Publications *Books: Unternehmensverwaltung und Angestelltenschaft am Beispiel Siemens 1847–1914,* 1969; *Facing Total War. Geman Soc. 1914–1918,* Leamington Spa/Cambridge Mass., 1984; *Arbeitsverhältnisse und Arbeiterexistenzen,* Bonn, 1990. *Articles:* 'Entrepreneurs and Managers in German Indust. Revolution', *The Cambridge Econ. Hist. of Europe,* vol. 7, Cambridge, 1978.; 'White Collar Workers in Amer. 1890–1940', *SAGE Studies in 20th Century Hist.,* 10, London/Beverly Hills, 1980.

Koda, Ryoichi

Assoc. Prof., Fac. of Econ., Saga Univ., Honjo-machi 1, 840 Saga, Japan. Tel.: 0952 24 5191. Fax: 0952 26 3457.

Year and Place of Birth 1954, Kumamoto, Japan.

Degrees and Qualifications M.Econ. Kyoto Univ., 1980.

Fields of Expertise *Industry Fields:* mechanical engineering. *Bus. Dimensions:* production management; bus. and technology. *Scope:* national; internat.; Germany. *Period:* early twentieth century; inter-war years, 1919–39. *Teaching:* undergrad.; post grad.

Publications *Articles:* 'Doitsu niokeru kousakukikai-kogyo no seirit-su' [The Establishment of the German Machine Tool Industry], *Tochiseidoshigaku* [J. of Agrarian Hist.], 133, 1991, 1–18; '19-seikimatsu doitsu niokeru tairyo-seisan no kaishi to kousakukikai-kogyo' [The Initiation of Mass Production Technology: A Study on the Machine Tool Industry in Germany], *Keieishigaku* [Japan Bus. Hist. Rev.], 27(2), 1992, 31–62; 'Technologietransfer in der Werkzeugmaschinenbauindustrie von Deutschland nach Japan vor dem Zweiten Weltkrieg', *Technologie-transfer Deutschland-Japan von 1850 bis zur Gegenwart,* Erich Pauer pub., Indicium Verlag, Munich, 1992, 185-206; 'Die Entwicklung der deutschen Maschinenbauindustrie aus japanischer Sicht - ein Vergleich der Entwicklungsgeschichte der deutschen und japanischen Werkzeugmaschinen-bauindustrie', *Sagadaigaku Keizaironshu* [Saga Univ. Econ. Rev.], 23(3), 1989, 1–23.

Köhne-Lindenlaub, Renate

Head of the Krupp Hist. Archives, Fried. Krupp AG Hoesch-Krupp,

Historisches Archiv Krupp, Villa Hügel, Postfach 45.117, D-45143 Essen, Germany. Tel.: 49 201 1884821. Fax: 49 201 1884859.
Year and Place of Birth 1942, Willingen, Germany.
Degrees and Qualifications Dr. phil. Tübingen Univ., 1977.
Fields of Expertise *Teaching:* Hist. of the Krupp-Konzern.
Publications *Books: Nationalliberale und Koalitionsrecht: Struktur und Verhalten der nationalliberalen Reichstagsfraktion 1890–1914*, Frankfurt/Bern, 1977; *Archivbestände zur Wirtschafts- und Sozialgeschichte der Weimarer Republik: Übersicht über Quellen in Archiven der Bundesrepublik Deutschland*, with Thomas Trumpp, Boppard, 1979. *Articles:* 'Krupp', *Neue Deutsche Biographie*, vol. 13, Berlin, 1982, 128–45; 'Private Kunstförderung im Kaiserreich am Beispiel Krupp', *Kunstpolitik und Kunstförderung im Kaiserreich*, E. Mai et al. eds., Berlin, 1982, 55–82; 'Fried. Krupp GmbH', *Internat. Directory of Co. Histories*, Adele Hast ed., vol. 4, Chicago & London, 1991.

Kohno, Shozo

Prof., Dept. of Bus. Admin., Fac. of Econ., Tohoku Univ., Kawauchi Aoba-ku, Sendai, Miyagi-ken 980, , Japan. Tel.: 022 222 1800. Fax: 022 221 6018.
Year and Place of Birth 1948, Kanagawa-ken, Japan.
Degrees and Qualifications B.Com. Hitotsubashi Univ., 1973; M. Com. Hitotsubashi Univ., 1975.
Previous Post Assoc. Prof., Dept. of Bus. Admin., Fac. of Econ., Tohoku Univ., 1985–9.
Fields of Expertise *Industry Fields:* electronics and computers: manufacture; software industry. *Bus. Dimensions:* personnel management;

co. admin.; strategy formation; bus. organization; bus. and technology. *Scope:* national. *Period:* mid-twentieth century, 1940–70; late twentieth century, 1970–present. *Teaching:* undergrad.; post grad. *Consultancy:* corporate strategy.
Publications *Books: Johoka e no Kigyo Senryaku* [Corporate Strategy for Information Soc.], co-auth., Dobunkan Press, 1990; *FA kara CIM e* [From FA to CIM], co-auth., Dobunkan Press, 1990.

Kohtoh, Isuke

Prof., Fac. of Management and Bus., Rissho Univ., 4-2-16 Oosaki, Shinagawaku, Tokyo 141, Japan. Tel.: 03 3492 1031. Fax: 03 5487 3351.
Year and Place of Birth 1943, Tokyo, Japan.
Degrees and Qualifications BA Waseda Univ., 1966; MA Waseda Univ., 1968.
Fields of Expertise *Industry Fields:* vehicle construction; electronics and computers: manufacture. *Bus. Dimensions:* entrepreneurs and entrepreneurship; co. admin.; bus.–state relations; markets and bus. *Scope:* internat. *Period:* twentieth century as a whole. *Teaching:* undergrad.
Publications *Books: Nihon ni okeru Amerika Keieigaku no Dounyuu to Tenkai, So-no Tokuchou* [Management Theory in Japan and the US, Comparative Theory of Management], co-auth., Seibundo Pub. Co., May, 1984; *Kigyou Bunkaron* [Corporate Culture, Management Theory], 2nd edn., co-auth., Seibundo Pub. Co., May, 1989. *Articles:* 'Kigyou no Shoyu, Shihai, Keiei to Koporatizumu' [Corporate Ownership, Control, Management and 'Corporatism'], *Rissho Management Rev.*, 24(1), Dec. 1991.

Kollmer-von Oheimb-Loup, Gert

Director of Archives, Baden-Württemberg Econ. Archives, Schloß Hohenheim, 70593 Stuttgart, Germany. Tel.: 49 711 459 3141. Fax: 49 711 459 3710.
Year and Place of Birth 1949, Esslingen, Germany.
Degrees and Qualifications Promotion Tübingen Univ., 1978; Staatsprüfung Marburg/Lahn College of Archives, 1980; Hon. Prof. Hohenheim Univ., 1991.
Previous Post Staatsarchiv-referendar, Central State Archives, Stuttgart, Oct., 1978–Oct., 1980.
Fields of Expertise *Industry Fields:* textiles; insurance, banking, finance,. *Bus. Dimensions:* entrepreneurs and entrepreneurship; co. finance and accounting; bus. and technology; bus.–state relations. *Scope:* regional; Germany, Baden-Württemberg. *Period:* early modern; eighteenth century; nineteenth century; twentieth century as a whole; early twentieth century. *Teaching:* undergrad. *Consultancy:* co. hist.
Publications *Books: Dokumentation zur Organisationsgeschichte des Hansa-Bundes. Quellensammlung*, Karl Erich Born, Otto Brunner et al. eds., supplement I(1.3), Wiesbaden, 1979; *Dokumentation zur Organisationsgeschichte der Deutschen Arbeitgeberverbände. Quellensammlung*, Karl Erich Born ed., Wiesbaden, 1985. *Articles:* 'Die Schwäbische Reichsritterschaft zwischen Westfälischem Frieden und Reichsdeputationshauptschluß', *Schriften zur südwestdeutschen Landeskunde*, vol. 17, Stuttgart, 1979; 'Die Familie Palm. Soziale Mobilität in ständischer Gesellschaft', *Beiträge zur südwestdeutschen Wirtschafts- und Sozialgeschichte*, vol. 1, Ostfildern, 1983; 'Folgen und Krisen des Zollvereins', *Vierteljahrschrift für Sozial- und Wirtschaftsgeschichte*, no. 80, Hans Pohl, Stuttgart, 1987, 198–220.

Kolltveit, Bård

Director, Norwegian Maritime Museum, Bygdøynesvn. 37, 0286 Oslo 2, Norway. Tel.: 47 22 43 82 40. Fax: 47 22 56 20 37.
Year and Place of Birth 1942, Odda, Norway.
Degrees and Qualifications MA Bergen Univ., 1969.
Current Offices and Honorary Posts Pres., internat. Congress of Maritime Museums, 1987–93.
Major Honours Cavalier, Order of Oranje Nassau (Netherlands); Cavalier, Order of Infante Dom Henrique (Portugal).
Fields of Expertise *Industry Fields:* transport and communication. *Bus. Dimensions:* bus. and technology. *Scope:* national. *Period:* twentieth century as a whole. *Teaching:* post grad. *Consultancy:* co. hist.
Publications *Books: Over Linjen S.A.L. 1913–1973* [Norwegian South-Amer. Line], 1976; *Over Fjord og Fjell. H.S.D. 1880–1980* [Hardanger Sunnhordland S.S. Co.], 1980; *La Oss Arbeide: A/S Laboremus 1910–1985*, 1985; new edn. 1910–1990 , 1990; *Fra Verdens Ende mot de Syv Hav. Anders Wilhelmsen & Co. 1939–1989*, 1989; *The Glolar Chronicle. Gotaar-Larsen Shipping Co. 1946–1991*, 1991.

Kolodziejczyk, Ryszard Antoni

Ordentlicher Prof. Doktor, Kielce Pedagogical College & Prof. Emeritus, Inst. of Hist., Polish Acad. of Sciences, 00-272 Warsaw, Rynek Starego Miasta 29/31 & Kielce Pedagogical College, ul. Zeromskiego 5, Kielce, Poland.
Year and Place of Birth 1922,

Witeradów, Poland.
Degrees and Qualifications MA Warsaw Univ., 1952; Ph.D. Inst. of Social Sciences, 1955; habilitation Inst. of Hist., Polish Acad. of Sciences, 1962.
Previous Post Prof. of Hist., Inst. of Hist., Polish Acad. of Sciences, Warsaw.
Major Honours Ministry of Education Prize, 1958 & 1968; Pres. of Warsaw Prize, 1972.
Fields of Expertise *Industry Fields:* transport and communication; bus. services. *Bus. Dimensions:* entrepreneurs and entrepreneurship; production management; co. finance and accounting. *Scope:* regional; national; internat. *Period:* nineteenth century; twentieth century as a whole; early twentieth century; inter-war years, 1919–39.
Publications *Books: Ksztaltowanie sie burzuazji w Królestwie Polskim 1815–1850*, Warsaw, 1957; *Bohaterowie nieromantyczni. O pionierach kapitalizmu w Królestwie Polskim*, Warsaw, 1961; *Piotr Steinkeller, Kupiec i przemyslowiec 1799–1854*, Warsaw, 1963; *Miasta polskie w okresie porozbiorowym*, Wroclaw, 1965; *Portret warszawskiego milionera Leopolda Kronenberga 1812–1878*, Warsaw, 1968.

Kondo, Akira

Prof. in General Econ. Hist., College of Econ., Rikkyo Univ., 3 Nishi-Ikebukuro, Toshima-ku, Tokyo, Japan. Tel.: 81 3 3985 2341/81 3 3985 2349.
Year and Place of Birth 1928, Yamaguchi, Japan.
Degrees and Qualifications BA Rikkyo Univ., 1951; MA Rikkyo Univ., 1953.
Previous Post Asst. Prof., College of Econ., Rikkyo Univ., 1958–68.
Current Offices and Honorary Posts

Mem. British Agricult. Hist. Soc.
Publications *Articles:* 'The Rise of the Petty-bourgeois Economy', *Econ. Structure of Civil Soc.*, H. Takahashi & A. Kondo eds., 1972, 123–50; 'The Rise of Market Economy in Rural Wiltshire, 1086–1461', *J. of Market Hist.*, 5, 1988, 35–53; 'The Rise of the Market Economy', *Rise of Modern Econ.*, A. Kondo ed., 1991, 13–44.

Kornblith, Gary J.

Assoc. Prof., Dept. of Hist., Oberlin College, 10 N. Prof. St, Rice Hall, Oberlin, OH 44074, , USA. Tel.: 1 216 775 8526. Fax: 1 216 775 8124.
Year and Place of Birth 1950, Chicago, USA.
Degrees and Qualifications BA Amherst College, 1973; MA Princeton Univ., 1975; Ph.D. Princeton Univ., 1983.
Previous Post Asst. Prof., Oberlin College, 1983–8.
Major Honours Special Article Award in Bus. Hist., Newcomen Soc., 1985; *Hist. Collections* Prize, Essex Inst., 1985.
Fields of Expertise *Industry Fields:* paper, printing, publishing; miscellaneous handicrafts. *Bus. Dimensions:* entrepreneurs and entrepreneurship; small bus. matters. *Scope:* local; regional; USA. *Period:* nineteenth century. *Teaching:* undergrad.
Publications *Articles:* 'The Rise of the Mechanic Interest and the Campaign to Develop Manufacturing in Salem; 1815–1830', *Essex Inst. Hist. Collections*, 121, Jan., 1985, 44–65; 'The Craftsman as Industrialist: Jonas Chickering and the Transformation of Amer. Piano Making', *Bus. Hist. Rev.*, 95, Autumn, 1985, 349–68; '"Cementing the Mechanic Interest": Origins of the Providence Assoc. of Mechanics and Manufacturers', *J. of*

the Early Republic, 8, Winter, 1988, 355–87; reprinted in *The New Amer. Nation 1775–1820*, Peter S. Onuf ed., vol. 10, Garland Publishing, Hamden, CT, 1991; 'The Artisanal Response to Capitalist Transformation', *J. of the Early Republic*, 10, Autumn, 1990, 315–21; 'The Making and Unmaking of an Amer. Ruling Class', *Beyond the Amer. Revolution: Further Explorations in the Hist. of Amer. Radicalism*, with John M. Murrin co-auth., Alfred F. Young ed., Northern Illinois Univ. Press, DeKalb, IL, 1993.

Kosacoff, Bernardo P.

Director of Indust. Development ECLAC, UN, Buenos Aires & Prof. of Indust. Econ., Buenos Aires Univ., Division ECLAC, United Nations - Buenos Aires, Corrientes 2554 5°, Buenos Aires (1046), Argentina. Tel.: 54 1 953 0074. Fax: 54 1 953 5382.

Year and Place of Birth 1950, Buenos Aires, Argentina.

Degrees and Qualifications M.Sc. (Econ.) Buenos Aires Univ., 1972.

Previous Post Prof. of Indust. Econ., Buenos Aires Univ., 1983–.

Current Offices and Honorary Posts Mem., Board of Directors, Instituto de Desarrollo Económico y Social (IDES), Buenos Aires.

Fields of Expertise *Industry Fields:* mechanical engineering. *Bus. Dimensions:* multinational bus. *Scope:* Argentina. *Period:* late twentieth century, 1970–present. *Teaching:* undergrad.

Publications *Books: Internacionalización de Empresas y Tecnologias de Origen Argentino*, Editorial Universitaria de B.A EUDE-BA, 1985; *La Industria Argentina: Desarrolla y Cambios Estructurales*, Centro Ed. de Amer. Latina, 1989; *El Proceso de Industrialización en Argentina: Evolucion, Retroceso y Prospectiva*, Centro Ed. de Amer. Latina, 1989; *Difusion de Tecnologías de Punta en Argentina. Algunas Reflexiones sobre la Organización de la Produccion Indust. de IBM*, CEPAL - Naciones Unidas, 1991; *Exportaciones Industriales en una Economia en Transformacion*, CEIAL, Naciones Unidas, 1993.

Kovaleff, Theodore P.

Chair, Community Board 9, NY, 454 Riverside Drive, New York, NY 10027, USA. Tel.: 1 212 749 2251.

Year and Place of Birth 1943, New York, USA.

Degrees and Qualifications BA Columbia Univ., 1964; MA Columbia Univ., 1966; Ph.D. (Hist. - Legal & Econ.) New York Univ., 1972.

Previous Post Asst. Dean, School of Law, Columbia Univ., 1980–92.

Current Offices and Honorary Posts Law School Admission Council com. mem.: Services Com. (two terms), Legal Affairs Com. (two terms), Sub-com. on Misconduct in the Admissions Process (one term); Assoc. of Amer. Law Schools: Section on Student Services, Summer 1993 Program Planning Com.; mem., Columbia Univ. Seminar: Hist. of Legal and Polit. Thought.

Major Honours City of New York Certification of Appreciation for Service on Behalf of Community Boards, 1987; Borough President's Citation for Service to the community, 1983; Borough President's Certificate of Service, 1977; Summer Research Grant, Eleutherian Mills-Hagley Foundation, 1974; Founders Day Award, New York Univ., 1983.

Fields of Expertise *Industry Fields:* transport and communication; insurance, banking, finance. *Bus. Dimensions:* merger movement and issues; markets and bus. *Scope:*

national. *Period:* twentieth century as a whole. *Teaching:* undergrad.; post grad. *Consultancy:* co. hist.

Publications *Books: The Antitrust Impulse,* M.E. Sharpe & Co, 1993, forthcoming; *Bus. and Government during the Eisenhower Admin.,* Ohio Univ. Press, 1980; *Poland and the Coming of World War II,* co-auth., Ohio State Univ. Press, 1977. *Articles:* 'The Two Sides of the Kennedy Antitrust Policy', *The Antitrust Bull.,* XXXVII, Spring, 1992, 35–56; '', *The Antitrust Bull.,* Guest Ed., XXXV, 1990, (four issues).

Koyama, Hiroyuki

Editorial Writer, Nihon Keizai Shimbun, 1-9-5 Otemachi, Chiyodku, Tokyo 100-06, Japan. Tel.: 03 3270 0251. Fax: 03 5255 2607.

Year and Place of Birth 1938, Aichi, Japan.

Degrees and Qualifications BA Aichi Gakugei Univ., 1961; MA Waseda Univ., 1963.

Fields of Expertise *Industry Fields:* vehicle construction; electronics and computers: manufacture. *Bus. Dimensions:* personnel management; co. admin.; bus. organization; Bus. values; co. culture; boardroom issues. *Scope:* national; internat.; global. *Period:* mid-twentieth century, 1940–'70; late twentieth century, 1970–present. *Consultancy:* corporate strategy.

Publications *Books: Nihon no Kaisha* [Japanese Companies in the Showa Era], Nihon Keizai Shimbun, 1988; *Nihon no Keiei* [Management in Japanese Companies], Nihon no Kigyou Group [Keiretsu in Japanese Bus. Circles]; co-auth., Nihon Keizai Shimbun, 1991.

Kozuki, Naoto

Researcher, Hamagin Research Inst. Ltd, 3-1-1 Minatomirai, Nishi-ku, Yokohama, PC220, Japan. Tel.: 81 45 313 2134. Fax: 81 45 313 2235.

Year and Place of Birth 1965, Kanagawa, Japan.

Degrees and Qualifications MBA, Yokohama Nat. Univ., 1989.

Fields of Expertise *Industry Fields:* distributive trades. *Bus. Dimensions:* bus. organization. *Scope:* national. *Period:* inter-war years, 1919–39. *Consultancy:* co. hist.

Publications *Articles:* 'Suzuki Shoten no Keieishaso' [The Managerial Hierarchy of Suzuki Shoten], *Japan Bus. Hist. Rev.,* 25, 1990.

Kraft, James P.

Asst. Prof. of Hist., Univ. of Hawaii, Manoa, 2530 Dale St, Honolulu, HI 96822–2383, USA. Tel.: 1 808 956 7151. Fax: 1 808 956 9600.

Year and Place of Birth 1951, Waco, USA.

Degrees and Qualifications Ph.D. (Hist.) Univ. of Southern California, 1990.

Fields of Expertise *Industry Fields:* entertainment industries. *Bus. Dimensions:* bus. and technology; labour relations. *Scope:* national. *Period:* twentieth century as a whole. *Teaching:* undergrad.; post grad.

Publications *Articles:* 'The Fall of Job Harriman's Socialist Party: Violence, Gender and Polit. in Los Angeles, 1911', *S. California Q.,* Spring, 1988, 9–44; 'The Pit Musicians: Mechanization in the Movie Theatres, 1926–1933', *Labor Hist.,* forthcoming, 1993; 'Musicians in Hollywood: Work and Technological Change in Entertainment Industries, 1926–1940', *Technology and Culture,* forthcoming, 1994.

Kristensen, Peer Hull

Assoc. Prof., Inst. of Organisation and Indust. Sociology, Copenhagen Bus. School, Blågårdsgade 23B, 4, 2200 Copenhagen N, Denmark. Tel.: 038152815. Fax: 038152828.

Year and Place of Birth 1951, Denmark.

Degrees and Qualifications School of Architecture, Acad. of Fine Arts, Copenhagen, 1970–2; BA (Soc. Sc.) Roskilde Univ. Centre, Denmark, 1972–4; BA (Administrative Econ.) Roskilde Univ. Centre, 1974–6; MA (Polit. Sc.) Roskilde Univ. Centre, 1976–8.

Previous Post Assoc. Prof., Bachelor of Science Programmes, Roskilde Univ. Centre.

Current Offices and Honorary Posts Mem., European Science Foundation's programme on European Management and Organisations in Transition (EMOT), 1992–; participant, CEDE-FOP's project on 'Formalized' continuing vocational training, 1991–; chairman/mem. of judging coms. for Ph.D. students, the Tietgen Prize, Asst. Professorships & Assoc. Professorships.

Fields of Expertise *Industry Fields:* mechanical engineering; instrument engineering; textiles; timber, furniture. *Bus. Dimensions:* entrepreneurs and entrepreneurship; production management; strategy formation; small bus. matters; co. culture. *Scope:* regional; national. *Period:* nineteenth century; twentieth century as a whole. *Teaching:* undergrad.; post grad.

Publications *Books: The Small Country Squeeze*, with Jørn Levinsen co-auth., Forlaget for Samfundsøkonomi & Planlægning, 1983; *Technological Innovation and Organizational Change. Danish Patterns of Knowledge, Networks and Culture*, with Finn Borum co-ed., Copenhagen, 1990; own contribution 'Denmark's Concealed Production Culture, its Sociohistorical Construction and Dynamics at Work'. *Articles:* 'Virksomhedsperspektiver på industripolitikken: Industrimodernister og industriens husmænd' [Bus. Perspectives on Indust. Policy: Indust. Modernists and Indust. Farmers], *Politica*, 20(3), 1988; 'Strategies against Structure: Institutions and Econ. Organization in Denmark', *European Bus. Systems. Firms and Markets in their National Contexts*, R. Whitley ed., Sage Publications, London, 1992, 117–36; 'Industrial Districts in West Jutland', *Indust. Districts and Local Econ. Regeneration*, Frank Pyke & Werner Sengenberger eds., 1992 (Spanish translation under preparation).

Kryger Larsen, Hans

Sen. Lect., Inst. of Hist., Univ. of Copenhagen, Njalsgade 102, 2300 Copenhagen S, Denmark. Tel.: 45 31 54 22 11. Fax: 45 32 96 44 06.

Year and Place of Birth 1947, Odense, Denmark.

Degrees and Qualifications MA Odense Univ.

Previous Post Research Fellow, NOS-S-Project on Nordic Industrialization, 1989–93.

Fields of Expertise *Industry Fields:* professional and scientific services. *Bus. Dimensions:* research and development. *Scope:* national. *Period:* nineteenth century; early twentieth century. *Teaching:* post grad.

Publications *Books: Merkantilismen* [Mercantilism in Danish Historiography 1890–1940: A Study], Copenhagen, 1983; *Forbrug og Produktion.* [Consumption and Production of Indust. Projects], with Carl-Axel Nilsson, Dansk Industri efter 1870, vol. 2, Odense, 1989. *Articles:* 'Nationalist Attitudes towards Econ.

Development 1888–1914' [Det Nationale Synspunkt.], *Dansk Identitetshistorie*, vol. 3, Copenhagen, 1992; 'Some Remarks on the Use of Prices when Constructing Volume Series', *Scandinavian Econ. Hist. Rev.*, with Carl-Axel Nilsson, 1, 1992.

Kudo, Akira

Prof., Tokyo Univ., Inst. of Soc. Sc., Hongo 7-3-1, Bunkyo-ku, Tokyo 113, Japan. Tel.: 81 3 3812 2111. Fax: 81 3 3816 6864.
Year and Place of Birth 1946, Tokyo, Japan.
Degrees and Qualifications BA Tokyo Univ., 1969; MA Tokyo Univ., 1972.
Previous Post Assoc. Prof., Dept. of Social & Internat. Relations, Tokyo Univ., 1979–91.
Current Offices and Honorary Posts Chairman of the Organizing Com. of the Fifth Series of the Fuji Conf., Bus. Hist. Soc. of Japan; edit. board mem., *Japanese Bus. Hist. Rev.*
Fields of Expertise *Industry Fields:* chemicals and allied industries; metal manufacture; mechanical engineering; electrical engineering; insurance, banking, finance. *Bus. Dimensions:* production management; co. finance and accounting; personnel management; research and development; strategy formation; bus. and technology; multinational bus.; bus.–state relations; co. culture. *Period:* twentieth century as a whole. *Teaching:* undergrad.; post grad.
Publications *Books: A Hist. of Japan-German Business Relations*, Yuhikaku, 1992, (in Japanese); *I.G. Farben's Japan Strategy: A Hist. of Japan-German Bus. Relations during the Interwar Period*, Univ. of Tokyo Press, 1992, (in Japanese); *Internat. Cartels in Bus. Hist.*, co-ed., Univ. of Tokyo Press, 1992; *The Unification of*

Germany and Changing Eastern Europe, co-ed., Minerva, 1992, (in Japanese); *The Hundred Year Hist. of Kao Corporation*, co-auth., Kao Corp., 1993, (in Japanese).

Kuisma, Markku

Sen. Lect., Dept. of Hist., Helsinki Univ., P.O.B. 4 (Hallitusk 15), 00014 Helsingin Yliopisto, Finland. Tel.: 358 0 1911. Fax: 358 0 1913217.
Year and Place of Birth 1952, Hyvinkaa, Finland.
Degrees and Qualifications Hum. kand., 1974; Fil. kand., 1978; Fil. lis., 1980; Ph.D. Helsinki Univ., 1983.
Previous Post Acting Prof. of Finnish Hist., Helsinki Univ., 1989–91.
Current Offices and Honorary Posts Edit. council mem., *Finnish Hist. Rev.*
Fields of Expertise *Industry Fields:* mining and quarrying; timber, furniture; paper, printing, publishing. *Bus. Dimensions:* entrepreneurs and entrepreneurship; strategy formation; bus.–state relations. *Scope:* national; internat.; Finland. *Period:* eighteenth century; twentieth century as a whole. *Teaching:* undergrad.; post grad. *Consultancy:* co. hist.
Publications *Books: Kauppa sahojen perustaminen Suomessa 1700-luvulla. Tutkimus päätöksen tekoprosessista* [The Establishment of the Sawmill Industry in Finland in the 18th Century. A Study of the Decision-making Process], Finska Vetenskapsakademin, 1983; *Kupari kaivoksesta suuryhtiöksi. Outokumpu 1910–1985* [From Copper Mine to Major Corporation. Outokumpu 1910–1985], Forssan Kirjapaino-Outokumpu, 1985; *Teollisuuden vuosisata. Teollisuusvakuutus ja sen edeltajayhtiot 100 vuotta* [A Century of Industry 1890–1990. The Past 100 Years of Indust. Mutual Insurance and its Predecessor Companies], Otavan

Kirjapaino-Teollisuusvakuutus, 1990, (shorter edn. in English). *Articles:* 'When Country Dwellers became Staple Town Burghers. The Establishment of the First Export Sawmill in Eastern Finnish Hinterland and the Granting of Privileges to the Export Sawmill Industry of Savo in the 1760s and 1770s', *Scandinavian J. of Hist.*, 7, 1982, 233–54; 'The New Entrepreneurs, the Old Bourgeoisie. Industry, Soc. and State in Eighteenth Century Finland', *State, Culture and the Bourgeoisie. Aspects of the Peculiarity of the Finnish*, publications of the Research Unit for Contemporary Culture, Univ. of Jyväskylä, 1989, 13–32.

Kunz, Andreas

Deputy Director, Dept. of World Hist., Inst. for European Hist., Alte Universitätsstrasse 19, 55116 Mainz, Germany. Tel.: 49 6131 399363. Fax: 49 6131 237988.

Year and Place of Birth 1948, Leipzig, Germany.

Degrees and Qualifications Dipl. Freiburg Univ., 1973; MA Massachusetts-Amherst Univ., 1974; Ph.D. Univ., of California, Berkeley, 1983.

Previous Post Assistant, Econ. & Social Hist. Dept., Free Univ. of Berlin, 1984–9.

Fields of Expertise *Industry Fields:* transport and communication. *Bus. Dimensions:* bus.–state relations. *Scope:* national. *Period:* nineteenth century. *Teaching:* post grad. *Consultancy:* computer-based research; historical statistics.

Publications *Articles:* 'Database Applications in Econ. Hist.: German Transport Stats., 1835–1985', *Computers in the Humanities and the Social Sciences*, H. Best et al., eds., K.K. Saur, 1991, 148–55; 'Voies Navigables e Développement Économique', *Histoire, Economie e Société*, 11, 1/1992, 13–17; 'La Modernisation d'un Transport encore Préindustriel pendant l'Ère Industrielle: Le Cas des Voies Navigables de l'Allemagne Impériale de 1871 à 1918', *Histoire, Economie et Société*, 11, 1/1992, 19–32; 'Mapping 19th Century Transport. The Application of Computer Cartography to Hist.-Statistical Data', *Histore et Informatique*, J. Smets ed., Montpellier, 1992, 325–31; '"Binnenschiffahrt" und "Seeschiffahrt"', *Technik und Wirtschaft*, U. Wengenroth ed., VDI-Verlag, 1993.

Kuwahara, Tetsuya

Prof., Fac. of Bus. Admin., Kyoto Sangyo Univ., Kamigamo, Kitaku, Kyoto, Japan. Tel.: 81 75 701 2151. Fax: 81 75 712 6881.

Year and Place of Birth 1947, Gifu, Japan.

Degrees and Qualifications B.Ed. Nagasaki, 1969; MBA Kobe, 1972; MBA Syracuse, 1972; DBA Kobe, 1993.

Previous Post Assoc. Prof., Fac. of Bus. Admin., Kyoto Sangyo Univ., 1981–8.

Current Offices and Honorary Posts Sec., Japan Bus. His. Soc., 1980–4; Council mem., Japan Bus. Hist. Soc., 1984–8; editorial board mem., Japan Bus. Hist. Soc., 1984–; sec., Acad. of Management Philo., 1991–.

Fields of Expertise *Industry Fields:* textiles. *Bus. Dimensions:* entrepreneurs and entrepreneurship; production management; personnel management; strategy formation; multinational bus.; bus. values. *Scope:* regional; national; internat. *Period:* nineteenth century; twentieth century as a whole. *Teaching:* undergrad. *Consultancy:* co. hist.; corporate strategy.

Publications *Books: Kigyou Kokusaika no Siteki-bunseki: Senzenki Nihon Boseki-kigyo no Chuugoku Toushi*

[Japanese Bus. Abroad in Hist. Perspective: Japanese Cotton Spinners' Direct Investment in China before World War II], Moriyama Shoten, 1990, (in Japanese). *Articles:* 'The Bus. Strategy of Japanese Cotton Spinners: Overseas Operations 1890–1931', *The Textile Industry and its Bus.*, S. Yonekawa & A Okouchi eds., Tokyo Univ. Press., 1982, 139–66; 'The Establishment of Oligopoly in the Japanese Cotton Spinning Industry and the Bus. Strategies of Latecomers: the Case of Naigaiwata & Co.', *Japanese Yearbook on Bus. Hist.*, 3, 1986, 103–34; 'The Japanese Cotton Spinners' Direct Investment into China before World War II', *Hist. Studies in Internat. Corporate Bus.*, A. Teichova, M. Levy-Leboyer & H. Nussbaum eds., CUP, 1988, 151–62; 'Local Competitiveness and Management of Japanese Cotton Spinning Mills in China in the Inter-war Years', *The Transfer of Internat. Technology*, David Jeremy ed., Edward Elgar Pub. Ltd., 1992, 147–66.

Kuwata, Masaru

Prof., Kobe Internat. Univ., 5-1-1 Manabigaoka, Tarumi-ku, Kobe 655, Japan. Tel.: 078 709 3851. Fax: 078 707 3500.

Year and Place of Birth 1945, Hyogo, Japan.

Degrees and Qualifications M.Litt. Kansei Gakuin Grad. School of Litt., 1970.

Fields of Expertise *Industry Fields:* coal and petroleum products; metal goods. *Bus. Dimensions:* marketing. *Scope:* local; national. *Period:* early modern. *Teaching:* undergrad.

Publications *Books: Miki Kanamono Tonyashi* [The Hist. of Miki Hardware Wholesale Merchant], Chamber of Commerce & Industry, Miki, 1984; *Banshu Takasago*

Kishimoto-ke no Kenkyu [The Study of the Kishimoto Family in Takasago, Harima Province], *Junku-do, 1989; Nihon no Kokusaika o Kangaeru* [The Nationalization of Japan], co-ed., Mineruva-shoho, 1992. *Articles:* 'Kinsei Kouki ni Okeru Osaka Edo Shizyo to Miki Kanamonos' [Osaka and Edo Markets for Miki Hardware in the Late Edo Period], *Socio-Econ. Hist.*, 46(1), 1980.

Lacina, Vlastislav

Sen. Researcher, Inst. of Hist. Sciences, Czech Acad. of Sciences, Vysehradská 49, 128 26 Prague 2, Czechland. Tel.: 42 2 29 64 51.

Year and Place of Birth 1931, Blazenice, Czechland.

Degrees and Qualifications Ph.Dr. Charles Univ., Prague, 1961; docent, Inst. of Hist. Sciences, Prague, 1965.

Previous Post Researcher, Inst. of Czechoslovak & World Hist., Prague, 1970–90.

Current Offices and Honorary Posts V-P, Assoc. of Bus. Historians, Czechland.

Major Honours Czechoslovak Acad. of Sciences Prize, 1985.

Fields of Expertise *Industry Fields:* agriculture, forestry, fishing; insurance, banking, finance. *Bus. Dimensions:* co. finance and accounting; bus.–state relations. *Scope:* national; Czechland; Czechoslovakia. *Period:* twentieth century as a whole. *Teaching:* post grad. *Consultancy:* co. hist.

Publications *Books: Krize Ceskoslovenského Zemedelství (1928–34)* [Depression in the Agric. of the Czech Lands], Acad. Press, 1974; *Velká hospodárská krize v Ceskoslovensku (1929–1934)* [Great Depression in Czechoslovakia], Academia, 1984; *Formování ceskoslovenské ekonomiky, 1918–1924* [Formation of the

Czechoslovak Economy], Academia, 1990; *Economy in the Czech Lands, 1880–1914*, HIU Prague Press, 1990; *Alois Rasín, První ministr financí* [Alois Rasín, the First Minister of Finance], Mladá Fronta Press, 1992.

Lamard, Pierre

Prof. of Indust. Hist., Institut Polytechnique de Sévenans, 90010 Belfort Cedex, France. Tel.: 33 84 58 30 29. Fax: 33 84 58 30 27.

Year and Place of Birth 1954, Belfort, France.

Degrees and Qualifications Ph.D. (Bus. Hist.).

Previous Post Lect./researcher, Institut Polytechnique de Sévenans.

Fields of Expertise *Industry Fields:* metal manufacture. *Bus. Dimensions:* entrepreneurs and entrepreneurship; co. culture. *Scope:* local; regional. *Period:* nineteenth century. *Teaching:* undergrad.; post grad.

Publications *Articles:* 'Histoire d'un capital familial au XIXe siècle: le capital Japy de 1777 à 1910. Fondateur Japy (1749–1812)', *Mem. Sté. belfortaine émul.*, Franche-Comté Univ., thesis, 1988; 'L'école Japy; cours primaire supérieur à caractère professionel spécial', *Les agents de l'industrialisation et de l'innovation dans une région française: La Franche-Comté*, C.N.R.S., A.T.P. Histoire Industrielle de la France, Franche-Comté Univ., 1988; 'La technicité Japy: une révolution méconnue', *Inter-universitaires de l'Est. Innovations et renouveaux techniques de l'Antiquité à nos jours*, summary of meeting, Mulhouse, 1989, 193–202; 'Pouvoirs et Maîtres de Forges au Siècle des Lumières: Des Rapport Paradoxaux. La tréfilerie de Morvillars (1759–1789)', *Actes de la 22ème Semaine d'Etudes de l'Institut Francesco Datini* [L'impresa industria

commercio banca, secc. XIIIe-XVIIIe], 1991, 943–53; 'Les Entrepreneurs-, Montbéliard du Wurtemberg à la France', *S.E.M.*, series publication, 1992, 208–23.

Landau, Zbigniew

Chair of Econ. & Social Hist., Warsaw School of Econ., Ul. Wisniowa 41 room 74, Warsaw, Poland. Tel.: 48 22 39 17 31. Fax: 48 22 49 55 05.

Year and Place of Birth 1931, Warsaw, Poland.

Degrees and Qualifications Magister, Central School of Planning & Stats. (SGPiS), 1955; Ph.D. SGPiS, 1960; Doktor habilitowany SGPis, 1963; Extraordinary Prof., 1972; Ordinary Prof. (full), 1980;.

Current Offices and Honorary Posts Mem. of Senate, Warsaw School of Econ.; editor-in-chief, *Encyclopaedia of Polish Interwar Hist. & Econ.*

Major Honours Ministry of Education Science Award, 1965, 1967, 1971, 1975, 1976, 1978, 1981, 1987; *Polityka* award, 1972, 1986; Literni Fond Award, 1978.

Fields of Expertise *Industry Fields:* insurance, banking, finance. *Bus. Dimensions:* multinational bus. *Scope:* national; internat. *Period:* inter-war years, 1919–39; mid-twentieth century, 1940–70. *Teaching:* undergrad.; post grad. *Consultancy:* co. hist.

Publications *Books: Gospodarka Polski Miedzywojennej* [The Economy of Interwar Poland], with J. Tomaszewski, 4 vols., Ksiazka i Wiedza, 1967–89; *Wirtschaftsgeschichte Polens im 19. und 20 Jahrhundert*, with J. Tomaszewski, Akademie Verlag, Berlin; *The Polish Economy in the Twentieth Century*, with J. Tomaszewski, Croom Helm, 1985; *Bank Polska Kasa Opieki S.A. 1929–1989* [Polish Social Welfare Bank SA 1929–1989], with J. Tomaszewski, Bank PKO, 1991.

Landry, John

Grad. Student, Dept. of Hist., Brown Univ., Providence, RI 02912, USA. Tel.: 1 401 863 2131.
Degrees and Qualifications MA Brown Univ., 1988.
Fields of Expertise *Industry Fields:* metal manufacture. *Bus. Dimensions:* personnel management; co. culture. *Scope:* national; USA. *Period:* nineteenth century; early twentieth century.

Lange, Even

Director, Inst. for Bus. Hist., The Norwegian School of Management, POB 580, 1301 Sandvika, Norway. Tel.: 47 67 57 05 00. Fax: 47 67 57 05 70.
Year and Place of Birth 1943, Oslo, Norway.
Degrees and Qualifications MA Oslo Univ., 1974; Dr.phil. Oslo Univ., 1987.
Previous Post Research Director, Centre for Bus. Hist., Norwegian National Archives, 1980–8.
Current Offices and Honorary Posts Norwegian ed., *Scandinavian Econ. Hist. Rev.*
Fields of Expertise *Industry Fields:* timber, furniture; paper, printing, publishing; insurance, banking, finance,. *Bus. Dimensions:* entrepreneurs and entrepreneurship; bus. and technology. *Scope:* Norway; Scandinavia. *Period:* twentieth century as a whole. *Teaching:* post grad. *Consultancy:* co. hist.
Publications *Books: Growth and Development. The Norwegian Experience 1830–1980*, co-auth., Oslo, 1983. *Articles:* 'The Concession Laws of 1906–9 and Norwegian Indust. Development', *Scandinavian J. of Hist.*, 2, 1977; 'The Importance of Small Indust. Establishments in Norway over the last 100 Years', *Petite Entreprise et*

Croissance Industrielle dans le Monde aux XIXe et XXe Siècles, CNRS, Paris, 1980; 'Planning and Econ. Policy in Norway 1945–1960', *Scandinavian J. of Hist.*, with Helge Pharo, 16, 1991; 'Norwegian Pulp on the English Market', *Technology Transfer and Scandinavian Industrialisation*, Kristine Bruland ed., Berg Publishers, Oxford, 1991.

Langlois, Richard N.

Prof. of Econ., Dept. of Econ. U63, Univ. of Connecticut, 322 Monteith, 341 Mansfield Road, Storrs, CT 06269-1063, USA. Tel.: 1 203 486 3472. Fax: 1 203 486 4463.
Year and Place of Birth 1952, Putnam, USA.
Degrees and Qualifications BA (Physics & Eng. Lit) Williams College, 1974; MS (Astrophysics) Yale Univ., 1975; MS (Engineering-Econ. Systems) Stanford Univ., 1976; Ph.D. (Engineering-Econ. Systems) Stanford Univ., 1981.
Previous Post Assoc. Research Scientist, C.V. Starr Center for Applied Econ., Fac. of Arts & Sciences, and Research Asst. Prof., Center for Science & Technology Policy, Grad. School of Bus. Admin., New York Univ., 1980–3.
Fields of Expertise *Industry Fields:* instrument engineering; electrical engineering; other manufacturing industries; electronics and computers: manufacture. *Bus. Dimensions:* research and development; bus. organization; bus. and technology. *Scope:* internat. *Period:* late twentieth century, 1970–present. *Teaching:* undergrad.; post grad.
Publications *Books: Econ. as a Process: Essays in the New Institutional Econ.*, ed., CUP, 1986; paperback, 1989. *Articles:* 'Explaining Vertical Integration: Lessons from the

Amer. Automobile Industry', *J. of Econ. Hist.*, with Paul L. Robertson, 49(2), June, 1989, 361–75; 'Economic Change and the Boundaries of the Firm', *J. of Institutional and Theoretical Econ.*, 144(4), 1988, 635–57; reprinted in Bo Carlsson, ed., *Indust. Dynamics: Technological, Organizational and Structural Changes in Industries and Firms*, Kluwer Academic Publishers, Dordrecht, 1989, & in Geoffrey Hodgson, ed., *The Econ. of Institutions*, Edward Elgar Publishing, Aldershot, 1993; 'Transaction-Cost Econ. in Real Time', *Indust. & Corporate Change*, 1(1), 1992, 99–127; 'External Economies and Econ. Progress: The Case of the Microcomputer Industry', *Bus. Hist. Rev.*, 66(1), Spring, 1992, 1–50.

Latham, A.J.H.

Sen. Lect. in Internat. Econ. Hist., Univ. College, Swansea, SA3 1AA, UK. Tel.: 44 792 390055/44 792 205678. Fax: 44 792 295746.

Year and Place of Birth 1940, Wigan, UK.

Degrees and Qualifications BA Birmingham Univ., 1964; Ph.D. Birmingham Univ., 1970.

Fields of Expertise *Industry Fields:* agric., forestry, fishing; food, drink, tobacco. *Bus. Dimensions:* entrepreneurs and entrepreneurship; markets and bus. *Scope:* internat. *Period:* nineteenth century; twentieth century as a whole. *Teaching:* undergrad.; post grad.

Publications *Books: Old Calabar 1600–1891: The Impact of the Internat. Economy upon a Traditional Soc.*, Clarendon Press, Oxford, 1973, 2nd edn. 1978; translated into Japanese: Nihon-Hyoron-Sha, Tokyo, 1987; *The Internat. Economy and the Undeveloped World, 1865–1914*, Croom Helm, London; Rowman & Littlefield, Totowa N.J., 1978, 2nd

edn., 1983; *The Depression and the Developing World, 1914–1939*, Croom Helm, London; Barnes & Noble, Totowa N.J., 1981; *The Market in Hist.*, with B.L. Anderson co-ed., Croom Helm, London, 1986. *Articles:* 'From Competition to Constraint: The Internat. Rice Trade in the Nineteenth and Twentieth Centuries', *Bus. & Econ. Hist*, 17, 1988, 91–102.

Lazonick, William

Prof. of Policy & Planning, Univ. of Massachusetts Lowell, College of Management, One Univ. Ave., Lowell, MA 01854, USA. Tel.: 1 617 547 5632. Fax: 1 508 934 3000.

Year and Place of Birth 1945, Toronto, Canada.

Degrees and Qualifications B.Com. Toronto Univ., 1968; M.Sc. (Econ.) London School of Econ., 1969; Ph.D. Harvard Univ., 1975.

Previous Post Prof. of Econ., Barnard College, Columbia Univ., 1985–93.

Current Offices and Honorary Posts Research Assoc., Harvard Inst. for Internat. Development; edit. board mem., *Bus. Hist. Rev., Bus. Hist., Indust. & Corporate Change.*

Major Honours Hon. Doctor of Phil., Uppsala Univ., 1991; Pres., Bus. Hist. Conf., 1990–1; Harvard-Newcomen Bus. Hist. Fellow, 1983.

Fields of Expertise *Industry Fields:* textiles. *Bus. Dimensions:* bus. organization. *Scope:* internat. *Period:* twentieth century as a whole. *Teaching:* undergrad.; post grad. *Consultancy:* organizational restructuring.

Publications *Books: The Decline of the British Economy*, with Bernard Elbaum co-ed., Clarendon Press, 1986; *Competitive Advantage on the Shop Floor*, Harvard Univ. Press, 1990; *Bus. Organization and the Myth of the Market Economy*, CUP, 1991;

Organization and Technology in Capitalist Development, Edward Elgar, 1992; *Organizational Capability and Competitive Advantage*, with William Mass co-ed., Edward Elgar, 1993.

Le Heron, Richard B.

Assoc. Prof., Dept. of Geography, Massey Univ., Private Bag, Palmerston North, New Zealand. Tel.: 64 6 3569099. Fax: 64 6 3505644.
Year and Place of Birth 1947, Paparoa, New Zealand.
Degrees and Qualifications BA Massey Univ., 1968; MA Massey Univ., 1970; Ph.D. Washington Univ., Seattle, 1973.
Previous Post Sen. lect., Dept. of Geography, Massey Univ., 1979–90.
Current Offices and Honorary Posts Ed., *New Zealand Geographer*; full commission mem., Internat. Geographical Union Commission on 'The Organisation of Indust. Spaces'.
Major Honours Fulbright Hayes Travel Award, 1970; Claude McCarthy Travel Fellowship, 1986.
Fields of Expertise *Industry Fields:* agric., forestry, fishing; food, drink, tobacco. *Bus. Dimensions:* strategy formation. *Scope:* global. *Period:* late twentieth century, 1970–present. *Teaching:* post grad. *Consultancy:* corporate strategy.
Publications *Books: Changing Places in New Zealand. A Geography of Restructuring*, New Zealand Geographical Soc., Univ. of Canterbury, Christchurch, 1992 (1st edn.), 1993 (2nd edn.). *Articles:* 'The Diversified Corporation and Development Strategy - New Zealand's Experience', *Regional Studies*, 14(3), 1980, 201–18; 'The Internationalisation of New Zealand Forestry Companies and the Social Reappraisal of New Zealand's Exotic Forest Resource', *Environment and Planning*, 20, 1988, 489–515; 'Good Food Worldwide?

Internationalisation and Performance of Goodman Fielder Wattie Ltd', *The Corporate Firm in a Changing World Economy*, M. de Smidt & E. Wever eds., Routledge, London, 1990, 100–19; 'Reorganisation of the New Zealand Export Meat Freezing Industry: Polit. Dilemmas and Spatial Impacts', *The State and the Spatial Management of Indust. Change*, D. Rich & G.J.R. Linge eds., Routledge, London, 1990, 108–27.

Leménorel, Alain

Lect., Dept. of Modern Hist., Inst. of Hist., Rouen Univ., POB 138, 1 rue Thomas Becket, 76821 Mont-Saint-Aignan Cedex, France. Tel.: 33 35 14 61 45.
Year and Place of Birth 1949, Caen, France.
Degrees and Qualifications Agrégation (Hist.), 1973; Doctorat de troisième cycle, 1983.
Current Offices and Honorary Posts French Assoc. of Econ. Historians; Research Centre for Quantitative Hist., Caen; Hist. Research Group, Rouen; pres., Assoc. for the Hist. & Indust. Heritage of Lower Normany, Caen.
Fields of Expertise *Industry Fields:* mining and quarrying; metal manufacture; textiles. *Bus. Dimensions:* entrepreneurs and entrepreneurship; production management; bus. organization; markets and bus. *Scope:* regional; national. *Period:* nineteenth century; twentieth century as a whole. *Teaching:* post grad.
Publications *Articles:* 'L'Impossible Révolution Industrielle? Economie et Sociologie Minières en Basse-Normandie de 1800 à 1914', *Cahier des Annales de Normandie*, 21, 1988; 'The Land Registry: A Source of Demography for Bus. The Example of Lower Normandy in the 19th Century', *The Birth and Death of Companies, an Hist. Perspective*, P.

Jobert & M. Moss eds., The Parthenon Publishing Group Ltd, England, 1990; 'Les Trajectoires Ouvrières en Basse-Normandie aux XIX–XXe Siècles', Actes Colloque Québec 1985: Sociétés Villageoises et Rapports Villes-Campagnes au Québec et dans la France de l'Ouest, XVII–XXe, P.H. Rennes, Trois-Rivières Univ., 1987; 'Les Comités d'Entreprise et le Social: Paternalisme, néo-Paternalisme, Démocratie, 1945–1990', *De la Charité médiévale à Sécurité Sociale*, Ouvrières edn., 1992; 'Le Paternalisme, Version XXe Siècle: L'Exemple de la Société Métallurgique de Normandie 1910–1988', *Cahiers de la Recherche sur le Travail Social*, Le Musée Social, CEDIAS, 1991–3.

Levenstein, Margaret C.

Assistant Prof., Dept. of Econ., Michigan Univ., 205 Lorch Hall, Ann Arbor, MI 48109-1220, USA. Tel.: 1 313 764 5274. Fax: 1 313 764 2769.

Year and Place of Birth 1962, Cambridge, USA.

Degrees and Qualifications BA Barnard College, Columbia Univ., 1984; MA Yale Univ., 1986; Ph.D. Yale Univ., 1991.

Current Offices and Honorary Posts Fac. Research Fellow, National Bureau of Econ. Research.

Major Honours Herman Krooss Prize for the best dissertation in Bus. Hist., 1992.

Fields of Expertise *Industry Fields:* chemicals and allied industries. *Bus. Dimensions:* entrepreneurs and entrepreneurship; co. finance and accounting; marketing; research and development; strategy formation; merger movement and issues; bus. organization. *Scope:* regional; national; internat. *Period:* nineteenth century; early twentieth century. *Teaching:* undergrad.; post grad. *Consultancy:* co.

hist.; corporate strategy.

Publications *Articles:* 'The Use of Cost Measures: the Dow Chemical Co., 1890–1914', *Inside the Bus. Enterprise: The Use and Transformation of Information*, Peter Temin ed., Univ. of Chicago Press, 1991.

Lewchuk, Wayne A.

Assoc. Prof., Dept. of Econ., McMaster Univ., Hamilton, Ontario, L8S 4M4, Canada. Tel.: 1 416 525 9140.

Year and Place of Birth 1952, Canada.

Degrees and Qualifications MA Toronto Univ., 1977; Ph.D. Cambridge Univ., 1982.

Fields of Expertise *Industry Fields:* vehicle construction; metal goods. *Bus. Dimensions:* production management; bus. and technology; markets and bus. labour. *Scope:* internat. *Period:* nineteenth century; twentieth century as a whole. *Teaching:* undergrad.

Publications *Books: The British Motor Vehicle Industry 1896–1984: The British System of Mass Production and the Roots of Indust. Decline*, CUP, 1987. *Articles:* 'Worker Preference for Co-operatives versus Private Buy-outs', *J. of Econ. Behavior and Organization*, with Martin Browning co-auth., 14, 1990, 262–83; 'Industrialization and Occupational Mortality in France prior to 1914', *Explorations in Econ. Hist.*, 28, 1991, 344–66; 'Giving and Getting the Wrong Signals: Institutions, Technical Change and the Decline of British Productivity since 1850', *Bus. & Econ. Hist.*, 20, 1991, 77–88; 'Fordist Technology and Britain: The Diffusion of Labour Speed-up', *The Transfer of Internat. Technology: Europe, Japan and the USA in the Twentieth Century*, D. Jeremy ed., Edward Elgar, 1992, 3–27.

Lewis, David L.

Prof. of Bus. Hist., School of Bus. B3253, Michigan Univ., Ann Arbor, MI 48109-1234, USA. Tel.: 1 313 764 9540. Fax: 1 313 763 5688.

Year and Place of Birth 1927, Bethalto, USA.

Degrees and Qualifications BS Illinois Univ., 1948; MS Boston Univ., 1955; MA Michigan Univ., 1956; Ph.D. Michigan Univ., 1959.

Previous Post Staff Writer, General Motors Corporation, Detroit, 1959–65.

Current Offices and Honorary Posts Friend of Automotive Hist. Award, Soc. of Automotive Historians, 1991; Cugnot Award, Soc. of Automotive Historians, 1976.

Fields of Expertise *Industry Fields:* automobile. *Scope:* internat. *Period:* twentieth century as a whole. *Teaching:* post grad. *Consultancy:* co. hist.

Publications *Books: The Public Image of Henry Ford*, Wayne State Univ. Press, Detroit, 1976; *The Automobile and Amer. Culture*, Univ.of Michigan Press, Ann Arbor, MI, 1983; *Ford, 1903 to 1984*, co-auth., Beckman House, New York, 1983; *Ford Country*, Amos Press, Sidney, Ohio, 1987; *Ford Chronicle: A Pictorial Hist. from 1893*, co-auth., Publications Internat. Ltd., Lincolnwood, IL, 1992.

Lindenlaub, Dieter

Head of Library & Archive Dept., Bundesbank, & Privatdozent, Frankfurt Univ., Deutsche Bundesbank, 60431 Frankfurt, Wilhelm-Epstein-Str. 14; Dept. of Econ. Hist., Frankfurt Univ., 60325 Frankfurt-am-Main, Sencken-berganlage 31, Postfach 11932, Germany.

Tel.: 49 69 9566 3751. Fax: 49 69 9566 3104.

Year and Place of Birth 1937, Cologne, Germany.

Degrees and Qualifications Dr.phil. Cologne Univ., 1965; Dr.phil. & rer.pol.habil. Tübingen Univ., 1982.

Previous Post Researcher & lecturer, Tübingen Univ., 1983–6.

Current Offices and Honorary Posts Scientific council mem., Inst. for Research in the Hist. of Banking (Frankfurt).

Fields of Expertise *Industry Fields:* mechanical engineering; German central banking. *Bus. Dimensions:* co. admin.; bus. organization. *Scope:* national. *Period:* inter-war years, 1919–39. *Teaching:* undergrad.; post grad. *Consultancy:* corporate strategy.

Publications *Books: Richtungskämpfe im Verein für Sozialpolitik*, 2 vols., Steiner, 1967; *Maschinenbauunternehmen in der Inflation 1919–23. Unternehmenshistorische Untersuchungen zu einigen Inflationstheorien*, de Guyter, 1985. *Articles:* 'Firmengeschichte', *Handwörterbuch der Wirtschaftswissenschaft*, vol. 3, 1980, 294–302; 'Unternehmensgeschichte', *Zeitschrift für Betriebswirtschaft*, 53, 1983, 91–123; 'Die Weltwirtschaftskrise in Deutschland: Die gesamtwirtschaftliche, die einzelwirtschaftliche und die internationale Perspektive', *Wirtschafts- und sozialgeschichtliche Forschungen und Probleme. Karl Erich Born zum 65. Geburtstag*, contrib. & co-ed. with H. Henning & E. Wandel, Scripta Mercaturae, 1987, 375–441.

Lindgren, Håkan

Assistant Prof., Financial Hist. Unit, Dept. of Econ. Hist., Uppsala Univ., POB 513, 751 20 Uppsala, Sweden.

Tel.: 46 18 501550. Fax: 46 18 501585.

Year and Place of Birth 1941, Ängelholm, Sweden.

Degrees and Qualifications BA (Hist. & Polit.) Uppsala Univ., 1967; MA (Econ. Hist.) Uppsala Univ., 1972; Ph.D. (Econ. Hist.) Uppsala Univ., 1972.

Fields of Expertise *Industry Fields:* insurance, banking, finance. *Bus. Dimensions:* entrepreneurs and entrepreneurship; merger movement and issues; bus.–state relations. *Scope:* national; global. *Period:* nineteenth century; twentieth century as a whole. *Teaching:* undergrad.; post grad. *Consultancy:* co. hist.; corporate strategy.

Publications *Books: Corporate Growth. The Swedish Match Industry in its Global Setting*, Liber Förlag, Stockholm, 1979; series: Studies in Bus. Internationalisation; *Bank, investmentbolag, bankirfirma. Stockholms Enskilda Bank 1924–1945*, EHF, Stockholm School of Econ., Stockholm, 1988, (includes an extensive English summary); *European Industry and Banking between the Wars. A Rev. of Bank-Industry Relations*, P.L. Cottrell & Alice Teichova co-eds., Leicester Univ. Press, Leicester, 1992. *Articles:* 'Long-term Contracts in Financial Markets. Bank-Industry Connections in Sweden, illustrated by the Operations of the Stockholm Enskilda Bank, 1900–70', *The Firm as a Nexus of Treaties*, M. Aoki, B. Gustafsson & O.E. Williamson eds., Sage Publications, London, 1990; 'Swedish Hist. Research on Banking during the 1980s', *Scandinavian Econ. Hist. Rev.*, XXXIX(3), 1991.

Lipartito, Kenneth J.

Assoc. Prof. of Hist., Dept. of Hist., Houston Univ., Houston, TX 77204, USA. Tel.: 1 713 743 3106. Fax: 1 713 743 3216.

Year and Place of Birth 1957, USA.

Degrees and Qualifications BA (Hist. & Econ.) Delaware Univ., 1980; MA (Hist.) Johns Hopkins Univ., 1982; Ph.D. (Hist.) Johns Hopkins Univ., 1986.

Current Offices and Honorary Posts Pres., Econ. & Bus. Hist. Soc., 1992–3.

Major Honours Allan Nevins Prize for Outstanding Dissertation in Amer. Econ. Hist., 1986; Newcomen Fellowship, Harvard Bus. School, 1991–2.

Fields of Expertise *Industry Fields:* transport and communication. *Bus. Dimensions:* bus. and technology. *Scope:* internat. *Period:* twentieth century as a whole. *Consultancy:* co. hist.

Publications *Books: The Bell System and Regional Bus.: The Tel. in the South, 1877–1920*, Johns Hopkins Univ. Press, Baltimore, 1989; *Baker & Botts in the Development of Modern Houston*, with Joseph Pratt co-auth., Univ. of Texas Press, Austin, Texas, 1991. *Articles:* 'The Tel. in the South: A Comparative Analysis, 1877–1920', *J. of Econ. Hist.*, 48, 1988, 419–21; 'System-Building at the Margin: The Problem of Public Choice in Tel. Industry', *J. of Econ. Hist.*, 49, 1989, 323–36; 'What Have Lawyers Done for Amer. Bus.: The Case of Baker & Botts of Houston', *Bus. Hist. Rev.*, 64, 1990, 489–526.

Locke, Robert R.

Prof. of Hist., Dept. of Hist., Univ. of Hawaii at Manoa, 2530 Dole St, Honolulu, HI 96822, USA. Tel.: 1 808 956 7708. Fax: 1 808 956 9600.

Year and Place of Birth 1932, Montebello, USA.

Degrees and Qualifications BA (Hist.) UCLA, 1956; Ph.D. (Hist.) UCLA, 1966.

Previous Post Assoc. Prof., Dept. of Hist., Fordham Univ., 1970–4.

Major Honours Sen. Fulbright Research Fellowship - Germany, 1977; West European Fulbright Regional Research Fellowship, 1986; Visiting Prof., Dept. of Econ., Reading Univ., 1989–95.

Fields of Expertise *Bus. Dimensions:* entrepreneurs and entrepreneurship; management education; co. culture. *Period:* nineteenth century; twentieth century as a whole. *Teaching:* undergrad.; post grad. *Consultancy:* education.

Publications *Books: The End of the Practical Man: Entrepreneurship and Higher Education in Germany, France and Great Britain, 1880–1940,* JAI Press, Greenwich, CT, 1984; *Management and Higher Education since 1940: The Influence of Amer. and Japan on West Germany, Great Britain and France,* CUP, Cambridge, 1989. *Articles:* 'Bus. Education in Germany: Past Systems and Current Practice', *Bus. Hist. Rev.,* 59, Summer, 1985, 232–53; 'Industralisierung und Erziehungssystem in Frankreich und Deutschland vor dem 1. Weltkrieg', *Historische Zeitschrift,* 225, 1977, 265–96; 'Higher Education and Management: Their Relational Changes in the 20th Century', *Education and Training in the Development of Modern Corporations,* Nobuo Kawabe & Eisuke Daito eds., Univ. of Tokyo Press, Tokyo, 1993, 26–52.

Lorcin, Jean

Prof., Fac. of Geography, Hist., Hist. of Art & Tourism, Univ. Lumière-Lyon 2, C.P. 11–5, Avenue Pierre-Mendès-France, 69676 Bron Cedex, France. Tel.: 33 78 77 23 23. Fax: 33 78 77 23 36.

Year and Place of Birth 1929, Saint-Etienne, France.

Degrees and Qualifications Agrégation (Hist.) Lyons Univ., 1955; Doctorat d'Etat (Hist.) Paris 1 Univ., 1987.

Previous Post MC Mod. Hist., Univ. Lumière-Lyon 2, 1985–92.

Current Offices and Honorary Posts Director, Dept. of Hist., Univ. Lumière-Lyon 2.

Fields of Expertise *Industry Fields:* gas, electricity, water. *Bus. Dimensions:* entrepreneurs and entrepreneurship; private-public relations. *Scope:* regional. *Period:* early twentieth century. *Teaching:* undergrad. *Consultancy:* co. hist.

Publications *Books: Economie et Comportements Sociaux e Politiques. La Région de Saint-Etienne de la Grande Dépression à la 2éme Guerre Mondiale,* doctoral thesis, Paris 1, 1987, multig., 9 vols. *Articles:* 'La Distribution de l'Énergie Électrique à Saint-Etienne: Les Origines du "Monopole" de la Compagnie Electrique de la Loire', *Actes du 98e Congrès National des Sociétés Savantes (Saint-Etienne, 1973),* Section d'Histoire Moderne et Contemporaine, vol. 2, 205–20; 'Un Projet Régional: L'Exploitation des Forces Motrices du Lignon', *L'Aménagement du Bassin Ligérien,* Journées d'Étude du Centre Interdisciplinaire d'Études et de Recherches sur les Structures Régionales, Saint-Etienne Univ., 1978, 101–18; 'Houille Blanche contre Houille Verte: Du Projet du Lignon à l'Interconnexion entre "Loire et Centre" et les Alpes du Dauphiné', *Actes du 5e Colloque sur le Patrimoine Industriel (Alès 1983),* CILAC, 1984, 100–8; 'Du "Socialisme Municipal" au Libéralisme. Le Régime de la Production et de la Distribution de la Force Motrice à Saint-Etienne (Loire) avant 1914', *Bull. d'Histoire de l'Electricité,* 12, 1988, 61–81.

Lorenz, Edward H.

Assoc. Prof. of Econ., Dept. of Econ., Univ. of Notre Dame, Notre Dame, IN 46556, USA. Tel.: 1 219 631 7590. Fax: 1 219 631 8809.

Year and Place of Birth 1950, Boston, USA.

Degrees and Qualifications BS (Econ.) MIT, 1975; MA (Econ.) Univ. of California, Berkeley, 1977; Ph.D. Cambridge Univ., UK, 1983.

Previous Post ESRL Post-doctoral Fellow, Dept. of Applied Econ., Cambridge Univ., 1983–6.

Current Offices and Honorary Posts Fellow of the Helen Kellogg Inst. for Internat. Studies, Univ. of Notre Dame.

Fields of Expertise *Industry Fields:* mechanical engineering; shipbuilding and marine engineering. *Bus. Dimensions:* entrepreneurs and entrepreneurship; personnel management; strategy formation; bus. organization. *Scope:* internat. *Period:* nineteenth century; twentieth century as a whole. *Teaching:* post grad.

Publications *Books: Econ. Decline in Britain: The Shipbuilding Industry, 1890–1970,* OUP, 1991. *Articles:* 'Neither Friends nor Strangers: Informal Networks of Subcontracting in French Industry', *Trust: Making and Breaking Co-operative Relations,* D. Gambetta ed., Basil Blackwell, 1988; 'An Evolutionary Explanation for Competitive Decline; British Shipbuilding 1890–1970', *J. of Econ. Hist.,* 51(4), Dec., 1991, 911–935; 'Labor Supply and the Employment Strategies of French and British Shipbuilders, 1890–1970', *Internat. Contributions to Labour Studies,* vol. 2, 1992; 'Trust and the Flexible Firm: Internat. Comparison', *Indust. Relations,* 3(3), Fall, 1992, 455–72.

Lubar, Steven

Curator of Engineering & Industry, Museum of Amer. Hist., Room 5014, Smithsonian Inst., Washington, DC 20560, USA. Tel.: 1 202 357 3188. Fax: 1 202 357 4256.

Year and Place of Birth 1954, Philadelphia, USA.

Degrees and Qualifications BA, Massachusetts Inst. of Technology, 1976; MA Chicago Univ., 1977; Ph.D. Chicago Univ., 1983.

Major Honours Engines of Change exhibit won Soc. for the Hist. of Technology Dibner Prize.

Fields of Expertise *Industry Fields:* other manufacturing industries. *Bus. Dimensions:* bus. and technology. *Scope:* national. *Period:* nineteenth century. *Consultancy:* co. hist.

Publications *Books: The Philo. of Manufactures: Early Debate on Industry in the United States,* co-ed., MIT Press, 1982; *Engines of Change: The Amer. Indust. Revolution, 1790–1860,* co-auth., Smithsonian Press, 1986; *Hist. from Things: Essays on Material Culture,* co-ed., Smithsonian Press, 1993; *InfoCulture: The Smithsonian Book of Information Age Inventions,* Houghton Mifflin, 1993.

Lutz, John S.

Post Doctoral Fellow, Dept. of Hist., Washington Univ., Seattle, Washington 98195, USA. Tel.: 1 604 595 4960. Fax: 1 604 595 0204.

Year and Place of Birth 1959, Montreal, Canada.

Degrees and Qualifications BA Victoria Univ., 1983; MA Victoria Univ., 1988; Ph.D. Ottawa Univ., 1993.

Major Honours Fulbright Doctoral Fellowship; Social Sciences and Humanities Research Council of Canada Post-Doctoral Fellowship.

Fields of Expertise *Industry Fields:*

agric., forestry, fishing; mining and quarrying; food, drink, tobacco; metal goods; other manufacturing industries. *Bus. Dimensions:* small bus. matters; bus.–state relations; bus.–labour relations. *Scope:* regional; national. *Period:* nineteenth century; twentieth century as a whole. *Teaching:* undergrad.

Publications *Articles:* 'After the Fur Trade: The Aboriginal Labouring Class of British Columbia, 1849–90', *J. of the Canadian Hist. Assoc.*, new ser., 3, forthcoming; 'Shadows and Light. Canadian Capitalists in Latin Amer. and the Caribbean', *J. of Canadian Studies*, forthcoming; 'Losing Steam; The Boiler and Engine Industry as an Index of British Columbia's De-industrialization', *Hist. Papers*, 1989, 168–207; 'Technology in Canada through the Lens of Labour History', *Scientia Canadensis*. [J. of the hist. of Canadian science, technology & medicine], 15(1), 1991, 5–20; *Occasional Papers in the Teaching of Hist. in Canada*, ed.

Lyons, John S.

Assistant Prof., Dept. of Econ., Miami Univ., Oxford, OH 45056, USA. Tel.: 1 513 529 2853. Fax: 1 513 529 6992.

Year and Place of Birth 1944, Albany, USA.

Degrees and Qualifications BA Harvard Univ., 1966; Ph.D. Univ. of California, Berkeley, 1977.

Previous Post Lect., Dept. of Econ. & Soc. Hist., Edinburgh Univ., 1981–2.

Current Offices and Honorary Posts Assoc. ed., *The Newsletter of the Cliometric Soc.*

Fields of Expertise *Industry Fields:* textiles. *Bus. Dimensions:* bus. and technology. *Scope:* national; UK. *Period:* nineteenth century. *Teaching:* undergrad.

Publications *Articles:* 'Eighteenth Century British Trade: Homespun or Empire-made?', *Explorations in Econ. Hist.*, with T.J. Hatton & S.E. Satchell, 20, 1983, 163–82; 'Vertical Integration in the British Cotton Industry, 1825–1850: A Revision', *J. of Econ. Hist.*, 45, 1985, 419–26; 'Powerloom Profitability and Steam Power Costs: Britain in the 1830's', *Explorations in Econ. Hist.*, 24, 1987, 392–408; 'Family Response to Econ. Decline: Handloom Weavers in Early Nineteenth Century Lancashire', *Research in Econ. Hist.*, 12, 1989, 45–91; 'Technological Dualism, Rivalry and Complementarity: Handicrafts in the Transition to "Modern Industry"', forthcoming.

MacMurray, Robert R.

802 Country Club Drive, Bloomsburg, PA 17815, USA.

Year and Place of Birth 1925, Philadelphia, USA.

Degrees and Qualifications MBA (Indust. Relations) Wharton Grad. Division; Ph.D. (Econ.) Pennsylvania Univ.

Previous Post Dept. of Econ., Bloomsburg, Pennsylvania Univ., 1971–89.

Current Offices and Honorary Posts Board mem., National Soc. Sc. Assoc.; standing com. mem., Databases & Archives, EHA; standing com. mem., Technology Studies & Education, SIG.

Major Honours Amer. Philosophical Soc. Grant -Johnson Fund, 1982; National Science Foundation, 1987.

Fields of Expertise *Industry Fields:* patent hist. (over 20 fields). *Bus. Dimensions:* bus. and technology. *Scope:* national; USA. *Period:* nineteenth century. *Teaching:* undergrad. *Consultancy:* US patents, 1790–1836.

Publications *Books: Technological Change in the Amer. Cotton Spinning*

Industry, 1790–1836, The Arno Press, NY, 1977, (doctoral dissertation). *Articles*: 'Technological Change in a Soc. in Transition: Work in Progress on an unified Reference Work in Early Amer. Patent History', *J. of Econ. Hist.*, XLV(2), June, 1985, 299–303.

MacPherson, Ian

Dean of Humanities, Dept. of Hist., Univ. of Victoria, POB 1700, Victoria, British Columbia, V8W 3P4, Canada. Tel.: 1 604 721 7063. Fax: 1 604 721 7059.

Year and Place of Birth 1939, Toronto, Canada.

Degrees and Qualifications BA Windsor Univ., 1960; MA Western Ontario Univ., 1968; Ph.D. Western Ontario Univ., 1971.

Previous Post Prof. of Hist. & Chair, Dept. of Hist., Victoria Univ., 1985–91.

Current Offices and Honorary Posts Chair, Com. to Rev. the Basic Principles of the Internat. Co-operative Movement, Internat. Co-operative Alliance, Geneva.

Major Honours Served as Pres. of the Canadian Co-operative Assoc., 1988–92.

Fields of Expertise *Industry Fields*: agric., forestry, fishing; insurance, banking, finance; miscellaneous services. *Bus. Dimensions*: merger movement and issues; multinational bus.; bus.–state relations; markets and bus.; bus. values. *Scope*: global. *Period*: nineteenth century; twentieth century as a whole. *Teaching*: undergrad.; post grad. *Consultancy*: co. hist.; corporate strategy.

Publications *Books: Each for All: A Hist. of the Co-operative Movement in English Canada*, Macmillan, Toronto, 1979; *A Hist. of Co-operative Insurance Services*, Western Producer Press, Saskatoon, 1978; *Building and Protecting the Co-opera-*

tive Movement: A Brief Hist. of the Co-operative Union of Canada, Co-op Union, Ottawa, 1984; *A Hist. of Co-op Trust*, Western Producer, Saskatoon, 1980; *Building Beyond the Homestead*, Univ. of Calgary, Calgary, 1986.

Maggia, Giovanni

Assoc. Prof. of Econ. Hist., Fac. of Polit. Science, Dept. of Econ., Turin Univ., Via Po 53, 10124 Turin; Fondazione Adriano Olivetti, Archivio Storico del Gruppo Olivetti, Villa Casana, Via Miniere 31, 10015 Ivrea (TO), Italy. Tel.: 39 11 8127655. Fax: 39 11 879281.

Year and Place of Birth 1946, Ivrea, Italy.

Degrees and Qualifications Laurea (Polit. Sc.) Turin Univ., 1972.

Previous Post Assoc. Prof. of Econ. Hist., Fac. of Econ. & Bank Sc., Dept. of Econ., Siena Univ., Italy, 1978–91.

Current Offices and Honorary Posts Gen. sec., Fondazione Adriano Olivetti (Rome-Ivrea); scientific director, Olivetti Group Hist. Archives; scientific com. mem. ASSI (Associazione per la Storia e gli Studi sull'Impresa), Milan.

Fields of Expertise *Industry Fields*: mechanical engineering; metal goods; electronics and computers: manufacture. *Bus. Dimensions*: entrepreneurs and entrepreneurship; bus. and technology; multinational bus.; co. culture. *Scope*: global. *Period*: twentieth century as a whole. *Teaching*: undergrad.; post grad. *Consultancy*: co. hist.

Publications *Books: Bibliografia degli Scritti di Adriano Olivetti*, 2 vols., Pubblicazioni della Facoltà di Scienze Economiche e Bancarie, Siena Univ., 1983; *Le Lezioni ai Giovani Operai di F. Prat*, ed., Enrico, Ivrea, 1990. *Articles*: 'L'Intervento del Potere Pubblico nello Sviluppo Industriale Italiano dalla Unità alla II Guerra Mondiale', *Appunti sul Sistema dell*

Partecipazioni Statali in Italia, with G. Fornengo co-ed., Giappichelli, Turin, 1975; 'Sviluppo Economico e Condizione Operaia in un'Area in via di Industrializzazione: Il Canavese fra le due Guerre. Documentazione Statistica di Base', *Movimento Operaio e Sviluppo Economico in Piemonte negli ultimi 50 Anni*, E. Passerin ed., Cassa di Risparmio di Torino, Turin, 1978; 'L'Archivio Storico del Gruppo Olivetti', *Economia e Industria nella Guerra. Le Fonti e gli Archivi in Piemonte*, C. Dellavalle ed., F. Angeli, Milan, 1988.

Maitra, Priyatosh

Assoc. Prof. of Econ., Dept. of Econ., Univ. of Otago, POB 56, Dunedin, New Zealand. Tel.: 64 3 479 8649. Fax: 64 3 479 8174.

Year and Place of Birth 1930, India.

Degrees and Qualifications MA (Econ.) Calcutta Univ., 1949; MA (Polit. Sc.) Calcutta Univ., 1950.

Previous Post Research Technician & Lect., Indian Statistical Inst., Calcutta, 1957–68.

Current Offices and Honorary Posts Edit. board mem., *Soc. and Change*; edit. advisory board mem., *Internat. J. of Social Econ.*; mem., Council of the Internat. Centre for Middle East Bus. & Econ. Research Centre, Sydney.

Fields of Expertise *Industry Fields:* economic development, technological change and population and demography; internationalization of production and capitalism's dilemma. *Period:* nineteenth century; twentieth century as a whole.

Publications *Books: Import Subtitution Potential in East Africa*, OUP, Nairobi, 1967; *The Mainspring of Econ. Development*, Croom Helm, London, & St Martin's Press, NY, 1980; *Population, Technology and Development*, Gower Publications, London & Vermont, 1984; *Technological Change, Development and the Environment*, with Clem Tisdell co-ed., Routledge, London, 1988; *Indian Econ. Development - Population Growth and Technological Change*, A.P.H., New Delhi, 1991.

Marchildon, Gregory P.

Assistant Prof., Center for Canadian Studies, The Paul H. Nitze School of Advanced Internat. Studies, Johns Hopkins Univ., 1740 Massachusetts Avenue, N.W., Washington, DC 20036-1984, USA. Tel.: 1 202 663 5716. Fax: 1 202 663 5656.

Year and Place of Birth 1956, Saskatchewan, Canada.

Degrees and Qualifications BA Regina Univ., 1980; LLB Saskatchewan Univ., 1980; MA Regina Univ., 1984; Ph.D. London School of Econ., 1990.

Previous Post Lect., London School of Econ., 1988.

Current Offices and Honorary Posts Acting director, Center of Canadian Studies SAIS; mem., Law Soc. of Saskatchewan.

Major Honours George W. Robertson Memorial Scholarship, 1986–8; Invited Mem., Sloan Competitiveness Colloquia, 1992–3.

Fields of Expertise *Industry Fields:* insurance, banking, finance. *Bus. Dimensions:* merger movement and issues. *Scope:* internat. *Period:* early twentieth century. *Teaching:* post grad.

Publications *Books: Mergers and Acquisitions*, edn., no. 3 in Internat. Library of Critical Writings in Bus. Hist. series, Edward Elgar, 1991. *Articles:* 'The Role of Lawyers in Corporate Promotion and Management: A Canadian Case Study and Theoretical Speculations', *Bus. &*

Econ. Hist., 2nd ser., 19, 1990, 193–202; 'British Investment Banking and Indust. Decline before the Great War: A Case Study of Capital Outflow to Canadian Industry', *Bus. Hist.*, 33, July, 1991, 72–92; 'Canadian Multinationals and Internat. Finance', *Bus. Hist.*, D. McDowall co-ed., 34, July, 1992, theme issue; 'John F. Stairs, Max Aitken and the Scotia Group: Finance Capitalism and Indust. Decline in the Maritimes, 1890–1914', *Farm, Factory and Fortune: New Essays in the Econ. Hist. of the Maritimes*, K. Inwood ed., Acadiensis Press, 1993.

Markowski, Mieczyslaw B.

Prof. of Hist., Inst. of Hist., Univ. of Pedagogy in Kielce, ul. Zeromskiego 5, 25–369 Kielce, Poland. Tel.: 48 41 486 70. Fax: 48 41 488 05.

Year and Place of Birth 1936, Male Boze, Poland.

Degrees and Qualifications Doktor, 1974; Doktor Habilitowany, 1990; Prof., 1992.

Previous Post Deputy Manager, Inst. of Hist., 1986–9.

Current Offices and Honorary Posts Manager, post-grad. studies; mem., Polish Hist. Soc.; management mem., Kielce Scientific Soc.

Major Honours Ministry of Education Award.

Fields of Expertise *Industry Fields:* agric., forestry, fishing; mining and quarrying. *Bus. Dimensions:* entrepreneurs and entrepreneurship; production management; personnel management; bus. organization. *Scope:* regional; national; Poland. *Consultancy:* economic and social history.

Publications *Books: District of Olkusz in Independent Poland (1918–1939)*, in Hist. of Olkusz and Olkusz Province vol. II, Polish Scientific Publishers, Cracow, 1978; *Industrial Workpeople in the Kielce Province 1918–1939*, Kziazka i Wiedza Publishers, Warsaw, 1980; *Industrial Classes and Landed Aristocracy in the Province of Kielce 1918–1939*, Univ. of Pedagogy in Kielce Publishers, 1990. *Articles:* 'The Owners of the Industrial Works in Kielce Province in the Interwar Period', *The Hist. of the Bourgeoisie in Poland*, vol. 3, Ossolineum Publishers, 1983, 237–65; 'Jews in the Econ. Life of Kielce Province in the Interwar Period', *Jews in Malopolska*, Przemysl, 1991, 309–35.

Marriner, Sheila

Sen. Research Fellow, Liverpool Univ., POB 147, Liverpool, L69 3BX, UK. Tel.: 44 51 794 2413. Fax: 44 51 708 6502.

Year and Place of Birth 1925, Southport, UK.

Degrees and Qualifications BA Liverpool Univ., 1946; MA Liverpool Univ., 1948; Ph.D. Liverpool Univ., 1957.

Previous Post Reader in Econ. Hist., Liverpool Univ., 1974–83.

Fields of Expertise *Industry Fields:* transport and communication. *Bus. Dimensions:* entrepreneurs and entrepreneurship. *Scope:* national. *Period:* nineteenth century.

Publications *Books: Rathbones of Liverpool, 1845–73*, Liverpool Univ. Press, 1961; *The Sen. John Samuel Swire, 1825–98*, with F.E. Hyde, Liverpool Univ. Press, 1967; *Bus. and Bus.men. Studies in Bus., Econ. and Accounting Hist.*, ed., Liverpool Univ. Press, 1978; *The Econ. and Social Development of Merseyside, 1750–1960*, Croom, Helm, 1982. *Articles:* 'Co. Financial Statements as Source Material for Bus. Historians', *Bus. Hist.*, XXII(2), Jul., 1980, 203–35.

Marseille, Jacques

Inst. of Econ. and Social Hist., Univ. of Paris I - Sorbonne, 17 rue de la Sorbonne, 75005 Paris, France. Tel.: 33 40 46 28 21.
Year and Place of Birth 1945, Abbeville, France.
Degrees and Qualifications Docteur-ès-lettres; Agrégé.
Current Offices and Honorary Posts Edit. director (Nathan); assoc. pres., *Découvrir*; pres., Assoc. for the Development of Econ. Hist.
Fields of Expertise *Industry Fields:* capitalism - internat. relations. *Bus. Dimensions:* entrepreneurs and entrepreneurship; markets and bus.; co. culture. *Scope:* national; internat.; France. *Period:* twentieth century as a whole. *Teaching:* undergrad.; post grad. *Consultancy:* co. hist.; corporate strategy.
Publications *Books: Empire Colonial et Capitalisme Français. Histoire d'un Divorce*, Albin Michel, 1984; *L'Age d'Or de la France Coloniale*, Albin Michel, 1987; *La France Travaille Trop*, Albin Michel, 1989; *C'est Beau, la France, Essai sur le Masochisme Français*, Plon, 1993.

Martin, John E.

Sen. Historian, Hist. Branch, Dept. of Internal Affairs, POB 805, Wellington, New Zealand. Tel.: 64 4 712599. Fax: 64 4 991943.
Year and Place of Birth 1951, London, UK.
Degrees and Qualifications BA Victoria Univ. of Wellington, 1973; BA Victoria Univ. of Wellington, 1974; Ph.D. Lancaster Univ. (England), 1979.
Previous Post Lect./Sen. Lect. in Sociology, Canterbury Univ., Christchurch, 1986-9.
Fields of Expertise *Industry Fields:* agric., forestry, fishing; electrical engineering; gas, electricity, water. *Bus. Dimensions:* bus.–state relations; bus. and labour. *Scope:* national. *Period:* nineteenth century; twentieth century as a whole. *Consultancy:* public hist. contracts (esp. government departments concerned with science, engineering and construction, electricity generation, agric., etc..
Publications *Books: The Forgotten Worker: The Rural Wage Earner in 19th Century New Zealand*, Allen & Unwin, 1990; *People, Polit. and Power Stations: Electric Power Generation in New Zealand, 1880–1990*, Bridget Williams ed., Books/Electricity Corporation, 1991; *Labour and Kiwifruit*, Dept. of Scientific and Indust. Research, 1983. *Articles:* 'Control in the Shearing Shed: The Introduction of Machinery and Changing Workplace Relations in New Zealand', *Labour Hist.*, 62, May, 1992, 71–90.

Martin, Manuel

Catedratico de Economia Aplicada, Granada Univ., Facultad de Derecho, Pl. Campillo 5, 7°L, 18009 Granada, Spain. Tel.: 34 58 222729.
Year and Place of Birth 1941, Granada, Spain.
Degrees and Qualifications Ph.D. (Econ. Sc.) Complutense Univ., Madrid, 1975.
Major Honours Premio Andalucia de Economia, Junta de Andalucia, 1991.
Fields of Expertise *Industry Fields:* agric., forestry, fishing; food, drink, tobacco. *Bus. Dimensions:* entrepreneurs and entrepreneurship; bus. organization; bus. and technology. *Scope:* local; regional; national; Spain. *Period:* nineteenth century; twentieth century as a whole. *Teaching:* undergrad.; post grad.

167

Publications *Books: Azucar y Descolonizacion*, Granada Univ., 1982; *Pensamiento Economico Español sobre la Poblacion*, Piramide, Madrid, 1984; *La Gran Via de Granada*, Caja General de Ahorros de Granada, Granada, 1986; *El Azucar en el Encuentro entre dos Mundos*, Asociacion General de Fabricantes de Azucar de España, Madrid, 1992; *Estructura Economica de Andalucia*, Espasa Calpe, Madrid, 1993.

Martin-Aceña, Pablo

Director of Econ. Hist. Programme, Fundacion Empresa Publica, Plaza del Márqués de Salamanca 8, 28006 Madrid, Spain. Tel.: 34 1 5777909. Fax: 34 1 5755641.
Year and Place of Birth 1950, Madrid, Spain.
Degrees and Qualifications MA (Econ.) Toronto Univ., 1980; Ph.D. (Econ. & Econ. Hist.) Complutense Univ., Madrid, 1983.
Current Offices and Honorary Posts Dean, Faculdad de Ciencias Economicas y Empresariales, Alcala Univ.; director, Econ. Hist. Programme, Fundación Empresa Pública; gen. sec., Spanish Econ. Hist. Assoc.
Fields of Expertise *Industry Fields:* mining and quarrying; coal and petroleum products; chemicals and allied industries; metal manufacture; mechanical engineering; shipbuilding and marine engineering; vehicle construction; metal goods; gas, electricity, water; transport and communication; insurance, banking, finance; public industrial holdings. *Bus. Dimensions:* bus. organization; bus.–state relations; public policy and public owned companies. *Scope:* national. *Period:* inter-war years, 1919–39; mid-twentieth century, 1940–70. *Teaching:* undergrad.; post grad. *Consultancy:* co. hist.
Publications *Books: Empresa*

Publica e Industrializacion en España, ed., Alianza Editorial, 1990; *IWI. 50 Años de Industrializacion en España*, Espasa Calpe, 1991; *Historia de la Empresa Publica en España*, ed., Espasa Calpe, 1991.

Martuliak, Pavol

Mateja Bela Univ., Fac. of Humanities and Soc. Sc., Tajovského 40, 975 49 Banská Bystrica, Slovakia. Tel.: 42 88 34555.
Year and Place of Birth 1939, Dolny Tisovník, Slovakia.
Degrees and Qualifications Ph.D. Comenius Univ., Bratislava, 1970.
Previous Post High School Teacher, Gymnazium Bytca, 1963–7.
Current Offices and Honorary Posts Com. mem., Slovak Econ. Hist. Soc.
Fields of Expertise *Industry Fields:* agric., forestry, fishing. *Bus. Dimensions:* production management; merger movement and issues. *Scope:* national. *Period:* inter-war years, 1919–39. *Teaching:* undergrad. *Consultancy:* co. hist.
Publications *Books: The Evolution of Agric. in Slovakia in the 1920s*, Matica slovenská in Martin, 1982. *Articles:* 'The Specialities of the First Land Reform in Slovakia', *Slovácke Múzeum Uherské Hradiste J.*, 1991, 84–110; 'The Position of Gemer-Malohont at the Origin of the Slovak Unified Farmers' Co-operative', *Obzor Gemera-Malohontu*, no. 4, 1992, 178–91; 'The Unified Farmers'Co-operative in Slovakia at the Time of the First Czechoslovak Republic', *Slovácke Múzeum Uherské Hradiste J.*, 1992, 95–105.

Mason, Mark

Assistant Prof., School of Management, Yale Univ., Box 1A, 135 Prospect St, New Haven, CT 06520,

USA. Tel.: 0203 432 3235. Fax: 0203 432 6974.

Year and Place of Birth 1955, Norwalk, USA.

Degrees and Qualifications BA Haverford College, 1978; MA Columbia Univ., 1982; Ph.D. Harvard Univ., 1988.

Previous Post Post-doctoral Fellow, Harvard Acad. for Internat. & Area Studies, Harvard Univ., 1988–90.

Current Offices and Honorary Posts Assoc.-in-Research, Reischauer Inst., Harvard Univ.

Major Honours Fac. Research Award, Center for Internat. & Area Studies, Yale Univ.; Acad. Fellowship, Harvard Acad. for Internat. & Area Studies, Harvard Univ.; National Resource Fellowship, US Dept. of Education.

Fields of Expertise *Industry Fields:* vehicle construction. *Bus. Dimensions:* bus.–state relations. *Scope:* internat. *Period:* late twentieth century, 1970–present. *Teaching:* post grad. *Consultancy:* corporate strategy.

Publications *Books: Amer. Multinationals and Japan: The Polit. Economy of Japanese Capital Controls, 1899–1980,* Harvard Council on East Asian Studies, Harvard Univ., 1992; *Does Ownership Matter? Japanese Multinationals in Europe,* with Dennis J. Encarnation co-ed., OUP, Oxford, forthcoming. *Articles:* 'Neither MITI nor Amer.: The Polit. Economy of Capital Liberalization in Japan', *Internat. Organization,* with Dennis J. Encarnation, 44(1), Winter, 1990, 25–54; 'United States Direct Investment in Japan: Trends and Prospects', *Californian Management Rev.,* 35(1), Autumn, 1992, 48–115; 'The Origins and Evolution of Japanese Direct Investment in Europe', *Bus. Hist. Rev.,* 67(1), Spring, 1993.

Matejcek, Jirí

Leading Research Worker & Fellow, Czech Acad. of Science, Silesian Inst., Nádrazní Okruh 31, A746 48 Opava, Czechland.

Year and Place of Birth 1930, Hradec Králové, Bohemia.

Degrees and Qualifications Magister Charles Univ., 1962; Ph.Dr. Charles Univ., 1970; Dr.Sc. Prague Univ., 1991.

Previous Post Research Fellow, Silesian Inst., Opava, 1966–93.

Current Offices and Honorary Posts Central com. mem., Assoc. of Bus. Hist., Czechland; edit. board mem., *Prager Zeitschrift für Wirtschafts- und Sozialgeschichte;* edit. board mem., *Slezky sborník*[Silesian Research Rev.].

Publications *Books: Vyvoj uhelného prumyslu v ceskych zemích po prumyslové revoluci 1880–1914* [Development of Coal Mining in Czech Lands 1880–1914], Academia, Prague, 1984; *Uhelné hornictví v Ceskoslovensku* [Coalmining in Czechoslovakia], with J. Majer co-auth., Profil, Ostrava, 1985; *Hutnictví zeleza v Ceskoslovensku 2* [Iron-making in Czechoslovakia 1830–1914], co-auth., Academia, Prague, 1986; *Nástin vyvoje textilní vyroby v ceskych zemích 1781–1848* [Development of Textile Manufacturing in Czech Lands 1781–1848], with J. Machacová, Slezsky ústav CSAV, Opava, 3 vols., 1991–2. *Articles:* 'Vyznam tazvané velkovyroby v ceskych zemích v první polovine 19. století' [Impact of the So-called Great Industry on the Econ. and Social Development of the Czech Lands in the first Half of the 19th Century], *Studie k sociálním dejinám 19. století, 1* [Studies in Social Hist. of the 19th Century. 1], Slezzsky ústav, CSAV, Opava, 1992, 213–85.

Mathias, Peter

Master, Downing College, Cambridge, CB2 1DQ, UK. Tel.: 44 223 334868.
Year and Place of Birth 1928, UK.
Degrees and Qualifications BA Cambridge Univ., 1951; MA Cambridge Univ., 1954; Litt.D. Oxford Univ., 1985; D.Litt. Univ. of Cambridge, 1987.
Previous Post Chichele Prof. of Econ. Hist., Oxford Univ., 1969–87.
Major Honours CBE; FBA; Honorary doctorates from Cambridge, Oxford, Buckingham, Birmingham & Hull Universities; Foreign mem., Royal Danish Acad., Royal Belgian Acad.; mem., Academia Europaea.
Fields of Expertise *Industry Fields:* food, drink, tobacco. *Bus. Dimensions:* entrepreneurs and entrepreneurship. *Period:* eighteenth century; nineteenth century; twentieth century as a whole. *Teaching:* undergrad.; post grad. *Consultancy:* co. hist.
Publications *Books: The Brewing Industry in England, 1700–1830,* 1959; *Retailing Revolution,* Longman, 1967; *The First Indust. Nation,* Methuen, 1969, 1983; *Innovation and Technology in Europe,* with J.A. Davis co-ed. & contributor, 1991; *Growth and Change in the British Economy, 1815–1914,* Einaudi, forthcoming.

Mathis, Franz

Prof., Dept. of Hist., Univ. of Innsbruck, Innrain 52, A-6020 Innsbruck, Austria. Tel.: 43 512 507 3499. Fax: 43 512 507 3629.
Year and Place of Birth 1946, Hohenems, Austria.
Degrees and Qualifications Mag.phil. Innsbruck Univ., 1971; Dr.phil. Innsbruck Univ., 1973.
Previous Post Assoc. Prof., Dept. of Hist., Innsbruck Univ., 1979–93.
Current Offices and Honorary Posts Chairman, Studies Commission for Hist. at Innsbruck Univ.; vice-pres., Austrian Assoc. for Amer. Studies.
Major Honours Theodor-Körner Prize, Vienna; First Prize from Salzburg Province for scientific publications, 1978.
Fields of Expertise *Industry Fields:* mining and quarrying; industry in general. *Bus. Dimensions:* entrepreneurs and entrepreneurship; strategy formation; merger movement and issues; multinational bus.; bus.–state relations. *Scope:* national; internat.; global. *Period:* nineteenth century; twentieth century as a whole. *Teaching:* undergrad.; post grad. *Consultancy:* co. hist.
Publications *Books: Big Bus. in Österreich. Österreichische Großunternehmen in Kurzdarstellungen,* Verlag für Geschichte und Politik, Vienna, 1987; *Big Bus. in Österreich II. Wachstum und Eigentumsstruktur der österreichischen Großunternehmen im 19. und 20. Jahrhundert. Analyse und Interpretation,* Verlag für Geschichte und Politik, Vienna, 1990. *Articles:* 'Kartelle, Fusionen und multinationale Unternehmen in Großbritannien, Frankreich, Deutschland, den USA und den wichtigsten Staaten der übrigen Welt bis 1914', *Wettbewerbsbeschränkungen auf internationalen Märkten,* Zeitschrift für Unternehmensgeschichte, Beiheft 46, Stuttgart, 1988, 79–96; 'Abschied vom Klassenkampf. Zur Entwicklung der Sozialpartnerschaft im österreichischen Kohlenbergbau', *Arbeiter Unternehmer und Staat im Bergbau. Industrielle Beziehungen im internationalen Vergleich,* G.D. Feldman & K. Tenfelde eds., C.H. Beck, Munich, 1989, 256–91, (English version in *Workers, Owners and Polit. in Coalmining,* Berg, Oxford, 1990, 315–60); 'Erfolg und Mißerfolg der österreichischen Großunternehmen im 20. Jahrhundert', *Zeitschrift für Unternehmensgeschichte,* 37, 1992, 1–18.

Matis, Herbert W.

Prof., Inst. of Econ. and Social Hist., Vienna Univ. of Econ. and Bus. Admin., Augasse 2-6, A-1180 Vienna, Austria. Tel.: 43 1 31336 4709. Fax: 43 1 31336 710.
Year and Place of Birth 1941, Vienna, Austria.
Degrees and Qualifications Ph.D. Vienna Univ., 1965; Habilitation, Hochschule für Welthandel (Vienna), 1971.
Previous Post Lect. & Head of Dept. of Econ. Hist., Univ. of Econ. & Bus. Admin, 1971–2.
Current Offices and Honorary Posts V-P, Austrian Science Foundation; vice-director, Univ. of Econ. & Bus. Admin.; sec., Austrian Schumpeter Soc.; head of Boltzmann Inst. for Econ. Hist. Research.
Major Honours Corr. mem., Austrian Acad. of Sciences, 1988; Grand Cross of Honour, Republic of Austria, 1988.
Fields of Expertise *Industry Fields:* vehicle construction; metal goods; textiles; bricks, pottery, glass, cement; construction; transport and communication; distributive trades; insurance, banking, finance. *Bus. Dimensions:* entrepreneurs and entrepreneurship; production management; co. finance and accounting; personnel management; strategy formation; bus. organization; bus. and technology; small bus. matters; multinational bus.; management education; markets and bus.; co. culture. *Scope:* national; internat.; former Austrian monarchy and Austrian Republic. *Period:* eighteenth century; nineteenth century; twentieth century as a whole. *Teaching:* undergrad.; post grad. *Consultancy:* co. hist.
Publications *Books: Österreichs Wirtschaft 1848–1913*, Duncker & Humblot, 1972; *Der Österreichische Schilling*, K. Bachinger co-auth., Styria, 1974; *Geburt der Neuzeit*, L. Bauer co-auth., DTV, 1988; *Das Industriesystem*, Ueberreuter, 1988; *Die Weltwirtschaft*, D. Stiefel co-auth., Ueberreuter, 1991.

Matsuda, Tomoo

Emeritus Prof. of Tokyo Univ. & Director of Nomura Foundation for Science & Art, Nomura Foundation for Science & Art, Takaido Nishi 1-9-31, Suginami-ku, 168 Tokyo, Japan. Tel.: 81 3 3334 8597.
Year and Place of Birth 1911, Tokyo, Japan.
Degrees and Qualifications Dr of Econ., Tokyo Univ., 1957.
Previous Post Pres., National Univ. of Library and Information Science, 1978–84.
Current Offices and Honorary Posts Council mem., Assoc. of Bus. Hist. (Japan); council mem., Seijo Univ., Tokyo.
Major Honours Großer Kreuz - Verdienstorder (for cultural contribution), 1976.
Fields of Expertise *Industry Fields:* mechanical engineering; textiles; professional and scientific services. *Bus. Dimensions:* entrepreneurs and entrepreneurship; markets and bus. *Scope:* regional; internat. *Period:* nineteenth century; twentieth century as a whole. *Teaching:* post grad. *Consultancy:* co. hist.
Publications *Books: Comparative Econ. Hist. of Japan/Germany*, Iwanami Shoten, Tokyo, 1958; *Formation and Development of Social Sciences*, Univ. Press, Tokyo, 1986.

Matsumoto, Koji

Prof., Grad. School of Policy Science, Saitama Univ., Japan. Tel.: 048 855 5367. Fax: 048 852 0499.
Year and Place of Birth 1944,

Sizuoka pref., Japan.

Degrees and Qualifications BA (Econ.) Tokyo Univ., 1966.

Previous Post Gen. Director, Japan National Oil Corp.

Fields of Expertise *Bus. Dimensions:* entrepreneurs and entrepreneurship; personnel management; bus. organization; bus.–state relations. *Period:* late twentieth century, 1970–present. *Teaching:* post grad.

Publications *Books: Organizing for Higher Productivity: An Analysis of Japanese Systems and Practices*, Asian Productivity Organization, 1982; *Nikkan Keizai Masatsu* [The Econ. Dispute between Japan and Korea], Toyo Keizai Shimpo-sha, 1986; *The Rise of the Japanese Corporate System*, Kegan Paul Internat., 1991.

Matsumoto, Takanori

Assoc. Prof., Dept. of Econ., Seikei Univ., Kichijoji-Kitamachi, Musachino City, Tokyo 180, Japan. Tel.: 0422 37 3688. Fax: 0422 37 3866.

Year and Place of Birth 1961, Mie, Japan.

Degrees and Qualifications BA Doshisha Univ., 1985; MA Doshisha Univ., 1987; Ph.D. Osaka Univ., 1989.

Previous Post Assistant, Dept. of Econ., Osaka Univ., 1988–9.

Current Offices and Honorary Posts Sec., Bus. Hist. Soc. of Japan.

Fields of Expertise *Industry Fields:* textiles; clothing and footwear; other manufacturing industries; transport and communication; distributive trades. *Bus. Dimensions:* marketing; research and development; bus. organization; small bus. matters; multinational bus.; management education; markets and bus.; inter-firm organization. *Scope:* local; regional; national; internat.; global. *Period:* nineteenth century; twentieth century as a whole; early twentieth century; inter-war years, 1919–39; mid-twentieth century, 1940–70; late twentieth century, 1970–present. *Teaching:* undergrad.; post grad. *Consultancy:* co. hist.; corporate strategy.

Publications *Articles:* 'Taishouki niokeru Orimono Dogyo kumiai no Kinou' [Functions of Textile Local Trade Associations in the Taisho Era], *Osaka Econ. Papers*, 38(1–2), 1988; 'Handou Kyoukouki kara Showaki no Senshu Menmoufu Kougyou niokeru Dougyousha Sashiki no Kinou' [Functions of Trade Associations and Indust. Associations from the 1920s to the 1930s], *Osaka Econ. Papers*, 38(3–4), 1989; 'Ryotaisenkanki Senboku Kigyo niokeru Orimono Kojo Keiei no Doukou' [Study of the Trend of the Management of a Textile Weaving Factory in Senboku Textile Weaving Industry in the Inter-war Period], *Japan Bus. Hist. Rev.*, 26(4), 1991; 'Study of the Trend of the Management of a Textile Weaving Factory in Senboku Textile Weaving Industry in the Inter-war Period', *Japanese Yearbook on Bus. Hist.*, 9, forthcoming; 'Ryotaisenkanki Nihon no Seizougyo niokeru Dogyo Kumiai no Kinou' [Study of Functions of Local Trade Associations in the Local Manufacturing Industries in the Inter-war Period of Japan], *The Socio-Econ. Hist.*, forthcoming.

Matthiessen, Poul C.

Prof. of Demography, Copenhagen Univ., Inst. of Stats., Studiestræde 6, 1455 Copenhagen K, Denmark. Tel.: 45 35 323260. Fax: 45 35 323259.

Year and Place of Birth 1933, Odense, Denmark.

Degrees and Qualifications Master of Econ. Copenhagen Univ., 1957; Doctor of Econ. Copenhagen Univ., 1970.

Current Offices and Honorary Posts

Mem., Royal Danish Acad. of Sciences & Letters; founding mem., Academia Europaea.

Fields of Expertise *Industry Fields:* food, drink, tobacco. *Bus. Dimensions:* co. finance and accounting. *Scope:* internat. *Period:* late twentieth century, 1970–present. *Teaching:* undergrad.; post grad. *Consultancy:* co. hist.

Publications *Books: Some Aspects of the Demographic Transition,* Gads Forlag, Copenhagen, 1970; *The Growth of Population,* Munksgaards Forlag, Copenhagen, 1984, (in Danish); *The Limitation of Family Size in Denmark, Part 1 & 2,* The Royal Acad. of Sciences & Letters, Copenhagen, 1985; *Population and Soc.,* Handelshøjskolens Forlag, Copenhagen, 1992. *Articles:* 'Some Reflections on the Hist. and Recent Fertility Decline in Denmark', *Scandinavian Population Studies,* 6(2), Stockholm, 1983.

Mayer, Daniel

Univ. of West Bohemia, Fac. of Electrical Engineering, Americká 42, 306 14 Pilsen, Czechland. Tel.: 42 19 374 61. Fax: 42 18 22 00 19.

Year and Place of Birth 1930, Pilsen, Czechland.

Degrees and Qualifications Ing. Prague Univ., 1952; Ph.D. Prague Univ., 1958; Sen. Lect.-Soc. Pilsen Univ., 1959; Prof. Pilsen Univ., 1968; Dr.Sc. Prague Univ., 1979; C.Eng. FIEE London Univ., 1990.

Previous Post Head of Dept. of Theory of Electrical Engineering, 1990.

Current Offices and Honorary Posts FIEE; honorable mem., Soc. of Hist. of Science & Engineering (Prague).

Major Honours Ministry of Education and Publishers Prize for Best Textbook of the Year (electrical engineering), 1982.

Fields of Expertise *Industry Fields:* electrical engineering; gas, electricity, water; transport and communication; professional and scientific services; miscellaneous services; public admin. and defence; electronics and computers: manufacture. *Bus. Dimensions:* personnel management; research and development; strategy formation; bus. organization; bus. and technology; management education. *Scope:* national; internat.; global; Czechland. *Period:* eighteenth century; nineteenth century; twentieth century as a whole. *Teaching:* post grad. *Consultancy:* co. hist.; corporate strategy.

Publications *Articles:* 'George Green - zakladatel matematické teorie elektrickych a magnetickych jevu' [George Green - the Founder of the Mathematical Theory of Electrical and Magnetical Phenomena], *Dejiny ved a techniky,* 11, 1978, 208–15; 'Oliver Heaviside a teoretická elektrotechnika' [Oliver Heaviside and the Theory of Electrical Engineering], *Dejiny ved a techniky,* 20(1), 1987, 12–28; 'Uplynulo 100 let od smrti G.R. Kirchhoffa' [100 Years from the Death of G.R. Kirchhoff], *Elektrotechnicky obzor,* 76(10), 1987; 'Heinrich Hertz a soudobá elektrotechnika' [Heinrich Hertz and Contemporary Electrical Engineering], *Dejiny ved a techniky,* 22(4), 1989 209–22; 'Historicky pohled na vznik a vyvoj teoretické elektrotechniky' [Retrospect on Development on Theory of Electrical Engineering], *Prace z dejin prírodních ved,* Csl. spolecnost DVT, Prague, 279–97.

McCalla, Douglas

Dept. of Hist., Trent Univ., Peterborough, Ontario, K9J 7B8, Canada. Tel.: 1 705 748 1740. Fax: 1 705 748 1795.

Year and Place of Birth 1942,

Edmonton, Canada.

Degrees and Qualifications BA Queen's Univ., Canada, 1964; MA Toronto Univ., 1965; D.Phil. Oxford Univ., 1972.

Fields of Expertise *Industry Fields:* agric., forestry, fishing. *Bus. Dimensions:* bus. organization. *Scope:* regional; Canada. *Period:* nineteenth century. *Teaching:* undergrad. *Consultancy:* co. hist.

Publications *Books: The Upper Canada Trade, 1834–1872: A Study of the Buchanans' Bus.*, Univ. of Toronto Press, Toronto, 1979; *Perspectives on Canadian Econ. Hist.*, ed. & introduction, New Canadian Readings Series, Copp, Clark Pitman, Toronto, 1987; 2nd edn., revised, edited & introduced with Michael Huberman forthcoming 1994; *The Development of Canadian Capitalism: Essays in Canadian Bus. Hist.*, ed. & introduction, New Canadian Readings Series, Copp, Clark Pitman, Toronto, 1990; *Planting the Province: The Econ. Hist. of Upper Canada, 1784–1871*, Ontario Hist. Studies Series, Univ. of Toronto Press, Toronto, 1993.

McChesney, Robert W.

Assistant Prof., School of Journalism and Mass Communication, Univ. of Wisconsin-Madison, 5115 Vilas Communication Hall, 821 Univ. Avenue, Madison, WI 53706, USA. Tel.: 1 608 263 4365. Fax: 1 608 238 3013.

Year and Place of Birth 1952, Cleveland, USA.

Degrees and Qualifications BA Evergreen State College, 1977; MA Washington Univ., 1986; Ph.D. Washington Univ., Seattle, 1989.

Current Offices and Honorary Posts Pres., Madison Chapter, Cleveland Browns Backers Assoc.

Fields of Expertise *Industry Fields:*

electrical engineering; transport and communication. *Bus. Dimensions:* bus.–state relations. *Scope:* internat. *Period:* twentieth century as a whole. *Teaching:* undergrad.; post grad.

Publications *Books: Telecommunications, Mass Media and Democracy: The Battle for the Control of US Broadcasting, 1928–1935*, OUP, New York, 1993; *Ruthless Criticism: New Perspectives in US Communication Hist.*, with William S. Solomon co-ed., Univ. of Minnesota Press, Minneapolis, 1993.

McCraw, Thomas K.

Straus Prof. of Bus. Hist., Harvard Bus. School, Soldiers Field, Boston, MA 02163, USA. Tel.: 1 617 495 6364.

Year and Place of Birth 1940, Corinth, USA.

Degrees and Qualifications BA Missouri Univ., 1962; MA Wisconsin Univ., 1968; Ph.D. Wisconsin Univ., 1970.

Current Offices and Honorary Posts Trustee, Bus. Hist. Conf.; co-chair, Bus., Government & Competition Area, Harvard Bus. School.

Major Honours Pulitzer Prize (Hist.), 1985; Pres., Bus. Hist. Conf., 1989–90; Thos. Newcomen Book Award, 1985; William P. Lyons Master's Essay Award, 1970.

Fields of Expertise *Industry Fields:* transport and communication. *Bus. Dimensions:* bus.–state relations. *Scope:* internat. *Period:* twentieth century as a whole. *Teaching:* post grad. *Consultancy:* co. education.

Publications *Books: Morgan vs. Lilienthal: The Feud within TVA*, 1970; *TVA and the Power Fight, 1933–1939*, 1971; *Prophets of Regulation*, 1984; *Amer. vs. Japan*, ed. & contributor, 1986; *The Essential Alfred Chandler*, ed. & contributor, 1988.

McCullough, Alan B.

Historian, National Historic Sites, Environment Canada, Hull, Quebec, K1A 0H3, Canada. Tel.: 1 819 997 0506. Fax: 1 819 953 4909.

Year and Place of Birth 1945, Carman, Canada.

Degrees and Qualifications BA Manitoba Univ.

Fields of Expertise *Industry Fields:* agric., forestry, fishing; textiles. *Bus. Dimensions:* bus. and technology. *Scope:* national. *Period:* nineteenth century; early twentieth century. *Teaching:* research.

Publications *Books: Money and Exchange in Canada to 1900*, Dundurn Press Ltd, Toronto, 1984; *The Commercial Fishery of the Canadian Great Lakes*, Minister of Supply and Services, Ottawa, 1989; *The Primary Textile Industry in Canada: Hist. and Heritage*, Minister of Supply & Services, Canada, 1992.

McCusker, John J.

Ewing Halsell Distinguished Prof. of Amer. Hist. & Prof. of Econ., Trinity Univ., Dept. of Hist., 715 Stadium Drive, San Antonio, TX 78212–7200, USA. Tel.: 1 210 736 7625. Fax: 1 210 736 7305.

Year and Place of Birth 1939, Rochester, USA.

Degrees and Qualifications BA (Philo.) St Bernard's Seminary & College, Rochester, NY; MA (Hist.) Rochester Univ., 1963; Grad. Research Student, Univ. College London, 1966–7; Ph.D. (Econ. Hist.) Pittsburgh Univ., 1970.

Previous Post Prof., Dept. of Hist., Maryland Univ.

Current Offices and Honorary Posts Mem., Amer. Antiquarian Soc., 1988–;

Econ. Hist. Assoc.: nominating com., 1985–6, 1992–3; audit com., 1988; publications com. mem., Hist. Soc. of Pennsylvania, 1980–; editorial advisory board mem., *Bus. Hist. Rev.*, 1980–; editorial advisory com. mem., *Pennsylvania Magazine of Hist. & Biography*, 1980–; editorial board mem., *J. of Econ. Hist.*, 1985–9; mem., board of advisors, *Proceedings of the Amer. Antiquarian Soc.*, 1989–.

Major Honours Fellow, John Simon Guggenheim Memorial Foundation, 1982–3; Research Fellowship, Centrum voor Economische Studiën, Katholieke Universiteit, Leuven, Belgium, 1984–5; Fellowship, Fulbright-Hays Program, Western European Research Award, 1984–5; Christensen Visiting Fellowship, St Catherine's College, Univ. of Oxford, 1985.

Fields of Expertise *Industry Fields:* food, drink, tobacco; shipbuilding and marine engineering; transport and communication; insurance, banking, finance; distilling industry; sugar industry; bus. publishing. *Scope:* internat.; the Atlantic world. *Period:* early modern; eighteenth century. *Teaching:* undergrad.

Publications *Books: Money and Exchange in Europe and Amer., 1600–1775: A Handbook*, Chapel Hill, North Carolina, Univ. of North Carolina Press for the Inst. of Early Amer. Hist. and Culture, and London, Macmillan, 1978, corrected, paperback reprinted edn., Chapel Hill, North Carolina, Univ. of North Carolina Press for the Inst. of Early Amer. Hist. & Culture, 1992; *The Economy of British Amer., 1607–1789*, Russell R. Menard co-auth., Chapel Hill, North Carolina, Univ. of North Carolina Press for the Inst. of Early Amer. Hist. & Culture, 1985, paperback edn., 1986, paperback reprinted edn. with supplementary bibliography, 1991; *Rum and the Amer. Revolution: The Rum Trade and the Balance of*

Payments of the Thirteen Continental Colonies, 2 vols., Garland Publishing Co., New York & London, 1989; *The Beginnings of Commercial and Financial Journalism: The Commodity Price Currents, Exchange Rate Currents and Money Currents of Early Modern Europe*, Cora Gravesteijn co-auth., Nederlandsch Economisch-Historisch Archief, III ser., (11) (Amsterdam: Nederlandsch Economisch-Historisch Archief, 1991; *How Much is that in Real Money? A Hist. Price Index for Use as a Deflator of Money Values in the Economy of the United States*, Amer. Antiquarian Soc., Worcester, MA, 1992, reprinted, 1993.

McDermott, Kathleen

Principal, Winthrop Group, The Winthrop Group Inc., 1100 Massachusetts Ave., Cambridge, MA 02139, USA. Tel.: 1 617 497 0777. Fax: 1 617 661 6497.

Year and Place of Birth 1956, New York, USA.

Degrees and Qualifications BA Alfred Univ.; JD SUNY, Buffalo; LL M Harvard Law School.

Fields of Expertise *Industry Fields:* chemicals and allied industries; clothing and footwear; insurance, banking, finance; professional and scientific services. *Bus. Dimensions:* co. finance and accounting; co. culture; corporate hist. *Scope:* national. *Period:* twentieth century as a whole. *Consultancy:* co. hist.; corporate strategy.

Publications *Books: America's Paint Co.: A Hist. of Sherwin-Williams*, with Dyer co-auth., Sherwin-Williams, Cleveland, 1991; *Accounting for Success: One Hundred Years of Price Waterhouse in Amer.*, with Allen co-auth., Harvard Bus. School Press, Boston, 1993; *Underwriting America's Success: 125 Years of Metropol. Life,*

Metropol. Life, New York, 1993. *Articles:* 'The Development of the Massachusetts District Courts: 1821–1922', *Hist. J. of Massachusetts*, 15, June, 1987.

McDowall, Duncan L.

Prof. of Hist., Dept. of Hist., Carleton Univ., Ottawa, Ontario, K1S 5B6, Canada. Tel.: 1 613 788 2600. Fax: 1 613 788 2819.

Year and Place of Birth 1949, Victoria, Canada.

Degrees and Qualifications BA Queen's Univ., 1972; MA Queen's Univ., 1973; Ph.D. Carleton Univ., 1978.

Previous Post Sen. Research Assoc., Conf. Board of Canada, 1980–7.

Fields of Expertise *Industry Fields:* insurance, banking, finance. *Bus. Dimensions:* multinational bus.; bus.–state relations; co. culture; boardroom issues. *Scope:* national; internat. *Period:* early twentieth century; interwar years, 1919–39; mid-twentieth century, 1940–70; late twentieth century, 1970–present. *Teaching:* undergrad.; post grad. *Consultancy:* public affairs; co. hist.

Publications *Books: Steel at the Sault: Francis H. Clergue, Sir James Dunn: The Algoma Steel Corporation, 1901–1956*, Univ. of Toronto Press, 1984, paperback, 1988; *The Light: Brazilian Traction, Light Power Co. Ltd. 1899–1945*, Univ. of Toronto Press, 1988; *Quick to the Frontier: Canada's Royal Bank 1864–*, McLlelland, Stewart, Toronto, 1993, French translation: Sogides, Montreal.

McKay, John P.

Dept. of Hist., Univ. of Illinois, 309 Gregory Hall, 810 S. Wright St, Urbana, IL 61821, USA. Tel.: 1 217

244 2594. Fax: 1 217 333 2297.

Year and Place of Birth 1938, St Louis, USA.

Degrees and Qualifications BA Wesleyan Univ., 1961; MA Fletcher School of Law & Diplomacy, 1962; Ph.D. Univ. of California, Berkeley, 1968.

Previous Post Assoc. Prof. of Hist., Illinois Univ., 1971–6.

Current Offices and Honorary Posts Edit. board mem, *Bus. Hist. Rev.*

Major Honours Herbert Baxter Adams Prize from Amer. Hist. Assoc., 1970.

Fields of Expertise *Industry Fields:* coal and petroleum products. *Bus. Dimensions:* entrepreneurs and entrepreneurship. *Scope:* internat. *Period:* nineteenth century. *Teaching:* undergrad.

Publications *Books: Pioneers for Profit: Foreign Entrepreneurship and Russian Industrialization, 1885–1913,* Univ. of Chicago Press, 1970; *Tramways and Trolleys: The Rise of Urban Mass Transport in Europe,* Princeton Univ. Press, 1976; *A Hist. of Western Soc.; Vol. 2, From Absolutism to the Present,* Houghton Mifflin, 1979, 2nd edn., 1983, 3rd edn., 1987, 4th edn., 1991. *Articles:* 'The House of Rothschild (Paris) as a Multinational Indust. Enterprise', *Multinational Enterprise in Hist. Perspective,* Alice Teichova, Maurice Lévy-Leboyer & Helga Nussbaum eds., CUP, 1986, 74–86; 'Restructuring the Russian Petroleum Industry in the 1890s: Government and Market Forces', *Economy and Soc. in Russia and the Soviet Union 1860–1930,* Linda Edmundson & Peter Waldron eds., Macmillan, 1992, 85–106.

McKinlay, Alan

Colquhoun Lect. in Bus. Hist., Centre for Bus. Hist. in Scotland, Univ. of Glasgow, 4 Univ. Gardens, Glasgow,

G12 8QQ, UK. Tel.: 44 41 339 8855. Fax: 44 41 330 4889.

Year and Place of Birth 1957, UK.

Degrees and Qualifications BA Caledonian Univ., 1981; D.Phil. Oxford Univ., 1986.

Previous Post Conoco Lect. in Management, St Andrews Univ., 1988–9.

Fields of Expertise *Industry Fields:* mechanical engineering; shipbuilding and marine engineering; vehicle construction; electronics and computers: manufacture. *Bus. Dimensions:* strategy formation; bus. organization; multinational bus.; markets and bus. *Scope:* regional; global. *Period:* inter-war years, 1919–39; mid-twentieth century, 1940–70; late twentieth century, 1970–present. *Teaching:* undergrad.; post grad. *Consultancy:* corporate strategy.

Publications *Books: Strategy and the Human Resource: Ford's Search for Competitive Advantage,* Blackwell, Oxford, 1993.

McLean, Gavin

Historian, New Zealand Historic Places Trust, POB 2629, Wellington, New Zealand. Tel.: 64 4 472 4341. Fax: 64 4 499 0669.

Year and Place of Birth 1957, Oamaru, New Zealand.

Degrees and Qualifications BA Otago Univ., 1979; Ph.D. Otago Univ., 1984.

Previous Post Publisher, New Zealand Government Printing Office, 1987–90.

Current Offices and Honorary Posts National com., New Zealand Ship & Marine Soc.

Major Honours James Scott Prize, Otago Univ., 1979; Ross Fellow, Knox College, Dunedin, 1980–2.

Fields of Expertise *Industry Fields:* transport and communication. *Bus. Dimensions:* entrepreneurs and entrepreneurship; bus. organization. *Scope:* national. *Period:* nineteenth century; twentieth century as a whole. *Consultancy:* co. hist.

Publications *Books: The Southern Octopus*, New Zealand Ship & Marine Soc./Wellington Maritime Museum, Wellington, 1990; *Local Hist.: A Short Guide to Researching, Writing and Publishing a Local Hist.*, Bridget Williams Books/Hist. Branch, Dept. of Internal Affairs, Wellington, 1992; *Otago Harbour: Currents of Controversy*, Otago Harbour Board, Dunedin, 1985; *NZ Tragedies: Shipwrecks and Maritime Disasters*, Grantham House, Wellington, 1991.

McQuaid, Kim

Prof. of Hist., Lake Erie College, Painesville, OH 44077, USA. Tel.: 1 216 352 3361. Fax: 1 216 352 3533.

Year and Place of Birth 1947, Norwalk, USA.

Degrees and Qualifications BA Antioch College, 1970; MA Northwestern Univ., 1973; Ph.D. Northwestern Univ., 1975.

Fields of Expertise *Industry Fields:* public admin. and defence. *Bus. Dimensions:* bus.–state relations. *Period:* late twentieth century, 1970–present. *Teaching:* undergrad.; post grad.

Publications *Books: Creating the Welfare State: The Polit. Economy of Twentieth Century Reform*, with Edward D. Berkowitz, 1980, 1988, 2nd. revised ed. 1992, Univ. Press of Kansas; *Big Bus. and Presidential Power: From FDR to Reagan*, William Morrow & Co., New York, 1982; *The Anxious Years: Amer. in the Vietnam–Watergate Era*, Basic Books, New York, 1989; *Uneasy Partners: Big Bus. in Amer. Polit., 1945–1990*, Johns Hopkins Univ. Press, Baltimore, 1993.

McRoberts, Mary L.

Ph.D. Student/Teaching Assistant, Dept. of Hist., 2140 Vari Hall, York Univ., 4700 Keele St, North York, Ontario, M3J 1P3, Canada. Tel.: 1 416 736 5123. Fax: 1 416 736 5836.

Place of Birth Kelowna, Canada.

Degrees and Qualifications BA Victoria Univ., 1984; B.Ed. Victoria Univ., 1984; MA Victoria Univ., 1986; Ph.D. York Univ., Ontario, in progress.

Major Honours Social Sciences and Humanities Research Council of Canada, 1986/7–1989/90 (4 years).

Fields of Expertise *Industry Fields:* timber, furniture, international lumber trade. *Bus. Dimensions:* bus. organization; markets and bus. *Scope:* internat.; Canada. *Period:* twentieth century as a whole. *Teaching:* undergrad. *Consultancy:* corporate strategy.

Publications *Articles:* 'Corporate Structures and Local Economies: The Case of the Williams Lake Lumber Industry', *Canadian Papers in Rural Hist.*, 6, 1988, 154–71; 'Why Good Intentions Fail: A Case of Forest Policy in the British Columbia Interior, 1945–1956', *J. of Forest Hist.*, 32(3), July, 1988, 138–49.

Meixner, Wolfgang

Inst. of Hist., Dept. of Econ. and Social Hist., Innsbruck Univ., Innrain 52, A-6020 Innsbruck, Austria. Tel.: 43 512 507 3375. Fax: 43 512 507 3629.

Year and Place of Birth 1961, Jenbach, Austria.

Degrees and Qualifications Mag.phil. Innsbruck Univ., 1989.

Previous Post Researcher, 'Austrian Industrialists in the 19th Century', Fonds zur Forderung der Wissenschaftlichen Forschung, Vienna, 1989–91, 1991–93.

Current Offices and Honorary Posts
Correspondent, Österreichischen
Zeitschrift für Geschichts-
wissenschaften.
Fields of Expertise *Industry Fields:*
paper, printing, publishing. *Bus.*
Dimensions: entrepreneurs and entre-
preneurship. *Scope:* national; Austria.
Period: nineteenth century. *Teaching:*
undergrad. *Consultancy:* collective
biography.
Publications *Books:*
Ausstellungskatalog 'Transit'. Die
Überwindung der Alpenbarriere in der
Photographie, Brixen, 1991. *Articles:*
'Quantitative Sozialgeschichte österre-
ichischer Unternehmer',
Österreichische Zeitschrift für
Geschichtswissenschaften, with Bettina
Kessler & Rupert Pichler, 1, 1990,
113–18; 'Austrian Entrepreneurs in the
19th Century', *Hist. Social Research*,
with Rupert Pichler, 16, 1991, 208–9;
'Die Wirtschaft im 19. Jahrhundert',
Tiroler Wirtschaftschronik, with
Elisabeth Dietrich & Bettina Kessler,
Vienna, 1992; 'Zum Sozialprofil
Tiroler Unternehmer im 19.
Jahrhundert', *Bericht zum 19. österre-*
ichischen Historikertag 1992,Graz,
1993.

Melling, Joseph

Lect. in Econ. and Social Hist. &
Management Studies, Dept. of Econ.
and Social Hist., Exeter Univ., Exeter,
EX4 4RJ, UK. Tel.: 44 392 263289.
Fax: 44 392 263305.
Year and Place of Birth 1954, UK.
Degrees and Qualifications B.Sc.
(Soc. Sc.) Bradford Univ.; Ph.D.
Glasgow Univ.
Fields of Expertise *Industry Fields:*
mining and quarrying; coal and petro-
leum products; mechanical engineering;
shipbuilding and marine engineering.
Bus. Dimensions: production manage-
ment; management education;

bus.–state relations; bus. values; co.
culture. *Scope:* regional; national;
internat. *Period:* nineteenth century;
twentieth century as a whole; early
twentieth century; inter-war years,
1919–39; mid-twentieth century,
1940–70. *Teaching:* undergrad.; post
grad.; consultancies. *Consultancy:*
management strategy.
Publications *Books: Culture and*
Hist., Exeter Press, 1992; *European*
Management, Edward Elgar, forthcoming. *Articles:* 'Capitalism and Welfare
States', *Sociology*, 1991; 'Employers
and Welfare States', *Soc. Hist.*, 1992;
'British Productivity 1945-Present',
Econ. Hist. Rev., forthcoming.

Mercer, Helen

Lect. in Econ. and Social Hist., School
of Bus. & Econ. Studies, Leeds Univ.,
Leeds, LS2 9JT, UK. Tel.: 44 532
431751.
Year and Place of Birth 1956,
London, UK.
Degrees and Qualifications BA
(Hist.) Bristol Univ., 1978; M.Sc.
(Econ. Hist.) London School of Econ.,
1984; Ph.D. (Econ. Hist.) London
School of Econ., 1989.
Fields of Expertise *Bus.*
Dimensions: entrepreneurs and entre-
preneurship; co. law; merger move-
ment and issues; bus. organization;
multinational bus.; bus.–state relations.
Scope: national; internat. *Period:*
twentieth century as a whole; inter-war
years, 1919–39; mid-twentieth century,
1940–70. *Teaching:* undergrad.; post
grad.
Publications *Books: Labour*
Governments and Private Industry:
The Experience of 1945–1951, with N.
Rollings & J. Tomlinson co-eds.,
Edinburgh Univ. Press, 1992. *Articles:*
'Labour Governments of 1945–51 and
Private Industry', *The Attlee Years*, N.
Tiratsoo ed., Pinter, 1991, 71–89; 'The

Monopolies and Restrictive Practices Commission, 1949–56: A Study in Regulatory Failure', *Competitiveness and the State. Government and Bus. in Twentieth Century Britain*, G. Jones & M. Kirby eds., Manchester, 1991, 78–99; 'Anti-monopoly Policy', *Labour Governments and Private Industry: The Experience of 1945–1951*, 55–73.

Merger, Michèle

CNRS Researcher, Inst. of Modern & Contemporary Hist., 45 rue d'Ulm, 750011 Paris, France. Tel.: 33 1 44323152. Fax: 33 1 43295352.

Year and Place of Birth 1947, Brethenay, France.

Degrees and Qualifications Agrégation (Hist.), 1972; Ph.D. Paris IV Univ. Sorbonne, 1979.

Previous Post Substitute Prof., Paris IV Univ. Sorbonne, 1986–7.

Current Offices and Honorary Posts Mem., Executive Com., Assoc. pour l'Histoire des Chemins de Fer en France (A.H.I.C.F.); mem., Lecture Com., *Histoire Economie et Société*, 1993–.

Fields of Expertise *Industry Fields:* transport and communication. *Bus. Dimensions:* co. admin.; bus. organization; bus. and technology; bus.–state relations. *Scope:* national; internat.; Italy; Europe. *Period:* nineteenth century; twentieth century as a whole.

Publications *Articles:* 'Un modello di Sostituzione: la Locomotiva Italiana al 1850 al 1914', *Rivista di Storia Economica*, 5(3), Feb., 1986, Einaudi, Turin, 66–108; 'Les Transports Terrestres en France XIXe–XXe Siècles et la Concurrence Rail-navigation Intérieure en France', *Histoire Économie et Société*, special issue, 1, 1990, 3–7, 65–94; 'Les Transports Terrestres en Europe Continentale XIXe–XXe Siècles', *Histoire Économie et Société*, ed., special issue, 1, 1992, 184; 'Mutations Techniques e Commerciales: Les Relations Ferroviaires entre l'Italie et l'Europe Occidentale de 1867 au Début du XXe Siècle', *Revue d'Histoire des Chemins de Fer*, special issue, 3, Paris, 1992, 211–252; 'Origini e Sviluppo del Management Ferroviario Italiano 1850–1905', *Annali di Storia sull'Impresa*, 8, 1992, Fondazione A.S.S.I., Il Mulino, Bologna, 379–417.

Merrett, D.T.

Assoc. Prof., Dept. of Econ. Hist., Fac. of Econ. and Commerce, Melbourne Univ., Parkville, VIC 3052, Australia. Tel.: 61 3 344 5337. Fax: 61 3 347 3770.

Year and Place of Birth 1944, Melbourne, Australia.

Degrees and Qualifications M.Com Monash Univ., 1970; B.Econ. Monash Univ., 1986.

Previous Post Sen. Lect., Dept. of Econ. Hist., Fac. of Econ. & Commerce, Melbourne Univ., 1990–92.

Current Offices and Honorary Posts Edit. adviser, *Bus. Hist.*

Fields of Expertise *Industry Fields:* insurance, banking, finance. *Bus. Dimensions:* strategy formation. *Scope:* national. *Period:* twentieth century as a whole. *Consultancy:* co. hist.

Publications *Books: ANZ Bank*, Allen & Unwin, Australia, 1985. *Articles:* 'The Victorian Licensing Court 1906–68: A Study of Role and Impact', *Australian Econ. Hist. Record*, XIX(2), 1979, 123–50; 'Australian Banking Practice and the Crisis of 1893', *Australian Econ. Hist. Rev.*, XXIX(1), 1989; 'Paradise Lost? British Banks in Australia', *Banks as Multinationals*, Geoffrey Jones ed., Routledge, London, 1990, 62–84.

Michelsen, Karl-Erik

Researcher, Helsinki Univ., Dept. of Hist., Hallituskatu 15, P.O.B. 4, SF-00014 Helsinki, Finland. Tel.: 358 0 1912845. Fax: 358 0 1913217.
Year and Place of Birth 1957, Ähtäri, Finland.
Degrees and Qualifications BA Helsinki Univ., 1985; MA Pennsylvania Univ., 1988; L.phil. Helsinki Univ., 1991; Ph.D. Helsinki Univ., 1993.
Previous Post Asst., Helsinki Univ., 1988–92.
Fields of Expertise *Industry Fields:* agric., forestry, fishing; chemicals and allied industries; timber, furniture; paper, printing, publishing. *Bus. Dimensions:* entrepreneurs and entrepreneurship; production management; research and development; strategy formation; bus. and technology; multinational bus.; co. culture. *Scope:* national; internat. *Period:* nineteenth century; twentieth century as a whole. *Teaching:* undergrad.; post grad. *Consultancy:* co. hist.; corporate strategy.
Publications *Books: Teknologinen Muutos Suomen Teollisuudessa, 1880–1920* [Technological Change in Finnish Industry, 1880–1920], with Timo Myllyntaus & Timo Herranen co-auths., Suomen Tiedeseura, Helsinki, 1987; *Sähköstä ja Suolasta Syntynyt, Finnish Chemicals Oy-Nokia Chemicals 1937–1987* [Made of Salt and Electricity, Finnish Chemicals Oy-Nokia Chemicals 1937–1987], Gummerus, Jyväskylä, 1989; *Valtio, Teknologia, Tutkimus, VTT ja Kansallisen Tutkimusjärjestelmän Kehitys* [State, Technology, Research, State Technical Research Centre and the Development of the National Innovation System], Vapk, Helsinki, 1993. *Articles:* 'The Power of System, Zellstoffabrik Waldhof in Pernau, Livonia, 1898–1915', *Scandinavian J.*

of Hist., 16, 1992, 189–204; 'Nationalism and Indust. Development in Finland', *Bus. & Econ. Hist.*, with Markku Kuisma co-auth., 2nd ser., XXI, 1992, 343–53.

Mierzejewski, Alfred C.

Assistant Prof., Athens State College, 200 Beaty St, Athens, AL 35611, USA. Tel.: 1 205 233 8292. Fax: 1 205 233 8164.
Year and Place of Birth 1953, New Bedford, USA.
Degrees and Qualifications BA (Hist.) Southeastern Massachusetts Univ., 1978; MA (Hist.) Univ. of North Carolina-Chapel Hill, 1981; Ph.D. (Hist.) Univ. of North Carolina-Chapel Hill, 1985.
Previous Post Command Historian, US Army Test and Experimentation Command, Aug., 1987–Jul., 1990.
Major Honours Fulbright Scholar, Germany, 1992–3; National Intelligence Study Center, Best Intelligence Article by an Amer. published in 1989 for *Intelligence and the Combined Strategic Targets Committee*, May, 1990.
Fields of Expertise *Industry Fields:* transport and communication. *Bus. Dimensions:* co. finance and accounting; strategy formation; bus. organization; bus.–state relations; co. culture. *Scope:* national; Germany. *Period:* inter-war years, 1919–39. *Teaching:* undergrad. *Consultancy:* co. hist.
Publications *Books: Collapse of the German War Economy 1944–1945,* Chapel Hill, 1988. *Articles:* 'The Deutsche Reichsbahn and Germany's Supply of Coal, 1939–1945', *J. of Transport Hist.*, VIII(2), Sept., 1987, 111–25; 'Intelligence and the Strategic Bombing of Germany: The Combined Strategic Targets Committee', *J. of Intelligence and Counterintelligence,* III(1), Jul., 1989, 83–104; 'The German National Railway between the

World Wars: Modernisation or Preparation for War?', *J. of Transport Hist.*, XI(1), March, 1990, 40–60; 'The Doppmüller Controversy of 1926: Cabinet Polit., Reparations and Railways in the Weimar Republic', *Internat. Hist. Rev.*, XIV(4), Nov., 1992, 701–16.

Mikami, Atsufumi

Prof., Internat. Dept., Osaka-Gakuin Univ., 2-36-1 Kishibe-minami, Suita, Osaka 582, Japan. Tel.: 06 381 8434. Fax: 06 382 4363.
Year and Place of Birth 1941, Tottori pref., Japan.
Degrees and Qualifications MA Osaka Univ., 1972.
Previous Post Assoc. Prof., Fac. of Econ., Fukuyama Univ.
Current Offices and Honorary Posts Council mem., sec., Bus. Hist. Soc. of Japan, 1987–91; council mem., The Socio-Econ. Hist. Soc.
Fields of Expertise *Industry Fields:* industry as a whole. *Bus. Dimensions:* entrepreneurs and entrepreneurship; co. admin.; bus. organization. *Scope:* national; internat.; India. *Period:* twentieth century as a whole. *Teaching:* undergrad. *Consultancy:* co. hist.
Publications *Books: Nihon no Kigyoka (2) Taisho-hen* [Japan's Industrialists (2) Taisho Era], co-auth., Yuhikaku, 1978, 36–72. *Articles:* 'Old and New Zaibatsu in the Hist. of Japan's Chemical Industry', *Development and Diffusion of Technology*, A. Okochi ed., Univ. of Tokyo Press, 201–218; 'Indo Zaibatsu no Shoyu to Keiei' [Ownership and Management of Indian Zaibatsu], *Japan Bus. Hist. Rev.*, 22(3), 1–28; 'Bajaj Zaibatsu no Keisei to Hatten' [Development of Bajaj Zaibatsu in India], *Bull. of the Research Center for Human Science*, 3, Fukuyama Univ., 1988; 'Birla Zaibatsu no Keisei to

Hatten' [Development of Birla Zaibatsu in India], *Osaka Econ. Papers*, 39(1).

Milkereit, Gertrud

Hans-Luther-Allee 9, D-45131 Essen 1, Germany. Tel.: 49 201 790788.
Year and Place of Birth 1916, Gotha, Germany.
Degrees and Qualifications Librarian 1937; stud.phil. Jena Univ., 1946; stud.phil. Münster Univ., 1948; Dr.phil. Cologne Univ., 1957.
Previous Post Head of Co. Archives, Thyssen Stahl Aktiengesellschaft, Duisburg 11.
Fields of Expertise *Industry Fields:* mining and quarrying; metal manufacture: iron and steel industry. *Bus. Dimensions:* entrepreneurs and entrepreneurship; co. finance and accounting; bus. organization; bus.–state relations; co. culture. *Scope:* Germany; western Europe. *Period:.* *Consultancy:* co. history; co. research and biography.
Publications *Books: Lebensbilder aus dem Rhein.-Westfäl. Industriegebiet. Jg. 1973–1976*, Volks- und Betriebwirtschaftliche Vereinigung im Rhein.- Westfälischen Industriegebiet, Nomos Verlagsgesellschaft, Baden-Baden, 1984. *Articles:* 'Das Projekt der Moselkanalisierung. Ein Problem der westdeutschen Eisen- und Stahlindustrie', *Schr. z. rhein. Wirtschaftsgeschichte*, 14, Rheinland-Westf. Wirtschaftsarchiv, Cologne, 1967, 111–303; 'Das Unternehmerbild im zeitkrit. Roman d. Vormärz', *Kölner Vortr. zur Sozial- und Wirtschaft.- Geschichte*, 10, Cologne Univ. Research Inst. for Social & Econ. Hist.; 'Die Anfänge der Eisen- und Stahlherstellung für die Hochseeschiffahrt 1844–80', *Schr. Dt. Schiffahrtsmus.*, vol. 5, Stalling Verl., Oldenburg, 1975, 91–102; 'Zum

Verhältnis zwischen Wissenschaft und Praxis im westdeutschen Eisenhüttenw. zwischen 1870–1910 am Beispiel der Lehrst. für Eisenhüttenkde. an der Technischen Hochsch. Aachen und seine Beziehungen z. Ver. Dt. Eisenhüttenl.', *Technikgeschichte*, 44(4), Ver. Dt. Ingenieure, Düsseldorf, 1977.

Millard, Andre

Assoc. Prof. of Hist., Dept. of Hist., Univ. of Alabama at Birmingham, Ullman 402G, 1212 Univ. Blvd., Birmingham, AL 35294, USA. Tel.: 1 205 934 0901. Fax: 1 205 934 9896.
Year and Place of Birth 1947, London, UK.
Degrees and Qualifications Ph.D. Emory Univ., Atlanta, 1983.
Previous Post Director of Amer. Studies, Univ. of Alabama at Birmingham, 1991.
Fields of Expertise *Industry Fields:* electrical engineering; other manufacturing industries. *Bus. Dimensions:* bus. and technology. *Scope:* internat. *Period:* nineteenth century; early twentieth century. *Teaching:* undergrad. *Consultancy:* co. hist.
Publications *Books: A Technological Lag, Diffusion of Electrical Technology in England, 1879–1914*, Garland, New York, 1987; *Edison and the Bus. of Innovation*, Johns Hopkins, Baltimore, 1990. *Articles:* 'Machine Shop Culture and Menlo Park', *Working at Inventing: T.A. Edison and the Menlo Park Experience*, W. Pretzer ed., Henry Ford Museum, 1989.

Millward, Robert

Prof. of Econ. Hist., Dept. of Hist., Manchester Univ., Oxford Road, Manchester, M13 9PL, UK. Tel.: 44 61 275 3086. Fax: 44 61 275 3098.
Year and Place of Birth 1939, Rawtenstall, UK.
Degrees and Qualifications B.Sc. (Econ.) Hull Univ., 1961; Ph.D. Manchester Univ., 1966.
Previous Post Prof. of Econ., Dept. of Econ., Salford Univ., Lancs.
Current Offices and Honorary Posts Council mem., Econ. Hist. Soc.
Fields of Expertise *Industry Fields:* gas, electricity, water. *Bus. Dimensions:* bus. organization. *Scope:* national. *Period:* nineteenth century; twentieth century as a whole. *Teaching:* undergrad. *Consultancy:* economic analysis.
Publications *Books: Public Sector Econ.*, with M.T. Sumner, Longman, 1983. *Articles:* 'Productivity in the UK Services Sector, 1850–1985', *Oxford Bull. of Econ. & Stats.*, Nov., 1990, 423–6; 'From Private to Public Gas Undertakings in England and Wales', *Bus. Hist.*, 35(3), July, 1993, 1–21; 'Industry and Commerce since 1950', *Econ. Hist. of Britain, 1700–1973*, R. Floud & D. McClosky, new edn., Cambridge, 1993.

Misa, Thomas J.

Assoc. Prof. of Hist., Dept. of Humanities, Illinois Inst. of Technology, Chicago, IL 60616, USA. Tel.: 1 312 567 7967. Fax: 1 312 567 3493.
Place of Birth USA.
Degrees and Qualifications Ph.D. Pennsylvania Univ., 1987.
Major Honours SHOT/IEEE Life Members Prize in Electrical Hist., 1987.
Fields of Expertise *Industry Fields:* metal manufacture. *Bus. Dimensions:* research and development; bus. and technology; bus.–state relations. *Scope:* national; USA. *Period:* nineteenth century; early twentieth century.

Teaching: undergrad.

Publications *Articles:* Military Needs, Commercial Realities and the Development of the Transistor, 1948–1958', *Military Enterprise and Technological Change*, Merritt Roe Smith ed., MIT Press, Cambridge, MA, 1985, 253–87; 'How Machines make Hist. and how Historians (and others) Help Them to Do so', *Science, Technology and Human Values*, 13, Summer & Autumn, 1988, 308–31; 'Theories of Technological Change: Parameters and Purposes', *Science, Technology and Human Values*, 17, Winter, 1992, 3–12; 'Controversy and Closure in Technological Change: Constructing "Steel"', *Shaping Technology/Building Soc.: Studies in Sociotechnical Change*, Wiebe E. Bijker & John Law eds., MIT Press, Cambridge, MA, 1992, 109–39; 'Retrieving Sociotechnical Change from Technological Determinism', *Machines and Hist.: The Question of Technological Determinism*, Merritt Roe Smith & Leo Marx eds., MIT Press, Cambridge, MA, 1993.

Mishima, Yasuo

Prof., Fac. of Commerce, Nara Prefectural Univ., 10 Funabashi-cho, Nara City 630, Japan. Tel.: 0742 22 4978. Fax: 0742 22 4991.

Year and Place of Birth 1926, Aichi pref., Japan.

Degrees and Qualifications BA Kyoto Univ., 1956; Ph.D. Osaka Univ., 1970.

Previous Post Prof., Fac. of Bus. Admin., Konan Univ., 1970–92.

Current Offices and Honorary Posts Bus. Hist. Soc. of Japan: council mem. 1965–74, 1983–6; exec. council mem. 1975–8; exec. off. 1979–82; Socio-Econ. Hist. Soc.: council mem. 1968–; Fisher Econ. Soc.: exec. off. 1965–7; exec. comm. mem. 1967–70; Konan

Univ. Hon. Prof. 1992–.

Major Honours Fisheries Econ. Soc. Academic Prize, 1973.

Fields of Expertise *Industry Fields:* agric., forestry, fishing; shipbuilding and marine engineering; textiles. *Bus. Dimensions:* strategy formation; bus. organization; bus.–state relations. *Scope:* local; national. *Period:* nineteenth century; early twentieth century; inter-war years, 1919–39. *Teaching:* undergrad.; post grad. *Consultancy:* co. hist.

Publications *Books: Hokuyo Gyogyo no keieishi teki Kenkyu* [Research on the Bus. Hist. of the Salmon Fishing Industry in the Northern Sea of Japan], Minerva Shobo, 1972; *Mitsubishi Zaibatsu Shi* [The Hist. of Mitsubishi Zaibatsu], 2 vols., Kyoikusha, 1979–80; *Hanshin Zaibatsu (Nomura, Yamaguchi and Kawasaki Zaibatsus in Osaka-Kobe District*, Nippon Keizai Shinbun Sha, 1984; *The Mitsubishi: Its Challenge and Strategy*, J.A.I. Press, 1989; *Zosenkyo Kawasaki Shozo no Shogai* [The Biography of Shozo Kawasaki as a Shipbuilder], Dobunkan Shuppan, 1992.

Mitsugi, Yoshio

Prof., Sapporo Univ., Women's Junior College, Fac. of Management, 3-1, 3-7 Chome, Nishioka, Toyohira-ku, Sapporo 062, Japan. Tel.: 81 11 852 1181. Fax: 81 11 852 1181.

Year and Place of Birth 1948, Tochigi Pref., Japan.

Degrees and Qualifications BA Tokyo Econ. Univ., 1971; MA Nihon Univ. Grad. School, 1973; Ph.D. Nihon Univ. Grad. School, 1976.

Previous Post Instructor (p-t), Fac. of Econ., Obirin Univ., 1976–82.

Current Offices and Honorary Posts Sec., Nihon Keiei Kyoiku Soc., 1991–.

Fields of Expertise *Industry Fields:*

agric., forestry, fishing. *Bus. Dimensions:* entrepreneurs and entrepreneurship; bus. organization; bus. values; co. culture. *Scope:* local; national. *Period:* eighteenth century; late twentieth century, 1970–present. *Teaching:* undergrad.

Publications *Articles:* 'Tayouto Riyou mai no Seisan to Ryutsu udoko' [Trends in the Production and Distribution of Processed Rice in Hokkaido], *Sapporo Univ. Women's Junior College Bull.*, 12, 1988; 'Bashoukeoinin Hidaya Kyubei ni Kansuru Kenkyu' [Bashoukeoinin: The Case of Hidaya Kyubei], *Sapporo Univ. Women's Junior College Bull.*, 1st edn., 14, 1989, 2nd edn., 16, 1990, 3rd edn., 19, 1992; 'Kinsei ki Hidaya ni Okeru Sanrinjigyo Keiei no Tenkai' [Bus. Management in Hidaya during the Edo Era], *Sapporo Univ. Women's Junior College Bull.*, 18, 1991; 'Kigyo to Kankyo' [Corporation and Environment], *Introduction to Bus. Management*, Ishii Taketoshi ed., Keieigaku Nyumon, 1992; 'Kigyo Bunka' [Corporate Culture], *Introduction to Bus. Management*, Ishii Taketoshi ed., 1992.

Mitsui, Takashige

Prof., Matsusho Gakuen Junior College, 2117-3 Niimura, Matsumoto 390-12, Japan. Tel.: 0263 47 6200. Fax: 0263 47 7190.

Year and Place of Birth 1925, Osaka, Japan.

Degrees and Qualifications BA Tokyo Univ., 1952.

Previous Post Prof., National Defence Acad., 1968–91.

Fields of Expertise *Industry Fields:* insurance, banking, finance. *Bus. Dimensions:* entrepreneurs and entrepreneurship; merger movement and issues. *Scope:* local; regional. *Period:* nineteenth century; early twentieth century. *Teaching:* undergrad. *Consultancy:* co. hist.

Publications *Articles:* 'Ginkoho no Seitei to Ginko-Godo' [Enactment of the Banking Act and Bank Merger], *Matsusho-Tandai Ronso* [J. of Matsusho Gakuen Junior College], 9, 1961; 'Dai 19 Kokuritsu-Ginko no Setsuritsu' [Foundation of the 19th National Bank], *Matsusho-Tandai Ronso* [J. of Matsusho Gakuen Junior College], 11, 1963; 'Sogyoki no Dai 117 Kokuyitsu-Ainko' [The 117th National Bank in its Founding Stage], *Matsusho-Tandai Ronso* [J. of Matsusho Gakuen Junior College], 15, 1966; 'Dai 24 Kokuritsu-Ginko no Shiteki-Bunseki' [Hist. Analysis of the 24th National Bank], *Chukyo Shogaku Ronso* [J. Fac. of Commerce Chukyo Univ.], 14(4), 1967; 'Kokuritsu-Ginko no Setsuritsu-Shutai – "Shizoku-ginko"' [Founders of National Banks in Japan – Significance of 'Bank for the ex-Military Class'], *Boei Daigakko Kiyo* [Memoirs of National Defense Acad.], 25, 1972.

Miyamoto, Matao

Prof. of Japanese Econ. & Bus. Hist., Osaka University, 1–1 Machikaneyama-cho, Toyonaka, Osaka 560, Japan. Tel.: 81 6 844 1151. Fax: 81 6 841 6631.

Year and Place of Birth 1943, Fukuoka Pref., Japan.

Degrees and Qualifications BA Kobe Univ., 1967; MA Kobe Univ., 1969; Ph.D. Osaka Univ., 1988.

Current Offices and Honorary Posts Exec. officer, Socio-Econ. Hist. Soc., 1990–; exec. officer, Bus. Hist. Soc. of Japan, 1987–90; sec., Socio-Econ. Hist. Soc., 1987–90.

Major Honours 31st Nikkei Prize, 1988; 5th Tohata Memorial Prize, 1989.

Fields of Expertise *Industry Fields:* textiles; distributive trades; insurance, banking, finance. *Bus. Dimensions:* entrepreneurs and entrepreneurship; co. law; marketing; bus. organization; markets and bus. *Scope:* regional; national. *Period:* early modern; eighteenth century; nineteenth century; twentieth century as a whole; early twentieth century. *Teaching:* undergrad.; post grad. *Consultancy:* co. hist.

Publications *Books: The Market Economy of Tokugawa Japan*, Yuhikaku, 1988, (in Japanese); *Trade Associations in Bus. Hist.*, co-ed., Univ. of Tokyo Press, 1988, (in English); *The Formation of Econ. Soc. - Japanese Econ. Hist. Vol. I*, co-ed., Iwanami Shoten, 1988, (in Japanese); *Hist. of Japanese Commerce*, co-ed., Yuhikaku, 1978, (in Japanese); *Entrepreneurial Activities of Tokugawa Merchants*, co-ed., Yuhikaku, 1978, (in Japanese).

Møller, Anders Monrad

Museumskonsulent, Told - Og Skattestyrelsen, Amaliegade 44, 1256 Copenhagen K, Denmark. Tel.: 45 33 75 51 81.

Year and Place of Birth 1942, Aalborg, Denmark.

Degrees and Qualifications BA (Musicology) Copenhagen Univ., 1969; MA (Hist.) Copenhagen Univ., 1972; Dr.Phil. Odense Univ., 1981.

Previous Post Lect., Copenhagen Univ., 1981–5.

Current Offices and Honorary Posts Co-ed., *Historisk Tidsskrift*; ed., *Told-Og Skattehistorisk Tidsskrift*.

Major Honours Mem., Det Kongelige Danske Selskab for Fedrelandets Historie.

Fields of Expertise *Industry Fields:* transport and communication. *Bus. Dimensions:* markets and bus. *Scope:* national. *Period:* eighteenth century; nineteenth century; twentieth century as a whole. *Teaching:* post grad.

Publications *Books: Frederik den Fjerdes Kommercekollegium*, Akademisk Forlag, Copenhagen, 1983; *Jagt og skonnert* [A Study of the Provincial Shipping Industry in Denmark during the Period 1814–1864], Falcon Bøger, Copenhagen, 1988. *Articles:* 'Fra galeoth til galease' [A Study of the Provincial Shipping Industry in 18th Century Denmark], Fiskeri-og Søfartsmuseet, Esbjerg, 1981, dissertation; 'Etaten og Traditionerne', *Dansk Toldhistorie Vol. 5, 1914–1945*, Toldistorisk Selskab, Copenhagen, 1990; 'Postrytter, Dagvogn og Fodpost', *P&Ts Historie Vol. 2, 1711–1850*, Generaldirektoratet for Post- og Telegrafvæsenet, Copenhagen, 1992.

Mori, Tetsuhiko

Prof., Nagoya Municipal Women's College, 464 Kitachikusa 2-1-10, Chikusa-ku, Nagoya, Japan. Tel.: 052 721 1371. Fax: 052 721 3110.

Year and Place of Birth 1943, Kyoto, Japan.

Degrees and Qualifications MA Ritsumeikan Univ., 1965.

Fields of Expertise *Industry Fields:* instrument engineering; insurance, banking, finance. *Bus. Dimensions:* entrepreneurs and entrepreneurship; co. finance and accounting; co. law. *Scope:* national. *Period:* nineteenth century; early twentieth century. *Teaching:* undergrad. *Consultancy:* co. hist.

Publications *Books: Doitsu Denki Kogyo Kigyo no Keisei* [Formation of the German Electrical Machinery Enterprise], 1984; *Keieigakushi no Kenkyuhoho to Kadai* [The Method of Study and the Subject about the Hist. of Bus. Econ.], 1985; *Doitsu Taisyakutaishohyo no Ichi Keitai* [One Form of German Balance Sheet Theory], 1987; *Doitsu Shihonsyugi to*

Shikeizaigaku [German Capitalism and Private Econ.], 1988; *Waiyaman. Shenizu to Shumalenbbaha no Shikeizaigaku* [Management Ideas of Weyermann-Schönitz and Schmalenbach], 1989.

Mori, Yasuhiro

Prof., Fac. of Bus. Admin., Kwansei Gakuin Univ., 1-155 Uegahara-Ichiban-cho, Nishinomiya 662, Japan. Tel.: 0798 53 6111.

Year and Place of Birth 1931, Osaka, Japan.

Degrees and Qualifications BA Osaka Univ., 1954; M.Econ. Osaka Univ., 1956; Ph.D.(Econ). Osaka Univ., 1971.

Previous Post Assist. Prof., Fac. of Econ., Osaka Univ., 1970–5.

Current Offices and Honorary Posts Council mem., exec. off., Bus. Hist. Soc. of Japan.

Fields of Expertise *Industry Fields:* insurance, banking, finance. *Bus. Dimensions:* entrepreneurs and entrepreneurship; co. admin. *Scope:* national. *Period:* early modern; eighteenth century; nineteenth century; twentieth century as a whole. *Teaching:* undergrad.; post grad.

Publications *Books: Daimyo Kin yushiron* [Borrowings by Daimyos from the Osaka Money Changers], Ohara-Shinsei-sha, 1970. *Articles:* 'Loans to Daimyos by the Osaka Money Changers', *Osaka Econ. Paper*, 15(29), 1967; 'Sogo-shoken-gaisha no Seiritsu Katei' [Formation of the Full Line Securities Co.], *Syogaku Ronkyu* [Kwansei Gakuin Univ. J. of Bus. Admin.], 31(1), 1983; 'Funai-han Osaka Kurayashiki no Gyomu' [Bus. in the Osaka Kuraya-shiki of the Funai Baronial Government], *Osaka no Rekishi* [The Hist. of Osaka], 25, 1988; 'Sogo-shoken-gaisha no Kigen' [Origin of the Full Line Securities Co.], *Kindaika no Shoso* [Phases of the Modernization], M. Yunoki ed., Seibun-sha, 1992.

Morikawa, Hidemasa

Prof., Keio Univ., Grad. School of Bus. Admin., 2-1-1 Hiyoshi-Honcho, Kohoku-ku, Yokohama 223, Japan. Tel.: 045 562 1185. Fax: 045 562 3502.

Year and Place of Birth 1930, Nagasaki, Japan.

Degrees and Qualifications BA Tokyo Univ.; MA Tokyo Univ.

Previous Post Prof., Keio Univ., 1990–2.

Current Offices and Honorary Posts Bus. Hist. Soc. of Japan: sec., exec. com. mem., exec. off. & pres.

Fields of Expertise *Bus. Dimensions:* entrepreneurs and entrepreneurship; strategy formation; bus. and technology. *Scope:* national. *Period:* twentieth century as a whole. *Consultancy:* co. hist.

Publications *Books: Zaibatsu no Keieishiteki Kenkyu* [Bus. Hist. of Zaibatsu], Toyo-keizai Shimpo sha, 1980; *Nihon Keieishi* [Japanese Bus. Hist.], Nihon Keizai Shimbunsha, 1981; *Makita Tamaki Denki Shiryo* [Hist. Materials on Tamaki Makita], Japan Bus. Hist. Instit., 1982; *Chiho Zaibatsu* [Local Zaibatsu], Nihon Keizai Shimbunsha, 1985; *Zaibatsu*, Univ. of Tokyo Press, 1992.

Moss, Michael Stanley

Archivist, Univ. of Glasgow, G12 8QQ. Tel.: 041 330 5516. Fax: 041 330 4158.

Year and Place of Birth 1947, Harrogate, UK.

Degrees and Qualifications MA, Oxford, 1969.

Previous Post Registrar of National

Register Archives (Western Survey), 1970–1974.

Current Offices and Honorary Posts Chairman of Scottish Univ. Special Collections of Archive Group; Scottish Representative on the European Univ. Hist. Project.

Fields of Expertise *Industry Fields:* agric., forestry, fishing; food, drink, tobacco; chemicals and allied industries; metal manufacture; mechanical engineering; instrument engineering; shipbuilding and marine engineering; construction; transport and communication; insurance, banking, finance; public administration and defence. *Business Dimensions:* entrepreneurs and entrepreneurship; company finance and accounting; company law; marketing; research and development; business organization; small business matters; business–state relations; company culture. *Scope:* national; international. *Period:* eighteenth century; nineteenth century; twentieth century as a whole. *Teaching:* ; undergrad.; post grad. *Consultancy:* company history.

Publications *Books: Workshop of the British Empire: Engineers and Shipbuilding in the West of Scotland*, with John R. Moss, Heinemann Educational Books Ltd, 1977; *A History of William Beardmore and Co: The History of a Scottish Industrial Giant*, with John R. More, Heinemann Educational Books Ltd, 1979; *A Business of National Importance: The Royal Mail Shipping Group 1903–1937*, with Edwin Green, Methuen, 1982; *The First Hundred Years of Bar and Stroud*, with I. F. Russell, Mainstream Publishing Co. Ltd, Edinburgh, 1988; *A Legend of Retailing: House of Fraser*, with A. M. Turton, Weidenfeld & Nicolson, 1989.

Mosser, Alois

Prof., Inst. of Econ. and Soc. Hist., Vienna Univ. of Econ. and Bus. Admin., Augasse 2-6, A-1090 Vienna, Austria. Tel.: 43 222 3136 4710. Fax: 43 222 347541 709.

Year and Place of Birth 1937, Laakirchen, Austria.

Degrees and Qualifications Dr.phil. Vienna Univ., 1965; univ. doz. Vienna Univ., 1976; ao. prof. Vienna Univ., 1983; o. prof. Vienna Econ. Univ., 1991.

Current Offices and Honorary Posts Mem., Austrian Hist. Research Inst., Vienna; chair, Austrian Assoc. for Bus. Hist., Vienna.

Major Honours Kardinal-Innitzer-Förderungs Prize, 1976.

Fields of Expertise *Industry Fields:* insurance, banking, finance. *Bus. Dimensions:* entrepreneurs and entrepreneurship. *Scope:* national. *Period:* twentieth century as a whole. *Teaching:* undergrad. *Consultancy:* co. hist.

Publications *Books: Der Unternehmer und die Geschichte; Festschrift für Alois Brusatti*, ed., Vienna, 1979; *Die Industrieaktiengesellschaft in Österreich 1880–1913. Versuch einer historischen Bilanz- und Betriebsanalyse*, Vienna, 1980; *Wiener Allianz. Gegründet 1860*, with Marita Roloff, Vienna, 1992. *Articles:* 'Die Entwicklung des Böhler-Konzerns von seinen Anfängen bis zum Ausbruch des Ersten Weltkrieges', *1870–1970: 100 Jahre Böhler Edelstahl*, Vienna, 1970, 8–48; 'Geschichte der Interessenvertretung der Maschinen- und Stahlbauindustrie', *Hundert Jahre Interessenvertretung der Maschinen- und Stahlbauindustrie Österreichs*, with Roland Löffler, Vienna, 1985, 14–69.

Mumford, Michael J.

Sen. Lect. in Accounting, Dept. of Accounting & Finance, Univ. of Lancaster Management School, Gillow House, Bailrigg, Lancaster, LA1 4TT, UK. Tel.: 44 524 65201. Fax: 44 524 847321.

Year and Place of Birth 1939, Purley, UK.

Degrees and Qualifications B. Com. Liverpool Univ., 1963; MA (Econ.) McMaster Univ., Canada, 1967; FCCA, 1966.

Previous Post Sen. lect. in accounting, Nairobi Univ., Kenya, 1970–2.

Current Offices and Honorary Posts Council mem., Chartered Assoc. of Certified Accountants (ACCA); chair, ACCA Technical & Research Com.; mem., Internat. Accounting Com.; mem., Consultative Com. of Accountancy Bodies.

Fields of Expertise *Industry Fields:* other manufacturing industries; insurance, banking, finance; professional and scientific services; rubber (especially tyres). *Bus. Dimensions:* co. finance and accounting; markets and bus.; boardroom issues. *Scope:* national; internat.; UK. *Period:* twentieth century as a whole. *Teaching:* undergrad.; post grad. *Consultancy:* corporate strategy.

Publications *Books: Distributable Profits - the Auditor's Role*, with Andrew McGee co-auth., ACCA, London, 1991; *Philosophical Perspectives on Accounting: Essays in Honour of Edward Stamp*, contributor & co-ed. with Ken Peasnell, Routledge, London, (chapter 'Users, Characteristics and Standards', 7–29).

Munn, Charles W.

Chief Executive, The Chartered Inst. of Bankers in Scotland, 19 Rutland Square, Edinburgh, EH1 2DE, UK.

Tel.: 44 31 229 9869. Fax: 44 31 229 1852.

Year and Place of Birth 1948, Glasgow, UK.

Degrees and Qualifications BA Strathclyde Univ., 1972; Ph.D. Glasgow Univ., 1976; FCIBS 1993.

Previous Post Sen. Lect., Dept. of Econ. Hist., Glasgow Univ., 1986–8.

Current Offices and Honorary Posts Chief executive, Chartered Inst. of Bankers in Scotland.

Fields of Expertise *Industry Fields:* insurance, banking, finance; professional and scientific services. *Bus. Dimensions:* co. finance and accounting; co. law; management education. *Scope:* national. *Period:* eighteenth century; nineteenth century; twentieth century as a whole. *Teaching:* undergrad.; post grad. *Consultancy:* co. hist.

Publications *Books: The Scottish Provincial Banking Companies 1747–1864*, John Donald, 1981; *The Clydesdale Bank: The First 150 Years*, Collins, 1988; *The Scottish Dictionary of Bus. Biography*, assoc. ed., Aberdeen Univ. Press, vol. I, 1986, vol. II, 1990.

Munro, J. Forbes

Prof. in Econ. Hist. & Clerk of Senate, Dept. of Econ. Hist., Glasgow Univ., 4 Univ. Gardens, Glasgow, G12 8QQ, UK. Tel.: 44 41 339 8855. Fax: 44 41 330 4920.

Year and Place of Birth 1940, Grantown-on-Spey, UK.

Degrees and Qualifications MA (Hist.) Edinburgh Univ.; Ph.D. (Hist.) Wisconsin Univ.

Previous Post Reader in Econ. Hist., Glasgow Univ., 1985–90.

Current Offices and Honorary Posts Edit. board, *Internat. J. of Maritime Hist.*

Fields of Expertise *Industry Fields:* transport and communication. *Bus.*

Dimensions: entrepreneurs and entrepreneurship. *Scope:* internat. *Period:* nineteenth century. *Teaching:* undergrad.; post grad.

Publications *Articles:* 'Scottish Overseas Enterprise and the Lure of London: The Mackinnon Shipping Group, 1847–1893', *Scottish Econ. & Social Hist.*, 8, 1988, 73–87; 'Suez and the Shipowner: The Response of the Mackinnon Group to the Opening of the Canal, 1869–1884', *Shipping and Trade, 1750–1950*, R. Lewis, R. Fischer & Helge Nordvick eds., Lofthouse Pubs., Pontefract, 1990, 97–117; '"The Gilt of Illusion": The Mackinnon Group's Entry into Queensland Shipping, 1880–1895', *Internat. J. of Maritime Hist.*, III(2), 1991, 1–37; 'The "Scrubby Scotch Screw Co.": British India Steam Navigation Co.'s Coastal Services in South Asia, 1867–1870', *From Wheel House to Counting House: Essays in Maritime Bus. Hist. in Honour of Prof. Peter Neville Davies*, R. Lewis R. Fischer ed., St John's Internat. Maritime Econ. Hist. Assoc., 1992, 43–72.

Munting, Roger

Lect., School of Econ. and Social Studies, Univ. of East Anglia, Norwich, NR4 7TJ, UK. Tel.: 44 603 592069. Fax: 44 603 250434.

Year and Place of Birth 1945, Welwyn Garden City, UK.

Degrees and Qualifications BA (Econ.) Sheffield Univ., 1966; Ph.D. Birmingham Univ., 1974.

Previous Post Sen. Lect., Dept. of Econ., Auckland Univ., New Zealand.

Fields of Expertise *Industry Fields:* entertainment and leisure. *Bus. Dimensions:* entrepreneurs and entrepreneurship. *Scope:* internat. *Period:* twentieth century as a whole. *Teaching:* undergrad. *Consultancy:* co.

hist.

Publications *Books: Econ. Development of the USSR*, Croom Helm, 1982. *Articles:* 'Ramsomes in Russia - an English Agric. Engineering Co.'s Trade with Russia before 1917', *Econ. Hist. Rev.*, XXXI, 1978, 257–69; 'Soviet Food Supply and Allied Aid in the War 1941–45', *Soviet Studies*, 36, 1984, 582–93; 'Agric. Engineering and European Exports to 1914', *Bus. Hist.*, 27, 1985, 125–45; 'Betting and Bus.: The Commercialisation of Gambling in Britain', *Bus. Hist.*, 31, 1989, 67–85.

Murkison, Eugene C.

Assoc. Prof. of Management, College of Bus. Admin., The Georgia Southern Univ., Hollis Hall, Statesboro, GA 30460-8152, USA. Tel.: 1 912 681 5931. Fax: 1 912 681 0292.

Year and Place of Birth 1936, Donalsonville, USA.

Degrees and Qualifications BS Georgia Univ., 1959; MBA Rochester Univ., 1970; Ph.D. Missouri Univ., 1986.

Previous Post Officer, US Army, 1959–81.

Current Offices and Honorary Posts Membership chairman, Optimist Club, Statesboro; div. chairman, Human Resource Management Div., Internat Acad. of Bus. Disciplines.

Fields of Expertise *Industry Fields:* food, drink, tobacco; metal manufacture; vehicle construction; transport and communication; public admin. and defence. *Bus. Dimensions:* personnel management; merger movement and issues; bus. organization; small bus. matters; management education; co. culture. *Scope:* local; regional; national; internat. *Period:* nineteenth century; twentieth century as a whole. *Teaching:* undergrad.; post grad. *Consultancy:* co. hist.

Publications *Articles:* 'How

Managers Influence Superiors: A Study of Upward Influence Tactics', *Leadership & Organization Development J.*, with Tom Case, Lloyd & Bernie Keys, 9(4), 1988, 25–31; 'Difficult Management Training: Will it Fly in the USA?', *Mid-Amer. J. of Bus.*, 4(2), 1989, 45–49; 'The Predisposition toward Organizational Commitment of Future Managers', *Lander College Bus. Rev.*, 4(2), 1990, 13–16; 'Small Bus. Failure Rates and Learning', *J. of Bus. & Econ. Studies*, with R.J. Stapleton, 3(4), Oct., 1990; 'Scripts and Decisions: An Empirical Analysis', *Transactional Analysis J.*, with R.J. Stapleton, 20(3), Jul., 1990.

Myers, Michael D.

Lect., Dept. of Management Science and Information Systems, Univ. of Auckland, Private Bag 92019, Auckland 1, New Zealand. Tel.: 64 9 3737999. Fax: 64 9 3737430.

Year and Place of Birth 1954, UK.

Degrees and Qualifications BA Auckland Univ., 1975; MA Auckland Univ., 1978; Ph.D. Auckland Univ., 1987.

Previous Post Marketing Representative, IBM, 1975–8.

Major Honours Sen. Scholar in Anthropology, 1975.

Fields of Expertise *Industry Fields:* information systems - dairy industry; health. *Bus. Dimensions:* bus. and technology. *Scope:* global; New Zealand. *Period:* late twentieth century, 1970–present. *Teaching:* undergrad.; post grad. *Consultancy:* information systems.

Publications *Books: New Zealand Cases in Information Systems*, 2nd edn., Pagination Publishers, 1992; *Australian and New Zealand Cases in Information Systems*, Pagination Publishers, 1992.

Myllyntaus, Timo

Sen. Lect., Dept. of Econ. and Soc. Hist., Univ. of Helsinki, POB 33 (Aleksi 7), FIN-00 014 Helsinki Univ., Finland. Tel.: 358 0 191 2081. Fax: 358 0 191 2180.

Year and Place of Birth 1951, Jyväskylä, Finland.

Degrees and Qualifications M.Soc.Sc. Helsinki Univ., 1978; L.Soc.Sc. Helsinki Univ., 1980; Ph.D. (Econ.) London School of Econ., 1989.

Previous Post Research fellow, Helsinki Univ., 1988–93.

Current Offices and Honorary Posts Internat. Scholar, Soc. for the Hist. of Technology, USA.

Major Honours Award for merit, Finnish Soc. for the Hist. of the Press, 1980.

Fields of Expertise *Industry Fields:* electrical engineering; timber, furniture; gas, electricity, water. *Bus. Dimensions:* bus. and technology. *Scope:* national; Finland. *Period:* nineteenth century; twentieth century as a whole. *Teaching:* undergrad. *Consultancy:* co. hist.

Publications *Books: Electrifying Finland. The Transfer of a new Technology into a late Industrialising Economy*, Macmillan & ETLA, London, 1991, xvi. *Articles:* 'The Finnish Model of Technology Transfer', *Econ. Development & Cultural Change*, 38(3), Chicago, 1990, 625–43; 'The Role of Industry in the Electrification of Finland', *Électricité et électrification dans le monde. Actes du deuxième colloque internàt. D'histoire de l'électricité*, Monique Trédé ed., Assoc. pour l'histoire de l'électricité en France, 1992, 235–49; 'Technology Transfer and the Contextual Filter in the Finnish Setting. Transfer Channels and Mechanisms in an Hist. Perspective', *Mastering Technology Diffusion - The Finnish Experience*, Synnöve Vuori & Pekka

Ylä-Anttila eds., ETLA-Series B 82, The Research Inst. of the Finnish Econ., Helsinki, 1992, 195–251; 'Technological Change in Finland', *Technology and Industry, a Nordic Heritage,* Jan Hult & Bengt Nyström eds., Nantucket, Science Hist. Pubs., USA, 1992, 29–52.

Nader, John S.

Assoc. Prof. of Econ. and Hist., 713 Evenden Tower, SUNY at Delhi, Delhi, NY 13753, USA. Tel.: 1 607 746 4204.
Year and Place of Birth 1955, Oneonta, USA.
Degrees and Qualifications BA Ithaca College, 1978; MA New School for Soc. Research, 1980; Ph.D. New School for Soc. Research, 1991.
Fields of Expertise *Industry Fields:* agric., forestry, fishing; agricultural implements and machines. *Bus. Dimensions:* research and development. *Scope:* regional; USA. *Period:* nineteenth century; twentieth century as a whole. *Teaching:* undergrad.

Nakagawa, Keiichiro

Prof., School of Internat. Polit., Econ. & Bus., Aoyama Gakuin Univ., Shibuya, Tokyo 106, Japan. Tel.: 81 3 3409 8111. Fax: 81 3 5485 0782.
Year and Place of Birth 1920, Shiga pref., Japan.
Degrees and Qualifications BA Tokyo Univ., 1948.
Previous Post Prof., Fac. of Econ., Tokyo Univ., 1951–81.
Current Offices and Honorary Posts Adviser to Japan Bus. Hist. Soc.; director, Japan Bus. Hist. Inst.; director, Japan Maritime Research Inst.; mem., Japan Acad.
Major Honours Kun Nito Zuiho

Sho [the Second Grade Order of the Sacred Treasure].
Fields of Expertise *Industry Fields:* shipbuilding and marine engineering. *Bus. Dimensions:* strategy formation. *Scope:* internat.; USA; UK; Japan. *Period:* nineteenth century. *Teaching:* undergrad.; post grad. *Consultancy:* co. hist.
Publications *Books: Ryotaisenkan no Nihon Kaiungyo* [Japanese Shipping in the Interwar Period], Nihonkeizai Shinbunsha, 1980; *Nihonteki Keiei* [Japanese Bus. Management], NHK Publishing Co., 1981; *Hikaku Keieishi Josetsu* [An Introduction to Comparative Bus. Hist.], Tokyo Univ. Press, 1981; *Igirisu Keiei Shi* [British Bus. Hist.], Tokyo Univ. Press, 1986; *Sengo Nihon no Kaiun to Zosen* [Postwar Japanese Shipping and Shipbuilding], Nihon keizai Hyoron Sha, 1992.

Nakagawa, Seishi

Assoc. Prof., Fac. of Commerce, Fukuoka Univ., Nanakuma, Jonan-ku, Fukuoka 814-01, Japan.
Year and Place of Birth 1954, Fukuoka, Japan.
Degrees and Qualifications M.Econ. Kyushu Univ., 1981.
Previous Post Research Asst., Fac. of Econ., Kyushu Univ., 1985–7.
Current Offices and Honorary Posts Sec., Assoc. of Management Philo.
Fields of Expertise *Industry Fields:* metal manufacture; mechanical engineering. *Bus. Dimensions:* production management; personnel management. *Scope:* national; internat.; USA. *Period:* nineteenth century; twentieth century as a whole; early twentieth century. *Teaching:* undergrad.
Publications *Books: Teira-Shugi-Seisei-Shiron* [Hist. Analysis of the Formation of Taylorism], Moriyama-Shoten, 1992. *Articles:* 'The

Introduction and Development of Scientific Management and the Rise of Japanese Management (I) (II) - from the Viewpoint of Separation of Planning and Execution', *Fukuoka Univ. Rev. of Commercial Sciences*, 36(1), July, 1991; 'The Japan that Mammon Rules: Where have our Bus. Ethics gone?', *Perspectives, the Center for the Study of Ethics in the Professions*, Illinois Instit. of Technology, 12(1), Aug., 1992.

Nakatsukasa, Ichiro

Prof. of Bus. Hist., Fac. of Commerce and Econ., Chiba Univ. of Commerce, 1-3-1 Konodai, Ichikawa-shi, Chiba 272, Japan. Tel.: 0473 72 4111. Fax: 0473 71 6881.
Year and Place of Birth 1932, Tokyo, Japan.
Degrees and Qualifications MA Aoyamagakuin Univ., 1959.
Current Offices and Honorary Posts Council mem.
Fields of Expertise *Industry Fields:* transport and communication. *Bus. Dimensions:* entrepreneurs and entrepreneurship. *Scope:* internat.; national. *Period:* nineteenth century; twentieth century as a whole. *Teaching:* undergrad.; post grad. *Consultancy:* co. hist.
Publications *Articles:* 'Interstate Commerce Act 1887 and the Entrepreneur of the Railroad', *Chiba Univ. of Commerce Rev.*, 1970; 'The Ina Electric Railway - a Bus. Hist. of Japanese Railroads (I)', *Chiba Univ. of Commerce Rev.*, 1980; 'A Bus. Hist. of Japanese Railroads (2)', *Chiba Univ. of Commerce Rev.*, 1981.

Nasuno, Kimito

Lect., Dept. of Bus. Admin., Sakushin Gakuin Univ., Takeshita-cho 908, Utsunomiya, Tochigi 321–32, Japan.

Tel.: 0286 67 7111. Fax: 0286 67 7110.
Year and Place of Birth 1954, Nagano pref., Japan.
Degrees and Qualifications B.Econ. Chiba Univ. of Commerce, 1977; M.Econ. Chiba Univ. of Commerce, 1983; Ph.D. (Bus. & Commerce) Keio Gijuku Univ. Grad. School, 1987.
Fields of Expertise *Industry Fields:* mechanical engineering; electronics and computers: manufacture. *Bus. Dimensions:* bus. and technology. *Scope:* national; internat. *Period:* nineteenth century; early twentieth century; late twentieth century, 1970–present. *Teaching:* undergrad. *Consultancy:* co. hist.
Publications *Articles:* 'Nihon Kindaika to kosaku-kikai seisan' [The Modernization of Japan and the Production of Machine Tools], *Keio Shogaku Ronshu* [Keio Bus. & Commerce Rev.], 1, 1987, 66–101; 'Mekatoronikusu to sofutouea' [Mechatronics and Software], *Sofutouea no keiei-kanri* [Managerial Admin. of Software], Noguchi Tasuku ed., Zeimu-keiri-kyokai Pub., 1989, 3–29; 'Kosaku-kikai no sofutoka to kosaku-kikai seisan' [Development of Numerical Control and Production of the Machine Tools], *Sofutouea no keiei-kanri* [Managerial Admin. of Software], Noguchi Tasuku ed., Zeimu-keiri-kyokai Pub., 1989, 285–314; 'Kyodai-kigyo no kigyo-kanri' [Management of Japanese Big Bus.], *Gendai nihon keieishi* [Modern Bus. Hist. in Japan], Fujii Mituo & Maruyama Yoshinari eds., Minerva Pub., 1991, 166–98.

Naylor, R. Thomas

Prof. of Econ., Dept. of Econ., McGill Univ., Montreal, Quebec, H3A 2T6, Canada. Tel.: 1 514 398 4828. Fax: 1 514 398 4938.

Year and Place of Birth 1945, Canada.

Degrees and Qualifications BA Toronto Univ.; M.Sc. London School of Econ.; Ph.D. Cambridge Univ.

Major Honours *Hist. of Canadian Bus.* selected by Soc. Sc. Federation of Canada as one of twenty most outstanding works in Canadian Soc. Sc. in the last fifty years (1990).

Fields of Expertise *Industry Fields:* coal and petroleum products; insurance, banking, finance. *Bus. Dimensions:* bus. organization; multinational bus.; bus. values; black markets and corporate crime. *Scope:* internat. *Period:* nineteenth century; twentieth century as a whole. *Teaching:* undergrad.; post grad.

Publications *Books: Hist. of Canadian Bus. 1867–1914,* Lorimer, 1975; *Hot Money and the Polit. of Debt,* Unwin, 1987; *Canada in the European Age 1453–1919,* New Star, 1987.

Scholarship, 1958–62; Ford Foundation Dissertation Fellowship, 1966; Clio Award for *Service to Cliometrics,* 1990.

Fields of Expertise *Industry Fields:* insurance, banking, finance. *Bus. Dimensions:* co. finance and accounting; merger movement and issues. *Scope:* internat. *Period:* eighteenth century; nineteenth century; twentieth century as a whole. *Teaching:* undergrad.; post grad.

Publications *Books: Explorations in Econ. Hist.,* ed.; *The Rise of Financial Capitalism: Internat. Capital Markets in the Age of Reason,* CUP, Cambridge, 1990; *War Finance,* ed., Edward Elgar Publishing, forthcoming. *Articles:* 'The Rise of a Financial Press: London and Amsterdam, 1681–1810', *Bus. Hist.,* 30, April, 1988, 163–78; 'A Tale of Two Revolutions: Internat. Capital Flows, 1789–1819', *Bull. of Econ. Research,* 43, 1991, 307–37.

Neal, Larry D.

Prof. of Econ., Dept. of Econ., Univ. of Illinois at Urbana-Champaign, 328A DKH, 1407 W. Gregory, Urbana, IL 61801, USA. Tel.: 1 217 333 2686. Fax: 1 217 244 6678.

Year and Place of Birth 1941, Twin Falls, USA.

Degrees and Qualifications BA (Hist.), Stanford Univ., 1962; Ph.D. (Econ.) Univ. of California at Berkeley, 1968.

Previous Post Assoc. ed., *Explorations in Econ. Hist.,* 1981; Director, Office of West European Studies, Univ. of Illinois, 1977–80.

Current Offices and Honorary Posts *ex officio* trustee, the Cliometrics Soc.; Alexander von Humboldt Fellow, 1982; ODE Award for Excellence in Grad. Teaching, 1990–1; vice-pres., Econ. Hist. Assoc., 1991–2.

Major Honours Nat. Merit

Neiva, Elizabeth MacIver

Grad. student, Dept. of Hist., Harvard Univ., Robinson Hall, Cambridge, MA 02138, USA. Tel.: 1 617 495 2556. Fax: 1 617 496 3425.

Year and Place of Birth 1964, Hartford, USA.

Degrees and Qualifications BA Williams College, 1986; MA Harvard Univ., 1990; Ph.D. Harvard Univ., 1993.

Previous Post Research Assoc., Harvard Bus. School, 1990 & teaching fellow, 1992.

Major Honours Josephine de Karman Fellowship in the Humanities, 1992; Harvard Bus. School's Doctoral Fellowship in Bus. Hist., 1988–92; the Alfred D. Chandler Jr. Grant for Bus. Hist., 1991; the Charles Warren Center Dissertation Grant, 1991 & 1992.

Fields of Expertise *Industry Fields:* paper, printing, publishing. *Bus. Dimensions:*

strategy formation; bus. and technology; boardroom issues. *Scope:* national. *Period:* mid-twentieth century, 1940–70; late twentieth century, 1970–present. *Teaching:* undergrad.

Publications *Books: Pawns or Potentates: The Reality of America's Corporate Boards*, with Jay W. Lorsch, Harvard Bus. School Press, 1989. *Articles:* 'Corporate Governance and Investment Time Horizons', *Capital Choices: Changes in the Way Amer. Invests in Industry*, with Jay W. Lorsch, Michael Porter ed., Harvard Bus. School Press, 1993.

Nelson, Daniel

Prof. of Hist., Dept. of Hist., Akron Univ., Akron, OH 44325-1902, USA. Tel.: 1 216 972 7125. Fax: 1 216 374 8795.

Year and Place of Birth 1941, USA.

Degrees and Qualifications BA Ohio Wesleyan Univ.; Ph.D. Wisconsin Univ.

Major Honours Phi Beta Kappa.

Fields of Expertise *Industry Fields:* vehicle construction; professional and scientific services. *Bus. Dimensions:* personnel management; bus. and technology. *Scope:* regional; national. *Period:* early twentieth century; interwar years, 1919–39; mid-twentieth century, 1940–'70. *Teaching:* undergrad.; post grad.

Publications *Books: Unemployment Insurance*, Univ. of Wisconsin Press, 1969; *Managers and Workers*, Univ. of Wisconsin Press, Madison, 1975; *Frederick W. Taylor*, Univ. of Wisconsin Press, Madison, 1980; *Amer. Rubber Workers and Organized Labor*, Princeton Univ. Press, Princeton, 1988; *A Mental Revolution*, ed., Ohio State Press, Columbus, 1992.

Neufeld, Edward P.

Exec. Vice Pres., Econ. and Corporate Affairs, The Royal Bank of Canada, Royal Bank Plaza, 200 Bay St, Toronto, Ontario, M5J 2J5, Canada. Tel.: 1 416 974 3340. Fax: 1 416 974 3343.

Year and Place of Birth 1927, Nipawin, Canada.

Degrees and Qualifications BA Saskatchewan Univ., 1951; Ph.D. London School of Econ. & Polit. Science, 1954.

Previous Post Asst. Deputy Minister, Tax Policy & Legislation Branch, Government of Canada, 1973–80.

Current Offices and Honorary Posts Advisory board mem., Centre for Internat. Studies, Toronto Univ.; dir., C.D. Howe Inst.

Major Honours Hutchinson Silver Medal, London School of Econ., 1954; Honorary Fellow, London School of Econ.

Fields of Expertise *Industry Fields:* insurance, banking, finance. *Bus. Dimensions:* research and development. *Scope:* national; internat. *Period:* twentieth century as a whole. *Consultancy:* co. hist.

Publications *Books: Bank of Canada Operations and Policy*, Univ. of Toronto Press, 1958; *Money and Banking in Canada*, McClelland & Stewart Ltd., 1964; *A Global Corporation*, Univ. of Toronto Press, 1969; *The Financial System of Canada*, Macmillan Co. of Canada Ltd., 1972.

Newby, Sonja

Senior Lect., Dept. of Accounting and Finance, Auckland Univ., Private Bag 92019, Auckland 1, New Zealand. Tel.: 64 9 3737599. Fax: 64 9 3737406.

Year and Place of Birth 1957, Invercargill, New Zealand.

Degrees and Qualifications M.Com. (Accounting) Auckland Univ., 1984; ACA New Zealand Soc. of Accountants, 1988; ACIS Inst. of Chartered Secretaries & Administrators, 1988.

Previous Post National Director of Professional Practice, KPMG Peat Marwick, 1988–90.

Current Offices and Honorary Posts New Zealand Pres., Accounting Assoc. of Australia & New Zealand, 1993–.

Fields of Expertise *Industry Fields:* bus. services; professional and scientific services. *Bus. Dimensions:* co. finance and accounting; bus.–state relations. *Scope:* national. *Period:* late twentieth century, 1970–present. *Teaching:* undergrad. *Consultancy:* corporate strategy.

Publications *Articles:* 'Opportunities for Growth Companies on the Second-Board Market', *New Zealand Soc. of Accountants' Publication*, with R. Higham, S.258, 1987; 'Financial Reporting in New Zealand: Towards Internat. Harmonisation', *The Proceedings of the Sixth Internat. Conf. on Accounting Education*, Kyojiro Someya ed., Greenwood Press Inc., Westport, CT, 1988, 660–70; 'The Use of a Statement of Changes in Financial Position to Interpret Financial Data: An Empirical Investigation', *ABACUS*, with M. Bradbury, 25(1), 1989, 31–8; 'SSAP Update', *New Zealand Soc. of Accountants' Publication*, S.321, August, 1989; 'Financial Reporting in New Zealand', *Financial Reporting in the West Pacific Rim*, R.H. Parker ed., Routledge, London, 1993.

Newell, Dianne

Assoc. Prof., Dept. of Hist., Univ. of British Columbia, 2075 Westbrook Pl., Vancouver, British Columbia, V6T 1Z1, Canada. Tel.: 1 604 822 2561. Fax: 1 604 822 6658.

Year and Place of Birth 1943, Ottawa, Canada.

Degrees and Qualifications BA Ottawa Univ., 1966; BA Carleton Univ., 1970; MA Carleton Univ., 1974; Ph.D. Western Ontario Univ., 1981.

Current Offices and Honorary Posts Head of Grad. Programme, Dept. of Hist., Univ. of British Columbia.

Major Honours Isaak Walton Killam Research Fellowship, 1990; Assoc. of Canadian Studies Writer's Award, 1990.

Fields of Expertise *Industry Fields:* agric., forestry, fishing. *Bus. Dimensions:* bus. and technology. *Period:* twentieth century as a whole. *Teaching:* post grad.

Publications *Books: Technology on the Frontier: Mining in Old Ontario*, Univ. of BC Press, Vancouver, 1986; *Survivals: Aspects of Industrial Archaeology in Ontario*, with Ralph Greenhill, Boston Mills Press, Erin, Ont., 1989; *The Development of the Pacific Salmon-Canning Industry: A Grown Man's Game*, ed., McGill-Queen's Univ. Press, Montreal /Kingston, 1989; *Tangled Webs of Hist.: Indians and the Law in Canada's Pacific Coast Fisheries*, Univ. of Toronto Press, Toronto, forthcoming. *Articles:* 'The Rationality of Mechanization in the Pacific Salmon-Canning Industry before the Second World War', *Bus. Hist. Rev.*, 62(4), Winter, 1988, 626–55*f*.

Nicholas, Stephen

Prof., Dept. of Econ. Hist., Melbourne Univ., Parkville, VIC 3052, Australia. Tel.: 61 3 344 5340. Fax: 61 3 347 3770.

Year and Place of Birth 1946, Ontario, Canada.

Degrees and Qualifications BA Syracuse Univ., 1967; MA Iowa Univ., 1969.

Previous Post Assoc. Prof. of Econ., Univ. of New South Wales, 1989–93.

Fields of Expertise *Industry Fields:* manufacturing and trade. *Bus. Dimensions:* bus. organization; multinational bus.; co. culture. *Scope:* internat. *Period:* eighteenth century; nineteenth century; twentieth century as a whole. *Teaching:* undergrad.; post grad.

Publications *Articles:* 'Agency Contracts, Institutional Modes and the Transition to Foreign Direct Investment by British Manufacturing Multinationals before 1939', *J. of Econ. Hist.*, 43, 1983, 675–86; 'The Overseas Marketing Performance of British Industry, 1870–1914', *Econ. Hist. Rev.*, 37, 1984, 489–506; 'Locational Choice, Performance and Growth of British Multinational Firms', *Bus. Hist.*, 31, 1989, 122–41; 'Agency Problems in the Early Charter Companies: The Case of the Hudson's Bay Co.', *J. of Econ. Hist.*, with Ann Carlos, 50, 1990, 853–76; 'Managing the Manager: An Application of the Principal Agent Model to the Hudson's Bay Co.', *Oxford Econ. Papers*, 45, 1993, 791–806.

Nishikawa, Hiroshi

Ph.D. Candidate, Ryukoku Univ. Grad. School, 67 Fukakusa-Tsukamoto-cho, Fushimi-ku, Kyoto, Japan. Tel.: 81 75 642 1111.

Year and Place of Birth 1964, Osaka, Japan.

Degrees and Qualifications MBA Ryukoku Univ., 1989.

Fields of Expertise *Industry Fields:* bricks, pottery, glass, cement. *Bus. Dimensions:* production management; bus. and technology; co. culture. *Scope:* internat. *Period:* nineteenth century; twentieth century as a whole.

Publications *Articles:* 'Jidosha sangyo ni okeru gijutsu joho chikuseki katei no kokusai hikaku' [A Comparative Study on a Formative Process of the Production System in the Automobile Industry], Master's, Ryukoku Univ., 1989; 'Kigyo no paradaimu tenkan ni kansuru hikakushiteki kousatsu' [A Hist. Study on the Paradigm Shift], *Ryukoku Univ. J. of Econ. & Bus. Studies*, 29(3), Dec., 1989.

Nishikawa, Junko

Prof. of Bus. Hist., Fac. of Bus. Management, Tokyo Metropol. College of Commerce, Harumi 1-2-1, Chuo-ku, Tokyo, Japan. Tel.: 03 3533 4372.

Year and Place of Birth 1934, Hokkaido, Japan.

Degrees and Qualifications Ph.D. Tokyo Univ., 1980.

Previous Post Asst. Prof. of Econ. Hist., Kantogakuin Univ.

Current Offices and Honorary Posts Exec. com. mem., Agrarian Hist. Soc.

Fields of Expertise *Industry Fields:* gas, electricity, water; insurance, banking, finance. *Bus. Dimensions:* co. finance and accounting; merger movement and issues. *Scope:* national; USA. *Period:* nineteenth century; inter-war years, 1919–39. *Teaching:* undergrad. *Consultancy:* co. hist.

Publications *Books: Amerika kigyokinyu no kenkyu, 1920 nendai o chushin ni* [Amer. Corporation Financing during the 1920s], Univ. of Tokyo Press, 1980; *Amerika Kinyushi* [Amer. Financial Hist.], Kazuo Matsui co-auth., Yuhikaku, 1989 & 1990. *Articles:* 'Amerika Keizaigaku to Seidogakuha' [American Institutionalism, Past and Present], *Kindaika no Kokusaihikaku* [Comparative Studies of

Modernization], Nishikawa, Junko &
Takaura Tadahiko eds., Sekaishoin,
1991.

Nishikawa, Noboru

Prof. of Accounting, Kanagawa Univ.,
Fac. of Econ., 3-27-1 Rokkakubashi,
Kanagawa-ku, Yokohama 221, Japan.
Tel.: 81 45 481 5661. Fax: 81 45 413
2678.
Year and Place of Birth 1952,
Ichikawa, Chiba Pref., Japan.
Degrees and Qualifications BA
Kyoto Univ., 1975; MA Hitotsubashi
Univ., 1977; Ph.D. (Econ.) Kyoto
Univ., 1993.
Previous Post Asst. Prof.,
Kanagawa Univ., 1987–90.
Current Offices and Honorary Posts
Sec., Bus. Hist. Soc. of Japan,
1989–92.
Fields of Expertise *Bus.
Dimensions:* co. finance and account-
ing. *Scope:* national; Japan. *Period:*
early modern; eighteenth century; nine-
teenth century; early twentieth century.
Teaching: undergrad.; post grad.
Publications *Books: Puroguramu
Gakusyuu niyoru Kiso Boki Kaikei*
[Essentials of Book-keeping and
Accounting by Programmed Learning],
Hakuto Shobo, 1991; *Mitui-ke
Kanzyou Kanken: Edo Zidai no Mitui-
ke niokeru Naibu Kaikei Houkou-seid
oyobi Kaikei Syori-gihou no Kenkyuu*
[Accounting of Mitsui: A Study on
Internal Financial Reporting Systems
and Book-keeping Procedures of the
House of Mitsui in the Tokugawa
Period], Hakuito Shobo, Tokyo, 1993.
Articles: 'Genesis of Divisional
Management and Accounting Systems
in the House of Mitsui, 1710–1730',
The Accounting Historians' J., with
Prof. Sadao Takatera co-auth., 11(1),
Spring, 1984.

Nishimura, Shizuya

Prof. in Monetary Econ., Fac. of Bus.
Admin., Hosei Univ., 2–17–1 Fujimi,
Chiyoda-ku, Tokyo 102, Japan. Tel.:
81 3 3264 9359. Fax: 81 3 3264
9326.
Year and Place of Birth 1929,
Tokyo, Japan.
Degrees and Qualifications B.Econ.
Tokyo Univ., 1953; M.Econ. Tokyo
Univ., 1955; Ph.D. London School of
Econ., 1969.
Current Offices and Honorary Posts
Ed.-in-chief, *Rev. of Monetary &
Financial Studies*, Japan Soc. of
Monetary Econ.; exec. com. mem.,
Japan Soc. of Monetary Econ.
Fields of Expertise *Industry Fields:*
insurance, banking, finance. *Bus.
Dimensions:* relationships between
banks and industry; internat. banking.
Scope: national; internat.; UK; France;
China. *Period:* early twentieth century.
Teaching: undergrad.; post grad.
Consultancy: co. hist.
Publications *Books: The Decline of
Inland Bills of Exchange in the
London Money Market, 1855–1913*,
CUP, 1971. *Articles:* 'The Mechanism
of the Supply of Money in the UK,
1973–1913', *Money and Power*, P.L.
Cottrell & D.E. Moggridge eds.,
Macmillan, London, 1988; 'Bill of
Exchange', *The New Palgrave
Dictionary of Money and Banking*, P.
Newman, M. Milgate & J. Eatwell
eds., Macmillan, London, 1992.

Nishimura, Takao

Emeritus Prof., Osaka Pref. Univ.,
Sakai Osaka-fu, Japan. Tel.: 0722 52
1161.
Year and Place of Birth 1921,
Kyoto, Japan.
Degrees and Qualifications Ph.D.
(Econ.) Kyoto Univ., 1961.

Previous Post Prof., Setsunan Univ., 1982–92.

Current Offices and Honorary Posts Council mem., Socio-Econ. Hist. Soc.

Fields of Expertise *Industry Fields:* shipbuilding and marine engineering; textiles; distributive trades. *Bus. Dimensions:* entrepreneurs and entrepreneurship; co. admin.; multinational bus. *Scope:* internat. *Period:* early modern; eighteenth century; nineteenth century. *Teaching:* undergrad.; post grad. *Consultancy:* co. hist.

Publications *Books: Hist. Research on the English East India Company*, Univ. of Osaka Pref. Press, 1960; *The Hist. of the Indian Cotton Industry*, Miraisha, Tokyo, 1966; *A Study of the Calico Controversy*, Kazamashobo, Tokyo, 1967; *A Study in Anglo-Asian Trade in Modern Times*, Kazamashobo, 1972; *A Short Hist. of the French East India Company*, Univ. of Osaka Pref. Press, 1977.

Nonaka, Izumi

Lect., Josai Univ., Fac. of Econ., 1-1 Keyakidai, Sakado-city, Saitama-pref. 350-02, Japan. Tel.: 0492 71 7606. Fax: 0492 85 7167.

Year and Place of Birth 1958, Sapporo, Japan.

Degrees and Qualifications MBA Aoyama Gakuin Univ. Grad. School of Bus. Admin., 1982.

Fields of Expertise *Bus. Dimensions:* production management. *Scope:* internat. *Period:* mid-twentieth century, 1940–70. *Teaching:* undergrad.

Publications *Articles:* 'Soshiki to Kanri' [Management and Organization], *Technology and Organization*, Masahiro Sakai & Masahiko Yoshihara eds., Bunshin-do, 1987; 'Kagakuteki Kanri no Donyu to Tenkai' [The Hist. Process of Introducing Scientific Management to

the World: Case Histories in Japan, Amer., England, France, Russia and Italy].

Noort, Jan van den

Sint Mariastraat 144 A, 3014 SR Rotterdam, Netherlands. Tel.: 010 4866014.

Year and Place of Birth 1949, Made, Netherlands.

Degrees and Qualifications MA (Hist., Econ., Sociology, Geography), Leyden Univ.; Ph.D. (Hist.) Leyden Univ.

Previous Post Freelance historian, NV GEB Rotterdam, 1992.

Current Offices and Honorary Posts Chairman, 'Net Werk voor de geschiedenis van hygiene en Milieu'; org. mem., Dutch Urban Hist. Group.

Fields of Expertise *Industry Fields:* coal and petroleum products; electrical engineering; gas, electricity, water; transport and communication; public admin. and defence. *Bus. Dimensions:* entrepreneurs and entrepreneurship; production management; co. finance and accounting; co. admin.; merger movement and issues; bus. organization; bus. and technology; bus.–state relations; co. culture; boardroom issues. *Scope:* local; regional; national; internat. *Period:* nineteenth century; twentieth century as a whole. *Teaching:* post grad. *Consultancy:* co. hist.; corporate strategy.

Publications *Books: Licht op het GEB, geschiedenis van het Gemeente-Energiebedriff Rotterdam*, Rotterdam, 1993. *Articles:* 'Bedrijfsgeschiedenis en bedrijfswaarde', *Jaarboek voor de geschiedenis van bedriff en techniek*, 5, 1988, 469–81; 'Gemengde gevoelens, vijftig jaar in de relatie NS-Overheid', *Het Spoor, Honderdviftig jaar spoorwegen in Nederland*, Utrecht, 1989, (Jubileumboek NS); 'Pion of Pionier, Rotterdam - gemeentelijke bedrijvigheid in de negentiende eeuw', thesis, Leyden Univ., Rotterdam, 1990; 'Foresight is not the essence of government', *Econ. Policy in Europe since the Middle Ages: the Visible Hand and the Fortune of Cities*, Herman Diederiks, Paul Hohenberg & Michael Wagenaar eds., Leicester, 1992.

Norberg, Arthur L.

Assoc. Prof., Dept. of Computer Science, 4–192 EE/CS Building, Minnesota Univ., Minneapolis, MN 55455, USA. Tel.: 1 612 625 1067. Fax: 1 612 625 0572.

Year and Place of Birth 1938, Providence, USA.

Degrees and Qualifications BS (Physics) Providence College, 1959; MS (Physics) Vermont Univ., 1962; Ph.D. (Hist. of Sci. & Tech.) Univ. of Wisconsin, Madison, 1974.

Previous Post Director, Charles Babbage Inst., Minnesota Univ., 1981–93.

Major Honours Engineering Research Associates Inc., Land-Grant Chair in Hist. of Technology, Minnesota Univ., 1989–93; Fellow, Amer. Assoc. for the Advancement of Science, 1992; Soc. of the Sigma Xi, National Lect., 1989–91.

Fields of Expertise *Industry Fields:* electrical engineering; electronics and computers: manufacture; bricks, pottery, glass, cement. *Bus. Dimensions:* research and development; bus. and technology. *Scope:* internat. *Period:* twentieth century as a whole. *Teaching:* undergrad.; post grad. *Consultancy:* co. hist.

Publications *Books: A Hist. of the Information Processing Techniques Office of the Defense Advanced Research Projects Agency*, with Judy E. O'Neill & Kerry J. Freedman, Charles Babbage Inst., Minneapolis, 1992. *Articles:* 'The Origins of the Electronics Industry on the Pacific Coast', *Proc. IEEE*, 64, 1976, 1314–1322; 'High-Technology Calculation in the Early 20th Century: Punched Card Machinery in Bus. and Government', *Technology and Culture*, 31, 1990, 753–79; 'New Engineering Companies and the Evolution of the United States Computer Industry', *Bus. & Econ. Hist.*, 22, 2nd ser., 1993; 'The Contexts for the Development of Radar: A Comparison of Efforts in the United States and the United Kingdom in the 1930s', *Hist. of Radar: An Internat. Pespective*, with Robert W. Seidel co-auth., Blumtritt & Petzold eds., IEEE Press, Piscataway, NJ, 1994, forthcoming.

Nordvik, Helge W.

Prof. of Maritime Studies, The Norwegian School of Management, Inst. for Bus. Hist., POB 580, 1301 Sandvika, Norway. Tel.: 47 67570752. Fax: 47 67570854.

Year and Place of Birth 1943, Fredrikstad, Norway.

Degrees and Qualifications Siviløkonom, The Norwegian School of Econ. & Bus. Admin., 1966; M.Sc. London School of Econ., 1969.

Previous Post Assoc. Prof. of Econ. Hist., Norwegian School of Econ. & Bus. Admin., 1986–91.

Current Offices and Honorary Posts Vice-pres., Norwegian Commission of Maritime Hist.

Fields of Expertise *Industry Fields:* transport and communication; insurance, banking, finance. *Bus. Dimensions:* strategy formation. *Scope:* national. *Period:* inter-war years, 1919–39. *Teaching:* post grad. *Consultancy:* co. hist.

Publications *Books: Penger Spart, Penger Tjent*, co-auth. with G. Nerheim & T. Brandal, SR Bank, 1989; *Across the Broad Atlantic: Essays in Comparative Canadian-*

Norwegian Maritime Hist., 1850–1914, co-ed. with Lewis R. Fischer, St John's, 1993. *Articles:* 'Norwegian Maritime Hist. Research during the past Twenty Years: A Critical Survey', *Norwegian Yearbook of Maritime Hist.*, Bergen, 1991, 241–78; 'Entrepreneurship and Risk-taking in the early Part of the Twentieth Century: The Case of Lauritz Kloster Stavanger', *From Wheel-house to Counting House: Essays in Maritime Bus. Hist. in Honour of Prof. Peter Neville Davies*, Lewis R. Fischer ed., St John's, 1992, 323–48; 'Bankkrise, Bankstruktur og Bankpolitikk i Norge i Mellomkrigstiden', *Historisk Tidsskrift*, 2, 1992, 171–92.

Novotny, Jirí

Director of Archives for the Governor of the Czech National Bank, Na prlkope 28, 110 03 Prague 1, Czechland.

Year and Place of Birth 1941, Cerny Les, Czechland.

Degrees and Qualifications C.Sc. Charles Univ., Prague, 1964; Ph.D., 1975.

Publications *Books: The Agrarian Bank in the Years 1911–1929*, Ph.D. Thesis, Prague, 1975. *Articles:* 'The Inst. of Banking for the Ministry of Finance - its Role in Monetary Policy 1919–1922', *Silesian Reports*, 72, 1974, 274–85.

Nuñez Romero-Balmas, Gregorio

Lect. in Econ. Hist., Dept. of Econ. Hist., Fac. of Econ. and Management, Granada Univ., Granada, Spain. Tel.: 34 58 243730. Fax: 34 58 243728.

Year and Place of Birth 1953, Almeria, Spain.

Degrees and Qualifications Ph.D.

(Contemporary Hist.).

Current Offices and Honorary Posts Dean, Fac. of Econ. & Management, Granada Univ.

Fields of Expertise *Industry Fields:* gas, electricity, water; urban services supply (tramways). *Bus. Dimensions:* merger movement and issues; small bus. matters. *Scope:* local; regional; Spain; Andalucia. *Period:* early twentieth century. *Teaching:* undergrad.; post grad. *Consultancy:* co. hist.; corporate strategy.

Publications *Articles:* 'Distribucion y Venta de Combustibles Liquidos en Andalucia en 1934', *Revista de Estudios Regionales*, Malaga, 1989; 'Développement et Intégration Régionale de l'Industrie Électrique en Andaloussie', *Electricité et Electrification dans le Monde*, Paris, PUF, 1990; 'Notas para una Tipología de las Empresas Eléctricas', *V. Coloquio de Asepelt-España*, Granada, forthcoming; 'Origen e Integración de la Industria Eléctrica en Andalucia y Badajoz', *Un Siglo de Historia de Sevillana de Electricidad*, Madrid, forthcoming.

O'Brien, Anthony Patrick

Assoc. Prof. of Econ., Dept. of Econ., 621 Taylor St, Lehigh Univ., Bethlehem, PA 18015, USA. Tel.: 1 215 758 3442. Fax: 1 215 758 4499.

Year and Place of Birth 1954, San Francisco, USA.

Degrees and Qualifications BA Univ. of California, Berkeley, 1976; Ph.D. Univ. of California, Berkeley, 1987.

Previous Post Visiting Asst. Prof. of Econ., Univ. of California, Santa Barbara.

Fields of Expertise *Industry Fields:* vehicle construction; insurance, banking, finance. *Bus. Dimensions:* entrepreneurs and entrepreneurship; merger movement and issues; bus. organization. *Scope:* national. *Period:* twentieth century as a whole; inter-war years, 1919–39. *Teaching:* undergrad.; post grad.

Publications *Articles:* 'The Cyclical Sensitivity of Wages', *Amer. Econ. Rev.,* 75, Dec., 1985, 1124–32; 'Factory Size, Economies of Scale and the Great Merger Wave of 1898–1902', *J. of Econ. Hist.,* 48, Sept., 1988, 639–49; 'The I.C.C., Freight Rates and the Great Depression', *Explorations in Econ. Hist.,* 26, Jan., 1989, 73–98; 'A Behavioral Explanation for Nominal Wage Rigidity during the Great Depression', *Q. J. of Econ.,* 104, Nov., 1989, 719–35; 'How to Succeed in Bus.: Lessons from the Struggle between Ford and General Motors during the 1920s and 1930s', *Bus. & Econ. Hist.,* 2nd ser., 18, 1989, 19–28.

O'Connor, Richard

Historian, HABS/HAER, POB 37127, Washington, DC 20013–7127, USA. Tel.: 1 412 731 4145.

Year and Place of Birth 1952, Lockport, USA.

Degrees and Qualifications BA SUNY at Buffalo; MA (Hist.) SUNY at Bufalo; Ph.D. (Hist.) Pittsburgh Univ.

Major Honours Andrew Mellon Fellowships.

Fields of Expertise *Industry Fields:* mining and quarrying; coal and petroleum products; metal manufacture; bricks, pottery, glass, cement. *Bus. Dimensions:* entrepreneurs and entrepreneurship; merger movement and issues; bus. and technology. *Period:* eighteenth century; nineteenth century; early twentieth century. *Teaching:* undergrad. *Consultancy:* co. hist.

Ohno, Akira

Lect., Fac. of Econ., Kyoto Gakuen Univ., Nanjo Sogabe-cho, Kameoka-shi, Kyoto 621, Japan. Tel.: 07712 2 2001. Fax: 07712 4 8150.

Year and Place of Birth 1955, Osaka-fu, Japan.

Degrees and Qualifications M.Econ. Kwansei Gakuin Univ., 1980.

Fields of Expertise *Industry Fields:* textiles. *Bus. Dimensions:* bus. and technology; markets and bus. *Scope:* internat. *Period:* nineteenth century; early twentieth century. *Teaching:* undergrad. *Consultancy:* co. hist.

Publications *Articles:* 'Daiichijitaisengo no Sekai ki-ito Sujo no Kouzou oyobi ki-ito Soba no Hendo ni Tsuite' [The Structure and Changes in Raw Silk Prices of the World-wide Silk Market after World War I], *J. of Econ. of Kwansei Gakuin Univ.,* 38(2), 1984, 103–28; 'The Japanese Raw Silk Industry in Relation to the Amer. and French Silk Industries', *Kwansei Gakuin Univ. Annual Studies,* 34, 1985, 137–62; 'Amerika Shijo niokeru Sansigyo no Kokusaikyoso ni Tsuite' [Internat. Competition amongst the Silk Producing Countries in the Amer. Market, 1900–1925], *Kwansei Gakuin Econ. Rev.,* 18, 1985, 1–16; 'Kinuorimono Seizo kosuto no Kokusaihikaku' [Comparison of Manufacturing Costs in Countries which produced Silk Goods], *Kwansei Gakuin Econ. Rev.,* 20, 1987, 1–20; 'Wagakuni ni Okeru Yoshiki Seishi Gijutsu no Tekiseika wo Meguru Syomondai' [Adaptation of Western-style Silk-reeling to the Requirements in Japan], *Kyoto Gakuen Univ. Fac. of Econ. Rev.,* 1(3), 1991, 41–59.

Oikawa, Yoshinobu

Assoc. Prof., Rikkyo Univ., Fac. of Econ., 3-34-1 Nishi Ikebukuro, Toshima-ku, Tokyo 171, Japan. Tel.: 03 3985 2332. Fax: 03 3985 4096.
Year and Place of Birth 1950, Saitama pref., Japan.
Degrees and Qualifications MA Rikkyo Univ., 1974; Ph.D. Rikkyo Univ., 1982.
Previous Post Assoc. Prof., Fac. of Econ., Teikyo Univ.
Current Offices and Honorary Posts Exec. com. mem., Railway Hist. of Japan; mem. of standing com., Japanese Soc. of the Hist. of Transport and Communication; council mem., Socio-Econ. Hist. Soc.
Major Honours Transport Soc. of Japan Prize, 1986.
Fields of Expertise *Industry Fields:* transport and communication. *Bus. Dimensions:* entrepreneurs and entrepreneurship; co. admin.; bus. organization; bus.–state relations; markets and bus. *Scope:* local; regional; national. *Period:* nineteenth century; twentieth century as a whole; inter-war years, 1919–39. *Teaching:* undergrad. *Consultancy:* co. hist.
Publications *Books: The Railway Hist. in Saitama Prefecture*, Saitama Shinbun Press, 1982; *A Study of Rural Railway Hist. in Japan during the Meiji Era*, Nihon Keizai Hyoronsha, 1983; *The Railway Hist. of Japan*, ed., Nihon Keizai Hyoronsha, 1986; *Hist. and Culture in the Management of Privately-owned Railways*, ed., Koon shoin, 1992; *Japanese Rural Transportation in the Period of Industrial Revolution*, Nihon Keizai Hyoronsha, 1992.

Oita, Akira

Assoc. Prof., Fac. of Commerce, Univ. of Marketing & Distribution Sciences, 651-21 Gakuen-Nishimachi 3-1, Nishi-ku, Kobe, Japan. Tel.: 078 794 3555. Fax: 078 794 3510.
Year and Place of Birth 1949, Hyogo, Japan.
Degrees and Qualifications BA Keio Univ., 1973; MA Keio Univ., 1975.
Previous Post Asst. Prof., Fac. of Lib. Arts, Tamagawa Univ., 1981–7.
Current Offices and Honorary Posts Exec. sec./sec., Japan Indust. Archaeology Soc.; sec., Japan Soc. for the Hist. of Indust. Technology; subscribing mem., Assoc. of German Engineers.
Fields of Expertise *Industry Fields:* mechanical engineering; instrument engineering; vehicle construction; transport and communication; education of engineering. *Bus. Dimensions:* entrepreneurs and entrepreneurship; research and development; bus. and technology; co. culture. *Scope:* regional; internat. *Period:* eighteenth century; nineteenth century; twentieth century as a whole. *Teaching:* undergrad. *Consultancy:* cities; museums of technology.
Publications *Articles:* 'The Diffusion of Technologies', *Technologies in the Industrial Revolution*, M. Arai, H. Uchida & K. Toba eds., Yuhikaku, 1981, 277–317; 'Industrial Heritage and Museums', *Deutschland Heute*, T. Ohnishi & U. Lins, eds., 10, Sanshusha, 1982, 207–30; 'The Industrial Revolution and Machines', *Machine and Man*, K. Takeuchi ed., Univ. of Tokyo Press, 1985, 215–44; 'Technikgeschichte, Industriearchaeologie und technische Museen - ein kleiner Überblick unter zeitgeschichtlicher Fragestellung', *Internat. J. of the Hist. of Science Soc. of Japan*, Historia Scientarum, 23, 1982, 99–109; 'Tradition of Creativity and Technology: A Life of Rudolf Diesel', *Onko Chisin* [Researches into Hist. and Getting at the Truth], M. Terao ed., Keio Univ. Press, 1990, 27–52.

Okayama, Reiko

Prof. of Bus. Admin. & Dean of Women's College, Meiji Univ., 1-1 Kanda-Surugadai, Chiyoda-ku, Tokyo 101, Japan. Tel.: 81 3 3296 4260/81 3 3296 4545. Fax: 81 3 3296 4351.

Place of Birth Okayama, Japan.

Degrees and Qualifications B.Com. Meiji Univ., 1952; MBA Meiji Univ., 1954.

Current Offices and Honorary Posts Ex-council mem. & treas. sec., Japan Bus. Hist. Soc.

Fields of Expertise *Industry Fields:* chemicals and allied industries; shipbuilding and marine engineering; vehicle construction. *Bus. Dimensions:* personnel management; bus. and technology; industrial relations. *Scope:* national; UK. *Period:* inter-war years, 1919–39; mid-twentieth century, 1940–70; late twentieth century, 1970–present. *Teaching:* undergrad.; post grad.

Publications *Articles:* 'Industrial Relations in Great Britain and Japan from the 1880s to the 1920s', *Labour and Management*, Univ. of Tokyo Press, 1979; 'Employers' Labour Policy and Craft Unions', *Bull. of the Instit. of Social Sciences*, Meiji Univ., 1980; 'Japanese Employers' Labour Policy: The Heavy Engineering Industry in 1900–1930', *Managerial Strategies and Industrial Relations*, Heinemann, 1983; 'Industrial Relations in the Japanese Automobile Industry 1945–1970: The Case of Toyota', *Between Fordism and Flexibility: The Automobile Industry and its Workers*, Polity Press, 1986, 1st edn., Berg Publishers, 1992, 2nd edn.; 'Industrial Training in Britain and Japan: An Overview', in *Industrial Training and Technological Innovation*, Howard F. Gospel co-auth., Routledge, 1991.

Okochi, Akio

Prof., Fac. of Econ., Tokyo Univ., 7-3-1 Hongo, Bunkyo-ku, Tokyo 113, Japan. Tel.: 81 3 3812-2111.

Year and Place of Birth 1932, Tokyo, Japan.

Degrees and Qualifications BA Tokyo Univ., 1955; MA Tokyo Univ., 1957; D.Econ. Tokyo Univ., 1961.

Previous Post Prof., Rikkyo Univ., 1969–70.

Current Offices and Honorary Posts Council mem., Socio-Econ. Hist. Soc., 1979–; exec. com. mem., Bus. Hist. Soc. of Japan, 1979–82; advisory board mem., Bus. Hist. Rev., 1979–82.

Major Honours Acad. Book of the Year Prize, Instit. of Chart. Accountants of Japan, 1980.

Fields of Expertise *Industry Fields:* metal manufacture; mechanical engineering; electrical engineering; transport and communication; electronics and computers: manufacture. *Bus. Dimensions:* entrepreneurs and entrepreneurship; research and development; bus. and technology. *Scope:* regional; national. *Period:* eighteenth century; nineteenth century; twentieth century as a whole. *Teaching:* undergrad.; post grad. *Consultancy:* co. hist.

Publications *Books: Entrepreneurial Activities during the Industrial Revolution*, Iwanami Shoten, 1978, published in Japanese; *Entrepreneurial Perception in Hist. Perspective*, Univ. of Tokyo Press, 1979, published in Japanese; *Japan Airlines 1971–1981*, Japan Airlines Co. Ltd., 1985, published in Japanese; *Development of Modern Enterprise*, Univ. of Tokyo Press, 1991, published in Japanese; *Inventive Activities and Technological Perception*, Univ. of Tokyo Press, 1992, published in Japanese.

Olien, Diana Davids

Sen. Lect. in Hist., Univ. of Texas -
Permian Basin, 4901 E. Univ., Odessa,
Texas 79762, USA. Tel.: 1 915 367
2325.
Year and Place of Birth 1943,
Oceanside, NY, USA.
Degrees and Qualifications BA
(Hist.) Swarthmore College, 1964; MA
(Hist.) Yale Univ., 1966; M.Phil. Yale
Univ., 1967; Ph.D. Yale Univ., 1969.
Previous Post Asst. Prof. of Hist.,
Southern Methodist Univ., 1969–73.
Current Offices and Honorary Posts
Mem., Hist. Advisory Com., NASA;
fellow, Texas State Hist. Assoc..
Major Honours Phi Beta Kappa,
High Honors, Swarthmore College;
Woodrow Wilson Fellow; Woodrow
Wilson Dissertation Fellow; Phi Alpha
Theta.
Fields of Expertise *Industry Fields:*
petroleum products. *Bus. Dimensions:*
entrepreneurs and entrepreneurship;
bus. and technology; bus.–state rela-
tions; bus. values; bus. and the envi-
ronment. *Scope:* local; regional;
national. *Period:* twentieth century as
a whole. *Teaching:* undergrad.; post
grad. *Consultancy:* corporate strategy;
media.
Publications *Books: Oil Booms:
Social Change in Five Texas Towns,*
with Roger M. Olien, Univ. of
Nebraska Press, 1982; *Morpeth: A
Victorian Public Career,* Univ. Press of
Amer., 1983; *Wildcatters: Texas
Independent Oil Men,* with Roger M.
Olien, Texas Monthly Press, 1984; *Life
in the Oilfields,* with Roger M. Olien,
Texas Monthly Press, 1986; *Easy
Money: Promoters and Investors dur-
ing the Jazz Age,* with Roger M. Olien,
Univ. of North Carolina Press, 1990.

Olien, Roger M.

J. Conrad Dunagan Prof. of Regional
& Bus. Hist., Univ. of Texas - Permian
Basin, 4901 East Univ. Blvd., Odessa,
Texas 79762, USA. Tel.: 1 915 367
2232/1 915 694 0793.
Year and Place of Birth 1938, New
Richmond, USA.
Degrees and Qualifications BA St
Olaf College, 1960; Ph.D. Brown
Univ., 1973.
Previous Post Asst. Prof. of Hist.,
Southern Methodist Univ., Dallas,
1967–73.
Current Offices and Honorary Posts
Hon. Fellow, Texas State Hist. Assoc.;
pres., Permian Honors Scholarship
Foundation.
Major Honours Univ. Fellow,
Brown Univ., 1963–5; Phi Alpha
Theta; President's Research Prize,
Univ. of Texas-Permian Basin, 1988.
Fields of Expertise *Industry Fields:*
coal and petroleum products; gas, elec-
tricity, water. *Bus. Dimensions:* entre-
preneurs and entrepreneurship; bus.
and technology; bus.–state relations;
bus. values; co. culture; bus. and the
environment. *Scope:* local; regional;
national; internat. *Teaching:* under-
grad.; post grad. *Consultancy:* corpo-
rate strategy.
Publications *Books: From Token to
Triumph: Texas Republicans since
1920,* Southern Methodist Univ. Press,
1982; *Oil Booms: Social Change in
Five Texas Towns,* with Diana Davids
Olien, Univ. of Nebraska Press, 1982;
*Wild Catters: Texas Independent Oil
Men,* with Diana Davids Olien, Texas
Monthly Press, 1984; *Life in the
Oilfields,* with Diana Davids Olien,
Texas Monthly Press, 1986; *Easy
Money: Promoters and Investors dur-
ing the Jazz Age,* with Diana Davids
Olien, Univ. of North Carolina Press,
1990.

Ollerenshaw, Philip G.

Principal Lect. in Econ. & Bus. Hist., Dept. of Humanities, Univ. of the West of England, Oldbury Court Road, Fishponds, Bristol, BS16 2JP, UK. Tel.: 44 272 656261.
Year and Place of Birth 1953, Hyde, UK.
Degrees and Qualifications BA Leeds Univ., 1975; M.Sc. London Univ., 1976; Ph.D. Sheffield Univ., 1982.
Previous Post Lect. in Hist., Univ. of Ulster, 1979–85.
Fields of Expertise *Industry Fields:* textiles; insurance, banking, finance. *Bus. Dimensions:* co. finance and accounting; entrepreneurs and entrepreneurship; small bus. matters. *Scope:* regional; national; UK; Ireland. *Period:* nineteenth century; twentieth century as a whole. *Teaching:* undergrad.; post grad.
Publications *Books: An Econ. Hist. of Ulster, 1820–1939*, Liam Kennedy co-ed., Manchester UP, 1985; *Banking in Nineteenth Century Ireland*, Manchester UP, 1987. *Articles:* 'The Development of Banking in the Bristol Region 1750–1914', *Studies in the Bus. Hist. of Bristol*, Charles Harvey & Jon Press eds., Bristol Academic Press, 1988, 55–82; 'British Bus. Hist.: A Rev. of Recent Periodical Literature', *Bus. Hist.*, 32, 1990, 76–99; 'Textiles and Regional Econ. Decline: Northern Ireland 1914–70', *Economy & Soc.: European Industrialisation and its Social Consequences; Essays Presented to Sidney Pollard*, Colin Holmes & Alan Booth eds., Leicester UP, 1991, 58–83.

Olsson, Ulf

Prof. of Econ. Hist., Dept. of Econ. Hist., Stockholm School of Econ., POB 6501, S-113 83 Stockholm, Sweden.

Tel.: 46 8 736 9204. Fax: 46 8 313207.
Year and Place of Birth 1939, Lysekil, Sweden.
Degrees and Qualifications Ph.D. Göteburg Univ., 1970; Docent, Göteburg Univ., 1971.
Previous Post Full prof., Umeå Univ., 1977–89.
Current Offices and Honorary Posts Chairman, Scandinavian Assoc. of Econ. & Social Hist.; academic advisory board mem., European Banking Hist. Assoc.; V.P., Swedish Hist. Assoc.
Fields of Expertise *Industry Fields:* insurance, banking, finance. *Bus. Dimensions:* bus.–state relations. *Scope:* national. *Period:* twentieth century as a whole. *Teaching:* undergrad. *Consultancy:* co. hist.
Publications *Books: L.M. Ericsson 150 Years*, Stockholm, 1976; *The Creation of a Modern Arms Industry. Sweden 1939–1974*, Göteburg, 1977. *Articles:* 'Bank, Familj och Företagande' [Bank, Family and Entrepreneurship], *Stockholms Enskilda Bank 1946–1971*, Stockholm School of Econ., Stockholm, 1986; 'Securing the Markets. Swedish Multinationals in Hist. Perspective', *The Rise of Multinationals in Continental Europe*, G. Jones & H.G. Schröter eds., Edward Elgar Publishing, 1993; 'Sweden and Europe in the Twentieth Century. Econ. and Politics', *Scandinavian J. of Hist.*, 1, 1993.

Ommer, Rosemary E.

Research Director, Inst. of Soc. & Econ. Research & Prof. of Hist., Memorial Univ. of Newfoundland, Dept. of Hist., Memorial Univ. of Newfoundland, St. John's, Newfoundland, A1C 5S7, Canada. Tel.: 1 709 737 8156. Fax: 1 709 737 2041.

Year and Place of Birth 1943, Glasgow, UK.

Degrees and Qualifications BA (Modern Studies) Glasgow Univ., 1964; Teacher's Training Certificates, Notre Dame College of Education, Glasgow, 1965 & Ontario College of Education, 1968; MA (Hist. Geography) Memorial Univ. of Newfoundland, 1974; Ph.D. (Econ. Hist. Geography) McGill Univ., Montreal, 1979.

Current Offices and Honorary Posts Mem., Board of Directors, Vanier Inst. on the Family, 1990, 1991; chair of its Programme (Research) Com.; mem., Nominations Com.; mem., Exec. Com.; vice-pres. of the Inst. (on-going); mem., Board of Directors, Gorsebrook Inst., Halifax; project manager, Eco-research team on Sustainability in Cold Coastal Communities, Memorial Univ. of Newfoundland, 1991–; mem., Maritime Hist. Archive Board, 1987–; mem., Maritime Studies Research Unit, 1988–; chair, vice-pres. (research) com. on Conflict of Interest, 1992–3; mem., Hist. Com., SSHRCC Research grants, 1992, 1993.

Major Honours Awarded ISER Team Research Grant (with Dr D. May, Econ.) 1987/8; ISER Grant 1988/9 for research on the Newfoundland economy; External Affairs grant to do background research for the Canada/France boundary dispute; SSHRCC grant (with Robert Sweeny) for research on fisheries mercantile accounting records, 1991/3; invited to give MacNutt Lecture, Univ. of New Brunswick, Oct., 1993; vice-pres., Vanier Inst. of the Family (on-going).

Fields of Expertise *Industry Fields:* agric., forestry, fishing. *Bus. Dimensions:* entrepreneurs and entrepreneurship; bus. organization. *Scope:* local; regional; Canada. *Period:* nineteenth century; twentieth century as a whole. *Teaching:* post grad.; undergrad.

Publications *Books: Merchant Credit in Hist. Perspective*, ed. & contributor, Acadiensis Press, 1990; *From Outpost to Outport: A Structural Analysis of the Jersey-Gaspe Codfishery, 1767–1886*, McGill-Queen's Univ. Press, 1991. *Articles:* 'What's Wrong with Canadian Fish', *A Question of Survival*, Peter R. Sinclair ed., Inst. of Social & Econ. Research, 1988, 23–44; reprinted from *J. of Canadian Studies*, 20(3), 1985, 122–42; 'Capitalism in a Cold Climate', *Acadiensis*, XIX(2), Spring, 1990, 197–212; 'An Inshore Fishery: A Commercially Viable Industry or an Employer of Last Resort', *Ocean Development and Internat. Law*, with W.E. Schrank, N. Roy & B. Skoda co-auths., 23, 1992, 335–67.

Onozuka, Tomoji

Assoc. Prof. of Econ. Hist., Fac. of Econ. & Bus. Admin., Yokohama City Univ., 22–2 Seto, Kanazawa-ku, Yokohama 236, Japan. Tel.: 81 45 787 2125. Fax: 81 45 787 2096.

Year and Place of Birth 1957, Yokohama, Japan.

Degrees and Qualifications BA Tokyo Univ., 1981.

Previous Post Research Assoc., Inst. of Soc. Sc., Tokyo Univ., 1987–90.

Current Offices and Honorary Posts Edit. com. mem., Agrarian Hist. Soc.

Fields of Expertise *Industry Fields:* mechanical engineering; instrument engineering; electrical engineering; shipbuilding and marine engineering; vehicle construction. *Bus. Dimensions:* entrepreneurs and entrepreneurship; production management; personnel management; bus. organization; bus. and technology. *Scope:* local; regional; national; internat.; UK; Germany; Sweden; Japan. *Period:* nineteenth century; twentieth century as a whole. *Teaching:* undergrad.; post grad.

Publications *Articles:* 'Keieiken to Rodokumiai' [The Power to Manage and Trade Unions - Labour Problems for British Engineering Managers in the First Half of the Nineteenth Century], *J. of Social Science,* 40(6), Tokyo Univ., 1989, 303–34; 'Roshikankei niokeru Ruru' [Rules in Industrial Relations in the British Engineering Industry, 1851–71], *J. of Social Science,* 41(3), Tokyo Univ., 1989, 1–102, (Pt. I); *J. of Social Science,* 41(5), Tokyo Univ., 1990, 87–138, (Pt. II); *J. of Social Science,* 42(1), Tokyo Univ., 1990, 97–178, (Pt. III); 'Shiyoshadantai no Saihen to Chiiki' [Reorganization of the Local Employers' Associations in the British Engineering Industry, 1871–1872], *Shijo to Chiiki* [Markets and Localities], I. Hirota et al. eds., Nihonkeizai-Hyoron-Sha, Tokyo, 1993.

Orbell, John

Archivist, Baring Brothers & Co. Ltd., 8 Bishopsgate, London, EC2N 4AE, UK. Tel.: 44 71 280 1401. Fax: 44 71 283 2224.

Year and Place of Birth 1950, Kiel, Germany.

Degrees and Qualifications BA York Univ., 1972; Ph.D. Nottingham Univ., 1977.

Previous Post Head of Advisory Service, Bus. Archives Council.

Current Offices and Honorary Posts Executive Com., Bus. Archives Council; Hist. Com., Royal Soc. of Arts.

Fields of Expertise *Industry Fields:* food, drink, tobacco; transport and communication; insurance, banking, finance. *Scope:* national. *Period:* eighteenth century; nineteenth century; twentieth century as a whole. *Consultancy:* co. hist.; corporate strategy; bus. archives.

Publications *Books: From Cape to Cape: A Hist. of Lyle Shipping,* Paul Harris Pub., 1979; *Baring Brothers & Co. Limited. A Hist. to 1939,* privately published, 1985; *A Guide to the Hist. Records of British Banking,* with L.S. Pressnell, Gower, 1985; *A Guide to Tracing the Hist. of a Bus.,* Gower, 1987. *Articles:* 'The Corn Milling Industry, 1750–1820', *Studies in Capital Formation in the United Kingdom 1750–1820,* Charles H. Feinstein & Sidney Pollard eds., OUP, 1988.

Orsenigo, Luigi

Assoc. Prof. of Econ. Policy, Dept. of Econ., Bocconi Univ., Via Sarfatti 25, 20136 Milan, Italy. Tel.: 39 2 5836 5339. Fax: 39 2 5836 5349.

Year and Place of Birth 1954, Milan, Italy.

Degrees and Qualifications Laurea (Econ.) Bocconi Univ., 1982; Ph.D. Sussex Univ., 1989.

Previous Post Research Fellow, Bocconi Univ., Milan, 1989–92.

Current Offices and Honorary Posts Assoc. ed., *Industrial and Corporate Change;* scientific com. mem. & exec. com. mem., Fondazione ASSI, Milan.

Fields of Expertise *Industry Fields:* coal and petroleum products; chemicals and allied industries; genetic engineering: manufacture. *Bus. Dimensions:* research and development; bus. and technology. *Scope:* global. *Period:* late twentieth century, 1970–present. *Teaching:* undergrad.

Publications *Books: The Emergence of Biotechnology. Institutions and Markets in Industrial Innovation,* Pinter Pub., 1989; *Nascita e Trasformazione d'Impresa. La Storia di AGIP Petroli,* with G. Sapelli, P. Toninelli & C. Corduas, Il Mulino, Bologna, 1993. *Articles:* 'Innovation, Diversity and Diffusion: A Self-organisation Model', *The Econ. J.*, with G. Silverberg & G. Dosi co-auths., 98(393), 1988, 1932–54; 'Technological Regimes and Firm Behaviour', *Industrial and Corporate Change*, with F. Malerba, 2(1), 1993; 'Innovative Learning and Institutions in the Process of Development: On the Microfoundations of Growth Regimes', *Learning and Technological Change*, with F. Chiaromonte & G. Dosi co-auths., R. Thompson ed., Macmillan, 1993.

Ostrolucká, Milena

Státny Oblastny Archív, Bacíkova 1, 041 56 Kosice, Slovakia. Tel.: 42 62 224 15. Fax: 42 62 208 40.
   Year and Place of Birth 1953, Vsetín, Czechland.
   Degrees and Qualifications Ph.D. (Hist.) Comenius Univ., Bratislava.
   Previous Post Main special archivist, Kosice Urban Archives.
   Fields of Expertise *Industry Fields:* food, drink, tobacco. *Bus. Dimensions:* small bus. matters; co. culture. *Scope:* local; regional; national. *Period:* early modern; eighteenth century; nineteenth century. *Teaching:*
   Publications *Articles:* 'Beiträge zur Geschichte der Lebkuchenbäckerzunft von Kosice' [Contribution to the Hist. of the Gingerbreadmakers' Guild in the City of Kosice], *II. Internazionales Handwerksgeschichtliches Symposium*, vol. II, Veszprém, 1982, 309–20; 'Die Beziehungen zwischen der Stadt und den Zünften im 16. und 17. Jahrhundert in Kosice' [Relations between the City of Kosice and Guilds in the 16th and 17th Century], *III Internationales Handwerksgeschichtliches Symposium*, vol. III, Veszprém, 1986, 73–90; 'Der Alltag der Handwerksgesellen in Kosice im 15. und 16. Jahrhundert' [Everyday Life of Artisan's Apprentices in the

City of Kosice in the 15th and 16th Century], *Jahrbuch für Regionalgeschichte und Landeskunde*, 17, Pt. II, 1990, 93–9; 'Mestské hospodárenie v Kosiciach v 17. storocí v zrkadle pramenov Archívu mesta Kosíc' [The Management of the City of Kosice in the 17th Century], *Slovenská Archivistika*, I, 1993, forthcoming.

Otruba, Gustav

Prof. Emeritus, 1238 Marktgemeindg. 63/E7, A-4045 Linz-Auhof, Austria. Tel.: 43 222 8866593.
   Year and Place of Birth 1925, Kritzendorf, Austria.
   Degrees and Qualifications Ph.D., 1948; univ. lect. Vienna Univ., 1965; sen. univ. prof. Linz Univ., 1967; ordinary prof. Linz Univ., 1970; emeritus prof., 1986.
   Fields of Expertise *Industry Fields:* metal manufacture; mechanical engineering; instrument engineering; textiles; other manufacturing industries. *Scope:* regional; national. *Period:* early modern; eighteenth century; nineteenth century; twentieth century as a whole.
   Publications *Books: Berufsstruktur und Berufslaufbahn vor der industr. Revolution*, 1952; *Die Wirtschaftspolitik Maria Theresias*, 1963; *Österreichs Wirtschaft im 20. Jahrhundert*, 1968; *Österreichische Fabriksprivilegien vom 16. bis zum 18. Jahrhundert*, 1981.

Ozawa, Katsuyuki

Prof., Fac. of Commerce, Takachiho Univ., 2-19-1 Ohmiya, Suginamiku, Tokyo 168, Japan. Tel.: 81 3 3313 0146.
   Place of Birth Niigata, Japan.
   Degrees and Qualifications BA Niigata Univ., 1967.
   Current Offices and Honorary Posts Council mem., 1989–92.

Fields of Expertise *Industry Fields:* chemicals and allied industries; distributive trades. *Bus. Dimensions:* co. admin.; marketing; strategy formation; bus. organization; markets and bus. *Scope:* national; internat. *Period:* twentieth century as a whole. *Teaching:* undergrad. *Consultancy:* co. hist.

Publications *Books: A Bus. Hist. of the Du Pont Company*, Nihon Hyoronsha, 1986. *Articles:* 'Organizational Change of Japanese Chainstores', *Japanese Commercial Conf. Annual Report*, Dobunkan, 1973; *Bus. Hist. - Europe and Amer.*, Yukio Yamashita ed., Nihon Hyoronsha, 1977, chaps. 6, 7 & 8; 'Japanese Bus. Organization and Econ.-Culture Conditions', *Contemporary Bus. Organization*, Chokki Toshiaki ed., 1983, Yuhikaku, chap. 7; 'The Delay of Management Modernization in the US Rubber Co.', *Takachiho Ronso*, March, 1988.

Ozolina, Dzidra

Sen. Research Assoc., Inst. of Hist., Latvian Acad. of Sciences, 19 Turgenew St, 1518 Riga, Latvia. Tel.: 7 132 225044.

Year and Place of Birth 1933, Riga, Latvia.

Degrees and Qualifications Dip.Ed., BA. Riga Univ., 1957; Cand. of Hist. Sciences Riga Univ., 1969; Ph.D. Riga Univ., 1992.

Previous Post Junior Research Assoc., Inst. of Hist., Latvian Acad. of Sciences, 1958–78.

Current Offices and Honorary Posts Mem., Latvian Scientific Assoc.

Major Honours Presidium Acad. of Sciences Prize, 1977 & 1979; Latvian State Prize, 1982.

Fields of Expertise *Industry Fields:* gas, electricity, water; transport and communication; insurance, banking, finance; bus. services; public admin.

and defence. *Scope:* national. *Period:* nineteenth century; early twentieth century; inter-war years, 1919–39.

Publications *Books: The 'City Fathers' of Riga and Their Communal Policy 1877–1913*, Zinatne, 1976, (in Latvian); *Liepaja City Municipality, 1877–1913*, Zinatne, 1990, (in Latvian). *Articles: Treatise on the Econ. Hist. of Latvia, 1860–1900: The City of Latvia in the second half of the 19th Century*, Zinatne, 1972, 446–79, (in Latvian); *Riga 1860–1917: The Admin. of Riga City and its Public Utility*, Zinatne, 1978, 77–122 & 175–218, (in Latvian).

Palme, Rudolf

Prof. Inst. for Austrian Legal Hist., Innrain 52, A-6020 Innsbruck, Austria. Tel.: 43 512 507 2606. Fax: 43 512 507 2777.

Year and Place of Birth 1942, Berlin, Germany.

Degrees and Qualifications Dr. Vienna Univ., 1969.

Previous Post Univ. Doz., Inst. for Austrian Legal Hist., 1982–7.

Current Offices and Honorary Posts Gen. sec., Commission for the Hist. of Salt; Pres., Tiroler Geschichtsverein.

Major Honours Theodor-Körner Prize, 1978.

Fields of Expertise *Industry Fields:* mining and quarrying; food, drink, tobacco; transport and communication. *Bus. Dimensions:* entrepreneurs and entrepreneurship; co. law; co. admin.; bus. organization; bus. and technology. *Scope:* local; national; internat.; Austria. *Period:* medieval; early modern. *Teaching:* undergrad.; post grad. *Consultancy:* co. hist.

Publications *Books: Die landesherrlichen Salinen- und Salzbergrechte. Eine vergleichende Studie*, Institut für Sprachwissenschaft, Innsbruck, 1974; *Die Messinghütte in Pflach bei Reutte. Ein bedeutendes Industrieunternehmen zu Beginn der Neuzeit*, RTW, 1976; *Rechts-, Wirtschafts- und Sozialgeschichte der inneralpinen Salzwerke bis zu deren Monopolisierung*, Lang, 1983; *Stollen, Schächte, fahle Erze. Zur Geschichte des Schwazer Bergbaus*, 3rd edn., Berenkamp, 1993. *Articles:* 'Die Salzordnungen Maximilians I für Hall in Tirol und ihre Auswirkungen auf die Produktion', *Das Salz in der Rechts- und Handelsgeschichte*, with Jean-Claude Hocquet co-ed., Berenkamp, 1991, 323–40.

Pantelakis, Nicos

Researcher & Archivist, Hist. Archives, National Bank of Greece, 112A Vas. Sofias Ave, 112.54 Athens, Greece. Tel.: 30 1 7785186.

Year and Place of Birth 1953, Geneva, Switzerland.

Degrees and Qualifications Maîtrise de Sociologie Grenoble Univ., 1977; Diplome d'Etudes Approfondies de Sociologie Paris V Rene Descartes Univ., 1978; Doctorat en Sociologie Paris V Rene Descartes Univ., 1980.

Current Offices and Honorary Posts Pres., Assoc. of Hellenic Archivists.

Fields of Expertise *Industry Fields:* gas, electricity, water; insurance, banking, finance; public admin. and defence. *Bus. Dimensions:* entrepreneurs and entrepreneurship; strategy formation; bus.–state relations. *Scope:* national. *Period:* early twentieth century; inter-war years, 1919–39; mid-twentieth century, 1940–70.

Publications *Books: Crédits de Guerre Alloués par les Alliés. État et Banque Nationale de Grèce (1917–1928) Athenes*, National Bank of Greece Press, 1988; *Histoire de l'Électricité en Grèce (1889–1956)*, National Bank of Greece Press, 1991; *Les Societés de Production de l'Électricité e l'Intervention de l'État en*

Grèce entre 1889 et 1950, l'Entreprise en Grèce et en Europe XIX–XX Siècles, Assoc. Interdisciplinaire Franco-Hellenique, 1991.

Papalexandris, Nancy

Asst. Prof. of Management, Athens Univ. of Econ. & Bus., 76 Patission St, Athens 10434, Greece. Tel.: 30 1 8223802. Fax: 30 1 8228419.

Year and Place of Birth 1944, Athens, Greece.

Degrees and Qualifications MA New York Univ., 1972; Ph.D. Bath Univ., 1986.

Fields of Expertise *Bus. Dimensions:* entrepreneurs and entrepreneurship; personnel management; marketing; small bus. matters; management education. *Scope:* national; Greece. *Period:* late twentieth century, 1970–present. *Teaching:* undergrad.; executive training. *Consultancy:* human resources.

Publications *Articles:* 'Factors Affecting Management Staffing and Development: The Case of Greek Firms', *European Management J.*, 6(1), Spring, 1988; 'A Comparative Study of Human Resource Management in Selected Greek and Foreign-owned Subsidiaries in Greece', *Internat. Comparisons in Human Resource Management*, C. Brewster & S. Tyson eds., Pitman Publishing, London, 1991; 'Greece', *Human Resource Management Guide*, C. Brewster et al. eds., Academic Press, London, 1992, 229–60; 'Human Resource Management in Greece', *Employee Relations*, 14(4), 1992, 38–53; 'Environmental Constraints on Management in Greek Manufacturing Firms', *L'Entreprise en Grèce et en Europe XIXe–XXe Siècles*, A. Teikova, H. Lindgren & M. Dritsas eds., SO.FH.I.S., Athens, 1992, 169–84.

Papathanassopoulos, Konstantinos

Assoc. Prof. of Hist., Dept. of Sociology, Panteion Univ. of Social and Polit. Science, Leoforos A. Syngrou 136, 176 71 Athens, Greece. Tel.: 30 1 9220100. Fax: 30 1 9223690.
Year and Place of Birth 1950, Peireaus, Greece.
Degrees and Qualifications BA (Polit. Sc.) Panteion Univ., 1973; DEA Ecole des Hautes Etudes en Sciences Sociales, 1977; Ph.D. (Hist.) Panteion Univ., 1982.
Previous Post Asst. Prof. of Hist., Panteion Univ., 1985–8.
Fields of Expertise *Industry Fields:* agric., forestry, fishing; mining and quarrying; shipbuilding and marine engineering; gas, electricity, water; transport and communication; distributive trades; insurance, banking, finance. *Bus. Dimensions:* entrepreneurs and entrepreneurship; production management; co. finance and accounting; personnel management; co. admin.; bus. and technology. *Scope:* national; internat.; global. *Period:* nineteenth century; twentieth century as a whole. *Teaching:* undergrad.; post grad. *Consultancy:* co. hist.; corporate strategy.
Publications *Books: The Greek Commercial Navy (1833–1856): Development and Restructuring,* M.I.E.T., Athens, 1983 (in Greek); *The Greek Steamshipping Company (1857–1869): The Difficulties of Protectionism,* M.I.E.T., Athens, 1987, 1st edn., 1988, 2nd edn. (in Greek); *Alexandros Koumoundouros: Towards a Biography,* Lenis, Athens, 1993 (in Greek). *Articles:* 'Contribution to the Hist. of Greek Steamshipping (1849–1857): Shareholders and Distribution of the Original Capital Shares', *Mnemon,* X, 1984 (in Greek); 'European Steamshipping and the Commercial Activities of Syros (1833–1853)',

Historica, 3, 1985 (in Greek).

Pátek, Jaroslav

Prof., Charles Univ., Fac. of Philo., Dept. of Econ. Hist., Nám. J. Palacha 2, 116 38 Prague 1, Czechland. Tel.: 42 2 228 441/42 2 228 291. Fax: 42 2 325 016.
Year and Place of Birth 1934, Horní Lhotka, Czechland.
Degrees and Qualifications Ph.Dr. Prague Univ., 1968; C.Sc. Prague Univ., 1968; Sen. Lect. - Doc., Prague Univ., 1972; Prof., Prague Univ., 1986.
Current Offices and Honorary Posts Pres., ICOTHEC National Group; mem., Hist. of Science & Technology Soc.
Fields of Expertise *Industry Fields:* agric., forestry, fishing; metal manufacture; mechanical engineering; insurance, banking, finance. *Bus. Dimensions:* entrepreneurs and entrepreneurship; bus. organization; bus. and technology; multinational bus.; bus.–state relations. *Scope:* national; internat.; Czechland. *Period:* nineteenth century; twentieth century as a whole; early twentieth century; interwar years, 1919–39; mid-twentieth century, 1940–'70. *Teaching:* undergrad.; post grad.
Publications *Books: Prehled dejin ceskoslovenské techniky do 18. století* [Hist. of Czechoslovakian Technology to the 18th Century], Kapitoly o zemedelské technice [chapters concerning agricultural technology], Czechoslovak Acad. of Sciences, Prague, 1971; *Vyvoj mechanizace semedelské vyroby v ceskych semích v 1. polovine 20. století* [The Development of the Mechanisation of Agric. in Czechland in the first Half of the 20th Century], Zemedelské Muzeum [Museum of Agric.], 1972; *Ceské zemedelství v 19. a 20. století* [Czech Agric. in the 19th and 20th Centuries], Charles Univ., Hist. IV,

Prague, 1974. Articles: 'Ceskoslovensko-rakouské hospodárské a zahranicní vztahy v letech 1929–34' [Czechoslovak-Austrian Econ. and Foreign Relations 1929–34], *Sborník Historie* [Hist.Yearbook], II, Prague, 1959, 37–71.

Pauer, Erich

Prof., Centre for Japanese Studies, Universität Marburg, Biegenstrasse 9, D-35037 Marburg, Germany. Tel.: 49 6421 284953. Fax: 49 6421 284934.
Year and Place of Birth 1943, Vienna, Austria.
Degrees and Qualifications Ph.D. Vienna Univ.
Previous Post Director, Centre for Jap. Studies, Marburg Univ., Germany.
Current Offices and Honorary Posts Ed., Foerderverein 'Marburger Japan-Reihe'.
Fields of Expertise *Industry Fields:* coal and petroleum products; chemicals and allied industries; mechanical engineering; shipbuilding and marine engineering; vehicle construction. *Bus. Dimensions:* entrepreneurs and entrepreneurship; research and development; bus. and technology; small bus. matters; bus.–state relations. *Scope:* national; Japan. *Period:* twentieth century as a whole. *Teaching:* post grad. *Consultancy:* co. hist.
Publications *Books: Technologietransfer Deutschland Japan von 1850 bis zur Gegenwart*, ed., Iudicium-Verlag, Munich, 1992. *Articles:* 'Japans industrielle Lehrzeit', *Bonner Zeitschrift für Japanologie*, 8, Bonn, 1986; 'Silkworms, Oil and Chips', *Bonner Zeitschrift für Japanologie*, 8, Bonn, 1986; 'Schwarzes Gold in Japan', *Marburger Japan-Reihe*, 5, Marburg, 1991; 'Nachbarschaftsgruppen und Versorgung in den japanischen Städten während des Zweiten Weltkriegs',

Marburger Japan-Reihe, 9, Marburg, 1993.

Pavese, Claudio

Sen. Lect., Dept. of Social and Bus. Hist., Fac. of Social Sciences, Università degli Studi di Milano, Via del Conservatorio 7, 20122 Milan, Italy. Tel.: 39 2 76074207. Fax: 39 2 76004700.
Year and Place of Birth 1944, Voghera (PV), Italy.
Degrees and Qualifications Laurea Università degli Studi, Milan, 1973.
Previous Post Sen. Research Fellow, Fac. of Polit. Sc., Università degli Studi, Milan, 1981–91.
Current Offices and Honorary Posts Exec. & scientific com. mem., Fondazione ASSI di Storia e Studi sull'Impresa, Milan; scientific com. mem., Centro sulla Storia dell'Impresa e dell'Innovazione, Milan.
Major Honours Levi-Cases Prize, Padua Univ., for best dissertation on energy econ., 1974; 'DANECO' Prize for the Hist. of Entrepreneurship, 1989, (joint winner).
Fields of Expertise *Industry Fields:* gas, electricity, water. *Bus. Dimensions:* bus. and technology. *Scope:* national. *Period:* nineteenth century; twentieth century as a whole. *Teaching:* undergrad. *Consultancy:* co. hist.
Publications *Articles:* 'Between Financiers and Entrepreneurs: Some Notes on the Growth of the Electric Industry in Italy from its Origins to World War I', *Annali della Facoltà di Scienze Politiche dell'Università degli Studi di Milano*, 1, 1981, 367–95; 'Le Origini della Società Edison e il suo Sviluppo fino alla Costituzione del "Gruppo" (1881–1919)', *Energia e Sviluppo. L'Industria Elettrica Italiana e la Società Edison*, B. Bezza ed., Einaudi, Turin, 1986, 23–169, 2nd edn., Il Mulino, Bologna, 1991; 'La

Naissance et le Développement de la Société Génerale Italienne Edison d'Électricité jusqu'à la Constitution de son "Groupe" (1881–1919)', *1880–1980 Un Siècle d'Électricité dans le Monde*, Actes du premier colloque internationale d'histoire de l'électricité, Paris, 15–17 Avril, 1986, Presses Universitaires de France, Paris, 1987, 391–403; 'Anagrafe della Società Elettriche: La Documentazione di Base', *Storia dell'Industria Elettrica in Italia*, with P.A. Toninelli, vol. I *Le origini (1882–1914)*, 1992, 761–827; vol. II *Il potenziamento tecnico e finanario (1914–1925)*, 1993, 719–804; vol. III *Espansione e oligopolio (1926–1945)*, 1994; vol. IV *Dal dopoguerra alla nazionalizzazione (1945–1962)*, forthcoming, Laterza, Roma-Bari.

Payne, Peter L.

Prof. of Econ. Hist., Dept. of Hist. & Econ. Hist., Kings College, Univ. of Aberdeen, Aberdeen, AB9 2UB, UK. Tel.: 44 224 272195. Fax: 44 224 487048.

Year and Place of Birth 1929, London, UK.

Degrees and Qualifications BA Nottingham Univ., 1951; Ph.D. Nottingham Univ., 1954.

Previous Post Colquhoun Lect. in Bus. Hist., Glasgow Univ., 1959–69.

Current Offices and Honorary Posts Hon. mem., Bus. Archives Council (London).

Major Honours California Inst. of Technology: Sherman Fairchild Distinguished Scholar (Econ.), 1977–8; Wadsworth Prize in Bus. Hist., Bus. Archives Council, 1980.

Fields of Expertise *Industry Fields:* metal manufacture; gas, electricity, water. *Bus. Dimensions:* entrepreneurs and entrepreneurship; bus. and technology. *Scope:* national. *Period:* nineteenth century; twentieth century as a whole. *Teaching:* undergrad.; post grad. *Consultancy:* co. hist.

Publications *Books: Rubber and Railway in the Nineteenth Century*, Liverpool Univ. Press, 1961; *British Entrepreneurship in the Nineteenth Century*, Macmillan, London, 1st edn., 1974, 2nd edn., 1988; *Colvilles and the Scottish Steel Industry*, Clarendon Press, Oxford, 1979; *The Hydro: A Study of the Development of the Major Hydro-Electric Schemes undertaken by the North of Scotland Hydro-Electric Board*, Aberdeen Univ. Press, 1988; *Growth & Contraction: Scottish Industry c. 1860–1990*, Econ. & Social Hist. Soc. of Scotland, Glasgow, 1992.

Pearson, Robin

Lect. in Econ. & Social Hist., Dept. of Econ. and Social Hist., School of Econ. Studies, Univ. of Hull, Hull, HU6 7RX, UK. Tel.: 44 482 466301. Fax: 44 482 466205.

Year and Place of Birth 1955, Dunfermline, UK.

Degrees and Qualifications MA Edinburgh Univ., 1979; Ph.D. Leeds Univ., 1986.

Previous Post Lect. (temp.) in econ. & soc. hist., Hull Univ., 1988–91.

Fields of Expertise *Industry Fields:* insurance, banking, finance. *Bus. Dimensions:* markets and bus. *Scope:* internat. *Period:* nineteenth century. *Teaching:* undergrad. *Consultancy:* co. hist.

Publications *Articles:* 'Thrift or Dissipation? The Bus. of Life Assurance in the early 19th C.', *Econ. Hist. Rev.*, 2nd ser., XLIII(2), May, 1990, 236–54; 'Collective Diversification: Manchester Cotton Merchants and the Insurance Bus. in the early 19th C.', *Bus. Hist. Rev.*, 65(2), Summer, 1991, 379–414; 'Fire Insurance and the British Textile Industries during the Industrial Revolution', *Bus. Hist.*, 34(4), Oct.,

1992, 1–19; 'Taking Risks and Containing Competition: Diversification and Oligopoly in the Fire Insurance Markets of the North of England in the early 19th C.', *Econ. Hist. Rev.*, 2nd ser., XLVI(1), Feb., 1993, 39–64; 'Capital Formation in the Industrial Revolution Revisited: Insurance Valuations and some new Sectoral Estimates', *Explorations in Econ. Hist.*, forthcoming, 1993.

Pedersen, Erik Helmer

Prof., Inst. of Econ. Hist., Univ. of Copenhagen, Njalsgade 102, 2300 Copenhagen S, Denmark. Tel.: 45 31542211.

Year and Place of Birth 1932, Skovby, Denmark.

Degrees and Qualifications Dr.Phil., 1979.

Previous Post Sen. Lect., Copenhagen Univ., 1972.

Current Offices and Honorary Posts Council mem., Danish & Nordic Econ. Hist. Assoc.

Fields of Expertise *Industry Fields:* agric., forestry, fishing. *Bus. Dimensions:* bus.–state relations. *Scope:* national. *Period:* twentieth century as a whole. *Teaching:* post grad. *Consultancy:* co. hist.

Publications *Books: Landbrugsrådet som Erhverspolitisk Toporgan 1919–33* [The Danish Agric. Board and its Econ. Policy 1919–33], 1979; *Drømmen om Amerika* [The Amer. Dream (The Danish Emigration to Amer.)], 1985; *Pionererne* [The Pioneers (The Danish Emigration to Overseas Countries)], 1986; *Det Danske Landbrugs Historie 1914–1988* [Hist. of Danish Agric. 1914–1988], 1988; *Landbosamfundet og Danmarks Historien 1880–1993* [Hist. of the Danish Farmers' Unions 1880–1993], 1993.

Perkins, Edwin J.

Prof., Dept. of Hist., Univ. of Southern California, Los Angeles, CA 90089-0034, USA. Tel.: 1 213 740 1671. Fax: 1 213 740 6999.

Year and Place of Birth 1939, Charlottesville, USA.

Degrees and Qualifications BA William & Mary Univ., 1961; MBA Virginia Univ., 1963; Ph.D. Johns Hopkins Univ., 1972.

Current Offices and Honorary Posts Pres.-elect, Bus. Hist. Conf.

Major Honours Annual Book Award, Soc. of Colonial Wars, 1981.

Fields of Expertise *Industry Fields:* insurance, banking, finance. *Bus. Dimensions:* entrepreneurs and entrepreneurship; co. finance and accounting. *Scope:* national. *Period:* eighteenth century; nineteenth century; twentieth century as a whole. *Teaching:* undergrad.; post grad.

Publications *Books: Financing Anglo-Amer. Trade: The House of Brown, 1800–1880*, Harvard Univ. Press, 1975; *Economy of Colonial Amer.*, Columbia Univ. Press, 1980 & 1988; *Amer. Public Finance and Financial Services, 1700–1815*, Ohio State Univ. Press, 1994, forthcoming; *Articles:* 'The Emergence of a Futures Market for Foreign Exchange in the United States', *Explorations in Econ. Hist.*, 1978, 193–211; 'Conflicting Views on Fiat Currency: Britain and its North Amer. Colonies', *Bus. Hist.*, vol. 33, 1991, 8–30.

Petersen, Peter B.

Prof. of Management and Organization Theory, Johns Hopkins Univ., 6740 Alexander Bell Drive, Columbia, Maryland 21046-2100, USA. Tel.: 1 410 290 1935. Fax: 1 410 290 0007.

Year and Place of Birth 1932,

Chicago, USA.

Degrees and Qualifications BS Nebraska Univ., 1962; MBA George Washington Univ., 1967; DBA George Washington Univ., 1971.

Previous Post Director, Div. of Bus. & Management, Johns Hopkins Univ., 1979–92.

Current Offices and Honorary Posts Book Rev. Ed., *The Executive*, Acad. of Management Publication; edit. rev. board, three management journals; past chair, Management Hist. Division, Acad. of Management.

Major Honours John F. Mee Memorial Prize, Management Hist., 1991 & 1992; Sigma Iota Epsilon Honorary Management Fraternity - selected by Peers; Richard D. Irwin Best Paper Award, 1988.

Fields of Expertise *Industry Fields:* mechanical engineering; textiles; paper, printing, publishing; other manufacturing industries, all within a management hist. framework. *Bus. Dimensions:* production management; personnel management; co. admin.; strategy formation; management history. *Scope:* USA; Japan. *Period:* nineteenth century; early twentieth century; inter-war years, 1919–39. *Teaching:* post grad. *Consultancy:* total quality management circa 1993.

Publications *Books: Against the Tide*, Arlington House Publishers, New Rochelle, NY, 1974. *Articles:* 'Comparison of Behavioral Styles between Entering and Graduating Students in Officer Candidate School', *J. of Applied Psychology*, with Gordon L. Lippitt, 52(1), part 1, Feb., 1968, 66–70; 'Correspondence from Henry L. Gantt to an old Friend Reveals New Information about Gantt', *J. of Management*, 12(3), Fall, 1986, 339–50; 'The Evolution of the Gantt Chart and its Relevance Today', *J. of Managerial Issues*, III(2), Summer, 1991, 131–55; 'Management Amer. Style: The Old Fashioned Way', *Rev. of Bus. Studies*, with Frank A.

Cappiello, I(1), Spring, 1992, 1–8.

Petrás, Milan

Director, Museum of Western Slovakia, Múzejné Nám. 3, 918 09 Trnava, Slovakia. Tel.: 42 805 27585. Fax: 42 805 27585.

Year and Place of Birth 1941, Martin, Slovakia.

Degrees and Qualifications Dipl. Ing. Nitra Univ., 1963; C.Sc. (Hist.) Bratislava Univ., 1981.

Previous Post Research Fellow, Slovak Museum of Agric. in Nitra, 1970–90.

Current Offices and Honorary Posts Mem., Internat. Assoc. of Agric. Museums (1981); mem., Slovak Historic Soc.; mem., Slovak Soc. for Science & Technology Hist.

Major Honours Matej Bel Medal, Slovak Acad. of Sciences, 1984.

Fields of Expertise *Industry Fields:* agric., forestry, fishing; food, drink, tobacco. *Scope:* local; regional; national. *Period:* nineteenth century; twentieth century as a whole.

Publications *Books: Matej Bel on Agric.*, Slovak Museum of Agric., Nitra, 1984; *Ivan Houdek 1887–1985. Life - Work - Bibliography*, Slovak National Museum, Bratislava, 1988; *Václav Vrany 1851–1929. Life - Work - Bibliography.*, Slovak National Museum, Bratislava, 1990. *Articles:* 'Martin Szentiványi's Natural Sciences and Agric. Opinions', *The Agric.*, 16, 1979, 165–203; 'Die Landwirtschaftliche Fachliteratur in der Slowakei bis zum Beginn der 19. Jahrhunderts', *Acta Historicae Necnon Technicarum*, special issue 19, Prague, 1981, 293–305.

Pettersen, Lauritz

Museum Director, Bergen Maritime Museum, P.B. 2637 Møhlenpris, 5026

Bergen, Norway. Tel.: 05 327980. Fax: 05 329137.

Year and Place of Birth 1926, Bergen, Norway.

Degrees and Qualifications Cand. philol. Oslo Univ.

Current Offices and Honorary Posts Chairman, Norwegian Commission for Maritime Hist.; exec. board mem., Internat. Commission of Maritime Hist.; trustee, Internat. Congress of Maritime Museums; ed., *Norwegian Yearbook of Maritime Hist.*

Fields of Expertise *Industry Fields:* shipbuilding and marine engineering; shipping. *Bus. Dimensions:* entrepreneurs and entrepreneurship; co. admin. *Scope:* internat. *Period:* twentieth century as a whole. *Consultancy:* co. hist.

Publications *Books: A/S J. Ludwig Mowinckels Rederi 1898–1960,* Bergen, 1960; *Bergens Skipperforening I 1867–1914,* Bergen, 1968; *Bergen og Sjøfarten III 1860–1914,* Bergen, 1981; *Bergens Skibsassuranseforening 1850–1987,* Bergen, 1987; *Handelsflåten i krig 5. Hjemmeflåten,* Dreyer-Grøndahl, Oslo, 1992.

Phillips, William H.

Assoc. Prof. of Econ., Dept. of Econ., College of Bus. Admin., Univ. of South Carolina, Columbia, SC 29208, USA. Tel.: 1 803 777 4930. Fax: 1 803 777 6876.

Year and Place of Birth 1953, Montgomery, USA.

Degrees and Qualifications BA Alabama Univ., 1975; Ph.D. Massachusetts Inst. of Technology, 1980.

Fields of Expertise *Industry Fields:* agric., forestry, fishing; textiles; transport and communication. *Bus. Dimensions:* entrepreneurs and entrepreneurship; bus. and technology. *Scope:* regional. *Period:* nineteenth century; early twentieth century.

Teaching: undergrad.; post grad.

Publications *Articles:* 'Induced Innovation and Econ. Performance in Late Victorian British Industry', *J. of Econ. Hist.,* 42, Mar., 1982, 97–103; 'Textile Mill Villages on the Eve of World War II: The Courtenay Mill of South Carolina', *J. of Econ. Hist.,* 45, June, 1985, 269–75; 'The Labor Market of Southern Textile Mill Villages: Some Micro Evidence', *Explorations in Econ. Hist.,* 23, Apr., 1986, 103–23; 'The Econ. Performance of Late Victorian Britain: Traditional Historians and Growth', *J. of European Econ. Hist.,* 18, Autumn, 1989, 292–414; 'Patent Growth in the Old Dominion: The Impact of Railroad Integration before 1880', *J. of Econ. Hist.,* 52, June, 1992, 389–400.

Pierenkemper, Toni

Full Prof. of Econ. & Social Hist., Senckenberganlage Univ., Senckenberganlage 31, 60054 Frankfurt, Germany. Tel.: 49 69 798 2369. Fax: 49 69 798 8383.

Year and Place of Birth 1944, Wiedenbrück, Germany.

Degrees and Qualifications Dipl. Volkswirt, 1972; MA (Sociology), 1975; Dr (Econ.), 1977.

Previous Post Full Prof., Saarland Univ., Saarbrücken, 1989–90.

Current Offices and Honorary Posts Managing ed., *Jahrbuch für Wirtschaftsgeschichte.*

Fields of Expertise *Industry Fields:* coal and petroleum products. *Bus. Dimensions:* entrepreneurs and entrepreneurship; bus. and technology. *Scope:* regional; internat. *Period:* nineteenth century. *Teaching:* post grad. *Consultancy:* co. hist.

Publications *Books: Die westfälischen Schwerindustriellen, 1852–1913. Soziale Struktur unternehmerischer Erfolg,* Vandenhoek & Ruprecht, Göttingen, 1979;

Wirtschaftssoziologie. Eine proble-morientierte Einführung, Bund-Verlag, Cologne, 1980; *Allokationsprozesse im Arbeitsmarkt. Das Beispiel des Arbeitsmarktes für Angestelltenberufe im Kaiserreich 1880–1913*, Westdeutscher Verlag, Cologne, 1982; *Angestellte und Arbeitsmarkt im Deutschen Kaiserreich 1880–1913. Interessen und Strategien als Instrumente der Integration eines segmentierten Arbeitsmarktes*, special issue no. 82 of *Vierteljahrschrift für Sozial- und Wirtschaftsgeschichte*, Steiner Verlag, Stuttgart, 1987; *Die Geschichte der Drahtweberei. Dargestellt am Beispiel der Firma Haver & Boecker, Oelde*, with R. Tilly, special issue no. 51 of the *Zeitschrift für Unternehmensgeschicte*, Steiner Verlag, Stuttgart, 1987.

Pierson Doti, Lynne

Prof. of Econ. and Bus., School of Bus., Chapman Univ., Orange, CA 92666, USA. Tel.: 1 714 997 6805. Fax: 1 714 532 6081.

Year and Place of Birth 1948, New Jersey, USA.

Degrees and Qualifications MA (Econ.) California State Uni., Fullerton, 1971; Ph.D. (Econ.) Univ. of California-Riverside, 1978.

Current Offices and Honorary Posts Pres., Econ. & Bus. Hist. Soc.

Major Honours Charles Kennedy Award for Previously Unpublished Econ. Hist.

Fields of Expertise *Industry Fields:* insurance, banking, finance. *Bus. Dimensions:* co. admin. *Scope:* regional. *Period:* nineteenth century. *Teaching:* undergrad. *Consultancy:* corporate strategy.

Publications *Books: Banking in the Amer. West*, with Larry Schweikart, Univ. of Oklahoma Press; 'The Postwar Land Boom in Phoenix and Los Angeles 1945–1960', *Pacific Hist.*

Rev., with Larry Schweikart, April, 1989. *Articles:* 'Nationwide Branching: Some Lessons from California', *Essays in Econ. & Bus. Hist.*, IX, May, 1991.

Pinsdorf, Marion K.

Assoc. Prof., Center for Communications and Media Management, Grad. School of Bus. Admin., Fordham Univ., Fordham Road, Bronx, NY 10458, USA. Tel.: 1 212 579 2000.

Place of Birth Teaneck, USA.

Degrees and Qualifications BA (Polit. Sc.) Drew Univ., 1954; MA New York Univ., 1967; Ph.D. New York Univ., 1967; hon. doctorate of science in Bus. Management Nichols College, 1982.

Current Offices and Honorary Posts Edit. advisory board mem., *Public Relations Q.*, Amer. Hist. Soc.

Fields of Expertise *Industry Fields:* communications; public relations. *Bus. Dimensions:* entrepreneurs and entrepreneurship; crisis communications. *Scope:* national. *Period:* late twentieth century, 1970–present. *Teaching:* MBA/grad. bus. *Consultancy:* corporate strategy.

Publications *Books: Communicating when your Company is under Siege. Surviving Public Crises*, Lexington Books/D.C. Heath, Lexington, 1987; *German-speaking Entrepreneurs: Builders of Bus. in Brazil South*, Peter Lang Publishing Inc., New York, 1990. *Articles:* 'Mavericks on the Market Roller Coaster, Daniel Drew and Michael Milken', *Drew Magazine*, June. 1991; 'Varig Airlines of Brazil: An Enterprising German Investment', *Bus. & Econ. Hist.*, Summer, 1992; 'How Hype and Glory Gull', *Risk Management Reports*, Nov., 1992.

Pix, Manfred

Verbandsdirektor, Bayerischer Sparkassen- und Giroverband, Karolinenplatz 5, 80333 Munich, Germany. Tel.: 49 89 21731299. Fax: 49 89 21731245.

Year and Place of Birth 1934, Donauwörth, Germany.

Previous Post Vorstandsvorsitzender der Sparkasse im Landkreis Neustadt/Aisch & Bad Windsheim, 1972–84.

Major Honours Bundesverdienstkreuz.

Fields of Expertise *Industry Fields:* insurance, banking, finance. *Bus. Dimensions:* entrepreneurs and entrepreneurship. *Scope:* regional. *Period:* nineteenth century; twentieth century as a whole. *Teaching:* undergrad. *Consultancy:* co. hist.

Plessis, Alain

Prof. of Econ. Hist., Dept. of Hist., Univ. of Paris X, 200 Av. de la République, 92001 Nanterre Cedex, France. Tel.: 33 1 42 25 87 18.

Year and Place of Birth 1932, Paris, France.

Degrees and Qualifications Agrégé d'Histoire; Docteur d'Etat.

Previous Post Prof., Paris VII Univ., 1980–6.

Current Offices and Honorary Posts Pres., French Assoc. of Econ. Historians; director, Centre for Modern French Hist.; director, Centre d'Etudes des Croissances, Paris X Univ.

Fields of Expertise *Industry Fields:* insurance, banking, finance; bus. services. *Bus. Dimensions:* entrepreneurs and entrepreneurship; co. finance and accounting; bus.–state relations; money. *Scope:* national; internat. *Period:* nineteenth century; twentieth century as a whole. *Teaching:* post grad.

Publications *Books: La Banque de France et Ses Deux Cents Actionnaires sous le Second Empire*, DROZ, 1982; *Vive la Crise e l'Inflation*, Hachette, 1983; *Régents e Governeurs de la Banque de France sous le Second Empire*, DROZ, 1985; *La Politique de la Banque de France de 1850 à 1870*, DROZ, 1985; *Articles:* 'La Culture Bourgeoise en France', *La Culture en France*, Le Seuil, Histoire de la France IV, 1993.

Pohl, Hans

Prof., Historisches Seminar, Bonn Univ., Dept. of Constitutional, Social and Econ. Hist., Konviktstr. 11, 53113 Bonn, Germany. Tel.: 49 228 735172. Fax: 49 228 733778.

Year and Place of Birth 1935, Bärdorf, Silesia.

Degrees and Qualifications Dr.Phil. Cologne Univ., 1961; Habilitation (Econ. & Soc. Hist.) Cologne Univ., 1968.

Current Offices and Honorary Posts Chairman, Academic Board, Bus. Hist. Soc., Cologne; chairman, Inst. of Banking Hist., Frankfurt; mem., Academic Board, Deutsches Museum, Munich; ed., *Vierteljahrschrift für Sozial- und Wirtschaftsgeschichte*; ed., *Zeitschrift für Unternehmensgeschichte*; ed., *German Bus. Hist. Yearbook*.

Fields of Expertise *Industry Fields:* chemicals and allied industries; metal manufacture; metal goods; insurance, banking, finance. *Bus. Dimensions:* entrepreneurs and entrepreneurship; small bus. matters; multinational bus. *Scope:* regional; national; internat. *Period:* nineteenth century; twentieth century as a whole. *Teaching:* undergrad.; post grad. *Consultancy:* co. hist.

Publications *Books: Die Portugiesen in Antwerpen (1567–1648). Zur Geschichte einer Minderheit*, Vierteljahrschrift für

Sozial- und Wirtschaftsgeschichte, Beiheft no. 63, Franz Steiner Verlag, Wiesbaden, 1977; *Aufbruch der Weltwirtschaft. Geschichte der Weltwirtschaft von der Mitte des 19. Jahrhunderte bis zum Ersten Weltkrieg*, Wissenschaftliche Paperbacks Sozial- und Wirtschaftsgeschichte, vol. 24, Franz Steiner Verlag, Stuttgart, 1989; *Vom Stadtwerk zum Elektrizitätsgroßunternehmen, Gründung, Aufbau und Ausbau der Rheinisch-Westfälischen Elektrizitätswerk AG (RWE) 1898–1918*, Zeitschrift für Unternehmensgeschichte, Beiheft 73, Franz Steiner Verlag, 1992; *Verbandsgeschichte und Zeitgeschichte. Bd.1: VDMA - 100 Jahre im Dienste des Maschinenbaus*, with Joh. Markner co-ed., Maschinenbauverlag, Frankfurt, 1992. *Articles:* 'Betrachtungen zum wissenschaftlichen Standort von Wirtschafts- und Unternehmensgeschichte', *Vierteljahrschrift für Sozial- und Wirtschaftsgeschichte*, Beiheft 78, Franz Steiner Verlag, Stuttgart, 1991, 326–43.

Pohl, Manfred

Director of Hist. Archives, Deutsche Bank AG, Zentrale Frankfurt/GS/HA, Taunusanlage 12, 6000 Frankfurt-a-Main, Germany. Tel.: 49 69 71 50 31 33. Fax: 49 69 71 50 83 36.

Year and Place of Birth 1944, Bliesransbach, Germany.

Degrees and Qualifications Ph.D. (Hist.) Saarbrücken Univ., 1972; hon. prof., Frankfurt Univ., 1992.

Previous Post Hon. Prof., Frankfurt Univ., 1992.

Current Offices and Honorary Posts Managing board mem., Soc. for Bus. Hist., 1976–; exec. board mem., European Assoc. for Banking Hist., 1990–; exec. chairman, Deutsche Bank Hist. Assoc., 1991–; mem., Research Council of the Inst. for Bank Hist.

Research, 1973–.

Major Honours Prix des Editeurs des 'Syndicat National des Editeurs', 1970.

Fields of Expertise *Industry Fields:* insurance, banking, finance. *Bus. Dimensions:* co. culture. *Scope:* internat. *Period:* twentieth century as a whole. *Teaching:* undergrad. *Consultancy:* co. hist.

Publications *Books:* Konzentration im Deutschen Bankwesen (1848–1980), Fritz Knapp Verlag, Frankfurt a.M., 1982; *Hist. Research*, Fritz Knapp Verlag, Frankfurt a.M., 1982/3; *Emil Rathenau und die AEG*, v. Hase & Koehler Verlag, Mainz, 1988; *Baden-Württembergische Bankgeschichte*, Verlag W. Kohlhammer, Stuttgart, Berlin, Cologne, 1992; *Unternehmen und Geschichte*, v. Hase & Koehler Verlag, Mainz, 1992. *Articles: Deutsche Bankengeschichte*, Banking Inst. ed., three articles.

Pollard, Sidney

Honorary Senior Fellow, Dept. of Hist., Sheffield Univ., Sheffield, S10 2TN, UK. Tel.: 44 742 76855. Fax: 44 742 788304.

Year and Place of Birth 1925, Vienna, Austria.

Degrees and Qualifications B.Sc. (Econ.) London Univ., 1948; Ph.D. London Univ., 1951.

Previous Post Prof. of Econ. Hist., Bielefeld Univ., Germany, 1980–90.

Major Honours Newcomen Soc. Prize for best book on Bus. Hist., 1964–6 for *The Genesis of Modern Management;* Corresponding Fellow of the British Acad.; Hon. Litt.D., Sheffield Univ.

Fields of Expertise *Industry Fields:* shipbuilding and marine engineering. *Bus. Dimensions:* entrepreneurs and entrepreneurship. *Scope:* internat.

Period: nineteenth century. *Consultancy:* co. hist.

Publications *Books: Three Centuries of Sheffield Steel*, Marsh Brothers, 1954; *Shirley Aldred & Co. Ltd., 1796–1858*, Aldred, 1958; *The Genesis of Modern Management*, Edward Arnold & Harvard Univ. Press, 1965, Penguin, 1968; *The British Shipbuilding Industry 1870–1914*, with Paul L..Robertson, Harvard Univ. Press, 1979; *Von der Heimarbeit in die Fabrik*, with Karl Ditt co-ed., Schöning, Paderborn, 1992.

Pollins, Harold

Year and Place of Birth 1924, London, UK.

Degrees and Qualifications B.Sc. (Econ.) London School of Econ., 1949.

Previous Post Sen. Tutor, Ruskin College, Oxford, 1964–89.

Fields of Expertise *Industry Fields:* mining and quarrying; transport and communication. *Bus. Dimensions:* entrepreneurs and entrepreneurship; co. finance and accounting; personnel management; bus. values; industrial relations. *Scope:* local; regional; national; UK. *Period:* eighteenth century; nineteenth century; twentieth century as a whole. *Teaching:* undergrad. adult further.

Publications *Books: Britain's Railways: An Industrial Hist.*, David & Charles, 1971. *Articles:* 'Aspects of Railway Accounting before 1868', *Studies in the Hist. of Accounting*, A.C. Littleton & B.S. Yamey eds., Sweet & Maxwell, 1956; 'Trade Unions', *The Hist. of Technology. Vol. 6: The Twentieth Century c. 1900–1950, Part I*, T.I Williams ed., Clarendon Press, 1978; 'Immigrants and Minorities: The Outsiders in Bus.', *Immigrants & Minorities*, 8(3), Nov., 1989, 252–70; 'British Horse Tramway Co. Accounting Practices, 1870–1914', *Accounting, Bus. & Financial Hist.*, 1(3), 1991, 280–302.

Pope, Daniel

Assoc. Prof., Dept. of Hist., Univ. of Oregon, Eugene, OR 97403, USA. Tel.: 503 346 4015. Fax: 503 346 4895.

Year and Place of Birth 1946, Brooklyn, New York, USA.

Degrees and Qualifications BA Swarthmore College, 1966; MA Columbia Univ., 1968; Ph.D. Columbia Univ., 1973.

Previous Post Research Assoc., Harvard Bus. School, 1980–2.

Major Honours Harvard Newcomen Post-doctoral Fellowship, 1980–1.

Fields of Expertise *Industry Fields:* gas, electricity, water. *Bus. Dimensions:* bus.–state relations. *Scope:* regional. *Period:* late twentieth century, 1970–present. *Teaching:* undergrad.

Publications *Books: The Making of Modern Advertising*, Basic Books, 1983. *Articles:* 'American Economists and the High Cost of Living', *J. of the Hist. of the Behavioral Sciences*, 17, 1981, 75–87; 'We Can Wait, We Should Wait: Eugene's Nuclear Power Controversy 1968–1970', *Pacific Hist. Rev.*, 59, 1990, 349–73; 'Advertising as a Consumer Issue: An Hist. View', *J. of Social Issues*, 47, 1991, 41–56; 'We Tried Harder: Jews and Amer. Advertising', *Amer. Jewish Hist.*, 72, 1992, 26–51.

Poznanska, Barbara

Inst. of Hist., Polish Acad. of Sciences (PAN), 00-272 Warsaw, Rynek Starego Miasta 29/31, Poland. Tel.: 48 22 31 02 61. Fax: 48 22 31 36 42.

Year and Place of Birth 1936,

Warsaw, Poland.

Degrees and Qualifications Ph.D. (Hist.) Inst. of Hist., Polish Acad. of Sciences, 1976.

Current Offices and Honorary Posts Mem., Polish Soc. of Historians.

Fields of Expertise *Industry Fields:* . *Bus. Dimensions:* research and development. *Scope:* local. *Period:* interwar years, 1919–39.

Publications *Articles:* 'The Social Division of the Warsaw Bourgeoisie during the Interwar Years 1918–1939', *Hist. of the Bourgeoisie in Poland*, study & materials, vol. I, Wroclaw, 1974, 205–35; 'The Warsaw Bourgeoisie in the Interwar Years 1918–1939', *The Warsaw Community in Hist. Development*, Warsaw, 1977, 435–55; 'The Hist. of the Bourgeoisie in Poland in the 19th and 20th Centuries', *Hist. of Contemporary Times*, research thesis, 1st edn., 1977, 121–35; 'The Number and Placement of the Warsaw Bourgeoisie in the Interwar Years 1918–1939', *Hist. of the Bourgeoisie in Poland*, study & materials, vol. II, Wroclaw, 1980, 65–95 plus supplements; 'Image of the Warsaw Bourgeoisie in the Interwar Years', *Image of Bus.men in Poland in the 19th & 20th Centuries*, conf. organized by the Inst. of Hist., Polish Acad. of Science, Jan., 1992, forthcoming.

Press, Jon

Modular Programmes Director, Bath College of Higher Education, Newton Park, Bath, BA2 9BN, UK. Tel.: 44 225 873701. Fax: 44 225 874082.

Year and Place of Birth 1953, Watford, UK.

Degrees and Qualifications BA (Hist.) Bristol Univ., 1974; Ph.D. (Econ./Soc. Hist.) Bristol Univ., 1987.

Previous Post Principal Lect., Bath College, 1990–3.

Current Offices and Honorary Posts Com. mem., Assoc. for Hist. &

Computing.

Major Honours Cass Prize 1991, Wadsworth Prize 1992, shortlisted for Nat. Art Book Prize 1992.

Fields of Expertise *Industry Fields:* mining and quarrying. *Bus. Dimensions:* multinational bus. *Scope:* internat. *Period:* nineteenth century. *Teaching:* undergrad.

Publications *Books: Studies in the Bus. Hist. of Bristol*, with C.E. Harvey eds., Bristol Academic Press, 1988; *The Footwear Industry in Ireland, 1922–1973*, Irish Academic Press, 1989; *William Morris: Design and Enterprise in Victorian Britain*, with C.E. Harvey, Manchester Univ. Press, 1991. *Articles:* 'Overseas Expansion and the Professional Advance of British Mining Engineers, 1851–1914', *Econ. Hist. Rev.*, with C.E. Harvey, 2nd ser., 42(1), 1989, 64–86; 'The City and Internat. Mining, 1870–1914', *Bus. Hist.*, with C.E. Harvey, 32(3), 1990, 98–119.

Previts, Gary John

Prof. of Accountancy, Weatherhead School of Management, Case Western Reserve Univ., 625 Enterprise Hall, Cleveland, OH 44106–7235, USA. Tel.: 1 216 368 2074.

Year and Place of Birth 1942, Cleveland, USA.

Degrees and Qualifications B.Sc. (Bus. Admin.) John Carroll Univ., 1963; Master of Accounting, Ohio State Univ., 1964; Certified Public Accountant, Ohio, 1965; Ph.D. Florida Univ., 1972.

Previous Post Alabama Univ., 1973–9.

Current Offices and Honorary Posts Pres., Ohio Soc. of CPA's, 1993–4; pres., Acad. of Accounting Historians, 1973–5; mem., exec. comm. and director of education, Amer. Accounting Assoc., 1987–9; mem., Governing

Council, Amer. Inst. of CPA's, 1985–7, 1989–.

Major Honours Hourglass Award (Literature Achievement in Accounting Hist.), 1980.

Fields of Expertise *Industry Fields:* . *Bus. Dimensions:* accountancy. *Teaching:* undergrad.; post grad. *Consultancy:* hist. of bus. and 'professions'. ·

Publications *Books: A Hist. of Accounting in Amer.*, B.D. Merino co-auth., John Wiley & Sons, NYC, 1979; *The Accounting Historians*, journal ed., 1974–8, 1985–8.

Prúcha, Václav

Dept. of Econ. Hist., Fac. of National Economy, Prague Econ. Univ., Námestí W. Churchilla 4, 130 67 Prague 3, Czechland. Tel.: 42 2 2125265. Fax: 42 2 236014.

Year and Place of Birth 1931, Prague, Czechland.

Degrees and Qualifications Ing. Prague Econ. Univ., 1954; C.Sc. Prague Econ. Univ., 1961; Doktor, Prague Econ. Univ., 1966; Prof. Prague Econ. Univ., 1991.

Previous Post Dept. of Econ. Hist., Prague Econ. Univ., 1957–93.

Current Offices and Honorary Posts Head of Dept. of Econ. Hist., Prague Econ. Univ., 1990–; chairman, Czech Econ. Hist. Soc., 1990–.

Major Honours Slovak Literary Fund Prize, 1969; Czech Literary Fund (3 prizes), 1978–9; Czechoslovak publishing houses prizes, 1975, 1978, 1983, 1985.

Fields of Expertise *Industry Fields:* metal manufacture; other manufacturing industries; branch structure of econ. and industry (armament industry); agric. *Bus. Dimensions:* entrepreneurs and entrepreneurship; bus.–state relations; co-operative stores (in agric.). *Scope:* national; internat.; Czech and Slovak Republics; central,

east and south-east Europe. *Period:* twentieth century as a whole; inter-war years, 1919–39; mid-twentieth century, 1940–70; late twentieth century, 1970–present. *Teaching:* undergrad.; post grad.

Publications *Books: Hospodárské dejiny Ceskoslovenska v 19. a 20. Století* [Econ. Hist. of Czechoslovakia in the 19th and 20th Century], et al. eds., Svoboda, Prague, 1974; in Slovak: Pravda, Bratislava, 1974; *Hospodárské dejiny evropskych socialistickych zemí* [Econ. Hist. of European Socialist Countries], Svoboda, Prague, 1977; in Polish: Ksiazka i Wiedza, Warsaw, 1981; *Dejiny hutnictví v Ceskoslovensku* [Hist. of Czechoslovak Metallurgy], joint-auth., 3 vols., Academia, Prague, 1984, 1986, 1988. *Articles:* 'The Integration of Czechoslovakia in the Econ. System of Nazi Germany', *Making the New Europe. European Unity and the Second World War*, M.L. Smith & P.M.R. Stirk eds., Pinter Publishers, London & New York, 1990; 'Changes in the Structure of Manufacturing Industry in the Countries of Central-East and South-East Europe after the Second World War', *Sectoral Changes in Industry*, W. Falk co-ed., Inst. of Hist., Prague, 1991.

Raaschou-Nielsen, Agnete

Chief Economist, Carlsberg Internat., Strandvejen 50, 2900 Hellerup, Denmark. Tel.: 45 33272003. Fax: 45 33274809.

Year and Place of Birth 1957, Copenhagen, Denmark.

Degrees and Qualifications MA, 1985; Ph.D. (Econ.) Copenhagen Univ., 1989.

Previous Post Asst. Prof., Copenhagen Bus. School, 1989–91.

Fields of Expertise *Industry Fields:* food, drink, tobacco; clothing and footwear. *Bus. Dimensions:* bus. organization. *Scope:* national; Denmark. *Period:* nineteenth century. *Teaching:* post grad.

Publications *Articles:* 'Danish Agrarian Reform and Econ. Theory', *Scandinavian Econ. Hist. Rev.*, XXXVIII(3), 1990; 'The Organisational Hist. of the Firm: The Putting-out System in Denmark around 1900', *Scandinavian Econ. Hist. Rev.*, forthcoming, 1993.

Rauck, Michael

Research Asst., Fac. of Econ., Tokyo Metropolitan Univ., 1-1 Minami Osawa, Hachioji-City, Tokyo 192-03, Japan. Tel.: 81 426 77 1386. Fax: 81 426 77 3002.

Year and Place of Birth 1957, Munich, Germany.

Degrees and Qualifications Diplom-Handelslehrer Friederich-Alexander-Univ. Erlangen-Nuremberg, 1980; Dr. rer. pol. Friederich-Alexander Univ. Erlangen-Nuremberg, 1989; Assessor Bavarian State Min. of Ed., 1982.

Previous Post Visiting Research Fellow, Fac. of Econ., Tokyo Metropol. Univ., 1989–91.

Fields of Expertise *Industry Fields:* vehicle construction; transport and communication; distributive trades; insurance, banking, finance; German-Japanese technology transfer; mining and quarrying; chemicals and allied industries; metal manufacture; mechanical engineering; electrical engineering; shipbuilding and marine engineering; textiles; bricks, pottery, glass, cement; paper, printing, publishing; construction. *Bus. Dimensions:* entrepreneurs and entrepreneurship; research and development; bus. and technology; multinational bus.; management education; bus.–state relations. *Scope:* internat.; Austria; Germany; Japan; Switzerland; China. *Period:* nineteenth century; twentieth century as a whole. *Teaching:* undergrad.; post grad.

Consultancy: co. hist.

Publications *Articles:* 'Karl Freiherr Drais von Sauerbronn. Erfinder und Unternehmer (1985–1851)', *Beiträge zur Wirtschafts- und Sozialgeschichte*, 24, Franz-Steiner-Verlag Wiesbaden GmbH, Stuttgart, 1983; 'Daiichiji taisen-zen ni okeru doitsu kigyo no tainichi toshi katsudo' [Investment Activities of German Companies in Japan before World War I], *Keizai to keizaigaku*, 71, 1992; 'Technologie-transfer Deutschland-Japan (1870–1914), dargestellt anhand konkreter Industrieprojekte', *Technologietransfer Deutschland-Japan von 1850 bis zur Gegenwart.*, 2, Monographien aus dem Deutschen Institut für Japanstudien der Philipp-Franz-von-Siebold-Stiftung, vol. 2, iudicium-Verlag, Munich 1992.

Reagan, Patrick D.

Prof., Dept. of Hist., POB 5064, Tennessee Technical Univ., Cookeville, TN 84057-4864, USA. Tel.: Work: 0615 372 3332; home: 0615 528 3998.

Year and Place of Birth 1953, St Paul, USA.

Degrees and Qualifications BA (Hist.) Kenyon College, Ohio, 1975; MA (Hist.) Ohio State Univ., 1976; Ph.D. (Hist.) Ohio State Univ., 1982.

Previous Post Assoc. Prof., Dept. of Hist., Tennessee Technological Univ., 1987–92.

Major Honours National Endowment for the Humanities Summer Fellow, Iowa Univ., 1984.

Fields of Expertise *Industry Fields:* public admin. and defence; professional services. *Bus. Dimensions:* bus.–state relations. *Scope:* national; USA. *Period:* twentieth century as a whole. *Teaching:* undergrad. *Consultancy:* Houghton Mifflin (Boston, MA); D.C. Heath (Lexington, MA).

Publications *Books: Voluntarism, Planning and the State: The Amer. Planning Experience, 1914–1946*, co-ed. & contributor, Greenwood Press, Westport, CT, 1988; *For the General Welfare: Essays in Honor of Robert H. Bremner*, co-ed. & contributor, Peter Lang, New York, Bern, Frankfurt, Paris, 1989; *Introduction to Horace Coon, Money to Burn: Great Amer. Foundations and their Money*, Transaction Publishers, New Brunswick, NJ, 1990. *Articles:* 'From Depression to Depression: Hooverian National Planning, 1921–33', *Mid-Amer.*, 70, 1988, 35–60; 'Strategy and Hist.: Paul Kennedy's The Rise and Fall of the Great Powers', *J. of Military Hist.*, 53, July, 1989, 291–306.

Regehr, Theodore D.

Prof. of Hist., Dept. of Hist., Univ. of Saskatchewan, 512 Quance Ave., Saskatoon, Saskatchewan, S7N 0W0, Canada. Tel.: 0306 966 5809. Fax: 0306 966 5852.

Year and Place of Birth 1937, Coaldale, Canada.

Degrees and Qualifications BA Alberta Univ., 1959; MA Carleton Univ., Ottawa, 1963; Ph.D. Alberta Univ., Edmonton, 1967.

Previous Post Head, Government Records Div., National Archives of Canada, Ottawa, 1960–8.

Fields of Expertise *Industry Fields:* agric., forestry, fishing; paper, printing, publishing; gas, electricity, water; transport and communication; insurance, banking, finance. *Bus. Dimensions:* entrepreneurs and entrepreneurship; bus. and technology; bus.–state relations. *Scope:* national; internat. *Period:* early twentieth century; inter-war years, 1919–39. *Teaching:* undergrad.; post grad. *Consultancy:* co. hist.

Publications *Books: The Possibilities of Canada are Truly Great. Memoirs 1906–1924 by Martin Nordegg*, Macmillan, Toronto, 1971; *The Canadian Northern Railway. Pioneer Road of the Northern Prairies, 1895–1918*, Macmillan, Toronto, 1976; *The Beauharnois Scandal. A Story of Canadian Entrepreneurship and Polit.*, Univ. of Toronto Press, Toronto, 1990. *Articles:* 'High-powered Lawyers, Veteran Lobbyists, Cunning Propagandists: Canadian Lawyers and the Beauharnois Scandal', *Beyond the Law: Lawyers and Bus. in Canada, 1830–1930*, Carold Wilton ed., The Osgoods Soc., Toronto, 1990; 'The Irish Childhood and Youth of a Canadian Capitalist', *The Irish World Wide: Hist., Heritage, Identity. Vol. I. Patterns of Migration*, Patrick O'Sullivan ed., Leicester Univ. Press, Leicester, UK, 1992.

Reinert, Erik S.

Research Scientist, Step-Group, Studies in Technology, Innovation & Econ. Policy, Norwegian Computing Centre, POB 114, Blindern, N-0314 Oslo, Norway. Tel.: 47 22 85 26 26. Fax: 47 33 393 502.

Year and Place of Birth 1949, Oslo, Norway.

Degrees and Qualifications BA St Gallen Univ., Switzerland, 1973; MBA Harvard Univ., 1976; Ph.D. (Econ.) Cornell Univ., 1980.

Fields of Expertise *Industry Fields:* manufacturing in general. *Bus. Dimensions:* bus. and technology. *Scope:* global. *Period:* twentieth century as a whole. *Teaching:* undergrad. *Consultancy:* national industrial policy.

Publications *Books: Internat. Trade and the Econ. Mechanisms of Underdevelopment*, university microfilm, Ann Arbor, 1980; *Catching up from Way Behind - a Third World Perspective on First World Hist.*, Step-Group, Oslo, 1993.

Renz, Regina

Prof. of Hist., Inst. of Hist., Univ. of Pedagogy in Kielce, ul. Żeromskiego 5, 25–369 Kielce, Poland. Tel.: 48 41 48670. Fax: 48 41 48805.
Year and Place of Birth 1948, Siemieradz, Poland.
Degrees and Qualifications Ph.D., 1982; Habilitation (Asst. Prof.), 1990; Prof. (Univ. of Pedagogy in Kielce), 1992.
Previous Post Deputy Dean, Fac. of Humanities.
Current Offices and Honorary Posts Mem., Polish Hist. Soc.; mem., Kielce Scientific Soc.
Major Honours Ministry of Education Award, 1981.
Fields of Expertise *Industry Fields:* distributive trades; bus. services. *Bus. Dimensions:* small bus. matters; co. culture; economic activity of the Jewish community, 1918–1939. *Scope:* regional; national. *Period:* inter-war years, 1919–39. *Teaching:* undergrad.; post grad. *Consultancy:* econ. and social hist.
Publications *Books: Crafts in the Kielce Provice in the Interwar Period. Social and Econ. Aspects*, Polish Scientific Publishers, 1984; *Little Town Community in the Kielce Province in the Years 1918–1939*, Univ. of Pedagogy in Kielce Publishers, 1990. *Articles:* 'Urban Population in the Kielce Province in the Interwar Period. Social Aspects', *Studia Kieleckie*, 1(53), 1987, 99–112; 'Petty Bourgeoisie of the Kielce Province in the Interwar Period', *Petty Bourgeoisie of the 19th and 20th Century Studies*, Stefania Kowalska-Glikman ed., III, Warsaw, 1992, 180–253, (dissertation); 'Jews in the Small-town Community in the Kielce Province in the Interwar Period in the Light of Memoirs', *Culture of Polish Jews in the 19th and 20th Century*, with M. Meducka co-ed., Kielce, 1992, 101–116.

Resch, Andreas

Asst., Inst. of Econ. and Social Hist., Vienna Univ. of Econ. and Bus. Admin., Augasse 2-6, A-1090 Vienna, Austria. Tel.: 43 313 36 4245. Fax: 43 313 36 710.
Year and Place of Birth 1962, Gmunden, Austria.
Degrees and Qualifications Mag. phil. Vienna Univ., 1986; Dr. phil. Vienna Univ., 1993.
Previous Post Collaborator, Vienna Museum of Technology, 1990.
Fields of Expertise *Industry Fields:* metal manufacture; mechanical engineering; metal goods; construction. *Bus. Dimensions:* entrepreneurs and entrepreneurship; production management; co. finance and accounting; bus. and technology; bus.–state relations. *Scope:* regional; national; internat. *Period:* nineteenth century; twentieth century as a whole. *Teaching:* undergrad.
Publications *Articles:* 'Mächtig dröhnt der Hämmer Klang. Sensenindustrie und regionale Entwicklung', Scharnstein ed., *Linzer Schriften zur Sozial- und Wirtschaftsgeschichte*, Gustav Otruba & Roman Sandgruber eds., 1991; 'Unternehmer und Arbeiter in der österreichischen Sensenbranche um 1900. Industrialisierung und regionale Entwicklung am Beispiel der größten Sensenfabrik der Habsburgermonarchie, des Redtenbacher-Werks', *Oberösterreich*, Scharnstein (dissertation, Vienna, 1993).

Reulecke, Jürgen

Prof., Fachbereich 1, Universität-Gesamthochschule Siegen, D-57068 Siegen, Germany. Tel.: 49 271 7404606. Fax: 49 271 7404586.
Year and Place of Birth 1940, Düsseldorf, Germany.
Degrees and Qualifications Dr.phil. Bochum Univ., 1972; Habilitation Bochum Univ., 1979.
Previous Post Univ. Prof. of Modern & Contemporary Hist., Siegen Univ.
Current Offices and Honorary Posts Director, Inst. of European Regional Research, Siegen Univ.
Major Honours Freiherr-vom-Stein Prize, 1990.
Fields of Expertise *Industry Fields:* textiles; industry and regional identity. *Bus. Dimensions:* co. culture. *Scope:* regional; Germany (West). *Period:* nineteenth century; early twentieth century. *Teaching:* undergrad.; post grad.
Publications *Books: Sozialer Frieden durch soziale Reform. Der Centralverein für das Wohl der arbeitenden Klassen,* Hammer, 1983; *Geschichte der Urbanisierung in Deutschland,* Suhrkamp, 1985; *Bevölkerung, Wirtschaft, Gesellschaft seit der Industrialisierung,* with D. Petzina co-ed., Gesellschaft für Westfälische Wirtschaftsgeschichte, 1990; *Vom Kohlenpott zu Deutschlands 'starkem Stück',* Beiträge zur Sozialgeschichte des Ruhrgebiets, Bouvier, 1990; *Metropolis Berlin. Berlin als deutsche Hauptstadt im Vergleich europäischer Hauptstädte,* with G. Brunn co-ed., Bouvier, 1992.

Riis, Thomas

Visiting Prof., Inst. of Hist., Kiel Univ., Olshausenstrasse 40, D-24098, Kiel, Germany. Tel.: 49 431 880 2298.
Fax: 49 431 880 1524.
Year and Place of Birth 1941, Copenhagen, Denmark.
Degrees and Qualifications MA Copenhagen Univ., 1968; Dr.Phil. Odense Univ., 1977.
Previous Post Soc. for Danish Language and Literature (from 1985) & ed., *The Diplomatarium Danicum,* Copenhagen.
Current Offices and Honorary Posts Chairman, Danish Com. for Urban Hist.; v.-p., Internat. Commission for the Hist. of Towns.
Fields of Expertise *Industry Fields:* transport and communication; distributive trades; public admin. and defence; fishing. *Bus. Dimensions:* bus.–state relations; markets and bus. *Scope:* regional; national; internat. *Period:* medieval; early modern; eighteenth century. *Teaching:* undergrad.; post grad.
Publications *Books: Les Institutions Politiques Centrales du Danemark 1100–1332,* Odense, 1977; *Le Temps du Travail. Une Esquisse,* Diogène, no. 149, Paris, 1990; *Aspects of Poverty in Early Modern Europe I–III,* ed., Stuttgart-Odense, 1981–90; *Should Auld Acquaintance be Forgot. Scottish-Danish Relations c. 1450–1707 I–II,* Odense, 1989; *Articles:* 'La Baltique et le Monde Baltique au XVe. Siècle', *Critica Storica,* XXV, 1988, 713–28.

Roberts, William I.

2013 Parkview Ave, Abington, PA 19001, USA.
Year and Place of Birth 1924, Philadelphia, USA.
Degrees and Qualifications BS Temple Univ., 1946; MA Temple Univ., 1948; Ph.D. Pennsylvania Univ., 1958.
Previous Post Assoc. Prof. of Hist., Pennsylvania State Univ., 1955–88.

Fields of Expertise *Industry Fields:* chemicals and allied industries. *Bus. Dimensions:* bus. and technology. *Scope:* internat.; transatlantic. *Period:* nineteenth century. *Teaching:* undergrad. *Consultancy:* co. hist.

Publications *Articles:* 'American Potash Manufacture before the Amer. Revolution', *Proceedings of the Amer. Philosophical Soc.*, 116(5), Oct., 1972; 'Potash and Pearlash',. *Encyclopaedia of Amer. Forest and Conservation Hist.*, Macmillan, 1983.

Roche, Michael

Sen. Lect., Dept. of Geography, Massey Univ., Private Bag 11-222, Palmerston North, New Zealand. Tel.: 64 6 356 9099. Fax: 64 6 350 5644.

Year and Place of Birth 1956, Ashburton, New Zealand.

Degrees and Qualifications BA Canterbury Univ., 1978; MA Canterbury Univ., 1980; Ph.D. Canterbury Univ., 1983.

Previous Post Contract Researcher, Hist. Publications Branch, Dept. of Internal Affairs.

Current Offices and Honorary Posts Rev. ed., *New Zealand Geography*; New Zealand co-ordinator, Australian Forest Hist. Soc.

Major Honours 1993 Symes Award, Royal Australian Geographical Soc.

Fields of Expertise *Industry Fields:* agric., forestry, fishing; food, drink, tobacco; timber, furniture; paper, printing, publishing. *Bus. Dimensions:* bus.–state relations; entrepreneurs and entrepreneurship; bus. organization; boardroom issues. *Scope:* national; local; regional; internat.; New Zealand. *Period:* nineteenth century; twentieth century as a whole. *Teaching:* undergrad.; post grad.

Publications *Books: Hist. of Forestry in New Zealand*, Government

Print, Wellington, 1990. *Articles:* 'The New Zealand Timber Economy 1845–1935', *Hist. Geography*, 16(3), 1990, 295–313; 'Perspectives on the post 1984 Restructuring of State Forestry in New Zealand', *Environment and Planning*, A22(7), 1990, 941–959; 'Internationalisation as Co. and Industry Colonialization: The Frozen Meat Industry in New Zealand in the 1900's', *New Zealand Geographer*, 49(1), 1993, forthcoming; 'New Zealand Afforestation Policy in Eras of State Regulation and Deregulation', *Afforestation, Policies, Planning and Progress*, with R.B. Le Heron co-auth., A.S. Mather ed., Belhaven, London, 1993, 140–61.

Rockoff, Hugh T.

Prof. of Econ., Dept. of Econ., Rutgers Univ., New Brunswick, NJ 08903-5055, USA. Tel.: 1 908 932 7857. Fax: 1 908 932 7416.

Year and Place of Birth 1945, Dayton, USA.

Degrees and Qualifications BA Earlham College, 1967; MA Chicago Univ., 1969; Ph.D. Chicago Univ., 1972.

Previous Post Assoc. Prof., Rutgers Univ., New Brunswick, 1976–83.

Fields of Expertise *Industry Fields:* insurance, banking, finance. *Bus. Dimensions:* bus. organization. *Scope:* internat. *Period:* nineteenth century; twentieth century as a whole. *Teaching:* undergrad.; post grad.

Publications *Books: The Free Banking Era: A Re-examination*, Arno Press, 1975; *Drastic Measures: A Hist. of Wage and Price Controls in the United States*, CUP, 1984; *Strategic Factors in Nineteenth Century Amer. Econ. Hist.: A Volume to honor Robert W. Fogel*, with Claudia Goldin, co-ed. Univ.of Chicago Press, 1992; *Price Controls*, ed., Edward Elgar

Publishing, 1992; *Sinews of War: Essays on the Econ. Hist. of World War II and its Aftermath*, with Geofrey Mills, co-ed., Iowa State Univ. Press, 1993.

Rose, Mark H.

Prof. of Hist., Dept. of Hist., Florida Atlantic Univ., 2912 College Ave., Davie, FL 33314, USA. Tel.: 1 305 476 4587. Fax: 1 305 476 4582.

Year and Place of Birth 1945, Chicago, USA.

Degrees and Qualifications BA (Hist.) Roosevelt Univ., 1967; Ph.D. (Hist.) Ohio State Univ., 1973.

Previous Post Assoc. Prof. of the Hist. of Science, Technology & Soc., Michigan Technological Univ., 1980–90.

Current Offices and Honorary Posts Advisory com. mem, Soc. for the Hist. of Technology.

Major Honours Gen. ed., *Technology and Urban Growth*, a monographic series published by Temple Univ. Press, 1979–90.

Fields of Expertise *Industry Fields:* gas, electricity, water; transport and communication. *Bus. Dimensions:* bus. and technology; bus.–state relations. *Scope:* national. *Period:* twentieth century as a whole. *Teaching:* undergrad.; post grad.

Publications *Books: Interstate: Express Highway Polit., 1939–1989*, Univ. of Tennessee Press, Knoxville, 1990, 2nd edn.; *Cities of Light and Heat*, Penn State Univ. Press, Univ. Park, 1994, forthcoming. *Articles:* 'Building the Interstate Highway System: Road Engineers and the Implementation of Public Policy', *J. of Policy Hist.*, 2, Jan., 1990, 23–55; 'The Hist. of Kansas City Projects and the Origins of Amer. Urban Hist.', *J. of Urban Hist.*, 18, Aug., 1992, 371–94; 'Street Smarts: The Polit. of Numbers

in Shaping the Amer. City, 1900–1990', *Amer. City Hist: Modes of Inquiry*, Kathleen Conzen et al. eds., Univ. of Chicago Press, Chicago, 1993.

Rose, Mary B.

Sen. Lect. in Bus. Hist., Dept. of Econ., School of Management, Univ. of Lancaster, Lancaster, LA1 4YX, UK. Tel.: 44 524 594214. Fax: 44 524 594244.

Year and Place of Birth 1953, Altrincham, UK.

Degrees and Qualifications BA (Econ.) Liverpool Univ., 1974; Ph.D. Manchester Univ., 1977.

Previous Post Research/Education Officer, Quarry Bank Mill Museum, 1978.

Current Offices and Honorary Posts Book reviews ed., *Bus. Hist.*; vice-pres., Assoc. of Bus. Historians.

Major Honours Cass Prize for best article in *Bus. Hist.* in 1989, ('Social Policy and Bus.').

Fields of Expertise *Industry Fields:* textiles. *Bus. Dimensions:* entrepreneurs and entrepreneurship; bus. organization; small bus. matters; co. culture; family firms. *Scope:* internat. *Period:* eighteenth century; nineteenth century; twentieth century as a whole. *Teaching:* undergrad.; post grad. *Consultancy:* museums (work on exhibitions, etc.).

Publications *Books: The Gregs of Quarry Bank Mill: The Rise and Decline of a Family Firm, 1750–1914*, CUP, 1986; *Internat. Competition and Strategic Response in the Textile Industries since 1870*, ed., Frank Cass & Co., 1991. *Articles:* 'The Role of the Family in the Provision of Capital and Managerial Talent in Samuel Greg and Co.', *Bus. Hist.*, 19, 1977, 37–54; 'The Diversification of Investment by the Gregs, 1800–1900', *Bus. Hist.*, 21, 1979, 79–96; 'Social Policy and Bus.:

Parish Apprenticeship and the Early Factory System, 1750–1834', *Bus. Hist.*, 31, 1989, 5–32.

Rosenbloom, Richard S.

David Sarnoff Prof. of Bus. Admin., Grad. School of Bus. Admin., Harvard Univ., Morgan Hall 213, Soldiers Field, Boston, MA 02163, USA. Tel.: 1 617 495 6295. Fax: 1 617 495 8030.

Year and Place of Birth 1933, Springfield, USA.

Degrees and Qualifications BA (Chemistry) Harvard Univ., 1954; MBA (Bus. Admin.) Harvard Univ., 1956; DBA (Bus. Admin.) Harvard Univ., 1960.

Previous Post Visiting Prof., Stanford Univ., Dept.of Industrial Engineering & Engineering Management, 1986.

Current Offices and Honorary Posts Mem., Amer. Assoc. for the Advancement of Science; mem., Soc. for the Hist. of Technology; mem., Bus. Hist. Conf.; mem., Econ. Hist. Assoc.

Fields of Expertise *Industry Fields:* electronics and computers: manufacture. *Bus. Dimensions:* research and development. *Scope:* global. *Period:* late twentieth century, 1970–present. *Teaching:* post grad. *Consultancy:* corporate strategy.

Publications *Books: Research on Technological Innovation, Management and Policy*, with Robert A. Burgelman co-ed., vol. 4, JAI Press Inc., 1989. *Articles:* 'Technological Pioneering and Competitive Advantage: The Birth of the VCR Industry', *California Management Rev.*, with Michael Cusumano, Summer, 1987, 57–76; 'The Climate for Innovation in Industry: The Role of Management Attitudes and Practices in Consumer Electronics', *Research Policy*, with William Abernathy, 11, 1982, 209–25; 'Nurturing Corporate Research', *Harvard Bus. Rev.*, with Alan Kantrow, Jan./Feb., 1982; 'Men and Machines: An Essay on 19th Century Analyses of Mechanization', *Technology and Culture*, Autumn, 1964.

Rothstein, Morton

Prof. in Hist., Univ. of California, Davis & Editor, *Agric. Hist.*, Univ. of California, Davis, CA 95616, USA. Tel.: 1 916 752 3046. Fax: 1 916 752 5611.

Year and Place of Birth 1926, Omaha, USA.

Degrees and Qualifications BA Brooklyn College, 1954; Ph.D. Cornell Univ., 1960.

Previous Post Prof. in Hist., Univ. of Wisconsin, Madison, WI, 1961–84, (Dept. Chair, 1969–72).

Current Offices and Honorary Posts Ed., *Agric. Hist.*, 1984–; past pres., Agric. Hist. Soc., 1974–5; past pres., Bus. Hist. Conf., 1985–6.

Major Honours Cartensen Prize for best article in *Agric. Hist.*, 1983; pres., Agric. Hist. Soc., 1975; pres., Bus. Hist. Conf., 1986; Social Science Research Council Training Fellowship 1956–7 for research in UK; National Endowment for the Humanities Fellowship, Newberry Library, Chicago, July-Dec., 1976; National Endowment for the Humanities Fellowship, 1983.

Fields of Expertise *Industry Fields:* agric., forestry, fishing; food, drink, tobacco; transport and communication; distributive trades. *Bus. Dimensions:* marketing; entrepreneurs and entrepreneurship; multinational bus.; markets and bus. *Scope:* internat.; local; regional; national; USA; UK; Canada. *Period:* nineteenth century; eighteenth century; early twentieth century. *Teaching:* undergrad.; post grad. *Consultancy:* co. hist.

Publications *Articles:* 'The New South and the Internat. Economy', *Agric. Hist.*, LVII, Oct., 1983, 385–402; 'The Rejection and Acceptance of a Marketing Innovation: Hedging in the late 19th Century', *Rev. of Research in Futures Markets*, 1983; 'Technological Change and Amer. Farmer Movements', *Technology, Econ. & Soc.: The Amer. Experience*, S. Bruchey & J. Colton eds., Columbia Univ. Press. 1987, 186–222; 'Centralizing Firms and Widening Markets: The World of Internat. Grain Traders, 1846–1914', *Bus. & Econ. Hist*, 2nd ser., 1988; 'The United States and the United Kingdom as Centers of the World Wheat Trade, 1846–1914', *Internat. Congress of Hist. Sciences*, Proceedings, Madrid, 1993.

Rubner, Heinrich

Prof. of Demographic & Social Hist., Fac. of Hist., Social Sciences & Geography, D 93040 Regensburg Univ., Germany. Tel.: 49 941 9431. Fax: 49 941 943 2305.

Year and Place of Birth 1925, Grafrath, Germany.

Degrees and Qualifications Dr.phil. Munich Univ., 1955; Dr.nat.habil. Freiburg Univ., 1963; Prof., Regensburg Univ. (tenure), 1969.

Previous Post European co-ordinator of subject group 'Forest Hist.', Internat. Union of Forest Research Organization, 1990–5 congress period.

Current Offices and Honorary Posts Fellow, Forest Hist. Soc., Durham, N.C., USA, 1985; corresponding mem., French Acad. of Agric., 1988.

Major Honours Heinrich Cotta Medal, Tharandt Forestry College, 1991; French Forest Law Medal, 1979.

Fields of Expertise *Industry Fields:* agric., forestry, fishing. *Bus. Dimensions:* entrepreneurs and entre-

preneurship. *Scope:* internat. *Period:* twentieth century as a whole. *Consultancy:* biography; currently: Bavarian Dept. of Agriculture (biographies of important German foresters:1870/1970).

Publications *Books: Forest Hist. in the Age of Industrial Revolution*, Duncker & Humblot, Berlin, 1967; *Adolph Wagner: Letters, Documents and Oral Reports, 1851–1917*, Duncker & Humblot, West Berlin, 1978; *German Hist. of Forestry, 1933–1945*, Scripta Mercaturae, D-W-6551 St. Katharinen, 1985. *Articles:* 'The French Forest Régime during the Middle Ages', *Beiheft Vierteljahrschrift für Sozial- und Wirtschaftsgeschichte*, Steiner, Wiesbaden, 1965; 'Forty Years of Forest Polit. and Forest Economy in the GDR 1949–1989', *Compte Rendu de l'Académie d'Agriculture Française*, 79, 1990, 59–65.

Rugman, Alan M.

Prof. of Internat. Bus., Fac. of Management, Univ. of Toronto, 246 Bloor St West, Toronto, Ontario, M5S 1V4, Canada. Tel.: 1 416 978 4063. Fax: 1 416 928 6694.

Year and Place of Birth 1945, Bristol, UK.

Degrees and Qualifications BA (Econ.) Leeds Univ., 1966; M.Sc. (Econ.) London Univ.; Ph.D. (Econ.) Simon Fraser Univ., 1974.

Previous Post Research Dir., Ontario Center for Internat. Bus., 1989–92.

Current Offices and Honorary Posts Fellow, Acad. of Internat. Bus., (V-P, 1989); pres., N. Amer. Econ. & Finance Assoc., 1984.

Fields of Expertise *Industry Fields:* timber, furniture. *Bus. Dimensions:* multinational bus. *Scope:* global; Canada. *Period:* late twentieth century, 1970–present. *Teaching:* post grad.

Ryant

Consultancy: corporate strategy.

Publications *Books: Multinationals in Canada: Theory, Performance and Econ. Impact*, Martinus Nijhoff, Boston, 1980, reprinted 1983; *Inside the Multinationals: The Econ. of Internal Markets*, Croom Helm, London/Columbia Univ. Press, New York, 1981, translated into Japanese; *Administered Protection in Amer.*, with Andrew Anderson, Croom Helm, London/St Martin's Press, New York, 1985; *Multinationals and Canada-United States Free Trade*, Univ. of South Carolina Press, Columbia, 1990; *Research in Global Strategic Management: Volume IV: Beyond the Three Generics*, Alain Verbeke co-ed., JAI Press, Greenwich, Conn., 1993.

Ryant, Carl G.

Prof. of Hist., Dept. of Hist., Univ. of Louisville, Louisville, KY 40292, USA. Tel.: 1 502 588 6817. Fax: 1 502 588 0770.

Year and Place of Birth 1942, Cleveland, Ohio, USA.

Degrees and Qualifications BA Case Western Reserve Univ., 1964; MA Wisconsin Univ., 1965; Ph.D. Wisconsin Univ., 1968.

Current Offices and Honorary Posts Chair, Internat. Com., Oral Hist. Assoc. (USA).

Fields of Expertise *Industry Fields:* food, drink, tobacco; distributive trades; insurance, banking, finance. *Bus. Dimensions:* entrepreneurs and entrepreneurship; marketing; co. culture. *Scope:* local; regional; national; internat.; UK; USA. *Period:* twentieth century as a whole. *Teaching:* undergrad.; post grad. *Consultancy:* co. hist.

Publications *Books: Profit's Prophet: Garet Garrett, 1878–1954*, Assoc. Univ. Presses, 1989; *Insuring the Future: The Holyoke Mutual Insurance Company in Salem, 1843–1993*, with

John J. Fox, Tapestry Press, 1993. *Articles:* 'Oral Hist. and Bus. Hist.', *J. of Amer. Hist.*, 75, Sept., 1988, 560–66; 'The Public Historian and Bus. Hist.', *Ethics and the Use of Hist.*, Theodore Karamanski ed., Kreiger, 1990.

Saalfeld, Diedrich

Retired. Gehrenring 17, D-37085 Göttingen, Germany. Tel.: 49 551 794 695.

Year and Place of Birth 1927, Hengsterholz, Germany.

Degrees and Qualifications Dip. in Agric. Sc. Göttingen Univ., 1953; Dr.sc.agr. Göttingen Univ., 1957; Dr.rer.pol.habil. Göttingen Univ., 1979.

Previous Post Prof. for Agric. Science, Göttingen Univ. until 1992.

Current Offices and Honorary Posts Mem., Econ. Hist. Branch of the Assoc. for Econ. & Social Sciences, (Germany); mem., Hist. Commission for Lower Saxony, (Hanover); mem., Internat. Union of Agric. Museums.

Fields of Expertise *Industry Fields:* food, drink, tobacco; agric. *Bus. Dimensions:* production management. *Scope:* national; internat.; Germany; Europe. *Period:* early modern; eighteenth century. *Teaching:* post grad.

Publications *Books: Bauernwirtschaft und Gutsbetrieb in der vorindustriellen Zeit*, Quellen und Forschungen zur Agrargeschichte, vol. 6, G. Franz, 1960. *Articles:* 'Handwerkereinkommen in Deutschland vom ausgehenden 18. bis zur Mitte des 19. Jahrhunderts', *Göttinger Beitrag zur Wirtschafts- und Sozialgeschichte 1*, W. Abel & K.H. Kaufhold eds., 1978, 65–120; 'Die ständ. Gliederung d. Ges. Deutschlands im Zeitalter d. Absolutismus. Ein Quantifizierungsversuch', *Vierteljahrschrift für sozial- und wirtschaftliche Geschichte*, 67, 1980, 457–83; 'German Peasantry on the Eve

232

of the French Revolution', *Hist. of European Ideas*, March, 1990, 351–62; 'Wandlungen der bäuerlichen Konsumgewohnheiten vom Mittelalter zur Neuzeit', *Essen und Trinken in Mittelalter und Neuzeit*, X. von Ertzdorff ed., 1990, 59–75.

Preußens vor 1850, with Karl Heinrisch Kaufhold ed., St Katharinen, 1989. *Articles*: 'Familienunternehmen in Wirtschaft und Gesellschaft bis zur Mitte des 20. Jahrhunderts', *Zeitschrift für Unternehmensgeschichte*, 36(1), 1991, 9–25.

Sachse, Wieland

Wissenschaftlicher Assistent, Inst. of Econ. and Social Hist., Göttingen Univ., Platz der Göttinger Sieben 3, D-37073 Göttingen, Germany. Tel.: 49 551 397236.
Year and Place of Birth 1952, Hanover, Germany.
Degrees and Qualifications Dr.phil. Göttingen Univ., 1987.
Current Offices and Honorary Posts Director, Assoc. for Econ. & Social Hist., Niedersachsen, 1986–.
Major Honours Mem., Hist. Commission for Niedersachsen & Bremen since 1983.
Fields of Expertise *Industry Fields:* mining and quarrying; coal and petroleum products; chemicals and allied industries; metal manufacture; mechanical engineering; instrument engineering; textiles; leather; clothing and footwear; miscellaneous services. *Bus. Dimensions:* entrepreneurs and entrepreneurship; personnel management-family enterprises. *Scope:* local; regional; national; internat.; Germany. *Period:* early modern; eighteenth century; nineteenth century; twentieth century as a whole. *Teaching:* undergrad.; post grad. *Consultancy:* co. hist.; corporate strategy.
Publications *Books: Bibliographie der preußischen Gewerbestatistik 1750–1850*, Göttingen, 1981; *Joachim Friedrich Markus und die deutsche Arbeiterbewegung 1806–1877*, with John Brailly, Göttingen, 1984; *Göttingen im 18. und 19. Jahrhundert*, Göttingen, 1987; *Gewerbestatistik*

Saito, Takenori

Prof. of Bus. Management, Fac. of Econ. and Bus. Admin., Yokahama City Univ., 22–2 Seto, Kanazawa-ku, Yokohama City, Japan. Tel.: 045 788 2105.
Year and Place of Birth 1942, Tokyo, Japan.
Degrees and Qualifications B.Com. Waseda Univ., 1966; M.Com. Waseda Univ., 1968; Ph.D.Com. Waseda Univ., 1987.
Current Offices and Honorary Posts Exec. com. mem., Bus. Hist. Soc. of Japan.
Major Honours Nippon Office Management Assoc. Prize.
Fields of Expertise *Industry Fields:* professional and scientific services. *Bus. Dimensions:* personnel management; co. admin.; bus. organization; management education. *Scope:* national. *Period:* twentieth century as a whole. *Teaching:* undergrad.; post grad.
Publications *Books: Yoichi Ueno - His Career and Personality*, Sanno Instit. of Bus. Admin., 1983; *Yoichi Ueno and the Pioneers of Management Theory*, Sanno Instit. of Bus. Admin., 1985.

Saito, Tomoaki

Prof. of Bus. Hist., Fac. of Management, Tokyo Univ. of Science, 500 Shimokiyoku kuki, Saitama 346, Japan. Tel.: 81 480 21 7618. Fax: 81

480 21 7613.

Year and Place of Birth 1948, Tokyo, Japan.

Degrees and Qualifications BA Seijyo Univ., 1972; MA Hitotsubashi Univ., 1977.

Previous Post Assoc. Prof. of Management, Kogabui Univ.

Current Offices and Honorary Posts Council mem., Japan Bus. Hist. Soc.

Fields of Expertise *Industry Fields:* coal and petroleum products; transport and communication; distributive trades; insurance, banking, finance; security; brokerage. *Bus. Dimensions:* co. finance and accounting; co. admin.; marketing; strategy formation; merger movement and issues; bus. organization; multinational bus.; bus.–state relations; markets and bus.; bus. values; co. culture. *Scope:* national; internat.; global. *Period:* early twentieth century; inter-war years, 1919–39; mid-twentieth century, 1940–70; late twentieth century, 1970–present. *Teaching:* undergrad. *Consultancy:* co. hist.

Publications *Books: Sengo Nihon Keieishi (2)* [Bus. Hist. of Japan after World War II, Vol. II], co-auth., Toyo-keizai-shinpo-sha, 1990; *Keieisha kigyo no Jidai* [The Era of Managerial Bus.], co-auth., Yuhikaku, 1991; *Sengo keieishi Nyumon* [Introduction of Japanese Bus. Hist. after World War II], co-auth., Nihon-keizai-shinbun-sha, 1992.

Sakamoto, Takuji

Prof. of Bus. Hist., Fac. of Econ., Kobe-Gakuin Univ., 518 Arise, Ikawadani, Nishi-ku, Kobe 651-21, Japan. Tel.: 81 78 974 1551. Fax: 81 78 795 7346.

Year and Place of Birth 1944, Fukuoka Pref., Japan.

Degrees and Qualifications BA Yokohama National Univ., 1969; MA Hitotsubashi Univ., 1972.

Previous Post Prof. of Bus. Hist., Himeji-Dokkyo Univ., 1989–93.

Current Offices and Honorary Posts Bus. Hist. Soc. of Japan: sec, 1979–83; council mem., 1983–7; exec. com. mem., 1989–92; chairman, internat. com., 1993–.

Fields of Expertise *Industry Fields:* mechanical engineering; electrical engineering; shipbuilding and marine engineering; gas, electricity, water; transport and communication; public admin. and defence; electronics and computers: manufacture. *Bus. Dimensions:* entrepreneurs and entrepreneurship; production management; co. finance and accounting; co. admin.; marketing; research and development; strategy formation; merger movement and issues; bus. organization; bus. and technology; multinational bus.; bus.–state relations; markets and bus.; co. culture. *Scope:* regional; national; internat. *Period:* nineteenth century; twentieth century as a whole. *Teaching:* undergrad.; post grad. *Consultancy:* corporate strategy.

Publications *Books: Igirisu denryoku sangyo no seisei hatten to denki jigyoho no hensen* [The Formation and Development of the British Electricity Industry and Changes in Legislation], Nagasaki Univ., ser. no. 19, 1983. *Articles:* 'GEC no keiei senryaku to hatten katei' [The Strategy and Development of GEC], *Japan Bus. Hist. Rev.*, 13(3), 1979; 'Technology and Bus. in the British Electrical Industry 1880–1914', *Development and Diffusion of Technology*, A. Okochi & H. Uchida eds., Univ. of Tokyo, 1980; 'Dai Ichi lji taisenzen niokeru Ferranti sha no tenkaikatei' [De Ferranti and his co. before World War II], *Econoinformatics Rev.*, 1, Himeji Dokkyo Univ., 1991; 'Dai lji taisenzen niokeru eibei denki kogyo no hikakukosatsu' [Comparative Study of British and Amer. Electrical Industries before World War I], *Kikaikogyo* *niokeru shingijutsu no kaihatsu to donyu* [Development and Introduction of New Technologies in the Mechanical Engineering Industry], Y. Takeoka et al. eds., Dobunkan, 1993.

Sakudo, Jun

Assoc. Prof., Fac. of Econ., Kobe Gakuin Univ., Arise, Igawadani-cho, Nishi-ku, Kobe-shi, Hyogo 651-21, Japan. Tel.: 81 78 974 1551. Fax: 81 78 974 5689.

Year and Place of Birth 1953, Osaka, Japan.

Degrees and Qualifications MA (Econ.) Kobe Univ., 1978; DEA, Paris X Univ., 1985.

Current Offices and Honorary Posts Sec., com. mem of internat. relations of Fuji conf.; com. mem of Bus. Hist. Soc. of Japan.

Fields of Expertise *Industry Fields:* chemicals and allied industries; textiles. *Bus. Dimensions:* entrepreneurs and entrepreneurship; personnel management; co. law; co. admin.; research and development; strategy formation; merger movement and issues; bus. organization; bus. and technology; multinational bus.; management education; bus.–state relations; markets and bus. *Scope:* internat. *Period:* nineteenth century; early twentieth century; inter-war years, 1919–39. *Teaching:* undergrad.

Publications *Articles:* '19 seiki Furansu niokeru kabushiki kaisya no hatten (1807–1867) I, II' [The Development of the Joint-stock Co. in Nineteenth Century France, 1807–1867, I & II], *Kobe-Gakuin Econ. Papers*, 12(3), 1980, 45–88, 13(1.2), 1981, 159–206; 'Daiichiji Taisen Zenya no Fransu Kaglen - Kogyo' [The French Chemical Industry on the Eve of the First World War], *Kobe-Gakuin Econ. Papers*, 19(2.3), 221–43, 19(4), 261–81, 20(2), 205–22,

20(3), 265–84, 1987–88; '19 Seiki kohan kara Daiichiji Taisenki no Furansu Yukikagaku-kogyo' [France's Organic Chemical Industry from the Second Half of the 19th Century to the First World War], *Japan Bus. Hist. Rev.*, 24(2), 1989, 1–32; '19 seiki Furansu niokeru Kigyosha-katsudo no syotokucho' [Some Aspects of French Entrepreneurship in the Nineteenth Century], *Japan Bus. Hist. Rev.*, 25(4), 1991, 29–58; '19 seiki kohan kara Daiichiji Taisen ki no Furansu Seiyaku-Sangyo' [The French Pharmaceutical Industry from the Second Half of the Nineteenth Century to the First World War], *Kobe Gakuin Econ. Papers*, 23(4), 1992, 67–93.

Sampson, Cezley

Director, Mona Inst. of Bus., Univ. of the West Indies, Mona, Kingston 7, Jamaica. Tel.: 1 809 92 72775. Fax: 1 809 92 77147.

Year and Place of Birth 1939, Annotto Bay, Jamaica.

Degrees and Qualifications HND (Bus. Studies) Welsh Inst. of Science & Technology, 1965; Cert. Eng. Management College of Aeronautics, Bedford, 1966; MA (Marketing) Lancaster Univ., 1967.

Previous Post Special advisor to the Deputy Prime Minister, Jamaica, 1989–91.

Current Offices and Honorary Posts Chairman, Jamaica Inst. of Management Fellows Board.

Fields of Expertise *Industry Fields:* transport and communication. *Bus. Dimensions:* competition, privatization and utility regulation. *Scope:* regional. *Period:* nineteenth century. *Teaching:* post grad. *Consultancy:* corporate strategy.

Publications *Articles:* 'Institution Building for Transport Development with Special Reference to Jamaica',

Third World Planning Rev., vol. 2, Liverpool Univ. Press, 1979; 'Regulation, Institutions and Commitment. The Jamaica Telecommunication Sector', , with Pablo T. Spiller, prepared for the World Bank, June, 1992; 'Strategic Marketing Cases in a Developing Country', forthcoming, 1993.

Sanchez Suarez, Alejandro

Prof. Titular, Fac. of Econ. Sciences, Dept. of Econ. Hist., Univ. of Barcelona, Avda. Diagonal 690, 08034-Barcelona, Spain. Tel.: 34 93 4021930. Fax: 34 93 2802378.
Year and Place of Birth 1953, Barcelona, Spain.
Degrees and Qualifications Licenciado (Mod. Hist.) Barcelona Univ., 1981; Doctorado (Econ. Hist.) Barcelona Univ., 1987.
Previous Post Prof. of Contemporary Hist., Lleida Univ., 1981–9.
Current Offices and Honorary Posts Sec., *Revista de Historia Industrial*; mem., Asociacion de Historia Economica de España.
Fields of Expertise *Industry Fields:* textiles. *Bus. Dimensions:* entrepreneurs and entrepreneurship; bus. and technology. *Scope:* local; regional. *Period:* eighteenth century; nineteenth century. *Consultancy:* co. hist.
Publications *Books: La Formacion de una Politica Economica prohibicionista en Cataluña, 1760–1840*, Espoi i Temps, 1988; *Proteccion, Orden y Libertad. El Pensamiento y la Politica Economica de la Comision de Fabricas de Barcelona (1820–1840)*, Altafulla, 1990. *Articles:* Los Inicios del Asociacionismo empresarial en España. La Cia. de Nicados de Algodon de Barcelona', *Hacienda Publica Española*, 1987, 108–9; 'La Era de la Manufactura Algodonera en

Barcelona, 1736–1839', *Estudios de Historia Social*, 1989, 48–9; 'L'Estructura comercial d'una Fabrica d'Indianes Barcelonina: Joan Rull y Cia (1790–1921)', *Recerques*, 22, 1989.

Sandgruber, Roman

Prof., Inst. of Social and Econ. Hist., Johannes Kepler Univ., 4040 Linz-Auhof, Austria. Tel.: 43 732 2468 844. Fax: 43 732 246810.
Year and Place of Birth 1947, Rohrback, Austria.
Degrees and Qualifications Dr.phil., 1971.
Previous Post Univ. Doz., Inst. of Econ. & Social Hist., Vienna Univ., 1972–88.
Fields of Expertise *Industry Fields:* agric., forestry, fishing; mining and quarrying; food, drink, tobacco; metal manufacture; transport and communication. *Bus. Dimensions:* entrepreneurs and entrepreneurship. *Scope:* national. *Period:* early modern; eighteenth century; nineteenth century; twentieth century as a whole. *Teaching:* undergrad.; post grad.
Publications *Books: Österreichische Agrarstatistik 1750–1918. Wirtschafts- und Sozialstatistik Österreich-Ungarns 2*, A. Hoffman & H. Matis, Vienna, 1978; *Die Anfänge der Konsumgesellschaft. Lebensstandard, Konsumgüterverbrauch und Alltagskultur in Österreich im 18. und 19. Jahrhundert*, Vienna, 1982; *Bittersüße Genüsse. Kulturgeschichte der Genußmittel*, Vienna, 1986; *Strom der Zeit. Das Jahrhundert der Elektrizität*, Linz, 1992. *Articles:* 'Österreich 1650–1850', *Handbuch der europäischen Wirtschafts- und Sozialgeschichte, Bd. 4, Europäische Wirtschafts- und Sozialgeschichte von der Mitte des 17. Jahrhunderts bis zur Mitte des 19. Jahrhunderts*, Ilja Mieck,

Stuttgart, 1993, 619–87.

Sapelli, Giulio

Fondazione ASSI, Corso di Porta Romana 57 6, 20122 Milan, Fondazione Feltrinelli, via Romagnosi 3, 20121 Milan, Italy. Tel.: Fondazione ASSI: 39 2 .55191679; Fondazione Feltrinelli: 39 2 874175. Fax: Fondazione ASSI: 39 2 55191683; Fondazione Feltrinelli: 39 2 86461855.
Year and Place of Birth 1947, Turin, Italy.
Degrees and Qualifications Professore Ordinario.
Previous Post The Goubelkian Foundation, Lisbon, 1991.
Current Offices and Honorary Posts Scientific Director, Fondazione Feltrinelli, 1981–; pres., Fondazione ASSI di Storia e Studi sull'Impresa, 1983–; steering com. mem., Fondazione Olivetti; steering com. mem., Scientific Com. of the Ministry of Labour.
Major Honours Scanno Prize for best publication on industrial relationships, 1983.
Fields of Expertise *Industry Fields:* coal and petroleum products; vehicle construction; construction; gas, electricity, water; insurance, banking, finance; nuclear engineering: manufacture. *Bus. Dimensions:* entrepreneurs and entrepreneurship; bus. organization; bus. and technology; small bus. matters; management education; bus.–state relations; bus. values; co. culture. *Scope:* local; national; internat.; global. *Period:* eighteenth century; nineteenth century; twentieth century as a whole. *Teaching:* post grad.
Publications *Articles:* 'A Hist. Typology of Group Enterprises: The Debate on the Decline of Popular Sovereignty', *Regulating Corporate Groups in Europe*, D. Sugarmon & G. Teubner eds., Nemas Verlag-

gesellschaft, Baden, 1990; 'Netzwerke, Kulturen, Betrieb', *Netzwerk Dimensionen. Kulturelle Konfigurationen und Management Perspektiven*, J. Ehrhardt ed., Bergheim, 1992, 86–105; 'Technical Change. Microeconomic Evolution and Growth: An Introductory View of Italian Industrial Development', *Technology and Enterprise in a Hist. Perspective*, G. Dosi, R. Giannetti & P.A. Toninelli eds., Clarendon Press, Oxford, 1992, 291–313; 'The Evolution of the Strategy and Structure of a State owned Co.: The Case of AGIP Petroli S.p.A. 1960–1990', *Bus. & Econ. Hist.*, with L. Orsenigo & P.A.Toninelli, 2nd ser., 21, 1992, 129–37.

Sasaki, Satoshi

Lect., School of Admin. & Informatics, Univ. of Shizuoka, 52–7 Yada, Shizuoka-shi, Shizuoka-ken 422, Japan. Tel.: 054 264 5421/054 264 5449. Fax: 054 264 5446.
Year and Place of Birth 1957, Aomori, Japan.
Degrees and Qualifications MA Meiji Univ., Grad. School.
Fields of Expertise *Industry Fields:* mechanical engineering; electrical engineering; shipbuilding and marine engineering; vehicle construction; textiles; construction. *Bus. Dimensions:* production management; co. admin.; marketing; bus. and technology; management education. *Scope:* national; internat. *Period:* nineteenth century; twentieth century as a whole. *Teaching:* undergrad.
Publications *Articles:* 'On Materials of Scientific Management in Japan in the Meiji-Taisyo Era', *Japan Bus. Hist. Rev.*, 21(1), Univ. of Tokyo Press, April, 1986; 'Scientific Management Movements in pre-War Japan', *Japanese Yearbook on Bus. Hist.*, 4,

Aug., 1987; 'An Aspect of Scientific Management during the Pacific War', *Admin. and Informatics*, 4(1), Univ. of Shizuoka, Jan., 1992; 'The Introduction of Scientific Management by Mitsubishi Electric Engineering Co. and the Formation of an organized Scientific Management in Japan in the 1920s', *Bus. Hist.*, 34(2), April, 1992; 'An Endeavour to Rationalize the Production Management System in Japan during World War II: A Case Study of the Nakajima Aircraft Co., Musashino Works', *Japan Bus. Hist. Rev.*, 27(3), Univ. of Tokyo Press, Oct., 1992.

Saunders Jr., Richard

Assoc. Prof. of Hist., Dept. of Hist., Clemson Univ., Hardin Hall, Clemson, SC 29634, USA. Tel.: 1 803 656 5373.

Year and Place of Birth 1940, Buffalo, NY, USA.

Degrees and Qualifications BA Northwestern Univ., 1962; Ph.D. Univ. of Illinois at Urbana, 1971.

Fields of Expertise *Industry Fields:* transport and communication. *Bus. Dimensions:* co. finance and accounting; co. admin.; merger movement and issues; bus. and technology; bus.–state relations; co. culture. *Scope:* national. *Period:* inter-war years, 1919–39; mid-twentieth century, 1940–70; late twentieth century, 1970–present. *Teaching:* undergrad.; post grad.

Publications *Books: The Railroad Mergers and the Coming of Conrail*, Greenwood Press, Westport, CT, 1978.

Savage, Deborah A.

Lect. in Econ., The Univ. of Connecticut at Avery Point, 97 Bridge St, Willimantic, CT 06226-3201, USA. Tel.: 1 203 456 4180. Fax: 1 203

4864463.

Year and Place of Birth 1953, Everett, USA.

Degrees and Qualifications BS (Econ.) George Mason Univ., 1982; MA (Econ.) Connecticut Univ., 1984; Ph.D. (Econ.) Connecticut Univ., 1993.

Previous Post Visiting Instructor, Connecticut College, New London, Connecticut, Jan., 1990 to June 1991.

Fields of Expertise *Industry Fields:* bus. services; professional and scientific services; miscellaneous services; history of the professions. *Bus. Dimensions:* bus. organization; bus. and technology; small bus. matters; markets and bus. *Scope:* national. *Period:* eighteenth century; nineteenth century; twentieth century as a whole. *Teaching:* undergrad. *Consultancy:* co. hist.

Publications *Articles:* 'Change and Response: An Essay on the Hist. of the Pharmacy Profession', *Working Paper 91–9901*, Dept. of Econ., Univ. of Connecticut, Nov., 1991; 'An Econ. Theory of Professions', *Working Paper 93–991*, Dept. of Econ., Univ. of Connecticut, Feb., 1993.

Sawai, Minoru

Assoc. Prof., Fac. of Econ., Osaka Univ., 1-1 Machikaneyama, Toyonaka, Osaka, Japan. Tel.: 06 844 1151. Fax: 06 841 6631.

Year and Place of Birth 1953, Wakayama pref., Japan.

Degrees and Qualifications BA Internat. Christian Univ., 1978.

Previous Post Assoc. Prof., Fac. of Econ., Hokusei Gakuen Univ., 1988–91.

Fields of Expertise *Industry Fields:* mechanical engineering; instrument engineering; vehicle construction. *Bus. Dimensions:* entrepreneurs and entrepreneurship; production management; co. finance and accounting; personnel management; research and development; bus. and technology; labour relations. *Scope:* regional; national. *Period:* early twentieth century; interwar years, 1919–39; mid-twentieth century, 1940–70. *Teaching:* undergrad.; post grad.

Publications *Articles:* 'The Development of Machine Industries and the Evolution of Production and Labor Management', *Japanese Management in Hist. Perspective*, Tsunehiko Yui & Keiichiro Nakagawa eds., Univ. of Tokyo Press, 1989, 199–236; 'Tetsudo sharyo kogyo to Manshu Shijo' [The Rolling Stock Industry and the Manchurian Market, 1930–7], *Senkanki Nippon no Taigai Keizai Kankei* [Foreign Relations of the Japanese Economy between the Wars], Kaichiro Oishi ed., Nihon Keizai Hyoronsha, 1992, 132–70; 'Kagaku Gijustu Shintaisei koso no Tenkai to Gijutsu-In no Tanjo' [The New Order of Science and Technology and the Establishment of Gijutsu-In (Agency of Technology)], *Osaka Econ. Papers*, 41(2.3), 1992, 367–95; 'Senji Keizai to Zaibatsu' [Wartime Economy and Zaibatsu], *Nihon Keizai no Hatten to kigyo Shudan* [The Development of the Japanese Economy and the Corporate Groupings], Juro Hashimoto & Haruto Takeda eds., Univ. of Tokyo Press, 1992, 149–202.

Scheiber, Harry N.

Riesenfeld Prof. of Law Hist., School of Law, Univ. of California, Boalt Hall, Berkeley, CA 94720-2499, USA. Tel.: 1 510 642 4038. Fax: 1 510 642 2951.
Year and Place of Birth 1935, USA.
Degrees and Qualifications BA Columbia Univ., 1955; MA Cornell Univ., 1957; Ph.D. Cornell Univ., 1962.
Previous Post Prof. of Hist., Univ. of California, San Diego, 1971–80.

Current Offices and Honorary Posts Pres., Agric. Hist. Soc.
Major Honours Guggenheim Fellow, 1970–1 & 1988–9; Fulbright Distinguished Sen. Lect. to Australia, 1983.
Fields of Expertise *Bus. Dimensions:* entrepreneurs and entrepreneurship; bus. and technology.
Publications *Books: Ohio Canal Era: A Case Study of Government and the Economy, 1820–1861*, Ohio Univ. Press, Athens, Ohio, 2nd. edn., 1987; *Power Divided: Essays on the Theory and Practice of Federalism*, with M. Feeley co-ed., Inst. of Governmental Studies Press, UC Berkeley, 1989. *Articles:* 'Occupation Policy and Econ. Planning in Postwar Japan', *Econ. Planning in the Post-1945 Period*, E. Aerts & A. Milward eds., Univ. of Leuven Press, Belgium, 1990, 100–9; 'The New Deal and the Constitution', *Encyclopaedia of the Amer. Constitution*, Suppl., Macmillan, NY, 1993; 'Race Radicalism and Reform: Hist. Perspectives on the 1879 California Constitution', *Hastings Consitutional Law Q.*, 17, 1989.

Schmitz, Christopher J.

Lect. in Econ. Hist., Dept. of Modern Hist., Univ. of St. Andrews, St. Andrews, Fife, KY16 9AL, Scotland, UK. Tel.: 44 334 76161. Fax: 44 334 76884.
Year and Place of Birth 1950, London, UK.
Degrees and Qualifications BA Exeter Univ., 1972.
Previous Post Lect. in Econ. Hist., Bath Univ., 1974–8.
Fields of Expertise *Industry Fields:* mining and quarrying; metal manufacture; insurance, banking, finance. *Bus. Dimensions:* bus. organization; bus. and technology; multinational bus.; bus.–state relations; foreign direct

Schönert-Röhlk

investment (from UK). *Scope:* national; internat.; global; USA. *Period:* nineteenth century; twentieth century as a whole. *Teaching:* undergrad.; post grad. *Consultancy:* co. hist.

Publications *Books: World non-Ferrous Metal Production and Prices, 1700–1976,* Frank Cass, 1979; *The Teign Valley Silver-Lead Mines, 1806–1880,* Northern Mine Research Soc., 1980; *Output and Employment in the New South Wales Coal Industry, 1805–1923,* Australian Reference Pubs.: Hist. Stats. No. 7, 1988; *The Growth of Big Bus. in the United States and Western Europe, 1850–1939,* Macmillan: Studies in Econ. & Soc. Hist., 1993. *Articles:* 'The Rise of Big Bus. in the World Copper Industry, 1870–1930', *Econ. Hist. Rev.,* 2nd. ser., 39, 1986, 392–410.

Schönert-Röhlk, Frauke

Akademische Oberrätin, Abt. Verfassungs-, Sozial- und Wirtschaftsgeschichte, Historisches Seminar, Konviktstr. 11, 53113 Bonn, Germany. Tel.: 49 228 735381.

Year and Place of Birth 1936, Rendsburg, Germany.

Degrees and Qualifications Dipl. Handelslehrer Cologne Univ., 1964; Dr.rer.pol. Cologne Univ., 1969.

Fields of Expertise *Industry Fields:* chemicals and allied industries; textiles. *Bus. Dimensions:* entrepreneurs and entrepreneurship; small bus. matters. *Scope:* regional; internat. *Period:* nineteenth century. *Teaching:* undergrad.

Publications *Books: Schiffahrt und Handel zwischen Hamburg und den Niederlanden in der zweiten Hälfte des 18. und zu Beginn des 19. Jahrhunderts,* 2 vols., Steiner Verlag, 1973; *Die chemische Industrie in den Rheinlanden während der industriellen Revolution. Vol. I: Die Farben-*

industrie, with Hans Pohl & Ralf Schaumann, Steiner Verlag, 1983. *Articles:* 'Die räumliche Verteilung der chemischen Industrie im 19. Jahrhundert', *Gewerbe- und Industrielandschaften vom Spätmittelalter bis ins 20. Jahrhundert,* Hans Pohl ed., Steiner Verlag, 1986.

Schröter, Harm G.

Lect., Free Univ. of Berlin, Inst. of Econ. Polit. and Hist., Hittorfstr. 2–4, D14195 Berlin, Germany. Tel.: 49 30 8383620. Fax: 49 30 838 2140.

Year and Place of Birth 1948, Hamburg, Germany.

Degrees and Qualifications 1st Erstes Staatsexamen Hamburg Univ., 1976; 2nd Erstes Staatsexamen Hamburg Univ., 1981; Ph.D. Hamburg Univ., 1981; Habilitation Berlin Free Univ., 1992.

Previous Post Asst., Berlin Free Univ., 1985–91.

Current Offices and Honorary Posts Scientific employee, Berlin Free Univ.

Fields of Expertise *Industry Fields:* chemicals and allied industries; electrical engineering. *Bus. Dimensions:* entrepreneurs and entrepreneurship; research and development; strategy formation; merger movement and issues; multinational bus. *Scope:* national; internat. *Period:* nineteenth century; twentieth century as a whole. *Teaching:* post grad.

Publications *Books: Außenpolitik und Wirtschaftsinteresse. Skandinavien im außenwirtschaftlichen Kalkül Deutschlands und Großbritanniens 1918–1939,* P. Lan, 1983; *Politik, Wirtschaft und internazionale Beziehungen, Studien zu ihrem Verhältnis in der Zeit zwischen den Weltkriegen,* co-ed., Ph. v. Zabern, 1991; *The Rise of Multinationals in Continental Europe,* co-ed., Edward Elgar, 1993; *Aufstieg der Kleinen,*

Multinationale Unternehmen aus 5 kleinen Staaten bis 1914, Duncker & Humblot, 1993.

Schuler, Peter-Johannes

apl. Prof. Ruhr-Bochum Univ; Thüringer Allee 131, D-53757 St. Augustin 2, Germany.
Place of Birth Germany.
Degrees and Qualifications Dr.phil., 1972; Habilitation, 1982.
Previous Post Secretary of State, Ministry of Culture, Thürigen, 1991.
Current Offices and Honorary Posts Mem., Kuratorium für Vergleichende Städtegeschichte in Münster.
Fields of Expertise *Industry Fields:* insurance, banking, finance; professional and scientific services; public admin. *Bus. Dimensions:* personnel management; co. admin.; management education. *Scope:* regional; national. *Period:* medieval. *Teaching:* post grad. *Consultancy:* co. hist.
Publications *Books: Südwestdeutsche Notarszeichen,* 1972; *Geschichte des Südwestdeutschen Notariats. Von seinen Anfängen bis zur Reichsnotariatsordnung von 1512,* 1976; *Familie als historischer and sozialer Verband,* 1988; *Grundbibliographie zur mittelalterlichen Geschichte,* 1990.

Schulz, Günther

Prof. of Econ. & Social Hist., Seminar für Wirtschafts- und Sozialgeschichte, Cologne Univ., Albertus-Magnus-Platz, D-50931 Cologne, Germany. Tel.: 49 221 4704274.
Year and Place of Birth 1950, Morsbach/Sieg, Germany.
Degrees and Qualifications Erstes Staatsexamen Bonn Univ., 1974; Dr.phil. Bonn Univ., 1977;

Privatdozent Bonn Univ., 1990; Univ. Prof. of Econ. & Social Hist., Cologne, 1992.
Previous Post Privatdozent, Bonn, 1990–2; Gastdozent, Dresden, 1991.
Fields of Expertise *Industry Fields:* metal goods; distributive trades. *Bus. Dimensions:* entrepreneurs and entrepreneurship; personnel management; bus.–state relations; co. culture. *Scope:* regional; national. *Period:* nineteenth century; twentieth century as a whole. *Teaching:* undergrad.; post grad. *Consultancy:* co. hist.
Publications *Books: Die Arbeiter und Angestellten bei Felten & Guilleaume. Sozialgeschichtliche Untersuchung eines Kölner Industrieunternehmens im 19. und beginnenden 20. Jahrhundert,* Steiner-Verlag, Wiesbaden, 1979; *Wiederaufbau in Deutschland. Die Wohnungspolitik in den Westzonen und der Bundesrepublik Deutschland 1945–1957,* Droste-Verlag, Düsseldorf, 1993. *Articles:* 'Die industriellen Angestellten. Zum Wandel einer sozialen Gruppe im Industrialisierungsprozeß', *Sozialgeschichtliche Probleme in der Zeit der Hochindustrialisierung,* Hans Pohl ed., Schöning-Verlag, Paderborn, 1979; 'Industrial Patriarchalism in Germany', *Liberalism and Paternalism in the 19th Century,* E. Aerts, C. Beaud & J. Stengers eds., Leuven Univ. Press, 1990; 'Betriebliche Sozialpolitik seit der Mitte des 19. Jahrhunderts', *Staatliche, städtische, betriebliche and kirchliche Sozialpolitik,* Hans Pohl ed., Steiner-Verlag, Stuttgart, 1991.

Schvarzer, Jorge

Researcher, CISEA, Dragones 2486, (1428) Buenos Aires, Argentina. Tel.: 01 781-7077/01 781 790. Fax: 01 781-0387.
Year and Place of Birth 1938,

Buenos Aires, Argentina.
Degrees and Qualifications Ing. Univ. of Buenos Aires, 1962; Director, CISEA, 1983–91.
Current Offices and Honorary Posts Edit. board, LARR (Latin Amer. Research Rev.); advisory board, FLCSO (Facultad Latinoamericana de Ciencias Sociales); director, CLACSO (Consegno Latinoamericano di Ciencias Sociales).
Fields of Expertise *Industry Fields:* food, drink, tobacco; vehicle construction. *Bus. Dimensions:* entrepreneurs and entrepreneurship; bus. organization; multinational bus. *Scope:* national; Argentina. *Period:* twentieth century as a whole. *Consultancy:* corporate strategy.
Publications *Books: La Politica Económica de Martinez de Hoz*, Editorial Hyspanierica, Buenos Aires, 1986; *Un Modelo sin Retorno*, Ediciones CISEA, Buenos Aires, 1989. *Articles:* 'Empresarios del Pasado. La Union Industrial Argentina', Imago Mundi ed., Buenos Aires, 1991.

Schybergson, Per

Sen. Lect. in Econ. & Social Hist., Dept. of Econ. & Social Hist., Helsinki Univ., SF-00014, POB 33, Helsinki, Finland. Tel.: 358 1912542. Fax: 358 01912180.
Year and Place of Birth 1933, Turku, Finland.
Degrees and Qualifications Dr.phil. (Hist.) Åbo Akademi, 1973.
Previous Post Asst. Prof., Helsinki Univ., 1989–92.
Current Offices and Honorary Posts Pres., Finnish Econ. Hist. Soc.
Fields of Expertise *Industry Fields:* food, drink, tobacco; chemicals and allied industries; mechanical engineering; instrument engineering; shipbuilding and marine engineering; textiles; leather; bricks, pottery, glass, cement;

timber, furniture; paper, printing, publishing. *Bus. Dimensions:* entrepreneurs and entrepreneurship; co. finance and accounting; co. admin.; bus. organization; co. culture; boardroom issues. *Scope:* national. *Period:* nineteenth century; twentieth century as a whole. *Teaching:* undergrad. *Consultancy:* co. hist.
Publications *Books: Aktiebolagsformens Genombrott i Finland* [The Coming of Incorporation in Finland (1762–1895)], Bidrag till Kännedom av Finlands Natur och Folk. H.109, Helsingfors, 1964; *Hantverk och Fabriker Vols. I - III* [Handicrafts and Factories. The Growth of the Consumer Goods Industry in Finland 1815–1870], Bidrag till Kännedom av Finlands Natur och Folk, H. 114, 116, 117, Helsingfors, 1973–4; *Med Rötter i Skogen. Schauman 1883–1983. Vols. I & II,* [Roots in the Forests], Helsingfors, 1983, (also in Finnish); *Verk och Dagar. Ahlströms Historia 1851–1981* [Works and Days], Helsingfors, 1992, (also in Finnish).

Scott, Roy V.

Distinguished Prof. of Hist., POB 1018, Mississippi State Univ., MS 39762, USA. Tel.: 1 601 325 7077.
Year and Place of Birth 1927, Wrights, IL, USA.
Degrees and Qualifications BS Iowa State Univ., 1952; MA Univ. of Illinois, 1953; Ph.D. Univ. of Illinois, 1957.
Fields of Expertise *Industry Fields:* transport and communication. *Bus. Dimensions:* strategy formation. *Scope:* national. *Period:* twentieth century as a whole. *Teaching:* post grad.
Publications *Books: Railroad Development Programs in the Twentieth Century*, Iowa State Univ. Press, 1985; *Great Northern Railway: A Hist.*, Harvard Bus. School Press,

1988. *Articles:* 'Sam Walton and Wal-Mart Stores, Inc.: A Study in Modern Southern Entrepreneurship', *J. of Southern Hist.*, Sandra S. Vance co-auth., 58, 1992, 231–52.

Scranton, Philip B,

Prof. of Hist., Rutgers Univ. & Director, Center for the Hist. of Bus., Technology and Soc., Hagley Museum & Library, Dept. of Hist., Rutgers Univ., Camden, NJ 08102, Hagley Museum & Library, POB 3630, Wilmington, DE 19807, USA. Tel.: Rutgers Univ.: 1 609 225 6080; Hagley Museum & Library: 1 302 658 2400. Fax: Hagley Museum & Library: 1 302 658 0568.

Year and Place of Birth 1946, New Brighton, USA.

Degrees and Qualifications BA Pennsylvania Univ., 1968; MA Pennsylvania Univ., 1971; Ph.D. Pennsylvania Univ., 1975.

Previous Post Instructor to Assoc. Prof., Hist., Philadelphia College of Textiles & Science, 1974–84.

Current Offices and Honorary Posts Edit. boards, *Bus. Hist. Rev.* & *Technology and Culture*; program com., Soc. for the Hist. of Technology, (chair, 1992–3).

Major Honours Shear Prize (for *Proprietary Capitalism*), 1984; Philip Taft Prize (for *Figured Tapestry*), 1990; Woodrow Wilson Fellow, Smithsonian Inst., 1989–90.

Fields of Expertise *Industry Fields:* metal goods; textiles; paper, printing, publishing; other manufacturing industries; clothing; furniture; jewellery; silverware. *Bus. Dimensions:* entrepreneurs and entrepreneurship; production management; marketing; bus. and technology; small bus. matters; bus.–state relations; inter-firm relations; trade associations. *Scope:* national. *Period:* nineteenth century;

twentieth century as a whole. *Teaching:* undergrad.; post grad. *Consultancy:* museums.

Publications *Books: Proprietary Capitalism*, CUP, 1983, paperback: Temple Univ. Press, 1987; *Work Sights: Philadelphia, 1890–1950*, Temple Univ. Press, 1986; *Figured Tapestry*, CUP, 1989. *Articles:* 'Diversity in Diversity', *Bus. Hist. Rev.*, 65, 1991, 27–90; 'Build a Firm, Start Another', *Bus. Hist. (UK)*, Summer, 1993, forthcoming.

Seavoy, Ronald E.

Visiting Prof., Dept. of Bus. Econ. & Public Policy, School of Bus., Indiana Univ., Bloomington, IN 47405, USA. Tel.: 1 812 855 9125.

Year and Place of Birth 1931, New York City, USA.

Degrees and Qualifications BS (Geology) Michigan Univ., 1953; MA (Hist.) Michigan Univ., 1963; Ph.D. (Hist.) Michigan Univ., 1969.

Previous Post Dept. of Bus. Econ. & Public Policy, Indiana Univ., 1992–3.

Fields of Expertise *Industry Fields:* agric., forestry, fishing; mining and quarrying. *Bus. Dimensions:* bus.–state relations. *Scope:* internat.; USA. *Period:* nineteenth century. *Teaching:* undergrad. *Consultancy:* exploration geology (base metals & industrial minerals).

Publications *Books: The Origins of the Amer. Bus. Corporation, 1784–1855: Broadening the Concept of Public Service during Industrialization*, Greenwood Press, Westport, CT, 1982. *Articles:* 'Laws to Encourage Manufacturing: New York Policy and the 1811 General Incorporation Statute', *Bus. Hist. Rev.*, 46, 1972, 85–95; 'Borrowed Laws to Speed Development: Michigan, 1835–1863', *Michigan Hist.*, 59, 1975,

38–68; 'Laissez-Faire: Bus. Policy, Corporations and Capital Investment in the Early National Period', *Encyclopedia of Amer. Polit. Hist.*, Jack P. Greene ed., 2, Scribners, New York, 1984, 728–37; 'The Constitutionalization of Laissez-Faire Bus. Policy in the United States', *Econ. & Bus. Hist.*, 9, 1991, 35–50.

Seely, Bruce E.

Assoc. Prof., Dept. of Social Sciences, Michigan Technological Univ., Houghton, MI 49931-1295, USA. Tel.: 1 906 487 2459. Fax: 1 906 487 2468.

Year and Place of Birth 1953, Chicago, USA.

Degrees and Qualifications BA (Hist.) St Lawrence Univ., 1975; MA (Hist. of Technology) Delaware Univ., 1977; Ph.D. (Hist. of Technology) Delaware Univ., 1982.

Previous Post Asst. Prof., Texas A&M Univ., 1981–6.

Current Offices and Honorary Posts Sec., Soc. for the Hist. of Technology, 1990–; trustee, Bus. Hist. Conf., 1992–; trustee, Public Works Hist. Soc., 1992–4.

Major Honours Abel Wolman Award of the Public Works Hist. Soc. & Amer. Public Works Assoc. Book Prize, 1988 for *Building the Amer. Highway System: Engineers as Policy Makers*; Abbott Payson Usher Prize, Soc. for the Hist. of Technology, 1987 for 'The Scientific Mystique in Engineering: Highway Research in the Bureau of Public Roads, 1918–1940' in *Technology & Culture*, 25, Oct., 1984; Railroad Hist. Article Award, Railway & Locomotive Hist. Soc., 1987, for 'Railroads, Good Roads and Technological Change', *Railway Hist. Bull.*, no. 155, Autumn, 1986; Norton Prize, Soc. for Indust. Archaeology, 1984 for best article in the society's

journal from 1981 to 1983, awarded for 'Blast Furnace Technology in the Nineteenth Century: A Case Study', *Industrial Archaeology*, 7, 1981, 27–54.

Fields of Expertise *Industry Fields:* transport and communication. *Bus. Dimensions:* bus.–state relations. *Scope:* national. *Period:* twentieth century as a whole. *Teaching:* undergrad. *Consultancy:* trade and professional associations.

Publications *Books: Building the Amer. Highway System: Engineers as Policy Makers*, Temple Univ. Press, 1987; *The Iron & Steel Industry in the 20th Century*, ed., in *Encyclopedia of Amer. Bus. Hist. & Biography* series, Bruccoli Clark Layman, forthcoming.

Segreto, Luciano

Sen. Lect., Ancona Univ., Fac. of Econ., Dept. of Econ. Hist. and Sociology, Via Pizzecolli 37, 60121 Ancona, Italy. Tel.: 39 71 2203967 80. Fax: 39 55 2345486.

Year and Place of Birth 1954, Glarus, Switzerland.

Degrees and Qualifications BA Florence Univ., 1981.

Current Offices and Honorary Posts Prof. of Econ. Hist., Dipartimento di Studi sullo Stato, Fac. of Polit. Sciences, Florence Univ; member of scientific board of 'Studi storici'.

Fields of Expertise *Industry Fields:* mining and quarrying; mechanical engineering; electrical engineering; gas, electricity, water; insurance, banking, finance. *Bus. Dimensions:* entrepreneurs and entrepreneurship; multinational bus.; bus.–state relations; markets and bus. *Scope:* national; internat. *Period:* twentieth century as a whole. *Teaching:* undergrad. *Consultancy:* co. hist.

Publications *Books: Monte Amiata. Il Mercurio Italiano. Strategie*

Internazionali e Vincoli Extraeconomici, Angeli, Milan, 1991. *Articles:* 'More Trouble than Profit: Vickers' Investments in Italy (1905–1939)', *Bus. Hist.*, 27, Nov., 1985, 316–37; 'La City e la "Dolce Vita" Romana. La Storia della Banca Italo Britannica (1916–1930)', *Passato e Presente*, 6, 1987; 'Du "Made in Germany" au "Made in Switzerland". Les Sociétés financières suisses pour l'Industrie électrique dans l'Entre-deux-guerres', *1880–1980. Électricité et Électrification dans le Monde*, Presses Universitaires de France, Paris; 'Imprenditori e Finanzieri' and 'Elettricità ed Economia in Europa', *Storia dell'Industria elettrica in Italia. 1. Le Origini. 1882–1914*, Giorio Mori ed., Laterza, Bari, 1992, 249–337 and 697–750.

Sejersted, Francis

Prof. & Director, TMV -Centre, Research Park, Oslo Univ., Gaustadalleen 21, 0371 Oslo, Norway. Tel.: 47 2 2958836. Fax: 47 2 2958845.
Year and Place of Birth 1936, Oslo, Norway.
Degrees and Qualifications Cand.philol., 1965.
Current Offices and Honorary Posts Ed., *Historisk Tidsskrift* [Norwegian Hist. Rev.], 1971–5; mem., Norwegian Acad. of Sciences, 1976–; mem., Academia Europae, 1989–.
Fields of Expertise *Industry Fields:* timber, furniture; insurance, banking, finance. *Bus. Dimensions:* research and development; bus. values. *Scope:* national. *Period:* nineteenth century; twentieth century as a whole. *Teaching:* undergrad.; post grad.
Publications *Books: Fra Linderud til Eidsvold Værk*, vol. II & III, Oslo, 1972 & 1978; (two volumes (covering the 19th century) of a hist. of one of

the leading Norwegian timber firms; *Historisk introduksjon til økonomien* [Hist. Introduction to Econ.], Oslo, 1973, 2nd edn., 1985; *Demokratisk Kapitalisme* [Democratic Capitalism], Oslo, 1993, (theoretical & empirical articles on the development of Norwegian capitalist institutions); *Vekst gjennom krise* [Growth through Depression. Studies in the Hist. of Technology in Norway], ed. & co-auth., Oslo, 1982; *En storbank i blandingsøkonomien* [A Hist. of the Largest Norwegian Private Bank], Oslo, 1982.

Shiba, Takao

Prof., Dept. of Bus. Admin., Kyoto Sangyo Univ., Kamigamo-motoyama Kita Ku, Kyoto 603, Japan. Tel.: 81 75 701 2151. Fax: 81 75 705 1742.
Year and Place of Birth 1950, Hyogo, Japan.
Degrees and Qualifications MBA Konan Univ., 1978.
Current Offices and Honorary Posts Sec., Bus. Hist. Soc. of Japan, 1985–8; auditor, Bus. Hist. Soc. of Japan, 1993–.
Fields of Expertise *Industry Fields:* shipbuilding and marine engineering. *Bus. Dimensions:* strategy formation. *Scope:* national. *Period:* inter-war years, 1919–39. *Teaching:* undergrad. *Consultancy:* corporate strategy.
Publications *Books: Nihon Zaibatsu keieishi: Mitsubishi Zaibatsu* [Bus. Hist. of Japanese Zaibatsu: Mitsubishi Zaibatsu], co-auth., Nihon Keizai Shinbusha, 1981; *Dai niji taisen to Mitsubishi Zaibatsu* [Mitsubishi Zaibatsu during World War II], co-auth., Nihon Keizai Shinbunsha, 1987; *Succeeding against the Odds, Courting Collapse: How Mitsubishi Shipbuilding and the Kawasaki Dockyard managed the Post World War I Slump*, Japanese Yearbook on

Bus. Hist., 1985. *Articles:* 'A Comparative Study of the Development of the Managerial Structure of two Japanese Shipbuilding Firms: Mitsubishi Shipbuilding and Engineering Co. and Kawasaki Dockyard Co., 1896–1927', *Development of Managerial Enterprise*, Kesaji Kobayashi & Hidemasa Morikawa eds., Univ. of Tokyo Press, 1986; 'Senji taisei-ka no kigyo boei senriyaku' [A Strategy for Corporate Defence during Wartime], *Keieishigaku* [Japan Bus. Hist. Rev.], 23(2), 1988.

Shiman, Daniel R.

Asst. Prof., Dept. of Econ., SUNY - Oswego, Oswego, NY 13126, USA. Tel.: 1 315 341 3487.

Year and Place of Birth 1959, Middletown, USA.

Degrees and Qualifications BS Yale Univ., 1981; MA (Econ.) Northwestern Univ., 1986; Ph.D. (Econ.) Northwestern Univ., 1992.

Fields of Expertise *Industry Fields:* chemicals and allied industries; electrical engineering; gas, electricity, water. *Bus. Dimensions:* entrepreneurs and entrepreneurship; bus. organization; bus. and technology. *Scope:* internat. *Period:* nineteenth century; early twentieth century. *Teaching:* undergrad.

Publications *Articles:* 'Managerial Inefficiency and Technological Decline in Britain 1860–1914', *Bus. & Econ. Hist.*, 2nd ser., 20, 1991, 89–98.

Shimokawa, Koichi

Prof., Hosei Univ., Fac. of Bus. Admin., 2-17-1 Fujimi, Chiyoda-ku, Tokyo, Japan. Tel.: 81 3 3264 9741.

Year and Place of Birth 1930, Tokyo, Japan.

Degrees and Qualifications Ph.D.

(Econ.) Kyushu Univ., 1981.

Previous Post Vice-pres., Hosei Univ., 1988–90.

Current Offices and Honorary Posts Mem., board of directors, Japanese Soc. of Organization Science.

Fields of Expertise *Industry Fields:* vehicle construction; transport and communication; distributive trades. *Bus. Dimensions:* production management; marketing; multinational bus. *Scope:* national; internat.; global; USA; Japan; Asia. *Period:* nineteenth century; twentieth century as a whole; late twentieth century, 1970–present. *Teaching:* undergrad.; post grad. *Consultancy:* co. hist.; corporate strategy.

Publications *Books: Development of Mass Marketing*, co-ed., Tokyo Univ. Press, 1981, (in English); *The Amer. Automobile Civilization and Japan*, Bunshindo, Tokyo, 1982; *The Automobile Industry toward Dematured Age*, Tokyo, 1985; *Development of the Japanese Company after the Postwar Period*, Tokyo, 1990; *The Rise and Fall of the World Automobile Industry*, Tokyo, 1992.

Shimono, Katsumi

Prof. of Econ. Hist., Fac. of Econ., Okayama Univ., 3-1-1 Tsushima-naka, Okayama-shi 700, Japan. Tel.: 086 251 7536. Fax: 086 253 1449.

Year and Place of Birth 1943, Okayama, Japan.

Degrees and Qualifications B.Econ. Kyoto Univ., 1966; M.Econ. Kyoto Univ., 1968; Ph.D. (Econ.) Kyoto Univ., 1988.

Fields of Expertise *Industry Fields:* chemicals and allied industries; textiles; clothing and footwear; regional industry. *Bus. Dimensions:* bus. and technology; small bus. matters; industrial structure. *Scope:* local; regional;

national. *Period:* twentieth century as a whole. *Teaching:* undergrad.; post grad. *Consultancy:* co. hist.

Publications *Books: Sengo Nihon Sekitan Kagaku Kogyoshi* [The Coal-Chemical Industry in post-War Japan], Ochanomizu Shobo ed., Dept. of Econ., Okayama Univ., 1984, reprinted 1987. *Articles:* 'The Growth of the Spinning Mill in Japan', *J. of Japanese Hist.*, 105, 1969, 39–59; 'On the Production Technology of the Textile Factory System in post-War Japan', *J. of Agrarian Hist.*, 51, 1971, 53–63; 'Features of Region and Direction of Industrial Promotion of Okayama Prefecture', *Contemporary Regional Development*, Meibun Shobo, 1987, 139–60; 'The Industrial Revival and Development of Okayama City in the post-War Showa Era', *A Centennial Hist. of Okayama City*, 2, 1991, 454–506.

Shimotani, Masahiro

Prof., Fac. of Econ., Kyoto Univ., Yoshidahonmachi, Sakyo, Kyoto, Japan. Tel.: 075 753 3437. Fax: 075 751 1532.

Year and Place of Birth 1944, Kanazawa, Japan.

Degrees and Qualifications Ph.D. Kyoto Univ., 1982.

Previous Post Assoc. Prof., Osaka Keizai Univ.

Fields of Expertise *Industry Fields:* chemicals and allied industries. *Bus. Dimensions:* bus. organization. *Scope:* internat. *Period:* twentieth century as a whole. *Teaching:* undergrad.; post grad.

Publications *Books: Nihon kagaku kogyo shiron* [The Development of the Chemical Industry in Japan], Ochanomizu shobo, 1982; *Gendai Nihon no kigyo-Group* [The Corporate Group in Japan], Toyo keizai, 1987; *Senji keizai to Nihon kigyo* [The War-time Economy in Japan], Showado, 1990. *Articles:* 'Corporate Groups and Industrial Fusion', *The Kyoto Univ. Econ. Rev.*, 124, 1988; 'Corporate Groups and Keiretsu in Japan', *Japanese Yearbook on Bus. Hist.*, 8, 1992.

Shinomiya, Toshiyuki

Prof., Dept. of Econ., Fac. of Humanities, Hirosaki Univ., 1 Bunkyo-cho, Hirosaki, Aomori 036, Japan. Tel.: 81 172 36 2111. Fax: 81 172 32 5340.

Year and Place of Birth 1947, Tokyo, Japan.

Degrees and Qualifications BA Meiji Univ., 1971; MBA Meiji Univ., 1973.

Current Offices and Honorary Posts Council mem. & mem. of edit. com., Bus. Hist. Soc. of Japan, 1991–; sec., Japan Indust. Archaeology Soc., 1989–; sec., Bus. Hist. Soc. of Japan, 1979–82.

Fields of Expertise *Industry Fields:* paper, printing, publishing. *Bus. Dimensions:* entrepreneurs and entrepreneurship; co. admin. *Scope:* internat. *Period:* nineteenth century; twentieth century as a whole. *Teaching:* undergrad. *Consultancy:* co. hist.

Publications *Articles:* 'The Japan Paper Assoc. and the Japanese Paper Manufacturing Bus. during and after World War I', *Studies in Humanities: Econ.*, published in Japanese, Hirosaki Univ., 18(1), 1982, 1–48; 'The Rivalry between the Cartel of Japan's Newsprint Manufacturers and Imported Newsprint before World War II', *Japan Bus. Hist. Rev.*, published in Japanese, 23(3), 1988, 1–28; 'Political Manœuvering with regard to Import Duty on Newsprint in Japan before World War II', *Hirosaki Econ. Rev.*, published in Japanese, 11, 1988, 14–34; 'Shiro Kubota and the Fuji

Paper Co.: on his Behaviour and Performance as a Salaried Professional Manager', *Studies in the Humanities: Econ.*, published in Japanese, Hirosaki Univ., 24(2), 1989, 63–95; 'Heizaburo Okawa and the Fuji Paper Co.: on his Behaviour and Performance as a part-time big Stockholding Top Manager', *Soka Keiei Ronshu*, published in Japanese, Soka Univ., 15(2), 1991, 39–52. ·

Shioji, Hiromi

Assoc. Prof. of Bus. Hist., Fac. of Commerce, Kyushu Sangyo Univ., 2-3-1 Matsukadai, Higashi-ku, Fukuoka 813, Japan. Tel.: 092 673 5269/092 673 5200. Fax: 092 673 5299.

Year and Place of Birth 1955, Wakayama pref., Japan.

Degrees and Qualifications B.Econ. Kyoto Univ., 1982; M.Econ. Kyoto Univ., 1984.

Fields of Expertise *Industry Fields:* mechanical engineering. *Bus. Dimensions:* production management; marketing; merger movement and issues; bus. organization; small bus. matters; markets and bus. *Scope:* internat.; Japan; USA; Korea. *Period:* inter-war years, 1919–39; mid-twentieth century, 1940–70; late twentieth century, 1970–present. *Teaching:* undergrad. *Consultancy:* co. hist.

Publications *Books: Gendai Nihon no Kigyo Group* [The Current Japanese Big Bus. Group], Sakamoto Kazuichico-auth., Toyokezaishinposhya, 1987. *Articles:* 'Toyota jiko no Kojo tenkai' [The Factory Development of the Toyota Motor Co. in the 1960s], *The Econ. Rev.*, Kyoto Univ. Econ. Soc., 137(6), 1986; 'Toyota jiko niokeru itaku seisan no tenkai' [The Subcontracting of Car Assembly: An Aspect of the Development of the Full-line-wide Selection Production System by Toyota in the 1960s], *The Econ. Rev.*, Kyoto Univ. Econ. Soc., 138(5.6), 1986; 'Hino Toyota teikei no shiteki kosatsu' [An Hist. Study of the Hino-Toyota Tie-up], *Japan Bus. Hist. Rev.*, 23(2), 1988; 'Jidoshya Dealer no nich bei kan kokusai hikaku - "Keiretsu" o hikaku shiza toshite' [A Comparative Study of Car Dealers in the US, Korea and Japan in relation to the 'Keiretsu' Problem], *Rev. of Econ. & Bus.*, Kyushu Sangyo Univ., 32(2), 1991.

Shumilo, Erica

Assoc. Prof., Dept. of Internat. Econ. Relations, Latvia Univ., 5 Aspazijas Blvd, 2150 Riga, Latvia. Tel.: 7 132 226180.

Year and Place of Birth 1958, Riga, Latvia.

Degrees and Qualifications Ph.D. Moscow State Univ., 1986.

Fields of Expertise *Industry Fields:* manufacturing industry. *Bus. Dimensions:* bus. organization; industrial policy. *Scope:* national; Latvia. *Period:* inter-war years, 1919–39. *Teaching:* undergrad. *Consultancy:* corporate strategy.

Publications *Books: Monetary Policy in the Republic of Latvia in the 1920s*, Riga, LVU Publishers, 1982, (in Russian); *The Development of Latvian Industry (1920–1929)*, Moscow, 1986 (in Russian); *Towards the Baltic Market*, Kaunas, 1991; *Conditions and Prospects of Internat. Bus. in the Republic of Latvia. Management Education and Training: An Eastern European Dilemma*, Krieger Publishing Co., 1993. *Articles:* 'The Trade Treaty of 1927 between Latvia and the USSR and its Influence on the Development of Latvian Industry', *LPSR 2A Vestis*, 12, Riga, 1985, (in Russian).

Sicilia, David B.

Charles Warren Fellow, Dept. of Hist., Harvard Univ., Cambridge, MA 02138, USA. Tel.: 1 617 495 9945. Fax: 1 617 496 3425.

Year and Place of Birth 1955, Cape May Court House, New Jersey, USA.

Degrees and Qualifications BA Hofstra Univ. New York, 1976; Ph.D. Brandeis Univ., Massachusetts, 1991.

Previous Post Visiting Asst. Prof., Ohio State Univ., 1991–2.

Major Honours Charles Warren Fellow, Harvard Univ., 1992–3; Samuel B. Davis Fellow in Bus. Hist., Ohio State Univ., 1990–1; John E. Rovenshy Fellow in Bus. & Econ. Hist., 1987–8; winner of the 1991 Herman E. Krooss Prize for the best dissertation presented at the Bus. Hist. Conf.

Fields of Expertise *Industry Fields:* gas, electricity, water. *Bus. Dimensions:* marketing. *Scope:* national. *Period:* twentieth century as a whole. *Teaching:* undergrad. *Consultancy:* co. hist.

Publications *Books: The Entrepreneurs: An Amer. Adventure,* with Robert Sobel co-auth., Houghton-Mifflin, 1986; *Labors of a Modern Hercules: The Evolution of a Chemical Company,* with Davis Dyer co-auth., Harvard Bus. School Press, 1990.

Simmons III, F. Bruce

Assoc. Prof., Dept. of Management, The Univ. of Akron, Akron, OH 44325–4801, USA. Tel.: 0216 972 6979.

Degrees and Qualifications Ph.D. Cincinnati Univ., 1981; J.D. Akron Univ., 1986; LL M Cleveland State Univ., 1991.

Fields of Expertise *Industry Fields:* . *Bus. Dimensions:* entrepreneurs and entrepreneurship. *Scope:* national;

internat. *Period:* late twentieth century, 1970–present. *Teaching:* undergrad.; post grad. *Consultancy:* corporate strategy.

Sinclair, F.R.J.

Historian, Treaty Issues Unit, Crown Law Office, POB 5012, Wellington, New Zealand. Tel.: 64 4 4721 719. Fax: 64 4 473 3482.

Year and Place of Birth 1963, Otago, New Zealand.

Degrees and Qualifications BA Otago Univ., 1986; LL B Otago Univ., 1988.

Fields of Expertise *Industry Fields:* agric., forestry, fishing; insurance, banking, finance. *Bus. Dimensions:* entrepreneurs and entrepreneurship; bus.–state relations; bus. values. *Scope:* regional; national. *Period:* nineteenth century.

Publications *Articles: Dictionary of New Zealand Biography,* vol. 2, 3 essays.

Singleton, John

Lect., Econ. Hist. Group, Fac. of Commerce and Admin., Victoria Univ. of Wellington, POB 600, Wellington, New Zealand. Tel.: 64 4 471 5385. Fax: 64 4 471 2200.

Year and Place of Birth 1960, Preston, UK.

Degrees and Qualifications BA Lancaster Univ., 1981; M.Sc. London School of Econ., 1982; Ph.D. Lancaster Univ., 1986; BD Edinburgh Univ., 1989.

Previous Post Temp. Lect. in Econ. Hist., Dept. of Hist., Manchester Univ., 1991–3.

Fields of Expertise *Industry Fields:* textiles; transport and communication; public admin. and defence. *Bus. Dimensions:* research and development; strategy formation; merger movement and issues; bus. organization; bus. and technology; multinational bus.; bus.–state relations; markets and bus. *Scope:* local; regional; national; internat.; global; UK. *Period:* twentieth century as a whole. *Teaching:* undergrad.; post grad.

Publications *Books: Lancashire on the Scrapheap: The Cotton Industry 1945-70,* OUP for Pasold Research Fund, 1991. *Articles:* 'Showing the White Flag: The Lancashire Cotton Industry, 1945-70', *Bus. Hist.,* XXXII, 1990, 129–49; 'Future Relations between Defence and Civil Science and Technology: A Report for the Parliamentary Office of Science and Technology', co-auth., Defence Science & Technology Policy Team, Science Policy Support Group, 1991; 'Full Steam Ahead? The British Arms Industry and the Market for Warships in Britain, 1850–1914', *Entrepreneurship, Networks and Modern Bus.,* J. Brown & M.B. Rose eds., Manchester Univ. Press, 1993, 229–58; 'Britain's Military Use of Horses, 1914–1918', *Past and Present,* 139, May, 1993.

Sklar, Martin J.

Prof. of Hist., Dept. of Hist., Bucknell Univ., Lewisburg, PA 17837, USA. Tel.: 1 717 238 2790. Fax: 1 717 524 3760.

Year and Place of Birth 1935, New York City, USA.

Degrees and Qualifications BA Wisconsin-Madison Univ., 1955; MA Wisconsin-Madison Univ., 1962; Ph.D. Rochester Univ., NY, 1982.

Major Honours MacArthur Chair of Bucknell, 1983–8; Law & Soc. Association's 1990 J. Willard Hurst Prize in Legal Hist. for *The Corporate Reconstruction of Amer. Capitalism.*

Fields of Expertise *Bus. Dimensions:* merger movement and issues; bus.–state relations; markets and bus. *Scope:* national; internat.

Period: nineteenth century; twentieth century as a whole; early twentieth century. *Teaching:* undergrad.; post grad. *Consultancy:* policy.

Publications *Books: The Corporate Reconstruction of Amer. Capitalism, 1890–1916: The Market, the Law, and Polit.,* CUP, 1988; *The United States as a Developing Country: Studies in US Hist. in the Progressive Era and the 1920s,* CUP, 1992. *Articles:* 'Woodrow Wilson and the Polit. Economy of Modern United States Liberalism', *A New Hist. of Leviathan: Essays on the Rise of the Amer. Corporate State,* Ronald Radosh & Murray N. Rothbard eds., E.P. Dutton, 1972; 'Le Socialisme et la Tradition Politique Américaine', *Encrages,* 11/12, Winter, 1983–4, Université Paris VIII-Vincennes a Saint Denis, 32–53; 'Periodization and Historiography: Studying Amer. Polit. Development in the Progressive Era, 1890s–1916', *Studies in Amer. Polit. Development,* 5, Fall, 1991, 173–213, 221–223.

Slaven, Anthony

Prof. of Bus. Hist. & Director of the Centre for Bus. Hist. in Scotland, Centre for Bus. Hist., Univ. of Glasgow, 4 Univ. Gardens, Glasgow, G12 8QQ, UK. Tel.: 44 41 330 4669. Fax: 44 41 330 4889.

Year and Place of Birth 1937, Blantyre, UK.

Degrees and Qualifications MA Glasgow Univ., 1960; B.Litt Glasgow Univ., 1967.

Previous Post Sen. Lect. in Econ. Hist. & Colquhoun Lect. in Bus. Hist., Glasgow Univ., 1969–79.

Current Offices and Honorary Posts Chairman, Scottish Records Assoc.; sec.-treasurer, Assoc. of Bus. Historians; council mem., Econ. Hist. Soc.

Fields of Expertise *Industry Fields:*

shipbuilding and marine engineering. *Bus. Dimensions:* entrepreneurs and entrepreneurship; strategy formation; bus. organization; bus.–state relations. *Scope:* local; regional; national; internat.; Scotland. *Period:* twentieth century as a whole. *Teaching:* undergrad.; post grad. *Consultancy:* co. hist.; public policy.

Publications *Books: Econ. Development of the West of Scotland, 1750–1960,* Routledge & Kegan Paul, London, 1975; *Studies in Bus., Banking and Urban Hist.,* with D.H. Aldcroft co-ed., John Donald, Edinburgh, 1982; *Shipbuilding: Review of UK Statistical Sources,* Pergamon, London, 1983; *Dictionary of Scottish Bus. Biography,* with S.G. Checkland co-ed., 2 vols., Aberdeen Univ. Press, Aberdeen, 1985 & 1990.

Slinn, Judy

Sen. Lect., School of Bus., Brookes Univ., Oxford, UK. Tel.: 44 865 880323. Fax: 44 865 883005.

Year and Place of Birth 1943, Scarborough, UK.

Degrees and Qualifications BA Oxford Univ., 1965.

Current Offices and Honorary Posts Sen. Lect., School of Bus., Oxford, Brookes Univ.

Fields of Expertise *Industry Fields:* food, drink, tobacco; chemicals and allied industries; professional and scientific services. *Bus. Dimensions:* co. law; strategy formation; merger movement and issues. *Scope:* internat. *Period:* nineteenth century; twentieth century as a whole. *Teaching:* undergrad. *Consultancy:* co. hist.

Publications *Books: A Hist. of May & Baker,* Hobson, Cambridge, 1984; *Linklaters & Paines, The First 150 Years,* Longman, 1987; *Engineers in Power, 75 Years of the EPEA,* Laurence & Wishart, 1989.; *Glaxo: A Hist. to 1962,* with R.P.T. Davenport

Hines, CUP, 1992; *Clifford Chance: Origins and Development,* Granta, 1993.

Sluyterman, Keetie E.

Freelance Bus. Historian, Centre for Bus. Hist., Erasmus Univ., POB 1738, 3000 DR Rotterdam, Netherlands. Tel.: 31 10 408 2500.

Year and Place of Birth 1949, Amsterdam, Netherlands.

Degrees and Qualifications BA (Hist.) Leiden Univ., 1974; Dissertation (Econ.) Brabant Univ., 1983.

Previous Post Lect., Erasmus Univ., Rotterdam, 1989–90.

Current Offices and Honorary Posts Board mem., Netherlands Econ. Hist. Archives.

Fields of Expertise *Industry Fields:* chemicals and allied industries; bus. services; tobacco; accountancy. *Bus. Dimensions:* small bus. matters; multinational bus. *Scope:* national; internat. *Period:* twentieth century as a whole; inter-war years, 1919–39. *Consultancy:* co. hist.

Publications *Books: Ondernemen in Sigaren. Analyse van Bedrijfsbeleid in vijf Nederlandse Sigarenfabrieken in de Perioden 1856–1865 en 1925–1934,* Stichting Zuidelijk Historisch Contact, Tilburg, 1983; *Winnen met Papier. Proost en Brandt 1942–1992,* Proost en Brandt, Diemen, 1992. *Articles:* 'Uitvinden en Verdienen', *Van Boterkleursel naar Kopieersystemen. De ontstaansgeschiedenis van Océ-van der Grinten, 1988–1956,* H.F.J.M. van den Eerenbeemt ed., Martinus Nijhoff, Leiden, 1991, 171–268; 'From Licensor to Multinational Enterprise. The small Dutch Firm Océ-van der Grinten in the Internat. World, 1920–1966', *Bus. Hist.,* 34(2), 1992, 28–49; 'Outward Bound. The Rise of Dutch Multinationals', *The Rise of*

Multinationals in Continental Europe, with Ben P.A. Gales; Geoffrey Jones & Harm G. Schröter eds., Edward Elgar, Aldershot, 1993.

Smith, Bernard

Asst. Prof., Dept. of Econ., Drew Univ., Madison, NJ 07940, USA. Tel.: 1 201 408 3595. Fax: 1 201 408 3768.

Year and Place of Birth 1955, Havana; Cuba.

Degrees and Qualifications BS & BA Florida Univ.; MA, M.Phil. & Ph.D. Yale Univ.

Fields of Expertise *Industry Fields:* clothing and footwear. *Bus. Dimensions:* markets and bus. *Scope:* national. *Period:* early twentieth century. *Teaching:* undergrad. *Consultancy:* co. hist.

Publications *Articles:* 'Market Development, Indust. Development: The Case of the Amer. Corset Trade', *Bus. Hist. Rev.*, 65, Spring, 1991, 91–129.

Smith, George David

Pres., The Winthrop Group & Clinical Prof. of Econ., New York Univ., Winthrop Group Inc., 1100 Massachusetts Ave, Cambridge, MA 02138, USA. Tel.: Winthrop: 1 617 497 0777. Fax: Winthrop: 1 617 661 6497.

Year and Place of Birth 1946, Du Quoin, IL, USA.

Degrees and Qualifications BA Fairleigh Dickinson Univ., 1968; MA Harvard Univ., 1970; Ph.D. Harvard Univ., 1976.

Previous Post Assoc., Cambridge Research Inst., 1978–81.

Major Honours Co-winner, Best Book in Industry & Bus., Scholarly Division, Amer. Publishers Assoc.,

1985; Glucksman Inst. Fac. Fellow, 1991–2.

Fields of Expertise *Industry Fields:* metal manufacture; transport and communication; insurance, banking, finance. *Bus. Dimensions:* entrepreneurs and entrepreneurship; co. admin.; bus. and technology; multinational bus.; management education; markets and bus.; bus. values; co. culture; boardroom issues. *Scope:* internat.; global. *Period:* nineteenth century; twentieth century as a whole. *Teaching:* post grad.; executive education. *Consultancy:* co. hist.; corporate strategy; corporate organization and culture.

Publications *Books: Anatomy of a Bus. Strategy: Bell, Western Electric and the Origins of the Amer. Tel. Industry*, Johns Hopkins Univ. Press, 1985; *From Monopoly to Competition: The Transformations of Alcoa, 1888–1986*, CUP, 1988; *The Transformation of Financial Capitalism: An Essay on the Hist. of the Amer. Capital Markets*, with Richard Sylla, co-auth., Blackwell Press, Salomon Brothers Center, 1993. *Articles:* 'The Bell-Western Union Patent Agreement of 1879: A Study in Corporate Imagination', *Readings in the Management of Innovation*, Michael Toshman & William Moore eds., Ballinger, 1988.

Smith, John Kenly

Assoc. Prof. of Hist., Dept. of Hist., Maginnes Hall No. 9, Lehigh Univ., Bethlehem, PA 18015, USA. Tel.: 1 215 758 3365.

Year and Place of Birth 1951, Baltimore, USA.

Degrees and Qualifications BS (Chem. Eng.) Delaware Univ., 1974; BA (Hist.) Delaware Univ., 1974; MS (Chem. Eng.) Virginia Univ., 1976; Ph.D. (Hist.) Delaware Univ., 1986.

Previous Post Newcomen Fellow, Harvard Bus. School, 1986–7.

Current Offices and Honorary Posts Head of Chemical Technology Interest Group (Pelicans), Soc. for Hist. of Technology.

Major Honours Newcomen Prize in Bus. Hist. for Best Book published in Amer., 1986–8.

Fields of Expertise *Industry Fields:* chemicals and allied industries; textiles. *Bus. Dimensions:* bus. and technology. *Scope:* internat. *Period:* eighteenth century; nineteenth century; twentieth century as a whole. *Teaching:* undergrad.; post grad. *Consultancy:* co. hist.

Publications *Books: Science and Corporate Strategy: DuPont R & D, 1902–1980*, with David A. Hounshell co-auth., CUP, 1988. *Articles:* 'The Scientific Tradition in Amer. Indust. Research', *Technology and Culture*, 31(1), Jan., 1990, 121–31; 'National Goals, Industry Structure and Corporate Strategy: Chemical Cartels between the Wars', *Proceedings of 18th Annual Fuji Conf. on Internat. Bus. Hist.*, Tokyo Univ. Press, Tokyo, 1991; 'America vs. Japan: Competition, Co-operation and Competitiveness', *Competitiveness and Amer. Soc.*, Steven L. Goldman ed., research in Technology Studies, vol. 7, Lehigh Univ. Press, Bethlehem, PA, 1993.

Smith, Merritt Roe

Prof. of the Hist. of Technology and Director, Program in Science, Technology and Soc., Room E51-110, MIT, Cambridge, MA 02139, USA. Tel.: 1 617 253 4008. Fax: 1 617 258 8118.

Year and Place of Birth 1940, Waverly, USA.

Degrees and Qualifications BA Georgetown Univ., 1963; MA Pennsylvania State Univ., 1965; Ph.D.

Pennsylvania State Univ., 1971.

Previous Post Assoc. Prof., Dept. of Hist., Ohio State Univ., 1974–8.

Current Offices and Honorary Posts Past pres., Soc. for the Hist. of Technology; mem., Amer. Acad. of Arts & Sciences; fellow, Amer. Assoc. for the Advancement of Science; board of trustees, Hagley Museum & Library; board of trustees, Museum of Amer. Textile Hist.

Major Honours Frederick Jackson Turner Award from the Organization of Amer. Historians, 1977; Pfizer Award from the Hist. of Science Soc., 1978; Certificate of Commendation, Amer. Assoc. for State and Local Hist.; Distinguished Teaching Award, Ohio State Univ., 1978.

Fields of Expertise *Industry Fields:* metal manufacture; public admin. and defence. *Bus. Dimensions:* production management; bus. and technology. *Scope:* national. *Period:* nineteenth century. *Teaching:* undergrad.; post grad. *Consultancy:* Government agencies and museums.

Publications *Books: Harpers Ferry Armory and the New Technology*, Cornell Univ. Press, 1977; *Military Enterprise and Technological Change*, ed. & contributor, MIT Press, 1985; *Machines and Hist. The Dilemma of Technological Determinism*, ed. & contributor, MIT Press, forthcoming. *Articles:* 'Technology, Industrialization and the Idea of Progress in America',*Responsible Science: The Impact of Technology on Soc.*, K.B. Byrne ed., Harper & Row, 1986.

Smith, Michael S.

Assoc. Prof., Dept. of Hist., Univ. of South Carolina, Columbia, SC 29208, USA. Tel.: 1 803 777 7421. Fax: 1 803 777 4494.

Year and Place of Birth 1944, Kansas City, USA.

Degrees and Qualifications BA

Oklahoma Univ., 1965; MA Cornell Univ., 1968; Ph.D. Cornell Univ., 1972; MBA Univ. of South Carolina, 1981.

Previous Post Asst. Prof., St Louis Univ., 1970–3.

Major Honours Kress Fellowship, Harvard Bus. School, Summer, 1974; William Koren Jr. Prize, Soc. for French Historical Studies, 1977; Charles J. Kennedy Award of Excellence, Econ. & Bus. Historical Soc., 1993.**Fields of Expertise** *Industry Fields:* general industrial hist. *Bus. Dimensions:* bus.–state relations. *Scope:* national; France. *Period:* nineteenth century. *Teaching:* undergrad.; post grad. *Consultancy:* co. hist.

Publications *Books: Tariff Reform in France, 1860–1900: The Polit. of Econ. Interest*, Cornell Univ. Press, Ithaca & London, 1980. *Articles:* 'Free Trade versus Protection in the Early Third Republic: Econ. Interests, Tariff Policy and the Making of the Republican Synthesis', *French Historical Studies*, X(2), Autumn, 1977, 293–314; 'Entrepreneurial Mentalities, Government Policies and National Econ. Performance: The Case of French Export Promotion, 1871–1914', *Proceedings of the Western Soc. for French Hist.*, XIV, 1986, 255–63; 'The Méline Tariff as Social Protection: Rhetoric or Reality?', *Internat. Rev. of Soc. Hist.*, XXXVIII(2), 1992, 230–43; 'The Beginnings of Big Bus. in France, 1880–1920: A Chandlerian Perspective', *Essays in Econ. & Bus. Hist.*, Edwin J. Perkins ed., XI, 1993.

Smith, Victor C.

Asst. Prof., Dept. of Hist., Lakehead Univ., Thunder Bay, Ontario, P7B 5E1, Canada. Tel.: 0807 343 8475/0807 346 7725. Fax: 0807 343 8023.

Year and Place of Birth 1942, Dundee, UK.

Degrees and Qualifications MA (Eng. & Hist.) St Andrews Univ., 1964; MA (Hist.) Univ. of Western Ontario, 1966; Ph.D. (Hist.) Duke Univ., 1969.

Fields of Expertise *Industry Fields:* paper, printing, publishing. *Bus. Dimensions:* bus.–state relations. *Scope:* regional. *Period:* twentieth century as a whole. *Teaching:* undergrad.

Publications *Articles:* 'Lumbering, Pulp and Paper and Forestry', *A Vast and Magnificent Land: An Illustrated Hist. of Northern Ontario*, Matt Bray & Ernie Epp eds., Lakehead & Laurentian Univ., 1984, 75–83; 'Factories in the Forest: A Hist. of Pulp and Paper in Northwestern Ontario', delivered & published in proceedings of a conference on The Engineering Heritage of Northwestern Ontario, Thunder Bay, March, 1987, 83–90; 'Thomas Macfarlane', *Dictionary of Canadian Biography/Dictionnaire Biographique du Canada*, Univ. of Toronto Press, vol. XIII, (forthcoming).

Smitka, Michael J.

Assoc. Prof. of Econ., Commerce School, Washington & Lee Univ., Lexington, VA 24450, USA. Tel.: 1 703 463 8625. Fax: 1 703 463 8639.

Year and Place of Birth 1953, USA.

Degrees and Qualifications BA (E. Asian Studies) Harvard Univ., 1975; Ph.D. (Econ.) Yale Univ., 1989.

Previous Post Japan Foundation Fellow & Visiting Prof., Law Fac., Rikkyo Univ., Tokyo, 1991–2.

Fields of Expertise *Industry Fields:* vehicle construction. *Bus. Dimensions:* bus. organization; production management; personnel management. *Scope:* internat.; Japan; USA. *Period:* mid-twentieth century, 1940–70; late twentieth century, 1970–present; inter-war years, 1919–39. *Teaching:* undergrad. *Consultancy:* contemporary Japanese economy and automobile industry.

Publications *Books: Competitive Ties: Subcontracting in the Japanese Automotive Industry,* Columbia Univ. Press, 1991. *Articles:* 'The Invisible Handshake: The Development of the Japanese Automotive Parts Industry', *Bus. & Econ. Hist.,* 2nd ser., 19, 1990, 163–171; 'American Management: Reformation or Revolution? The Transfer of Japanese Management Technology to the US', *The Globalization of Japanese Economy,* Komagawa Univ., 1990; (working paper no. 37, Center on the Japanese Economy, Grad. Bus. School of Bus., Columbia Univ., 1989); 'Contracting without Contracts', *The Legalistic Organization,* Sim Sitkin & Robert Bies eds., Sage, 1993.

Sobel, Robert

Lawrence Stessin Prof. of Bus. Hist., Hofstra Univ., Roosevelt Hall, Hempstead, NY 11550, USA. Tel.: 1 516 463 5827. Fax: 1 516 564 4296.

Year and Place of Birth 1931, New York, USA.

Degrees and Qualifications BSS City College of New York, 1951; MA New York Univ., 1952; Ph.D. New York Univ., 1957.

Fields of Expertise *Industry Fields:* insurance, banking, finance. *Bus. Dimensions:* bus. organization. *Scope:* internat. *Period:* twentieth century as a whole. *Teaching:* undergrad. *Consultancy:* co. hist.

Publications *Books: IBM Colossus in Transition,* Timesbooks, 1981; *ITT: The Management of Opportunity,* Timesbooks, 1982; *Car Wars,* Dutton, 1984; *The New Game on Wall St,* Wiley, 1988; *The Life and Times of Dillon Read,* Dutton, 1991.

Soltow, James H.

Prof. of Hist. Emeritus, POB 422, Isle of Palms, SC 29451, USA. Tel.: 1 803 886 4656.

Year and Place of Birth 1924, Chicago, USA.

Degrees and Qualifications BA Dickinson College, 1948; Ph.D. Pennsylvania Univ., 1954.

Previous Post Prof. of Hist., Michigan State Univ., 1959–84.

Major Honours Bus. Hist. Fellow, Harvard Univ., Grad. School of Bus. Admin., 1958–9; Fulbright Research Scholarship, Louvain Univ., Belgium, 1965–6; Econ. and Bus. Historical Soc.: pres., 1982, ed. & trustee, 1978–84; Bus. Hist. Conf.: trustee, 1980–6.

Fields of Expertise *Industry Fields:* metal manufacture; metal goods; timber, furniture; other manufacturing industries; distributive trades; insurance, banking, finance; electronics and computers: manufacture. *Bus. Dimensions:* entrepreneurs and entrepreneurship; strategy formation; small bus. matters; markets and bus. *Scope:* local; regional; national; USA; Belgium. *Period:* eighteenth century; twentieth century as a whole. *Teaching:* undergrad.; post grad. *Consultancy:* co. hist.

Publications *Books: Origins of Small Bus.: Metal Fabricators and Machinery Makers in New England, 1890–1957,* Amer. Philosophical Soc., 1965; *The Econ. Role of Wiliamsburg,* Univ. Press of Virginia, 1965; *Ninety Years: A Hist. of CTS Corporation, 1896–1986,* CTS Corporation, 1988; *The Hon Story: A Hist. of Hon Industries, 1944–1985,* with C. Maxwell Stanley co-auth., Iowa State Univ. Press, 1991; *The Evolution of the Amer. Economy: Growth, Welfare and Decision Making,* with Sidney Ratner & Richard Sylla co-auths., 1st edn., Basic Books, 1979; 2nd edn., Macmillan, 1993.

Sommer, Karel

Leading Research Worker & Fellow, Czech Acad. of Sciences, Silesian Inst., Nádrazní okruh 31, 746 48 Opava, Czechland.
Year and Place of Birth 1929, Malé Hradisko, Bohemia.
Degrees and Qualifications C.Sc., 1963; Ph.Dr. Palackeho Univ., 1965; Docent, Olomouc Univ., 1966.
Previous Post Docent, Palackeho Univ., 1966–9.
Current Offices and Honorary Posts Chairman, Research Council, Silesian Inst.; edit. board mem., *Slezsky sborník* [Silesian Research Rev.].
Major Honours Czech Literature Fund Prize 1990, (section for research & special literature).
Publications *Books: Z dejin odevníiho prumyslu na Prostojovsku* [Hist. of the Clothing Industry], with Emíl Gímes, Prostejov, 1970; *UNRRA a Ceskoslovensko* [UNRRA and Czechoslovakia], OPTYS, Opava, 1993. *Articles:* 'Evropsky ocelársky kartel a ceskoslovensky hutní prumysl' [European Steel Making Cartels and the Czechoslovak Metallurgical Industry], *Zájem rísskonemeckych koncernu o ceskoslovenské prumyslové oblasti* [Interest of German Concerns about Czechoslovak Indust. Regions], Opava, 1974, 25–69; 'Kontinentální kartel válcoven tru a ceskoslovenské zelezárské koncerny' [Continental Cartel Rolling Pipes and the Czechoslovak Iron Industry], *Hospodárské dejiny* [Econ. Hist.], 5, UCSD, Prague, 1980, 5–86; 'Hospodárská politika ceskoslovenské vlády a hutní prumysl v letach 1918–1923' [Econ. Polit. of the Czechoslovak Government and the Metallurgical Industry in the Years 1918–1923], *Slezsky sborník* [Silesian Research Rev.], 3-4, 1991, 219–30.

Sorrenson, M.P.K.

Prof. of Hist., Dept. of Hist., Univ. of Auckland, Private Bag 92019, Auckland 1, New Zealand. Tel.: 64 9 3737 999. Fax: 64 9 3737 438.
Year and Place of Birth 1932, Upper Papamoa, New Zealand.
Degrees and Qualifications MA Auckland Univ., 1954; D.Phil. Oxford Univ., 1962.
Previous Post Assoc. Prof., Auckland Univ., 1966.
Current Offices and Honorary Posts Mem., Waitangi Tribunal; council mem., New Zealand Geographic Board.
Fields of Expertise *Bus. Dimensions:* research and development. *Scope:* New Zealand. *Period:* nineteenth century; twentieth century as a whole. *Teaching:* undergrad.; post grad. *Consultancy:* New Zealand hist. maori hist.
Publications *Books: Land Reform in the Kikuyu Country*, OUP, East Africa, 1967; *Origins of European Settlement in Kenya*, OUP, East Africa, 1968; *Maori Origins and Migrations*, Auckland Univ. Press, 1979, 1993; *Na to Hoa Aroha: The Correspondence of Sir Abrana Ngata and Sir Peter Buck*, ed., 3 vols., 1986, 1987 & 1988; *Manifest Duty: The Polynesian Soc. over a Hundred Years*, Auckland Univ. Press, 1992.

Spender, J.-C.

Prof. of Strategy, Chair of Small Bus. & Enterprise, Grad. School of Management, Rutgers Univ., 180 Univ. Avenue, Newark, NJ 07102, USA. Tel.: 1 212 759 6451. Fax: 1 212 759 6451.
Year and Place of Birth 1936, Bishops Stortford, UK.
Degrees and Qualifications BA

(Eng.) Oxford, 1960; MA Oxford Univ., 1965; Ph.D. Manchester Bus. School, 1980.

Previous Post Chair of Bus. Policy, Glasgow Univ., 1988–91.

Major Honours Acad. of Management Ktarney Prize for Outstanding Research, 1980.

Fields of Expertise *Industry Fields:* mechanical engineering; shipbuilding and marine engineering; vehicle construction; paper, printing, publishing; transport and communication; insurance, banking, finance; professional and scientific services; electronics and computers: manufacture. *Bus. Dimensions:* entrepreneurs and entrepreneurship; research and development; strategy formation; bus. organization; bus. and technology; small bus. matters; management education; bus.–state relations; markets and bus.; co. culture. *Scope:* national; UK; USA. *Period:* nineteenth century; twentieth century as a whole; early twentieth century; inter-war years, 1919–39; late twentieth century, 1970–present; mid-twentieth century, 1940–70. *Teaching:* undergrad.; post grad.; exec. *Consultancy:* corporate strategy.

Publications *Books: Industry Receipts: The Nature and Sources of Managerial Judgement*, Blackwell, Oxford, 1989; *Turnaround, the Fall and Rise of the Newton Chambers Group*, with P.H. Grinyer, Associated Bus. Press, London, 1979. *Articles:* 'Some Frontier Activities around Strategy Historizing', *J. of Management Studies*, 30(1), 1993, 11–30.

Spitzer, Paul G.

Co. Historian, Boeing M/S 1R-24, POB 3707, Seattle, WA 98124, USA. Tel.: 1 206 655 4822. Fax: 1 206 655 3000.

Year and Place of Birth 1937, Vienna, Austria.

Degrees and Qualifications BA (Physics) Reed College, 1959; Ph.D. (Hist. of Sc.) Johns Hopkins Univ., 1970.

Previous Post Curator, Museum of Hist., Seattle, 1978–9.

Fields of Expertise *Industry Fields:* transport and communication; aviation and aerospace. *Bus. Dimensions:* bus. and technology; markets and bus. *Scope:* regional; USA. *Period:* twentieth century as a whole. *Teaching:* undergrad.; post grad. hist. sc., technology and aerospace. *Consultancy:* Boeing co. hist. (as employee not consultant).

Publications *Books: Boeing Logbook, 1916–1991*, 1991; *Boeing Year by Year*, 1991.

Spree, Reinhard

Prof., Munich Univ., Fac. of Polit. Econ., Dept. of Social & Econ. Hist., Ludwigstr. 33, 80539 Munich, Germany. Tel.: 49 89 2180 2229. Fax: 49 89 2180 3168.

Year and Place of Birth 1941, Arnsdorf, Germany.

Degrees and Qualifications Diplom (Econ.) Free Univ. Berlin, 1969; Dr.rer.pol. Free Univ. Berlin, 1975; Habilitation (Econ. & Soc. Hist.) Berlin Technical Univ., 1981.

Previous Post Prof. of Econ. Hist., Konstanz Univ., 1986–92.

Current Offices and Honorary Posts Advisory board, Inst. for European Population Studies, Liverpool Univ.; overseas mem. of edit. board, *Social Hist. of Medicine*, OUP.

Fields of Expertise *Industry Fields:* professional and scientific services. *Bus. Dimensions:* markets and bus. *Scope:* national. *Period:* nineteenth century; early twentieth century. *Teaching:* undergrad.; post grad.

Publications *Books: Die Wachstumszyklen der deutschen*

Wirtschaft von 1840 bis 1880, Duncker & Humblot, Berlin, 1977; *Wachstumstrends and Konjunkturzyklen in der deutschen Wirtschaft von 1820 bis 1913*, Vandenhoeck & Ruprecht, Göttingen, 1978; *Health and Social Class in Imperial Germany. A Hist. of Mortality, Morbidity and Inequality*, Berg Publishers, Oxford, 1988; *Lange Wellen wirtschaftlicher Entwicklung in der Neuzeit*, Centre for Historical Research, Cologne, 1991, (Historical Social Research Suppl. 4); *Der Rückzug des Todes. Der Epidemiologische Übergang in Deutschland seit dem späten 18. Jahrhundert*, Universitätsverlag, Konstanz, 1992.

Statham, Pamela C.

Dean of Econ. & Commerce, Dept. of Econ., The Univ. of Western Australia, Nedlands, WA 6009, Australia. Tel.: 61 9 380 2930. Fax: 61 9 380 1086.

Year and Place of Birth 1944, Sydney, Australia.

Degrees and Qualifications B.Econ. Monash Univ., 1966; Ph.D. Univ. of Western Australia, 1980.

Previous Post Research Fellow RSSS, Australian National Univ., 1987–8.

Fields of Expertise *Industry Fields:* general industry - rural and manufacture sectors. *Bus. Dimensions:* entrepreneurs and entrepreneurship; merger movement and issues; bus. organization; markets and bus. *Scope:* local; regional; national; internat.; Australia. *Period:* nineteenth century; twentieth century as a whole. *Teaching:* undergrad.

Publications *Books: Dictionary of Western Australians. Vol. I 1829–1850*, UWA Press, 1981; *The Tanner Letters - A Pioneer Saga of Swan River & Tasmania 1831–1845*, UWA Press, 1982; *The Origin of*

Australia's Capital Cities, ed., CUP, 1989; *A Colonial Regiment. New Sources Relating to the NSW Corps 1798–1810*, ANU Tech, 1993. *Articles:* 'The Sandalwood Industry in Australia - A History', *Sandalwood in the Pacific US Dept. of Agric.*, Hamilton & Conrad eds., Forrest Service, 1990.

Steiner, Jan

Head of Dept. of Social Sciences & Vice-Dean for Student Affairs, Silesian Univ., Fac. of Bus. Studies, Univerzitní Nám. 76, 733 40 Karviná, Czechland. Tel.: 42 6993 49951. Fax: 42 6993 46451.

Year and Place of Birth 1932, Orlová, Czechland.

Degrees and Qualifications BA (Czech. Hist.) Palacky Univ., Olomouc, 1956; Ph.D. (Hist.) Palacky Univ., 1970; Cand., Science Inst. of Hist., Prague, 1966.

Previous Post Research Fellow, Selesian Inst. of Czechoslovak Acad. of Sciences, Opava, 1966–90.

Current Offices and Honorary Posts Mem., Assoc. of Bus. Historians, Acad. of Sciences, Prague.

Fields of Expertise *Bus. Dimensions:* entrepreneurs and entrepreneurship. *Scope:* national; internat. *Teaching:* undergrad. *Consultancy:* co. hist.

Publications *Books: Kaptioly z dejin podnikani v Ceskoslovensko. I. 1918–1938* [Chapters from the Hist. of Bus. Enterprises in Czechoslovakia], with J. Gerslová, Karviná, 1992. *Articles:* 'Komparacní vyzkun vyvoje ostravské a hornoslezské prumyslové oblasti' [Comparative Research of the Development of Ostrava and the Upper Silesian Indust. Area], *Slezky Sborník*, 1990, 241–52; 'Rozmístení tezkého prumyslu na Ostravsku a Horním Slezsku po první svetové válce' [The Allocation of Heavy Industry in the

Ostrava Region and Upper Silesia after the First World War], *Slezsky Sborník,* 1991, 80–93; 'Hospodársky vyvoj prumyslovych oblastí ceskych zemí v období první republiky' [Econ. Development of Indust. Areas in Czechoslovakia in the Period of the First Republic], *Prumyslové oblasti ceskych zemí (1780–1945),* II, cést 1.Opava, SÚ CSAV-obchodne podnikatelská fakulta SU, 1991; 'Wirtschaftliche und soziale Zusammenhänge der technischen Entwicklung im Kohlenbergbau der Tschechoslowakei in der 1. Hälfte des 20. Jahrhunderts' [Econ. and Social Relations of Technical Development in the Czechoslovakian Mining Industry in the first Half of the 20th Century], *Sozialgeschichte des Bergbaus im 19. und 20. Jahrhundert,* C.H. Beck, Munich, 492–503.

Stiefel, Dieter

Prof., Inst. of Econ. and Social Hist., Vienna Univ. of Econ. and Bus. Admin., Augasse 2-6, A-1090 Vienna, Austria. Tel.: 43 222 31336 4243. Fax: 43 222 31336 710.

Year and Place of Birth 1946, Linz, Austria.

Degrees and Qualifications Dr. Hist.; Dr. Econ. & Bus. Admin.

Fields of Expertise *Industry Fields:* food, drink, tobacco; construction; transport and communication; insurance, banking, finance; public admin. and defence. *Bus. Dimensions:* entrepreneurs and entrepreneurship; production management; co. finance and accounting; personnel management; co. admin.; marketing; merger movement and issues; bus. organization; multinational bus.; bus.–state relations; markets and bus.; co. culture. *Scope:* national; internat.; global; Austria. *Period:* nineteenth century; twentieth century as a whole. *Teaching:* undergrad.; post grad. *Consultancy:* co.

hist.

Publications *Books: Die große Krise in einem kleinen Land, Österreichische Finanz- und Wirtschaftspolitik 1929–1938,* Böhlau Verlag, Vienna, 1988; *Finanzdiplomatie und Weltwirtschafskrise. Die Krise der Credit-Anstalt 1931,* Knapp Verlag, Frankfurt, 1989; *Zusammen mit Herbert Matis: Unternehmenskultur in Österreich,* Service Verlag, Vienna, 1987; *Die Weltwirtschaft. Struktur und Entwicklung im 20. Jahrhundert,* Verlag Ueberreuter, Vienna, 1991.

Stone, R.C.J.

Emeritus Prof. of Hist., Dept. of Hist., Univ. of Auckland, Private Bag, Auckland 1, New Zealand. Tel.: 0373 799. Fax: 0373 7438.

Year and Place of Birth 1923, Auckland, New Zealand.

Degrees and Qualifications MA New Zealand; Ph.D., Auckland Univ.

Previous Post Personal Chair in Hist., Auckland Univ., 1987–9.

Fields of Expertise *Industry Fields:* insurance, banking, finance; professional and scientific services. *Bus. Dimensions:* entrepreneurs and entrepreneurship. *Scope:* regional. *Period:* nineteenth century; twentieth century as a whole. *Teaching:* post grad. *Consultancy:* co. hist.

Publications *Books: Makers of Fortune,* Univ. of Auckland Press, 1973; *In the Time of Age,* Selwyn Foundation, Auckland, 1979; *Young Logan Campbell,* Univ. of Auckland Press, 1982; *The Father and his Gift,* Univ. of Auckland Press, 1987; *The Making of Russell McVeagh,* Univ. of Auckland Press, 1992.

Stromberg, Raymond

Adjunct Prof., Dept. of Bus. and Econ., Montgomery College, 2001551 Mannakee St, Rockville, Maryland 20850, USA. Tel.: 1 301 279 5137.

Year and Place of Birth 1911, Philadelphia, USA.

Degrees and Qualifications BA Central High School, Philadelphia, 1928; BS Temple Univ., Philadelphia, 1934; MA, Catholic of Univ. of Amer., Colombia District, 1948.

Previous Post US Army Dept., 1943–63.

Fields of Expertise *Industry Fields:* insurance, banking, finance. *Bus. Dimensions:* wage policy. *Scope:* UK. *Period:* inter-war years, 1919–39. *Teaching:* undergrad.

Publications *Articles:* 'Some British Theories on Wage Policy during the Interwar Period', MA, Catholic Univ. of Amer., 1948.

Sturchio, Jeffrey L.

Assoc. Director, Information Resources & Publishing, Merck & Co. Inc., One Merck Drive/WS1A-40, Whitehouse Station, NJ 08889–0100, USA. Tel.: 1 908 423 3981. Fax: 1 908 735 1182.

Year and Place of Birth 1952, Newark, USA.

Degrees and Qualifications BA Princeton Univ., 1973; MA Pennsylvania Univ., 1976; Ph.D. Pennsylvania Univ., 1981.

Previous Post Sen. Research Assoc., AT&T Archives, Feb. 1988–May 1989.

Current Offices and Honorary Posts Chair, Division of the Hist. of Chemistry, Amer. Chemical Soc., 1993; council mem., Hist. of Science Soc., 1993; council mem., Amer. Inst. of the Hist. of Pharmacy, 1993–6; sen.

fellow, National Museum of Amer. Hist., Smithsonian Inst.; research associate, Dept. of Hist. & Sociology of Science, Pennsylvania Univ.

Major Honours Smithsonian Inst. Post-doctoral Fellowship, 1980–1.

Fields of Expertise *Industry Fields:* chemicals and allied industries; pharmaceuticals. *Bus. Dimensions:* research and development; bus. and technology; co. culture. *Scope:* internat. *Period:* nineteenth century; twentieth century as a whole. *Consultancy:* co. hist.; corporate archives.

Publications *Books: Corporate Hist. and the Chemical Industries: A Resource Guide*, ed., CHOC, Philadelphia, 1985; *Chemistry in Amer. 1876–1976: Historical Indicators*, with W. Thackray, P.T. Carroll & R.F. Bud, D. Reidel, Dordrecht/Boston, 1985; paperback, 1988; *Values and Visions: A Merck Century*, ed., Merck & Co. Inc., Rahway, NJ, 1991, (also published in French, German, Italian & Spanish). *Articles:* 'Chemistry and Corporate Strategy at Du Pont', *Research Management*, 27, 1984, 10–18; 'Chemistry in Action: Penicillin Production in World War II', *Today's Chemist*, 1(1), Feb., 1988, 20–2, 35–6.

Sudrià, Carles

Prof., Fac. of Econ. Sciences, Dept. of Hist. and Econ. Institutions, Univ. of Barcelona, Av. Diagonal 690, 08034-Barcelona, Spain. Tel.: 34 3 40 1929/34 3 40 1930. Fax: 34 3 280 2376.

Year and Place of Birth 1953, Barcelona, Spain.

Degrees and Qualifications BA (Econ.) Autonomous Univ., Barcelona, 1975; Ph.D. (Econ.) Autonomous Univ., Barcelona, 1981.

Previous Post Assoc. Prof., Barcelona Univ., 1983–91.

Fields of Expertise *Industry Fields:* mining and quarrying; coal and petroleum products; textiles; gas, electricity, water; insurance, banking, finance. *Bus. Dimensions:* entrepreneurs and entrepreneurship; co. finance and accounting. *Scope:* local; regional; national; internat.; Spain. *Period:* nineteenth century; twentieth century as a whole. *Teaching:* undergrad.; post grad. *Consultancy:* co. hist.

Publications *Books: Historia de la Caja de Pensiones,* with Jordi Nadal, Edicions 62, Barcelona, 1983; *Una Societat Plenament Indust.,* ser.: Història Econòmica de la Catalunya Contemporània, vol. IV, Enciclop. Catalana, Barcelona, 1988. *Articles:* 'Un Factor Determinante: La Energía', *La Economia Española en el Siglo XX. Una Perspectiva Historica,* co-ed. with J. Nadal & A. Carreras, Ariel, Barcelona, 1987, 313–63; 'El Sector Energético: Condicionamientos y Posibilidades', *España. Economia,* J.L. García Delgado ed., Espasa Calpe, Madrid, 1988, 177–96; 'Los Beneficios de España durante la Gran Guerra. Una Aproximación a la Balanza de Pagos Española, 1914–1920', *Revista de Historia Economica,* VIII(2), 1990, Madrid, 363–96.

Sugimoto, Kimihiko

Prof., Fac. of Commerce, Osaka Gakuin Univ., 2-36-1 Kishibe-Minmi, Suita-City, Osaka 564, Japan. Tel.: 06 381 8434.

Year and Place of Birth 1944, Osaka, Japan.

Degrees and Qualifications B.Econ. Kobe Univ. of Commerce; M.Econ. Kobe Univ. of Commerce.

Current Offices and Honorary Posts V-P., Japanese Assoc. for Canadian Studies; council mem., Socio-Econ. Hist. Soc.

Fields of Expertise *Industry Fields:* transport and communication. *Bus. Dimensions:* entrepreneurs and entrepreneurship. *Scope:* regional; national. *Period:* nineteenth century; early twentieth century. *Teaching:* undergrad. *Consultancy:* co. hist.

Publications *Articles:* 'A Study of Canadian Hist. in Canada: An Introduction', *Osaka Gakuin Bus. Rev.,* 13(1), 1987, 109–23; 'A Study of Canadian Hist. in Canada (II)', *Osaka Gakuin Bus. Rev.,* 13(3), 1987, 83–103; 'A Study of Concepts of Canada', *Osaka Gakuin Bus. Rev,* 16(3), 1990, 129–64; 'A Study of the Rediscovery of Canadian History', *Osaka Gakuin Bus. Rev.,* 17(3), 1992, 121–37; 'A Note on the Study of Canadian Hist. (I) (II)', *Osaka Gakuin Bus. Rev.,* 18(1), 1992, 95–113 & 18(2), 1992, 115–38.

Sugisaki, Takamoto

Assoc. Prof., Dept. of Internat. Relations, Tsuda Univ., 2–1–1 Tsuda-machi, Kodaira-shi, Tokyo 187, Japan. Tel.: 81 423 42 5155. Fax: 81 423 41 2444.

Year and Place of Birth 1949, Tokyo, Japan.

Degrees and Qualifications BA Tokyo Univ., 1974; MA Tokyo Univ., 1977.

Previous Post Assoc. Prof., Dept. of Bus. Admin., Hakuoh Univ., 1992.

Current Offices and Honorary Posts Mem., various publications; mem., Assoc. of Bus. Historians.

Fields of Expertise *Industry Fields:* chemicals and allied industries; metal manufacture; electronics and computers: manufacture. *Bus. Dimensions:* personnel management; co. admin.; multinational bus. *Scope:* national; internat. *Period:* early twentieth century; inter-war years, 1919–39; mid-twentieth century, 1940–70. *Teaching:* undergrad.; post grad.

Publications *Articles:* 'Restructuring the "Internal Labour Markets" in the British Iron and Steel Industry between the Wars', *Hakuoh Univ. J.*, 3(1), Mar., 1989; 'The British Steel Industry and the Internat. Steel Cartel between the Wars', *The Study of Internat. Relations*, Tsuda, 16, 1989; '"Internal Labour Market" and Indust. Relations - the Case of the British Iron and Steel Industries', *Hakuoh Univ. J.*, 4(1), Mar., 1990; 'The British Iron and Steel Industry and the Internat. Cartel under the Great Depression', *The Study of Internat. Relations*, 17, 1991; 'ICI's Labour Management Policy and the Introduction of the Bedaux System in the 1930s', *The Hakuoh Women's Junior College J.*, 14(2), Mar., 1992.

Sugiyama, Shinya

Prof. of Econ. Hist., Dept. of Econ., Keio Univ., 2-15-45 Mita, Minato-ku, Tokyo 108, Japan. Tel.: 03 3453 4511. Fax: 03 3798 7480.

Year and Place of Birth 1949, Shizuoka-ken, Japan.

Degrees and Qualifications BA Waseda Univ., 1972; MA Waseda Univ., 1975; Ph.D. London Univ., 1981.

Previous Post Research Officer, ICERD, London School of Econ., 1981–4.

Current Offices and Honorary Posts Sec., Shakai Keizaishi Gakkai, 1985–.

Major Honours Nikkei Award, Econ. & Bus. Studies, 1989.

Fields of Expertise *Industry Fields:* food, drink, tobacco; coal and petroleum products; shipbuilding and marine engineering; textiles; transport and communication; distributive trades. *Bus. Dimensions:* entrepreneurs and entrepreneurship; production management; co. finance and accounting; marketing; bus. and technology; multinational bus.; bus.–state relations; mar-

kets and bus. *Scope:* regional; national; internat.; Japan; China. *Period:* nineteenth century; early twentieth century; inter-war years, 1919–39. *Teaching:* undergrad.; post grad.

Publications *Books: Japan's Industrialization in the World Economy, 1859–1899: Export Trade and Overseas Competition*, Athlone Press, London, 1988; *Senkanki Tonan-Ajia no keizai masatsu* [Internat. Commercial Rivalry in Southeast Asia in the Interwar Period], co-ed., Dobunkan Press, Tokyo, 1990. *Articles:* 'Thomas B. Glover: A British Merchant in Japan, 1861–1870', *Bus. Hist.*, 26(2), July 1984, 115–38; 'A British Trading Firm in the Far East: John Swire & Sons, 1867–1914', *Bus. Hist. of General Trading Cos.*, S. Yonekawa & H. Yoshihara eds., Univ. of Tokyo Press, 1987, 171–202; 'Textile Marketing in East Asia, 1860–1914', *Textile Hist.*, 19(2), Oct. 1988, 279–98.

Sullivan, Timothy E.

Asst. Prof. of Econ., Towson State Univ., Dept. of Econ., Baltimore, MD 21204, USA. Tel.: 1 410 830 2338. Fax: 1 410 830 3424.

Year and Place of Birth 1955, Oak Park, USA.

Degrees and Qualifications BA Eastern Illinois Univ., 1977; MA Eastern Illinois Univ., 1977; MS Univ. of Illinois at Urbana-Champaigne, 1987; Ph.D. Univ. of Illinois at Urbana-Champaigne, 1987.

Previous Post Asst. Prof. of Econ., Elon College, North Carolina, 1987–9.

Fields of Expertise *Industry Fields:* other manufacturing industries. *Bus. Dimensions:* entrepreneurs and entrepreneurship; production management; research and development; bus. organization; markets and bus. *Scope:* regional. *Period:* nineteenth century.

Teaching: undergrad. *Consultancy:* co. hist.

Publications *Articles:* 'Industrial Transformation and Market Integration along the Amer. Manufacturing Frontier: The Midwest from 1850 to 1880', *Bus. & Econ. Hist.*, 2nd ser., 17, 1988, 201–6; 'Comparative Perspectives on Nineteenth Century Growth: Ontario in the Great Lakes Region', *Canadian Papers in Bus. Hist.*, with Inwood, 2, 1993, 71–101.

Sunaga, Kinzaburo

Prof., Dept. of Econ., Kokugakuin Univ., 4–10–28 Higashi, Shibuya-ku, Tokyo 150, Japan. Tel.: 81 3 5466 0317.

Year and Place of Birth 1943, Kita-ku, Japan.

Degrees and Qualifications M.Com., Chuo Univ., 1971.

Current Offices and Honorary Posts Director, Japanese Bus. Hist. Soc.

Fields of Expertise *Industry Fields:* metal manufacture; mechanical engineering; electronics and computers: manufacture. *Bus. Dimensions:* entrepreneurs and entrepreneurship; production management; co. admin.; bus. and technology. *Scope:* regional; national. *Period:* nineteenth century; twentieth century as a whole; inter-war years, 1919–39. *Teaching:* undergrad.; post grad. *Consultancy:* corporate strategy.

Publications *Books: Hist. of Commerce*, co-auth., Yuhikaku, 1981. *Articles:* 'The Acceptance Conditions of the Mass Production System - A Comparative Study of the Machine Tool Industry between Amer. and the United Kingdom', *Japan Bus. Hist. Rev.*, 16(2), 1981; 'On the Major Management Problem in Amer. Industry', *Kokugakuin Econ. Rev.*, 33(1), 1985; 'On the Labor Problem during the Formation Period of Management Systems in America', *Kokugakuin Econ. Rev.*, 36(1), 1988.

Supple, Barry

Director, Leverhulme Trust, 15–17 New Fetter Lane, London, EC4A 1NR, UK. Tel.: 44 71 822 6938. Fax: 44 71 822 5084.

Year and Place of Birth 1930, London, UK.

Degrees and Qualifications B.Sc. (Econ.) London Univ., 1952; Ph.D. Cambridge Univ., 1955; Litt.D. Cambridge Univ., 1993.

Previous Post Prof. of Econ. Hist., Cambridge Univ., 1981–93.

Current Offices and Honorary Posts Pres., Econ. Hist. Soc.

Fields of Expertise *Industry Fields:* mining and quarrying; insurance, banking, finance. *Bus. Dimensions:* bus.–state relations. *Scope:* national. *Period:* twentieth century as a whole. *Teaching:* undergrad.; post grad. *Consultancy:* co. hist.

Publications *Books: Commercial Crisis and Change in England, 1600–42*, CUP, 1959; *Boston Capitalists and Western Railroads*, with Arthur M. Johnson, Harvard Univ. Press, 1967; *The Royal Exchange Assurance: A Hist. of British Insurance, 1720–1970*, CUP, 1970; *The Hist. of the British Coalmining Industry, 1913–46: The Polit. Economy of Decline*, OUP, 1987; *The Rise of Big Bus.*, ed., Edward Elgar Publishing, 1992.

Sutet, Marcel

Teacher of Econ. and Social Sciences, Lycée Polyvalent Régional, Place Mathias, 71321 Chalon-sur-Saône, France. Tel.: 33 85 41 44 43.

Year and Place of Birth 1939, Montceau-les-Mines, France.

Degrees and Qualifications Dip. d'Etudes Supérieures (Econ. Hist.), Lyon Univ., 1963; Agrégation (Soc. Sc.).

Fields of Expertise *Industry Fields:* mining and quarrying; metal manufacture. *Bus. Dimensions:* entrepreneurs and entrepreneurship. *Scope:* local; regional. *Period:* nineteenth century. *Teaching:* comprehensive school. *Consultancy:* co. hist.; corporate strategy.

Publications *Books: Montceau-les-Mines. Essor d'une Mine. Naissance d'une Ville.*, Editions Horvath, Roanne, 1981, 2nd edn., 1987; *Le Creusot. Montceau-les-Mines autrefois: Du Terroir à l'Usine*, Editions Horvath, Roanne, 1981, 2nd edn., 1991. *Articles:* 'Un grand Capitaine d'Industrie: Jules Chagot, Fondateur de la Compagnie des Mines de Blanzy (1801–1877). Etude de Mentalité patronale au XIXe Siècle', *Actes du 89. Congrès National des Sociétés Savantes*, Lyon, 1964, Imprimerie Nationale, Paris, 1965; 'La Communauté Urbaine. Le Creusot. Montceau-les-Mines', *La Saône et Loire*, Editions de la Taillanderie, Bourg, 1989; 'Bourgogne', *Les Patrons du Second Empire.*, vol. II, Philippe Jobert ed., Picard Editeur Paris, Editions Cénomane, Le Mans, 1991.

Suyenaga, Kunitoshi

Prof., Fac. of Econ., Doshisha Univ., Karasuma-Imadegawa, Kamigyo-ku, Kyoto, Japan. Tel.: 075 251 3657. Fax: 075 251 3060.

Year and Place of Birth 1943, Fukuoka, Japan.

Degrees and Qualifications B.Econ. Doshisha Univ., 1967; M.Econ, Doshisha Univ., 1970.

Previous Post Prof. of Japanese Econ. Hist., Fac. of Econ., Doshisha

Univ., 1990–2.

Current Offices and Honorary Posts Council mem., Socio-Econ. Hist. Soc.

Fields of Expertise *Industry Fields:* textiles. *Bus. Dimensions:* entrepreneurs and entrepreneurship. *Scope:* national. *Period:* early modern; eighteenth century; nineteenth century. *Teaching:* undergrad.; post grad. *Consultancy:* co. hist.

Publications *Books: Henkakuki no Shonin Shihon-Ohmi Shonin Chogin no Kenkyu* [A Study of the Ohmi Merchant House Chogin in the 19th Century], co-auth., Yoshikawa Press, 1984; *Ohmi Shonin no Keiei Isan* [The Managerial Legacy of Ohmi Merchants in Japan], co-auth., Dobunkan Press, 1992.

Suzuki, Toshio

Assoc. Prof., Fac. of Management, Chukyo Univ., 101-2 Yagoto-honmachi, Showa-ku, Nagoya City 466, Japan. Tel.: 81 52 832 2151. Fax: 81 52 835 7196.

Year and Place of Birth 1948, Yamagata pref., Japan.

Degrees and Qualifications BA Keio Univ., 1971; MA Keio Univ., 1973; Ph.D. London School of Econ., 1991.

Previous Post Lect., Fac. of Commerce, Chukyo Univ.

Fields of Expertise *Industry Fields:* insurance, banking, finance; electronics and computers: manufacture. *Bus. Dimensions:* co. finance and accounting; co. law; multinational bus. *Scope:* national; internat.; UK. *Period:* nineteenth century; early twentieth century. *Teaching:* undergrad. *Consultancy:* co. hist.

Publications *Books: Eikoku Jushoshugi Kosai Seiri Keikaku to Nankai Gaisha* [The South Sea Co.], Chukyo Univ., 1986. *Articles:* 'Baring Brothers to Nichiro Senji Kosai Hakko' [The Baring Brothers and Russo-Japanese War Loan Issues], *Mita Econ.*

J., 82(special II), 1988; 'Eikoku Kindai Kabushiki Kaisha no Keisei Katei' [The Formation of the Modern Joint Stock Co. in England 1–3], *J. of Monetary Econ.*, 155, 163–4, 181–2, 1975–80; 'Foreign Government Loan Issues on the London Capital Market, 1870–1913, with Special Reference to Japan', Ph.D. thesis, London Univ., 1991.

'Postwar Development of General Trading Companies', *General Trading Companies*, S. Yonekawa ed., United Nations Univ. Press, 1990; 'Gosei Seni' [A Synthetic Fibre Industry], *Sengo Nihon Keieishi I* [Japanese Bus. Hist. after World War II, Vol. I], S. Yonekawa, K. Shimokawa & H. Yamazaki eds., Toyokeizai Shinposha, 1991.

Suzuki, Tsuneo

Prof. of Indust. Economy, Gakushuin Univ., Fac. of Econ., 1-5-1 Mejiro, Toshima, Tokyo 171, Japan. Tel.: 81 3 3986 0221. Fax: 81 3 5992 1007.

Year and Place of Birth 1947, Tokyo, Japan.

Degrees and Qualifications BA Yokohama Nat. Univ., 1972; MA (Econ.) Hitotsubashi Univ., 1977.

Previous Post Assoc. Prof., Fac. of Econ., Wako Univ.

Current Offices and Honorary Posts Edit. board mem., *Yearbook*, 1991–; council mem., Japan Bus. Hist. Soc., 1993–; council mem., Socio-Econ. Hist. Soc., 1991–.

Fields of Expertise *Industry Fields:* chemicals and allied industries; textiles; distributive trades. *Bus. Dimensions:* research and development; bus. and technology. *Scope:* internat. *Period:* inter-war years, 1919–39; mid-twentieth century, 1940–70. *Teaching:* undergrad.; post grad. *Consultancy:* co. hist.

Publications *Books: Nihon Ryuan Kogyoshiron* [A Historical Study of the Japanese Nitrogen Industry], Krume Univ., Sangyo-Keizai Kenkyusho. *Articles:* 'Kyushu niokeru Kagaku Sangyo no Hatten' [The Development of Chemical Industries in Kyushu District], *Kyushu niokeru Sangyo no Hatten* [The Development of Modern Industries in Kyushu District], T. Kojima ed., Kyushu Univ. Press, 1988;

Suzuki, Yoshitaka

Prof. of Bus. Hist., Fac. of Econ., Tohoku Univ., Kawauchi, Sendai 980, Japan. Tel.: 022 222 1800.

Year and Place of Birth 1944, Tokyo, Japan.

Degrees and Qualifications BA Hitotsubashi Univ.; MA (Econ). Hitotsubashi Univ.

Previous Post Assoc. Prof. of Bus. Hist., Tohoku Univ., 1973–86.

Current Offices and Honorary Posts Exec. com. mem., Japan Bus. Hist. Soc., 1989–90; exec. officer, Japan Bus. Hist. Soc., 1991–2; council mem., Socio-Econ. Soc., 1990–.

Fields of Expertise *Industry Fields:* instrument engineering; distributive trades; insurance, banking, finance. *Bus. Dimensions:* production management; co. finance and accounting; co. admin.; merger movement and issues; bus. organization. *Scope:* internat. *Period:* mid-twentieth century, 1940–70. *Teaching:* undergrad.; post grad. *Consultancy:* co. hist.

Publications *Books: Keieishi* [Bus. Hist.], co-auth., Yuhikaku, Tokyo, 1987; *Keieishi* [Entrepreneurship in the early Phase of Industrialization], Dobunkan Press, Tokyo, 1987; *Japanese Management Structures 1920–80*, Macmillan Press, London, 1991. *Articles:* 'Igirisu Dai Kigyo to Naibu Shihon Shijo, 1920–40 nen' [The Internal Capital Market and British large-scale Companies,

1920–40], *Kenkyu nenpo Keizaigaku* [Annals of Econ.], 1991; 'The Rise and Decline of Steel Industries', *Changing Patterns of Internat. Rivalry*, Suzuki & Abe eds., Tokyo Univ. Press, 1991.

Svorc, Peter

Sen. Lect., P.J. Safárik Univ. Presov, Fac. of Philo., Dept. of Hist. and Archives, ul. 17. novembra, c. 1, 081 16 Presov, Slovakia. Tel.: 42 91 332 31. Fax: 42 91 332 68.

Year and Place of Birth 1957, Strba, Liptovsky Mikulas, Slovakia.

Degrees and Qualifications MA Presov Univ., 1981; Ph.Dr. Presov Univ., 1981; Ph.D. Bratislava Univ., 1990.

Previous Post Historian/Research Fellow, East Slovakian Museum Kosice, 1981–3.

Current Offices and Honorary Posts Scholarly sec., Dept. of Hist. & Archives; mem., P.J. Safarik Univ., Academic Senate; com. mem., bus. section, Slovak Acad. of Sciences.

Major Honours Slovak Literary Fund Prize for Scholarly Writings, 1980; Univ. Rector's Prize for Monograph Podtatranske Premeny, 1988.

Fields of Expertise *Industry Fields:* agric., forestry, fishing; emigration. *Scope:* local; regional; national. *Period:* twentieth century as a whole. *Teaching:* undergrad.

Publications *Books: Podtatranské Premeny* [Transformations of the Lower High Tatras Region], Vychodoslovenské vydavatelstvo Kosice, 1988; *Zrod Republiky. Dobové Dokumenty, Spomienky a Stanoviská 1914–1918* [The Birth of the Republic. Documents, Reminiscences and Attitudes of the 1914–1918 Period], Slovo Kosice, 1991; *Rozbíjali monarchiu. Populárny slovník osobností cesko-slovenského odboja 1914–1918* [They were break-

ing the Monarchy. A Popular Dictionary of Personalities of Czecho-Slovak Resistance 1914–1918], Vychodoslovenské vydavatel'stvo Kosice, 1992. *Articles:* 'Pociatky kolektivizácie v byvalom Popradskom a Kezmarskom okrese 1949–1953' [The Beginnings of the Process of Collectivization of Agric. Land in the Former Districts of Poprad and Kezmarok 1949–1953], *Historica Carpatica*, 13, East Slovakian Museum Kosice, 1982, 13–36; 'Druhá etapa kolektivizácie v byvalych okresoch Poprad a Kezmarok 1956–1960' [Second Period of the Process of Collectivization of Agric. Land in the Former Districts of Poprad and Kezmarok 1956–1960], *Historica Carpatica*, 15, East Slovakian Museum Kosice, 1984, 69–94.

Sweeny, Robert C.H.

Asst. Prof., Dept. of Hist., Memorial Univ. of Newfoundland, Elizabeth Avenue, POB 4200, St John's, Newfoundland, A1C 5S7, Canada. Tel.: 1 719 737 8420. Fax: 1 719 737 2164.

Year and Place of Birth 1952, Montreal, Canada.

Degrees and Qualifications BA Sir George Williams Univ., 1975; MA Québec Univ. at Montreal, 1980; Ph.D. McGill Univ., 1985.

Previous Post Montreal Bus. Hist. Project, McGill Univ., 1976–89.

Fields of Expertise *Industry Fields:* insurance, banking, finance. *Bus. Dimensions:* merger movement and issues. *Scope:* national; Canada: Quebec, Newfoundland. *Period:* nineteenth century. *Teaching:* undergrad.

Publications *Books: A Guide to the Hist. and Records of Selected Montreal Bus.es before 1947*, HEC, Montreal, 1978; *Les Relations Ville/Campagne: Le Cas du Bois de Chauffage*, Editions du MBHP, Montreal, 1988. *Articles:*

'Paysan et Ouvrier: Du Féodalisme laurentien au Capitalisme québécois', *Sociologie et Sociétés*, XXII(1), April, 1990, 143–61.

Sylla, Richard

Henry Kaufman Prof. of the Hist. of Financial Institutions and Markets & Prof. of Econ., New York Univ., 44 West 4th St, New York, NY 10012-4218, USA. Tel.: 1 212 998 0869. Fax: 1 212 995 4218.

Year and Place of Birth 1940, Illinois, USA.

Degrees and Qualifications BA Harvard Univ., 1962; MA Harvard Univ., 1965; Ph.D. Harvard Univ., 1969.

Previous Post Prof. of Econ. & Bus., North Carolina State Univ., 1968–90.

Current Offices and Honorary Posts Trustee, Bus. Hist. Conf.

Major Honours Arthur H. Cole Prize, Econ. Hist. Assoc.; Research Assoc., Nat. Bureau of Econ. Research.

Fields of Expertise *Industry Fields:* insurance, banking, finance. *Bus. Dimensions:* markets and bus. *Scope:* internat. *Period:* nineteenth century. *Teaching:* post grad. *Consultancy:* co. hist.

Publications *Books:* Routledge, 1991; *The Amer. Capital Market, 1846–1914*, Arno, 1975; *Patterns of European Industrialization - the Nineteenth Century*, co-ed., Routledge, 1991; *A Hist. of Interest Rates*, co-auth., 3rd edn., Rutgers, 1991; *The Evolution of the Amer. Economy*, co-auth., 2nd edn., Macmillan, New York, 1993.

Takahashi, Yasutaka

Assoc. Prof., Fac. of Econ., Kanto Gakuen Univ., 200 Fujiagu Ota Gumma 373, Japan. Tel.: 81 276 31 2711.

Year and Place of Birth 1946, Saitama, Japan.

Degrees and Qualifications Dip. Waseda Univ., 1969; MBA Waseda Univ., 1972.

Previous Post Lect., Rikkyo Univ.

Fields of Expertise *Industry Fields:* mechanical engineering; vehicle construction; transport and communication. *Bus. Dimensions:* entrepreneurs and entrepreneurship; production management. *Scope:* global. *Period:* interwar years, 1919–39; late twentieth century, 1970–present. *Teaching:* undergrad. *Consultancy:* co. hist.

Publications *Books: Nihonteikokushugika no Chugoku* [China under Japan], Rakuyushobou, 1981; *Nihonteikokushugi no Manshushihai* [Manchuria under Japan], Jichosha, 1986; *Nakajimahikoki no Kenkyu* [A Study on the Nakajima Aircraft Co.], Nihonkeizaihyoronsha, 1988. *Articles:* 'Taiwan Tetudo no Seiritu' [The Construction of the Taiwan Railway], *Management Hist. Science*, 13(2), 1979; 'Ryo Taisen kan ni okeru Taiwan Tou Gyo' [The Sugar Industry in Taiwan, 1912–39], *Social Econ. Hist. Science*, 51(6), 1986.

Takechi, Kyozo

Prof., Fac. of Bus. & Econ., Kinki Univ., 3-4-1 Kowakae Higashiosaka-city, Osaka, Japan. Tel.: 06 721 2332. Fax: 06 729 2493.

Year and Place of Birth 1940, China.

Degrees and Qualifications M.Econ. Univ. of Osaka pref., 1967.

Previous Post Asst. Prof., Hanazono Univ., 1977–80.

Fields of Expertise *Industry Fields:* other manufacturing industries; transport and communication. *Bus. Dimensions:* entrepreneurs and entrepreneurship; small bus. matters.

Scope: local; regional. *Period:* twentieth century as a whole; early twentieth century; inter-war years, 1919–39. *Teaching:* undergrad.; post grad. *Consultancy:* co. hist.

Publications *Books: Meijizenki Yusoshi no Kisoteki Kenkyu* [A Hist. of Transport in the Early Meiji Era], Yazankaku Press, 1978; *Toshikinko Tetsudo no Shiteki Tenkai* [A Historical Study of the Suburban Railways of Japan], Nihonkeizaihyoronsha, 1986; *Nihon Shihonsyugi to Jibashihon* [Local Capital under Japanese Capitalism], Yuzankaku, 1990; *Nihon no Chihotetsudono Keiseishi* [The Formation of Local Railway Networks in Japan], Kashiwa Syobo, 1990; *Kindai Nihon Kotsu Rodoshi Kenkyu* [A Hist. of Modern Labour in the Japanese Transport Industry], Nihonkeizaihyoronsha, 1992.

Tanaka, Toshihiro

Prof. of Foreign Econ. Hist., Fac. of Econ., Fukuoka Univ., 8-19-1 Nanakuma, Jonan-ku, Fukoka-shi, Japan. Tel.: 092 871 6631. Fax: 092 864 2904.

Year and Place of Birth 1946, Osaka, Japan.

Degrees and Qualifications BA Wakayama Univ.; MA Kobe Univ.

Current Offices and Honorary Posts Sec. & ed., Japanese Bus. Hist. Soc.

Fields of Expertise *Industry Fields:* transport and communication. *Bus. Dimensions:* entrepreneurs and entrepreneurship; co. finance and accounting; bus. organization. *Scope:* internat.; France. *Period:* nineteenth century; early twentieth century. *Teaching:* undergrad.; post grad. *Consultancy:* co. hist.

Publications *Articles:* 'An Analysis of "Groups" and "Control" among French Railway Companies under the Hornachie Juillet', *Japan Bus. Hist.*

Rev., 14(2), 1979, 31–53; 'Note on the Relationship between English and French Interests in the French Railway Companies of the 1840s', *J. of Econ. of Fukuoka Univ.*, 27, 1982, 281–316; 'The Formation and Activities of English Finance Companies in the 1860s', *J. of Econ. of Fukuoka Univ.*, 26, 1981, 1–34 & 27, 1982, 1–25.

Taniguchi, Akitake

Assoc. Prof. of Bus. Hist., Fac. of Bus. Admin., Osaka Keizai Univ., 2-Chome, Osumidori, Higashiyodogawa-ku, Osaka 533, Japan. Tel.: 06 328 2431.

Year and Place of Birth 1949, Tottori pref., Japan.

Degrees and Qualifications M.Econ. Kyoto Univ., 1975.

Current Offices and Honorary Posts Mem. of edit. com., Bus. Hist. Soc. of Japan, 1991–.

Fields of Expertise *Industry Fields:* food, drink, tobacco; coal and petroleum products; chemicals and allied industries; metal manufacture; mechanical engineering; instrument engineering; electrical engineering; shipbuilding and marine engineering; vehicle construction; metal goods; textiles; leather; clothing and footwear; bricks, pottery, glass, cement; timber, furniture; paper, printing, publishing; other manufacturing industries. *Bus. Dimensions:* strategy formation; merger movement and issues; bus. organization; bus. and technology. *Scope:* national; USA. *Period:* nineteenth century; twentieth century as a whole. *Teaching:* undergrad.

Publications *Books: Amerika Syoki Torasuto no Kenkyu* [A Study of the Early Trusts in the United States], Osaka Keizai Univ., 1984; *Amerika Biggu Bizinesu Seiritushi* [Hist. of the Formation of Big Bus. in the United States], co-auth., Toyokeizaishinposha, 1986. *Articles:* 'Amerika Godokigyo no Ruikeibunseki, 1882–1904' [A Study of Consolidations in the United States, 1882–1904], *Japan Bus. Hist. Rev.*, 25 (3), 1990.

Tanimoto, Masayuki

Asst. Prof., Fac. of Econ., Sendai Aobaku, Kawauchi, Japan. Tel.: 81 22 222 1800. Fax: 81 22 221 6018.

Year and Place of Birth 1959, Hokkaido, Japan.

Degrees and Qualifications B.Econ. Tokyo Univ., 1982.

Previous Post Asst. Prof., Fac. of Econ., Toyama Univ.

Publications *Books: The Study of the Soy Brewing Industry*, co-auth., Yoshikawa Kobunkan, 1990, 231–340. *Articles:* 'The Development of Cotton Weaving in the Bakumatsu and Early Meiji Periods', *Socio-Econ. Hist.*, 52(2), 1986, 1–34; 'The Development of the Cotton Weaving Market in the Bakumatsu and Meiji Periods', *J. of Agrarian Hist.*, 115, 54–67; 'The Opening of the Port and Meiji Restoration', *Econ. Hist. of Japan*, 3, ch. 5, Iwanami Shoten, 1989, 224–83.

Tatsuki, Mariko

Prof., Keisen Jogakuen College, 2-10 Minamino, Tama-shi, Tokyo, Japan Bus. Hist. Inst., Fuji Building, 2-12-4 Hirakawa-cho, Chiyoda-ku, Tokyo, Japan. Tel.: 81 3 3262 1090 (Japan Bus. Hist. Inst.). Fax: 81 3 3239 5090.

Year and Place of Birth 1944, Tokyo, Japan.

Degrees and Qualifications B.Econ. Tokyo Univ., 1968; M.Econ. Tokyo Univ., 1971.

Current Offices and Honorary Posts Council mem., Bus. Hist. Soc., 1988–.

Fields of Expertise *Industry Fields:* transport and communication; distrib-

utive trades; insurance, banking, finance. *Bus. Dimensions:* co. finance and accounting; marketing; strategy formation; merger movement and issues; markets and bus. *Scope:* national; internat. *Period:* twentieth century as a whole; early twentieth century; inter-war years, 1919–39; mid-twentieth century, 1940–70; late twentieth century, 1970–present. *Teaching:* undergrad. *Consultancy:* co. hist.

Publications *Books: Nihon Sangyo Kinyu Shi Kenkyu* [Hist. of Japanese Indust. Finance], co-auth., Tokyo Univ. Press, 1974; *Kogyo-ka to Kigyosha Katudo* [Industrialization and Entrepreneurship], co-auth., Nihon Keizai Shinbun Sha, 1976; *Kigyo Keiei no Rekishi-teki Kenkyu* [Historical Inquiry on Managerial Industries], co-auth., Iwanami Shoten, 1991. *Articles:* 'Kaiun Fukyo to Teiki sen no Gorika' [The Streamlining of O.S.K. under Depressive Econ. Conditions], *Shakai Keizai Shigaku* [Socio-Econ. Hist], 52(3), 1986; 'Competition and Streamlining on the Pacific Routes in the 1920s and 1930s', *Bus. Hist.*, July 1993.

Tedesco, Paul H.

Lect. in Hist., Government and Bus., Maryland Univ. Asian Division, The Univ. of Maryland Asian Division, Unit 5060, POB 0100, APO AP 96328–0100, USA. Tel.: 011 81 0425 52 2511. Fax: 011 81 0425 51 8305.

Year and Place of Birth 1928, Nashua, USA.

Degrees and Qualifications BA (Hist.) Harvard College, 1952; MA (Hist.) Boston Univ., 1955; Ph.D. (Amer. Econ./Bus. Hist.) Boston Univ., 1970; CAGS (Educational Admin.) Northeastern Univ., 1974.

Previous Post Chairman, Dept. of Education & Prof. of Education (Sen.

Lect./Adjunct Prof. of Hist.), Northeastern Univ., Boston, 1965–87.

Current Offices and Honorary Posts National co-ordinator/mem., board of directors, Bus. Hist. & Econ. Life Program, Inc. (BHelp, Inc.).

Major Honours Financial Executive Institute's National Collegiate Award, 1985; Freedom Foundation George Washington Medal of Honor for Econ., 1984; Horace Kidger Award - New England Hist. Teachers Assoc.

Fields of Expertise *Industry Fields:* metal goods; textiles; clothing and footwear; bus. services. *Bus. Dimensions:* trade associations; case development. *Scope:* local; regional; national. *Period:* nineteenth century; twentieth century as a whole. *Teaching:* undergrad.; post grad. *Consultancy:* co. hist.

Publications *Books: Econ. Change and the Community: Canton, Massachusetts, 1797–1965,* General Learning Corp., Morristown, NJ, 1970; *The Hub of the Jewelry World: Attleboro, Massachusetts, 1894–1975,* Attleboro Historical Commission, Atteleboro, 1979; *Thunder of the Mills: A New England Bus. and Econ. Hist. Casebook, 1690–1965,* ed., Northeastern Univ. Pub., Boston, 1981; *Patriotism, Protection and Prosperity: James M. Swank, the Amer. Iron and Steel Assoc. and the Tariff, 1872–1913,* Garland Pub., New York, 1985;*A New England City: Haverhill, Massachusetts, 1890–1990,* Windsor Publications, Northridge, CA, 1987.

Degrees and Qualifications BA Yale Univ., 1969; MA Columbia Univ., 1971; Ph.D. Columbia Univ., 1976.

Previous Post Assoc. Prof., Harvard Bus. School, 1985–90.

Current Offices and Honorary Posts Director, Research Div., Harvard Bus. School; mem., Board of Trustees, Bus. Hist. Conf.

Major Honours Newcomen Fellowship for the Study of Bus. Hist. at the Harvard Bus. School, 1978–79; Newcomen Award for the best article in Vol. 55 of *Bus. Hist. Rev.,* 1981; Honorary MA. Harvard Univ., 1990.

Fields of Expertise *Industry Fields:* distributive trades. *Bus. Dimensions:* marketing. *Scope:* national; USA. *Period:* twentieth century as a whole. *Teaching:* post grad. *Consultancy:* corporate strategy.

Publications *Books: Keeping the Corporate Image: Public Relations and Bus., 1900–1950,* JAI Press, Greenwich, CT., 1979; *The Coming of Managerial Capitalism: A Casebook on the Hist. of Amer. Econ. Institutions,* with Alfred D. Chandler Jr. co-auth., Irwin, Homewood, IL, 1985; *New and Improved: The Story of Mass Marketing in Amer.,* Basic Books, New York, 1990; most recent edn. translated into Japanese & published by Mirnerva Shobo, 1993; *The Rise and Fall of Mass Marketing,* with G. Jones co-ed., Routledge, London, 1993. *Articles:* 'From Competitor to Consumer: The Changing Focus of Federal Regulation of Advertising', *Bus. Hist. Rev.,* 55(1), Spring, 1981.

Tedlow, Richard S.

Prof. of Bus. Admin., Grad. School of Bus., Harvard Univ., Soldiers Field, Boston, MA 02163, USA. Tel.: 1 617 495 6688. Fax: 1 617 496 5994.

Year and Place of Birth 1947, Orange, NJ, USA.

Terachi, Takashi

Assoc. Prof. of Bus. Hist., School of Bus. Admin., Kwansei Gakuin Univ., 1-1-155 Uegahara, Nishinomiya-shi, Hyogo 662, Japan. Tel.: 0798 53 6111. Fax: 0798 51 0903.

Year and Place of Birth 1959,

Hiroshima pref., Japan.

Degrees and Qualifications BA Kwansei Gakuin Univ., 1982; MBA Kwansei Univ., 1984.

Previous Post Asst. Prof. of Bus. Hist., School of Bus. Admin., Kwansei Gakuin Univ., 1988–92.

Fields of Expertise *Industry Fields:* insurance, banking, finance. *Bus. Dimensions:* co. admin.; strategy formation; bus. organization. *Scope:* national; internat. *Period:* nineteenth century. *Teaching:* undergrad. *Consultancy:* co. hist.

Publications *Articles:* 'Merchant Bankers in the Panic of 1837', *Kwansei Gakuin J. of Bus. Admin.*, 35(1), 1987;'The Bank of England as a Central Bank in the Panic of 1839', *Kwansei Gakuin J. of Bus. Admin.*, 35(3), 1988; 'Central Banking in the Second Bank of the United States', *Kwansei Gakuin J. of Econ.*, 44(3), 1990; 'The Role of the United States Treasury in the early 19th Century', *Kwansei Gakuin J. of Bus. Admin.*, 38(4), 1991; 'Modernization and the Monetary System', *Aspects of Modernization*, M. Yunoki ed., ch. 2, Seibunsha, 1992.

Teuteberg, Hans Jürgen

Prof. of Modern Econ. and Social Hist., Münster Univ., Dept. of Hist., 48165 Münster, Germany. Tel.: Office: 49 251 834317; home 49 2501 1855. Fax: 49 251 832090.

Year and Place of Birth 1929, Düsseldorf, Germany.

Degrees and Qualifications Dr.phil. Göttingen Univ., 1958.

Previous Post Research Fellow, Nankai Univ., (China), 1985.

Current Offices and Honorary Posts Mem., pres. & publications, Internat. Commission for Research into European Food Hist.; head & mem., working group of German Transport

Hist.; head, mem. & publications, Research Unit, Comparative Historical Urban Research, Münster Univ.

Fields of Expertise *Industry Fields:* food, drink, tobacco; vehicle construction; textiles; distributive trades; agric. and forestry; chemicals; bricks; electricity and water; transport; packaging. *Bus. Dimensions:* entrepreneurs and entrepreneurship; production management; co. finance and accounting; personnel management; marketing; co. culture. *Scope:* local; regional; national; internat. *Period:* nineteenth century; twentieth century as a whole.

Publications *Books: Geschichte der industriellen Mitbestimmung in Deutschland*, J.C.B. Mohr, Tübingen, 1961; *Westfalens Wirtschaft am Beginn des 'Maschinenzeitalters'*, ed., Gesellschaft für Westfälische Wirtschaftsgeschichte, Dortmund, 1988; *Bischof & Klein 1892–1992. Jahrhundertbilanz eines westfälischen Verpackungsunternehmens*, Kleins Druck- und Verlagsanstalt, Lengerich, 1992; *European Food Hist.: A Research Rev.*, ed., Leicester Univ. Press, Leicester, London, New York, 1992.

Thackray, Arnold

Exec. Director, Chemical Heritage Foundation & Joseph Priestley Prof., Pennsylvania Univ., Chemical Heritage Foundation, 3401 Walnut St, Philadelphia, PA 19104, & Univ. of Pennsylvania, Univ. Park, Pennsylvania 16802, USA. Tel.: 1 215 898 1805. Fax: 1 215 898 3327.

Year and Place of Birth 1939, Manchester, UK.

Degrees and Qualifications Ph.D. Cambridge Univ., 1966.

Current Offices and Honorary Posts Treasurer & exec. com. mem., Amer. Council of Learned Societies.

Major Honours Dexter Award,

Amer. Chemical Soc.; Fellow, Amer. Acad. of Arts & Sciences.

Fields of Expertise *Industry Fields:* chemicals and allied industries. *Bus. Dimensions:* entrepreneurs and entrepreneurship; multinational bus.; co. culture. *Scope:* national; internat.; USA; UK. *Period:* inter-war years, 1919–39; mid-twentieth century, 1940–70; late twentieth century, 1970–present. *Teaching:* post grad. *Consultancy:* co. hist.

Publications *Books: Gentlemen of Science,* Oxford, 1981; *Chemistry in Amer.,* Reidel, 1985; *Science after '40,* Chicago, 1992; *Chemical Sciences in Modern Soc.,* ed., Univ. of Pennsylvania Press.

Thomes, Paul

Privatdozent, Dept. of Hist., Saarland Univ., POB 1150, 66041 Saarbrücken, Germany. Tel.: 49 681 3022219.

Year and Place of Birth 1953, Wittlich, Germany.

Degrees and Qualifications Erstes Staatsexamen Saarbrücken Univ., 1979; Dr.phil. Saarbrücken Univ., 1984; Habilitation Saarbrücken Univ., 1991/2.

Previous Post Oberassistent, Saarland Univ.

Fields of Expertise *Industry Fields:* mining and quarrying; insurance, banking, finance. *Bus. Dimensions:* entrepreneurs and entrepreneurship. *Scope:* regional; national. *Period:* eighteenth century; nineteenth century; early twentieth century. *Teaching:* post grad. *Consultancy:* co. hist.

Publications *Books: Die Kreissparkasse Saarbrücken (1854–1914),* Knapp, Frankfurt, 1985; *Kommunale Haushalte zwischen Mittelalter und Moderne,* Steiner, Stuttgart, 1993. *Articles:* 'Die Diffusion der Sparkassen in Preußen', *Invention - Innovation - Diffusion,* M.

Pix & H. Pohl eds., Steiner, Stuttgart, 1992, 187–205; 'Zwischen Staatsmonopol und privatem Unternehmertum', *Jahrbuch für Wirtschaftsgeschichte,* 1992, 57–78; 'Sozialpolitik des preussischen Bergfiskus', *Sozialgeschichte des Bergbaus,* K. Tenfelde ed., Beck, Munich, 1992, 1082–101.

Thompson, Gregory L.

Asst. Prof., Dept. of Urban & Regional Planning, R-117, Florida State Univ., Tallahassee, FL 32306, USA. Tel.: 1 904 644 8514. Fax: 1 904 644 6041.

Year and Place of Birth 1946, Huntingdon Park, USA.

Degrees and Qualifications BA(Geography) Univ. of California, Davis, 1968; Master of City Planning Univ. of California, Berkeley, 1970; Ph.D. (Soc. Sc.) Univ. of California, Irvine, 1987.

Previous Post Andrew W. Mellon/National Endowment for the Humanities Advanced Research Fellow, Hagley Museum and Library, Wilmington, Delaware, 1987–8.

Major Honours Mellon – NEH Fellow.

Fields of Expertise *Industry Fields:* transport and communication. *Bus. Dimensions:* entrepreneurs and entrepreneurship; co. admin.; marketing; research and development; strategy formation; bus. organization; bus. and technology; management education; bus.–state relations; markets and bus.; bus. values; co. culture. *Scope:* regional; national; USA. *Period:* nineteenth century; early twentieth century; inter-war years, 1919–39; mid-twentieth century, 1940–'70. *Teaching:* undergrad.; post grad.

Publications *Books: The Passenger Train in the Motor Age: California's Rail and Bus Industries 1910–1941,*

Ohio State Univ. Press, Columbus, 1993. *Articles:* 'Management's Role in US Rail Passenger Decline 1920–1941', *Transportation Research*, A 21A, 1987, 95–108; 'Misused Product Costing in the Amer. Railroad Industry: Southern Pacific Passenger Service between the Wars', *Bus. Hist. Rev.*, 63, Autumn, 1989, 510–54; 'Myth and Rationality in Management Decision-making: The Evolution of Amer. Railroad Product Costing 1870–1940', *J. of Transport Hist.*, 12, 1991, 1–10; 'Pacific Greyhound Lines in the 1930s: A Case where Planning beat the Market', *J. of Planning Education and Research*, Dec., 1993, forthcoming.

Thomson, Ross

Assoc. Prof., Dept. of Econ., Vermont Univ., 479 Main St, Burlington, VT 05405, USA. Tel.: 1 802 656 0182. Fax: 1 802 656 8405.

Year and Place of Birth 1948, Detroit, USA.

Degrees and Qualifications BA Arizona State Univ., 1970; Ph.D. Yale Univ., 1976.

Previous Post Asst. Prof., New School for Social Research, New York City, 1970–91.

Fields of Expertise *Industry Fields:* mechanical engineering; electrical engineering; clothing and footwear. *Bus. Dimensions:* bus. and technology; markets and bus. *Scope:* national; USA. *Period:* nineteenth century; early twentieth century. *Teaching:* undergrad.

Publications *Books: The Path to Mechanized Shoe Production in the United States,* Univ. of North Carolina Press, 1989; *Learning and Technological Change,* ed., Macmillan, 1993. *Articles:* 'Learning by Selling and Invention: The Case of the Sewing Machine', *J. of Econ. Hist.*, XLVII(2), June, 1987, 433–45; 'Invention,

Markets and the Scope of the Firm: The Nineteenth Century US Shoe Machinery Industry', *Bus. & Econ. Hist.*, 2nd ser., 18, 1989, 140–9; 'Crossover Inventors and Technological Linkages: Amer. Shoemaking and the Broader Economy', *Technology and Culture,* 32(4), Oct., 1991, 1018–46.

Thowsen, Atle

Assoc. Prof., Bergen Maritime Museum/Norwegian Research Fund for Maritime Hist., POB 2736, Møhlenpris, 5026 Bergen, Norway. Tel.: 47 5 327980. Fax: 47 5 329137.

Year and Place of Birth 1940, Bergen, Norway.

Degrees and Qualifications MA Bergen Univ., 1965; Ph.D. Bergen Univ., 1984.

Current Offices and Honorary Posts Exec. council mem., Internat. Commission of Maritime Hist.; ed., *Norwegian Yearbook of Maritime Hist.*

Fields of Expertise *Industry Fields:* shipbuilding and marine engineering; transport and communication; insurance, banking, finance. *Bus. Dimensions:* entrepreneurs and entrepreneurship; co. finance and accounting; co. admin.; bus. organization; markets and bus. *Scope:* national; internat. *Period:* early twentieth century; inter-war years, 1919–39; mid-twentieth century, 1940–70. *Teaching:* post grad. *Consultancy:* co. hist.

Publications *Books: Den Norske Krigsforsikring for Skib 1935–1985* [The Norwegian War Risks Club for Ships 1935–1985], vol. 1, Bergen, 1984. *Articles:* 'Vekst og Strukturendringer i Krisetider 1914–1939' [Growth and Structural Changes in Times of Crisis 1914–1939], *Bergen og Sjøfarten* [Maritime Bergen], vol. IV, Bergen,

273

1983; 'Nortraship-Profitt og Patriotisme 1939–1945' [Notraship - Profit and Patriotism 1939–1945], *Handelsflåten i Krig* [The Norwegian Merchant Marine at War], vol. 1, Oslo, 1992.

Tilly, Richard

Münster Univ., Inst. of Econ. and Social Hist., D-48165 Münster, Hüfferstraße 1a, Germany. Tel.: 49 251 832906/49 251 832905. Fax: 49 251 838399/49 251 834831.
Year and Place of Birth 1932, Chicago, USA.
Degrees and Qualifications Ph.D. (Econ.) Wisconsin Univ., 1964.
Current Offices and Honorary Posts Co-ed., *Geschichte und Gesellschaft*.
Major Honours Edwin Gay Prize for Econ. Hist., 1966; Fritz Redlich Prize for Econ. Hist., 1982.
Fields of Expertise *Industry Fields:* insurance, banking, finance; public admin. and defence. *Bus. Dimensions:* entrepreneurs and entrepreneurship; co. finance and accounting; merger movement and issues. *Scope:* national; internat.; global. *Period:* nineteenth century; twentieth century as a whole. *Teaching:* undergrad.; post grad.
Publications *Books: Financial Institutions and Industrialization in the Rhineland, 1915–70,* Univ. of Wisconsin Press, Madison, 1966; *Kapital, Staat und sozialer Protest in der deutschen Industrialisierung,* Göttingen, 1980; *Vom Zollverein zum Industriestaat. Die Wirtschaftlich-soziale Entwicklung Deutschlands 1834 bis 1914,* dtv, Munich, 1990; *The Rebellious Century,* with C. & L. Tilly, Harvard Univ. Press, 1975; *Beiträge zur quantitativen vergleichenden Unternehmensgeschichte,* Stuttgart, 1985.

Titos-Martinez, Manuel

Titular Prof. of Contemporary Hist., Dept. of Hist., Granada Univ., Granada, Spain. Tel.: 34 58 223980.
Year and Place of Birth 1948, Granada, Spain.
Degrees and Qualifications Licenciado Granada Univ., 1973; Ph.D. Granada Univ., 1977.
Current Offices and Honorary Posts Mem. Spanish Assoc. of Econ. Hist.; mem., Centre for Historical Studies, Granada; mem., Econ. Soc. of the Friends of Pais de Granada.
Fields of Expertise *Industry Fields:* insurance, banking, finance. *Bus. Dimensions:* co. finance and accounting. *Scope:* regional. *Period:* nineteenth century; twentieth century as a whole. *Teaching:* undergrad.; post grad. *Consultancy:* co. hist.
Publications *Books: Crédito, Ahorro en Granada en el siglo XIX,* 2 vols., Bank of Granada, Granada, 1978; *Bancos y Banqueros en la Historiografia Andaluza,* Instituto de Desarrollo Regional, Granada, 1980; *La Cámara de Comercio, Industria y Navegación de Granada,* Granada, 1987; *La Obra Social de las Cajas de Ahorro Espaniolas,* CECA, Madrid, 1990; *Historia de la Caja General de Ahorros de Granada,* 2nd edn., Granada, 1987.

Todd, Edmund N.

Assoc. Prof., Univ. of New Haven, 300 Orange Ave., West Haven, CT 06516-1999, USA. Tel.: 1 203 932 7287.
Year and Place of Birth 1944, Miami Beach, USA.
Degrees and Qualifications BA Florida Univ., 1970; MA Florida Univ., 1974; Ph.D. Pennsylvania Univ., 1984.

Previous Post Visiting Prof., State Univ. College of New York, Potsdam, 1984–5.

Current Offices and Honorary Posts Advisory board mem., Soc. for the Hist. of Technology.

Fields of Expertise *Industry Fields:* electrical engineering; gas, electricity, water. *Bus. Dimensions:* bus.–state relations. *Scope:* regional; Germany. *Period:* early twentieth century. *Teaching:* undergrad.

Publications *Articles:* 'A Tale of Three Cities: Electrification and the Structure of Choice in the Ruhr, 1886–1990', *Social Studies of Science*, 17, 1987, 387–412; 'Industry, State and Electrical Technology in the Ruhr circa 1900', *Osiris*, 5, 1989, 243–59; 'Electric Ploughs in Wilhelmine Germany: Failure of an Agric. System', *Social Studies of Science*, 22, 1992, 263–81.

Toensberg, Jeppe E.

Archivist, Byhistorisk Samling for Lyngby-Taarbæk, Lyngby Hovedgade 2, 2800 Lyngby, Denmark. Tel.: 45 4288 4383.

Year and Place of Birth 1950, Copenhagen, Denmark.

Degrees and Qualifications Cand.Mag. Copenhagen Univ., 1976.

Fields of Expertise *Industry Fields:* metal goods; textiles; paper, printing, publishing; gas, electricity, water. *Scope:* regional. *Period:* nineteenth century; twentieth century as a whole.

Publications *Books: Industrialiseringen af Lyngby*, 1984; *Handel i Kongens Lyngby*, 1987; *Københavnsegnen gennem 800 år*, Københavnsegnen og lokalarkiverne, 1990; *Brede Klædefabriks bygninger*, Industri og Bolig I, 1992; *Mølleåværkernes bygninger og drivkraft*, Registrant over danske møller, 1993.

Tokushima, Tatsuro

Prof., Fac. of Econ., Nagasaki Prefectural Univ., Kawashimo-cho, Sasebo, Nagasaki 858, Japan. Tel.: 0956 47 2191. Fax: 0956 47 6941.

Year and Place of Birth 1933, Tokyo, Japan.

Degrees and Qualifications BA Tokyo Metropolitan Univ., 1957; MS Kokugakuin Univ., 1977; Ph.D. Kokugakuin Univ., 1983.

Previous Post Asst. Prof., Fac. of Econ., Tohoku-Gakuin Univ., 1985–92.

Current Offices and Honorary Posts Sec., Market Hist. Soc. of Japan.

Fields of Expertise *Industry Fields:* food, drink, tobacco; distributive trades. *Bus. Dimensions:* markets and bus. *Scope:* regional; national. *Period:* early modern; eighteenth century; nineteenth century. *Consultancy:* co. hist.

Publications *Books: Kindai Igirisu Kourishogyo no Taito* [The Rise of Modern British Retailing], Azusa-shuppansha, 1986. *Articles:* 'Ribapuhru siei Mahkettono seiritu to tenkai' [The Establishment of Liverpool Municipal St. John's Market], *Socio-Econ. Hist.*, 54(1), 1988, 66–95; 'Gurasugou itiba bekken' [An Aspect of Glasgow Markets], *J. of Market Hist.*, 9, 1991, 101–12; 'Miyagi-ken kohsetsu kouri ichiba no kaisetsu (Taisho 8 nen) to nankyo' [A Study of the Establishment and Reputation of the First Municipal Retail Market in Miyagi Prefecture in 1919], *Nagasaki Kenritsu Daigaku Ronshu*, 25(3.4), 1992.

Tolliday, Steven W.

Prof. of Econ. & Social Hist., School of Bus. and Econ. Studies, Leeds Univ., Leeds, LS2 9JT, UK. Tel.: 44 532 334474. Fax: 44 532 334465.

Year and Place of Birth 1951, London, UK.

Degrees and Qualifications BA Cambridge Univ., 1972; Ph.D. Cambridge Univ., 1979.

Previous Post Asst. Prof., Grad. School of Bus. Admin., Harvard Univ., 1987–92 & ed., *Bus. Hist. Rev.*

Fields of Expertise *Industry Fields:* metal manufacture; vehicle construction. *Bus. Dimensions:* strategy formation; bus.–state relations; industrial relations. *Scope:* national; global. *Period:* twentieth century as a whole. *Teaching:* undergrad.; post grad. *Consultancy:* co. hist.; corporate strategy.

Publications *Books: The Automobile Industry and its Workers. Between Fordism and Flexibility*, with J. Zeitlin ed., Polity Press, 1986; 2nd edn., Berg Press, 1992; *Shopfloor Bargaining and the State. Historical and Comparative Perspectives*, with J. Zeitlin co-ed., CUP, 1985; *Bus., Banking and Polit. The Case of British Steel, 1918–39*, Harvard Univ. Press, 1987; *The Power to Manage? Employers and Indust. Relations in Comparative-Historical Perspective*, with J. Zeitlin co-ed., Routledge, 1991.

Tomlinson, Jim

Reader in Econ. Hist., Dept. of Econ., Brunel Univ., Uxbridge, Middlesex, UB8 3PH, UK. Tel.: 44 895 274000. Fax: 44 895 203384.

Year and Place of Birth 1951, London, UK.

Degrees and Qualifications B.Sc. (Econ.), London School of Econ., 1973; Ph.D. London School of Econ., 1977.

Current Offices and Honorary Posts Visiting Researcher, Bus. Hist. Unit, London School of Econ.

Fields of Expertise *Industry Fields:* textiles. *Bus. Dimensions:* bus. organization. *Scope:* national. *Period:* mid-twentieth century, 1940–70. *Teaching:* undergrad.

Publications *Books: The Unequal Struggle? British Socialism and the Capitalist Enterprise*, Methuen, 1982; *Employment Policy: The Crucial Years, 1939–55*, OUP, 1987; *Public Policy and the Economy since 1900*, OUP, 1990; *State Intervention and Indust. Efficiency: Labour 1939–51*, N. Tiratsoo co-auth., Routledge, 1993. *Articles:* 'Mr Attlee's Supply-side Socialism', *Econ. Hist. Rev.*, 46, 1993, 1–22.

Toninelli, PierAngelo

Sen. Lect., Inst. of Econ. Hist., LIUC (Free Univ. Inst. Carlo Cattaneo), Corso Matteotti 22, 21053 Castellanza (VA), Italy. Tel.: 39 331 480 747. Fax: 39 331 480 746.

Year and Place of Birth 1948, Milan, Italy.

Degrees and Qualifications Laurea (Pol. Sc.-Econ. Hist.) Milan Univ. degli Studi, 1971.

Previous Post Sen. Research Fellow, Dept. of Social & Institutional Hist., Milan Univ.

Current Offices and Honorary Posts Exec. com. mem. & scientific com. mem., Fondazione ASSI di Storia e Studi sull'Impresa, Milan; managing board, 'Indust. and Corporate Change'.

Major Honours DANECO Prize for Corporate Hist., 1989 (joint-winner).

Fields of Expertise *Industry Fields:* coal and petroleum products; gas, electricity, water. *Bus. Dimensions:* co. finance and accounting. *Scope:* internat. *Period:* nineteenth century; twentieth century as a whole. *Teaching:* undergrad. *Consultancy:* corporate strategy.

Publications *Books: La Edison. Contabilità e Bilanci di una Grande Impresa Elettrica (1884–1916)*, Il Mulino, Bologna, 1990; *Innovazione, Impresa e Sviluppo Economico*, with R. Giannetti co-ed., Il Mulino,

Bologna, 1991; *Technology and Enterprise in a Historical Perspective*, co-ed. with G. Dosi & R. Giannetti, Clarendon Press, Oxford, 1992; *Schiavi, Pionieri e Macchine. Alle Origini dello Sviluppo Economico Americano, 1776–1914*, Il Mulino, Bologna, 1993. *Articles:* 'Anagrafe delle Società Elettriche in Italia: La Documentazione di Base "Prima Parte (1893–1914)" - "Parte Seconda (1914–1925)"', *Storia dell'Industria Elettrica Italiana*, with C. Pavese co-auth., Laterza, Bari, vol. I, 1992, 761–888 & vol. II, 1993, 719–804.

Topp, Niels-Henrik

Assoc. Prof., Inst. of Polit. Science, Univ. of Copenhagen, Rosenborggade 15, 1130 Copenhagen K, Denmark. Tel.: 45 35 32 34 14. Fax: 45 35 32 33 99.

Year and Place of Birth 1951, Copenhagen, Denmark.

Degrees and Qualifications MA (Econ.) Copenhagen Univ., 1977; Dr.phil. (Econ.) Copenhagen Univ., 1987.

Previous Post Asst. Prof., Inst. of Econ., Copenhagen Univ., 1986–7.

Current Offices and Honorary Posts Director, Inst. of Polit. Science; vice-dean, Fac. of Social Science, Copenhagen Univ., 1993–; exec. com. mem., Danish Assoc. of Polit. Science, 1988–.

Fields of Expertise *Industry Fields:* mining and quarrying; chemicals and allied industries. *Bus. Dimensions:* entrepreneurs and entrepreneurship; bus. and technology; bus.–state relations. *Scope:* local; internat. *Period:* twentieth century as a whole. *Teaching:* undergrad.; post grad. *Consultancy:* co. hist.

Publications *Books: Udviklingen i de finanspolitiske ideer i Danmark 1930–1945* [The Introduction of New Ideas on Fiscal Policy in Denmark

1930–1945], Copenhagen, 1987; *Kryolitindustriens historie 1847–1990* [The Danish Cryolite Industry 1847–1990], Copenhagen, 1990; *Innovationer i kryolitindustrien* [Innovations within the Danish Cryolite Industry], Inst. for Statskundskab Københavns Universitet, Forskningsrapport, 1992/4. *Articles:* 'A Nineteenth Century Multiplier and its Fate. Julius Wulff and the Multiplier Theory in Denmark 1896–1932', *Hist. of Polit. Econ.*, 13(4), 1981, 824–45; 'Fiscal Policy in Denmark 1930–1945', *European Econ. Rev.*, 32, 1988, 512–18.

Torres Villanueva, Eugenio

Prof. Titular, Facultad de Ciencias Politicas y Sociologia, Depto. de Economía Aplicada V, Universidad Complutense de Madrid, Campus de Somosaguas, 28223 Madrid, Spain. Tel.: 34 91 3942808. Fax: 34 91 3942810.

Degrees and Qualifications Licenciado (Polit. Sc. & Sociology) Complutense Univ., 1979; Doctorado (Polit. Sc. & Sociology) Complutense Univ., 1989.

Previous Post Prof. of Macro and Microeconomics, Complutense Univ., 1982–92.

Current Offices and Honorary Posts Mem., Spanish Assoc. of Econ. Hist.

Major Honours Ramón Carande Prize, Econ. Hist. Soc., 1990.

Fields of Expertise *Industry Fields:* metal manufacture; shipbuilding and marine engineering; insurance, banking, finance. *Bus. Dimensions:* entrepreneurs and entrepreneurship; bus. organization. *Scope:* regional; national. *Period:* nineteenth century; twentieth century as a whole. *Teaching:* post grad. *Consultancy:* co. hist.

Publications *Books: Ramón de la Sota: Historia Económica de un*

Empresario, 1857–1936, Complutense Univ. Press, Madrid, 2 vols., 1989; *Catálogo de Publicaciones sobre la Historia Empresarial española de los Siglos XIX y XX*, Fundación Empresa Pública, Madrid, 1993. *Articles:* 'Barcos, Carbón y Mineral de Hierro. Los Vapores de Sota y Aznar y los Orígenes de la Moderna Flota Mercante de Bilbao, 1889–1900', *Revista de Historia Económica*, IX(1), 1991, 11–32; 'La Storia d'Impresa in Spagna. Una Rassegna Bibliografica', *Annali di Storia dell'Impresa*, 8, 1992, 27–45.

Tortella, Gabriel

Prof., Fac. of Econ. Science, Alcala Univ., 28802 Alcala de Henares, Madrid, Spain. Tel.: 34 1 8854202. Fax: 34 1 8854206.

Year and Place of Birth 1936, Barcelona, Spain.

Degrees and Qualifications Ph.D. (Econ.) Wisconsin Univ., 1971; Doctorate in Law Madrid Univ., 1973.

Previous Post Prof., Fac. of Econ. Sc., Valencia Univ., 1979–80.

Current Offices and Honorary Posts Exec. com. mem., Internat. Econ. Hist. Assoc.; V.P., Econ. Hist. Assoc., Spain; academic council mem., European Assoc. of Banking Hist.

Major Honours Research Prize, Alcala Univ., 1992.

Fields of Expertise *Industry Fields:* insurance, banking, finance. *Bus. Dimensions:* entrepreneurs and entrepreneurship. *Scope:* national. *Period:* nineteenth century; twentieth century as a whole. *Teaching:* undergrad.; post grad. *Consultancy:* co. hist.

Publications *Books: Banking, Railroads and Industry in Spain, 1829–1874*, Arno Press, New York, 1977; *Introducción a la Economía para Historiadores*, Tecnos, Madrid, 1986, 1991, (German translation: Transfer Verlag, Regensburg, 1992);

Historia del Banco de Credito Indust., with J.C. Jimenez, Alianza, Madrid, 1986; *Education and Econ. Development since the Indust. Revolution*, ed., Generalitat Valenciana, Valencia, 1990.

Traves, Tom

Vice-pres. (academic), New Brunswick Univ., POB 4400, Fredericton, New Brunswick, E3B 5A3, Canada. Tel.: 1 506 453 4801. Fax: 1 506 453 4599.

Year and Place of Birth 1948, Winnipeg, Canada.

Degrees and Qualifications BA Manitoba Univ., 1970; MA York Univ., 1971; Ph.D. York Univ., 1976.

Previous Post Dean of Arts, York Univ., Toronto, 1974–91.

Fields of Expertise *Industry Fields:* vehicle construction; paper, printing, publishing; transport and communication. *Bus. Dimensions:* entrepreneurs and entrepreneurship; production management; personnel management; bus. organization; bus.–state relations. *Scope:* national. *Period:* nineteenth century; inter-war years, 1919–39. *Teaching:* undergrad.; post grad.

Publications *Books: The State and Enterprise: Canadian Manufacturers and the Federal Government, 1917–1931*, Univ. of Toronto Press, 1979; *Essays in Canadian Bus. Hist.*, McLelland & Stewart, 1984. *Articles:* 'The Development of the Ontario Automobile Industry to 1939', *Progress without Planning: Econ. Hist. of Ontario*, I.M. Drummond ed., Univ. of Toronto Press, 1987; 'Railways as Manufacturers 1850–1890', *Canadian Historical Assoc. Historical Papers*, co-auth. with Paul Craven, 1984; reprinted in *Perspectives on Canadian Econ. Hist.*, D. McCalla ed.; 'The Law, the Bus. Corporation and Social Change', *U.N.B. Law J.*, vol. 42, 1993.

Trout, Andrew P.

Prof. of Hist., Indiana Univ. Southeast, New Albany, Indiana 47150, USA. Tel.: 1 812 948 9345.

Year and Place of Birth 1930, Des Moines, USA.

Degrees and Qualifications Ph.D. Univ. of Notre Dame, USA, 1968.

Previous Post Asst. Prof. of Hist., Lamar State Univ., Beaumont, Texas, 1965–8.

Fields of Expertise *Industry Fields:* tontines, government and private; public finance, France & USA. *Scope:* internat.; France; USA. *Period:* early modern. *Teaching:* undergrad.

Publications *Books: The Tontine: From the Reign of Louis XIV to the French Revolutionary Era*, with Robert M. Jennings co-auth., S.S. Huebner Foundation for Insurance Education, Wharton School, Philadelphia, (Monograph no. 12). *Articles:* 'Alexander Hamilton's Report on the Public Credit (1790) in a European Perspective', *J. of European Econ. Hist.*, with Donald F. Swanson co-auth., 19, 1990, 623–33; 'Alexander Hamilton, "The Celebrated Mr. Neckar" and Public Credit', *The William and Mary Q.*, with Donald F. Swanson, 3rd ser., 47, 1990, 422–30; 'Alexander Hamilton's Hidden Sinking Fund', *The William and Mary Q.*, with Donald F. Swanson co-auth., 3rd ser., 49, 1992, 108–16.

Tsuji, Setsuo

Prof., Fac. of Bus. Admin., Aichi Women's Junior College, 57 Takenoyama, Iwasaki, Nisshin-cho, Aichi-gun, Aichi-ken, Japan. Tel.: 05617 3 4111. Fax: 05617 3 8539.

Year and Place of Birth 1937, Kyoto, Japan.

Degrees and Qualifications BA Osaka Univ. of Econ.

Fields of Expertise *Industry Fields:* textiles; distributive trades. *Bus. Dimensions:* entrepreneurs and entrepreneurship; co. admin.; strategy formation; co. culture. *Scope:* national. *Period:* nineteenth century; twentieth century as a whole. *Teaching:* undergrad. *Consultancy:* co. hist.

Publications *Books: Kansai-kei Sogo Shosha* [Kansai General Trading Companies], Koyo-shobo, 1992. *Articles:* 'Ataka Yakichi no Kigyosha Katsudo' [A Study on Yakichi Ataka and his Entrepreneurship], *Aichi Women's Junior College Research Bull.*, 20, 1987; 'Senkanki ni okeru Iwai to Nissho' [Iwai Inc. and Nissho Inc. in the inter-War Period], *Aichi Women's Junior College Research Bull.*, 21, 1988; 'Marubeni no Sogo Shosha-ka katei no Kenkyu' [A Study of the Developing Process to Sogo Shosha of 'Marubeni'], *Aichi Women's Junior College Research Bull.*, 24, 1991; 'Sumitomo-shoji no Shiteki Kenkyu' [A Study on the Bus. Hist. of Sumitomo Shoji Kaisha], *Aichi Women's Junior College Research Bull.*, 25, 1992.

Tsunoyama, Sakae

Prof., Fac. of Econ., Nara Sangyo Univ., Tatsuno-kita, Sango-cho, Ikoma-gun, Nara-ken, Japan. Tel.: 0787 78 7800. Fax: 0745 72 0822.

Year and Place of Birth 1921, Osaka, Japan.

Degrees and Qualifications Ph.D. (Econ.) Kyoto Univ., 1961.

Previous Post Prof., Wakayama Univ.

Current Offices and Honorary Posts Council mem., 1965–8; exec. com. mem., 1969–80 & 1983–6; exec. off., 1975–80; advisor, 1992–.

Fields of Expertise *Bus. Dimensions:* entrepreneurs and entrepreneurship; marketing; bus.–state relations. *Scope:* internat.; global; UK; Japan. *Period:* nineteenth century. *Teaching:* undergrad.

Publications *Books: Koza Seiyo Keizaishi* [The Western Econ. Hist.], ed., 5 vols., Dobunkan Press, 1979–80; *Cha no Sedai-shi* [World Hist. of Tea Drinking], Chuo-koron-sha, 1979; *Tokei no Shakai-shi* [Social Hist. of Timepieces], Chuo-koron-sha, 1984; *Nihon·Ryoji-hokoku no Kenkyu* [Studies in Japanese Consular Reports], ed., Dobunkan Press, 1988; *Tsusho Kokka Nihon no Joho Senryaku* [The Information Strategy of Overseas Trade in Modern Japan], NHK, 1989.

Tucker, Albert V.

Prof. of Hist., Dept. of Hist., Glendon College, 2275 Bayview Ave., Toronto, Ontario, M4N 3M6, Canada. Tel.: 1 416 487 6724. Fax: 1 416 487 6728.

Year and Place of Birth 1923, Toronto, Canada.

Degrees and Qualifications BA Toronto Univ., 1951; MA Toronto Univ., 1952; Ph.D. Harvard Univ., 1958.

Current Offices and Honorary Posts Univ. Prof. Emeritus, York Univ.

Fields of Expertise *Industry Fields:* food, drink, tobacco. *Bus. Dimensions:* entrepreneurs and entre- preneurship; strategy formation; merg- er movement and issues; bus. organiza- tion. *Scope:* national. *Period:* inter- war years, 1919–39; mid-twentieth century, 1940–70. *Teaching:* under- grad. *Consultancy:* co. hist.

Publications *Books: Steam into Wilderness. A Hist. of the Ontario Northland Transportation Commis- sion,* Fitzhenry & Whiteside, Toronto, 1978; *'A Hist. of John Labatt Ltd',* commissioned as a co. hist. but unpublished, 1986.

Tulchinsky, Gerald J.J.

Prof. of Hist., Dept. of Hist., Queen's Univ., Kingston, Ontario, K7L 3N6, Canada. Tel.: 1 613 545 2150. Fax: 1 613 545 6298.

Year and Place of Birth 1933, Canada.

Degrees and Qualifications BA (Polit.Sc. & Econ.) Toronto Univ., 1957; MA (Hist.) McGill Univ., 1960; Ph.D. (Hist.) Toronto Univ., 1971.

Fields of Expertise *Industry Fields:* clothing and footwear. *Bus. Dimensions:* entrepreneurs and entre- preneurship; marketing. *Scope:* inter- nat. *Period:* nineteenth century; twen- tieth century as a whole. *Teaching:* undergrad.

Publications *Books: The River Barons: Montreal Bus.men and the Growth of Industry and Transportation 1837–53,* Univ. of Tronto Press, 1977; *Taking Root: The Origins of the Canadian Jewish Community,* Lester Publishing, Toronto, 1992. *Articles:* 'The Jewish Experience in Ontario to 1960', *Patterns of the Past: Interpreting Ontario's Hist.,* Roger Hall et al. eds., Dundurn Press, Toronto, 1988, 301–27; '"Said to be a very Honest Jew": The R.G. Dun Credit Reports and Jewish Bus. Activity in Montreal, 1840–1880', *Urban Hist. Rev.,* 1989; 'Hidden Among the Smokestacks: Toronto's Clothing Industry, 1850–1900', *Old Ontario Essays in Honour of J.M.S. Careless,* Dundurn Press, Toronto, 1990.

Tull, Malcolm

Sen. Lect., Dept. of Econ., Murdoch Univ., Murdoch, WA 6150, Australia. Tel.: 61 9 360 2481. Fax: 61 9 310 7725.

Year and Place of Birth 1951, High

Wycombe, UK.

Degrees and Qualifications B.Sc. (Econ.) Hull Univ., 1972; Ph.D. Murdoch Univ., 1985.

Current Offices and Honorary Posts Exec. mem., Australian Assoc. for Maritime Hist.

Fields of Expertise *Industry Fields:* agric., forestry, fishing; transport and communication. *Bus. Dimensions:* entrepreneurs and entrepreneurship; bus. and technology. *Scope:* local; regional; national; Australia; Japan. *Period:* twentieth century as a whole. *Teaching:* undergrad.; post grad. *Consultancy:* co. hist.

Publications *Articles:* 'The Financial Performance of the Fremantle Harbour Trust, 1903 to 1939', *Australian Econ. Hist. Rev.*, XXVIII(1), 1988, 21–42; 'The Development of Port Admin. in Australia: The Case of Fremantle, 1903–1939', *J. of Transport Hist.*, 10(1), Mar., 1989, 41–58; 'The Australian Fishing Industry: A Select Historical Bibliography', with H. Smith, 1990, Dept. of Econ. Research Monograph; 'Profits and Lifestyle: Western Australian Fishers', *Studies in Western Australian Hist.*, XIII, 1992, 92–111; 'Shipping Ports and the Marketing of Australia's Wheat, 1900–1970', *Australian Econ. Hist. Rev.*, XXXII, 1992, 33–59.

Turton, Alison

Manager, Archives Dept., The Royal Bank of Scotland plc, 29 Gresham St, London, EC2V 7HN, UK. Tel.: 071 615 5583.

Year and Place of Birth 1957, Ormskirk, UK.

Degrees and Qualifications MA, Cambridge, 1978; MA, Univ. College, Univ. of London, 1987.

Previous Post Archivist, Babcock Internat. plc, 1987–8.

Fields of Expertise *Industry Fields:*

food, drink, tobacco; mechanical engineering; distributive trades; insurance, banking, finance. *Scope:* local; regional; national. *Period:* eighteenth century; nineteenth century; twentieth century as a whole. *Consultancy:* co. hist.

Tweedale, Geoffrey

Leverhulme Research Fellow, Dept. of Hist., Sheffield Univ., Sheffield, Yorks, S10 2TN, UK. Tel.: 44 742 768555. Fax: 44 742 788304.

Year and Place of Birth 1951, Coventry, UK.

Degrees and Qualifications BA (Hist.) London Univ., 1973; M.Sc. (Econ. Hist.), London School of Econ., 1975; Ph.D. (Econ.) London School of Econ., 1983.

Previous Post Research Fellow, Centre for Hist. of Science, Technology & Medicine, Manchester Univ., 1987–91.

Fields of Expertise *Industry Fields:* metal manufacture. *Bus. Dimensions:* bus. and technology. *Scope:* internat. *Period:* nineteenth century. *Consultancy:* co. hist.

Publications *Books: Sheffield Steel and Amer.: A Century of Commercial and Technological Interdependence, 1830–1930*, CUP, 1987; *Allen & Hanburys and the British Pharmaceutical Industry, 1715–1990*, John Murray, London, 1990.

Uchida, Hoshimi

Prof. of Hist. of Technology, Dept. of Bus., Tokyo Keizai Univ., Minamicho 1-7, Kokubunji-shi, 185 Tokyo, Japan. Tel.: 0423 21 1941. Fax: 0423 24 1354.

Year and Place of Birth 1926, Tokyo, Japan.

Current Offices and Honorary Posts Ex-chairman, Japan Indust.

Archaeology Soc.; board mem., Internat. Com. of Conservation of Indust. Heritage.

Fields of Expertise *Industry Fields:* chemicals and allied industries; instrument engineering; electrical engineering; textiles; electronics and computers: manufacture. *Bus. Dimensions:* entrepreneurs and entrepreneurship; research and development; bus. and technology. *Scope:* internat.; Japan. *Period:* nineteenth century; twentieth century as a whole. *Teaching:* undergrad.; post grad. *Consultancy:* co. hist.

Publications *Books: Tokei Kogyo no Hattatsu* [The Evolution of the Watch Industry], Hattori Seiko Co., 1985; *Nihon IBM Shashi* [Hist. of IBM Japan], IBM Japan, 1988, 81–206. *Articles:* 'Development and Diffusion of Technology: Electrical and Chemical Industries', *Proceedings of the Internat. Conf. on Bus. Hist.* 6, A. Okochi co-ed., Univ. of Tokyo Press, 1981; 'Japanese Technical Manpower in Industry, 1880-1930: A Quantitative Survey', *Indust. Training & Technological Innovation*, H.F. Gospel ed., Routledge, 1990, 112–35; 'The Transfer of Electrical Technologies from the United States and Europe to Japan, 1869-1914', *Internat. Technology Transfer in Hist. Perspective*, D. Jeremy ed., Edward Elgar, 1991.

Udagawa, Masaru

Prof. of Bus. Hist., Fac. of Bus. Admin., Hosei Univ., 2-17-1 Fujimi, Chiyoda-ku, Tokyo, Japan. Tel.: 03 3264 9714. Fax: 03 3222 6425.

Year and Place of Birth 1944, Chiba, Japan.

Degrees and Qualifications B.Bus. Admin. Hosei Univ., 1968; M.Econ. Hosei Univ., 1971; Ph.D. (Econ.) Hosei Univ., 1988.

Current Offices and Honorary Posts

Sec., Bus. Hist. Soc. of Japan, 1975–8 & 1983–6; council mem., Bus. Hist. Soc. of Japan, 1987–90; exec. com. mem., Bus. Hist. Soc. of Japan, 1991–; council mem., Socio-Econ. Hist. Soc. of Japan, 1991–.

Fields of Expertise *Industry Fields:* coal and petroleum products; electrical engineering; vehicle construction. *Bus. Dimensions:* entrepreneurs and entrepreneurship; multinational bus.; bus.–state relations. *Scope:* national; internat. *Period:* twentieth century as a whole; inter-war years, 1919–39. *Teaching:* undergrad.; post grad. *Consultancy:* co. hist.

Publications *Books: Shinko Zaibatsu* [The New Zaibatsu], Nippon Keizai Shimbunsha, 1984; *Foreign Bus. in Japan before World War II*, co-ed., Univ. of Tokyo Press, 1990. *Articles:* 'The pre-War Japanese Automobile Industry and Amer. Manufacturers', *Japanese Yearbook on Bus. Hist*, 2, Japan Bus. Hist. Instit., 1985; 'The Move into Manchuria of the Nissan Combine', *Japanese Yearbook on Bus. Hist.*, 7, Japan Bus. Hist. Instit., 1991; 'Hitachi Seisakusho ni okeru Ouna to Senmon Keieisha' [Owners and Salaried Managers of the Hitachi Works Co. Ltd.], *Kigyo Keieisha no Jidai* [The Age of Managerial Enterprise], Hiedmasa Morikawa ed., Yuhikaku, 1991.

Ueda, Kinji

Prof., Soka Univ., Fac. of Management and Bus., 1-236 Tangicho, Hachiojishi, Tokyo, Japan. Tel.: 0426 91 2211.

Year and Place of Birth 1944, Yamaguchi, Japan.

Degrees and Qualifications Ph.D. Tokyo Univ., 1990.

Previous Post Researcher, Inst. for Banking & Financial Research Inc., 1974–89.

Fields of Expertise *Industry Fields:* insurance, banking, finance. *Bus.*

Dimensions: co. finance and accounting. *Scope:* regional; national. *Period:* early twentieth century; inter-war years, 1919–39; mid-twentieth century, 1940–70. *Teaching:* undergrad.; post grad.

Publications *Articles:* 'Kinyukyoko to Toshiginko no Keieisenryaku' [Financial Panic and the Nagoya Bank], *Kinyu Keizai*, 219, Oct. 1986, 89–132; 'Ginkogappei to Oguchikashidashi' [Amalgamation Movements of Commercial Banks and Succession of Large Loans 1930-1940'], *Kinyu Keizai*, 221, April 1987, 55–109; 'Senkanki ni okeru Fudosankinyu to Fudosanginko' [On the Hypothec Banks during the inter-war years in Japan], *Kinyu Keizai*, 222, Nov. 1987, 71–179; 'Chukyo Zaibatsu' [Chukyo Zaibatsu], *Local Zaibatsu and Banks*, Feb. 1989, 567–612; 'Toshiginko to Gunju-kinyu' [Commercial Banks in the Pacific War Era], *Hist. Analysis of Japanese Finan. Structure during World War II*, Feb. 1991, 477–508.

Uemura, Motokaku

Prof., Nanao Junior College, Fujibashi-machi, Nanao City, Ishikawa 926, Japan. Tel.: 0767 52 2236. Fax: 0767 52 2237.

Year and Place of Birth 1916, Toyama, Japan.

Degrees and Qualifications Ph.D. (Econ.) Osaka Univ., 1958.

Previous Post Director, Nanao Junior College, 1988–92.

Current Offices and Honorary Posts Council mem., Assoc. of Bus. Hist.

Fields of Expertise *Industry Fields:* distributive trades. *Bus. Dimensions:* bus. organization. *Scope:* regional. *Period:* nineteenth century. *Teaching:* undergrad. *Consultancy:* corporate strategy.

Publications *Books: Gyosho-ken to Ryoiki-keizai - Toyama Baiyaku-gyo*

Shi no Kenkyu [The Peddling Sphere and the Landlord Economy - A Historical Study of Toyama Drug Peddling], Minerva, 1957; *Toyama-Baiyaku-gyo si Siryo-shusei* [Historical Materials of Toyama Drug Peddlers], Toyama-ken Maruzen, 1982; *Toyama-Baiyakugyo-si zu-si* [The Hist. of Toyama Drug Peddlers], Toyama-ken Maruzen, 1984; *Historical Materials of Yankee Peddlers*, Vol. 27, Uemura ed. & pub., 1984. *Articles:* '1850 nendai New England ni okeru Yankee Gyosho-nin no Tabi-nikki' [Diary of a Yankee Peddler in New England in the 1850s], *Nanao Ronso*, 1, 1988.

Ulicny, Ferdinand

Lect., P.J. Safárik Univ., Dept. of Hist. and Archives, Fac. of Arts, Ulica 17. novembra 1, 081 16 Presov, Slovakia. Tel.: 42 91 33231-2. Fax: 42 91 33268.

Year and Place of Birth 1933, Plostín, Slovakia.

Degrees and Qualifications C.Sc. Inst. of Hist. of the Slovak Acad. of Sciences, Bratislava, 1969; Ph.Dr. Comenius Univ., Bratislava, 1970; Doc. Sarárik Univ., Presov, 1991; Dr.Sc. Inst. of Hist. of the Slovak Acad. of Sciences, Bratislava, 1993.

Current Offices and Honorary Posts Vice-dean, Fac. of Arts, Presov; com. mem., Slovak Hist. Soc.; mem., Scientific College, Slovak Acad. of Sciences.

Fields of Expertise *Industry Fields:* agric., forestry, fishing; food, drink, tobacco; metal goods; textiles; leather; clothing and footwear; transport and communication. *Bus. Dimensions:* bus.–state relations; markets and bus. *Scope:* local; regional; national; internat. *Period:* medieval; early modern. *Teaching:* undergrad. *Consultancy:* co. hist.

Publications *Books: Dejiny Osídlenia Sarisa* [Hist. of Settlement of the Saris Region], East-Slovakia

Publisher, Kosice, 1990. *Articles: Dejíny Presova I* [Hist. of Presov I], East-Slovakia Publisher, Kosice, 1965, 58–107; 'Vysady Spisskych Miest z Roku 1271' [The Privileges of the Town in the Spis Region of 1271], *Slovenská Archivistika*, XVI(2), 1981, 88–96; '', *Dejiny Trebisova* [Hist. of Trebisov], East-Slovakia Publisher, Kosice, 1982, 72–148; *Dejiny Vranova* [Hist. of Vranov], East-Slovakia Publisher, Kosice, 1992, 39–110.

Ullenhag, Kersti Margareta

Assoc. Prof., Dept. of Econ. Hist., Fac. of Social Sciences, Uppsala Univ., POB 513, 751 20 Uppsala, Sweden. Tel.: 46 18 18 12 13. Fax: 46 18 18 12 23.

Year and Place of Birth 1936, Åtvidaberg, Sweden.

Degrees and Qualifications Ph.D. (Soc. Sc.) Uppsala Univ., 1970.

Current Offices and Honorary Posts Contributor & expert on branches of industry in the new Swedish encyclopaedia; board mem., Univ. Library, *Carolina Rediviva*, Uppsala; chairperson, Swedish Inst. Com. for Scholarships, Fellowships & Grants.

Fields of Expertise *Bus. Dimensions:* development, expansion, contraction & merger questions. *Scope:* national; Sweden. *Period:* twentieth century as a whole. *Teaching:* undergrad. *Consultancy:* co. hist.

Publications *Books: AB Åtvidabergs förenade industrier med föregångare*, Ekonomisk-historiska studier V - Scandinavian Univ. Books, Svenska bokförlaget, Uppsala, 1970, (with a summary in English); *Industriell utveckling och demokratisering, 1862–1921. Uppsala stads historia V*, Almqvist & Wiksell, Uppsala, 1984; *Förnyelse Förvandling Fusion Uplandsbanken 1965–1985*, Hallgren & Fallgren Studieförlag AB, Uppsala, 1990; *'Hundred Flowers Bloom'*

Essays in Honour of Bo Gustafsson, ed., Uppsala Studies in Econ. Hist., 33, Acta Universitatis Upsaliensis, Almqvist & Wiksell, Uppsala, 1991; *Nordic Bus. in the Long View: On Control and Strategy in Structural Change*, ed., Bus. Hist. Special Issue, 35(2), Apr., 1993, Frank Cass, London, 1993.

Umeno, Naotoshi

Assoc. Prof., Dept. of Internat. Bus. and Marketing, Kobe Univ. of Commerce, 8-2-1 Gakuen Nishimachi, Nishi-ku, Kobe 651-21, Japan. Tel.: 078 794 6161.

Year and Place of Birth 1960, Hokkaido, Japan.

Degrees and Qualifications M.Bus.Admin. Kobe Univ., 1984.

Fields of Expertise *Industry Fields:* mining and quarrying; coal and petroleum products. *Bus. Dimensions:* co. admin.; multinational bus.; bus.–state relations. *Scope:* regional. *Period:* twentieth century as a whole; mid-twentieth century, 1940–70; late twentieth century, 1970–present.

Publications *Books: Kokusai Shigenkigyo no Kokuyuka* [The Nationalization of Internat. Natural Resource Companies], Hakuto shobo, Tokyo, 1992.

Usselman, Steven W.

Assoc. Prof., Dept. of Hist., Univ. of North Carolina at Charlotte, Charlotte, NC 28223, USA. Tel.: 1 704 547 4643. Fax: 1 704 547 3218.

Year and Place of Birth 1956, Lynwood, USA.

Degrees and Qualifications BA Univ. of California at San Diego, 1979; MA Delaware Univ., 1981; Ph.D. Delaware Univ., 1985.

Previous Post Visiting Asst. Prof., Maine Univ., 1984–5.
Current Offices and Honorary Posts Edit. com., Soc. for the Hist. of Technology.
Major Honours Newcomen Prize, *Bus. Hist. Rev.*, 1984.
Fields of Expertise *Industry Fields:* transport and communication; electronics and computers: manufacture. *Bus. Dimensions:* bus. and technology. *Scope:* national. *Period:* nineteenth century; twentieth century as a whole. *Teaching:* undergrad.; post grad. *Consultancy:* co. hist.
Publications *Articles:* 'Air Brakes for Freight Trains: Technological Innovation on Amer. Railroads, 1869–1901', *Bus. Hist. Rev.*, 58, 1984, 30–50; 'Patents Purloined: Railroads, Inventors and the Diffusion of Innovation in Nineteenth Century America', *Technology and Culture*, 32, 1991, 1047–75; 'The Lure of Technology and the Appeal of Order: Railroad Safety Regulation in Amer., 1865–1914', *Econ. & Bus. Hist.*, 2nd ser., 21, 1992; 'From Novelty to Utility: George Westinghouse and the Bus. of Innovation in the Age of Edison', *Bus. Hist. Rev.*, 66, Spring, 1992; 'IBM and its Imitators: Organizational Capabilities and the Emergence of the Modern Computer Industry', *Econ. & Bus. Hist.*, Special vol., 1993.

Valdaliso, Jesús M.

Lect., Dept. of Econ. Hist., Facultad de Ciencias Económicas y Empresariales, Universidad del País Vasco, Avda. Lehendakari Agirre 83, 48015 Bilbao, Spain. Tel.: 34 94 4472800. Fax: 34 94 4475154.
Year and Place of Birth 1964, Eibar, Spain.
Degrees and Qualifications BA (Hist.) Universidad del País Vasco,

1986; Ph.D. Universidad del País Vasco, 1990.
Current Offices and Honorary Posts Sec., Dept. of Econ. Hist., Universidad del País Vasco; ed. board mem., *Internat. J. of Maritime Hist.*
Major Honours Ramón Carande Prize, Asociación Española de Historia Económica, 1987.
Fields of Expertise *Industry Fields:* shipbuilding and marine engineering; transport and communication. *Bus. Dimensions:* entrepreneurs and entrepreneurship; co. finance and accounting. *Scope:* regional; national. *Period:* nineteenth century; twentieth century as a whole. *Teaching:* undergrad.; post grad.
Publications *Books: Los Navieros Vascos y la Marina Mercante en España, 1860–1935. Una Historia Económica*, IVAP, Bilbao, 1991. *Articles:* 'Grupos Empresariales e Inversión de Capital en Vizcaya, 1886–1913', *Revista de Historia Económica*, VI, Madrid, 1988; 'Política Económica y Grupos de Presión: la Acción Colectiva de la Asociación de Navieros de Bilbao, 1900–1936', *Historia Social*, 7, Valencia, 1990; 'Growth and Modernization of the Spanish Merchant Marine, 1860–1935', *Internat. J. of Maritime Hist.*, III, St John's, Newfoundland, Canada, 1991; 'Spanish Shipowners in the British Mirror: Patterns of Investment, Ownership and finance in the Bilbao Shipping Industry, 1879–1913', *Internat. J. of Maritime Hist.*, V, St John's, Newfoundland, Canada, 1993.

Vallieres, Marc

Titular Prof. & Director, Dept. of Hist., Laval Univ., Québec, G1K 7P4, Canada. Tel.: 1 418 656 5197. Fax: 1 418 656 3603.
Year and Place of Birth 1946,

Québec, Canada.

Degrees and Qualifications Ph.D. (Hist.) Laval Univ., 1980; Diplôme en Admin. Laval Univ., 1982.

Previous Post Prof., Sherbrooke Univ., 1972–5.

Fields of Expertise *Industry Fields:* mining and quarrying; metal manufacture; bus. services; insurance, banking, finance; public admin. and defence. *Bus. Dimensions:* entrepreneurs and entrepreneurship; co. finance and accounting; co. admin.; bus.–state relations; markets and bus. *Scope:* local; regional; Québec. *Period:* nineteenth century; twentieth century as a whole. *Teaching:* undergrad.; post grad. *Consultancy:* co. hist.

Publications *Books: SSQ. Mutuelle d'Assurance-Groupe. L'Histore d'un Succès Collectif,* SSQ, Québec, 1986; *Des Mines et des Hommes. Histoire de l'Industrie Minérale Québecoise. Des Origines au Début des Années 1980,* Les Publications du Québec, 1989; *Articles:* 'Le Gouvernement du Québec et les Milieux Financiers de 1867 à 1920', *Actualité Économique,* 59(3), 1983, 531–51.

---

van den Eerenbeemt, H.F.J.M.

Prof., Tilberg Univ., Warandalaan 2, Tilburg, Netherlands. Tel.: 31 13 669111. Fax: 31 13 663019.

Year and Place of Birth 1930, Roosendaal, Netherlands.

Degrees and Qualifications Ph.D. Nijmegen Univ., 1955.

Previous Post Lect., 1956–61.

Current Offices and Honorary Posts Chief project ed., *Hist. of Noord-Brabant 1796–1996;* pres. editorship, *Bijdragen tot de Geschiedenis van het Zuiden van Nederland.*

Major Honours Ridder in de orde van de Nederlandse leeuw; commandeur in de orde van de H. Gregorius de Grote.

Fields of Expertise *Industry Fields:* insurance, banking, finance. *Bus. Dimensions:* entrepreneurs and entrepreneurship. *Scope:* national. *Period:* twentieth century as a whole. *Consultancy:* co. hist.

Publications *Books: Armoede en Arbeidsdwang: Werkinrichtingen voor 'Onnutte' Nederlanders in de Republik, 1760–1795,* 'S-Gravenhage, 1977; *Bankieren in Brabant in de Loop der Eeuwen,* ed., Tilburg, 1987; *Mens en Maatschappij in Beweging: Wortels, Patronen en Ontwikkelingslijnen in het sociaal-economisch Leven van West-Europa voor 1940,* 1st edn., Tilburg, 1987; 4th edn., Tilburg, 1992; *Van Boterkleursel naar Kopieersystemen; de Ontstaansgeschiedenis van Océ-van der Grinten, 1877–1956,* ed., Leiden, 1992; *Op zoek naar het Zachte Goud; Pogingen tot Innovatie via een Zijdeteelt in Nederland, 17e-20e eeuw,* Tilburg, 1993.

Van Der Wee, Herman

Prof. and Chair of Social and Econ. Hist., Leuven Univ., Centre for Econ. Studies, E. Van Evenstraat 2B, B-3000 Leuven, Belgium. Tel.: 016 28 31 01. Fax: 016 28 33 61.

Year and Place of Birth 1928, Lier, Belgium.

Degrees and Qualifications B.Phil. K.U. Leuven, 1949; LL D K.U. Leuven, 1950; MA (Soc. & Polit. Sc.) K.U. Leuven, 1951; Ph.D. (Econ. Hist.) K.U. Leuven, 1963.

Previous Post Director, J. Verbreyt-Weyn Ltd. (Netherlands), 1956–66.

Current Offices and Honorary Posts Mem., 'Comité consultatif de la Fondation Internat.e des Sciences Humaines', 1974–; mem., Royal Acad. of Belgium, Class of Letters (elected 1977); corresponding mem., Royal Acad. of the Netherlands, 1983–; mem., Board of Trustees of the

'Academia Belgica', Rome, 1980–92; council mem., Istituto Internazionale di Storia Economica Francesco Datini in Prato, 1986–; mem. of Scientific Com. & Giunta Esecutiva, 1987–; corresponding fellow, British Acad. (elected July 1987); director, Class of Letters, Royal Acad. of Belgium, 1987; external mem., Research Council of the European Univ. Inst. (Florence), 1985–; pres., Internat. Econ. Hist. Assoc. (1986–90); hon. pres. since 1990; chairman, Academic Advisory Council of the European Assoc. for Banking Hist., 1991–; mem., Board of Management of the European Assoc. for Banking Hist., 1991–; founding mem., Academia Europeae.

Major Honours De Stassart Prize for National Hist. (1961–7) of the Royal Acad. of Belgium, 1968; Fulbright Award, 1975–1981; Quinquennial Solvay Prize for the Humanities (1976) by the National Foundation for Scientific Research of Belgium, 1981; Amsterdam Prize for the Historical Sciences awarded by the Royal Acad. of Sciences of the Netherlands, 1992.

Fields of Expertise *Industry Fields:* textiles; clothing and footwear; bricks, pottery, glass, cement; insurance, banking, finance. *Bus. Dimensions:* entrepreneurs and entrepreneurship; bus. values. *Scope:* local; national. *Period:* medieval; early modern; eighteenth century; nineteenth century; twentieth century as a whole. *Teaching:* post grad.

Publications *Books: La Banque Nationale de Belgique et la Politique Monétaire entre les deux Guerres Mondiales,* National Bank of Belgium, Brussels, 1975; *Mensen Maken Geschiedenis. De Kredietbank en de economische opgang van Vlaanderen 1935–1985* [The Kredietbank and the Rise of the Flemish Economy, 1935–1985], Lannoo, Tielt, 1985. *Articles:* 'La Banque en Europe au moyen âge et aux temps modernes

(1476–1789)', *La Banque en Occident,* ed., Mercatorfonds, Antwerp, 1991; 'The Medieval and Early Modern Origins of European Banking', *Banchi Pubblici, Banchi Privati e Monti de Pietà nell'Europa Preindustriale,* Società di Storia Patria, Genova, 1991, 1157–73; 'Internat. Factors in the Formation of Banking Systems: Belgium', *Internat. Banking, 1870–1914,* R. Cameron & V.I. Bovykin eds., OUP, New York, 1991, 113–29.

Van Driel, Hugo

Asst. Prof. of Bus. Hist., Faculteit Bedrijfskunde, Erasmus Univ. of Rotterdam, POB 1738, 3000 DR Rotterdam, Netherlands. Tel.: 31 10 4081900. Fax: 31 10 4523166.

Year and Place of Birth 1962, Brielle, Netherlands.

Degrees and Qualifications MA (Social Hist.) Erasmus Univ. Rotterdam, 1984; Ph.D. Erasmus Univ. Rotterdam, 1990.

Previous Post Research Fellow, Erasmus Univ. Rotterdam, 1985–90.

Major Honours Research Prize, Erasmus Univ., 1990.

Fields of Expertise *Industry Fields:* transport and communication. *Bus. Dimensions:* merger movement and issues. *Scope:* national. *Period:* late twentieth century, 1970–present. *Teaching:* undergrad.

Publications *Books: Een Verenigde Nederlandse Scheepvaart. De Fusie Tussen Nedlloyd en K.N.S.M. in 1980–1981,* Eburon, Delft, 1988; *Samenwerking in Haven en Vervoer in het Containertijdperk,* Eburon, Delft, 1990, (dissertation); *Four Centuries of Warehousing. Pakhoed: The Origins and Hist. 1616–1967,* Pakhoed, Rotterdam, 1992; *Kooperation im Rhein-Containerverkehr. Eine historische Analyse,* Binnenschiffahrts-

Verlag, Duisburg, 1993. *Articles:* 'Co-operation in Dutch Container Transport Industry', *The Service Industries J.*, 12(4), 1992, 512–32.

van Eyll, Klara

Managing Director, Rhineland-Westfalian Regional Bus. Archives, Cologne & Lect. in Econ. & Social Hist., Cologne Univ., Industrie- und Handelskammer zu Köln, D-5060 Cologne, Germany. Tel.: 49 221 1640106. Fax: 49 221 1640312.
Year and Place of Birth 1938, Essen, Germany.
Degrees and Qualifications Dipl.Hdl. Cologne Univ., 1963; Dr.rer.pol. Cologne Univ., 1968; Hon.Prof. Cologne Univ., 1992.
Previous Post Archivist, Rhineland-Westfalian Regional Bus. Archives, 1963–71.
Current Offices and Honorary Posts Board mem., Assoc. of German Archivists; board mem., Assoc. of German Econ. Archivists; scientific consultant, Assoc. of Bus. Hist.
Major Honours Hon. Prof. for Econ. & Soc. Hist., Cologne Univ., 1992; Bundesverdienstkreuz am Bande, 1989.
Fields of Expertise *Industry Fields:* chemicals and allied industries; paper, printing, publishing; insurance, banking, finance; public admin. and defence. *Bus. Dimensions:* entrepreneurs and entrepreneurship; bus. organization; co. culture. *Scope:* local; regional. *Period:* nineteenth century; twentieth century as a whole. *Teaching:* undergrad.; post grad. *Consultancy:* co. hist.
Publications *Books: Voraussetzungen und Entwicklungslinien von Wirtschafts-archiven bis zum Zweiten Weltkrieg*, Cologne, 1969, (Schriften zur rheinisch-westfälischen Wirtschaftsgeschichte, vol. 20); *Die Geschichte der unternehmerischen Selbstverwaltung in Köln 1797–1914*, with Herman Kellenbenz, Cologne, 1972; *Wirtschaftsgeschichte Kölns 1815–1871*, Zwei Jahrtausende Kölner Wirtschaft , vol. II, Cologne, 1975; *In Kölner Adreßbüchern geblättert*, Cologne, 1978; *genannt Colonia. 150 Jahre Kölnische Feuerversicherungsgesellschaft*, Cologne, 1989.

Vance, Sandra S.

Instructor of Hist., Dept. of Social Sciences, Hinds Community College, Raymond, MS 39154, USA. Tel.: 1 601 857 3393. Fax: 1 601 978 3027.
Year and Place of Birth 1946, Washington DC, USA.
Degrees and Qualifications BA Helhaven College, 1968; MA Louisiana State Univ., 1970; Ph.D. Mississippi State Univ., 1976.
Fields of Expertise *Industry Fields:* retailing. *Bus. Dimensions:* discount merchandising. *Scope:* national. *Period:* late twentieth century, 1970–present. *Teaching:* undergrad. *Consultancy:* co. hist.
Publications *Articles:* 'Sam Walton and Wal-Mart Stores Inc.: A Study in Modern Southern Entrepreneurship', *J. of Southern Hist.*, with Roy V. Scott co-auth., vol., LVIII, May, 1992, 231–52; 'Wal-Mart Stores in the 1980s: Innovative Formats for Modern Retailing', *Essays in Econ. & Bus. Hist.*, with Roy V. Scott co-auth., X, 1992, 298–309; 'Butler Brothers and the Rise and Decline of the Ben Franklin Variety Stores: A Study in Franchise Retailing', *Essays in Econ. & Bus. Hist.*, with Roy V. Scott, XI, 1993, forthcoming.

Veenendaal, Augustus J. Jr.

Sen. Research Historian, Inst. of Netherlands Hist., Prins Willem-

Alexanderhof 7, POB 90755, 2509 LT
The Hague, Netherlands. Tel.: 31 70
3814771. Fax: 31 70 3854098.
Year and Place of Birth 1940,
Heemstede, Netherlands.
Degrees and Qualifications Ph.D.
Nijmegen Univ., 1976.
Fields of Expertise *Industry Fields:*
transport and communication. *Bus.
Dimensions:* co. finance and account-
ing. *Scope:* internat.; Netherlands;
USA. *Period:* nineteenth century; early
twentieth century. *Consultancy:* co.
hist.
Publications *Articles:* 'Railroads,
Oil and Dutchmen: Investing in the
Oklahoma Frontier', *The Chronicles of
Oklahoma*, 53, 1985, 4–27; 'The
Kansas City Southern Railway and the
Dutch Connection', *Bus. Hist. Rev.*,
61, 1987, 291–316; 'The Dutch
Connection: Salomon Frederik van
Oss and Dutch Investment in
Oklahoma', *The Chronicles of
Oklahoma*, 55, 1987, 252–67; 'The
Oklahoma Central Railway: A
"Dutch" Railroad in the United States',
Railroad Hist., 166, 1992, 88–102;
'An Example of "Other People's
Money": Dutch Capital in Amer.
Railroads', *Bus. & Econ. Hist.*, 2nd
ser., 21, 1992, 147–58.

Verhoef, Grietjie

Sen. Lect., Dept. of Hist., Rand
Afrikaans Univ., POB 524,
Aucklandpark 2006, South Africa.
Tel.: 27 11 489 2001/27 11 489 2008.
Fax: 27 11 489 2797.
Year and Place of Birth 1957,
Pretoria, South Africa.
Degrees and Qualifications BA
(Polit. Sc.) Rand Afrikaans Univ.,
1978; BA (Hist.) Rand Afrikaans
Univ., 1979; MA (Hist.) Rand
Afrikaans Univ., 1983; D.Litt. et Phil.
(Hist.) Rand Afrikaans Univ., 1987;
BA (Econ.) Rand Afrikaans Univ.,
1993.

Current Offices and Honorary Posts
Rev. ed., *CONTREE* (J. for Urban &
Regional Hist.), 1990–; treasurer,
Econ. Hist. Soc. of South Africa,
1986–.
Fields of Expertise *Industry Fields:*
mining and quarrying; insurance,
banking, finance. *Scope:* regional;
national. *Period:* twentieth century as
a whole; mid-twentieth century,
1940–70; late twentieth century,
1970–present. *Teaching:* undergrad.;
post grad. *Consultancy:* co. hist.
Publications *Articles:* 'The
Nederlandsche Bank voor Zuid-Afrika,
N.V. becomes a South African Bank,
1945–1973', *Bankhistorisches Archiv,
Zeitschrift für Bankgeschichte*, 13
Jahrgang, Heft Z, Berlin, December,
1988; 'Nedbank's Activities in the
Promotion of Foreign Trade,
1945–1973', *A Hist. of Banking and
Bus. in South Africa*, F.S. Jones ed.,
Macmillan, London, 1988; 'State
Involvement in the Rehabilitation of
Poor Whites by means of Land
Resettlement at the Hartebeest-poort-
dam Irrigation Scheme', *South African
J. of Econ. Hist.*, 5(1), March, 1990;
'Afrikaner Nationalism in South
African Banking. The Cases of
Volkskas and Trust Bank', *Financial
Enterprise in South Africa*, F.S. Jones
ed., Macmillan, London, 1992;
'Nedbank, 1945–1989: The
Continental Approach to Banking in
South Africa', *Financial Enterprise in
South Africa*, F.S. Jones ed.,
Macmillan, London, 1992.

Vietor, Richard H.K.

Prof., Harvard Grad. School of Bus.
Admin., 285 Morgan Hall, Soldiers
Field, Boston, MA 02163, USA. Tel.:
1 617 495 6460. Fax: 1 617 496
5994.
Year and Place of Birth 1945,
Minneapolis, USA.

Degrees and Qualifications BA Union College, 1967; MA Hofstra Univ., 1971; Ph.D. Pittsburgh Univ., 1975.

Previous Post Assoc. Prof., Harvard Univ., 1979–84.

Current Offices and Honorary Posts Pres., Bus. Hist. Conf., 1993–4; board of eds., *Bus. Hist. Rev.*; advisory board, IPADE (Mexico).

Major Honours Newcomen Award in Bus. Hist., 1981; Newcomen Postdoctoral Fellowship, Harvard Bus. School, 1978.

Fields of Expertise *Industry Fields:* transport and communication. *Bus. Dimensions:* bus.–state relations. *Scope:* internat. *Period:* late twentieth century, 1970–present. *Teaching:* post grad. *Consultancy:* corporate strategy.

Publications *Books: Environmental Polit. and the Coal Coalition*, Texas A&M Univ. Press, College Station, 1980; *Energy Policy in Amer. since 1945: A Study of Bus.-Government Relations*, CUP, New York, 1984; *Strategic Management in the Regulatory Environment*, Prentice Hall, Englewood Cliffs, 1989; *Contrived Competition: Regulation and Deregulation in Amer.*, Harvard Univ. Press, Cambridge, MA, 1994.

Ville, Simon P.

Sen. Lect. in Econ. Hist., Dept. of Econ. Hist., Fac. of Econ. and Commerce, Australian National Univ., Canberra, ACT 0200, Australia. Tel.: 61 6 249 3589. Fax: 61 6 249 5792.

Year and Place of Birth 1958, London, UK.

Degrees and Qualifications BA London Univ., 1979; Ph.D. London Univ., 1984.

Previous Post Sen. Lect. in Econ., Auckland Univ., 1990–1.

Current Offices and Honorary Posts Book rev. ed., *Australian Econ. Hist.*

Rev.; overseas correspondent, *J. of Transport Hist.*

Fields of Expertise *Industry Fields:* coal and petroleum products; ship-building and marine engineering; transport and communication. *Bus. Dimensions:* entrepreneurs and entre-preneurship; bus. organization. *Scope:* national. *Period:* nineteenth century. *Teaching:* undergrad.; post grad.

Publications *Books: English Shipowning during the Indust. Revolution, 1770–1830*, Manchester Univ. Press, Manchester, 1987; *Transport and the Development of the European Economy, 1750–1918*, Macmillan, London, 1990; *United Kingdom Shipbuilding in the Nineteenth Century*, ed., Internat. Maritime Econ. Hist. Assoc. & Liverpool Maritime Museum, Liverpool, 1993; *The European Economy, 1750–1914. A Thematic Approach*, D.H. Aldcroft co-ed., Manchester Univ. Press, Manchester, 1993; *Management, Finance & Labour in the Maritime Industries*, D. Williams co-ed., Internat. Econ. Hist. Assoc., 1993.

Virtanen, Sakari

Researcher, Inst. of Northern Finland, Kauppakatu 25A, SF-87100 Kajaani, Finland. Tel.: 358 86 121903. Fax: 358 86 29978.

Year and Place of Birth 1938, Suomussalmi, Finland.

Degrees and Qualifications M.Polit.Sc. (National Econ.) Helsinki Univ., 1965.

Previous Post Information Manager, Kajaani Oy, 1973–92.

Fields of Expertise *Industry Fields:* timber; paper. *Bus. Dimensions:* bus.–state relations. *Scope:* regional. *Period:* twentieth century as a whole. *Teaching:* personnel. *Consultancy:* co. hist.

Publications *Books: Kajaani Oy*

1907–1982 [A Hist. of Kajaani Oy 1907–1982], part I, 1982, part II, 1985, in Finnish; *Lapin Leivänisä* [Centenary Hist. of the Kemi Co.], Oy Metsä-Botnia Ab, 1993, in Finnish. *Articles:* 'The Ownership of Forest Industries and Regional Identity in Northern Finland 1860–1990', *The Future of Kainuu - Alternatives and Strategies*, Univ. of Oulu, Research Inst. of Northern Finland, 106, 1991, seminar report.

Vleesenbeek, H.H.

Prof. of Econ. & Bus. Hist. & Managing Director, Center of Bus. Hist., Fac. of Econ./Fac. of Hist. & Arts, Erasmus Univ. of Rotterdam;, Center of Bus. Hist. (Research Unit), c/o EUR, Postbus 1738, 3000 DR Rotterdam, Netherlands. Tel.: 010 4082500. Fax: 010 4532922.

Year and Place of Birth 1940, Dordrecht, Netherlands.

Degrees and Qualifications M.Econ.Sc. Rotterdam School of Econ., 1976; Ph.D. Erasmus Univ., 1981.

Current Offices and Honorary Posts Chairman, Assoc. of Bus. Hist. (Netherlands).

Fields of Expertise *Industry Fields:* food, drink, tobacco; textiles; insurance, banking, finance. *Bus. Dimensions:* entrepreneurs and entrepreneurship; merger movement and issues. *Scope:* regional; national. *Period:* eighteenth century; nineteenth century; twentieth century as a whole. *Teaching:* undergrad.; post grad. *Consultancy:* co. hist.

Publications *Books: De eerste grote Industriele Fusie in Nederland na 1945, het Ontstaan van Nyverdal-ten Cate, een Bedrijfshistorische Analyse* [The First Merger after 1945 in the Dutch Cotton Industry], Rotterdam, 1981; *Van oude naar nieuwe*

Hoofdpoort, Geschiedenis van het Assurantie-Concern 'Stad Rotterdam A° 1720 NV' [Hist. of the oldest Insurance Co. on the Continent, 1720–1990], with Dr. P.Th. van de Laar, Rotterdam, 1990; *Waakzaam aan de Waterweg, de Kamer van Koophandel Rotterdam, 1945–1990* [Hist. of the Rotterdam Chamber of Commerce after the Second World War], with M. Veenstra. *Articles:* 'Investeren, Winstdeling en Werkgelegenheid, een historische Visie' [Investment, Profit-sharing and Employment, a Historical View], *Nederland in Zaken*, Dr. A van der Zwan ed., Utrecht, 1985.

Vogt, Martin

Head of the Inst. of European Hist. Library, Mainz, Dept. of Universal Hist. and of the Inst. of Hist., Darmstadt Technical Univ., Fuchstraße 26, D-64291 Darmstadt, Germany. Tel.: 49 6131 399366. Fax: 49 6131 237988.

Year and Place of Birth 1936, Hannover, Germany.

Degrees and Qualifications Dr.phil. Göttingen Univ., 1963; Habilitation, Darmstadt Tech. Univ., 1980; apl. Prof., Darmstadt Tech. Univ., 1991.

Previous Post Scientific Ed. 'Akten der Reichskanzlei', 1964–75.

Fields of Expertise *Industry Fields:* public admin. and defence. *Bus. Dimensions:* multinational bus. *Scope:* national. *Period:* inter-war years, 1919–39. *Teaching:* undergrad.; post grad. *Consultancy:* corporate strategy.

Publications. *Books: Die Entstehung des Young-Plans*, Boldt, 1971; *Akten der Reichskanzlei: Kabinett Müller I, Kabinette Streseman I/II, Kabinett Müller II*, Boldt, 1970, 1971 & 1978; *Deutsche Geschichte von den Anfängen bis zur Wiedervereinigung*, ed., 2nd edn., Metzlar, 1991. *Articles:*

'Brandenburg in Übersee: Zur Kolonialpolitik dt. Fürsten im 17. Jh.', *Geschichte der Entdeckungen und der frühen Kolonisation*, Darmstadt Tech. Univ. J. Series, 1993.

von Stromer (Freiherr von Reichenbach), Wolfgang

Emeritus Prof. of Econ. & Technological Hist., Fac. of Social & Econ. Sciences, Erlangen Nuremberg Univ., Findelgasse 7, D-90402 Nuremberg, Germany. Tel.: 49 9187 41121 (private).
Year and Place of Birth 1922, Munich, Germany.
Degrees and Qualifications Dr.rer.pol. Nuremberg Univ., 1962; Habilitation (Econ. Hist.) Nuremberg Univ., 1967; Habilitation (Technological Hist.) Nuremberg Univ., 1977; Dr.rer.pol.habil. Nuremberg Univ., 1977.
Previous Post Prof., Fac. of Social Science, Nuremberg Univ., 1984–90.
Current Offices and Honorary Posts Spokesman, 'Regional Research', Zentralinstitut 6, Erlangen-Nuremberg Univ.; mem., Centro Tedesco di Studi Veneziani, Palazzo Barbarigo dela Terrazza, Venice.
Major Honours Willibald Pirckheimer Medal, 1969; commem. pub. for Wolfgang von Stromer, *Hochfinanz Wirtschaftsräume-Innovationen*, 3 vols., U. Bestmann, F. Irsigler, J. Schneider eds., Trier, 1987.
Fields of Expertise *Industry Fields:* mining and quarrying; mechanical engineering; paper, printing, publishing; construction; insurance, banking, finance. *Bus. Dimensions:* research and development; multinational bus. *Scope:* internat. *Period:* medieval; early modern. *Teaching:* post grad. *Consultancy:* co. hist.
Publications *Books: Die Handelsgesellschaft Gruber-Podmer-Stromer im 15. Jahrhundert*, disserta-

tion for rer.pol. degree, Nuremberg, 1963; *Oberdeutsche Hochfinanz 1350–1450*, dissertation for Habilitation degree in Econ. Hist., Wiesbaden, 1970, 3 vols.; *Die Gründung der Baumwollindustrie in Mitteleuropa - Wirtschaftspolitik im Spätmittelalter*, dissertation for Habilitation degree in Technol. Hist., Wiesbaden, 1978; *Technik des Kunsthandwerks im zwölften Jahrhundert - Des Theophilus presbyter Diversarum Artium Schedula*, ed., Düsseldorf, 1984; *Venedig und die Weltwirtschaft um 1200*, ed., Sigmaringen, 1993.

Vozár, Jozef

Historicky ústav SAV, Klemensova 19, 813 64 Bratislava, Slovakia. Tel.: 42 7 326321.
Year and Place of Birth 1926, Nová Bana, Slovakia.
Degrees and Qualifications Ph.Dr. Komenského Univ., Bratislava, 1960; Dr.Sc. Slovenskej Académie Vied, Bratislava, 1991.
Current Offices and Honorary Posts Pres., Nat. Com. ICOHTEC, 1990.
Major Honours Mateja Bela Medal, 1984; L. Stura Gold Medal, 1986.
Fields of Expertise *Industry Fields:* mining and quarrying; coal and petroleum products; metal manufacture; mechanical engineering; transport and communication. *Bus. Dimensions:* bus. and technology. *Scope:* national; internat.; Slovakia. *Period:* early modern; eighteenth century.
Publications *Books: Európska nepriama amalgamácia a slovenské baníctvo*, Veda Vydavatelstvo SAV, Bratislava, 1988; *Zlatá kniha banícka - Das Goldene Bergbuch*, Veda Vydavatelstvo SAV, Bratislava, 1983; *Dejiny hutnictví zeleza v Ceskoslovensku I*, Academia Praha, 1984; *Denník Princa Leopolda. Das*

Tagebuch des Erzherzogs Leopold, Osveta Martin, 1990. *Articles:* 'English Mechanic Osaac Potter Constructor of the First Fire-engines in Slovakia', *Studia Historica Slovaca,* 7, 1974, 102–40.

Vrooman, David M.

Prof. of Bus. Admin., Bus. Admin., Wittenberg Univ., POB 720, Springfield, OH 45501, USA. Tel.: 1 513 327 7905. Fax: 1 513 327 6340.

Year and Place of Birth 1947, Marietta, USA.

Degrees and Qualifications BA Northwestern Univ., 1969; MS Northwestern Univ., 1974; Ph.D. Northwestern Univ., 1975.

Fields of Expertise *Industry Fields:* transport and communication. *Bus. Dimensions:* personnel management. *Scope:* national. *Period:* inter-war years, 1919–39. *Teaching:* undergrad. *Consultancy:* corporate strategy.

Publications *Books: Daniel Willard and Progressive Management on the Baltimore & Ohio Railroad,* Ohio State Univ. Press, 1991.

Wada, Kazuo

Assoc. Prof. of Bus. Hist., Tokyo Univ., Fac. of Econ., 7-3-1 Hongo, Bunkyo-ku, Tokyo, Japan. Tel.: 81 3 3812 2111. Fax: 81 3 3818 7082.

Year and Place of Birth 1949, Nigata pref., Japan.

Degrees and Qualifications MA Hitotsubashi Univ., Ph.D. London Univ., 1989.

Previous Post Assoc. Prof. of Bus. Hist., Nanzan Univ.

Current Offices and Honorary Posts Internat. Relations Com. mem., Japan Bus. Hist. Soc.

Fields of Expertise *Industry Fields:*
coal and petroleum products; vehicle construction; gas, electricity, water. *Bus. Dimensions:* production management; bus. organization; bus. and technology. *Scope:* regional; national; internat. *Period:* nineteenth century; twentieth century as a whole. *Teaching:* undergrad.; post grad.

Publications *Books: The Development of the British Electricity Supply Industry: A Case Study Approach. Articles:* 'The Development of Tiered Inter-firm Relationships in the Automobile Industry: A Case Study of the Toyota Motor Corporation', *Japanese Yearbook on Bus. Hist.,* 8, 1991.

Wale, Judith M.

Research Fellow, School of Bus. and Econ. Studies, Leeds Univ., Leeds, LS2 9JT, UK. Tel.: 44 532 332614. Fax: 44 532 332640.

Year and Place of Birth 1952, Cambridge, UK.

Degrees and Qualifications BA (Mod. Hist.) Oxford Univ., 1973; MA (Mod. Hist.) Oxford Univ., 1987; D.Phil. (Econ.) Oxford Univ., 1987; mem., Inst. of Chartered Accountants in England & Wales (ACA), 1980.

Previous Post Lect. in Accounting, Buckingham Univ., 1987–90.

Fields of Expertise *Industry Fields:* coal and petroleum products. *Bus. Dimensions:* co. finance and accounting. *Scope:* national. *Period:* early twentieth century. *Teaching:* undergrad. *Consultancy:* co. hist.

Publications *Articles:* 'The Griff Colliery Co. Limited, Warwickshire, 1882–1914: A Case Study in Bus. History', *Midland Hist.,* 14, 1989, 95–119; 'The Cramlington Coal Co. Limited, Northumberland, 1824–1914: A Case Study in Bus. History', *Bus. Archives,* 58, 1989, 1–21; 'How Reliable Were Reported Profits and Asset Values in the Period 1890–1914?

Case Studies from the British Coal Industry', *Accounting & Bus. Research*, 20(79), 1990, 253–68.

Waller, David S.

Lect. in Marketing, Univ. of Newcastle, Central Coast Campus, POB 127, Ourimbah, NSW 2258, Australia. Tel.: 61 43 622077. Fax: 61 43 622044.
Year and Place of Birth 1962, Sydney, Australia.
Degrees and Qualifications BA Sydney Univ., 1985; M.Com. New South Wales Univ., 1988.
Previous Post Lect. in Marketing, Charles Sturt Univ., Riverina, 1989–90.
Fields of Expertise *Industry Fields:* bus. services. *Bus. Dimensions:* marketing. *Scope:* national. *Period:* twentieth century as a whole. *Teaching:* undergrad.; post grad.
Publications *Articles:* 'A Tale of Truth Truthfully Told: The Early Development of the Advertising Industry and Ethics in Australia', *Proceedings* of the Marketing Educators Conf., Perth, 3, Feb., 1992, 831–45.

Walsh, Margaret

Sen. Lect., Dept. of Econ. & Social Hist., Univ. of Birmingham, POB 363, Birmingham, B15 2TT, UK. Tel.: 44 21 414 6635. Fax: 44 21 414 6625.
Year and Place of Birth 1942, Wigton, UK.
Degrees and Qualifications MA St Andrews Univ.; MA Smith College; Ph.D. Wisconsin-Madison Univ.
Previous Post Lect. in Amer. Studies, Keele Univ., 1969–71.
Major Honours Amer. Council for Learned Societies Research Fellowship, 1974–5; Nuffield Research Fellowship, 1990–1.

Fields of Expertise *Industry Fields:* food, drink, tobacco; transport and communication. *Bus. Dimensions:* small bus. matters; bus. evolution. *Scope:* regional; national; USA. *Period:* nineteenth century; twentieth century as a whole. *Teaching:* undergrad.
Publications *Books: The Manufacturing Frontier: Pioneer Industry in Antebellum Wisconsin 1830–1860*, State Historical Soc. of Wisconsin, 1972; *The Amer. Frontier Revisited (Studies in Econ. and Social Hist.)*, Macmillan, London, 1981; *The Rise of the Midwestern Meat Packing Industry*, Univ. Press of Kentucky, 1982. *Articles:* 'The Democratization of Fashion: The Emergence of Women's Paper Dress Patterns', *J. of American Hist.*, 66(2), 1979, 299–313; 'The Intercity Bus and its Competitors in the US in the mid Twentieth Century', *On the Move: Essays in Labour and Transport Hist. Presented to Philip Bagwell*, C. Wrigley & J. Shepherd eds., Hambledon Press, 1991, 231–51.

Walter, Rolf

Prof. of Econ. & Social Hist., Fac. of Econ., Univ. of Jena, Fürstengraben 11, 07743 Jena, Germany. Tel.: 49 3641 82 22607. Fax: 49 3641 82 22140.
Year and Place of Birth 1953, Kirchheim, Germany.
Degrees and Qualifications Dr.rer.pol. Nuremberg Univ., 1982; Dr.rer.pol.habil., 1988; Prof., 1991.
Current Offices and Honorary Posts Exec. board mem., German Soc. for Econ. & Soc. Hist.
Fields of Expertise *Industry Fields:* textiles; transport and communication; distributive trades; insurance, banking, finance. *Bus. Dimensions:* entrepreneurs and entrepreneurship; co. finance and accounting. *Scope:* region-

al; internat.; global. *Period:* medieval; early modern; eighteenth century; nineteenth century; early twentieth century; inter-war years, 1919–39. *Consultancy:* co. hist.

Publications *Books: Einführung in die Wirtschafts- und Sozialgeschichte,* UTB, (Schöningh 1717), 1993. *Articles:* 'Geld und Wechselbörsen vom Spätmittelalter bis zur Mitte des 17. Jahrhunderts', *Deutsche Börsengeschichte,* Fritz Knapp Verlag, Frankfurt, 1992, 13–76; 'Jüdische Unternehmer in der deutschen Textilindustrie bis 1932', *Jüdische Unternehmer in Deutschland im 19. und 20. Jahrhundert,* W.E. Mosse & H. Pohl eds., ZUG-Beiheft 64, Franz Steiner-Verlag, Stuttgart, 1992, 132–52; 'Jüdische Bankiers in Deutschland bis 1932', *ibid,* 78–99.

Watanabe, Hisashi

Prof., Fac. of Econ., Kyoto Univ., 606-01 Kyoto-shi, Sakyo-ku, Yoshidahommachi, Japan. Tel.: 075 753 3432. Fax: 075 751 1532.

Year and Place of Birth 1937, Tokyo, Japan.

Degrees and Qualifications B.Econ. Tokyo Univ., 1962; M.Econ. Tokyo Univ., 1964; D.Econ. Kyoto Univ., 1987.

Previous Post Assoc. Prof., Fac. of Econ., Kyoto Univ., 1975–86.

Current Offices and Honorary Posts Exec. com. mem., Bus. Hist. Soc. of Japan; council mem., Socio-Econ. Hist. Soc. of Japan; council mem., Agrarian Hist. Soc. of Japan.

Fields of Expertise *Industry Fields:* coal and petroleum products; metal manufacture; mechanical engineering; electrical engineering; textiles; clothing and footwear; transport and communication. *Bus. Dimensions:* entrepreneurs and entrepreneurship; strategy formation; bus. organization; bus. and

technology; small bus. matters; multinational bus.; bus.–state relations. *Scope:* regional; national; internat.; Germany; Taiwan. *Period:* nineteenth century; twentieth century as a whole. *Teaching:* undergrad.; post grad.

Publications *Books: Rain no Sangyo-Kakumei: Genkeizaiken no Keisei-Katei* [The Indust. Revolution on the Rhine: the Process Leading to the Formation of Proto-economic Areas], Toyokeizaishimposha, 1987. *Articles:* 'Die Industrielle Revolution in Japan und Deutschland - ein Vergleich', *Wirtschaftskräfte und Wirtschaftswege,* 5, Jürgen Schneider ed., Klett-Cotta, 1981; 'A Hist. of the Process leading to the Formation of Fuji Electric', *Japanese Yearbook on Bus. Hist.,* 1, 1984; 'On the so-called "Kolonialwaren" (1), (2), (3) & (4)', *Econ. Rev.,* 132(1/2), 1983; 133(1/2), 1984; 135(1/2), 1985, & 136(1), 1985; 'Gründungsjahre der Rheinkamerunion - unter besonderer Berücksichtigung der Industrie- und Handelskammer zu Köln (1), (2)', *Kyoto Univ. Econ. Rev.,* 57(2), 1987 & 58(2), 1988.

Watanabe, Kishichi

Prof. of Bus. Hist., Fac. of Bus. Admin., Kyoto Sangyo Univ., Kamigamo, Kita-ku, Kyoto 603, Japan. Tel.: 81 75 701 2151.

Year and Place of Birth 1927, Niigata pref., Japan.

Degrees and Qualifications B.Sc. Meiji Univ., 1957; M.Sc. Meiji Univ. Grad. School, 1960.

Current Offices and Honorary Posts Bus. Hist. Soc. of Japan: sec., 1973–8; council mem., 1979–84; exec. com. mem., 1985–8; auditor, 1989–92.

Fields of Expertise *Industry Fields:* vehicle construction; metal goods; textiles; other manufacturing industries; gas, electricity, water; transport and communication. *Bus. Dimensions:*

entrepreneurs and entrepreneurship; production management; personnel management; co. admin.; marketing; strategy formation; bus. organization; bus. and technology; small bus. matters; multinational bus.; management education; markets and bus.; bus. values; co. culture; bus. ideology. *Scope:* regional; national; internat.; USA; UK; Japan. *Period:* early modern; eighteenth century; nineteenth century; twentieth century as a whole; early twentieth century.

Publications *Articles:* 'The Bus. Organization of the Boston Manufacturing Company', *KSU Econ. & Bus. Rev.*, 1, Kyoto Sangyo Univ., 1974, 46–69; 'American Industrialization and the Slater Companies', *KSU Econ. & Bus. Rev.*, 10, Kyoto Sangyo Univ., 1983, 41–66; 'Keiei Kakumei: Chandler no Kindai Kigyoron' [Managerial Revolution: An Essay on Alfred D. Chandler's Modern Bus. Enterprise], *Econ. & Bus. Admin. Rev.*, 20(2), Kyoto Sangyo Univ., 1985, 609–29; 'The Bus. Ideology of Benjamin Franklin and Japanese Values of the 18th Century', *Bus. & Econ. Hist.*, 17, The Bus. Hist. Conf., 1988, 79–90; 'Keiei Rinen no Genryu: 18 Seiki no Nippon to Amerika' [The Origin of Bus. Ideology in the United States and Japan], *Japan Bus. Hist. Rev.*, 25(4), 1991, 1–28.

Watson, Katherine

Lect. in Econ. Hist., Dept. of Econ. and Related Studies, York Univ., Heslington, York, Y01 5DD, UK. Tel.: 44 904 433776.

Year and Place of Birth 1965, UK.

Degrees and Qualifications B.Sc. (Econ.) Univ. College, Swansea, 1986; MA (Econ.) Warwick Univ., 1987; Ph.D. (Econ. Hist.) Oxford Univ., 1990.

Previous Post Prize Research Fellow, Nuffield College, Oxford, Oct.

1989–Sept. 1991.

Fields of Expertise *Industry Fields:* drink. *Bus. Dimensions:* co. finance and accounting. *Scope:* national. *Period:* nineteenth century. *Teaching:* undergrad.

Watson, Nigel

10 St Matthews Terrace, Leyburn, N. Yorks, DL8 5EC, UK. Tel.: 44 969 22878. Fax: 44 969 22878.

Year and Place of Birth 1960, UK.

Degrees and Qualifications BA (Mod. Hist.) Durham Univ., 1981.

Fields of Expertise *Industry Fields:* transport and communication; construction; paper, printing, publishing; timber, furniture. *Bus. Dimensions:* family bus.es. *Scope:* national; UK. *Period:* nineteenth century; twentieth century as a whole. *Consultancy:* co. hist.

Publications *Books: The Last Mill on the Esk - 150 Years of Papermaking*, Scottish Academic Press, 1987; *The Bibby Line 1807–1990*, James & James, 1990; *Excellence by Caring - The Continuing Story of Silcock Express*, James & James, 1991.

Webb, Arthur C.M.

Assoc. Prof. of Econ. Hist., Dept. of Econ. & Econ. Hist., Rhodes Univ., POB 94, Grahamstown 6140, South Africa. Tel.: 27 461 26090. Fax: 27 461 25049.

Year and Place of Birth 1948, Bethal, South Africa.

Degrees and Qualifications MA & Ph.D. Rhodes Univ., 1982.

Previous Post Sen. Lect., Rhodes Univ., 1984–8.

Major Honours Founders' Medal & Prize of the Econ. Soc. of South Africa for Ph.D. dissertation 'Witwatersrand Genesis: A

Comparative Study of some early Gold Mining Companies 1886–1894', 1983.
Fields of Expertise *Industry Fields:* insurance, banking, finance. *Bus. Dimensions:* bus. organization. *Scope:* national. *Period:* nineteenth century. *Teaching:* post grad.
Publications *Books: The Roots of the Tree. A Study in Early South African Banking: The Predecessors of First National Bank 1838–1926*, First National Bank of Southern Africa Ltd., Cape Town, 1992; *Wilfit Oddy Ltd: 100 Years in South Africa*, Wilfit Oddy Ltd., Port Elizabeth, 1992. *Articles:* 'The Early Hist. of the Witwatersrand Gold Mining Company', *South African J. of Econ.*, 48(2), 1980, 144–66; 'Mining', *Econ. Hist. of South Africa*, F.I. Coleman ed., HAUM, Pretoria, 1983; 'Early Capitalism in the Cape: The Eastern Provence Bank 1839–73', *Banking and Bus. in South Africa*, S. Jones ed., Macmillan, 1988.

Weber, Wolfhard

Prof., Inst. of Hist., Bochum Univ., D-44780 Bochum, Germany. Tel.: 49 234 7002548. Fax: 49 234 7094128.
Year and Place of Birth 1940, Bremen, Germany.
Degrees and Qualifications Dr. phil., 1966; Privatdozent, 1974.
Current Offices and Honorary Posts Board mem., Gesellschaft für Technikgeschichte; pres., German National Com. of JUHPS/DHS.
Fields of Expertise *Industry Fields:* agric., forestry, fishing; mining and quarrying; coal and petroleum products; metal manufacture; mechanical engineering; vehicle construction; gas, electricity, water; transport and communication; genetic engineering: manufacture. *Bus. Dimensions:* entrepreneurs and entrepreneurship; production management; co. admin.; bus. and technology; markets and bus.

Scope: regional; national; internat. *Period:* medieval; early modern; eighteenth century; nineteenth century. *Teaching:* post grad. *Consultancy:* co. hist.
Publications *Books: Innovationen im frühindustriellen deutschen Bergbau and Hüttenwesen*, Vandenhoek & Ruprecht, Göttingen, 1976; *Technik. Von den Anfängen bis zur Gegenwart*, ed. & auth., Westermann, Brunswick, 1982, 1987, 1989; *Arbeitssicherheit. Historische Beispiele - aktuelle Analysen.*, Rowohlt, Reinbek, 1989; *Netze von Stahl und Strom*, with Wolfgang Köning co-auth., Propyläen, Berlin, 1990; *Das Ruhrgebiet im Industriezeitalter*, ed. & auth., 2 vols., Schwann, Düsseldorf.

Weil, François

Maître de Conférences, Centre d'Études Nord-Américaines, École des Hautes Études en Sciences Sociales, 12–14 rue Corvisart, 75013 Paris, France. Tel.: 33 1 44085170.
Year and Place of Birth 1961, Paris, France.
Degrees and Qualifications École Normale Supérieure, 1981; agrégation d'histoire, 1984; doctorat d'histoire, E.H.E.S.S., Paris, 1991.
Previous Post Fellow, Fondation Thiers, Paris, 1988–91.
Fields of Expertise *Industry Fields:* textiles. *Bus. Dimensions:* entrepreneurs and entrepreneurship. *Scope:* USA. *Period:* nineteenth century. *Teaching:* post grad.
Publications *Books: Les Franco-Américains*, Belin, Paris, 1989; *Naissance de l'Amérique urbaine, 1820–1920*, Sedes, Paris, 1992. *Articles:* 'L'Essor industriel du Nouveau Sud: L'Exemple de Gadsden, Alabama, 1880–1900', *Revue d'Histoire moderne et contemporaine*, 37, 1990, 268–82; 'A la Recherche

d'un Patronat: Les Bostoniens et l'Industrialisation de la Nouvelle-Angleterre', *De la Charité à la Sécurité Sociale*, André Gueslin & Pierre Guillaume eds., Les Éditions ouvrières, Paris, 1992, 215–22.

Weinberger, Hans

Ph.D. Student, Dept. of Hist. of Science & Technology, Royal Inst. of Technology, 10044 Stockholm, Sweden. Tel.: 46 8 7908799. Fax: 46 8 246263.

Year and Place of Birth 1962, Stockholm, Sweden.

Degrees and Qualifications M.Sc.Eng. (Eng. Physics) Royal Inst. of Technology, 1991.

Fields of Expertise *Industry Fields:* mechanical engineering; instrument engineering; nuclear engineering: manufacture; public admin. and defence; professional and scientific services. *Bus. Dimensions:* entrepreneurs and entrepreneurship; research and development; bus. organization. *Scope:* national; Sweden. *Period:* mid-twentieth century, 1940–70. *Consultancy:* research policy hist.

Publications *Books: Sievert: enhet och mångfald: En biografioverden svenska radiofysikens, radiobiologins och strålskyddets grundare Rolf Sievert*, Stockholm, 1990; *Technology and Industry: A Nordic Heritage*, Jan Hult & Bengt Nystrom co-eds., Science Hist. Publications, Canton, MA, 1992. *Articles:* 'Samarbete mellan FFA och KTH inom hogre utbildung', *Flygteknisk forsousaustalten 1940–1990*, with Janne Carlsson co-auth., Magnus Soderberg ed., Stockholm, 1990.

Wermiel, Sara E.

Doctoral Student, Massachusetts Inst. of Technology, Cambridge, MA 02139, USA. Tel.: 1 617 524 9483.

Year and Place of Birth 1950, Washington DC, USA.

Degrees and Qualifications BA Oberlin College, 1972; MUP Hunter College, 1977.

Fields of Expertise *Industry Fields:* construction. *Bus. Dimensions:* bus. and technology. *Scope:* national. *Period:* nineteenth century. *Consultancy:* writer on the hist. of building materials for building/architecture magazine.

Wessel, Horst A.

Manager of Mannesmann Archive, Mannesmann AG, Mannesmannufer 2, 40213 Düsseldorf, Germany. Tel.: 49 211 8202200. Fax: 49 211 8202822.

Year and Place of Birth 1943, Bonn, Germany.

Degrees and Qualifications Dipl. Bonn Univ., 1972; Ph.D. Bonn Univ., 1979.

Current Offices and Honorary Posts Manager, German Soc. for Bus. Hist., 1976–83; pres., Assoc. of German Econ. Archivists, 1986–92; lect., Düsseldorf Univ., 1989–.

Fields of Expertise *Industry Fields:* metal manufacture; mechanical engineering; electrical engineering. *Bus. Dimensions:* entrepreneurs and entrepreneurship; production management; multinational bus. *Period:* nineteenth century; twentieth century as a whole. *Teaching:* undergrad.; post grad.

Publications *Books: Hundert Thaler Preussische Courant. Industriefinanzierung in der Gründerzeit*, Vienna-Munich-Zurich-New York, 1981; *Kontinuität im Wandel. 100 Jahre Mannesman*

1890–1990, Düsseldorf, 1990; *Thyssen & Co., Mülheim a.d. Ruhr. Die Geschichte einer Familie und ihrer Unternehmung*, Stuttgart, 1991. *Articles:* 'Die Entwicklung des elektrischen Nachrichtenwesens in Deutschland und die rheinische Industrie', *Zeitschrift für Unternehmensgeschichte*, 25, 1983; 'Energie-Informationen-Innovation. 100 Jahre Verband Deutscher Elektrotechniker', *Geschichte der Elektrotechnik*, 12, 1993.

Westall, Oliver M.

Lect. in Econ., Dept. of Econ., Univ. of Lancaster, Management School, Lancaster, LA1 4YX, UK. Tel.: 44 524 594219. Fax: 44 524 381454.

Year and Place of Birth 1944, UK.

Degrees and Qualifications B.Sc. (Econ.) London School of Econ., 1966.

Major Honours Wadsworth Prize, 1993.

Fields of Expertise *Industry Fields:* insurance, banking, finance. *Bus. Dimensions:* entrepreneurs and entrepreneurship; co. finance and accounting; marketing; strategy formation; merger movement and issues; bus. organization; small bus. matters; multinational bus.; bus.–state relations; markets and bus.; bus. values; co. culture; boardroom issues; cartels and collusion. *Scope:* regional; national; internat.; global. *Period:* nineteenth century; twentieth century as a whole. *Teaching:* undergrad.; post grad. *Consultancy:* co. hist.; corporate strategy; U.N.C.T.C.

Publications *Books: The Historian and the Bus. of Insurance*, ed., Manchester Univ. Press, 1984; *Windermere in the Nineteenth Century*, ed., CNWRS Lancaster, 1991; *The Provincial Insurance Co., 1903–1938: Family Markets and Competitive Growth*, Manchester

Univ. Press, 1992. *Articles:* 'The Invisible Hand Strikes Back: Motor Insurance and the Erosion of Organised Competition in General Insurance, 1929–38', *Bus. Hist.*, XXX(4), 1988, 432–50; 'The Assumptions of Regulation in British General Insurance', *Competitiveness and the State*, G. Jones & M.W. Kirby eds., Manchester Univ. Press, 1991.

Whatley, Christopher A.

Lect., Dept. of Modern Hist., Dundee Univ., Dundee, DD1 4HN, UK. Tel.: 44 382 23181. Fax: 44 382 201604.

Year and Place of Birth 1948, Birmingham, UK.

Degrees and Qualifications BA Strathclyde Univ., 1972; Ph.D. Strathclyde Univ., 1975.

Previous Post Lect., Dept. of Scottish Hist., Univ. of St Andrews, 1988–92.

Current Offices and Honorary Posts Ed., *Abertay Historical Soc.*; ed. elect, *Scottish Econ. & Soc. Hist.*

Fields of Expertise *Industry Fields:* mining and quarrying; chemicals and allied industries; textiles. *Bus. Dimensions:* entrepreneurs and entrepreneurship. *Scope:* regional; national. *Period:* eighteenth century; nineteenth century. *Teaching:* undergrad.; post grad. *Consultancy:* co. hist.

Publications *Books: The Scottish Salt Industry: An Econ. and Social Hist., 1570–1850*, Aberdeen Univ. Press, Aberdeen, 1981; *Onwards from Osnaburghs: The Rise and Progress of a Scottish Textile Co.: Don-Low of Forfar, 1792–1992*, Mainstream, Edinburgh, 1992; *The Manufacture of Scottish Hist.*, with I.L. Donnachie co-ed., Polygon, Edinburgh, 1992. *Articles:* 'Salt, Coal and the Union of 1707: A Revision Article', *Scottish Historical Rev.*, 1987, 26–45; 'A Caste Apart? Colliers, Work, Community and Culture in the Era of Serfdom c. 1606–1799', *J. of Scottish Labour Hist. Soc.*, 1991, 3–20.

White, Christine A.

Asst. Prof. of History, Dept. of Hist., 601 Oswald Tower, Pennsylvania State Univ., Univ. Park, PA 16802, USA. Tel.: 1 814 865 1367. Fax: 1 814 863 7840.

Year and Place of Birth 1956, Pennsylvania, USA.

Degrees and Qualifications MA (Internat. Relations) Pennsylvania Univ., 1978; MA (Hist.) Pennsylvania Univ., 1980; Ph.D. (Hist.) Cambridge Univ., 1988.

Previous Post Video tape ed./engineer, The Amer. Broadcasting Co., New York, 1978–88.

Major Honours Phi Beta Kappa; State Dept. Title VIII Fellowship, the Hoover Inst., 1989–90; Guggenheim Fellowship, Smithsonian Inst., National Air & Space Museum, 1992 calendar year.

Fields of Expertise *Industry Fields:* mining and quarrying; coal and petroleum products; vehicle construction; transport and communication; insurance, banking, finance. *Bus. Dimensions:* entrepreneurs and entrepreneurship; bus. and technology; multinational bus. *Scope:* internat.; Russia; Soviet Union. *Period:* nineteenth century; early twentieth century; inter-war years, 1919–39. *Teaching:* undergrad.; post grad.

Publications *Books: British and Amer. Commercial Relations with Soviet Russia*, Chapel Hill, Univ. of North Carolina Press, 1992. *Articles:* 'Ford in Russia: In Pursuit of the Chimeral Market', *Bus. Hist.*, XXVIII(4), Oct., 1986, 77–104; 'British Bus. in Russian Asia since the 1860s: An Opportunity Lost?', *British Bus. in Asia since 1860*, R.P.T. Davenport-Hines & G.G. Jones eds., CUP, Cambridge, 1989, 68–91; 'Riches have Wings: The Use of Russian Gold in Soviet Foreign Trade, 1918–1922', *Studia Baltical Stockholmiensia No. 8, Contact or Isolation? Soviet-Western Relations in the Interwar Period*, John Hiden & A. Loit eds., Acta Universitatis Stockholmiensis, Stockholm, 1991, 117–36.

White, Eugene N.

Prof., Dept. of Econ., Rutgers Univ., New Brunswick, NJ 08903, USA. Tel.: 1 908 932 7486. Fax: 1 908 932 7416.

Year and Place of Birth 1952, USA.

Degrees and Qualifications BA Oxford Univ., 1976; BA Harvard Univ., 1974; Ph.D. Illinois Univ. Urbana, 1980.

Major Honours Redlich Prize for best article in Econ. Hist., 1991–2.

Fields of Expertise *Industry Fields:* insurance, banking, finance. *Bus. Dimensions:* co. finance and accounting; merger movement and issues. *Scope:* national; internat. *Period:*eighteenth century; nineteenth century; twentieth century as a whole. *Teaching:* undergrad.; post grad. *Consultancy:* co. hist.

Publications *Books: The Regulation and Reform of the Amer. Banking System, 1900–1929*, Princeton, 1983; *Crashes and Panics: The Lessons of Hist.*, ed., Dow-Jones-Irwin, 1991; *The Comptroller of the Currency and the Transformation of Amer. Banking*, OCC, 1992. *Articles:* 'Was there a Solution to the Financial Dilemma of the Ancien Regime?', *J. of Econ. Hist.*, 1989.

Whitten, Bess E.

Ed., *Bus. Library Rev.*, Bus. Building 209, Auburn Univ., AL 36849-5242, USA. Tel.: 1 205 844 2928. Fax:

1 205 844 4016.
Year and Place of Birth 1945, Opelika, USA.
Degrees and Qualifications Gen. Studies, Auburn Univ., 1963–7.
Previous Post Supervisor, Manuscript Preparation Center, Coll. of Bus., Auburn Univ., 1979–92.
Publications *Books: Manufacturing: A Historical and Bibliographical Guide. Vol. I. Handbook of Amer. Bus. Hist.*, asst. ed., Greenwood Press, 1990; *A Hist. of Econ. and Bus. at Auburn Univ.*, ed., Gordon & Breach, 1992; *Bus. Library Rev.*, ed., Gordon & Breach.

Whitten, David O.

Prof. of Econ., Dept. of Econ., Auburn Univ., Bus. Building 209, Auburn, AL 36849-5242, USA. Tel.: 1 205 844 2928. Fax: 1 205 844 4016.
Year and Place of Birth 1940, Beaver Falls, USA.
Degrees and Qualifications BS (Econ.) Charleston College, 1962; MA (Econ.) Univ. of South Carolina, 1963; Ph.D. Tulane Univ., 1970.
Current Offices and Honorary Posts Pres., Econ. & Bus. Hist. Soc., 1991–2.
Major Honours Louisiana Library Soc. Hasor Award for *Andrew Durnford, a Black Sugar Planter in Antebellum Louisiana*, (1982).
Fields of Expertise *Industry Fields:* construction. *Bus. Dimensions:* entrepreneurs and entrepreneurship. *Scope:* internat. *Period:* nineteenth century. *Teaching:* undergrad. *Consultancy:* co. hist.
Publications *Books: Andrew Durnford, A Black Sugar Planter in Antebellum Louisiana*, NSU Press, 1981; *Emergence of Giant Enterprise, 1860–1914: Amer. Commercial Enterprise and Extractive Industries*, Greenwood Press, 1983; *Manufacturing: A Historical and Bibliographical Guide. Vol. I Handbook of Amer. Bus. Hist.*, ed., Greenwood Press, 1990; *A Hist. of Econ. and Bus. at Auburn Univ.*, Gordon & Breach, 1992; *Bus. Library Rev.*, ed., Gordon & Breach.

Wijtuliet, Coz A.M.

Publisher/Journalist/Bus. Historian, The Dutch Inst. for Banking and Stockbroking, Herengracht 205, 1016 Amsterdam, Netherlands. Tel.: 31 20 5200520. Fax: 31 20 5200603.
Year and Place of Birth 1954, Breda, Netherlands.
Degrees and Qualifications DRS, Rijksuniversiteit Leiden, 1983; Ph.D. Katholieke Universiteit Brabant, 1993.
Fields of Expertise *Industry Fields:* insurance, banking, finance. *Bus. Dimensions:* markets and bus. *Scope:* national. *Period:* nineteenth century; twentieth century as a whole. *Consultancy:* co. hist.
Publications *Books: Veertig Jaar Nederlandse Bankiers - Vereniging 1949–1989*, Nibe, 1989; *De Geintegreerde Dealingroom in Nederland*, Nibe, 1992; *Nadenken over Exporteren. Uitdagingen en problemen voor het Midden en Kleinbedrijf in Nederland*, Nibe, 1992; *Expansie en Dynamiek: De Ontwikkeling van het Nederlands Handelsbankwezen*, Nibe, 1993.

Wilkins, Mira

Prof. of Econ., Dept. of Econ., Florida Internat. Univ., Miami, FL 33199, USA. Tel.: 1 305 348 2316. Fax: 1 305 348 3605.
Year and Place of Birth 1931, New York, USA.
Degrees and Qualifications BA Radcliffe College, Harvard Univ., 1953; Ph.D. Cambridge Univ., 1957.
Previous Post Smith College,

1968–70.

Current Offices and Honorary Posts
Pres., Bus. Hist. Conf., 1987–8;
trustee, Bus. Hist. Conf., 1990–3.

Major Honours 1993 Cass Prize for
best article in *Bus. Hist.* in 1992; *Bus.
Library Rev.* Editor's Award for
Exceptional Books (1992) for *Hist. of
Foreign Investment in the United States
to 1914*; Newcomen Prize for best arti-
cle in *Bus. Hist. Rev.* in 1982;
Guggenheim Fellowship, 1981–2;
National Book Award Nomination
(1975) for *Maturing of Multinational
Enterprise*.

Fields of Expertise *Bus.
Dimensions:* multinational bus. *Scope:*
global. *Period:* nineteenth century;
twentieth century as a whole.
Teaching: undergrad.; post grad.

Publications *Books: The Emergence
of Multinational Enterprise: Amer.
Bus. Abroad from the Colonial Era to
1914*, Harvard Univ. Press, 1970; *The
Maturing of Multinational Enterprise:
Amer. Bus. Abroad from 1914 to
1970*, Harvard Univ. Press, 1974; *The
Hist. of Foreign Investment in the
United States to 1914*, Harvard Univ.
Press, 1989. *Articles:* 'Japanese
Multinationals in the United States:
Continuity and Change, 1879–1990',
Bus. Hist. Rev., 64, Winter, 1990,
585–629; 'The Neglected Intangible
Asset: The Influence of the Trade
Mark on the Rise of the Modern
Corporation', *Bus. Hist.*, 34, Jan.,
1992, 66–95.

Williot, Jean-Pierre

Lect. and Researcher, Univ. of Paris IV
- Sorbonne, Centre for Historical and
Innovative Research, 1 rue Victor-
Cousin, 75230 Paris Cedex 05, France.

Year and Place of Birth 1957, Paris,
France.

Fields of Expertise *Industry Fields:*
chemicals and allied industries; gas.
Bus. Dimensions: bus. and technology.

Scope: national. *Period:* nineteenth
century; twentieth century as a whole.

Publications *Books: Annuaire
Statistique de l'Economie Française
aux XIX e XXe Siècles*, with D. Barjot,
Pens, Paris, 1991; *Le Noir et le Bleu,
Histoire du Gaz de France,
1946–1986*, with Alain Beltran,
Belfond, Paris, 1992. *Articles:* 'Un
Exemple de Recherche Industrielle au
XIXe Siècle: L'Usine Expérimentale de
la Compagnie Parisienne du Gaz',
Culture Technique, 18, 1988, 273–8;
'Naissance d'un Réseau gazier à Paris
au XIXe Siècle', *Histoire Economie
Société*, 4, 1989, 569–91; 'Nouvelle
Ville, Nouvelle Vie: Croissance et Rôle
du Réseau Gazier Parisien au XIXe
Siècle', *Actes du Colloque Paris et ses
Réseaux*, Paris, CRHI-BHUP, 1990,
213–32.

Wilson, John F.

Lect. in Econ. Hist., Dept. of Hist.,
Fac. of Arts, Univ. of Manchester,
Oxford Road, Manchester, M13 9PL,
UK. Tel.: 061 275 3092. Fax: 061
275 3098.

Year and Place of Birth 1955,
Preston, UK.

Degrees and Qualifications BA
Manchester Univ., 1977; Ph.D.
Manchester Univ., 1980.

Previous Post Research Assoc.,
Hist. Dept., Manchester Univ.,
1980–1.

Current Offices and Honorary Posts
Joint ed., *Transactions of the
Lancashire & Cheshire Antiquarian
Soc.*; management com. mem., North-
West Gas Historical Soc.

Fields of Expertise *Industry Fields:*
instrument engineering; electrical engineering; gas, electricity, water; insurance, banking, finance; bus. services;
electronics and computers: manufacture. *Bus. Dimensions:* entrepreneurs
and entrepreneurship; co. finance and
accounting; strategy formation; bus.

organization; bus. and technology; management education; co. culture. *Scope:* regional; national. *Period:* nineteenth century; twentieth century as a whole. *Teaching:* undergrad.; post grad. *Consultancy:* co. hist.; archives management.

Publications *Books: Ferranti and the British Electrical Industry, 1864–1930*, Manchester Univ. Press, 1988; *Lighting the Town: A Study of Management in the North-West Gas Industry, 1805–1880*, Paul Chapman Publishing, 1991; *The 'Manchester Experiment': A Hist. of Manchester Bus. School, 1965–1990*, Paul Chapman Publishing, 1992. *Articles:* 'A Strategy of Expansion & Consolidation: Dick, Kerr & Co., 1897–1914', *Bus. Hist.*, 27, 1985, 26–41; 'Ownership, Management & Strategy in Early North-West Gas Companies, 1815–30', *Bus. Hist.*, 33, 1991, 203–21.

Wilson, R.G.

Director, Centre of East Anglian Studies, Centre of East Anglian Studies, Univ. of East Anglia, Norwich, NR4 7TJ, UK. Tel.: 44 603 56161. Fax: 44 603 58553.

Year and Place of Birth 1938, Terrington, UK.

Degrees and Qualifications BA Leeds Univ.; Ph.D. Leeds Univ., 1964.

Previous Post Sen. lect., School of Econ. & Social Studies, East Anglia Univ., 1970–91.

Current Offices and Honorary Posts Mem., Econ. Hist. Soc. Council; governor, Pasold Research Fund.

Fields of Expertise *Industry Fields:* agric., forestry, fishing; food, drink, tobacco; textiles. *Bus. Dimensions:* entrepreneurs and entrepreneurship; bus. and technology; co. culture; boardroom issues. *Scope:* national. *Period:* eighteenth century; nineteenth century. *Teaching:* undergrad.; post

grad. *Consultancy:* co. hist.

Publications *Books: Gentleman Merchants: The Merchant Community in Leeds, 1700–1830*, Manchester Univ. Press, 1971; *Entrepreneurship in Britain, 1750–1939*, with R.H. Campbell eds., A. & C. Black, 1975; *Greene King: A Bus. and Family Hist.*, Jonathan Cape/The Bodley Head, 1983; *The British Brewing Industry, 1830–1980*, with T.R. Gourvish, CUP, 1993.

Winkelman, Hélène J.M.

Referee, Econ. Hist., Netherlands Econ. Hist. Archives, Cruquiusweg 31, 1019 AT Amsterdam, Netherlands. Tel.: 45 20 6685866. Fax: 45 20 6654181.

Year and Place of Birth 1968, The Hague, Netherlands.

Degrees and Qualifications M.Hist. Utrecht Univ., 1985; M.Library Sciences Amsterdam Univ., 1988.

Previous Post Documentalist, Federation of Patient Organizations, Utrecht, 1986–90.

Current Offices and Honorary Posts Edit. board mem., Netherlands Soc. of Bus. Archivists (NVBA); co-ordinator, NEMA Bus. Archives Register/Co. Record Information System.

Major Honours Van Schelven Prize, 1991, (for Textile Hist.).

Fields of Expertise *Industry Fields:* professional and scientific services. *Bus. Dimensions:* bus. organization; bus. archives/libraries. *Scope:* national. *Period:* nineteenth century; twentieth century as a whole. *Consultancy:* co. hist.

Publications *Books: Bestemming Semarang. Geschiedenis van de Textielfabrikanten Gelderman in Oldenzaal 1817–1970*, Gelderman Stichting/NEHA, Amsterdam, 1991. *Articles:* 'Familisme, falend management of generatiekloof? Het bestuursconflict bij de spinnenrijen en weverij en v/h Spanjaard to Borne, 1930–1939', *Textiel Historische Bijdragen*, 29, 1990; 'The Dutch Family Firm Confronted with Chandler's Dynamics of Indust. Capitalism, 1890–1940', *Bus. Hist*, Autumn, 1993.

Witthöft, Harald

Prof. of Econ. and Social Hist., Universität Gesamthochschule Siegen, Fachbereich 1, Adolf-Reichwein-Str., 57076 Siegen, Germany. Tel.: 49 271 740 4501/49 271 740 4511. Fax: 49 271 7402330.

Year and Place of Birth 1931, Lüneburg, Germany.

Degrees and Qualifications Matric, Johanneum, Lüneburg, 1951; Ph.D. Göttingen Univ., 1960.

Previous Post Lect. in Hist. & Didactics of Hist., Educational College, Lüneburg, 1965–70.

Current Offices and Honorary Posts Pres., Internat. Com. for Historical Metrology; vice-pres., Internat. Commission for the Hist. of Salt.

Fields of Expertise *Industry Fields:* salt and mining. *Bus. Dimensions:* bus. and technology. *Scope:* internat. *Period:* ancient; medieval; early modern; eighteenth century; nineteenth century. *Teaching:* undergrad.; post grad.

Publications *Books: Das Kaufhaus in Lüneburg als Zentrum von Handel und Faktorei, Landfracht, Schiffahrt und Warenumschlag bis zum Jahre 1637*, Museumverein f. d. Fst. Lüneburg, Lüneburg, 1962; *Industrie- und Handelskammer Hildesheim 1866–1966*, Musterschmidt, Göttingen, 1966; *Umrisse einer historischen Metrologie zum Nutzen der wirtschafts- und sozialgeschichtlichen Forschung. Maß und Gewicht in Stadt und Land Lüneburg, im Hanseraum und im Kurfürsten-* *tum/Königreich Hannover vom 13. bis zum 19. Jahrhundert*, Veröff. d. Max-Planck-Instituts f. Gesch., 60(1) u.2, 2 Bde., Vandenhoeck & Ruprecht, Göttingen, 1979. *Articles:* 'Struktur und Kapazität der Lüneburger Saline seit dem 12. Jahrhundert', *Vierteljahrschrift für Sozial- und Wirtschaftsgeschichte*, 63(1), 1976, 1–117; 'Auf den bibliographischen Spuren des kaufmännischen Münz-, Maß- und Gewichtswesens der Neuzeit', *Medien und Bildung*, Hans Dieter Erlinger & Winfried Leist eds., Festschrift für Walter Barton, Siegener Studien, 44, Essen, 1989, 201–21.

Woronoff, Denis

Prof. of Modern Hist., Paris I Univ. - Panthéon-Sorbonne, Inst. of Econ. & Social Hist., 17 rue de la Sorbonne, 75005 Paris, France.

Year and Place of Birth 1939, Paris, France.

Degrees and Qualifications Ecole Normale Supérieure, 1960; Agrégation d'histoire, 1964; Doctorat-ès-lettres, 1981.

Previous Post Research Director, CNRS, Ecole des Hautes Etudes en Sciences Sociales, 1986–92.

Current Offices and Honorary Posts Assoc. ed., *Hist. & Technology*; board mem., *Groupe d'histoire des mines et de la métallurgie*.

Major Honours Chevalier des Arts et Lettres.

Fields of Expertise *Industry Fields:* metal manufacture. *Bus. Dimensions:* bus. and technology. *Scope:* regional; national; France. *Period:* eighteenth century; nineteenth century. *Teaching:* post grad. *Consultancy:* industrial heritage (French Ministry of Culture).

Publications *Books: L'Industrie Sidérurgique en France pendant la Révolution et l'Empire*, ed., E.H.E.S.S., 1984; *Forges et Forêts*, ed., E.H.E.S.S.,

1990; *L'Homme et l'Industrie en Normandie*, ed., Société Historique de l'Orne, 1990.

Worthy, James C.

Prof. of Management, J.L. Kellogg Grad. School of Management, Northwestern Univ., Evanston, IL 60208, USA. Tel.: 1 708 467 1309. Fax: 1 708 467 1777.

Year and Place of Birth 1910, Midland, Texas, USA.

Degrees and Qualifications BS Northwestern Univ., 1933; LL D Lake Forest College, 1959; LL D Chicago Theological Seminary, 1960; DHL Sangamon State Univ., 1992.

Previous Post Prof. of Public Affairs & Management, Sangamon State Univ., 1972–8.

Major Honours Dean Emeritus; Fellow of the Acad. of Management; Fellow, Internat. Acad. of Management.

Fields of Expertise *Industry Fields:* distributive trades; bus. services. *Bus. Dimensions:* personnel management; co. admin.; bus. organization; management education; co. culture. *Scope:* national. *Period:* twentieth century as a whole. *Teaching:* undergrad.; post grad. *Consultancy:* co. hist.

Publications *Books: Research in Indust. Human Relations*, co-ed., Harper & Brothers, 1956; *Big Bus. and Free Men*, Harper & Brothers, 1959; *William C. Norris: Portrait of a Maverick*, Ballinger Publishing Co., 1987; *Shaping an Amer. Inst., Robert E. Wood and Sears, Roebuck*, Univ. of Illinois Press, 1989; *Lean but not Mean: Studies in Organization Structure*, Univ. of Illinois Press, forthcoming, 1994.

Wray, William D.

Assoc. Prof., Dept. of Hist., UBC, 1297-1873 East Mall, Vancouver, BC V6T 1Z1, Canada. Tel.: 1 604 822 2561. Fax: 1 604 822 6658.

Year and Place of Birth 1943, Winnipeg, Canada.

Degrees and Qualifications Ph.D. Harvard Univ., 1977.

Fields of Expertise *Industry Fields:* transport and communication; trade and commercial diplomacy. *Bus. Dimensions:* strategy formation; bus.–state relations; markets and bus. *Scope:* internat.; national; global. *Period:* twentieth century as a whole; early modern; eighteenth century; nineteenth century. *Teaching:* undergrad.; post grad.

Publications *Books: Mitsubishi and the N.Y.K., 1870–1914: Bus. Strategy in the Japanese Shipping Industry*, Harvard East Asian Monographs, Harvard Univ. Press, 1984; reprinted Feb., 1986; *Managing Indust. Enterprise: Cases from Japan's Pre-war Experience*, ed., Harvard East Asian Monographs, Harvard Univ. Press, 1989; *Japan's Economy: A Bibliography of its Past and Present*, Markus Wiener Publishers, New York, 1989. *Articles:* 'Shipping: From Sail to Steam', *Japan in Transition: From Tokugawa to Meiji*, Marius Jansen & Gilbert Rozman eds., Princeton Univ. Press, 1986, 248–70; 'Japan's Big Three Service Enterprises in China, 1896–1936', *The Japanese Informal Empire in China, 1895–1937*, Peter Duus, Ramon H. Myers & Mark R. Peattie eds., Princeton Univ. Press, 1989, 31–64.

Wren, Daniel A.

David Ross Boyd Prof. & Curator, Harry W. Bass Bus. Hist. Collection, Univ. of Oklahoma, Norman, OK

73019, USA. Tel.: 1 405 325 3941.

Year and Place of Birth 1932, Columbia, USA.

Degrees and Qualifications BS Missouri Univ., 1954; MS Missouri Univ., 1960; Ph.D. Illinois Univ., 1964.

Major Honours David Ross Boyd Prof., Oklahoma Univ.; Fellow of the Acad. of Management.

Fields of Expertise *Bus. Dimensions:* production management; personnel management; co. admin.; strategy formation; merger movement and issues; bus. organization; management education. *Scope:* global. *Period:* eighteenth century; nineteenth century; twentieth century as a whole. *Teaching:* undergrad.; post grad.

Publications *Books: The Evolution of Management Thought,* John Wiley & Sons, 1st edn., 1972, 4th edn., 1994; *White Collar Hobo: The Travels of Whiting Williams,* Iowa State Univ. Press, 1987.

Wrigley, Chris J.

Prof. of Modern British Hist., Dept. of Hist., Nottingham Univ., Nottingham, NG7 2RD, UK. Tel.: 44 602 515945. Fax: 44 602 513666.

Year and Place of Birth 1947, Woking, UK.

Degrees and Qualifications BA East Anglia Univ., 1968; Ph.D. London Univ., 1973.

Previous Post Reader in Econ. Hist, Loughborough Univ., 1984–8.

Current Offices and Honorary Posts Ordinary Vice Pres., Historical Assoc.; ed., *The Historian.*

Fields of Expertise *Industry Fields:* British toy industry. *Bus. Dimensions:* hist. of industrial relations. *Scope:* national. *Period:* twentieth century as a whole; nineteenth century. *Teaching:* undergrad.; post grad.

Publications *Books: David Lloyd George and the British Labour*

Movement, Harvester, Hassocks, 1976, 2nd edn., Gregg, 1992; *A Hist. of British Indust. Relations 1875–1914,* ed., Harvester, Brighton, 1982, Univ. of Massachussetts Press, 1982; *A Hist. of British Indust. Relations 1914–1939,* ed., Harvester, Brighton, 1986; 2nd edn., Gregg, 1993; *Lloyd George and the Challenge of Labour, 1918–1922,* Harvester, Hemel Hempstead, 1990; *Arthur Henderson,* Univ. of Wales Press, Cardiff, 1990.

Wysocki, Josef

Inst. of Hist., Salzburg Univ., Rudolfskai 42, Austria. Tel.: 43 662 80444760. Fax: 43 662 8044413.

Year and Place of Birth 1937, Leienkaul, Germany.

Degrees and Qualifications o.Prof.; Dr.phil.; Dr.rer.pol.

Previous Post Prof. of Econ., Soc., & Agrarian Hist., Hohenheim Univ., Stuttgart, 1971–74.

Major Honours Kardinal Innitzer-Prize, 1970.

Fields of Expertise *Industry Fields:* insurance, banking, finance. *Bus. Dimensions:* co. culture. *Scope:* regional; national. *Period:* nineteenth century; twentieth century as a whole. *Teaching:* undergrad.; post grad. *Consultancy:* co. hist.

Publications *Books: Heidelberg. Von Arbeit, Leben und Geld in 150 jähriger Geschichte der Sparkasse,* Stuttgart, 1981; *Spuren. 100 Jahre Waldhof - 100 Jahre Wirtschaftsgeschichte,* Mannheim, 1984; *Leben im Berchtesgadener Land 1800–1990,* Bad Reichenhall 1991. *Articles:* 'Infrastruktur und wachsende Staatsausgaben. Das Fallbeispiel Österreich 1868–1919', *Forschungen zur Sozial- und Wirtschaftsgeschichte,* 20, 1975; 'Untersuchungen zur Wirtschafts- und Sozialgeschichte der deutschen Sparkassen', *Forschungsberichte,* 11, 1980.

Yakura, Shintaro

Assoc. Prof., Documentation Center for Bus. Analysis, Research Inst. for Econ. and Bus. Admin., Kobe Univ., Rokkodai-cho, Nada-ku, Kobe 657, Japan. Tel.: 078 881 1212. Fax: 078 861 6434.

Year and Place of Birth 1944, Osaka, Japan.

Degrees and Qualifications Master Kwansei Gakuin Univ., 1972.

Fields of Expertise *Industry Fields:* textiles. *Bus. Dimensions:* entrepreneurs and entrepreneurship; co. admin. *Scope:* national. *Period:* twentieth century as a whole. *Consultancy:* co. hist.

Publications *Books: Shuyo kigiyo no keifuzu* [Genealogical Chart of Major Japanese Corporations], co-ed., Yushodo Press, 1986. *Articles:* 'Meijiki Menboseki Kigiyo no Keiei - Keiseiki Kanegafuci Boseki Kaisha no baai -' [The Management of the Cotton Spinning Co. in the Meiji Era - an Example of the Kanegafuchi Spinning Co. in its Formative Period], *Annual Report on Econ. & Bus. Admin.*, 38(I, II), 1988, 287–317; 'Meijikoki Kanegafuchi Boseki Kabushiki Kaisha no Kakucho to Takakuka ni tsuite' [The Enlargement and Diversification of the Kanegafuchi Spinning Co. in the later Meiji Era], *Annual Report on Econ. & Bus. Admin.*, 39 (I, II), 1989, 301–23; 'Meijiki Kanegafuchi Boseki Kabushiki Kaisha no Menshi Hanbai ni tsuite' [The Wholesale of Cotton Yarn of the Kanegafuchi Spinning Co. Ltd. in the Meiji Era], *Annual Report on Econ. & Bus. Admin.*, 40 (I, II), 1990, 129–47; 'Meiji 29 nen Hyogo Shiten Kaisetsuki ni okeru Kanegafuchi Boseki Kabushiki Kaisha no Keiei ni tsuite' [The Management of the Kanegafuchi Spinning Co. Ltd. in the period of the Establishment of its Hyogo Branch at the 29th of Meiji (1896)], *Annual Report on Econ. & Bus. Admin.*, 41, 1991, 71–95.

Yamada, Makiko

Prof. of Management, Nagaoka Community College, Niigata, Japan.

Year and Place of Birth 1938, Tokyo, Japan.

Degrees and Qualifications BA Rikkyo Univ., 1969; MA New York Univ., 1970.

Previous Post Assoc. Prof., Organization Management, Internat. Topics, Grad. School of Internat. Relations, Internat. Univ. of Japan, Niigata, Japan.

Current Offices and Honorary Posts Director, YMI Internat. Ltd., Japan.

Major Honours Research Fund Winner 'Econ. Growth in the '80s and Women's Careers', Nat. Inst. of Research Advancement, Tokyo; Walgreen Fellowship in Human Capital Projects, Univ. of Chicago.

Fields of Expertise *Industry Fields:* professional and scientific services. *Bus. Dimensions:* strategy formation. *Scope:* national; USA. *Period:* late twentieth century, 1970–present. *Teaching:* post grad. *Consultancy:* corporate strategy.

Publications *Books: The Amer. Bus. Elite*, Nihon Keizai Shimbun, Tokyo, 1976; *Amer. Professionalism*, Nihon Keizai Shimbun, Tokyo, 1979; *The Bus. Climate in the US*, Diamond, Tokyo, 1982; *Lobbying: Organizational Behavior on Governmental Regulation in the US*, Nihon Keizai Shimbun, Tokyo, 1982; *Top Management in the USA: Winners and Losers in the Money Game*, TBS, Britannica, Tokyo, 1988.

Yamada, Tetsuo

Prof., Fac. of Literature, Atomi-Gakuen Women's Univ., Nakano 1-9-6, Niiza-shi, Saitama-ken, Japan. Tel.: 0484 78 3333. Fax: 0484 79 8418.

Year and Place of Birth 1947,

Chigasaki, Japan.
Degrees and Qualifications BA
Waseda Univ., 1971; MBA Waseda
Univ., 1973.
Current Offices and Honorary Posts
Council mem., Socio-Econ. Hist. Soc.
of Japan.
Fields of Expertise *Industry Fields:*
transport and communication; distrib-
utive trades. *Bus. Dimensions:* mar-
kets and bus. *Scope:* Germany.
Period: nineteenth century. *Teaching:*
undergrad.
Publications *Articles:* 'Goods
Traffic on the Berg-Mark Railroad and
the Market Structure of Rhineland
Westphalia in the 1870s', *Rekishigaku
Kenkyu* [J. of Hist. Studies], 472,
1977; 'Die wirtschaftliche Bedeutung
des rheinisch-westfälischen Eisenbahn-
netzes im 19. Jh.', *Atomigakuen Kiyo*
[Bull. of Atomi-Gakuen Women's
Univ.], 14, 1981; 'The State and a
Private Railway in Prussia', *Keiei
Shigaku* [Japan Bus. Hist. Rev.], 16,
1981; 'Intra-German Commodity Flow
Analysis', *Atomigajuen Kiyo* [Bull. of
Atomi-Gakuen Women's Univ.], 15,
1982; 'A Perspective in Studies of
Railway Hist. in Germany', *Tetsudo
Shigaku* [Japan Railway Hist. Rev.], 8,
1990.

Yamaguchi, Fujio

Assoc. Prof., Fac. of Internat. Polit.,
Econ. & Bus., Aoyama Gakuin Univ.,
4-25-4 Shibuya, Shibuya-ku, Tokyo
150, Japan. Tel.: 81 3 3409 8111.
Year and Place of Birth 1957,
Chiba, Japan.
Degrees and Qualifications BA
Tokyo Univ.
Previous Post Assoc. Prof., Fac. of
Econ., Kanagwa Univ., 1987–92.
Fields of Expertise *Industry Fields:*
mining and quarrying; metal manufac-
ture; transport and communication.
Bus. Dimensions: production manage-
ment; co. finance and accounting.

Scope: national. *Period:* nineteenth
century; early twentieth century; inter-
war years, 1919–39; mid-twentieth
century, 1940–70. *Teaching:* undergrad.; post grad. *Consultancy:* co.
hist.; accounting hist.
Publications *Articles:* 'The Meiji
Era Budget System at N.Y.K.', *Shokei
Ronso* [Kanagawa Univ. Bull.], 24(1),
1988, 43–93; 'An Analysis of Profit
and Loss Statements for each Line at
N.Y.K. from 1897–1935', *Shokei
Ronso* [Kanagawa Univ. Bull.], 24(3),
1989, 108–64; 'Accounting Practices at
Nikko Copper Works of Furukawa
from 1906–1913', *Shokei Ronso*
[Kanagawa Univ. Bull.], 24(4), 1989,
221–68; 'Accounting Procedure of
Wrecked Ships at Nippon Yusen
Kaisha (N.Y.K.) under a Regulated
Economy', *Shokei Ronso* [Kanagawa
Univ. Bull.], 25(1), 1989, 105–61; 'The
Revaluation of Assets at N.Y.K. after
World War II', *Kaikei* [Accounting],
142(2), 1992, 69–81.

Yamamoto, Toru

Prof. of Econ. Hist., Kanagawa Univ.,
Rokkabubashi, Kanagawa-ku,
Yokohama, Japan. Tel.: 81 45 481
5661. Fax: 81 45 413 2678.
Year and Place of Birth 1946,
Miyazaki, Japan.
Degrees and Qualifications MA
Hitotsubashi Univ., 1972.
Previous Post Assoc. Prof. of Econ.
Hist., Kanagawa Univ.
Fields of Expertise *Industry Fields:*
metal manufacture. *Bus. Dimensions:*
entrepreneurs and entrepreneurship.
Scope: internat. *Period:* nineteenth
century. *Teaching:* undergrad.
Consultancy: co. hist.
Publications *Articles:* 'Economic
Ethics of the Quakers', *Shokei Ronsoh*,
14(3.4), 1990, 77–100 & 15(1), 1990,
97–115; 'From Quakerism to
Unitarianism: The Case of William
Rathbone the Fourth', *Shokei Ronsoh*,

25(3), 1990, 1–37, (in English); 'Quaker Bus.men and the Soc. of Friends in 19th Century England', *Socio-Econ. Hist.*, 57(3), 1991, 28–62, (in Japanese); 'Bus. Ideas of the Quaker Employers in the First Half of the 20th Century', *Shokei Ronsoh*, 28(1), 1992, 45–75, (in Japanese).

Yamamura, Mutsuo

Prof., Fac. of Econ., Wako Univ., 2160 Kanai-cho, Machida-shi, Tokyo 194, Japan. Tel.: 044 988 1431. Fax: 044 988 1435.

Year and Place of Birth 1946, Tokyo, Japan.

Degrees and Qualifications BA Waseda Univ., 1968; MA Waseda Univ., 1971.

Previous Post Assoc. Prof., Fac. of Econ., Asahikawa Univ., 1980–7.

Fields of Expertise *Industry Fields:* trade. *Bus. Dimensions:* strategy formation; multinational bus.; bus.–state relations. *Scope:* national; internat. *Period:* twentieth century as a whole; early twentieth century; inter-war years, 1919–39. *Teaching:* undergrad. *Consultancy:* co. hist.

Publications *Books: Gendai Nippon Keieishi* [Modern Japan Bus. Hist.], co-auth., Minerva-shobo, 1990. *Articles:* 'Nippon-teikokushugi Seiritsu-ki ni okeru Mitsui Bussan no Hatten' [The Development of Mistui Bussan Kaisha in China 1894-1910], *Tochi-seido Sigak* [J. of the Agrarian Hist. Soc.], 73, 1976; 'Daiichiji-Taisengo no Mitsui Bussan no Kaigai Shinshutsu' [The Development of Mitsui Bussan Kaisha in China 1914-1931], *Nippon Takokuseki-kigyo no Shiteki-tenkai (I)* [The Historical Analysis of Japanese Multinational Enterprises I], co-auth., Ohtsuki-shoten, 1979; 'Manshujihen-ki ni okeru Shanghai zairyu nippon-shonin to hainichi-undoh' [The Attitude of the Japanese Chamber of Commerce,

Shanghai, against the anti-Japan Movement 1927-1932], *Wako-keizai*, 20(2 & 3), 1988; 'Nissin-sengo ni okeru Mitsui Bussan Kaisha no Chugoku Shijo Ninshiki to 'China-ka' (Chinanization)' [The Attitude of Mitsui Bussan Kaisha in Competition between Chinese Merchants 1894-1907], *Wako-keizai*, 22(3), 1990.

Yamazaki, Hiroaki

Director and Prof., Inst. of Social Science, Tokyo Univ., 7-3-1 Hongo, Bunkyo-ku, Tokyo 113, Japan. Tel.: 81 3 3812 2111. Fax: 81 3 3816 6864.

Year and Place of Birth 1934, Fukuoka, Japan.

Degrees and Qualifications M.Econ. Tokyo Univ., 1960.

Previous Post Prof., Inst. of Soc. Sc., Tokyo Univ., 1975–92.

Current Offices and Honorary Posts Exec. director, Bus. Hist. Soc. of Japan.

Major Honours Economist Prize, Mainichi Newspaper Co., 1975.

Fields of Expertise *Industry Fields:* textiles; gas, electricity, water; distributive trades; insurance, banking, finance. *Bus. Dimensions:* entrepreneurs and entrepreneurship; marketing; strategy formation; multinational bus. *Scope:* local; national; internat. *Period:* inter-war years, 1919–39; mid-twentieth century, 1940–70; late twentieth century, 1970–present. *Teaching:* post grad. *Consultancy:* co. hist.

Publications *Books: Nihon Kasensangyo Hattatuschi Ron* [A Historical Study on the Development of the Japanese Rayon Industry], Univ. of Tokyo Press, 1975. *Articles:* 'The Logic of the Formation of General Trading Companies in Japan', *Bus. Hist. of General Trading Companies*, Shin'ichi Yonekawa & Hideki Yoshihara eds., Univ. of Tokyo Press, 1987, 21–64; 'The Development of Large Enterprises in Japan: An

Analysis of the top 50 Enterprises in the Profit Ranking Table (1929–1984)', *Japanese Yearbook on Bus. Hist.*, 5, Japan Bus. Hist. Inst., 1988, 12–55; 'Mitsùi Bussan during the 1920s', *Hist. Studies in Internat. Corporate Bus.*, Alice Teichova, Maurice Levy, Laboyer & Helga Nussbaum eds., CUP, 1989, 163–76; 'The Yokohama Specie Bank during the Period of the Restored Gold Standard in Japan', *Finance and Financiers in Econ. Hist. 1880–1960*, Youssef Cassis ed., CUP, 1991, 371–403.

Yamazaki, Ryuzo

Prof., Fac. of Commerce, Meijo Univ., 15 Yagoto, Tenpaku, Nagoya, Japan. Tel.: 81 52 832 1151.
Year and Place of Birth 1920, Osaka, Japan.
Degrees and Qualifications Ph.D. (Econ.) Osaka Municipal Commercial Univ., 1962.
Previous Post Prof., Fac. of Commerce, Osaka City Univ., 1962–81.
Current Offices and Honorary Posts Council mem., Agrarian Hist. Soc., 1948–; council mem., Socio-Econ. Hist. Soc.
Fields of Expertise *Industry Fields:* agric., forestry, fishing. *Bus. Dimensions:* entrepreneurs and entrepreneurship. *Scope:* regional; national. *Period:* eighteenth century; nineteenth century; inter-war years, 1919–39. *Teaching:* undergrad.
Publications *Books: The Japanese Farmer and Landowner in the 18th and 19th Century*, 1961, published in Japanese; *The Hist. of Amagasaki City (Modern Age) Vol. 3*, 1970, published in Japanese; *Japanese Capitalism in the inter-War Period*, 1978, published in Japanese; *The Hist. of Prices in the Edo Period*, 1983, published in Japanese.

Yanagisawa, Osamu

Prof., Tokyo Metropolitan Univ., Fac. of Econ., Minami Ohsawa 1-1, Hachi-oji-shi, Tokyo, Japan. Tel.: 81 426 77 2317. Fax: 81 426 77 2298.
Year and Place of Birth 1938, Tokyo, Japan.
Degrees and Qualifications Ph.D. (Econ.) Tokyo Univ., 1976.
Previous Post Asst. Prof., Fac. of Econ., Meiji Gakuin Univ., 1970–6.
Current Offices and Honorary Posts Chair, Publications Com., *J. of Agrarian Hist.*; council mem., Agrarian Hist. Soc.
Fields of Expertise *Industry Fields:* agric., forestry, fishing; metal manufacture; mechanical engineering; instrument engineering; metal goods; textiles; leather; clothing and footwear; timber, furniture; distributive trades; construction. *Bus. Dimensions:* entrepreneurs and entrepreneurship; bus. organization; bus. and technology; small bus. matters; bus. values. *Scope:* local; regional; national. *Period:* nineteenth century; twentieth century as a whole. *Teaching:* undergrad.; post grad. *Consultancy:* co. hist.
Publications *Books: Econ. and Social Problems during the German Revolution, 1848–1849*, Iwanami Shoten, Tokyo, 1974, 1987, (in Japanese); *The Development of Small and Medium-sized Enterprises in Germany from the end of the 19th Century to the 1930s*, Iwanami Shoten, Tokyo, 1989, (in Japanese). *Articles:* 'Die sozio-ökonomischen Forderungen dr preußischen Landbevölkerung im Jahre 1848 im Spiegel der Petitionsbewegung', *Wirtschaftskräfte und Wirtschaftswege*, Klett-Cotta, Stuttgart, 1978, 297–308; 'From the Rule of Fair Trade under Free Competition to the Governmental Regulation of Competition in Germany', *Socio-Econ. Hist.* [Shakai-Keizai-Shigaku], 56(2), June, 1990;

'Anti-monopole Policy and Small and Medium-sized Enterprises in Germany after World War II', *Transformation of the Modern World*, with Tanaka, Kobayashi & Matsuno co-eds., Libroport, Tokyo, 1991, 65–87, (in Japanese).

Yasumuro, Kenichi

Prof. of Internat. Bus., Kobe Univ. of Commerce, 2-1, 8 Gakuen Nishimachi, Nishiku, Kobe 651–21, Japan. Tel.: 81 78 794 6161. Fax: 81 78 794 6166.

Year and Place of Birth 1947, Yokohama, Japan.

Degrees and Qualifications BA (Engineering) Tokyo Univ. of Science, 1969; MBA Kobe Univ. of Commerce, 1971; Ph.D. Kobe Univ., 1993.

Previous Post Visiting Fellow, Bus. Hist. Unit., Dept. of Econ., Reading Univ., 1990–1.

Current Offices and Honorary Posts Director, Acad. of Multinational Enterprises (Japan).

Major Honours Management Science (Publication) Award, Japan Management Assoc., 1982.

Fields of Expertise *Industry Fields:* mechanical engineering; electrical engineering; distributive trades. *Bus. Dimensions:* entrepreneurs and entrepreneurship; personnel management; research and development; strategy formation; bus. organization; multinational bus.; markets and bus. *Scope:* internat.; global. *Period:* nineteenth century; twentieth century as a whole; late twentieth century, 1970–present. *Teaching:* undergrad.; post grad. *Consultancy:* internat. bus. management, especially human resource management.

Publications *Books: Internat. Bus. Behavior*, revised edn., Moriyama Shobo, 1986, (in Japanese); *Global Bus. Management*, Chikuta Shobo, 1993, (in Japanese). *Articles:* 'The

Contribution of Sogo Shosha to the Multinationalization of Japanese Indust. Enterprises in Historical Perspective', *Internat. Investment*, Peter J. Buckley ed., Edward Elgar Publishing Ltd., 1990; 'Engineers as Functional Alternatives to Entrepreneurs in Japanese Industrialization', *Entrepreneurship, Networks and Modern Bus.*, Jonathan Brown & Mary B. Rose eds., Manchester Univ. Press, 1993; 'Conceptualizing an Adaptable Marketing System - the End of Mass Marketing', *The Rise and Fall of Mass Marketing*, G. Jones & R. Tedlow eds., Praeger, 1993.

Yasuoka, Shigeaki

Prof., Fac. of Commerce, Doshisha Univ., Karasuma-Imadegawa, Kamigyo-ku, Kyoto 602, Japan. Tel.: 075 251 3122.

Year and Place of Birth 1928, Osaka, Japan.

Degrees and Qualifications Ph.D. (Econ.) Osaka Univ., 1959.

Current Offices and Honorary Posts Chairman, Bus. Hist. Soc. of Japan, 1987–91; adviser, Bus. Hist. Soc. of Japan, 1991–.

Fields of Expertise *Industry Fields:* distributive trades. *Bus. Dimensions:* bus. organization. *Scope:* internat. *Period:* eighteenth century; nineteenth century; early twentieth century. *Teaching:* undergrad.; post grad. *Consultancy:* co. hist.

Publications *Books: Nihon Hoken Keizai Seisaku Shiron* [Hist. of Econ. Policy in the Edo Period], Yuhikaku, 1959; *Zaibatsu Keiseishi no Kenkyu* [Studies on the Formation of Zaibatsu], Minverva Shobo, 1970; *Zaibatsu no Keieishi* [Bus. Hist. of Zaibatsu], Shakai Shisosha, 1978, 1990; *Mitsui Zaibatsu Shi, Edo-Meiji-Hen* [A Hist. of Mitsui Zaibatsu - Edo-

Meiji Period], Kyoikusha, 1979, 1984; *Family Bus. in the Era of Indust. Growth*, co-auth., Univ. of Tokyo Press, 1984.

Yates, Joanne

Assoc. Prof., Sloan School of Management, MIT E52-545, Cambridge, MA 02139, USA. Tel.: 1 617 253 7157. Fax: 1 617 253 2660.

Year and Place of Birth 1951, Wichita, USA.

Degrees and Qualifications BA (Eng. & Maths) Texas Christian Univ., 1974; MA (Eng.) North Carolina Univ., 1975; Ph.D. (Eng.) North Carolina Univ., 1980.

Current Offices and Honorary Posts Board of Directors, Bus. Hist. Conf.; ed. board mem. (& past ed.), *Management Communication Q.*

Major Honours Waldo Gifford Prize of the Soc. of Amer. Archivists for a book making an outstanding contribution to archival literature (for *Control through Communication*), 1990; Alpha Kappa Psi Award for Distinguished Publication in Bus. Communication (for *Control Through Communication*), 1990.

Fields of Expertise *Industry Fields:* transport and communication; insurance, banking, finance. *Bus. Dimensions:* bus. and technology; information and communication: technology and processes. *Scope:* national. *Period:* nineteenth century; twentieth century as a whole. *Teaching:* MBA students. *Consultancy:* corporate strategy.

Publications *Books: Control Through Communication: The Rise of System in Amer. Management*, Johns Hopkins Univ. Press, 1989; paperback edn., 1993. *Articles:* 'The Telegraph's Effect on Nineteenth Century Markets and Firms', *Bus. & Econ. Hist.*, 2nd ser., 15, 1986, 149–63; (proceedings of 1986 annual meeting of the Bus. Hist. Conf.); 'For the Record: The Embodiment of Organization Memory, 1850–1920', *Bus. & Econ. Hist.*, 2nd ser., 19, 1990, 172–82, (proceedings of the 1990 annual meeting of the Bus. Hist. Conf.); 'Investing in Information: Supply and Demand Forces in the Use of Information in Amer. Firms, 1850–1920', *Inside the Bus. Enterprise*, Peter Temin ed., NBER & Univ. of Chicago Press, Chicago, IL, 1991, 117–54; 'Evolving Information Use in Firms, 1850–1920: Ideology and Information Techniques and Technologies', *Information Acumen: The Understanding and Use of Knowledge in Modern Bus.*, Lisa Bud-Frierman ed., Routledge, London, forthcoming.

Yonekawa, Shin'ichi

Prof. of Bus. Hist., Fac. of Commerce, Hitotsubashi Univ., Naka 2-1, Kunitachi-shi, Tokyo, Japan. Tel.: 81 425 72 1101.

Year and Place of Birth 1931, Tokyo, Japan.

Degrees and Qualifications Ph.D. Hitotsubashi Univ., 1961.

Current Offices and Honorary Posts Exec. officer, Socio-Econ. Hist. Soc.; exec. officer, Japan Bus. Hist. Soc.

Publications *Articles:* 'Champion and Woodland Norfolk: The Development of Regional Differences', *J. of European Econ. Hist.*, 6(1) Spring 1977; 'The Development of Chinese and Japanese Bus. in an Internat. Perspective: A Bibliographical Introduction', *Bus. Hist. Rev.*, 56(2), Summer 1982; 'University Graduates in Japanese Enterprises before the Second World War', *Bus. Hist.*, 26(2), July 1984; 'Recent Writing on Japanese Econ. and Social History', *Econ. Hist. Rev.*, 2nd ser., 38(1), Feb., 1985; 'The

Emergence of the Large Firm in the Cotton Spinning Industries of the World, 1883-1938', *Textile Hist.*, D.A. Farnie & Y. Yonekawa, 19(2), Autumn, 1988.

Yonekura, Seiichiro

Assoc. Prof., Inst. of Bus. Research, Hitotsubashi Univ., 2-1 Naka, Kumitachi, Tokyo 186, Japan. Tel.: 81 425 72 1101. Fax: 81 425 77 2495.
Year and Place of Birth 1953, Tokyo, Japan.
Degrees and Qualifications Dip. Ed. BA Hitotsubashi Univ., 1977; M.Soc.Sc. Hitotsubashi Univ., 1981; Ph.D. Harvard Univ., 1990.
Fields of Expertise *Industry Fields:* mechanical engineering; metal goods; electronics and computers: manufacture. *Bus. Dimensions:* entrepreneurs and entrepreneurship; production management; research and development; strategy formation; bus. organization; bus. and technology; co. culture. *Scope:* internat.; global. *Period:* twentieth century as a whole; early twentieth century; inter-war years, 1919–39; mid-twentieth century, 1940–70; late twentieth century, 1970–present. *Teaching:* undergrad.; post grad. *Consultancy:* corporate strategy.
Publications *Books: Bus. Hist.* [Keiei shi], with Y. Suzuki & E. Abe co-auths., Yuhikaku, 1987; *Continuity and Discontinuity: The Japanese Iron and Steel Industry, 1850–1990*, Macmillan Press, forthcoming. *Articles:* 'Strategy of Externalization: Fuji Denki, Fujitsu and Fanuc', *Hitotsubashi Rev.*, 106(5), 1991, 36–69; 'The Postwar Japanese Iron and Steel Industry - Continuity and Discontinuity', *Changing Patterns of Internat. Rivalry*, E. Abe & Y. Suzuki eds., Univ. of Tokyo Press, 1991; 'The Postwar Reforms in Management and Labor', *Japanese Experience of Econ. Reforms*, Y. Kosai & J. Teranishi eds., Macmillan Press, 1993.

Yoneyama, Takau

Assoc. Prof., Fac. of Bus. Admin., Kyoto Sangyo Univ., Kamigamo Motoyama, Kita-ku, Kyoto 603, Japan. Tel.: 075 701 2151. Fax: 075 722 3034.
Year and Place of Birth 1953, Nagano, Japan.
Degrees and Qualifications M.Econ. Yokahama Nat. Univ.
Previous Post Lect., Kyoto Sangyo Univ., 1984–8.
Current Offices and Honorary Posts Membership sec., Japan Bus. Hist. Assoc.
Fields of Expertise *Industry Fields:* insurance, banking, finance; retailers. *Bus. Dimensions:* strategy formation; merger movement and issues; bus. organization. *Scope:* internat. *Period:* nineteenth century; early twentieth century; inter-war years, 1919–39. *Teaching:* undergrad. *Consultancy:* co. hist.
Publications *Books: The 100-Year Hist. of Nippon Life, its Growth and Socioeconomic Setting 1889–1989*, with M. Tatsuki & T. Siba, The Nippon Life Insurance Co., 1991.

Yoshida, Michael H.

Prof., Fac. of Econ., Kobe Internat. Univ., (St Michael's Univ.), 5-1-1 Manabigaoka, Tarumi-ku, Kobe 655, Japan. Tel.: 078 709 3851. Fax: 078 707 3500.
Year and Place of Birth 1945, Saitama, Japan.
Degrees and Qualifications BA Rikkyo Univ., 1968; MA Rikkyo Univ., 1970.
Previous Post Asst. Prof., Yashirogakuin Univ., 1984–91.
Fields of Expertise *Industry Fields:* agric., forestry, fishing; other manufacturing industries. *Bus. Dimensions:* entrepreneurs and entre-

preneurship; co. finance and accounting. *Scope:* local; regional; UK. *Period:* early modern; eighteenth century; nineteenth century. *Teaching:* undergrad. *Consultancy:* co. hist.

Publications *Articles:* 'A Record of Farm Management during the Indust. Revolution in England', *Japan Bus. Hist. Rev.*, 6(3), 1972, 78–93; 'The Ashworth Cotton Enterprise in Nineteenth Century Lancashire', *Yashirogakuin Univ. Annual Rev.* , 19, 1980, 129–42; "Ellis" Farm Management in early Nineteenth Century Leicestershire', *Yashirogakuin Univ. Econ. & Management Rev.*, 3(1), 1983, 135–46; 'Watkinson's Farm Management in early Nineteenth Century Essex', *Yashirogakuin Univ. Biannual Rev.*, 30, 1986, 45–59; 'Farm Management by T. Smith in Gloucestershire in the late Nineteenth Century', *Yashirogakuin Univ. Econ. & Management Rev.*, 10(1&2), 1991, 57–71.

Yoshihara, Hideki

Prof. and Director, Research Inst. for Econ. & Bus. Admin., Kobe Univ., 2-1 Rokkodai, Nada-ku, Kobe, Japan. Tel.: 078 881 1212. Fax: 078 861 6434.

Year and Place of Birth 1941, Osaka, Japan.

Degrees and Qualifications Ph.D. (Bus.) Kobe Univ., 1988.

Current Offices and Honorary Posts Exec. com. mem., Japanese Management Soc.; exec. com. mem., Soc. of Organizational Science; exec. committee mem., Bus. Hist. Soc. of Japan.

Fields of Expertise *Industry Fields:* electrical engineering. *Bus. Dimensions:* multinational bus. *Scope:* global. *Period:* late twentieth century, 1970–present. *Teaching:* post grad. *Consultancy:* corporate strategy.

Publications *Books: Senryakuteki Kigyo Kakushin* [Strategic Corporate Innovation], Toyo Keizai Shinposha, 1986; *Nihon Kigyo no Takakuka Senryaku* [Diversification Strategy of Japanese Companies], co-auth., Nihon Keizai Shinbunsha, 1981; *Bus. Hist. of General Trading Companies*, co-ed., Univ. of Tokyo Press, 1987.

Young, James Harvey

Candler Prof. of Amer. Social Hist. Emeritus, Emory Univ., 272 Heaton Park Drive, Decatur, GA 30030, USA. Tel.: 1 404 377 6341.

Year and Place of Birth 1915, Brooklyn, USA.

Degrees and Qualifications Ph.D. (Amer. Hist.) Univ. of Illinois, Champaign-Urbana, 1941.

Previous Post Emory Univ., 1941 until retirement in 1984.

Current Offices and Honorary Posts Council, Hon. Pres., Amer. Inst. of the Hist. of Pharmacy.

Major Honours Edward Kremers Award, Amer. Inst. of the Hist. of Pharmacy, 1962; William H. Welch Medal, 1982; Continuing Lifetime Achievement Award, 1992, Amer. Assoc. for the Hist. of Medicine; Pres., Southern Historical Assoc., 1982.

Fields of Expertise *Industry Fields:* proprietary and pharmaceutical drugs; food and drink. *Bus. Dimensions:* marketing; federal regulation. *Scope:* national; USA. *Period:* nineteenth century; twentieth century as a whole. *Consultancy:* US food and drug admin.

Publications *Books: The Toadstool Millionaires, A Social Hist. of Patent Medicines in Amer. before Federal Regulation*, Princeton Univ. Press, 1961; *The Medical Messiahs, A Social Hist. of Health Quackery in Twentieth Century Amer.*, Princeton Univ. Press, 1967 & 1992; *Amer. Self-dosage Medicines: An Historical Perspective*, Coronado Press, Lawrence, Kansas,

1974; *Pure Food: Securing the Federal Food and Drugs Act of 1906*, Princeton Univ. Press, 1989; *Amer. Health Quackery: Collected Essays of James Harvey Young*, Princeton Univ. Press, 1992.

Yui, Tsunehiko

Prof. of Bus. Hist., School of Bus. Admin., Meiji Univ., 1-1 Kanda-Surugadai, Chiyoda-ku, Tokyo, Japan. Tel.: 03 3296 4545. Fax: 03 3296 4350.

Year and Place of Birth 1931, Nagano-ken, Japan.

Degrees and Qualifications MA Tokyo Univ., 1957; Ph.D. Tokyo Univ., 1963.

Previous Post Invited Prof., Dept. of Econ., Tokyo Univ., 1989–90.

Current Offices and Honorary Posts Exec. director, Japan Bus. Hist. Inst.; edit. advisor, *Bus. Hist.*, UK.

Major Honours Prize for Literary Excellence, *Japanese Econ. J.*, 1978.

Fields of Expertise *Industry Fields:* food, drink, tobacco; textiles; electrical engineering. *Bus. Dimensions:* entrepreneurs and entrepreneurship; strategy formation; bus. values. *Scope:* national; internat. *Period:* twentieth century as a whole. *Consultancy:* co. hist.

Publications *Books: The Development of Japanese Bus.: 1600-1980*, Johannes Hirshmeier co-auth., Allen & Unwin, London, 1983, 2nd edn. *Articles:* 'The Development, Organization and Bus. Strategy of Indust. Enterprises in Japan, 1915-1935', *Japanese Yearbook on Bus. Hist.*, 5, 1985, 56–87; 'The Development, Organization and Internat. Competitiveness of Indust. Enterprises in Japan, 1880-1915', *Bus. & Econ. Hist.*, 2nd ser., 17, 1988, 31–48; 'Bus. Hist. of Shipping', *Proceedings of Fuji Internat. Conf. of Bus. Hist.*, Keiichiro Nakagawa co-

auth., Univ. of Tokyo Press, 1985; 'Japanese Management of Historical Perspective', *Proceedings of Fuji Internat. Conf. of Bus. Hist.*, Keiichiro Nakagawa co-auth., Univ. of Tokyo Press, 1989.

Yunoki, Manabu

Prof. of Japanese Econ. Hist., School of Econ., Kwansei Gakuin Univ., Uegahara, Nishinomiya 662, Japan. Tel.: 0798 53 6111. Fax: 0798 51 0944.

Year and Place of Birth 1929, Ishikawa, Japan.

Degrees and Qualifications M.Econ. Kwansei Gakuin Univ., 1956; Ph.D. (Econ.) Kwansei Gakuin Univ., 1964.

Current Offices and Honorary Posts Exec. officer, Socio-Econ. Hist. Soc.; vice-pres., Soc. of Saké Brewing Hist.; exec. com. mem., Japanese Soc. of Maritime Hist.; exec. com. mem., Japanese Soc. of the Hist. of Transport & Communications.

Major Honours Japanese Acad. Award, 1982; Sumita Prize for Maritime Promotion, 1979; Kobe Hist. Soc. Prize, 1985.

Fields of Expertise *Industry Fields:* shipbuilding and marine engineering; Japanese saké. *Bus. Dimensions:* production management; personnel management; bus. and technology; small bus. matters. *Scope:* local; regional; national. *Period:* medieval; early modern; eighteenth century; nineteenth century; early twentieth century. *Teaching:* undergrad.; post grad. *Consultancy:* co. hist.

Publications *Articles:* 'Ship Registration as Historical Material', *Study of Transportation Hist.*, 7, 1982; 'The Study and Problems of the Saké Brewing Industry in Modern Japan', *J. of Maritime Hist.*, 1, 1984; 'Japanese Saké', *Hist. of Indust. Technology*,

Dai-ichi Hoki Shuppan, 1988; 'The Development of the Saké Brewing Industry in Modern Japan', *J. of Socio-Econ. Hist.*, 55(2), 1989; 'Coastal Shipping in Japan before the Meiji Restoration', *Kwansei Gakuin Univ. Annual Studies*, 1991.

Yuzawa, Takeshi

Prof. of Bus. Hist. and Dean, Fac. of Econ., Gakushuin Univ., 1-5-1 Mejiro, Toshima, Tokyo 171, Japan. Tel.: 03 3986 0221. Fax: 03 5992 1007.

Year and Place of Birth 1940, Chiba pref., Japan.

Degrees and Qualifications BA Kyoto Univ., 1965; MA Hitotsubashi Univ., 1968.

Previous Post Assoc. Prof. of Bus. Hist., Fukushima Univ.

Current Offices and Honorary Posts Chairman, Fuji Conf. on Bus. Hist. (4th ser.); ed., *Japan Bus. Hist.*; ed., Socio-Econ. Hist.

Fields of Expertise *Industry Fields:* vehicle construction; textiles; transport and communication; distributive trades; insurance, banking, finance. *Bus. Dimensions:* entrepreneurs and entrepreneurship; production management; co. finance and accounting; personnel management; co. admin.; marketing; research and development; strategy formation; merger movement and issues; bus. organization; bus. and technology; multinational bus.; management education; bus.–state relations; bus. values; co. culture; boardroom issues. *Scope:* national; internat.; global; USA; UK. *Period:* nineteenth century; twentieth century as a whole. *Teaching:* undergrad.; post grad. *Consultancy:* co. hist.

Publications *Books: Igirisu Tetsudo Keieishi* [A Bus. Hist. of British Railways], Nihonkeizai-Hyoron-sha; *Foreign Bus. in Japan before World War II*, co-ed., Univ. of Tokyo Press,

1990. *Articles:* 'The Introduction of Electric Railways in Britain and Japan', *J. of Transport Hist.*, 3rd ser., 6(1), 1985; 'Das japanische Transportsystem als staatliches Unternehmen', *Wissenschaftliche Zeitschrift der Humboldt-Universität zu Berlin*, 1990; 'The Transfer of Railway Technologies from Britain to Japan', *Internat. Technology Transfer in Historical Perspective*, D. Jeremy ed., Edward Elgar, 1991.

Zacharias, Lawrence S.

Assoc. Prof., School of Management, Univ. of Massachusetts, Amherst, MA 01003, USA. Tel.: 1 413 545 5683.

Year and Place of Birth 1947, New York, USA.

Degrees and Qualifications BA Univ. of California, Berkeley, 1969; MA Columbia Univ., 1970; M.Phil. Columbia Univ., 1974; LL D Columbia Law School, 1973.

Previous Post Langdell Fellow, Harvard Law School, 1981–2.

Major Honours Fulbright Fellow (Germany), 1992; Langdell Fellow, Harvard Law School, 1981–2; Amer. Bar Foundation Legal Hist. Fellowship, 1981.

Fields of Expertise *Industry Fields:* professional and scientific services; distributive trades; public admin. *Bus. Dimensions:* co. law; bus. organization; bus.–state relations. *Scope:* national. *Period:* early modern; nineteenth century; twentieth century as a whole. *Teaching:* undergrad.; post grad. *Consultancy:* law regulation (corporate).

Publications *Books: The End of Managerial Ideology*, with Allen Kaufman & Marvin Karson, OUP, forthcoming. *Articles:* 'Local Power and Local Knowledge', *Amer. J. of Legal Hist.*, 30(2), 1986, 122–62; 'Case Method and Historical Inquiry', *The Legal Studies Forum*, 11(3), 1987,

317–36; 'Repaving the Brandeis Way: The Decline of Developmental Property', *Northwestern Univ. Law Rev.*, 82, Spring, 1988, 596–645; 'Opening Coase's Other Black Box: Why Workers submit to Vertical Integration into Firms', *J. of Corporation Law*, with Marc Linder, 1993, forthcoming.

Zahedieh, Nuala B.

Lect., Dept. of Econ. & Social Hist., Edinburgh Univ., Edinburgh, EH8 9JY, UK. Tel.: 44 31 650 3836. Fax: 44 31 668 3053.

Year and Place of Birth 1953, London, UK.

Degrees and Qualifications B.Sc. (Econ.) London School of Econ., 1975; M.Sc. (Econ.) London School of Econ., 1978; Ph.D. London School of Econ., 1984.

Previous Post Research Officer, London School of Econ., 1985–9.

Current Offices and Honorary Posts Council mem., Econ. Hist. Soc.

Fields of Expertise *Industry Fields:* food, drink, tobacco; textiles; clothing and footwear; insurance, banking, finance; bus. services. *Bus. Dimensions:* entrepreneurs and entrepreneurship. *Scope:* internat. *Period:* early modern. *Teaching:* undergrad.; post grad.

Publications *Articles:* 'Trade, Plunder and Econ. Development in early English Jamaica, 1655–89', *Econ. Hist. Rev.*, 2nd ser., XXXIX, 1986, 205–22; 'The Merchants of Port Royal, Jamaica and Spanish Contraband Trade, 1655–1689', *William & Mary Q.*, XLIII, 1986, 570–93; 'A Frugal, Prudential and Hopeful Trade. Privateering in Jamaica, 1655–1689', *J. of Imperial & Commonwealth Hist.*, 18, 1990, 145–68; 'London and the Colonial Consumer in the late Seventeenth Century', *Econ. Hist. Rev.*, 2nd ser., XLVII, 1994, forthcoming.

Zalite, Elga

Sen. Research Assoc., Inst. of Latvian Hist., Latvian Acad. of Sciences, 19 Turgenew St, 1518 Riga, Latvia. Tel.: 7 132 226924.

Year and Place of Birth 1959, Madona, Latvia.

Degrees and Qualifications Dr.hist. Latvian Acad. of Sciences, 1992.

Previous Post Research Assoc., Inst. of Latvian Hist., Latvian Acad. of Sciences, 1990–2.

Fields of Expertise *Industry Fields:* labour force and industry. *Scope:* national; Latvia. *Period:* inter-war years, 1919–39.

Publications *Articles:* 'The Socio-economic Characteristics of Workers of the Joint-stock Co. Fenikss Factory, 1923–1929 (enquiries)', *Proceedings of the Latvian Acad. of Sciences*, 12, 1987, 44–57; 'The Indust. Enterprise and the Indust. Worker in the 20s and 30s', *Proceedings of the Latvian Acad. of Sciences*, 4, 1988, 23–34; 'The Question of the Old Age Pension in the Social Policy of the Republic of Latvia', *Inst. of Hist. J.*, 2, 1991, 2, 581–708; 'The Unemployment Problem in the Republic of Latvia 1918–1940', *Inst. of Hist. J.*, 1, 1992, 81–102; 'Re-evacuation of Indust. Enterprises from Russia in the 20s and 30s', *Inst. of Hist. J.*, 3, 1993, 70–85.

Zamagni, Vera

Chair Prof., Dept. of Econ., Bologna Univ., Strada Maggiore 45, 40125 Bologna, Italy. Tel.: 39 51 6402614. Fax: 39 51 230197.

Year and Place of Birth 1943, Ponzone, Italy.

Degrees and Qualifications Laurea, Catholic Univ. of Milan, 1966; Ph.D. Oxford Univ., 1976.

Previous Post Assoc. Prof., Bologna

Univ., 1987–90.

Current Offices and Honorary Posts
Mem. of Scientific Board, ASSI.

Fields of Expertise *Industry Fields:*
chemicals and allied industries; distributive trades; insurance, banking, finance. *Bus. Dimensions:* research and development; bus. organization. *Scope:* local; national. *Period:* nineteenth century; twentieth century as a whole. *Teaching:* undergrad.; post grad.

Publications *Books: Dalla Periferia al Centro. La seconda Rinascita Economica dell'Italia 1861–1981,* Il Mulino, Bologna, 1990, English trans. *The Econ. Hist. of Italy 1860–1990,* Clarendon Press, OUP, 1993. *Articles:* 'Alle origini della grande Distribuzione in Italia', *Commercio,* 10, 1982, 71–95; 'L'industria Chimica in Italia dalle Origini agli Anni Cinquanta', *Montecatini. Capitoli di Storia di una Grande Impresa,* F. Amatori & B. Bezza eds., Il Mulino, Bologna, 1991; 'Le Dimensioni dell'IGD 1947–1964', *Dall'ammoniaca ai nuovi Materiali. Storia dell'Istituto di Ricerche Chimiche Guido Donegani di Novara,* with P.P. Saviotti & L. Simonin, Il Mulino, Bologna, 1991; 'La Cassa di Risparmio di Rimini tra Passato e Futuro', *Economia e Società a Rimini tra 800 e 900,* with A. Varni co-ed., Pizzi, Milan, 1992.

Zan, Stefano

Assoc. Prof. of Comparative Analysis of Organizations, Fac. of Polit. Science, Bologna Univ., Strada Maggiore 45, Bologna, Italy. Tel.: 39 51 238764. Fax: 39 51 234036.

Year and Place of Birth 1950, Transacqua, Italy.

Degrees and Qualifications Laurea Bologna Univ., 1973; Assoc. prof., Bologna Univ., 1987.

Current Offices and Honorary Posts

Pres., AROC (Associazione Ricerche sulle Organizzazioni Complesse); mem., ASSI (Associazione Storia e Studi sull'Impresa).

Fields of Expertise *Industry Fields:* agric., forestry, fishing; bricks, pottery, glass, cement; construction. *Bus. Dimensions:* bus. organization; small bus. matters; co-operatives. *Scope:* local. *Period:* late twentieth century, 1970–present. *Teaching:* undergrad.; post grad. *Consultancy:* co. hist.; corporate strategy.

Publications *Books: La Cooperazione in Italia,* De Donato, Bari, 1982; *Le Interdipendenze Organizzative in Agricoltura,* Edizioni della Regione Emilia-Romagna, Bologna, 1983; *Costruire l'Impresa. Storia della CMC di Ravenna dal 1945 al 1972,* with Giulio Sapelli co-auth., Il Mulino, Bologna, 1991.

Zembala, Dennis M.

Exec. Director, Baltimore Museum of Industry, 1415 Key Highway, Baltimore, Maryland 21230, USA. Tel.: 1 410 727 4808. Fax: 1 410 727 4869.

Year and Place of Birth 1942, Detroit, USA.

Degrees and Qualifications BA (Literature) Michigan Univ., 1964; Ph.D. (Amer. Civilization & Hist. of Technology) George Washington Univ., 1984.

Previous Post Historian, Baltimore Indust. & Engineering Survey, Baltimore Indust. Museum, 1978–80.

Current Offices and Honorary Posts US Rep. to the Board of Directors, Internat. Com. for the Conservation of the Indust. Heritage (TICCIH); board mem., Engineering Soc. of Baltimore; board mem., Historical Electronics Museum (Baltimore); mem., Maryland State Technology Education Advisory Com.

Major Honours Evans Scholarship, Michigan Univ.; Pre-professional Scholarship,Wayne State Univ., 1970–1; Grad. Teaching Fellowship, George Washington Univ., 1971–3; CINE Golden Eagle (documentary film award) for 'An Alleghany Glass Works'; Humanist of the Month, Maryland Com. for the Humanities, 1984.

Fields of Expertise *Industry Fields:* bricks, pottery, glass, cement. *Bus. Dimensions:* bus. and technology. *Scope:* national. *Period:* nineteenth century. *Teaching:* post grad. *Consultancy:* co. hist.

Publications *Articles:* 'The Preservation of Historic Public Works', *Amer. Public Works Reporter*, April, 1976; 'Baltimore and the Art of Work: The Emergence of the Indust. City', *Maryland Our Maryland*, Virginia Geiger ed., Univ. Press of Amer., Lanham, 1987; 'Industrial Hist. Moves Front and Center', *Museum News*, Nov./Dec., 1990, 34–37.

Zilák, Ján

Special Adviser, Státny Oblastny Archív, Sládkovicova 1, 974 05 Banská Bystrica, Slovakia. Tel.: 42 88 62017. Fax: 42 88 62017.

Year and Place of Birth 1952, Ceske Brezovo, Slovakia.

Degrees and Qualifications Ph.D.; C.Sc.

Previous Post Director of the State Regional Archive, Banska Bystrica, 1988–91.

Fields of Expertise *Industry Fields:* mining and quarrying; metal manufacture; bricks, pottery, glass, cement. *Scope:* local; regional. *Period:* eighteenth century; nineteenth century; twentieth century as a whole. *Consultancy:* co. hist.

Publications *Articles:* 'History of Mining in Lovinobana', *Book Lovinobana*, MNV, Lovinobana,

1986, 69–90; 'From the Hist. of the Metallurgical Plant in Rimavske Brezovo', *Vlastivedné Studie Gemera*, 6, Osveta Pub., 1988, 69–96; 'Mining and Metal Processing Enterprises in the Malohont Region in the Period 1750–1808', *Vlastivedne Studie Gemera*, 7, Osveta Pub., 1989, 81–102; 'From the Hist. of the Glass Factory in Katarinska Huta', *Stredne Slovensko*, 9, Osveta Pub., 1990, 7–33; 'Topographical Description of the Malohont Region', *Obzor Gemera Malohontu*, 22(4), 128–37.

Zuckerman, Mary Ellen

Assoc. Prof., SUNY-Geneseo, 206-C Welles, Geneseo, NY 14454, USA. Tel.: 1 716 245 5368. Fax: 1 716 245 5467.

Year and Place of Birth 1954, Gainesville, USA.

Degrees and Qualifications BA Simmons College, 1976; MBA Columbia Univ., 1982; Ph.D. Columbia Univ., 1987.

Previous Post Visiting Assoc. Prof., McGill Univ., 1991–2.

Major Honours Spencer Foundation Grant, 1992–5; Freedom Forum Media Studies Fellow, 1990–1.

Fields of Expertise *Industry Fields:* paper, printing, publishing. *Bus. Dimensions:* marketing; strategy formation; bus. organization. *Scope:* national. *Period:* eighteenth century; nineteenth century; twentieth century as a whole. *Teaching:* undergrad. *Consultancy:* co. hist.

Publications *Books: The Magazine in Amer.*, with John Tebbel co-auth., OUP, 1991; *Information Sources in the Hist. of Popular Women's Magazines*, Greenwood Press, 1991. *Articles:* 'Old Homes in a City of Perpetual Change: The Women's Magazine Industry, 1890–1917', *Bus. Hist. Rev.*, 63, Winter, 1989, 715–56; 'Pathway to

'Pathway to Success: Gertrude Battles Home and the Woman's Home Companion', *Journalism Hist.*, 16(3/4), Spring, 1990, 78–87; 'Contributions of Women to US Marketing Thought: The Consumer's Perspective, 1900–1940', *Journal of the Academy of Marketing Science*, with Mary Carsky co-auth., 18, Autumn, 1990, 313–18.

INDICES

Country

ARGENTINA

Kosacoff, Bernardo P.
Schvarzer, Jorge

AUSTRALIA

Boot, H.M.
Falkus, Malcolm E.
Howell, Paul M.
Merrett, D.T.
Nicholas, Stephen
Statham, Pamela C.
Tull, Malcolm
Ville, Simon P.
Waller, David S.

AUSTRIA

Eigner, Peter
Mathis, Franz
Matis, Herbert W.
Meixner, Wolfgang
Mosser, Alois
Otruba, Gustav
Palme, Rudolf
Resch, Andreas
Sandgruber, Roman
Stiefel, Dieter
Wysocki, Josef

BELGIUM

Van Der Wee, Herman

CANADA

Acheson, T.W.
Armstrong, Christopher
Armstrong, Fred H.
Austin, Barbara
Baskerville, Peter A.
Bothwell, Robert

Buchan, P. Bruce
Burley, David
Darroch, James L.
Davis, Donald F.
den Otter, A.A.
Fleming, Keith R.
Gerriets, Marilyn
Gilpin, John F.
Gingras, André
Hall, Roger D.
Huberman, Michael M.
Igartua, José E.
Ingham, John N.
Klassen, Henry C.
Lewchuk, Wayne A.
MacPherson, Ian
McCalla, Douglas
McCullough, Alan B.
McDowall, Duncan L.
McRoberts, Mary L.
Naylor, R. Thomas
Neufeld, Edward P.
Newell, Dianne
Ommer, Rosemary E.
Regehr, Theodore D.
Rugman, Alan M.
Smith, Victor C.
Sweeny, Robert C.H.
Traves, Tom
Tucker, Albert V.
Tulchinsky, Gerald J.J.
Vallieres, Marc
Wray, William D.

CHILE

Katz, Jorge M.

CZECHLAND

Efmertová, Marcela
Gerslová, Jana
Hájek, Jan
Jakubec, Ivan
Jancík, Drahomír
Jindra, Zdenek

Lacina, Vlastislav
Matejcek, Jirí
Mayer, Daniel
Novotny, Jirí
Pátek, Jaroslav
Prúcha, Václav
Sommer, Karel
Steiner, Jan

DENMARK

Bender, Henning
Boje, Per
Bonke, Jens
Burchardt, Jørgen
Eriksen, August Wiemann
Fink, Jørgen
Fode, Henrik
Goebel, Erik
Hansen, Per H.
Hansen, Povl A.
Hastrup, Knud Bjarne
Hyldtoft, Ole
Jensen, Jakob B.
Johansen, Hans Christian
Just, Flemming
Kjærgaard, Thorkild
Kristensen, Peer Hull
Kryger Larsen, Hans
Matthiessen, Poul C.
Møller, Anders Monrad
Pedersen, Erik Helmer
Raaschou-Nielsen, Agnete
Toensberg, Jeppe E.
Topp, Niels-Henrik

FINLAND

A'hvenainen, Jorma
Herranen, Timo
Hoffman, Kai J.
Karonen, Petri K.
Kuisma, Markku
Michelsen, Karl-Erik K.
Myllyntaus, Timo
Schybergson, Per

Iida, Takashi
Ikeda, Noritaka
Ikoma, Michihiro
Imakubo, Sachio
Inagaki, Yoshinari
Ioku, Shigehiko
Ishii, Kanji
Ito, Shoji
Itoh, Takashi
Kajimoto, Motonobu
Kaku, Sachio
Katoh, Kozaburo
Kawabe, Nobuo
Kawamura, Terumasa
Kawanami, Yoichi
Kawano, Aizaburo
Kazusa, Yasuyuki
Kikkawa, Takeo
Kimura, Masato
Kita, Masami
Kitabayashi, Masashi
Kiuchi, Kaichi
Kobayashi, Hiroshi
Kobayashi, Kesaji
Kobayashi, Tadashi
Kobayashi, Yoshiaki
Koda, Ryoichi
Kohno, Shozo
Kohtoh, Isuke
Kondo, Akira
Koyama, Hiroyuki
Kozuki, Naoto
Kudo, Akira
Kuwahara, Tetsuya
Kuwata, Masaru
Matsuda, Tomoo
Matsumoto, Koji
Matsumoto, Takanori
Mikami, Atsufumi
Mishima, Yasuo
Mitsugi, Yoshio
Mitsui, Takashige
Miyamoto, Matao
Mori, Tetsuhiko
Mori, Yasuhiro
Morikawa, Hidemasa
Nakagawa, Keiichiro
Nakagawa, Seishi
Nakatsukasa, Ichiro
Nasuno, Kimito
Nishikawa, Hiroshi

Nishikawa, Junko
Nishikawa, Noboru
Nishimura, Shizuya
Nishimura, Takao
Nonaka, Izumi
Ohno, Akira
Oikawa, Yoshinobu
Oita, Akira
Okayama, Reiko
Okochi, Akio
Onozuka, Tomoji
Ozawa, Katsuyuki
Rauck, Michael
Saito, Takenori
Saito, Tomoaki
Sakamoto, Takuji
Sakudo, Jun
Sasaki, Satoshi
Sawai, Minoru
Shiba, Takao
Shimokawa, Koichi
Shimono, Katsumi
Shimotani, Masahiro
Shinomiya, Toshiyuki
Shioji, Hiromi
Sugimoto, Kimihiko
Sugisaki, Takamoto
Sugiyama, Shinya
Sunaga, Kinzaburo
Suyenaga, Kunitoshi
Suzuki, Toshio
Suzuki, Tsuneo
Suzuki, Yoshitaka
Takahashi, Yasutaka
Takechi, Kyozo
Tanaka, Toshihiro
Taniguchi, Akitake
Tanimoto, Masayuki
Tatsuki, Mariko
Terachi, Takashi
Tokushima, Tatsuro
Tsuji, Setsuo
Tsunoyama, Sakae
Uchida, Hoshimi
Udagawa, Masaru
Ueda, Kinji
Uemura, Motokaku
Umeno, Naotoshi
Wada, Kazuo
Watanabe, Hisashi
Watanabe, Kishichi

Yakura, Shintaro
Yamada, Makiko
Yamada, Tetsuo
Yamaguchi, Fujio
Yamamoto, Toru
Yamamura, Mutsuo
Yamazaki, Hiroaki
Yamazaki, Ryuzo
Yanagisawa, Osamu
Yasumuro, Kenichi
Yasuoka, Shigeaki
Yonekawa, Shin'ichi
Yonekura, Seiichiro
Yoneyama, Takau
Yoshida, Michael H.
Yoshihara, Hideki
Yui, Tsunehiko
Yunoki, Manabu
Yuzawa, Takeshi

LATVIA

Barzdevica, Margarita
Gore, Ilga
Jakovleva, Marite
Ozolina, Dzidra
Shumilo, Erica
Zalite, Elga

NETHERLANDS

Blanken, Ivo J.
Bläsing, Josvhim F.E.
Broeke, W. van den
de Goey, F.M.M.
De Vries, Joh.
De Wit, Dirk
Hogesteeger, Gerardus
Jonker, Joost P.B.
Karsten, Luchien
Noort, Jan van den
Sluyterman, Keetie E.
van den Eerenbeemt,
  H.F.J.M.
Van Driel, Hugo
Veenendaal, Augustus
  J. Jr.

Brown, Kenneth D.
Bud-Frierman, Lisa
Burk, Kathleen
Burt, Roger
Campbell-Kelly, Martin
Capie, Forrest H.
Casson, Mark
Channon, Geoffrey
Chapman, Stanley David
Chick, Martin J.
Clay, Christopher
Coleman, D.C.
Collins, Michael
Coopey, Richard
Corley, T.A.B.
Cox, Howard
Crompton, G.W.
Davies, Peter N.
Donnelly, Tom
Dupree, Marguerite W.
Edgerton, D.E.H.
Edwards, John Richard
Farnie, D.A.
Fitzgerald, Robert
Foreman-Peck, James S.
French, Michael J.
Garside, W.R.
Godley, Andrew C.
Goodall, Francis
Goodchild, John
Gourvish, T.R.
Greenhill, Robert G.
Hannah, Leslie
Hart, Tom
Hawkins, Richard Adrian
Henderson, William Otto
Honeyman, Katrina
Jeremy, David J.
Johnman, Lewis
Jones, Charles A.
Jones, Edgar
Jones, Geoffrey
Katzenellenbogen, Simon E.
Killick, John Roper
King, Frank H.H.
Kirby, Maurice W.
Latham, A.J.H.
Marriner, Sheila

Mathias, Peter
McKinlay, Alan
Melling, Joseph
Mercer, Helen
Millward, Robert
Moss, Michael Stanley
Mumford, Michael J.
Munn, Charles W.
Munro, J. Forbes
Munting, Roger
Ollerenshaw, Philip G.
Orbell, John
Payne, Peter L.
Pearson, Robin
Pollard, Sidney
Press, Jon
Rose, Mary B.
Schmitz, Christopher J.
Slaven, Anthony
Slinn, Judy
Supple, Barry
Tolliday, Steven W.
Tomlinson, Jim
Turton, Alison
Tweedale, Geoffrey
Wale, Judith M.
Walsh, Margaret
Watson, Katherine
Watson, Nigel
Westall, Oliver M.
Whatley, Christopher A.
Wilson, John F.
Wilson, R.G.
Wrigley, Chris J.
Zahedieh, Nuala B.

USA

Aaronson, Susan Ariel
Alexander, James R.
Applebaum, Herbert A.
Atack, Jeremy
Barbezat, Daniel
Barsness, Richard W.
Bateman, Fred
Baughman, James L.
Beck, William O.
Blackson, Robert M.

Blicksilver, Jack
Bolton, Alfred A.
Bryant, Keith L. Jr.
Bugos, Glenn E.
Buss, Dietrich G.
Cain, Louis P.
Cameron, Rondo
Carlos, Ann M.
Carreras, Charles
Chandler, Alfred D. Jr.
Chatov, Robert
Cheape, Charles W.
Childs, William R.
Churella, Albert John
Collins, Theresa M.
Constant, Edward W. II
Coopersmith, Jonathan C.
Dicke, Thomas S.
Dintenfass, Michael
Doig, Jameson W.
Douglas, Alan
Downs, Jacques M.
Doyle, William M.
Dunlavy, Colleen A.
Dyer, Davis
Eakin, Marshall C.
Edmondson, Michael
Edwards, Pamela C.
Engelbourg, Saul
Engerman, Stanley L.
Englander, Ernest J.
Feldman, Gerald D.
Flesher, Dale L.
Friedricks, William B.
Furlong, Patrick J.
Galambos, Louis
Giebelhaus, August W.
Gordon, Nancy M.
Graham, Margaret B.W.
Harbaugh, Larry E.
Hausman, William J.
Hawley, Ellis W.
Heim, Carol E.
Helper, Susan
Henwood, James N.J.
Hessen, Robert
Hofsommer, Don L.
Hogler, Raymond L.
Hoke, Donald R.

FIELDS OF EXPERTISE

Industry Fields

Hapák, Pavel
Itoh, Takashi
Kaczynska, Elzbieta
Katoh, Kozaburo
Kikkawa, Takeo
Kirby, Maurice W.
Kobayashi, Yoshiaki
Kuwata, Masaru
Martin-Aceña, Pablo
McKay, John P.
Melling, Joseph
Naylor, R. Thomas
Noort, Jan van den
O'Connor, Richard
Olien, Diana Davids
Olien, Roger M.
Orsenigo, Luigi
Pauer, Erich
Pierenkemper, Toni
Sachse, Wieland
Saito, Tomoaki
Sapelli, Giulio
Sudrià, Carles
Sugiyama, Shinya
Taniguchi, Akitake
Toninelli, PierAngelo
Udagawa, Masaru
Umeno, Naotoshi
Ville, Simon P.
Vozár, Jozef
Wada, Kazuo
Wale, Judith M.
Watanabe, Hisashi
Weber, Wolfhard
White, Christine A.

COMMUNICATIONS

See Transport and
communication

CONSTRUCTION

Alberty, Július
Amatori, Franco
Applebaum, Herbert A.
Barker, T.C.

Bayerl, Günter J.
Bigazzi, Duccio
Bonke, Jens
Booth, Alan
Bowden, Sue
Chandler, Alfred D. Jr.
Christiansen, W.
 Kenneth S.
Davis, Donald F.
Demizu, Tsutomu
Donnelly, Tom
Dritsas, Margarita
Fabricius, Miroslav
Flik, Reiner
Foreman-Peck, James S.
French, Michael J.
Furlong, Patrick J.
Harada, Seiji
Hazama, Hiroshi
Helper, Susan
Ikoma, Michihiro
Inagaki, Yoshinari
Jackson, Kenneth E.
Kipping, Matthias
Kohtoh, Isuke
Koyama, Hiroyuki
Lewchuk, Wayne A.
Martin-Aceña, Pablo
Mason, Mark
Matis, Herbert W.
McKinlay, Alan
Moss, Michael Stanley
Murkison, Eugene C.
Nelson, Daniel
O'Brien, Anthony
 Patrick
Oita, Akira
Okayama, Reiko
Onozuka, Tomoji
Pauer, Erich
Rauck, Michael
Resch, Andreas
Sapelli, Giulio
Sasaki, Satoshi
Sawai, Minoru
Schvarzer, Jorge
Shimokawa, Koichi
Smitka, Michael J.
Spender, J.-C.
Stiefel, Dieter
Takahashi, Yasutaka

Taniguchi, Akitake
Teuteberg, Hans Jürgen
Tolliday, Steven W.
Traves, Tom
Udagawa, Masaru
von Stromer (Freiherr
 von Reichenbach),
 Wolfgang
Wada, Kazuo
Watanabe, Kishichi
Watson, Nigel
Weber, Wolfhard
Wermiel, Sara E.
White, Christine A.
Whitten, David O.
Yanagisawa, Osamu
Yuzawa, Takeshi
Zan, Stefano

DISTRIBUTIVE TRADES

Acheson, T.W.
Amatori, Franco
Barker, T.C.
Butel, Paul
Chapman, Stanley
 David
Daito, Eisuke
Dicke, Thomas S.
Dritsas, Margarita
Fabricius, Miroslav
Farnie, D.A.
Goodchild, John
Hagimoto, Shinichro
Hart, Tom
Hashimoto, Juro
Hazama, Hiroshi
Hodne, Fritz
Hoffman, Kai J.
Ioku, Shigehiko
Irsigler, Franz
Ishii, Kanji
Jacoby, Sanford M.
Jones, Charles A.
Kahn, Robert
Kawabe, Nobuo
Klassen, Henry C.
Kozuki, Naoto
Matis, Herbert W.

Gilpin, John F.
Goodchild, John
Gueslin, André
Hájek, Jan
Hall, Roger D.
Hannah, Leslie
Hansen, Per H.
Hapák, Pavel
Hardach, Gerd
Hashimoto, Juro
Hawke, G. R.
Hazama, Hiroshi
Hernandez-Esteve,
  Esteban
Hertner, Peter
Hildebrandt, Reinhard
Holtfrerich, Carl-
  Ludwig
Howell, Paul M.
Iida, Takashi
Irsigler, Franz
Ishii, Kanji
Jackson, Kenneth E.
Jaeger, Hans
Jimenez, Juan Carlos
Jindra, Zdenek
Jones, Charles A.
Jones, Geoffrey
Jones, Stuart
Jonker, Joost P.B.
Kawanami, Yoichi
Kawano, Aizaburo
Kemmerer, Donald L.
Khan, Zorina B.
Killick, John Roper
Kimura, Masato
King, Frank H.H.
Kitabayashi, Masashi
Klassen, Henry C.
Klebaner, Benjamin
  Joseph
Kobayashi, Tadashi
Kobayashi, Yoshiaki
Kollmer-von Oheimb-
  Loup, Gert
Kovaleff, Theodore P.
Kudo, Akira
Lacina, Vlastislav
Landau, Zbigniew
Lange, Even
Lindenlaub, Dieter

Lindgren, Håkan
MacPherson, Ian
Marchildon, Gregory
  P.
Martin-Aceña, Pablo
Matis, Herbert W.
McCusker, John J.
McDermott, Kathleen
McDowall, Duncan L.
Merrett, D.T.
Mitsui, Takashige
Miyamoto, Matao
Mori, Tetsuhiko
Mori, Yasuhiro
Moss, Michael Stanley
Mosser, Alois
Mumford, Michael J.
Munn, Charles W.
Naylor, R. Thomas
Neal, Larry D.
Neufeld, Edward P.
Nishikawa, Junko
Nishimura, Shizuya
Nordvik, Helge W.
O'Brien, Anthony
  Patrick
Ollerenshaw, Philip G.
Olsson, Ulf
Orbell, John
Ozolina, Dzidra
Pantelakis, Nicos
Papathanassopoulos,
  Konstantinos
Pátek, Jaroslav
Pearson, Robin
Perkins, Edwin J.
Pierson Doti, Lynne
Pix, Manfred
Plessis, Alain
Pohl, Hans
Pohl, Manfred
Rauck, Michael
Regehr, Theodore D.
Rockoff, Hugh T.
Ryant, Carl G.
Saito, Tomoaki
Sapelli, Giulio
Schmitz, Christopher
  J.
Schuler, Peter-
  Johannes

Segreto, Luciano
Sejersted, Francis
Sinclair, F.R.J.
Smith, George David
Sobel, Robert
Soltow, James H.
Spender, J.-C.
Stiefel, Dieter
Stone, R.C.J.
Stromberg, Raymond
Sudrià, Carles
Supple, Barry
Suzuki, Toshio
Suzuki, Yoshitaka
Sweeny, Robert C.H.
Sylla, Richard
Tatsuki, Mariko
Terachi, Takashi
Thomes, Paul
Thowsen, Atle
Tilly, Richard
Titos-Martinez,
  Manuel
Torres Villanueva,
  Eugenio
Tortella, Gabriel
Turton, Alison
Ueda, Kinji
Vallieres, Marc
van den Eerenbeemt,
  H.F.J.M.
Van Der Wee, Herman
van Eyll, Klara
Verhoef, Grietjie
Vleesenbeek, H.H.
von Stromer (Freiherr
  von Reichenbach),
  Wolfgang
Walter, Rolf
Webb, Arthur C.M.
Westall, Oliver M.
White, Christine A.
White, Eugene N.
Wijtuliet, Coz A.M.
Wilson, John F.
Wysocki, Josef
Yamazaki, Hiroaki
Yates, JoAnne
Yoneyama, Takau
Yuzawa, Takeshi
Zahedieh, Nuala B.

339

ENTERTAINMENT
INDUSTRIES

Kraft, James P.
Munting, Roger

PHOTOGRAPHY

Jenkins, Reese V.

RESTAURANTS

Harbaugh, Larry E.

NUCLEAR
TECHNOLOGY

NUCLEAR ENGINEERING:
MANUFACTURE

Bothwell, Robert
Ikeda, Noritaka
Sapelli, Giulio
Weinberger, Hans

OTHER
MANUFACTURING
INDUSTRIES

Amano, Masatoshi
Bateman, Fred
Brown, Kenneth D.
Churella, Albert John
Edmondson, Michael
Fabricius, Miroslav
French, Michael J.
Galambos, Louis
Graham, Margaret B.W.
Hapák, Pavel
Huberman, Michael M.
Jacoby, Sanford M.
Kiesewetter, Hubert
Langlois, Richard N.
Lubar, Steven
Lutz, John S.
Matsumoto, Takanori
Millard, Andre

Mumford, Michael J.
Otruba, Gustav
Petersen, Peter B.
Prúcha, Václav
Scranton, Philip B,
Soltow, James H.
Sullivan, Timothy E.
Takechi, Kyozo
Taniguchi, Akitake
Watanabe, Kishichi
Yoshida, Michael H.

RUBBER
(ESPECIALLY TYRES)

Mumford, Michael J.

TOY INDUSTRY
(BRITISH)

Brown, Kenneth D.
Wrigley, Chris J.

PAPER, PRINTING,
PUBLISHING

Ahvenainen, Jorma
Austin, Barbara
Bayerl, Günter J.
Chandler, Alfred D. Jr.
Fabricius, Miroslav
Fujita, Yukitoshi
Goodchild, John
Hapák, Pavel
Harasawa, Yoshitaro
Hazama, Hiroshi
Irsigler, Franz
Jensen, Jakob B.
Karonen, Petri K.
Karsten, Luchien
Kjærgaard, Thorkild
Kornblith, Gary J.
Kuisma, Markku
Lange, Even
McCusker, John J.
Meixner, Wolfgang
Michelsen, Karl-Erik
Neiva, Elizabeth
 MacIver

Petersen, Peter B.
Rauck, Michael
Regehr, Theodore D.
Roche, Michael
Schybergson, Per
Scranton, Philip B,
Shinomiya, Toshiyuki
Smith, Victor C.
Spender, J.-C.
Taniguchi, Akitake
Teuteberg, Hans Jürgen
Toensberg, Jeppe E.
Traves, Tom
van Eyll, Klara
Virtanen, Sakari
von Stromer (Freiherr
 von Reichenbach),
 Wolfgang
Watson, Nigel
Zuckerman, Mary Ellen

POPULATION AND
DEMOGRAPHY

Maitra Priyatosh

PROFESSIONAL AND
SCIENTIFIC SERVICES

Amdam, Rolv Petter
Andersen, Håkon With
Barker, T.C.
Bothwell, Robert
Bud-Frierman, Lisa
Bugos, Glenn E.
Chatov, Robert
Chiba, Junichi
Christiansen, W.
 Kenneth S.
Dritsas, Margarita
Dupree, Marguerite
 W.
Edgerton, D.E.H.
Fabricius, Miroslav
Galambos, Louis
Goodchild, John
Graham, Margaret B.W.

PUBLIC ADMINISTRA-TION AND DEFENCE

PUBLIC FINANCE

REAL ESTATE

See Insurance, banking
finance and business
services

SHIPBUILDING AND MARINE ENGINEERING

TEXTILES

Abe, Takeshi
Adelmann, Gerhard
Austin, Barbara
Bano, Sayeeda S.
Bartl, Július
Bartlová, Alena
Benaul, Josep M.
Bergeron, Louis
Blicksilver, Jack
Chandler, Alfred D. Jr.
Chapman, Stanley David
Chassagne, Serge
Chevalier, Jean-Joseph
Cizakca, Murat
Coleman, D.C.
Concato, Francis
Crouzet, François M.J.
Dritsas, Margarita
Dupree, Marguerite W.
Eakin, Marshall C.
Edwards, Pamela C.
Fabricius, Miroslav
Farnie, D.A.
Federico, Giovanni
Flik, Reiner
Fohlen, Claude
Fujita, Yukitoshi
Galambos, Louis
Garside, W.R.
Goodchild, John
Hapák, Pavel
Hara, Terushi
Harasawa, Yoshitaro
Hau, Michel
Hazama, Hiroshi
Hildebrandt, Reinhard
Hiramoto, Atsushi
Honeyman, Katrina
Huberman, Michael M.
Irsigler, Franz
Ishii, Kanji
Jeremy, David J.
Jones, Stephen R.H.
Katoh, Kozaburo
Kawamura, Terumasa
Kazusa, Yasuyuki
Killick, John Roper

Kobayashi, Kesaji
Kollmer-von Oheimb-Loup, Gert
Kristensen, Peer Hull
Kuwahara, Tetsuya
Lazonick, William
Leménorel, Alain
Lyons, John S.
Matis, Herbert W.
Matsuda, Tomoo
Matsumoto, Takanori
McCullough, Alan B.
Mishima, Yasuo
Miyamoto, Matao
Nishimura, Takao
Ohno, Akira
Ollerenshaw, Philip G.
Otruba, Gustav
Petersen, Peter B.
Phillips, William H.
Rauck, Michael
Reulecke, Jürgen
Rose, Mary B.
Sachse, Wieland
Sakudo, Jun
Sanchez Suarez, Alejandro
Sasaki, Satoshi
Schönert-Röhlk, Frauke
Schybergson, Per
Scranton, Philip B,
Shimono, Katsumi
Singleton, John
Smith, John Kenly
Sudrià, Carles
Sugiyama, Shinya
Suyenaga, Kunitoshi
Suzuki, Tsuneo
Taniguchi, Akitake
Tedesco, Paul H.
Teuteberg, Hans Jürgen
Toensberg, Jeppe E.
Tomlinson, Jim
Tsuji, Setsuo
Uchida, Hoshimi
Ulicny, Ferdinand
Van Der Wee, Herman
Vleesenbeek, H.H.
Walter, Rolf

Watanabe, Hisashi
Watanabe, Kishichi
Weil, François
Whatley, Christopher A.
Wilson, R.G.
Yakura, Shintaro
Yamazaki, Hiroaki
Yanagisawa, Osamu
Yui, Tsunehiko
Yuzawa, Takeshi
Zahedieh, Nuala B.

TIMBER, FURNITURE ETC.

Austin, Barbara
Deeks, John S.
Fabricius, Miroslav
Fitzgerald, Robert
Hapák, Pavel
Hodne, Fritz
Jackson, Kenneth E.
Kristensen, Peer Hull
Kuisma, Markku
Lange, Even
McRoberts, Mary L.
Michelsen, Karl-Erik
Myllyntaus, Timo
Roche, Michael
Rugman, Alan M.
Schybergson, Per
Scranton, Philip B.
Sejersted, Francis
Soltow, James H.
Taniguchi, Akitake
Virtanen, Sakari
Watson, Nigel
Yanagisawa, Osamu

TRADE

Bano, Sayeeda S.
Bud-Frierman, Lisa
Downs, Jacques M.
Wray, William D.

Thompson, Gregory L.
Thowsen, Atle
Traves, Tom
Tull, Malcolm
Ulicny, Ferdinand
Usselman, Steven W.
Valdaliso, Jesús M.
Van Driel, Hugo
Veenendaal, Augustus J. Jr.
Vietor, Richard H.K.
Ville, Simon P.
Vozár, Jozef
Vrooman, David M.
Walsh, Margaret
Walter, Rolf
Watanabe, Hisashi
Watanabe, Kishichi
Watson, Nigel
Weber, Wolfhard
White, Christine A.
Wray, William D.
Yamada, Tetsuo
Yamaguchi, Fujio
Yates, JoAnne
Yuzawa, Takeshi

See also Shipbuilding and marine engineering; Vehicle construction

VEHICLE CONSTRUCTION

Alberty, Július
Amatori, Franco
Barker, T.C.
Bayerl, Günter J.
Bigazzi, Duccio
Booth, Alan
Bowden, Sue
Chandler, Alfred D. Jr.
Davis, Donald F.
Demizu, Tsutomu
Donnelly, Tom
Fabricius, Miroslav
Flik, Reiner
Foreman-Peck, James S.
French, Michael J.
Furlong, Patrick J.
Harada, Seiji
Hazama, Hiroshi
Helper, Susan
Ikoma, Michihiro
Inagaki, Yoshinari
Kipping, Matthias
Kohtoh, Isuke
Koyama, Hiroyuki
Lewchuk, Wayne A.
Lewis, David L.
Martin-Aceña, Pablo

Mason, Mark
Matis, Herbert W.
McKinlay, Alan
Murkison, Eugene C.
Nelson, Daniel
O'Brien, Anthony Patrick
Oita, Akira
Okayama, Reiko
Onozuka, Tomoji
Pauer, Erich
Rauck, Michael
Sapelli, Giulio
Sasaki, Satoshi
Sawai, Minoru
Schvarzer, Jorge
Shimokawa, Koichi
Smitka, Michael J.
Spender, J.-C.
Takahashi, Yasutaka
Taniguchi, Akitake
Teuteberg, Hans Jürgen
Tolliday, Steven W.
Traves, Tom
Udagawa, Masaru
Wada, Kazuo
Watanabe, Kishichi
Weber, Wolfhard
White, Christine A.
Yuzawa, Takeshi

See also Transport and Communication

FIELDS OF EXPERTISE

Business Dimensions

Yanagisawa, Osamu
Yasumuro, Kenichi
Yonekura, Seiichiro
Yoshida, Michael H.
Yui, Tsunehiko
Yuzawa, Takeshi
Zahedieh, Nuala B.

**FAMILY BUSINESS
(FIRMS)**

Klassen, Henry C.
Rose, Mary B.
Sachse, Wieland
Watson, Nigel

See also Small business
matters

FINANCIAL FUNCTION

Ackrill, Margaret
Asajima, Shoichi
Banzawa, Ayumu
Barker, T.C.
Baskerville, Peter A.
Beaud, Claude
Boje, Per
Bonin, Hubert
Broeke, W. van den
Butel, Paul
Campbell-Kelly, Martin
Carlos, Ann M.
Chiba, Junichi
Cizakca, Murat
Collins, Michael
De Vries, Joh.
Doyle, William M.
Edwards, John
 Richard
Eigner, Peter
Fabricius, Miroslav
Flesher, Dale L.
Foreman-Peck, James
 S.
Fujimura, Daijiro
Fujita, Nobuhisa

Goodchild, John
Hájek, Jan
Hannah, Leslie
Hansen, Per H.
Harbaugh, Larry E.
Hernandez-Esteve,
 Esteban
Hildebrandt, Reinhard
Iida, Takashi
Ikoma, Michihiro
Irsigler, Franz
Ishii, Kanji
Jobert, Phillippe
Jonker, Joost P.B.
Kaczynska, Elzbieta
Kaku, Sachio
Katoh, Kozaburo
Katzenellenbogen, Simon
 E.
Kawamura, Terumasa
Kawanami, Yoichi
Kazusa, Yasuyuki
Kemmerer, Donald L.
Kikkawa, Takeo
Kiuchi, Kaichi
Klassen, Henry C.
Kobayashi, Tadashi
Kollmer-von Oheimb-
 Loup, Gert
Kolodziejczyk, Ryszard
 Antoni
Kudo, Akira
Lacina, Vlastislav
Levenstein, Margaret C.
Matis, Herbert W.
Matthiessen, Poul C.
McDermott, Kathleen
Mierzejewski, Alfred C.
Milkereit, Gertrud
Mori, Tetsuhiko
Moss, Michael Stanley
Mumford, Michael J.
Munn, Charles W.
Neal, Larry D.
Newby, Sonja
Nishikawa, Junko
Nishikawa, Noboru
Noort, Jan van den
Ollerenshaw, Philip G.
Papathanassopoulos,
 Konstantinos

Perkins, Edwin J.
Plessis, Alain
Pollins, Harold
Resch, Andreas
Saito, Tomoaki
Sakamoto, Takuji
Saunders Jr., Richard
Sawai, Minoru
Schybergson, Per
Stiefel, Dieter
Sudrià, Carles
Sugiyama, Shinya
Suzuki, Toshio
Suzuki, Yoshitaka
Tanaka, Toshihiro
Tatsuki, Mariko
Teuteberg, Hans Jürgen
Thowsen, Atle
Tilly, Richard
Titos-Martinez, Manuel
Toninelli, PierAngelo
Ueda, Kinji
Valdaliso, Jesús M.
Vallieres, Marc
Veenendaal, Augustus
 J. Jr.
Wale, Judith M.
Walter, Rolf
Watson, Katherine
Westall, Oliver M.
White, Eugene N.
Wilson, John F.
Yamaguchi, Fujio
Yoshida, Michael H.
Yuzawa, Takeshi

LABOUR

See Personnel manage-
ment

**MANAGEMENT
BOARDROOM ISSUES**

Ackrill, Margaret
Barker, T.C.
Buchan, P. Bruce

Martuliak, Pavol
Matis, Herbert W.
Melling, Joseph
Michelsen, Karl-Erik
Nakagawa, Seishi
Nishikawa, Hiroshi
Nonaka, Izumi
Noort, Jan van den
Onozuka, Tomoji
Papathanassopoulos,
 Konstantinos
Petersen, Peter B.
Resch, Andreas
Saalfeld, Diedrich
Sakamoto, Takuji
Sasaki, Satoshi
Sawai, Minoru
Scranton, Philip B,
Shimokawa, Koichi
Shioji, Hiromi
Smith, Merritt Roe
Smitka, Michael J.
Stiefel, Dieter
Sugiyama, Shinya
Sullivan, Timothy E.
Sunaga, Kinzaburo
Suzuki, Yoshitaka
Takahashi, Yasutaka
Teuteberg, Hans Jürgen
Traves, Tom
Wada, Kazuo
Watanabe, Kishichi
Weber, Wolfhard
Wessel, Horst A.
Wren, Daniel A.
Yamaguchi, Fujio
Yunoki, Manabu
Yuzawa, Takeshi
Yonekura, Seiichiro

**RELATIONS BETWEEN
BANKS AND INDUSTRY**

Nishimura, Shizuya

**RELATIONS BETWEEN
BUSINESS AND
LABOUR**

Deeks, John S.
Kraft, James P.
Lewchuk, Wayne A.
Lutz, John S.
Martin, John E.

BUSINESS AND STATE

Ackrill, Margaret
Adelmann, Gerhard
Amdam, Rolv Petter
Andersen, Håkon With
Arana, Ignacio
Armstrong, Christopher
Austin, Barbara
Banzawa, Ayumu
Barsness, Richard W.
Bartl, Július
Baskerville, Peter A.
Baughman, James L.
Beaud, Claude
Beltran, Alain
Booth, Alan
Bothwell, Robert
Bud-Frierman, Lisa
Bugos, Glenn E.
Bugra, Ayse
Burk, Kathleen
Bussière, Eric
Butterworth, Susan
Cain, Louis P.
Carreras, Charles
Chatov, Robert
Chiba, Junichi
Chick, Martin J.
Childs, William R.
Clay, Christopher
Crompton, G.W.
Davis, Donald F.
de Goey, F.M.M.
De Wit, Dirk
Deeks, John S.
Dritsas, Margarita
Dunlavy, Colleen A.
Dupree, Marguerite
 W.

Eakin, Marshall C.
Edgerton, D.E.H.
Edmondson, Michael
Englander, Ernest J.
Eriksen, August Wiemann
Espeli, Harald
Feldman, Gerald D.
Fleming, Keith R.
Foreman-Peck, James S.
Fridlund, Mats
Fujita, Nobuhisa
Galambos, Louis
Garside, W.R.
Giebelhaus, August W.
Gomez-Mendoza,
 Antonio
Gordon, Nancy M.
Gourvish, T.R.
Griset, Pascal
Haeberle, Eckehard
Hall, Roger D.
Hannah, Leslie
Hansen, Per H.
Harada, Seiji
Hardach, Karl W.
Hart, Tom
Hashimoto, Juro
Hausman, William J.
Hawke, G. R.
Hawley, Ellis W.
Helguera Quijada, Juan
Henning, Hansjoachim
Hertner, Peter
Hodne, Fritz
Hogesteeger, Gerardus
Howell, Paul M.
Ikeda, Noritaka
Ishii, Kanji
Jackson, Kenneth E.
Jacoby, Sanford M.
Jaeger, Hans
Jancík, Drahomír
Jimenez, Juan Carlos
Jindra, Zdenek
Johannessen, Finn
 Erhard
Johnman, Lewis
Jones, Charles A.
Just, Flemming
Karonen, Petri Kalevi
Kerr, K. Austin

Maggia, Giovanni
Martin, Manuel
Matis, Herbert W.
Mayer, Daniel
McCullough, Alan B.
Merger, Michèle
Michelsen, Karl-Erik
Millard, Andre
Misa, Thomas J.
Morikawa, Hidemasa
Myers, Michael D.

Myllyntaus, Timo
Nasuno, Kimito
Neiva, Elizabeth MacIver
Nelson, Daniel
Newell, Dianne
Nishikawa, Hiroshi
Noort, Jan van den
Norberg, Arthur L.
O'Connor, Richard
Ohno, Akira
Oita, Akira
Okayama, Reiko
Okochi, Akio
Olien, Diana Davids
Olien, Roger M.
Onozuka, Tomoji
Orsenigo, Luigi
Palme, Rudolf
Papathanassopoulos,
 Konstantinos
Pátek, Jaroslav
Pauer, Erich
Pavese, Claudio

Payne, Peter L.
Phillips, William H.
Pierenkemper, Toni
Rauck, Michael
Regehr, Theodore D.
Reinert, Erik S.
Resch, Andreas
Roberts, William I.
Rose, Mark H.
Sakamoto, Takuji
Sakudo, Jun
Sanchez Suarez, Alejandro
Sapelli, Giulio
Sasaki, Satoshi
Saunders Jr., Richard
Savage, Deborah A.
Sawai, Minoru
Scheiber, Harry N.
Schmitz, Christopher J.
Scranton, Philip B,
Shiman, Daniel R.
Shimono, Katsumi
Singleton, John
Smith, George David
Smith, John Kenly
Smith, Merritt Roe
Spender, J.-C.
Spitzer, Paul G.
Sturchio, Jeffrey L.
Sugiyama, Shinya
Sunaga, Kinsaburo
Suzuki, Tsuneo
Taniguchi, Akitake

Thompson, Gregory L.
Thomson, Ross
Topp, Niels-Henrik
Tull, Malcolm
Tweedale, Geoffrey
Uchida, Hoshimi
Usselman, Steven W.
Vozár, Jozef
Wada, Kazuo
Watanabe, Hisashi
Watanabe, Kishichi
Weber, Wolfhard
Wermiel, Sara E.
White, Christine A.
Williot, Jean-Pierre
Wilson, John F.
Wilson, R.G.
Witthöft, Harald
Woronoff, Denis
Yanagisawa, Osamu
Yates, JoAnne
Yonekura, Seiichiro
Yunoki, Manabu
Yuzawa, Takeshi
Zembala, Dennis M.

TRADE ASSOCIATIONS

Scranton, Philip B.
Tedesco, Paul H.

FIELDS OF EXPERTISE

Scope

GLOBAL

Bamberg, James H.
Bano, Sayeeda S.
Beaud, Claude
Burt, Roger
Cameron, Rondo
Cizakca, Murat
Coopersmith, Jonathan C.
Cox, Howard
Darroch, James L.
Demizu, Tsutomu
Dyer, Davis
Fabricius, Miroslav
Fitzgerald, Robert
Gilpin, John F.
Girvan, Norman Paul
Hannah, Leslie
Hastrup, Knud Bjarne
Helper, Susan
Hertner, Peter
Hiramoto, Atsushi
Inagaki, Yoshinari
Itoh, Takashi
Jones, Charles A.
Kajimoto, Motonobu
Katzenellenbogen, Simon E.
Kawabe, Nobuo
Kobayashi, Tadashi
Koyama, Hiroyuki
Le Heron, Richard B.
Lindgren, Håkan
MacPherson, Ian
Maggia, Giovanni
Mathis, Franz
Matsumoto, Takanori
Mayer, Daniel
McKinlay, Alan
Myers, Michael D.
Orsenigo, Luigi
Papathanassopoulos, Konstantinos
Reinert, Erik S.
Rosenbloom, Richard S.
Rugman, Alan M.
Saito, Tomoaki
Sapelli, Giulio
Schmitz, Christopher J.
Shimokawa, Koichi

Singleton, John
Smith, George David
Stiefel, Dieter
Takahashi, Yasutaka
Tilly, Richard
Tolliday, Steven W.
Tsunoyama, Sakae
Walter, Rolf
Westall, Oliver M.
Wilkins, Mira
Wray, William D.
Wren, Daniel A.
Yasumuro, Kenichi
Yonekura, Seiichiro
Yoshihara, Hideki
Yuzawa, Takeshi

INTERNATIONAL

Aaronson, Susan Ariel
Abé, Etsuo
Adelmann, Gerhard
Ahvenainen, Jorma
Amdam, Rolv Petter
Andersen, Håkon With
Applebaum, Herbert A.
Austin, Barbara
Bano, Sayeeda S.
Bansal, Pradeep Kumar
Barbezat, Daniel
Bartl, Július
Baskerville, Peter A.
Beaud, Claude
Beltran, Alain
Bennett, Neville
Blanken, Ivo J.
Bläsing, Josvhim F.E.
Bonin, Hubert
Bonke, Jens
Bostock, Frances G.
Bothwell, Robert
Braun, Hans-Joachim
Broeke, W. van den
Buchan, P. Bruce
Bud-Frierman, Lisa
Bugos, Glenn E.
Bugra, Ayse
Burk, Kathleen
Burt, Roger

Buss, Dietrich G.
Bussière, Eric
Butel, Paul
Butterworth, Susan
Campbell-Kelly, Martin
Capie, Forrest H.
Carlos, Ann M.
Carreras, Charles
Casado Alonso, Hilario
Cassis, Youssef
Casson, Mark
Chandler, Alfred D. Jr.
Channon, Geoffrey
Chassagne, Serge
Chiba, Junichi
Christiansen, W. Kenneth S.
Cizakca, Murat
Clay, Christopher
Coopey, Richard
Corley, T.A.B.
Cox, Howard
Crouzet, François M.J.
Daito, Eisuke
Davies, Peter N.
Davis, Donald F.
De Vries, Joh.
Demizu, Tsutomu
Dertilis, George B.
Dicke, Thomas S.
Doig, Jameson W.
Donnelly, Tom
Downs, Jacques M.
Dritsas, Margarita
Dunlavy, Colleen A.
Dupree, Marguerite W.
Eakin, Marshall C.
Edmondson, Michael
Eigner, Peter
Engerman, Stanley L.
Eriksen, August Wiemann
Espeli, Harald
Fabricius, Miroslav
Falkus, Malcolm Edward
Farnie, D.A.
Feldenkirchen, Wilfried
Flesher, Dale L.
Flik, Reiner
Foreman-Peck, James S.
Fraile Balbin, Pedro
Fraser, Maryna

Riis, Thomas
Roberts, William I.
Roche, Michael
Rockoff, Hugh T.
Rose, Mary B.
Rothstein, Morton
Rubner, Heinrich
Ryant, Carl G.
Saalfeld, Diedrich
Sachse, Wieland
Saito, Tomoaki
Sakamoto, Takuji
Sakudo, Jun
Sapelli, Giulio
Sasaki, Satoshi
Schmitz, Christopher J.
Schönert-Röhlk, Frauke
Schröter, Harm G.
Seavoy, Ronald E.
Segreto, Luciano
Shiman, Daniel R.
Shimokawa, Koichi
Shimotani, Masahiro
Shinomiya, Toshiyuki
Shioji, Hiromi
Simmons III, F. Bruce
Singleton, John
Sklar, Martin J.
Slaven, Anthony
Slinn, Judy
Sluyterman, Keetie E.
Smith, George David
Smith, John Kenly
Smitka, Michael J.
Sobel, Robert
Statham, Pamela C.
Steiner, Jan
Stiefel, Dieter
Sturchio, Jeffrey L.
Sudrià, Carles
Sugisaki, Takamoto
Sugiyama, Shinya
Suzuki, Toshio
Suzuki, Tsuneo
Suzuki, Yoshitaka
Sylla, Richard
Tanaka, Toshihiro
Tatsuki, Mariko
Terachi, Takashi
Teuteberg, Hans Jürgen
Thackray, Arnold

Thowsen, Atle
Tilly, Richard
Toninelli, PierAngelo
Topp, Niels-Henrik
Trout, Andrew P.
Tsunoyama, Sakae
Tulchinsky, Gerald J.J.
Tweedale, Geoffrey
Uchida, Hoshimi
Udagawa, Masaru
Ulicny, Ferdinand
Veenendaal, Augustus J. Jr.
Vietor, Richard H.K.
von Stromer (Freiherr von Reichenbach), Wolfgang
Vozár, Jozef
Wada, Kazuo
Walter, Rolf
Watanabe, Hisashi
Watanabe, Kishichi
Weber, Wolfhard
Westall, Oliver M.
White, Christine A.
White, Eugene N.
Whitten, David O.
Witthöft, Harald
Wray, William D.
Yamamoto, Toru
Yamamura, Mutsuo
Yamazaki, Hiroaki
Yasumuro, Kenichi
Yasuoka, Shigeaki
Yonekura, Seiichiro
Yoneyama, Takau
Yui, Tsunehiko
Yuzawa, Takeshi
Zahedieh, Nuala B.

LOCAL

Amano, Masatoshi
Ambrosius, Gerold
Andersen, Håkon With
Armstrong, Fred H.
Atack, Jeremy
Barker, T.C.
Bartl, Július

Barzdevica, Margarita
Beaud, Claude
Bergeron, Louis
Boje, Per
Burchardt, Jørgen
Burt, Roger
Butel, Paul
Butterworth, Susan
Cain, Louis P.
Chevalier, Jean-Joseph
Childs, William R.
Christiansen, W. Kenneth S.
Corley, T.A.B.
Dupree, Marguerite W.
Eakin, Marshall C.
Fabricius, Miroslav
Fode, Henrik
Fohlen, Claude
Fujita, Yukitoshi
Goodchild, John
Hiramoto, Atsushi
Irsigler, Franz
Jakovleva, Marite
Jequier, François
Kawamura, Terumasa
Kawano, Aizaburo
Klassen, Henry C.
Kornblith, Gary J.
Kuwata, Masaru
Lamard, Pierre
Martin, Manuel
Matsumoto, Takanori
Mishima, Yasuo
Mitsugi, Yoshio
Mitsui, Takashige
Murkison, Eugene C.
Noort, Jan van den
Nuñez Romero-Balmas, Gregorio
Oikawa, Yoshinobu
Olien, Diana Davids
Olien, Roger M.
Ommer, Rosemary E.
Onozuka, Tomoji
Ostrolucká, Milena
Palme, Rudolf
Petrás, Milan
Pollins, Harold
Poznanska, Barbara
Roche, Michael

Pollins, Harold
Pope, Daniel
Renz, Regina
Resch, Andreas
Reulecke, Jürgen
Riis, Thomas
Roche, Michael
Rothstein, Morton
Ryant, Carl G.
Sachse, Wieland
Sakamoto, Takuji
Sampson, Cezley
Sanchez Suarez, Alejandro
Sawai, Minoru
Schönert-Röhlk, Frauke
Schuler, Peter-Johannes
Schulz, Günther
Shimono, Katsumi
Sinclair, F.R.J.
Singleton, John
Slaven, Anthony
Smith, Victor C.
Soltow, James H.
Spitzer, Paul G.
Statham, Pamela C.
Stone, R.C.J.
Sudrià, Carles
Sugimoto, Kimihiko
Sugiyama, Shinya
Sullivan, Timothy E.
Sunaga, Kinzaburo
Sutet, Marcel
Svorc, Peter
Takechi, Kyozo
Tedesco, Paul H.
Teuteberg, Hans Jürgen
Thomes, Paul
Thompson, Gregory L.
Titos-Martinez, Manuel
Todd, Edmund N.
Toensberg, Jeppe E.
Tokushima, Tatsuro
Torres Villanueva, Eugenio
Tull, Malcolm
Turton, Alison
Ueda, Kinji
Uemura, Motokaku
Ulicny, Ferdinand
Umeno, Naotoshi
Valdaliso, Jesús M.
Vallieres, Marc

van Eyll, Klara
Verhoef, Grietjie
Virtanen, Sakari
Vleesenbeek, H.H.
Wada, Kazuo
Walsh, Margaret
Walter, Rolf
Watanabe, Hisashi
Watanabe, Kishichi
Weber, Wolfhard
Westall, Oliver M.
Whatley, Christopher A.
Wilson, John F.
Woronoff, Denis
Wysocki, Josef
Yamazaki, Ryuzo
Yanagisawa, Osamu
Yoshida, Michael H.
Yunoki, Manabu
Zilák, Ján

AFRICA

Bano, Sayeeda S.
Bostock, Frances G. (ex British Colonial)

ANDALUCIA

Nunez, Gregorio

ARGENTINA

Katz, Jorge M.
Kosacoff, Bernardo P.
Schvarzer, Jorge

ASIA

Shimokawa, Koichi

ATLANTIC WORLD

McCusker, John J.

AUSTRALIA

Statham, Pamela C.
Tull, Malcolm

AUSTRIA

Bartl, Július
Eigner, Peter
Hájek, Jan
Meixner, Wolfgang
Palme, Rudolf
Rauck, Michael
Stiefel, Dieter

BELGIUM

Jenkins, Reese V.
Soltow, James H.

BRAZIL

Eakin, Marshall C.

BRITISH EMPIRE

Acheson, T.W.

CANADA

Acheson, T.W.
Armstrong, Christopher
Bano, Sayeeda S.
Burley, David
Carlos, Ann M.

Merger, Michèle

JAPAN

Abé, Etsuo
Daito, Eisuke
Davies, Peter N.
Jacoby, Sanford M.
Jeremy, David J.
Nakagawa, Keiichiro
Nishikawa, Noboru
Onozuka, Tomoji
Pauer, Erich
Petersen, Peter B.
Rauck, Michael
Shimokawa, Koichi
Shioji, Hiromi
Smitka, Michael J.
Sugiyama, Shinya
Tsunoyama, Sakae
Tull, Malcolm
Uchida, Hoshimi
Watanabe, Kishichi

LATIN AMERICA

Eakin, Marshall C.
Katz, Jorge M.
Girvan, Norman Paul

LATVIA

Shumilo, Erica
Zalite, Elga

NETHERLANDS

Butel, Paul
Irsigler, Franz
Veenendaal, Augustus
 J. Jr.

NEWFOUNDLAND

Sweeny, Robert C.H.

NEW ZEALAND

Bano, Sayeeda S.
Bennett, Neville
Deeks, John S.
Jackson, Kenneth E.
Jones, Stephen R.H.
Myers, Michael D.
Roche, Michael
Sorrenson, M.P.K.

NORWAY

Amdam, Rolv Petter
Andersen, Håkon With
Lange, Even

POLAND

Markowski, Mieczyslaw
 B.

QUEBEC

Vallieres, Marc

RUSSIA

Beaud, Claude (before
 1914)
White, Christine A.

SCANDINAVIA

Hyldtoft, Ole

Lange, Even

SLOVAKIA

Bartl, Julius
Prucha, Vaclav
Vozar, Jozef

SOUTH AFRICA

Fraser, Maryna
Katzenellenbogen, Simon
 E.

SPAIN

Carreras, Albert
Comin Comin, Francisco
Hernandez-Esteve, Esteban
Martin, Manuel
Nuñez Romero-Balmas,
 Gregorio
Sudrià, Carles

SWEDEN

Fridlund, Mats
Onozuka, Tomoji
Ullenhag, Kersti Margareta
Weinberger, Hans

SWITZERLAND

Cassis, Youssef
Jequier, François
Rauck, Michael

FIELDS OF EXPERTISE

Period

ANCIENT

Applebaum, Herbert A.
Goodchild, John
Witthöft, Harald

MEDIEVAL

Alberty, Július
Applebaum, Herbert A.
Bartl, Július
Barty-King, Hugh
Burt, Roger
Cizakca, Murat
Goodchild, John
Graham, Margaret
  B.W.
Irsigler, Franz
Palme, Rudolf
Riis, Thomas
Schuler, Peter-Johannes
Ulicny, Ferdinand
Van Der Wee, Herman
von Stromer (Freiherr
  von Reichenbach),
  Wolfgang
Walter, Rolf
Weber, Wolfhard
Witthöft, Harald
Yunoki, Manabu

EARLY MODERN

Achilles, Walter
Alberty, Július
Amano, Masatoshi
Applebaum, Herbert A.
Badurík, Jozef
Barker, T.C.
Barty-King, Hugh
Barzdevica, Margarita
Bayerl, Günter J.
Burt, Roger
Butel, Paul
Carlos, Ann M.
Casado Alonso, Hilario
Cizakca, Murat

Clay, Christopher
Coleman, D.C.
Fujita, Yukitoshi
Glete, Jan
Goodchild, John
Hernandez-Esteve, Esteban
Hildebrandt, Reinhard
Irsigler, Franz
Jakovleva, Marite
Jones, Stephen R.H.
Kaufhold, Karl Heinrich
Kawamura, Terumasa
Kjærgaard, Thorkild
Kollmer-von Oheimb-
  Loup, Gert
Kuwata, Masaru
McCusker, John J.
Miyamoto, Matao
Mori, Yasuhiro
Nishikawa, Noboru
Nishimura, Takao
Ostrolucká, Milena
Otruba, Gustav
Palme, Rudolf
Riis, Thomas
Saalfeld, Diedrich
Sachse, Wieland
Sandgruber, Roman
Suyenaga, Kunitoshi
Tokushima, Tatsuro
Trout, Andrew P.
Ulicny, Ferdinand
Van Der Wee, Herman
von Stromer (Freiherr
  von Reichenbach),
  Wolfgang
Vozár, Jozef
Walter, Rolf
Watanabe, Kishichi
Weber, Wolfhard
Witthöft, Harald
Wray, William D.
Yoshida, Michael H.
Yunoki, Manabu
Zacharias, Lawrence S.
Zahedieh, Nuala B.

EIGHTEENTH
CENTURY

Achilles, Walter
Adelmann, Gerhard
Amano, Masatoshi
Amdam, Rolv Petter
Applebaum, Herbert A.
Barker, T.C.
Barty-King, Hugh
Barzdevica, Margarita
Bayerl, Günter J.
Bender, Henning
Burt, Roger
Butel, Paul
Carlos, Ann M.
Chapman, Stanley David
Chassagne, Serge
Chevalier, Jean-Joseph
Cizakca, Murat
Coleman, D.C.
Concato, Francis
Crouzet, François M.J.
De Vries, Joh.
Engerman, Stanley L.
Flik, Reiner
Fode, Henrik
Goebel, Erik
Goodchild, John
Helguera Quijada, Juan
Henning, Hansjoachim
Hodne, Fritz
Hoffman, Kai J.
Honeyman, Katrina
Hrabovec, Ivan
Irsigler, Franz
Jakovleva, Marite
Johannessen, Finn Erhard
Johansen, Hans Christian
Johnson, David
Jones, Stephen R.H.
Jonker, Joost P.B.
Kawamura, Terumasa
Kemmerer, Donald L.
Killick, John Roper
Kjærgaard, Thorkild
Kobayashi, Tadashi
Kobayashi, Yoshiaki
Kollmer-von Oheimb-
  Loup, Gert
Kuisma, Markku

Falkus, Malcolm Edward
Farnie, D.A.
Federico, Giovanni
Feldenkirchen, Wilfried
Fitzgerald, Robert
Flik, Reiner
Fode, Henrik
Fohlen, Claude
Foreman-Peck, James S.
Franaszek, Piotr
Fujimura, Daijiro
Galambos, Louis
Gerriets, Marilyn
Gilpin, John F.
Godley, Andrew C.
Gomez-Mendoza, Antonio
Goodchild, John
Goto, Shin
Greenhill, Robert G.
Griset, Pascal
Gueslin, André
Haeberle, Eckehard
Hagimoto, Shinichro
Hájek, Jan
Hall, Roger D.
Hansen, Per H.
Hapák, Pavel
Harasawa, Yoshitaro
Harbaugh, Larry E.
Hardach, Gerd
Hardach, Karl W.
Hastrup, Knud Bjarne
Hau, Michel
Hawke, G. R.
Heffer, Jean
Henning, Hansjoachim
Hertner, Peter
Hodne, Fritz
Hofsommer, Don L.
Hogesteeger, Gerardus
Hoke, Donald R.
Holtfrerich, Carl-Ludwig
Honeyman, Katrina
Horrocks, Sally M.
Howell, Paul M.
Hrabovec, Ivan
Huberman, Michael M.
Hyldtoft, Ole
Ichijo, Junya

Ikeda, Noritaka
Imakubo, Sachio
Ingham, John N.
Ioku, Shigehiko
Ishii, Kanji
Itoh, Takashi
Jackson, Kenneth E.
Jacoby, Sanford M.
Jakubec, Ivan
Jenkins, Reese V.
Jensen, Jakob B.
Jequier, François
Jindra, Zdenek
Jobert, Phillippe
Johannessen, Finn Erhard
John, Richard R.
Johnson, David
Jones, Charles A.
Jones, Edgar
Jones, Stephen R.H.
Jones, Stuart
Jonker, Joost P.B.
Kaczynska, Elzbieta
Kaelble, Hartmut
Kajimoto, Motonobu
Kaku, Sachio
Karsten, Luchien
Katoh, Kozaburo
Katzenellenbogen, Simon E.
Kawamura, Terumasa
Kazusa, Yasuyuki
Keenan, Michael G.
Kelly, Eileen P.
Kemmerer, Donald L.
Kennedy, Charles J.
Khan, Zorina B.
Kiesewetter, Hubert
Killick, John Roper
King, Frank H.H.
Kirby, Maurice W.
Kitabayashi, Masashi
Kjærgaard, Thorkild
Klassen, Henry C.
Klein, Daniel
Klein, Maury
Kobayashi, Hiroshi
Kobayashi, Kesaji
Kobayashi, Tadashi
Kobayashi, Yoshiaki

Kocka, Jürgen
Kollmer-von Oheimb-Loup, Gert
Kolodziejczyk, Ryszard Antoni
Kornblith, Gary J.
Kristensen, Peer Hull
Kryger Larsen, Hans
Kunz, Andreas
Kuwahara, Tetsuya
Lamard, Pierre
Landry, John
Latham, A.J.H.
Leménorel, Alain
Levenstein, Margaret C.
Lewchuk, Wayne A.
Lindgren, Håkan
Locke, Robert R.
Lorenz, Edward H.
Lubar, Steven
Lutz, John S.
Lyons, John S.
MacMurray, Robert R.
MacPherson, Ian
Maitra, Priyatosh
Marriner, Sheila
Martin, John E.
Martin, Manuel
Mathias, Peter
Mathis, Franz
Matis, Herbert W.
Matsuda, Tomoo
Matsumoto, Takanori
Mayer, Daniel
McCalla, Douglas
McCullough, Alan B.
McKay, John P.
McLean, Gavin
Meixner, Wolfgang
Melling, Joseph
Merger, Michèle
Michelsen, Karl-Erik
Millard, Andre
Millward, Robert
Misa, Thomas J.
Mishima, Yasuo
Mitsui, Takashige
Miyamoto, Matao
Møller, Anders Monrad
Mori, Tetsuhiko

Wijtuliet, Coz A.M.
Wilkins, Mira
Williot, Jean-Pierre
Wilson, John F.
Wilson, R.G.
Winkelman, Hélène J.M.
Witthöft, Harald
Woronoff, Denis
Wray, William D.
Wren, Daniel A.
Wrigley, Chris J.
Wysocki, Josef
Yamada, Tetsuo
Yamaguchi, Fujio
Yamamoto, Toru
Yamazaki, Ryuzo
Yanagisawa, Osamu
Yasumuro, Kenichi
Yasuoka, Shigeaki
Yates, JoAnne
Yoneyama, Takau
Yoshida, Michael H.
Young, James Harvey
Yunoki, Manabu
Yuzawa, Takeshi
Zacharias, Lawrence S.
Zamagni, Vera
Zembala, Dennis M.
Zilák, Ján
Zuckerman, Mary Ellen

TWENTIETH CENTURY AS A WHOLE

Abé, Etsuo
Ackrill, Margaret
Adelmann, Gerhard
Ahvenainen, Jorma
Aldcroft, Derek H.
Amatori, Franco
Ambrosius, Gerold
Amdam, Rolv Petter
Andersen, Håkon With
Applebaum, Herbert A.
Armstrong, Fred H.
Armstrong, John
Asajima, Shoichi
Austin, Barbara

Bamberg, James H.
Bano, Sayeeda S.
Barbezat, Daniel
Barker, T.C.
Barsness, Richard W.
Barty-King, Hugh
Baughman, James L.
Bayerl, Günter J.
Beaud, Claude
Beck, William O.
Beltran, Alain
Bender, Henning
Bennett, Neville
Bigazzi, Duccio
Bläsing, Josvhim F.E.
Boje, Per
Bonin, Hubert
Booth, Alan
Boyns, Trevor
Braun, Hans-Joachim
Brown, Jonathan
Brown, Kenneth D.
Bryant, Keith L. Jr.
Bud-Frierman, Lisa
Bugos, Glenn E.
Bugra, Ayse
Burk, Kathleen
Burt, Roger
Butterworth, Susan
Cain, Louis P.
Campbell-Kelly, Martin
Capie, Forrest H.
Carreras, Albert
Carreras, Charles
Cassis, Youssef
Casson, Mark
Chandler, Alfred D. Jr.
Channon, Geoffrey
Chapman, Stanley David
Cheape, Charles W.
Chevalier, Jean-Joseph
Chiba, Junichi
Childs, William R.
Churella, Albert John
Cizakca, Murat
Coleman, D.C.
Collins, Michael
Comin Comin, Francisco
Coopersmith, Jonathan C.
Coopey, Richard

Corley, T.A.B.
Cox, Howard
Davies, Peter N.
Davis, Donald F.
de Goey, F.M.M.
De Vries, Joh.
Demizu, Tsutomu
Dertilis, George B.
Dicke, Thomas S.
Dintenfass, Michael
Doig, Jameson W.
Dritsas, Margarita
Dupree, Marguerite W.
Dyer, Davis
Eakin, Marshall C.
Edgerton, D.E.H.
Edwards, Pamela C.
Espeli, Harald
Fabricius, Miroslav
Falkus, Malcolm Edward
Faltus, Jozef
Farnie, D.A.
Federico, Giovanni
Feldenkirchen, Wilfried
Fink, Jørgen
Fitzgerald, Robert
Fleming, Keith R.
Flesher, Dale L.
Flik, Reiner
Foreman-Peck, James S.
Fraile Balbin, Pedro
Fraser, Maryna
French, Michael J.
Fridlund, Mats
Friedricks, William B.
Fujita, Nobuhisa
Furlong, Patrick J.
Galambos, Louis
Gallo, Giampaolo
Garcia-Ruiz, José-Luis
Giannetti, Renato
Giebelhaus, August W.
Girvan, Norman Paul
Godley, Andrew C.
Goodall, Francis
Gordon, Nancy M.
Gore, Ilga
Goto, Shin
Gourvish, T.R.
Graham, Margaret B.W.

Otruba, Gustav
Ozawa, Katsuyuki
Papathanassopoulos,
 Konstantinos
Pátek, Jaroslav
Pauer, Erich
Pavese, Claudio
Payne, Peter L.
Pedersen, Erik Helmer
Perkins, Edwin J.
Petrás, Milan
Pettersen, Lauritz
Pix, Manfred
Plessis, Alain
Pohl, Hans
Pohl, Manfred
Pollins, Harold
Prúcha, Václav
Rauck, Michael
Reagan, Patrick D.
Reinert, Erik S.
Resch, Andreas
Roche, Michael
Rockoff, Hugh T.
Rose, Mark H.
Rose, Mary B.
Rubner, Heinrich
Ryant, Carl G.
Sachse, Wieland
Saito, Takenori
Sakamoto, Takuji
Sandgruber, Roman
Sapelli, Giulio
Sasaki, Satoshi
Savage, Deborah A.
Schmitz, Christopher J.
Schröter, Harm G.
Schulz, Günther
Schvarzer, Jorge
Schybergson, Per
Scott, Roy V.
Scranton, Philip B,
Seely, Bruce E.
Segreto, Luciano
Sejersted, Francis
Shimokawa, Koichi
Shimono, Katsumi
Shimotani, Masahiro
Shinomiya, Toshiyuki
Sicilia, David B.
Singleton, John

Sklar, Martin J.
Slaven, Anthony
Slinn, Judy
Sluyterman, Keetie E.
Smith, George David
Smith, John Kenly
Smith, Victor C.
Sobel, Robert
Soltow, James H.
Sorrenson, M.P.K.
Spender, J.-C.
Spitzer, Paul G.
Statham, Pamela C.
Stiefel, Dieter
Stone, R.C.J.
Sturchio, Jeffrey L.
Sudrià, Carles
Sunaga, Kinzaburo
Supple, Barry
Svorc, Peter
Takechi, Kyozo
Taniguchi, Akitake
Tatsuki, Mariko
Tedesco, Paul H.
Tedlow, Richard S.
Teuteberg, Hans Jürgen
Tilly, Richard
Titos-Martinez, Manuel
Toensberg, Jeppe E.
Tolliday, Steven W.
Toninelli, PierAngelo
Topp, Niels-Henrik
Torres Villanueva, Eugenio
Tortella, Gabriel
Tsuji, Setsuo
Tulchinsky, Gerald J.J.
Tull, Malcolm
Turton, Alison
Uchida, Hoshimi
Udagawa, Masaru
Ullenhag, Kersti Margareta
Umeno, Naotoshi
Usselman, Steven W.
Valdaliso, Jesús M.
Vallieres, Marc
van den Eerenbeemt,
 H.F.J.M.
Van Der Wee, Herman
van Eyll, Klara
Verhoef, Grietjie
Virtanen, Sakari

Vleesenbeek, H.H.
Wada, Kazuo
Waller, David S.
Walsh, Margaret
Watanabe, Hisashi
Watanabe, Kishichi
Watson, Nigel
Wessel, Horst A.
Westall, Oliver M.
White, Eugene N.
Wijtuliet, Coz A.M.
Wilkins, Mira
Williot, Jean-Pierre
Wilson, John F.
Winkelman, Hélène J.M.
Worthy, James C.
Wray, William D.
Wren, Daniel A.
Wrigley, Chris J.
Wysocki, Josef
Yakura, Shintaro
Yamamura, Mutsuo
Yanagisawa, Osamu
Yasumuro, Kenichi
Yates, JoAnne
Yonekura, Seiichiro
Young, James Harvey
Yui, Tsunehiko
Yuzawa, Takeshi
Zacharias, Lawrence S.
Zamagni, Vera
Zilák, Ján
Zuckerman, Mary Ellen

EARLY TWENTIETH
CENTURY

Abe, Takeshi
Applebaum, Herbert A.
Arana, Ignacio
Armstrong, Christopher
Banzawa, Ayumu
Barker, T.C.
Barty-King, Hugh
Baskerville, Peter A.
Bayerl, Günter J.
Bergeron, Louis
Blicksilver, Jack
Bolton, Alfred A.

Efmertová, Marcela
Eigner, Peter
Eriksen, August Wiemann
Faltus, Jozef
Feldenkirchen, Wilfried
Feldman, Gerald D.
Fujita, Nobuhisa
Fujita, Yukitoshi
Garside, W.R.
Giannetti, Renato
Gore, Ilga
Graham, Margaret B.W.
Hagimoto, Shinichro
Hara, Terushi
Harada, Seiji
Harbaugh, Larry E.
Hashimoto, Juro
Hawley, Ellis W.
Hertner, Peter
Iida, Takashi
Ishii, Kanji
Jancík, Drahomír
Johnman, Lewis
Jonker, Joost P.B.
Kajimoto, Motonobu
Katoh, Kozaburo
Kawanami, Yoichi
Kimura, Masato
Klassen, Henry C.
Klein, Maury
Kobayashi, Hiroshi
Koda, Ryoichi
Kolodziejczyk, Ryszard
 Antoni
Kozuki, Naoto
Landau, Zbigniew
Lindenlaub, Dieter
Martin-Aceña, Pablo
Martuliak, Pavol
Matsumoto, Takanori
McDowall, Duncan L.
McKinlay, Alan
Melling, Joseph
Mercer, Helen
Mierzejewski, Alfred C.
Mishima, Yasuo
Nelson, Daniel
Nishikawa, Junko
Nordvik, Helge W.
O'Brien, Anthony
 Patrick

Oikawa, Yoshinobu
Okayama, Reiko
Ozolina, Dzidra
Pantelakis, Nicos
Pátek, Jaroslav
Petersen, Peter B.
Poznanska, Barbara
Prúcha, Václav
Regehr, Theodore D.
Renz, Regina
Saito, Tomoaki
Sakudo, Jun
Saunders Jr., Richard
Sawai, Minoru
Shiba, Takao
Shioji, Hiromi
Shumilo, Erica
Sluyterman, Keetie E.
Smitka, Michael J.
Spender, J.-C.
Stromberg, Raymond
Sugisaki, Takamoto
Sugiyama, Shinya
Sunaga, Kinzaburo
Suzuki, Tsuneo
Takahashi, Yasutaka
Takechi, Kyozo
Tatsuki, Mariko
Thackray, Arnold
Thompson, Gregory L.
Thowsen, Atle
Traves, Tom
Tucker, Albert V.
Udagawa, Masaru
Ueda, Kinji
Vogt, Martin
Vrooman, David M.
Walter, Rolf
White, Christine A.
Yamaguchi, Fujio
Yamamura, Mutsuo
Yamazaki, Hiroaki
Yamazaki, Ryuzo
Yonekura, Seiichiro
Yoneyama, Takau
Zalite, Elga

MID-TWENTIETH
CENTURY, 1940–70

Aaronson, Susan Ariel
Abe, Takeshi
Ackrill, Margaret
Alberty, Július
Barty-King, Hugh
Berta, Giuseppe
Bostock, Frances G.
Bothwell, Robert
Bowden, Sue
Burchardt, Jørgen
Bussière, Eric
Capie, Forrest H.
Chick, Martin J.
Christiansen, W. Kenneth
 S.
Constant, Edward W. II
De Wit, Dirk
Demizu, Tsutomu
Donnelly, Tom
Dritsas, Margarita
Dupree, Marguerite W.
Efmertová, Marcela
Fujita, Nobuhisa
Garside, W.R.
Gomez-Mendoza, Antonio
Graham, Margaret B.W.
Hagimoto, Shinichro
Hansen, Povl A.
Hara, Terushi
Hashimoto, Juro
Hoffman, Kai J.
Johansen, Hans Christian
Johnman, Lewis
Karonen, Petri K.
Katoh, Kozaburo
Katz, Jorge M.
Kawanami, Yoichi
Kohno, Shozo
Koyama, Hiroyuki
Landau, Zbigniew
Martin-Aceña, Pablo
Matsumoto, Takanori
McDowall, Duncan L.
McKinlay, Alan
Melling, Joseph
Mercer, Helen
Neiva, Elizabeth MacIver
Nelson, Daniel

Nonaka, Izumi
Okayama, Reiko
Pantelakis, Nicos
Pátek, Jaroslav
Prúcha, Václav
Saito, Tomoaki
Saunders Jr., Richard
Sawai, Minoru
Seiichiro, Yonekura
Shioji, Hiromi
Smitka, Michael J.
Spender, J.-C.
Sugisaki, Takamoto
Suzuki, Tsuneo
Suzuki, Yoshitaka
Tatsuki, Mariko
Thackray, Arnold
Thompson, Gregory L.
Thowsen, Atle
Tomlinson, Jim
Tucker, Albert V.
Ueda, Kinji
Umeno, Naotoshi
Verhoef, Grietjie
Weinberger, Hans
Yamaguchi, Fujio
Yamazaki, Hiroaki

**LATE TWENTIETH
CENTURY,
1970–PRESENT**

Aaronson, Susan Ariel
Ackrill, Margaret
Bano, Sayeeda S.
Barty-King, Hugh

Beaud, Claude
Bonke, Jens
Bothwell, Robert
Buchan, P. Bruce
Chatov, Robert
Chick, Martin J.
Christiansen, W. Kenneth S.
Darroch, James L.
De Wit, Dirk
Deeks, John S.
Demizu, Tsutomu
Donnelly, Tom
Efmertová, Marcela
Englander, Ernest J.
Garside, W.R.
Gingras, André
Graham, Margaret B.W.
Hansen, Povl A.
Hashimoto, Juro
Helper, Susan
Hiramoto, Atsushi
Imakubo, Sachio
Johnson, G. Wesley
Karonen, Petri K.
Katz, Jorge M.
Kiuchi, Kaichi
Kohno, Shozo
Kosacoff, Bernardo P.
Koyama, Hiroyuki
Langlois, Richard N.
Le Heron, Richard B.
Mason, Mark

Matsumoto, Koji
Matsumoto, Takanori
Matthiessen, Poul C.
McDowall, Duncan L.
McKinlay, Alan
McQuaid, Kim
Mitsugi, Yoshio
Myers, Michael D.
Nasuno, Kimito
Neiva, Elizabeth MacIver
Newby, Sonja
Okayama, Reiko
Orsenigo, Luigi
Papalexandris, Nancy
Pinsdorf, Marion K.
Pope, Daniel
Prúcha, Václav
Rosenbloom, Richard S.
Rugman, Alan M.
Saito, Tomoaki
Saunders, Richard, Jr.
Shimokawa, Koichi
Shioji, Hiromi
Simmons III, F. Bruce
Smitka, Michael J.
Spender, J.-C.
Takahashi, Yasutaka
Tatsuki, Mariko
Thackray, Arnold
Umeno, Naotoshi
Van Driel, Hugo
Vance, Sandra S.
Verhoef, Grietjie
Vietor, Richard H.K.
Yamada, Makiko
Yamazaki, Hiroaki
Yasumuro, Kenichi
Yonekura, Seiichiro
Yoshihara, Hideki
Zan, Stefano

Teaching

EXECUTIVE

Graham, Margaret B.W.
Harbaugh, Larry E.
Melling, Joseph
Papalexandris, Nancy
Smith, George David
Spender, J.-C.

PERSONNEL

Virtanen, Sakari

POST GRADUATE

Abe, Takeshi
Ackrill, Margaret
Adelmann, Gerhard
Ahvenainen, Jorma
Amano, Masatoshi
Ambrosius, Gerold
Amdam, Rolv Petter
Andersen, Håkon With
Arana, Ignacio
Armstrong, Christopher
Armstrong, Fred H.
Armstrong, John
Badurík, Jozef
Bano, Sayeeda S.
Bansal, Pradeep Kumar
Barker, T.C.
Baskerville, Peter A.
Bateman, Fred
Baughman, James L.
Bayerl, Günter J
Beltran, Alain
Bergeron, Louis
Blicksilver, Jack
Boje, Per
Bolton, Alfred A.
Bonin, Hubert
Bonke, Jens
Boot, H.M.
Bothwell, Robert
Bowden, Sue
Boyce, Gordon
Brown, Jonathan

Bryant, Keith L. Jr.
Buchan, P. Bruce
Burk, Kathleen
Burt, Roger
Butel, Paul
Caban, Wieslaw
Cain, Louis P.
Capie, Forrest H.
Carlos, Ann M.
Carreras, Albert
Carter, Ian R.
Casado Alonso, Hilario
Cassis, Youssef
Chandler, Alfred D. Jr.
Channon, Geoffrey
Chapman, Stanley David
Chassagne, Serge
Chatov, Robert
Chiba, Junichi
Chick, Martin J.
Childs, William R.
Christiansen, W. Kenneth S.
Cizakca, Murat
Coleman, D.C.
Collins, Michael
Comin Comin, Francisco
Coopersmith, Jonathan C.
Coopey, Richard
Corley, T.A.B.
Cox, Howard
Crouzet, François M.J.
Daito, Eisuke
Darroch, James L.
Davies, Peter N.
Davis, Donald F.
de Goey, F.M.M.
De Vries, Joh.
Deeks, John S.
den Otter, A.A.
Dertilis, George B.
Dintenfass, Michael
Donnelly, Tom
Dritsas, Margarita
Dunlavy, Colleen A.
Dupree, Marguerite W.
Eakin, Marshall C.
Edgerton, D.E.H.
Engerman, Stanley L.
Englander, Ernest J.

Fabricius, Miroslav
Falkus, Malcolm Edward
Faltus, Jozef
Feldman, Gerald D.
Fink, Jørgen
Fitzgerald, Robert
Flesher, Dale L.
Flik, Reiner
Fode, Henrik
Foreman-Peck, James S.
Franaszek, Piotr
Fraser, Maryna
Fujimura, Daijiro
Galambos, Louis
Garside, W.R.
Giebelhaus, August W.
Gilpin, John F.
Gingras, André
Girvan, Norman Paul
Glete, Jan
Godley, Andrew C.
Goebel, Erik
Gomez-Mendoza, Antonio
Gourvish, T.R.
Graham, Margaret B.W.
Griset, Pascal
Gueslin, André
Haeberle, Eckehard
Hall, Roger D.
Hannah, Leslie
Hansen, Povl A.
Hara, Terushi
Harada, Seiji
Harasawa, Yoshitaro
Harbaugh, Larry E.
Hardach, Gerd
Hardach, Karl W.
Hau, Michel
Hawke, G. R.
Hawley, Ellis W.
Hayburn, Ralph H.C.
Hazama, Hiroshi
Heffer, Jean
Heim, Carol E.
Helguera Quijada, Juan
Helper, Susan
Henning, Hansjoachim
Henwood, James N.J.
Hernandez-Estev, Esteban
Hertner, Peter

Prúcha, Václav
Raaschou-Nielsen, Agnete
Rauck, Michael
Regehr, Theodore D.
Renz, Regina
Reulecke, Jürgen
Riis, Thomas
Roche, Michael
Rockoff, Hugh T.
Rose, Mark H.
Rose, Mary B.
Rosenbloom, Richard S.
Rothstein, Morton
Rugman, Alan M.
Ryant, Carl G.
Saalfeld, Diedrich
Sachse, Wieland
Saito, Takenori
Sakamoto, Takuji
Sampson, Cezley
Sandgruber, Roman
Sapelli, Giulio
Saunders Jr., Richard
Sawai, Minoru
Schmitz, Christopher J.
Schröter, Harm G.
Schuler, Peter-Johannes
Schulz, Günther
Scott, Roy V.
Scranton, Philip B,
Sejersted, Francis
Shimokawa, Koichi
Shimono, Katsumi
Shimotani, Masahiro
Simmons III, F. Bruce
Singleton, John
Sklar, Martin J.
Slaven, Anthony
Smith, George David
Smith, John Kenly
Smith, Merritt Roe
Smith, Michael S.
Soltow, James H.
Sorrenson, M.P.K.
Spender, J.-C.
Spitzer, Paul G.
Spree, Reinhard
Stiefel, Dieter
Stone, R.C.J.
Sudrià, Carles

Sugisaki, Takamoto
Sugiyama, Shinya
Sunaga, Kinzaburo
Supple, Barry
Suyenaga, Kunitoshi
Suzuki, Tsuneo
Suzuki, Yoshitaka
Sylla, Richard
Takechi, Kyozo
Tanaka, Toshihiro
Tedesco, Paul H.
Tedlow, Richard S.
Thackray, Arnold
Thomes, Paul
Thompson, Gregory L.
Thowsen, Atle
Tilly, Richard
Titos-Martinez, Manuel
Tolliday, Steven W.
Topp, Niels-Henrik
Torres Villanueva, Eugenio
Tortella, Gabriel
Traves, Tom
Tull, Malcolm
Uchida, Hoshimi
Udagawa, Masaru
Ueda, Kinji
Usselman, Steven W.
Valdaliso, Jesús M.
Vallieres, Marc
Van Der Wee, Herman
van Eyll, Klara
Verhoef, Grietjie
Vietor, Richard H.K.
Ville, Simon P.
Vleesenbeek, H.H.
Vogt, Martin
von Stromer (Freiherr von Reichenbach), Wolfgang
Wada, Kazuo
Waller, David S.
Watanabe, Hisashi
Webb, Arthur C.M.
Weber, Wolfhard
Weil, François
Wessel, Horst A.
Westall, Oliver M.
Whatley, Christopher A.
White, Christine A.
White, Eugene N.

Wilkins, Mira
Wilson, John F.
Wilson, R.G.
Witthöft, Harald
Woronoff, Denis
Worthy, James C.
Wray, William D.
Wren, Daniel A.
Wrigley, Chris J.
Wysocki, Josef
Yamada, Makiko
Yamaguchi, Fujio
Yamazaki, Hiroaki
Yanagisawa, Osamu
Yasumuro, Kenichi
Yasuoka, Shigeaki
Yates, J. Anne
Yonekura, Seiichiro
Yoshihara, Hideki
Yunoki, Manabu
Yuzawa, Takeshi
Zacharias, Lawrence S.
Zahedieh, Nuala B.
Zamagni, Vera
Zan, Stefano
Zembala, Dennis M.

UNDERGRADUATE

Abe, Takeshi
Achilles, Walter
Ackrill, Margaret
Adelmann, Gerhard
Alberty, Július
Aldcroft, Derek H.
Alexander, James R.
Amano, Masatoshi
Amatori, Franco
Ambrosius, Gerold
Amdam, Rolv Petter
Applebaum, Herbert A.
Arana, Ignacio
Armstrong, Christopher
Armstrong, Fred H.
Armstrong, John
Asajima, Shoichi
Austin, Barbara
Austin, John
Badurík, Jozef

Ichihara, Hiroshi
Ichijo, Junya
Igartua, José E.
Iida, Takashi
Ikeda, Noritaka
Ikoma, Michihiro
Imakubo, Sachio
Inagaki, Yoshinari
Ioku, Shigehiko
Irsigler, Franz
Ishii, Kanji
Ito, Shoji
Itoh, Takashi
Jackson, Kenneth E.
Jaeger, Hans
Jakubec, Ivan
Jancík, Drahomír
Jenkins, Reese V.
Jequier, François
Jeremy, David J.
Jimenez, Juan Carlos
Jindra, Zdenek
Jobert, Phillippe
Johannessen, Finn Erhard
Johansen, Hans Christian
Johnman, Lewis
Jones, Charles A.
Jones, Stephen R.H.
Jones, Stuart
Jonker, Joost P.B.
Kaczynska, Elzbieta
Kaelble, Hartmut
Kajimoto, Motonobu
Kaku, Sachio
Karonen, Petri Kalevi
Karsten, Luchien
Katoh, Kozaburo
Katz, Jorge M.
Katzenellenbogen, Simon E.
Kawabe, Nobuo
Kawamura, Terumasa
Kawanami, Yoichi
Kawano, Aizaburo
Kazusa, Yasuyuki
Kelly, Eileen P.
Kemmerer, Donald L.
Kennedy, Charles J.
Kerr, K. Austin
Kikkawa, Takeo
Killick, John Roper

Kimura, Masato
King, Frank H.H.
Kirby, Maurice W.
Kitabayashi, Masashi
Klassen, Henry C.
Klebaner, Benjamin Joseph
Klein, Maury
Kobayashi, Hiroshi
Kobayashi, Kesaji
Kobayashi, Yoshiaki
Koda, Ryoichi
Kohno, Shozo
Kohtoh, Isuke
Kollmer-von Oheimb-Loup, Gert
Kornblith, Gary J.
Kosacoff, Bernardo P.
Kovaleff, Theodore P.
Kraft, James P.
Kristensen, Peer Hull
Kudo, Akira
Kuisma, Markku
Kuwahara, Tetsuya
Kuwata, Masaru
Lamard, Pierre
Landau, Zbigniew
Langlois, Richard N.
Latham, A.J.H.
Lazonick, William
Levenstein, Margaret C.
Lewchuk, Wayne A.
Lindenlaub, Dieter
Lindgren, Håkan
Locke, Robert R.
Lorcin, Jean
Lutz, John S.
Lyons, John S.
MacMurray, Robert R.
MacPherson, Ian
Maggia, Giovanni
Marseille, Jacques
Martin, Manuel
Martin-Aceña, Pablo
Martuliak, Pavol
Mathias, Peter
Mathis, Franz
Matis, Herbert W.
Matsumoto, Takanori
Matthiessen, Poul C.

McCalla, Douglas
McChesney, Robert W.
McCusker, John J.
McDowall, Duncan L.
McKay, John P.
McKinlay, Alan
McQuaid, Kim
McRoberts, Mary L.
Meixner, Wolfgang
Melling, Joseph
Mercer, Helen
Michelsen, Karl-Erik
Mierzejewski, Alfred C.
Mikami, Atsufumi
Millard, Andre
Millward, Robert
Misa, Thomas J.
Mishima, Yasuo
Mitsugi, Yoshio
Mitsui, Takashige
Miyamoto, Matao
Mori, Tetsuhiko
Mori, Yasuhiro
Moss, Michael Stanley
Mosser, Alois
Mumford, Michael J.
Munn, Charles W.
Munro, J. Forbes
Munting, Roger
Murkison, Eugene C.
Myers, Michael D.
Myllyntaus, Timo
Nader, John S.
Nakagawa, Keiichiro
Nakagawa, Seishi
Nakatsukasa, Ichiro
Nasuno, Kimito
Naylor, R. Thomas
Neal, Larry D.
Neiva, Elizabeth MacIver
Nelson, Daniel
Newby, Sonja
Nicholas, Stephen
Nishikawa, Junko
Nishikawa, Noboru
Nishimura, Shizuya
Nishimura, Takao
Nonaka, Izumi
Norberg, Arthur L.
Nuñez Romero-Balmas, Gregorio

Wale, Judith M.
Waller, David S.
Walsh, Margaret
Watanabe, Hisashi
Watson, Katherine
Wessel, Horst A.
Westall, Oliver M.
Whatley, Christopher A.
White, Christine A.
White, Eugene N.
Whitten, David O.
Wilkins, Mira
Wilson, John F.
Wilson, R.G.

Witthöft, Harald
Worthy, James C.
Wray, William D.
Wren, Daniel A.
Wrigley, Chris J.
Wysocki, Josef
Yamada, Tetsuo
Yamaguchi, Fujio
Yamamoto, Toru
Yamamura, Mutsuo
Yamazaki, Ryuzo
Yanagisawa, Osamu

Yasumuro, Kenichi
Yasuoka, Shigeaki
Yonekura, Seiichiro,
Yoneyama, Takau
Yoshida, Michael H.
Yunoki, Manabu
Yuzawa, Takeshi
Zacharias, Lawrence S.
Zahedieh, Nuala B.
Zamagni, Vera
Zan, Stefano
Zuckerman, Mary Ellen

FIELDS OF EXPERTISE

Consultancy

ACCOUNTING

Hernandez-Estev, Esteban

ARCHIVES

Edgerton, D.E.H.
Orbell, John
Wilson, John F.

AUTOMOBILE INDUSTRY

Spitzer, Paul G.

BANKING

Hernandez-Estev, Esteban

COMPANY HISTORY

Abe, Takeshi
Achilles, Walter
Ahvenainen, Jorma
Alberty, Július
Alexander, James R.
Amano, Masatoshi
Amatori, Franco
Amdam, Rolv Petter
Andersen, Håkon With
Armstrong, Fred H.
Asajima, Shoichi
Austin, Barbara
Bamberg, James H.
Barker, T.C.
Barsness, Richard W.
Barty-King, Hugh
Beaud, Claude
Beck, William O.
Beltran, Alain
Benaul, Josep M.
Berta, Giuseppe
Bigazzi, Duccio

Blackson, Robert M.
Blanken, Ivo J.
Bläsing, Josvhim F.E.
Boje, Per
Bolton, Alfred A.
Bonin, Hubert
Bostock, Frances G.
Bothwell, Robert
Braun, Hans-Joachim
Broeke, W. van den
Bryant, Keith L. Jr.
Burchardt, Jørgen
Burk, Kathleen
Bussière, Eric
Butel, Paul
Butterworth, Susan
Cain, Louis P.
Cameron, Rondo
Carreras, Charles
Casado Alonso, Hilario
Cassis, Youssef
Chandler, Alfred D. Jr.
Chapman, Stanley David
Cheape, Charles W.
Chiba, Junichi
Clay, Christopher
Coleman, D.C.
Coll, Sebastián
Collins, Michael
Comin Comin, Francisco
Coopey, Richard
Corley, T.A.B.
Crouzet, François M.J.
Daito, Eisuke
Davies, Peter N.
de Goey, F.M.M.
De Vries, Joh.
Demizu, Tsutomu
Dicke, Thomas S.
Donnelly, Tom
Dritsas, Margarita
Dyer, Davis
Eakin, Marshall C.
Edmondson, Michael
Edwards, Pamela C.
Efmertová, Marcela
Fabricius, Miroslav
Falkus, Malcolm Edward
Feldenkirchen, Wilfried
Feldman, Gerald D.
Fitzgerald, Robert

Fleming, Keith R.
Flesher, Dale L.
Flik, Reiner
Foreman-Peck, James S.
Franaszek, Piotr
Fraser, Maryna
Fridlund, Mats
Friedricks, William B.
Fujita, Yukitoshi
Furlong, Patrick J.
Galambos, Louis
Gallo, Giampaolo
Garcia-Ruiz, José-Luis
Gerslová, Jana
Giannetti, Renato
Giebelhaus, August W.
Gilpin, John F.
Goebel, Erik
Gomez-Mendoza, Antonio
Goodall, Francis
Gordon, Nancy M.
Gourvish, T.R.
Graham, Margaret B.W.
Greenhill, Robert G.
Griset, Pascal
Gueslin, André
Haeberle, Eckehard
Hájek, Jan
Hall, Roger D.
Hapák, Pavel
Harasawa, Yoshitaro
Harbaugh, Larry E.
Hashimoto, Juro
Hayburn, Ralph H.C.
Heim, Carol E.
Henwood, James N.J.
Herranen, Timo
Hertner, Peter
Hildebrandt, Reinhard
Hiramoto, Atsushi
Hoffman, Kai J.
Hofsommer, Don L.
Hogesteeger, Gerardus
Hoke, Donald R.
Holtfrerich, Carl-Ludwig
Honeyman, Katrina
Ikeda, Noritaka
Ioku, Shigehiko
Irsigler, Franz
Jakubec, Ivan

ORGANIZATIONAL
DESIGN

Boyce, Gordon

ORGANIZATIONAL
RESTRUCTURING

Lazonick, William

POLICY

Girvan, Norman Paul
(governement)
Hart, Tom (frame-
works and strategies
for transport)
Hawke, G.R.
Klar, Martin J.
Reinert, Erik S. (nation-
al industrial)
Slaven, Anthony (pub-
lic)

PUBLIC AFFAIRS

McDowall, Duncan L

REGULATION

Armstrong, Christopher
Zacharias, Lawrence S.
(corporate)

RESEARCH

Kunz, Andreas (com-
puter-based)
Milkereit, Gertrud

THEATRE
DOCUDRAMA

Childs, William R.

TRADE AND
PROFESSIONAL
ASSOCIATIONS

Seely, Bruce E.

TRAINING

Boot, H.M.

STATISTICS

Kunz, Andreas (histori-
cal)

US CONTROLLER OF
THE CURRENCY

Klebaner, Benjamin
Joseph

US FOOD AND DRUG
ADMINISTRATION

Young, James Harvey

US PATENTS,
1790–1836

MacMurray, Robert R.

US TECHNOLOGY
STRATEGY

Aaronson, Susan Ariel

US TRADE POLICY

Aaronson, Susan Ariel